NTC's
Dictionary
of
CHANGES
in
MEANINGS

NTC's Dictionary of CHANGES in MEANINGS

Adrian Room

Printed on recyclable paper

NTC *Publishing Group*
Lincolnwood, Illinois USA

1996 Printing

This edition first published in 1991 by National Textbook Company,
a division of NTC Publishing Group, 4255 West Touhy Avenue,
Lincolnwood (Chicago), Illinois 60646-1975 U.S.A.
© Adrian Room 1986. Originally published by Routledge & Kegan Paul plc.
Library of Congress Catalog Card Number 89-64132
Manufactured in the United States of America

5 6 7 8 9 VP 9 8 7 6 5 4 3 2

CONTENTS

A language is never in a state of fixation, but is always changing; we are not looking at a lantern-slide but at a moving picture.

Arthur Lloyd James, *The Broadcast Word*, 1935.

INTRODUCTION

Consider the following:

'You should avoid *accidents* when lighting a *bonfire*, or your *career* could be in *danger*. This *entails* not having too many *friends* in the *gang* who are on *holiday*. They may seem *innocent* in their *japes*, and be *keen lads*, but some of them are rather *mischievous*, or at least *naughty*, and a few even enjoy some quite *obnoxious pranks*, and could be *quick* to *reduce* everything to a *shambles*. So keep your *temper* if they are *uncouth*. Don't *vilify* them. Just *watch* them with a *yawn*. They will then set to and work with *zest*.'

The italicized words in this admittedly contrived piece of fiction are not merely words that run in alphabetical order. They are all words whose meanings have changed over the years, whose senses have shifted in some way since they first entered the English language.

This may come as something of a shock. Surely 'friend' has never meant anything than what it means today, or 'quick' had a meaning other than 'fast', 'rapid'? Can such a basic verb as 'watch' have had any other sense?

Some people find it hard to believe that words can change their meanings. They accept that new words enter the language for new things and new concepts ('television', 'polythene', 'cybernetics'), and that many words refer to things and actions that are now historic ('arquebus', 'jousting', 'chariot'), and they recognize, too, that all apparently 'native English' words originally entered the language from the tongues of the people who successively settled in the British Isles – the Angles, Saxons and Jutes, the Scandinavians, and the Normans. But the fact that words change their *meaning* is less easy to comprehend. Why should a meaning change, or a sense shift? People find it hard to accept that an apparently historic or 'dead' sense can survive to apply to a new version or modern adaptation of the original, for example, and one annoyed reader of *The Times* even wrote a letter to the editor (2 March 1985) upbraiding the media for referring to the men who carry a coffin at a funeral as 'pallbearers'. This was incorrect, he claimed, since a 'pallbearer' was a 'bearer of a pall', that is the man who held one side of the 'pall' or heavy cloth that formerly covered a coffin. There was now no 'pall', he maintained, so the word was inaccurate. The worried reader overlooked the fact that the word has simply changed its original sense because the funeral ceremony has itself been modified (simplified in fact), and there are hundreds of similar instances where an original or literal sense has been overtaken by change and progress, but where the basic meaning or concept remains constant. Penknives are no longer used for repairing quill pens, and saucers no longer hold sauce. But penknives still basically *cut* and saucers still *contain*, and it is the sense that has altered as a result of the way we run our daily lives. The objects have simply been updated and modified over the years, and their uses adapted and altered.

The type of sense change illustrated by 'pallbearer' is only one of many, and at this point we should perhaps consider what other types there are, giving representative examples of words in a particular category that have their own entries in the dictionary. The categories are given in order of frequency, at least in the present dictionary, so that the 'pallbearer' one is easily the largest and heads the list. Similar categories have been devised by other linguists and lexicographers, but an overall unified agreed list of types of change has not yet been made. (Some, no doubt, would maintain that two separate categories below can easily be absorbed into a single category. Even so, I feel the different types are distinctive enough to be recognized, despite the occasional overlap, where a word can be classified in more ways than one.)

1   *Functional transfer of meaning*   These are words (such as the now familiar 'pallbearer') whose senses have altered because the thing or action they define or denote has itself changed. Among them are: *bayonet, busby, chorus, dock, flask, footman, grocer, hospital, lobby, match, pavilion, penknife, romance, rosary, saucer, secretary, shears, spanner, tennis, urinal, wardrobe, wife* and *yawn*. It will be noted that these are all nouns. There are some interesting subgroups in this category, such as the machines that have taken over from man (*calculator, computer*), masculine or 'male associated' words that have become feminine (*blouse, brothel, harlot, hoyden, tomboy*), and even some garments that have progressed from overwear, or top garments, to underwear (*camisole, corset, petticoat, vest*). Some food dishes, too, have substantially altered over the years (*blancmange, crumpet, custard, gravy, junket, lollipop, pastry, porridge, sherbet*). Additionally, people now sleep under a *quilt,* not on top of it, and a *midriff* is today usually on the outside of the body, not buried in the belly!

2   *Narrowing of meaning*   These are words, again mainly nouns but also including some adjectives, whose sense has progressed from the general to the specific. An 'accident' was originally simply an 'incident', an 'actor' a 'doer', a 'beam' an Old English word for 'tree', and so on. Among others are: *adder, affray, avenue, brown, cabin, cattle, cellar, coast, corpse, deer, engine, furniture, gestation, groom, knuckle, meat, parcel, passenger, science, stow, vegetable*.

3   *Deterioration of meaning*   This category, called 'pejoration of meaning' by some linguists, includes words whose meaning has gone from 'good', or at least 'neutral', to 'bad'. Thus such adjectives as 'artful', 'crafty', 'cunning'

and so on originally meant 'skilful' or 'clever', without any connotation of 'badness'. Among others are: *animosity, carp, cheat, daft, danger, devious, drab, err, gaudy, humiliate, hussy, knave* (compare 'knight' in category 7), *lewd, menial, minion* (which originally meant 'darling'), *poison, promiscuous, silly, smug, surly, terse, tinsel, uncouth, vulgar.*

4 *Expansion of meaning* This is the opposite of category 2, and contains words whose originally narrow or specialized meaning has become general or widespread. For example 'arrive' originally meant 'come to a shore', and 'bulb' originally denoted an onion. Among others are: *advent, beach, bedlam, bonfire, breeze, crisis, entail, evening, fellow, guess, holiday* (originally 'holy day'), *journey, manufacture, moth, panel, raid, regular, shambles, thug, vision, visit.*

5 *Associated transfer of meaning* This category is in a way similar to the first listed, since a functional development may well be involved. But the difference here is that a meaning arises by association with a prime sense and develops in that way. For example, a 'barbecue' was originally a framework of sticks where an animal such as a sheep could be roasted. Later, the word came to mean the meal made in order to eat the animal. Similarly, a 'bureau' was (and still is) an item of furniture, a writing desk. Later the word spread to include not only the room where such a desk stood but even a whole building or organization. In many ways, therefore, the category is also similar to no. 4, above, since frequently an 'expansion' will be involved. However, this is not always the case, as the entries for other words will show. Among them are: *bead, buccaneer, budget, cash, chest, counter, fairy* (here there is actually a diminution of meaning), *glamour, gossip, hearse, lavatory, mole, pantechnicon, seminary, siren, tabloid, toilet, treacle, urchin.*

6 *Abstraction of meaning* This category basically includes words whose 'concrete' sense has become abstract, or whose originally literal meaning became figurative. 'Aftermath', for example, originally meant 'second crop of grass', and 'bombast' meant 'cotton wool used as padding'. Among other examples are: *aspire, concur, deduce, depend, enhance, extol, hoodwink, imply, involve, polite, refund, repercussion, tact, thrill.*

7 *Improvement of meaning* This is the opposite of category 3, and is also known by some linguists as 'amelioration of meaning'. It includes words whose 'bad' sense has been improved to a 'good' one or at least a 'neutral'. For example, 'boy' originally meant 'low fellow', 'knave', and 'pretty' meant 'crafty' or 'wily' in Old English. Among other words in the group are: *ambition, bask, dogged, epicure, gourmand* (which later slipped back again), *knight* (compare 'knave'), *lad, luxury, nice, rapture, shrewd, spill, success.*

8 *Weakening of meaning* This category includes words whose original 'strong' sense has been toned down, weakened or trivialized. Well-known examples are the purely 'intensive' adjectives such as 'awful', 'chronic', 'dreadful', 'fearful', 'horrid', 'naughty' and 'terrible'. Among others are:

annoy, baffle, bane, bruise, confound, dismal, dreary, friend, hinder, prank, rascal, scamp, stale (quite literally), *truant, worry.*

The remaining three categories are much smaller.

9 *Scientific correction or adjustment of meaning* These are Greek-based words whose meanings changed as a result of the advance of scientific knowledge and a new thinking or 'consignment of category'. For example, 'planet' was originally the term for the heavenly bodies that revolved, so it was believed, round the Earth, including the Sun (!). Copernicus altered all that in the sixteenth century, whereupon the Sun was correctly redesignated as 'star' and the term 'planet' was properly applied to those celestial bodies, including the Earth, that revolved round it. Similarly 'astrology' and 'astronomy', which largely overlapped in medieval times, were redefined and redesignated. Other altered terms include: *geology, meteor, philology, physics, zoology.*

10 *Artificial deflection of meaning* This category, an interesting one, includes words whose senses have been altered through 'false etymology'. That is, the word has become wrongly associated with some other word, and the sense has acquired that association as its main meaning. For example, 'belfry' became associated with 'bell', so that in the end it actually was a structure containing bells, and 'elongate' became wrongly associated with 'long' to gain the sense 'lengthen'. Other such words include: *arbour, equerry* and (probably) *gingerbread.*

11 *Strengthening of meaning* This final category is the opposite of category 8. In this case, the word progressed from a 'weak' or neutral sense to a 'strong' one, not the other way round. Examples are not common, but include *disgust* (which originally meant 'not like') and *gale* (which was originally a light wind).

Of course, there are words that do not neatly fit into any of these categories, and 'buxom', for example, has done the reverse of category 6 and proceeded from an abstract sense ('tractable', 'pliable', 'obedient') to a 'concrete' one ('plump and good-looking'). But very many of the 1342 words in the dictionary will be seen to fall readily enough into one of the eleven categories mentioned. As members of the human race we may like to reflect on the fact that more 'bad' meanings have developed than 'good', and many more 'weak' than 'strong'.

The fact that such 'basic' and apparently immutable senses as 'evening', 'boy', 'moth', 'visit' and 'coast' have altered their meanings may shake our faith in the stability of things around us. But we live in an ever-changing and unstable world, where there is both construction and erosion in our society and environment, and where nothing remains constant. Such instability and impermanence is thus reflected in the language – it *has* to be, if words are to have a truthful meaning. Boys are now (mostly) no longer 'knaves', and visits are made for reasons other than purely religious ones. Saucers now hold teacups, not sauce, and pallbearers no longer carry the pall, even though they still bear the coffin.

If such radical sense changes seem shocking, then read no further! Not only did 'boy' mean 'knave' but 'girl' at one time even meant 'boy'. Similar 'volte-faces' may be seen for the words 'bully', 'chuckle', 'glimmer' (once a bright light), 'mere', 'quite' (which still has two virtually opposing senses), 'reprieve', 'restive', 'thrift', 'upset' (originally 'set up'), 'wan' and even 'with' (which meant 'against' in Old English). On another plane, some very common words have in certain cases taken over to oust former words. The present 'animal' superseded the former 'beast' in the sense, as it in turn had earlier ousted 'deer'. These two words have acquired a new meaning. Similarly, 'bird' replaced 'fowl', 'bread' took over from 'loaf', 'cloud' came in instead of 'hill' (!), as 'sky' did instead of 'welkin' (which also formerly meant 'cloud'), 'dog' kicked out 'hound', and 'hill' superseded 'down'. Even the homely 'rabbit' was originally a 'cony', and 'back' was the word that replaced 'ridge'. But perhaps enough is enough. . .

Most of the words just quoted are Old English ones, Old English being the now generally accepted name (formerly 'Anglo-Saxon') for the language spoken by some of the earliest settlers in the British Isles from the fifth century AD to about the eleventh. It existed in several dialects, although the chief literary form was West Saxon. Regarded overall, however, Old English was the language spoken by such dominant tribes as the Saxons, the Angles, and the Jutes, all from a part of Europe that is now in the north of West Germany and in Denmark (hence, as modern reminders of their provenance, the modern place-names Angeln, Saxony and Jutland in that part of the continent). The language of these settlers blended to produce what today is the 'Germanic' content of the English language, and the historic foundation on which later settlers built related or quite different language structures.

Next chronologically after the Anglo-Saxons came the Vikings, the Scandinavians. Their language (technically also Germanic) had a measured but significant impact on the form of English already existing when they arrived in the eighth century, but nothing like the impact that the language of the Normans had three centuries later. Even more important, *their* language was not a Germanic one but a Romance one, based on the Latin of Rome in its popular spoken form. To all intents and purposes, therefore, what had previously been exclusively Germanic 'English' (as it had then developed) was invaded or infiltrated by Romance 'French'. For the purposes of this dictionary this is interesting, since it means that many words of the eleventh century onwards that arose from French, at first only slowly, then increasingly down to the sixteenth century and even later, originally had the senses that in many cases they still retain in modern French today. The fact that the English meaning of such words altered, but the French sense did not, resulted in the many 'false friends' (or *faux amis*) that plague English-speaking learners of French today. Such words *look* as if they mean one thing, but actually mean another. Readers who have ever attempted to learn French (as the most common foreign language taught in Britain and many other English-speaking countries) may therefore be interested in the selection of words below. The column on the left shows the modern French word and its meaning; that on the right shows the corresponding English word that *originally* had the same sense as the modern French one. All these words were first recorded in English from the thirteenth century to the eighteenth, mostly in the fourteenth and fifteenth.

Modern French word and meaning	Corresponding English word
avertissement, 'warning'	*advertisement*
chasser, 'hunt'	*chase*
conforter, 'encourage'	*comfort*
délivrer, 'set free'	*deliver*
éditer, 'publish'	*edit*
engin, 'device', 'machine'	*engine*
expérience, 'experiment'	*experience*
fourniture, 'act of supplying'	*furniture*
grange, 'barn'	*grange*
hasard, 'chance'	*hazard*
ignorer, 'not to know'	*ignore*
industrieux, 'skilful'	*industrious*
injurier, 'insult'	*injure*
instamment, 'urgently'	*instantly*
labourer, 'plough', 'till'	*labour*
large, 'broad'	*large*
lecture, 'reading'	*lecture*
libeller, 'draw up a document'	*libel*
parent, 'relative'	*parent*
pétrole, 'petroleum'	*petrol*
pondérer, 'weigh'	*ponder*
prévenir, 'avoid', 'avert'	*prevent*
recette, 'recipe'	*receipt*
récupérer, 'regain'	*recuperate*
sauvage, 'wild'	*savage*
séculaire, 'age-old'	*secular*
sensible, 'sensitive'	*sensible*
truand, 'crook'	*truant*
veste, 'jacket'	*vest*
zeste, 'orange or lemon peel'	*zest*

Such problems will naturally also occur the other way round, and ensnare the French speaker learning English, so that initially 'advertisement', 'deliver', 'engine', 'ignore' and so on will conjure up the wrong association.

The dictionary, in the main, deals with past senses of a word that are now obsolete, charting their approximate century of appearance and disappearance. Some new meanings last little more than a hundred years before they become obsolete and leave the language. Others endure much longer, and may have been superseded only quite recently, in the nineteenth century. More than often a new meaning may develop while an earlier one is still current, so that the two (or more) run in parallel. This has annoyingly happened with 'quite', for example, so that the word today has two almost opposite meanings: 'entirely' (as 'quite complete') and 'fairly', 'rather' (as 'quite lucky'). This leads to ambiguity in such a sentence as, 'The box was quite full'. Completely full or only partly? (See the word itself for more considerations on this.)

Just as it has obviously not been possible to include *all* words in the English language that have undergone a change of meaning, so it has not proved always easy, or even desirable, to give all the former senses of a word. Even so, the most important will be mentioned, and their 'lifespan' indicated. At this point it may be wondered whether there are any words at all that have not had a change of meaning. There are, of course, although they are probably fewer than might be supposed. Amongst the most stable are those words that denote kinship, such as 'brother', 'sister', 'father', 'mother', as well as parts of the body such as 'head', 'eye', 'hand', 'foot', and colours such as 'red', 'blue', 'yellow', 'green'. Even here, however, this is only a general principle, since the sense of 'niece' and 'cousin' has not been stable, 'chest', 'gum' and 'midriff' (as mentioned) have had a changing history, and 'brown' has not always indicated the colour of earth and wood, just as 'purple' has also changed its hue over the years.

The various entries would not, of course, be complete if they restricted themselves to dates and meanings. What is needed is an illustrated backup, especially for some of the more important or surprising former meanings. This is given, in almost every entry, in the form of brief quotations from contemporary texts. The reader can thus see a phrase or whole sentence showing 'girl' meaning 'boy', 'knuckle' meaning 'knee', 'minion' meaning 'darling', and 'Dutch' meaning 'German'.

Most, but not all, of the quotations are taken from the *Oxford English Dictionary*, where occasionally they may have been slightly abridged or abbreviated. They have not been altered, however, and indeed appear in their original form, since the compilers of the *OED* were scrupulous in their exact transcription of the many texts. For this reason, some of the earlier quotations will look decidedly 'Olde Englishe', and occasionally I have felt it helpful to 'translate' or at any rate explain a word (in square brackets following it), in order to make the quotation intelligible as a whole. At times, this may seem superfluous to some readers, who can deduce the sense unaided. But the opposite may also hold, I fear, and some words, that I have not glossed, may appear hard to interpret or read. I apologize in advance in such cases, which I hope will be very few. I have tried to strike a balance between over-explaining like a pedantic schoolteacher on the one hand, and under-explaining like an impatient pedagogue on the other. In some cases it may help to try actually pronouncing the words, and regard the apparently eccentric spelling as merely a light camouflage for the 'real' word underneath.

The choice of quotation or quotations to illustrate a particular meaning was often a difficult one. To have given any quotation from a text much before 1100, for example, would be to offer the reader a sentence in neat Old English, and so in virtually a foreign language, complete with different letters in many cases. This would be clearly pointless. Again, other texts that might otherwise have been suitable were in early Scots or in a dialect of some kind. Here, also, the original would have been of little value, however helpful any accompanying translation. In some instances, too, there were simply too many meanings to provide an illustration for each, and in others the senses were purely technical and would have gained little from a supporting quotation. But all in all, there are more quotations than not, even where they are taken from texts several years or even centuries after the first experience of a new sense. (In a few cases I deliberately chose a later text for ease of comprehension. So long as the usage was accurate, I feel this is a legitimate course to take.)

There are, however, two important exceptions to the principle that the wording is exactly that of the original. For the most frequent quotations, from the Bible and Shakespeare, I have on the whole used the standard familiar texts of the Authorized Version of the Bible (the King James Bible of 1611) and a modern Shakespeare edition (in fact that of the Oxford Shakespeare edited by W.J. Craig and first published in 1905, with several subsequent reprinted editions in different formats). I made these exceptions not only because of the high frequency with which quotations from these works appear in the dictionary, but because if the reader is familiar with the Bible or Shakespeare at all, however foggily, it will probably be in such a 'standard' edition. At the same time, certain quotations from the Bible are made from an earlier English translation than the Authorized Version, and naturally the wording and spelling here will be as in the original. (For biblical quotations, too, chapter and verse of the appropriate book are always given, but for quotations from Shakespeare, I have merely 'placed' the words by indicating who is speaking to whom, and where necessary, by briefly explaining the subject of the speaker's words at that particular moment. To quote act and scene is not particularly helpful.)

Even a casual glance through the entries will show that some texts, apart from the Bible and Shakespeare, are quoted more frequently than others. This is the time to say a little about such texts.

In chronological order, the first major text to feature regularly in this respect is the early fourteenth-century one known as the *Cursor Mundi* (Latin for 'course of the world'). This is a vast religious poem in about 24,000 lines of rhyming couplets that was written in about 1300 (probably after rather than before.) We do not know who the author was, but the language shows it to be written in a northern dialect of what was at that time technically called Middle English (as it were, halfway between Old English and Modern). Its beauty for 'sense' quotations is that its subject matter is so wide-ranging. It is not only a 'world history' from the Creation to Doomsday, but it is packed full of colourful legends and saints' lives, so combining a wide spectrum of varied language on a factual and imaginative level.

The next milestone, one that will be frequently encountered by the reader, is that of by far the most important writer in Middle English, Chaucer, and thus of his monumental work, *The Canterbury Tales*. (Unfinished, alas, but monumental all the same for its subject matter, style, characterization and, most important from our point of view, its language.) The date given in the dictionary for the *Canterbury Tales* is always 1386, although this is an approximation and much of the work was written after this up to the author's death in about 1400. The earliest possible date is given, however, as with all other works quoted, since this is when the language quoted was actually written, rather than when the work was completed or published. Some quotations are also given from other works and translations by Chaucer.

The fourteenth century also contains the time of the first complete English translations of the Bible (from the Latin Vulgate of the fifth century in turn originally translated by St Jerome). These two English translations are ascribed to John Wyclif, and are now traditionally dated 1382 and 1388. Again, these years are approximate only and it is certain that Wyclif himself was not the translator of the entire Bible. For our purposes this does not really matter, however, since it is the language itself that is important and the usage of individual words that is of greatest interest. Where they occur in the dictionary, quotations from Wyclif's Bible are almost always matched with parallel quotations from the Authorized Version of 1611. In many cases an earlier word will have been altered, although in some others it will have been retained. Either way there will have been a change of meaning for the quotation to appear here at all.

The next landmark is another translation of the Bible, this time that of William Tyndale, whose New Testament, based on the Greek of Erasmus' edition, was printed in 1525, with his version of the Pentateuch (the first five books of the Old Testament) appearing about five years later. Tyndale's translation in essence formed the basis for the text of the Authorized Version nearly a century later. Closely following on Tyndale's Bible was the translation of the whole Bible that bears the name of Miles Coverdale, printed in 1535. This in turn was mostly based on Luther's German Bible as well as partly on the Latin Vulgate and even Tyndale's own version. Finally (for the purposes of this dictionary, although not in the history of Bible translation) the Authorized Version itself appeared in 1611, representing, as mentioned, a slightly altered rendering of Tyndale's text with a 'seasoning' of Wyclif's.

By now the English language was acquiring something like its current form, with a vocabulary and spelling that certainly seem more modern than 'ancient', and we have now reached the era of Shakespeare, whose value as a source of contemporary English usage is of supreme importance. Today, many people have a kind of ambivalent attitude to Shakespeare. On the one hand, they tend to 'write him off' as too remote, too 'high-falutin' or simply too difficult to understand. On the other, they recognize his genius and are perfectly ready to acknowledge his wonderful gift of characterization and sense of theatre (in the literal as well as the broader sense). Unfortunately, it is the 'antis' who react against his language. Inasmuch as it affects us, in this dictionary, this is a great pity, since Shakespeare's mastery of English was almost unparalleled, and his vocabulary ranges widely, incorporating meanings and nuances not only from English as it stood in his day, but from the past as well. And that is not all: Shakespeare was a true innovator, and if he felt that a word or phrase could be profitably and imaginatively exploited to enhance his text at a particular point, he did not hesitate to do so. He thus presents us with a true thesaurus of English words and meanings, from past, present and in effect future, since many current meanings today are first recorded in his writing. Thus, the following words (each entered in the dictionary) were all originally found in their modern sense in Shakespeare's works: 'bask', 'chaos', 'cur', 'deck' (of cards), 'emblem', 'excellent', 'favour' (in the sense 'token'), 'forfeit', 'gallant', 'gaudy', 'gossip' (as a verb), 'groom' (as a short form of 'bridegroom'), 'haunt', 'horrid', 'indiscreet', 'influence', 'jangle', 'meteor', 'miscarry' (in the sense 'go wrong'), 'portly', 'prime', 'probable', 'puny', 'puppy' (and 'puppy dog'), 'split', 'story', 'tall', 'thrill', 'tributary' (see *tribute*), 'trivial', 'upshot' and 'witty'.

The supreme value of Shakespeare's writing as a unique reference point in the development of the English language cannot therefore be overestimated. He was, too, not only a great and talented writer in any era and any language, but the first really important and gifted writer in what is now technically known as Modern English, that is, English as it has evolved in relatively recent times since the early sixteenth century.

Shakespeare lived from 1564 to 1616, and his almost exact contemporary was Spenser (1552–99), whose talent was fortunately not overshadowed by the greater and more prolific dramatist. Spenser's supreme work was *The Faerie Queene* (1590), and its language, too, will be seen to provide many valuable examples of newly emerging usage. After Spenser, it is the works of the twin giant poets Milton and Dryden that provide much useful material, some innovatory, some preserved from earlier usage. Both Milton and Dryden lived entirely within the seventeenth century (Milton died in 1674, Dryden in 1700), and the former's grandiose *Paradise Lost* (1667) similarly serves as a superb storehouse of contemporary English.

Both Milton and Dryden, as well as several other seventeenth- and eighteenth-century poets, made much use of the vocabulary of former centuries, in some cases, even resurrecting meanings that had become obsolete. This is especially true of words that had been adopted from French, and Dryden in particular made a vigorous attempt to promote French-based words. (He was very francophile in this respect, and bemoaned the fact that English was so 'barbarous' in comparison with elegant French). Hence some of the relatively late usages of earlier senses quoted from the works of this post-Elizabethan period.

Dryden also lamented the fact that the English had 'not so much as a tolerable dictionary, or a grammar'. Half a century after his death the lack he indicated was more than compensated for by the appearance in 1755 of Dr Johnson's great pioneering *Dictionary*.

Obviously, far and away the best guide to the contemporary sense of a word is a dictionary, which will not only define it but, if doing its job properly, illustrate it with quotations from contemporary sources. Johnson's *Dictionary* did both, and he explains in his Preface how his criteria for what should go into his work were based on the best conversation of contemporary London and the normal usage of literate writers after Sir Philip Sidney (1554–86). His emphasis was thus on the present and the relatively recent past, which means that his record preserves English as it was, and as it was understood, in the seventeenth century and first half of the eighteenth. Many of his etymologies are suspect, and some of his definitions wilfully idiosyncratic, but as a source of contemporary senses the work as a whole is more than valuable (and the etymologies of little relevance anyway). The present dictionary will therefore be found to contain a number of quotations and instances of usage taken from Johnson's work.

One final important literary innovator must be mentioned before proceeding to more modern 'wordbanks'. This is Sir Walter Scott (1771–1832). Today, perhaps understandably, Scott is little read. His writings, however, are in their way almost as important a source for vocabulary and language usage as those of Shakespeare, although admittedly on a less grandiose and 'charismatic' scale.

This is because Scott was not only a talented writer and poet, but a historian and (it goes without saying) a Scot. We therefore have language usage on three levels from him: contemporary (i.e. early nineteenth-century), historic (most of his novels are set several centuries earlier), and Scottish (especially relating to Scottish folklore). This unique amalgam therefore provides us with very many examples of 'esoteric' or even 'specialist' English meanings, as well as ordinary cultured usage. (The former element, undoubtedly, is what deters most people from reading him today. One English literature lecturer advised his students, who were reading Scott for examination purposes, to make their initial read-through of his books in a foreign language, if they knew one well enough. It was easier and quicker!) But Scott would not, presumably, have deliberately used antiquated or obscure or local words that his readers would not understand, so we must justifiably assume that most if not all usages found in his works would have been meaningful to his contemporaries, even if many of them are not now. To Scott, therefore, we look for special instances of historic or local (Scottish) words, as well as the general cultured English vocabulary that other writers of his day would have used.

The nineteenth century saw the emergence of the most important milestone of all in the recording of the English language over the centuries. This was the great *Oxford English Dictionary,* whose first part was published in 1884 and final part in 1928, with a Supplement added in 1933. The original complete title of the *OED* was *A New English Dictionary on Historical Principles,* and the last three words of this point to the work's unique value for any dictionary of sense changes, like the present one. The *OED* records the histories and meanings of all words known to have been in use since 1150, as well as hundreds more before this, with each different meaning, or shade of meaning, however fleeting, accompanied by a 'significant' quotation showing its use. The many readers working on the dictionary had amassed a staggering total of five million quotations by 1898, with doubtless at least a million more after that, but the completed work contains 'only' just under two million such citations. For our purposes, as mentioned, these proved a unique source of illustrative material, and I would like to express my thanks to the Copyright Department of the Oxford University Press for allowing me to plunder many of the supporting quotations which the *OED* compilers and readers had themselves so painstakingly gathered during the gradual fruition of their monumental work. The *OED,* too, has been my chief source for most of the actual sense changes themselves, and readers of this present dictionary who wish to discover further former senses of a word, or study a wider selection of relevant quotations than it has been possible to give here, are unconditionally recommended to turn to the pages of the *OED* itself where they will find a veritable feast of information.

It is thus self-evident (I hope!) that the language is changing all the time, and that not only are new words entering the language, but new meanings. Conversely, many words gradually become disused and fall out of use, while formerly current senses become obsolete, and similarly fossilize. Proof of this can be graphically seen in the four new supplementary volumes of the *OED* that have had to be compiled and published in the twentieth century to record such developments and changes. (See the Bibliography, p. 291, for the details of those volumes that have so far appeared.) So what we today readily know to be called a 'computer' may well have acquired some other name in a hundred years or so, when the machine itself has altered beyond all recognition from its present form. It is interesting to speculate what effect on the language the present revolutionary development in science and technology will have in a century or so. If, for example, we are moving towards a cashless society, as seems likely, many of the words now current to deal with the process of buying and selling may either become obsolete or change their meaning. If a purchase in a supermarket is effected through a simple debit to our bank account by means of a chargecard, for instance, the concept of 'change' (i.e. cash returned) will need revising, as may even that of 'coin' itself. Readers may like to speculate what could happen in other fields, such as those of transport, the working environment, and communications generally.

However, it is time to return to the present and to conclude this introduction by explaining briefly how the entries are arranged. Each word has its current main meaning or meanings added in brackets. The various past senses are then dealt with in chronological order, in centuries (occasionally, especially with a recent word or sense, by a precise year). Any special usages of a word, as in a set phrase or expression, are also often indicated, and in many cases etymologies are given to point to the original sense of a word. Mentions simply of 'the Bible', without any date, are of the Authorized Version of 1611. Mentions of the Book of Common Prayer (or just 'the Prayer Book') relate to the 'standard' one of 1662, not the so called 'Revised' one of 1927.

The method of dealing with quotations has already been explained, and the main milestones or landmarks have been considered. There are, of course, quotations from other important works, such as the translations of Caxton and his contemporaries, the most readable *Diary* of Pepys, and the sometimes less readily readable novels of Dickens, as well as from what might be called 'non-literary' sources such as cookery books, newspapers and magazines, agricultural and gardening manuals, ecclesiastical records and wills, and private letters. Other dictionaries besides Johnson's are quoted, too, including, very occasionally, the *OED* itself.

In short, *this* dictionary offers the English-speaking reader a historical panorama of the language, its gains and losses. I hope he or she will derive pleasure and interest from it.

Petersfield, Hampshire   Adrian Room

DICTIONARY

abeyance (state of temporary or permanent disuse)
The word originated as a legal term in the sixteenth century, meaning 'state of expectation', or more precisely, 'waiting for a claimant', as of a fee or title. (The ultimate root of the word is Old French *abeer*, 'to gape', 'aspire after', conjuring up an agreeable picture of an eager, open-mouthed would-be claimant.) A century later the word came to mean 'suspension', as of a person's honour or credibility, or a particular belief. From this developed the modern meaning, which has a rather more general sense.

abject (wretched, very miserable)
In the fifteenth century, the word was used literally, to mean 'rejected', 'cast away', from Latin *abjectus*, 'thrown away', 'cast off'. This sense then became obsolete, and a century later the present meaning of 'downcast' began to develop, as in Milton's 'To lowest pitch of abject fortune' (1671). Meanwhile, the 'wretched' sense also appeared, as in Shakespeare's 'paltry, servile, abject judges' in *Henry VI*, Part 2 (1593). For a time, the word was used as a noun, in the sense 'outcast', 'castaway', as in Psalm 35:15: 'yea, the abjects gathered themselves together against me', and Shelley's *Prometheus Unbound* (1818):

The subject of a tyrant's will
Became, worse fate! the abject of his own.

This use is now strictly limited to poetry and highly stylized literary writing.

abode (place of residence or habitation)
The word is related to 'abide' and originally meant 'delay', 'stay', especially in the phrase 'without abode' meaning 'without delay'. This sense continued in use down to the time of Shakespeare, although increasingly less frequently. Even so, it occurs in *The Merchant of Venice* (1596) in the 'delay' sense, where Lorenzo says to Gratiano and Salarino:

Sweet friends, your patience for my long abode:
Not I, but my affairs, have made you wait.

This sense of 'abode' then became obsolete, and the word continued with its present meaning of 'dwelling-place'.

abroad (out of the country)
In the thirteenth century, the word meant 'widely', 'at large', and it is used in this sense in the Bible: 'The love of God is shed abroad in our hearts by the Holy Ghost' (Romans 5:5). In the fourteenth century, the sense was extended to mean 'out of doors', as in Shakespeare's *Henry IV*, Part 2 (1597), where Falstaff says to the Lord Chief Justice: 'My good lord! God give your lordship good time of day. I am glad to see your lordship abroad; I heard say your lordship was sick'. After this, the modern sense of 'in a foreign country' prevailed.

abstract (not concrete)
In the fourteenth century, the meaning of the word was 'derived', 'withdrawn', much as 'abstracted' means today. The sense of 'not concrete' began to develop in the sixteenth century, when the word was used with such nouns as 'numbers', 'names' and 'substances' in a semi-technical sense. From this came the current use of the word to mean 'concerned with the idea of something

15

rather than with an actual example of it', as an 'abstract argument'.

abuse (use wrongly)

From the fourteenth century the word was often used to mean 'misrepresent', 'deceive', and this former sense still survives as late as 1749 in Fielding's *Tom Jones:* 'He hath been abused, grossly abused to you'. The sense 'deceive', or rather its opposite, still survives in the modern verb 'to disabuse', meaning 'tell someone the truth when he has been believing something untrue'. Otherwise, these old senses, which occurred in the noun as well as the verb, are now obsolete.

access (approach, admission)

One former sense of the word was 'attack of disease', and in particular 'ague', for which it was a synonym from about the fourteenth to the sixteenth century. For example in John de Trevisa's translation (1398) of Bartholomaeus Anglicus' *De proprietatibus rerum*, we read: 'Fyrste the cold and therafter the heete and euery daye axes, yet worse, for some daye comith double axes'. The modern meaning of the word was also in use, however, at this time, until the special sense ceased to apply.

accident (harmful and unexpected happening)

The original sense of the word was simply 'something that happens', whether harmful or not, as in Shakespeare's *The Tempest* (1611), where at the end of the play, just before he speaks the Epilogue, Prospero refers to:

> the story of my life
> And the particular accidents gone by
> Since I came to this isle.

Something of this former, wider sense survives in the phrase 'chapter of accidents' which means, unless used humorously, 'the unforeseen course of events', and a similar 'non-harmful' sense still exists in the expression 'by happy accident'. By the nineteenth century, however, the present, narrower sense of the word was generally well established.

accost (approach, go up to and speak to)

The ultimate origin of the word is in Low Latin *accostare,* 'to lie alongside' (Latin *ad,* 'to' and *costa,* 'rib'), and this was the first meaning of the verb in English, as in Spenser's *The Faerie Queene* (1596):

> All the shores, which to the sea accoste,
> He day and night doth ward both farre
> and wide.

Later, the literal sense gave way to the present general meaning of 'approach', without any basic idea of 'alongside'.

ace (playing card with value 'one'; person or thing that is the best)

The value of 'ace' in its different uses has ranged over the centuries from 'lowest' to 'highest'. Originally, in the thirteenth century, it was the throw of one at dice, when it was the lowest or worst number. Later, in the sixteenth century, it had become the highest or most valuable card in several card games, ranking even above the court cards, and this is the figurative sense of the 'ace' today in such terms as an 'ace player' or 'ace pilot'.

achieve (accomplish, manage to do)

The literal sense of the word in its Old French source was 'bring to a head', with the French verb *achever* representing Late Latin *ad capum venire,* 'to come to a head'. For this reason, one sense of 'achieve' down to Shakespeare's day was 'kill', since a person who has been killed has been 'brought to a head' or 'accomplished', and this use of the word occurs in *Henry V* (1599), where Henry says to the French herald, Montjoy:

> Bid them achieve me and then sell my
> bones.

acquiesce (agree tacitly)

The word is related to 'quiet', and its original sense was literally 'to remain quiet', 'stay at rest'. From this developed the sense 'submit quietly', and from these two meanings, now both obsolete, the modern meaning of 'agree tacitly' emerged. All three meanings were in use simultaneously in the seventeenth century.

across (from one side to the other, transversely)
In the thirteenth century, the sense of 'across' was more literal, as 'in the form of a cross' or 'crosswise', as in William Caxton's translation (1485) *The Lyf of Charles the Grete*, which tells at one point how Roland was found 'expryed, his hondes in crosse vpon hys vysage'. The use of the word as a preposition became popular only in the sixteenth century, with its earliest occurrence recorded in Shakespeare, as in *The Winter's Tale* (1611), where Florizel says to Perdita:

> I bless the time
> When my good falcon made her flight
> across
> Thy father's ground.

actor (stage player)
The original sense of the word in the fourteenth century was 'agent', i.e. referring to a person who takes action in order to manage or oversee. This translated the Latin *actor* with the same meaning. Later, an actor was simply a 'doer', 'one who acts', and is first recorded in this sense in Shakespeare's *Measure for Measure* (1603), where Angelo says:

> Condemn the fault and not the actor of it?

The modern sense, 'stage player', occurs about the same time, and one of its earliest uses is also in Shakespeare, this time in *Richard II* (1593), where the Duke of York, describing the king's arrival in London, says:

> As in a theatre, the eyes of men,
> After a well-grac'd actor leaves the stage,
> Are idly bent on him that enters next.

adamant (determined, firm in one's view)
The word originally meant 'diamond', 'lodestone', or some other hard rock or mineral, with this sense, common from the fourteenth century, found also in the Bible, as in Ezekiel 3:9: 'As an adamant harder than flint have I made thy forehead'. From this literal sense developed the modern figurative one, 'firm as rock', with the noun becoming an adjective. This became widely used only in the present century, so that although the word occurs in the sense

'inflexible', 'unshakeable' in *Webster's Collegiate Dictionary* of 1936, the common use of 'adamant' with the verb 'to be' is found only quite recently, as in the stories of Agatha Christie ('...she was quite adamant', *Moving Finger*, 1943) and Nevil Shute ('C.A.T.O. were adamant that they would not carry Mr. Honey back across the Atlantic', *No Highway*, 1948).

adder (viper)
'Adder' originally meant 'serpent' generally in Old English, and was figuratively used to mean 'the old serpent', i.e. the Devil. In early texts, however, the word appears as the equivalent of 'nadder', since the modern word arose through a wrong division of 'a nadder' as 'an adder'. Thus in the tenth-century *Lindisfarne Gospels*, the words that appear in the Authorized Version as 'Ye serpents, ye generation of vipers' (Matthew 23:33), occur as: 'Nedra, cynn ætterna!' (literally: 'Serpents, brood of venomous ones!'). The modern, more restricted meaning of 'viper' first appeared in the twelfth century, and occurs in Chaucer and Shakespeare.

address (speak to, apply oneself to)
From the fourteenth century down to about the eighteenth, 'to address' had additional meanings that are now obsolete. These included 'to make straight', 'to dress' and 'to direct the aim of', and reflect the literal origin of the word in Latin *directum*, 'straight', and the links with modern English 'direct' and 'dress' itself, of course. The last of the three obsolete senses quoted here occurs, for example, in Shakespeare's *Twelfth Night* (1601) where Orsino, speaking to Viola (disguised in man's clothes as Cesario), tells her (him) to go to 'his' love Olivia:

> Therefore, good youth, address thy gait
> unto her.

A survival of this sense of 'directing' can be seen in the golf expression 'to address the ball'. The modern sense of 'address' concerns the directing of words or speech to someone.

adjourn (defer, put off)
Modern French *jour*, 'day' can be seen

behind this word, which thus originally meant 'appoint a day for' in the fourteenth century. This sense died out in the early seventeenth century, and the modern meaning of 'put off' prevailed.

adjure (entreat solemnly)

The original fourteenth-century use of the word was to mean 'put a person to his oath', i.e. make him hold to the oath that he had made. Later, the modern sense came to apply to refer to the words of the speaker, as if the person addressed had made an oath (although he actually had not).

adjutant (army officer assisting a more senior officer)

The word originally meant 'assistant' in a general sense before it acquired its present specialized meaning, with this usage appearing as late as 1856 in Elisha Kane's *Arctic Explorations* ('. . .taking with me Morton, my faithful adjutant always'). The military sense developed from the seventeenth century.

admiral (senior naval officer and rank)

From the thirteenth to the fifteenth century, an admiral was an emir, or a Saracen chief, with 'admiral' itself actually based on the Arabic equivalent of 'emir', which means literally 'commander'. The title was also used fairly loosely of any 'infidel' ruler or commander, so that in a text of about 1430 Hannibal is described as 'chief Admirall' of Carthage (John Lydgate, *Bochas' Fall of Princes*). Later, the word came to apply to a naval Commander-in-Chief (the 'Lord High Admiral') and subsequently served as the designation of the highest naval rank.

admire (look at with pleasure)

An earlier sense of the word was 'wonder', 'be surprised', which was current mainly in the late seventeenth century but survived to the nineteenth century in one or two instances, as in Dickens' *Dombey and Son* (1848), which tells how Mrs Chick 'admires that Edith should be, by nature, such a perfect Dombey'. The current sense of the word came into popular use from the late sixteenth century, early enough to be used by Shakespeare.

adulterate (contaminate, make less pure)

The original sense of the verb in the sixteenth century was 'commit adultery'. Hence the use of the word by Shakespeare in *King John* (1595), when Constance tells her son Arthur how 'strumpet Fortune' '. . . adulterates hourly with thine uncle John'. The modern, less literal sense of the verb began to develop at about the same time.

advent (arrival)

The word was originally used from the twelfth century in its religious sense only, to mean 'Church season preceding Christmas'. In the fifteenth century this was extended to mean 'the Coming of Christ'. Only in the eighteenth century did the word acquire its present general sense of 'arrival', although even here the arrival itself is often an important or significant one.

adventure (dangerous or exciting enterprise)

In the thirteenth century, 'adventure' had a number of additional meanings, now all obsolete. Among them were 'chance', 'luck' and 'risk'. The second of these continued in poetic usage somewhat later, and occurs for example in Dryden's *Fables, Ancient and Modern* (1699):

> She smiled with sober cheer,
> And wished me fair adventure for the year.

The modern sense developed from the fourteenth century, but early enough to occur in Chaucer.

advertise (give public notice)

The modern sense was in use in the fifteenth century when, however, the verb also meant simply 'notice', as in the writings of the chronicler Robert Fabyan, published in 1494: 'Liuius Gallus, aduertysynge this myschief, and the great daunger that the Romaynes were in, drewe backe into the cytie'. A similar obsolete sense of the verb meant 'draw someone's attention to', as in the Bible: 'Naomi, that is come again out of the country of Moab, selleth a parcel of land, which was our brother Elimelech's; And I thought to advertise thee, saying, Buy it. . .' (Ruth 4:3-4). The noun 'advertisement' likewise had an earlier sense 'warning', 'attention', and survived in this sense down to the nineteenth century, notably in the 'advertisement to the reader' that was included in a number of books and publications of different kinds.

advice (counsel)

The original sense of the word in the thirteenth century was 'opinion', and this usage lasted in some cases to about the seventeenth century, so that in Thomas More's *Supplycacyon of Soulys* (1529), for example, it occurs in the sentence: 'He hath geuen hys aduise therto, and said that they haue to much'. Another obsolete meaning was 'consideration', 'deliberation', as in Shakespeare's *The Merchant of Venice* (1596), where Gratiano says to Portia:

My Lord Bassanio upon more advice
Hath sent you here this ring,

and in the Bible: 'Consider of it, take advice, and speak your minds' (Judges 19:30), where 'take advice' means 'deliberate', 'weigh it up'. Similar obsolete senses existed for the verb 'advise', which formerly meant 'observe' and 'take thought', and for the related adverb 'advisedly', which in the fifteenth century also meant 'warily', 'prudently' and even 'deliberately', as in Thomas Moffett and Christopher Bennet's *Healths Improvement* (1604): 'Mince or chew your Meat finely, eat leisurely, swallow advisedly'.

aerial (wire used for sending or receiving radio waves)

Originally, of course, the word was simply an adjective, meaning 'pertaining to the air', and it still survives in this sense to refer in particular to transportation through the air (as in 'aerial photography' and 'aerial ropeway'). The modern sense of 'antenna for transmitting or receiving radio waves' began to develop in the early twentieth century as an 'aerial wire' (as distinct from one that ran along the ground), and the shorter noun 'aerial' came to replace this within almost a matter of years.

aerodrome (base for aircraft)

In the nineteenth century, 'aerodrome', which literally (based on the Greek) means

'air runner', meant 'aeroplane', with this usage persisting some way into the twentieth century. A report in the learned scientific journal *Nature* in the issue for 29 October 1908 thus reads somewhat strangely: 'Mr. Farman mounted with M. Delagrange on the latter's aërodrome, which flew a considerable distance with a heavy load'. The word itself seems to have been devised in this sense by the American aeronautics pioneer Samuel Pierpoint Langley in the late nineteenth century. But 'aeroplane', already in use for the new flying machine, soon took over as the standard term, with 'aerodrome' coming to apply to the base.

affect (assume falsely)

The original sense of 'affect' in the fifteenth century was 'aim at', closely reflecting the Latin source verb *afficere*, 'put to', 'apply to'. This can be seen in Shakespeare's *Henry VI, Part 2*, where Lord Say says to Jack Cade:

Tell me wherein have I offended most?
Have I affected wealth, or honour?
    speak.

The sense development then continued as 'have a liking for', 'display openly' (both in the sixteenth century), and finally 'pretend falsely', from the seventeenth century. Compare **affectionate** in the next entry.

affectionate (fond, loving)

The original meaning of the adjective was 'affected', especially unduly so or even deliberately so. This sense can be seen, for example, in the martyrologist John Foxe's *Actes and Monuments* of 1553–87 (popularly known as 'Foxe's Book of Martyrs'), where he writes of 'judges not indifferent but very much affectionate against me', meaning that they were prejudiced or partial. The word then came to mean 'kindly inclined', 'favourable to', in such phrases as 'affectionate to a cause' or 'affectionate to a party', and finally developed from this now obsolete sense to have its present meaning, found from the sixteenth century and occurring in Shakespeare.

afflict (trouble severely)

In the fourteenth century the meaning of the word was close to the Latin original *affligere*, 'to throw down', whether literally or figuratively. This is the sense of the verb in the Bible: 'And this shall be a statute for ever unto you: that in the seventh month, on the tenth day of the month, ye shall afflict your souls, and do no work at all' (Leviticus 16:29), meaning 'humble your souls'. The modern sense began to be used in the sixteenth century, and occurs in Shakespeare.

afford (find time or money for; grant)
The Old English meaning of the verb was 'set forward', 'carry out', showing the word's basic connection with modern 'forth'. The two modern senses quoted above began to develop respectively in the fifteenth and sixteenth centuries.

affray (violent breach of the peace)
Before it acquired its present meaning, the word had the basic sense of 'attack', 'disturbance', and was commonly so used in the fourteenth and fifteenth centuries. Later, the meaning took on its narrower sense, referring to a breach of the peace in a public place.

affront (insult)
The Old French verb *afronter* from which the English word derived meant 'to hit in the face'. This literal sense was not transferred to English, but even so the verb 'affront' had a much more aggressive connotation in former times than it has today, often with an idea of physical opposition. This can be seen, for example, in Richard Grafton's *Abridgement of the Chronicles of England* (1563), which tells how 'King Philip and the French King with two most puyssaunt armies affronted eche other neer vnto the water of Some'. For a similar softening of the physical sense, compare **insult** and **offend**.

aftermath (consequence, resulting state)
The literal meaning of 'aftermath' is 'after mowing', i.e. a second crop of grass in autumn after the first crop has been cut in early summer. This was the original sense of the word in the fifteenth and sixteenth centuries, and even later at a local or more specialized level, so that the *Farmers' Magazine* was writing about 'a good aftermath' in 1860. The more common figurative meaning

of the word, however, was in use from the seventeenth century.

again (once more)
In Old English, 'again' meant 'back', 'in the opposite direction', and this sense came to be subsequently common with such verbs as 'go', 'wend', 'come' and 'turn', as when in Shakespeare's *The Taming of the Shrew* (1596) Petruchio says to Katharina, when she bids him farewell:

> What! with my tongue in your tail? nay, come again.

A more modern preservation of the same sense is in the famous quotation: 'Turn again, Whittington, thrice Lord Mayor of London' (i.e. 'turn back'). The current meaning of 'again' developed only from the fourteenth century.

aggravate (make worse, annoy)
In the sixteenth century, a sense of 'aggravate' was 'load', 'burden', relating to the origin of the word in the Latin base *gravis*, 'heavy', 'grave', with this usage applying both literally and figuratively (as 'aggravated with responsibility'). This then developed through 'add weight to', 'add gravity to' to the modern meaning, which first began to emerge in the seventeenth century.

agitator (political troublemaker)
The term was first used in 1647 in the sense of 'agent' for the delegates of private soldiers in the Parliamentary Army of 1647–9. Political agitators first emerged in the eighteenth century, and in the nineteenth the word was commonly used of the Irish nationalist leader, Daniel O'Connell ('the great popish leader and agitator' according to a report of 1828). After the Russian Revolution of 1917 the word came to mean more specifically 'Communist agitator', and this sense persisted for several years, so that the *Observer* of 29 March 1959, reporting the British Communist Party congress, quoted the words of a delegate who had said that 'the Communist aim should be: Every member a propagandist and agitator'. (For a similar political development, see **propaganda**.)

agree (be in harmony or of one mind)
In the fourteenth century, 'agree' was some-times used to mean 'please', 'become favourable', thus revealing the word's connection with modern 'grace'. Both these senses occur in Chaucer. The modern meaning began to be popularly used in the sixteenth century, and can be found in Shakespeare.

aground (of a ship: held where the water is too shallow for progress to be made)
The literal sense of the word is 'on the ground', and this was what the meaning was in the thirteenth century. From about 1500 the present sense meaning 'not afloat' began to develop, with specific reference to grounded boats or ships.

alarm (emergency signal)
In the fourteenth century, the word was an exclamation meaning 'to arms!', showing its origin in Italian *all' arme*, 'to the arms'. From this the modern sense developed, although for a while before the sixteenth century 'alarm' also meant 'surprise attack' (which would obviously require a sudden call to arms). This is the sense in Shakespeare's *Macbeth* (1605), where Menteith, speaking of the English forces, says:

Revenges burn in them; for their dear
  causes
Would to the bleeding and the grim
  alarm
Excite the mortified man.

alderman (borough magistrate)
In Old English, the word (*aldormann*) was used to designate a man of noble or high rank, especially the governor of a county. Later, the title was used for the warden of a guild, and from this developed the modern sense. The word basically means 'chief man', 'elder man'.

algebra (mathematical method of calculating by symbols)
The word is actually of Arabic origin, meaning 'the reunion' (Arabic *al-jabr*), referring to a 'reunion of broken parts'. The term also meant 'setting of bones', and even had this sense in some fourteenth-century medical texts, so that a surgical manual of 1541 deals with 'The helpes of Algebra & of dislocations'. The word still means 'bone-setting' in modern Spanish, as well as the mathematical system.

alibi (plea that a person was elsewhere when a crime was committed)
Originally, the word on its own was in legal use to mean 'elsewhere', (the meaning of Latin *alibi*), as in a report of 1727: 'The prisoner had little to say in his defence; he endeavoured to prove himself Alibi'. Subsequently, the word acquired its present sense, which in more recent times has been weakened to mean simply 'excuse', as in L.P. Hartley's *My Fellow Devils* (1951), where one of the characters says: 'I have an alibi because I'm going to have a baby'.

allude (refer indirectly)
The word is based on Latin *alludere*, 'to play with', 'dally with', and in the sixteenth century the word was used in English to mean 'make play with words', 'pun'. Thus in *Foxe's Book of Martyrs* (see **affectionate**), the reader learns that Christ, 'alluding to his [i.e. St Peter's] name, called him a rock'. This more literal use, however, did not last much beyond the early seventeenth century.

ally (friend, supporter in a cause)
In Chaucer's day, the word meant 'relative', 'kinsman', and it is used in this sense in his *Canterbury Tales* ('The Second Nun's Tale') (1386):

This day I take the for myn allye,
Sayde this blisful faire mayde.

The modern sense came into use from about the fifteenth century, some hundred years after this was written.

aloof (apart, at a distance)
The word is related to 'luff' in the naval sense, and was in fact originally a nautical command to the steersman of a ship to go to windward, i.e. to go 'a-luff'. A line from one of the poems by the sixteenth-century writer George Gascoigne thus runs:

Aloofe, aloofe then cryed the master out.

The modern sense of the word, in such phrases as 'to stand aloof', began to develop at about the same time as this, and occurs in its current sense in Shakespeare.

amaze (astonish, surprise greatly)
In Old English, 'amaze' meant 'stun', 'bewilder', and a text of 1530 preserves this sense: 'He was so amased with the stroke that he was redy to fall downe' (John Palsgrave, *Lesclarcissement de la langue françoyse*). Later, the word came to mean 'fill with panic', 'terrify', as in Izaac Walton's *The Compleat Angler* (1653), where the aspiring fisherman learns that 'the sight of any shadow amazes the fish'. After this, the verb came to have its more moderate sense of not much more than 'surprise'.

ambition (desire to be rich, famous or successful)
As originally used in English, the word implied an inordinate striving after high rank and wealth, and ambition was regarded as a vice and a sin. Something of this can be seen in the words of Brutus in Shakespeare's *Julius Caesar* (1601), when he is planning to kill Caesar and says:

But 'tis a common proof,
That lowliness is young ambition's
  ladder,
Whereto the climber-upward turns his
  face.

This undesirable sense comes from the Latin *ambitio*, 'going round' (i.e. canvassing for votes for oneself). In more recent times, ambition has come to be regarded as an honourable or creditable thing, with the positive moral attributes of self-improvement and 'local boy makes good'.

ambulance (vehicle for taking sick or injured to hospital)
The word came into English in the nineteenth century from modern French, where in turn it developed from *hôpital ambulant*, literally 'walking hospital'. As originally used in English, the word applied to a moving hospital that followed an army so as to provide medical treatment for the injured as rapidly as possible. By about the middle of the nineteenth century, the name came to be used of the actual vehicle (at first a wagon or cart) that took the injured from the battle field. After the First World War, the word came to have its modern sense to apply to a vehicle that took any injured or sick person to hospital.

amend (correct, improve)
In the thirteenth century, the word meant literally 'mend', applied to objects such as clothes and roads. At the same time, the present meaning began to develop and the literal sense was taken over by 'mend' from the fourteenth century.

amiable (likeable)
From the fourteenth century, the original sense of the word was 'friendly', 'lovable', and this is the meaning in Shakespeare's *Merry Wives of Windsor* (1598), when Ford tells Falstaff that he should 'lay an amiable siege to the honesty' of his own wife. (Today, the use of 'amiable' in this sense is usually restricted to such words as 'mood' and 'humour'.) The 'lovable' sense occurs in Shakespeare, too, when in *Othello* (1604), Othello says to Desdemona, speaking of his mother:

She [an Egyptian] was a charmer, and
  could almost read
The thoughts of people; she told her,
  while she kept it [a handkerchief],
'Twould make her amiable and subdue
  my father
Entirely to her love.

Both these usages of the word are now obsolete, and the modern meaning of 'likeable' emerged only in the eighteenth century.

ammunition (offensive missiles such as bullets, rockets etc.)
The word originally applied to military supplies generally, and continued in this sense for some time in the seventeenth century until the meaning narrowed to refer to shot and shells for guns and finally to offensive missiles of any kind.

amour (love affair)
When the French word was adopted by English in the thirteenth century, it meant simply 'love' pure and simple, and 'in amours' meant 'in love', as in this sentence from Lord Berners' translation (1523) of the *Chronicles* of Froissart: 'The kyng of Englande was in amours with the countesse of Salisbury'. This sense then became obsolete, and when the French word was reintroduced in the sixteenth century it

referred to love affairs and more specifically illicit love. The former of these is implied in an entry from Pepys' *Diary* of 15 August 1665, when he writes of leaving 'the young people together to begin their amours', and the latter is meant by Francis Bacon when he wrote (1626) that 'King Henry the Eighth was engaged in a new amour'.

amuse (please, entertain)
In its original fifteenth-century sense, 'amuse' meant 'delude', 'deceive', and this is the use of the verb in Caxton's translation (1489) of Ovid's *Metamorphoses*, where the line occurs: 'I never amused my husbonde, ne can not doo it'. Later, the sense became 'distract', 'divert', especially as defined by Johnson in his *Dictionary* (1755): 'To draw on from time to time, to keep in expectation'. This now obsolete use of the word occurs as late as the nineteenth century, when in Charles Merivale's *A History of the Romans under the Empire* (1850), for example, one reads: 'Silanus was directed to amuse and negotiate with both powers, and avoid an open rupture by all the arts of diplomacy'. The modern meaning of 'divert entertainingly' dates from the seventeenth century.

analyse (examine minutely)
The original sense of the word was 'dissect', and this is its meaning in the title 'The Phoenix Analysde' (1601) by Ben Jonson, which is the first record we have of the verb. In the eighteenth century the word came to apply to abstract things, and acquired its present sense from the early nineteenth century. However, the specific scientific use of 'analyse' ('ascertain the elements of' and the like) can be found from the seventeenth century, when it was first used by Boyle, and the literary sense (analysing a text, for example) dates from about the same time.

anarchy (absence of government, chaos)
The literal sense of the word (from Greek meaning 'without a leader') is 'absence of government', as stated above, and this was how the word was used in English when it first appeared in the sixteenth century. Although the secondary sense of 'political disorder' was also implicit, it soon transferred to refer to disorder in other spheres,

and by the twentieth century the word had acquired a generalized meaning of 'disorder', 'confusion'. Interestingly, however, in the mid-nineteenth century the word came to be used to apply to a social state in which, although there is no governing person, there is also no disorder, since theoretically each individual would have complete liberty. This particular sense was promoted in the writings of the contemporary French socialist philosopher Proudhon.

anatomy (science of the parts of the body)
For a time, the word also meant 'skeleton', and it occurs in the sense in Shakespeare's *King John* (1595), in Constance's powerful 'death' speech in Act 3, where she grieves for the loss of her young son Arthur, and the lines occur:

> Then with a passion would I shake the world,
> And rouse from sleep that fell anatomy
> Which cannot hear a lady's feeble voice.

This particular meaning was continued in the word 'atomy', which arose as a result of the first two letters of 'anatomy' being taken for the indefinite article ('an'). Thus also in Shakespeare, in the same sense 'skeleton', *Henry IV* Part 2 (1597) has Mistress Quickly saying to Doll Tearsheet: 'Thou atomy, thou!', and even Dickens in *Dombey and Son* (1848) wrote of 'withered atomies of teaspoons'. But this sense of 'anatomy' is now otherwise obsolete.

anecdote (short often amusing account)
The Greek source of the word literally means 'unpublished things', and the original seventeenth-century meaning of the word in English (in the plural) thus was 'secret history'. It was used by Swift in *Gulliver's Travels* (1727) in this sense, and was defined as such in Ephraim Chambers' *Cyclopaedia* of the same period: 'Anecdotes, Anecdota, a term used by some authors, for the titles of Secret Histories; that is, of such as relate the secret affairs and transactions of princes'. In the eighteenth century, this sense gave way to the current one applying to an isolated story about a particular incident.

anent (concerning)

This now old-fashioned word, used mostly humorously ('I would like a word anent the procedure here'), originally meant 'in company with' in Old English, a sense which survived in dialect use down to the nineteenth century. It also meant 'facing', 'towards', as in the *Voiage of Sir John Maundevile* (1366), which tells of 'Wylde Bestes' that 'slen and devouren alle that comen aneyntes hem'. However, the word does still have some Scottish usage in these senses, as well as the general one of 'concerning'.

anger (wrath, extreme annoyance)

In Old English, the verb 'anger' meant 'distress', 'vex', and the corresponding noun came to mean 'trouble', 'affliction' from the thirteenth century. These uses soon became obsolete, however, when the word passed into its present sense of 'rage', 'wrath' from the fourteenth century. A similar development took place with 'angry', which at first meant 'troublesome', and something of this old sense survives in an 'angry spot' or an 'angry rash'.

angina (disease of the heart)

The term is today almost exclusively used for so called 'angina pectoris', literally 'angina of the chest'. Originally, however, it meant 'quinsy', as a form of tonsillitis with abscesses. Hence Evelyn wrote in his *Diary* (1645) that he was 'afflicted with an angina and sore throat'. This sense continued in sporadic use down to the nineteenth century, by which time the meaning had on the whole transferred to the other disease of the heart. In many modern foreign languages, however, 'angina' (or the native equivalent) is still used to mean 'quinsy' or 'tonsillitis', even though it no longer has this sense in English.

animadvert (criticize, express censure)

The original basic sense of the word in English was 'observe', 'note', and it occurs as such in Fielding's *Tom Jones* (1749): 'Animadvert that you are in the house of a great lady'. Later, however, the word developed an unfavourable meaning, perhaps by association with Latin *adversus* or with 'adverse' itself (the literal sense of 'animadvert' is simply 'turn the mind').

animal (beast, living being)

Today, 'animal' is usually thought of by contrast with 'man' or with 'vegetable' and 'mineral'. Before the sixteenth century, it was used as an adjective by contrast with 'vital' and 'natural', so that 'animal' functions were those of the brain and nervous system, 'vital' those of the heart, lungs and other 'vital' organs, and 'natural' were those of nutrition and assimilation. A similar use of 'animal' occurred in the phrase 'animal spirits', which originally applied to the supposed 'spirit' of sensation and voluntary motion (a sort of 'nerve fluid' or 'nerve force'). This phrase has been preserved in modern English, although now meaning 'healthy liveliness', 'natural cheerfulness'. Otherwise, all the earlier 'animal' phrases and meanings are now obsolete.

animosity (active dislike, positive hatred)

In the fifteenth century, the word meant 'high spirit', 'courage', and it occurs in this sense, for example, in Richard Puttenham's *The Arte of English Poesie* (1589), where he writes: 'It was thought a decent countenance and constant animositie in the king to be so affected'. Later, however, the 'spirit' basis of the word came to be expressed in strong feeling towards a person, and in particular enmity, and this modern meaning developed from the early seventeenth century.

annoy (disturb, harass, displease)

The verb had a much stronger sense formerly, and even indicated physical hurt and destruction caused in war. This can be seen in Shakespeare, for example, where in *Henry VI*, Part 2 (1593) Henry says:

> The care you have of us,
> To mow down thorns that would annoy our foot,
> Is worthy praise.

Similarly, as late as the eighteenth century, historical writers were talking of an enemy who 'annoyed the coast' and who could 'annoy the town'. In the sixteenth century, too, there was a 'Jury of Annoyance' that reported on public nuisances (such as 'the corupte sauours and lothsom innoyaunces caused by slaughter of bestes within the cyte'). Since then, the word has taken on a weaker and more general sense, often hardly much stronger than 'bother'.

antelope (deerlike animal)
In the fifteenth century, the name was that of a heraldic animal, apparently originating as 'a creature haunting the banks of the Euphrates, very savage, hard to catch, having long saw-like horns, with which they cut in pieces and broke all "engines", and even cut down trees' (*Oxford English Dictionary*). From the early seventeenth century, the name came to be used of the much gentler, gazelle-like creature, as it is popularly known today.

anthem (hymn of praise)
The word is related to 'antiphon', and in Old English this is what an 'anthem' was, a church chant that alternated between the priest and the choir, or between two solo voices, or two choirs. Later, from about the sixteenth century, the term came to mean a religious song or hymn generally, and in poetry, simply a song. The 'National Anthem' is more accurately a hymn, and this is what the equivalent is called in most modern foreign languages, so that the Marseillaise, for example, is *l'hymne national français*, and 'God Save the Queen', to the Germans, is *die englische Nationalhymne*.

anthology (collection of selected poems or other literary pieces)
The word is derived from Greek *anthos*, 'flower', so really denotes a selection of 'literary flowers', i.e. of small, choice poems. Originally, the term applied to Greek selections of this kind, in particular the work that came to be called in English the 'Greek Anthology', comprising some six thousand short elegiac poems, inscriptions and the like by over three hundred writers (from the seventh century BC to the tenth century AD). In his *Dictionary* (1755), too, Johnson defined 'anthology', in the first sense of the word, as 'a collection of flowers'. Later, the word came to be used of any literary collection or selection, and in the mid-twentieth century 'anthology' also applied to other art forms, so that *The Listener* of 3 August 1967 spoke of the virtual 'anthologies of pop songs' recorded by Frank Sinatra. See also **rosary**.

antic (amusing action, ludicrous gesture)
As a noun, the original sense of the word was 'fantastic figure', especially a grotesque human one such as a caryatid (female figure representing a supporting column) or a gargoyle. From this developed a secondary sense, meaning 'clown', 'buffoon', as in the line from Milton's *Samson Agonistes* (1671):

> Jugglers and dancers, antics, mummers, mimics.

At the same time, an 'antic' was a grotesque pageant or theatrical display, as in Shakespeare's *Love's Labour's Lost* (1588), where Armado, speaking to Holofernes, says: 'I do implore secrecy, that the king would have me present the princess, sweet chuck, with some delightful ostentation, or show, or pageant, or antick, or fire-work'. Subsequently, the word took on its current sense. Its origin lies in Italian *antico*, 'ancient', and it originally applied to the grotesque figures found in ancient Roman remains.

antipodes (places on the opposite side of the globe, as Australia for Britain)
The literal meaning of the word is 'with feet opposite', and from the late fourteenth century the word applied to the inhabitants of the antipodes, rather than the places themselves. This is thus the meaning in Shakespeare's *The Merchant of Venice* (1596), when Bassanio says:

> We should hold day with the Antipodes,
> If you would walk in absence of the sun.

From the sixteenth century, the word came to be used of the places, and the sense of 'antipodean inhabitants' became obsolete.

Apocrypha (non-canonical books of the Old Testament)
From the fourteenth to the seventeenth century, 'apocrypha' was used adjectivally in English to mean 'of unknown authorship', as in John Capgrave's *The Chronicle of England* (1460), where he writes that '"The Penauns of Adam" be cleped [i.e. called] Apocriphum, whech is to sey, whanne the mater is in doute, or ellis whan men knowe not who mad the book'. The specific modern sense of the word, to denote those books of the Old Testament that were not originally

written in Hebrew and were not counted as genuine by the Jews, first occurs in the 'Great' Bible of 1539.

apothecary (druggist, pharmaceutical chemist)

The word ultimately derives from Greek *apothēkē*, 'storehouse', and originally an apothecary did indeed sell general merchandise down to the seventeenth century, as well as preparing and selling drugs for medicinal purposes. In 1617, however, the Apothecaries' Company of London was separated from the Grocers' and undertook to sell drugs only. Hence from about 1700 apothecaries were really medical practitioners, and 'apothecary' today is still the proper term for a dispensing chemist who has been examined and licensed by the Apothecaries' Company. As popularly understood, however, the word 'apothecary' is now old-fashioned, and belongs to history. Interestingly, though, the modern chemist's shop, and certainly the larger branches of chain stores, today sells a wide range of goods apart from drugs, and this is particularly true of the American 'drugstore', which now has its equivalent in Britain.

appal (dismay, shock)

The verb is directly related to 'pale', and in the fourteenth century thus meant literally 'to grow pale' or 'to make pale', with this sense even occurring as late as the sixteenth century in a few texts, for example the *Goodly Primer in Englyshe* of 1535: 'Would not even shortly thy mirth abate, thy colour apale, thy flesh faint'. The modern meaning of 'dismay' came into use from the same century, early enough to be used by Shakespeare.

applicable (able to be applied, pertinent)

In the sixteenth century, 'applicable' meant 'pliable', 'well-disposed' (i.e. 'compliant'). This sense soon gave way, however, to the modern meaning of 'capable of being applied', 'relevant'.

apprehend (understand)

The original sense of the verb in the fourteenth century was 'learn', as in modern French *apprendre*, with a contemporary meaning also being 'lay hold of', 'seize' as

in this text of 1572: 'A great quakyng and tremblyng dyd apprehende his hande' (John Bossewell, *Workes of Armorie*). This second sense later came to mean 'arrest', and the 'learn' sense developed in the sixteenth century to 'understand'.

aquatic (living or operating in water)

In the fifteenth century, the word meant simply 'watery', as in Caxton's *The Boke yf Eneydos* (1490), a translation of a French version of Virgil's *Aeneid*, where he writes of 'grete poundes and ryuers, alle thynges aquatyque'. The 'living in water' sense came into use from the seventeenth century.

arbitrary (random, capricious)

An 'arbiter' is a judge, of course, and the original sense of the word in English was thus 'depending on a person's discretion', as in this text of 1628: 'It is not left arbitrary to you that you may doe good if you will' (Bishop Joseph Hall, *The Righteous Mammon*). From this developed the legal sense, 'pertaining to the discretion of an official arbitrator', and hence the modern general sense of 'random'.

arbour (bower, place in a garden under the shade of trees and bushes)

The present sense of the word has been influenced by false association with both Latin *arbor*, 'tree' and English 'harbour', as a place of shelter. The original meaning was 'plot of grass', 'flower garden', showing the true origin of the word to be in Old French *erbier* (modern *herbier*), related to French *herbe*, 'grass' and English 'herb'. Here it is in a text of 1385: 'Faste thar-by was he, Sittynge on a grene erber' (*Sir Ferumbras*). But here it is again in the same year in more or less its modern sense, in Chaucer's *The Legend of Good Women*:

A litel herber that I have,
That benched was on turves fressh
  ygrave [i.e. dug].

archaeology (study of ancient and historic buildings and materials)

The word originally meant 'ancient history' or 'antiquities' in the seventeenth century, and only in the nineteenth century did the modern 'scientific' sense develop. Thus in

Holy Observations (1607), Bishop Joseph Hall wrote how the Greek church historian Sozomen narrated 'all the archaiology of the Jewes till Sauls gouernment'.

armature (piece of iron placed across the poles of a magnet to close the circuit)
In the fifteenth century, perhaps not surprisingly, the word meant simply 'arms', 'armour', and continued in this sense in some instances until the nineteenth century, when it had mostly been replaced by these two words. The 'magnet' sense developed in the eighteenth century, and a hundred years later the word was further used to apply to the metal core, wound with insulated wire, of an electric motor or generator. (The magnet's armature is now often popularly known as a 'keeper', as if its purpose was to 'keep' the magnetism in.)

armoury (place where weapons and ammunition are kept)
In the fourteenth century, 'armoury' meant simply 'armour', and the word even occurs in this sense in Spenser's *The Faerie Queene* (1596), where he writes of:

That armory,
Wherein ye have great glory wonne this day.

The modern sense developed from the sixteenth century, and occurs in Shakespeare's *Titus Andronicus* (1588), where the boy Lucius says to Aaron, Demetrius and Chiron:

My grandsire, well advis'd, hath sent by me
The goodliest weapons of his armoury.

arrange (put in order, make happen)
The sense was originally a purely military one, meaning 'draw up in battle array', and occurs from the fourteenth century to the nineteenth in this use, although decreasingly commonly. Thus, Spenser has it in *The Faerie Queene* (1596), where two knights are 'arraung'd in battell new'. The modern sense developed popularly, however, only from the eighteenth century, and although it is occasionally found before this, it does not occur in the Bible or Shakespeare, or in the works of Milton or Pope.

arrive (come to a place)
The word is based on Latin *ripa* (French *rive*), 'shore', 'bank', and so originally in English 'arrive' meant 'come to shore' or 'bring to shore', with this sense extended from the thirteenth century to much later times in poetry, so that Chapman in his *Homer's Hymn to Apollo* (1624) writes:

And made the sea-trod ship arrive them near
The grapeful Crissa.

This was in fact the common prevalent sense until about 1550, after which the verb was used to apply to places other than shores. In the seventeenth century 'arrive' was also used for a time to mean 'come to pass', 'happen' (compare modern French *arriver* in this sense), so that a text of 1653 reads: 'I will speak no further of him, but will deliver that which arrived in other Countries' (Henry Cogan, *The Voyages and Adventures of F. M. Pinto*).

arsenal (establishment where weapons and ammunition are stored or made)
The word (ultimately from Arabic, meaning 'house of art') was originally used in English to mean 'naval dock', in particular the one at Venice, and this is the sense in William Thomas's *The Historie of Italie* (1549), where he tells how: 'The Arsenale in myne eye excedeth all the rest: For there they haue well neere two hundred galeys'. At about the same time, the modern sense began to develop. The earlier use shows how the word came into English from Italian, although the present general sense owes much to the corresponding word in French, Spanish and Portuguese. The primary sense in Spanish, however, is still 'naval dockyard'.

artful (cunning, devious)
The original sense of the word was much more innocent, and meant simply 'skilful', 'artistic'. Thus Dryden, in his *Life of Virgil* (1697), says that he was 'too artful a writer to set down events in exact historical order', and Milton, in *Comus* (1637), has the lines:

Thyrsis! whose artful strains have oft delayed
The huddling brook.

The word gradually acquired its derogatory sense, however, and was well established in this by the nineteenth century and the era of Dickens' 'Artful Dodger', the young pick-pocket trained by Fagin in *Oliver Twist* (1838).

article (thing or object; piece of journalistic writing)
The word originated in English in the thirteenth century in the sense 'clause of the Apostles' Creed', with the same sense occurring for the 'Thirty-Nine Articles' included in the Prayer Book of the Church of England. In the fourteenth century, 'article' came to mean 'moment', 'nick of time', as in such phrases as 'the article of temptation' and 'the article of necessity' (and even 'the article of time'). In the fifteenth century, the word came to be used in the sense 'piece of business', 'matter', and this is what the word means in Shakespeare's *Hamlet* (1602), where Hamlet says that Laertes is 'a soul of great article' (i.e. of great importance). Both these two last senses are now obsolete. The sense 'journalistic piece' became widely used from the eighteenth century, although a dictionary 'article', like this one, is rather a different sense, and means more 'distinct entry', which is 'article' used in a much older meaning, dating from at least as early as the fifteenth century.

articulate (speak clearly and distinctly)
The early sense of this verb was 'formulate in articles', so that in the sixteenth century it was possible to 'articulate one's objections' (set them forth as articles), or 'articulate all the examples' (list them individually with a brief commentary on each). This sense then gave way to the current one. However, when 'articulate' was formerly used without a grammatical object, it meant 'capitulate', and this is the sense in Shakespeare's *Coriolanus* (1607), where Cominius says:

> Send us to Rome
> The best, with whom we may articulate,
> For their own good and ours.

Here, 'articulate' really means 'draw up articles for a peace settlement'. The adjective 'articulate', meaning 'explaining one's ideas well and clearly' developed in about the eighteenth century from the basic sense, 'having meaningful sounds in speech', i.e. divided into meaningful words and syllables.

artifice (cunning)
As with **artful** (which see, above), 'artifice' originally had a favourable meaning, in this case 'workmanship', 'work of art'. From this sense in the sixteenth century, the word came to acquire its present debased usage, which was commonly established by the end of the eighteenth century.

artillery (guns collectively)
Before the word acquired its present sense, it meant simply 'munitions', 'implements of war', or 'ammunition' generally. It could even include musical instruments, as shown in Henry Machyn's *Diary* of 1550–63, where he writes of 'all maner of artelere as drumes, flutes, trumpetes, gones [i.e. guns]', etc. Later, the term came to embrace all kinds of arms and weapons, but settled to the 'big guns' sense from the sixteenth century. Clearly, however, this is not the sense in the Bible, where in I Samuel 20:40 we read that 'Jonathan gave his artillery unto his lad, and said unto him, Go, carry them to the city'! (The preceding verses make it obvious that the reference was to arrows.)

asbestos (type of incombustible fabric)
The word (from the Greek, literally 'unquenchable') was originally used in the fourteenth century in English to apply to a fabulous 'unquenchable' stone, that is, one that once lit or kindled could not be 'quenched' (as quicklime could be by having cold water poured on it). A text of 1398 thus describes a 'candyll sticke' made from it 'on whiche was a lantern so brennynge that it myght not be quenched wyth tempeste nother with reyne' (John de Trevisa, translation of Bartholomaeus Anglicus' *De proprietatibus rerum*). From the early seventeenth century, however, the word came to have its present meaning, when the fibrous mineral was also known as 'amiant' or 'amiantus' (literally 'undefilable').

ascertain (establish, find out)
For some time from the fifteenth century, 'ascertain' could also mean 'make certain'

(it is after all based on 'certain' and until the seventeenth century was even pronounced with the same stress as this word, i.e. on its second syllable). Hence we find in Caxton's *The Boke yf Eneydos* (1490, see **aquatic**, above): 'Whan he was adcerteyned of the dooynge of dydo and of Eneas'. The present meaning of the verb became established from the eighteenth century.

asphyxia (suffocation)
In its origin, the word comes from the Greek for 'without pulse' (as in the doctor's sphygmomanometer, that measures arterial blood pressure). And thus 'stoppage of the pulse' was the original meaning of 'asphyxia' in English in the eighteenth century, this being a serious state of 'swooning' that was regarded as close to death. Later in the same century the present sense of the word evolved, referring to a state of unconsciousness and possibly death caused by interruption of breathing (not stoppage of the pulse). In fact the current usage is therefore really a misnomer, since a person or animal can be asphyxiated (by a lack of oxygen in the blood) and yet have a pulse that continues to beat.

aspire (aim for something above one)
For some time from the sixteenth century, 'aspire' meant 'rise up', 'mount' in a literal sense, in which it appears to have been influenced by 'spire'. Thus in Shakespeare's *The Merry Wives of Windsor* (1598), Anne Page's song (as the Fairy Queen) in the final scene of the play contains the lines:

Fed in heart, whose flames aspire,
As thoughts do blow them higher and
    higher,

and a similar sense occurs in his *Romeo and Juliet* (1592), where Benvolio says to Romeo:

O Romeo, Romeo! brave Mercutio's
    dead;
That gallant spirit hath aspir'd the
    clouds,

meaning that it has soared up to them. Except in poetry, however, this meaning of 'aspire' is now obsolete.

assist (help)
An additional meaning of the verb from the

sixteenth century was 'stand near', 'attend' (compare modern French *assister à*), as in these lines from Richard Crashaw's poem *Sospetto d'Herode* (1649), translated from the Italian:

Three vigorous virgins, waiting still
    behind,
Assist the throne of th'iron-sceptred
    king.

In the seventeenth century, the meaning of 'assist' was also 'be present at' (even closer to the modern French just mentioned), and occurred in this sense as late as the nineteenth century in Thackeray and Dickens, with the latter using it somewhat self-consciously in *The Seven Poor Travellers* (1854): ' . . . and assisted – in the French sense – at the performance of two waltzes'. Similarly, 'assistance' meant 'persons present', with one curiously late use of this occurring in a text of 1881, where George Gilbert Scott, in *An Essay on the History of English Church Architecture*, writes of an altar being 'in full view of all the assistance'. Otherwise, all these former senses are now obsolete, and 'assist' means simply 'aid', 'help'.

astonish (amaze, surprise greatly)
The earliest sense of the verb, from the fifteenth century, was 'shock', 'dumbfound', and even 'stun', 'stupefy' in a literal sense, as in a sentence in Philemon Holland's translation (1600) of Livy, which tells how 'the one smote the king upon the head, the other astonished his shoulder'. The powerful 'shock' sense is similarly found in Shakespeare, where in *Julius Caesar* (1601) Casca says to Cassius:

It is the part of men to fear and tremble
When the most mighty gods by tokens
    send
Such dreadful heralds to astonish us.

Even in the Bible, the word has a stronger sense than it has today, as in Matthew 7:28: 'And it came to pass, when Jesus had ended these sayings, the people were astonished at his doctrine'. A similar development occurred with **astound** (see next entry).

astound (amaze, astonish)
As with **astonish** (see previous entry), the

verb formerly had a much stronger sense, often meaning 'shock' or 'stun', as in Edward Fairfax's translation (1600) of Tasso's *Godfrey of Bulloigne:*

> No weapon on his hard'ned helmet bit,
> No puissant stroke his senses once
>   astound.

Etymologically, 'astonish' and 'astound' are related.

astrology ('divination by the stars')
It is only in comparatively recent times that a distinction has been made between 'astronomy' (as the scientific study of the stars and heavenly bodies) and 'astrology'. The division was formerly into so called 'judicial astrology' (which is astrology in the modern sense) and 'natural astrology', which was concerned with the prediction of natural phenomena such as the timing of Easter and the phases of the moon, and so corresponded to modern 'astronomy'. The 'split' between the two kinds of star-lores occurred at about the end of the seventeenth century. 'Astronomy' was anyway a later word than 'astrology'.

astronomy (science of the stars and heavenly bodies)
As mentioned for **astrology** (see previous entry), there was formerly a considerable overlap between 'astronomy' and the other term, so that for some time from the fourteenth century 'astronomy' actually meant 'astrology', and even occurs in this sense in one of Shakespeare's *Sonnets* (1600), as can be clearly seen in these lines:

> Not from the stars do I my judgment
>   pluck;
> And yet methinks I have astronomy,
> But not to tell of good and evil luck,
> Of plagues, of dearths, or seasons'
>   quality.

From the end of the seventeenth century, as mentioned above, the two types of 'astro' studies came to be distinctly differentiated.

atlas (book of maps)
The origin of the familiar word is in that of the Titan god Atlas who was said to support the pillars of the universe. As a common noun, an 'atlas' was originally a 'supporter'

or 'mainstay', for this reason, with this sense in use in the sixteenth century. Even as late as 1883, in *Harper's Magazine,* a writer stated that 'we brokers are the Atlases that bear the world upon our shoulders', and doubtless there have been subsequent uses of the name in this sense. The meaning 'book of maps' for 'atlas' arose in the seventeenth century, and is said to derive from the fact that early editions of such works had had a frontispiece depicting the Titan Atlas supporting the heavens, as was his traditional role. The word first occurs with this meaning on the title page of an atlas published in 1636, which ran: 'Atlas; or a Geographic Description of the World, by Gerard Mercator and John Hondt'. Only five years later, Evelyn was recording in his *Diary* that he had been to 'the famous Hondius and Bleaw's shop' to buy 'some maps, atlasses, etc.'.

atone (make amends for)
The verb is derived from the noun 'atonement', which means what it says, i.e. 'at-one-ment'. Not surprisingly, therefore, the original sense of 'atone' was 'reconcile' (as making 'at one'), and this is what the verb means in Shakespeare's *Richard II* (1593), where Richard says to Bolingbroke, at the end of Act I:

> Since we cannot atone you, we shall see
> Justice design the victor's chivalry.

After this, the sense gradually shifted to 'appease' and finally to its current meaning of 'expiate', in which it is first recorded in the second half of the seventeenth century.

attic (small room under the roof of a house)
The name, in full 'attic storey', properly applied originally to the top storey of a classical building above the cornice (the line of brickwork or moulding running between the eaves), with 'Attic' referring to the order of architecture so designated, which had square columns or pillars instead of round ones. The term arose in the late seventeenth century. From the nineteenth century, 'attic' came to apply to any top floor of a house (an 'attic floor') or simply a room in it.

attire (dress)
The earliest meaning of the word, from the thirteenth century, was 'put in order' or 'equip', as of a horse for war, for example, or a knight with armour. From this developed the wider sense of simply 'dress', although the verb is now only used in a literary or poetic context (while the noun is rather more common, as in 'everyday attire', 'splendid attire').

authentic (genuine, not false)
In the fourteenth century, 'authentic' meant 'authoritative', applied to both things and people, as an 'authentic book' or an 'authentic writer'. In Shakespeare's *All's Well That Ends Well* (1601), where Lafeu speaks of 'all the learned and authentic fellows', the sense is more 'authorised', 'duly qualified'. From this developed the modern sense, which occasionally occurred considerably earlier, however, so that Chaucer, in saying 'So her stories be autentike' (*The Boke of the Duchesse*, 1369), uses the word as we would use it today.

autograph (person's signature)
The original meaning of the word, still in specialized use today, was 'author's own manuscript'. The term was current from the seventeenth century. Some hundred years later, the word acquired its present popular meaning. The literal sense is 'self-writing', from the Greek.

avenue (tree-lined road or street)
As its French origin indicates, the basic meaning of the word is 'approach' (*avenir*, 'to arrive', 'to approach'), and this was the sense in English in the early seventeenth century, both literally and figuratively (in his *Life*, published in 1672, Anthony Wood wrote that a Colonel Legge ' ... with the reere guarded the towne and avenews', showing the common military use of the word). The word seems to have acquired its present sense of 'tree-lined road' through Evelyn, who in his 'Advertisement' (which see) to *Sylva, or a Discourse of Forest-Trees* (1664), specifically defined the word as follows: 'That this may yet be no prejudice to the meaner capacities let them read for *avenue*, the principal walk to the front of the house, or seat'. From this 'drive' sense came the modern 'street' one.

aviator (aeroplane pilot)
When the word originally came into use in the late nineteenth century, it meant not only 'aeroplane pilot' (as distinct from an 'aeronaut', who was a balloonist), but even 'flying machine', 'aeroplane', for a time. Thus, the *Brooklyn Morning Journal* of 22 July 1891 reported that 'Mr. Maxim's invention is called an Aviator', describing the early machine as 'like a huge kite of silk, to which hangs a platform carrying the engines and the screw propellers'. By the early twentieth century, however, the term had become obsolete, and 'aeroplane' took over. (Compare **aerodrome**, for a similar false take-off.) Today, even in its 'pilot' sense, 'aviator' is an old-fashioned word, and has given way to alternative terms such as 'flier' and 'pilot' itself.

avoid (keep away from)
The word is directly linked to 'void', so it is understandable that its original meaning was 'empty', 'make void'. This sense was extended to mean 'withdraw', 'retire', as in a Coventry mystery play of the early fifteenth century, which has the line: 'Avoyd, seres, and lete my lorde the buschop come'. From all these now obsolete senses developed the current meaning, also found in Shakespeare.

awful (terrible)
This is one of the most commonly used debased words in English, today meaning little more than 'bad', 'undesirable' (an 'awful pain', an 'awful man'). Some purists, rather unrealistically, deplore this use, maintaining that the word properly means 'full of awe', as indeed it originally did. Shakespeare's *Henry VI*, Part 2 (1593), for example, has York saying to Somerset:

Thy hand is made to grasp a palmer's staff,
And not to grace an awful princely sceptre.

The adjective frequently occurs, too, in eighteenth-century poetry (Pope talks of Homer's 'awful head' and James Thomson writes of the 'awful listening gloom'). But the present meaning of 'terrible' was already well established in the nineteenth century, and those who now wish to restore the former sense should really resign themselves to finding some other way of expressing the powerful original.

awkward (clumsy, difficult)
The word came into English from Old Norse, where it meant 'turned the wrong way', and this is virtually what it also meant in English, so that in the *Morte Arthure* of 1400 we read that:

> The emperour thane egerly at Arthure
> he strykez,
> Awkwarde on the umbrere.

(This means that he struck him with a back stroke on the visor of his helmet.) From this, the word came to mean 'perverse', 'cantankerous', and finally 'clumsy' (of a person), 'difficult' (of a thing).

baffle (puzzle, foil)
The earliest examples we have of this word refer to its Scottish sense of 'disgrace', with specific application to a perjured knight. This is best seen in Spenser's *The Faerie Queene* (1596), where:

> He by the heels him hung upon a tree,
> And bafful'd so, that all which passed
> by
> The picture of his punishment might see.

An unpleasant and disgraceful punishment indeed. It is possible, however, that this is a different word from the one we know in English today, which originally meant 'hoodwink' in the sixteenth century, as somewhat later in Milton's *Eikonoklastes* (1649), where he writes that 'the Scots would not be baffl'd with the pretence of a Coronation Oath'. From this, the sense of 'foil the plans of' developed, leading in turn to the much watered-down modern meaning 'puzzled', 'mystified'.

balderdash (nonsense, gibberish, rubbish)
In the sixteenth century, the word had a more concrete sense, 'froth', although admittedly this meaning appears to occur only in the writings of Thomas Nash, who in his burlesque *Lenten Stuffe* (1599), for example, tells of people who did not wish to 'have their heads washed with this bubbly spume or barbers balderdash'. A century later, the meaning had extended to refer to a mixture of drinks (e.g. milk and beer, beer and wine, or brandy and mineral water, in ascending order of palatability). The modern sense of the word then developed from this, to mean 'jumble of words' (like the mixed drinks) and so 'nonsense'. The precise origin of the colourful word is still unknown.

balk (hinder, frustrate)
A 'balk' was originally a ridge, and the verb 'balk' thus meant 'plough up in ridges'. This fourteenth-century sense then sidestepped, as it were, to mean 'pass by', 'miss out' in both a literal and a figurative sense, with this in turn leading to the modern meaning 'hinder', 'frustrate', the basic idea being that a person has been faced with a 'balk' or obstacle and must find some other way round or out.

balloon (light round bag filled with air or gas)
The word is Italian in origin, meaning literally 'big ball', and in English in the sixteenth century a 'balloon' was a large leather ball used in a game of the same name ('ballone') in which it was hit to and fro using either the hand or the whole arm. In the eighteenth century, the word came to designate the first of the great balloons in which early pioneers such as the Montgolfier brothers made their ascents. The child's toy balloon followed in the mid-nineteenth century.

banal (trite, commonplace)
In the eighteenth century, the word had a narrow legal sense, 'belonging to compul-

sory feudal service', and derived from a now obsolete noun 'ban' meaning 'proclamation', 'body of vassals summoned together'. (This old sense still survives in the 'banns' of marriage.) From this, the sense 'open to all' developed, with this finally giving the modern meaning of 'common', 'trite'.

bane (cause of worry, nuisance)
The original sense of 'bane' was 'murderer', from Old English times down to Shakespeare and even later. In *Titus Andronicus* (1588), for example, Marcus Andronicus speaks of Rome being 'bane unto herself'. From this, the sense 'poison' developed from the fourteenth century, and this survives in the names of various poisonous plants such as 'fleabane', 'henbane', 'ratsbane' and 'wolfsbane', implying that the respective plants could kill the creatures mentioned. The subsequent sense development was 'murder', 'destruction', 'disturbance', 'annoyance', a gradual weakening of the original.

bank (establishment for dealing in money)
In the fifteenth century, a 'bank' was simply the counter or shop of a money changer, showing the basic origin of the word in the related 'bench'. The next sense to develop was that of 'stock of money', still surviving in the 'bank' that is the stock of funds (whether money or chips) held by a banker or dealer in a gambling house or casino. This was in the sixteenth century. A hundred years later, the present meaning of the word was current, and was formally established with the foundation of the 'Bank of England' in 1694.

banquet (feast, formal meal)
The word had its present sense as early as the fifteenth century, so that Caxton in *The Golden Legend* (which he published in 1483), tells how a knight 'bayned [i.e. bathed] and made bankettis in etyng and drynkyng'. However, for a while the term seems to have been used to mean 'slight repast between meals', 'snack', or just the opposite of the modern concept of a banquet. This was also known as a 'running banquet' (as if a forerunner of the present 'running buffet'), and is referred to (figuratively) in Shakespeare's rarely read play *Henry VIII* (1613), where

the Porter talks of a whipping as 'the running banquet of two beadles that is to come'. A more specific description of the meal is given in Tobias Venner's *Via Recta ad Vitam Longam; also the true use of our famous Bathes at Bath* (1620), where he mentions 'banquets betweene meales, when the stomache is empty'. Possibly this 'diminutive' meaning comes from the fact that French *banquet* literally means 'little bench', as does the corresponding Italian *banchetto*. This particular meaning of 'banquet' soon became obsolete, however.

barbecue (outdoor meal or party at which roast meat is traditionally served)
The term itself originated in a native Haitian word used of a framework of sticks on posts where people could sleep or on which an animal such as a sheep could be roasted. This was the original meaning in English, and was what the traveller and explorer William Dampier was referring to in his *Voyages and Descriptions* (1699) when he reported: '. . .and lay there all night, upon our Borbecu's, or frames of sticks, raised about 3 foot from the Ground'. The word then came to apply to the animal, whatever it was, that was roasted, and finally in the early nineteenth century, and on American ground, the modern barbecue was born, with one of the first references to it in Washington Irving's *History of New York, by Diedrich Knickerbocker* (1809), where he writes: 'Engaged in a great "barbecue", a kind of festivity or carouse much practised in Merryland'. (However, an even earlier reference appears to have been made in the *Diary* of the American chief justice Benjamin Lynde, written in 1733, where he reports: 'Fair and hot; Browne, barbacue; hack overset'.)

baronet (title of nobility below rank of baron)
The present title of baronet was instituted in 1611. Before this, the word was used to mean simply 'lesser baron', 'little baron', and was applied to the gentlemen who, although not actually barons, were summoned to the House of Lords by Edward III. (In Ireland, however, a 'baronet' was originally the holder of a small barony.) After the 'Baronets of England'

(now 'of Great Britain') were instituted in 1611, the 'Baronets of Scotland' followed in 1625, and the 'Baronets of Ireland' in 1619.

barrow (type of cart on wheels)
A 'barrow' was originally simply a frame on which a load was carried, and this in early times included a stretcher and a bier. Thus, what in the Authorized Version of the Bible (1611) is called 'beds and couches' (Acts 5:15), in Miles Coverdale's Bible of 1535 is 'beddes and barowes'. But somewhat earlier than this, the word 'barrow' had come to be popularly restricted to the sense 'wheelbarrow' (from the fourteenth century) and later also 'handbarrow' (from the fifteenth). The word is itself related directly to 'bier'.

bask (lie in heat, especially that of the sun)
In the fourteenth century, the verb meant 'bathe in blood', which makes such works as John Lydgate's *Troy Book* (1412–20) read rather oddly in such phrases as 'seynge his brother baskynge in his bloud'. The earliest modern use of the word is recorded, as often the case, in Shakespeare, where in *As You Like It* (1600) Jaques tells how he met 'a fool in the forest' [i.e. Touchstone]:

> Who laid him down and bask'd him in the sun.

batch (group or set of things)
The word literally means 'baking', and originally referred to the quantity of bread produced at one baking. The sense then developed to mean 'quantity of flour or dough to be used at one baking' and finally, in the nineteenth century, 'quantity of things coming at the same time', 'instalment'. The 'baking' sense dates from the fifteenth century.

battery (device for producing an electric current)
The word has undergone various changes of meaning in order to arrive at the current sense. Originally, in the sixteenth century, it meant 'beating', as it still does in the legal sense of 'assault and battery'. At about the same time, it also came to mean 'battering', especially by artillery. From this, the word came to apply to the guns themselves, so that there were 'horse batteries', 'field batteries' and 'garrison batteries', for example. Such batteries, of course, discharged shells, and this 'discharge' is the semantic link that led to the word's adoption for the series of cells that, when interconnected, 'discharged' electricity, such basic batteries evolving out of the Leyden jars of the eighteenth century. One of the earliest records of the word in its present sense comes in a letter written in 1748 by the American statesman and scientist Benjamin Franklin, who told of 'an electrical battery, consisting of eleven panes of large sash-glass, armed with thin leaden plates'. In more recent times, 'battery' has come to be used for series or connected sets of other kinds, notably the cages and nesting boxes of 'battery' hens, which first appeared in the 1930s.

bawl (cry loudly, shout raucously)
Oddly enough, when the word first appeared in English in the fifteenth century, it meant 'bark', 'howl' (of a dog), so that Robert Burton, in his *Anatomy of Melancholy* (1621) wrote of 'a barking dog that always bawls, but seldome bites'. The 'human' sense developed almost simultaneously, however, and the verb occurs in Shakespeare's *Henry IV*, Part 2 (1597), where the Prince of Wales says to Poins: 'God knows whether those that bawl out the ruins of thy linen shall inherit his kingdom [i.e. his father's]'.

bayonet (stabbing weapon fixed to the end of a rifle)
The word also applied originally to a short dagger, and is so described (under the French word *Bayonnette*) in Randle Cotgrave's *A Dictionarie of the French and English Tongues* (1611): 'a kind of small flat pocket-dagger, furnished with kniues; or a great knife to hang at the girdle, like a dagger'. The name was used in English in this sense before being applied to the rifle-attached blade some hundred years later. The word itself apparently comes from the French city of Bayonne, where bayonets were originally manufactured or used.

beach (seashore)
The word originally meant just 'shingle', 'pebbles', and was a dialect term in use for

stretches of the coast in Sussex and Kent. Subsequently, the word extended its meaning to have the sense 'seashore' on the whole, although it is not quite clear when this transference occurred. The word 'beach' comes several times in Shakespeare, and even there it could mean either 'shingle' or 'shore'. For example, in *The Merchant of Venice* (1595), Antonio says:

You may as well go stand upon the beach,
And bid the main flood bate his usual height,

and in *King Lear* (1605), Edgar mentions

The fishermen that walk upon the beach,

while in *Coriolanus* (1608), Coriolanus says to his mother Volumnia:

Then let the pebbles on the hungry beach
Fillip the stars.

The first two of these appear to refer specifically to 'shingle' rather than the seashore as a whole. The word is still used locally in the 'shingle' sense in the counties mentioned, although Beachy Head has nothing to do with 'beach' but derives its name from the French for 'beautiful headland' (*beau chef*).

beacon (signal fire, light)
In Old English, 'beacon' meant just 'sign', 'standard', with no suggestion of a fire or signal light. This latter sense developed in the fourteenth century, while some hundred years later the word came to be used as the name of certain hills on which signal fires had been lit, or on which they could be lit, such as the Brecon Beacons, Dunkery Beacon on Exmoor, and so on.

bead (ornamental object on a chain or necklace)
The sense change of this word is quite dramatic. It originally meant 'prayer' (related to modern 'bid'), and lasted in this sense for several centuries, even occurring in a text as late as 1556: 'Went unto the crosse, & stode there alle the tyme, & whan he came unto the beddes they turnyd unto the precher & knelyd downe' (*Chronicle of the Grey Friars of London*). From this meaning,

the word was transferred to the rosaries on which 'telling beads' or saying prayers could be carried out, and from about the mid-sixteenth century 'beads' almost always refers to rosaries. From there, the transition to the ornamental beads on necklaces and the like was natural. (See also **rosary**.)

beadle (former minor parish official)
A 'beadle' (related to 'bid') was originally a herald or crier, and the words that appear as 'Then an herald cried aloud' in the Authorized Version of the Bible (1611) occur in Miles Coverdale's translation of 1535 as 'The bedell cried out with all his might' (Daniel 3:4). The word then came to be used in the sense 'messenger' before it acquired its settled meaning of 'parish constable', 'university official' and the like. All uses of the term however, have been recorded as early as the fourteenth century.

beaker (drinking glass, mug)
In the fourteenth century, 'beaker' was used as a word for a type of open goblet, especially a silver one. Only in the nineteenth century did the word acquire its modern meaning, which also includes the glass vessel used in scientific experiments.

beam (plank, long piece of heavy timber used in building)
The word had a basic sense 'tree' in Old English (compare modern German *Baum* and the names of such trees as 'hornbeam' and 'whitebeam'). The sense 'piece of timber used in building ships and houses', however, developed early, at least as long ago as the tenth century, and has survived since then in its original meaning.

beast (wild animal)
Originally, the general word for 'animal' in English was '**deer**' (which see). This was displaced by 'beast' (from Old French) in the thirteenth century, and was itself displaced by '**animal**' (which also see) some hundred years later. Hence the common occurrence of 'beast' in medieval texts and in the Bible (where it translated Greek *zōion* or Latin *animal*), for example in Revelation 4:6, with its 'four beasts full of eyes before and behind'. Even as late as the seventeenth century, the word was used where today we

would probably use 'animal', as in this text of 1691: 'Animate bodies are divided into four great genera or orders: Beasts, Birds, Fishes, and Insects' (John Ray, *The Wisdom of God Manifested in the Works of the Creation*). From the fifteenth century, the word had also acquired the sense 'human being like an animal', with one of the first indirect usages found in Shakespeare's *Merry Wives of Windsor* (1598), where Falstaff says: 'O powerful love! that, in some respects, makes a beast a man; in some other, a man a beast'.

become (come to be)
In Old English, 'become' meant simply 'come', 'arrive', a sense that was preserved by some writers as late as the seventeenth century, for example Bacon in his *Essays*, published in their final form in 1625, where he writes of 'Houses so full of Glasse, that one cannot tell, where to become, to be out of the Sunne'. This use is no longer found, however.

bedlam (uproar, chaos)
The word is an early spelling of 'Bethlehem', the biblical town in Judaea. In the sixteenth century, the name was used for an inmate of Bethlehem Hospital in London, a lunatic asylum (or mental hospital, as we would now say) whose full name was the Hospital of St Mary of Bethlehem, and which had originally been founded in 1247 as a priory for the 'entertainment' of the bishop and canons of the church of St Mary at Bethlehem, whenever they chanced to be in England. From the seventeenth century, a 'bedlam' was a term used of any such 'madhouse', and from about the same time the word came to apply to any scene of 'madness' or noisy disorder. Shakespeare uses 'bedlam' in the sense 'mad' in *Henry VI*, Part 2 (1592), where the Duke of Suffolk refers to Eleanor, Duchess of Gloucester, as 'the bedlam brain-sick duchess'.

bedstead (frame on which a bed is made)
Strictly speaking, a 'bedstead' is a place where a bed stands, and this was the original sense in English. The old, 'proper' sense occurs in Miles Coverdale's translation of the Bible (1535), where Song of Solomon 3:7 appears as: 'Aboute Salomons bedsteade there stonde LX. valeaunt men' (Authorized Version of 1611: 'Behold his bed, which is Solomon's; threescore valiant men are about it'). The modern, current sense itself appears in the Authorized Version, in Deuteronomy 3:11, where we are told of Og, king of Bashan, that 'his bedstead was a bedstead of iron'.

belfry (belltower)
The name of the building is actually misleading, since it originated not in 'bell' but in a Germanic word meaning 'defensive place' (compare modern German *Bergfried*, 'watch tower'). The earliest sense of the English word was thus 'siege tower', especially a movable one, and the term is found in fourteenth- and fifteenth-century texts with this meaning. The word came to be associated with 'bell', however, if only because a siege tower or watch tower came to have an alarm bell that could be sounded, and from this developed the modern sense, to denote a building that was part of a church, whether physically attached to it or not. The modern sense dates from the fifteenth century, and a hundred years later 'belfry' also came to be used of the actual bell chamber.

belly (stomach)
The modern meaning of the word dates from about the fourteenth century. Before this, 'belly' meant 'bag' or 'bellows' (to which latter word it is directly related). In Old English, thus, and allowing for the alteration in spelling (here modernized), a 'beanpod' was a 'bean belly', 'bellows' was a 'blast belly', and a 'wineskin' was a 'wine belly'. For a time from the thirteenth century, 'belly' meant 'body' in general.

benedicite (title of a hymn of praise to God)
The word, usually with a capital letter, is today normally regarded as the name of the church canticle or hymn that in Latin began with the words 'Benedicite omnia opera Domini Domino' and that is translated in English as 'O all ye works of the Lord, bless ye the Lord'. Originally, however, the word was simply an interjection meaning 'bless us!' or 'bless you!' (similarly from the

Latin), and it is used in this sense in Shakespeare's *Measure for Measure* (1603), where Vincentio, the Duke (disguised as a friar), bids farewell to Juliet with the words:

God's grace go with you! *Benedicite!*

This is a late use, however, and some time before this the word had also come to mean simply 'blessing', 'deliverance', in particular a blessing before food or 'grace', as in this example of 1225 in the *Ancren Riwle* or 'Rule of Nuns', where the blessing itself is given: 'Bitweone mete, hwo se drinken wule, sigge benedicite: potum nostrum filius Dei benedicat'. (That is: In between meals, whoever wishes to drink must say the blessing: 'May the Son of God bless our drink'.)

benefit (advantage, welfare, financial assistance)
As the Latin origin of the word suggests, the basic meaning is 'good deed' (*benefactum*), and this was what 'benefit' meant in English in the fourteenth century. Thus the phrase that occurs in the Authorized Version of the Bible (1611) as 'in that he did good' (Acts 14:17), occurs in Tindale's Bible (1526) as 'in that he shewed his benefaictes'. From the fifteenth century, the modern sense of 'advantage' began to develop, with the modern 'financial' use of the word, as in 'sickness benefit', occurring first in the late nineteenth century (initially in the wording of an act of 1875 relating to friendly societies).

bereave (deprive of by death)
The original sense of the word was rather different, meaning 'rob', 'strip', 'dispossess', with something of the former connotation in modern 'bereft' (as in 'He was bereft of all his property' or even 'bereft of speech'). From about the middle of the seventeenth century, 'bereave' has been chiefly confined to the loss of a person by death, and even 'bereft' has been limited to immaterial possessions such as 'life' and 'hope'.

berth (sleeping place on ship or train)
In its original seventeenth-century sense, 'berth' meant 'sea room', as in the still current expression 'give a wide berth to'. (The word is probably related to 'bear'.) Subsequently, the 'sleeping place' sense developed, first on ships, then on trains (but not on planes, since on the whole air passengers sleep where they sit, not in a separate bunk or bed).

bicker (quarrel)
In the thirteenth century, the verb meant 'fight', 'skirmish', as in this text of 1330: 'Than is tyme to bikere with the kyng of France' (Robert Manning of Brunne, *The Story of England*). From this physical fighting, the sense soon transferred to a verbal skirmishing, and the former use of the word became obsolete.

big (large)
As used in the thirteenth century, 'big' meant 'strong', 'stout', with the word apparently originating in the north of England. This sense of the word more or less survives in such phrases as 'big strong fellow' and 'big boy'. The early meaning survived down to Shakespeare's time, and even retains its connotation in his *Henry V* (1599), when Grandpré refers to 'Big Mars'. The adjective could be used of things in the 'strong' sense, too, so that fifteenth-century texts talk of a 'big' battle or a 'big' wind. The precise origin of the word is unknown.

bigot (person obstinately devoted to his religion)
Before it acquired its present sense in the seventeenth century, the word was used to apply to a hypocritical or superstitious professor of religion. The sense then widened to include any religious person, and today is sometimes used without any specific reference to religion.

bill (statement of charges or costs)
The word has been through a number of meanings since it first appeared in the fourteenth century. Its original sense was simply 'written document', either a general one or a legal statement of some kind. This is reflected in the more modern sense (of the sixteenth century) that means 'act of parliament'. The 'statement of charges' sense arose in the fifteenth century, as did the one that means 'poster', today more common in America. Most of the original meanings, however, are now obsolete, as is the fourteenth-century one of 'list' or 'catalogue',

although even this in a sense survives in such expressions as 'bill of fare'. The 'list' sense occurs in Shakespeare's *Macbeth* (1605), when Macbeth addresses the Murderers ('in the catalogue ye go for men') and talks of the 'bill' that lists the different characteristic of dogs.

bird (winged creature)

This was the word that came to supersede 'fowl' as the general term for the creature, so that in Old English (where 'fowl' was 'bird') it was restricted to the sense 'young bird', whether overall or of a specific kind, as 'chick', 'eaglet' and so on. This meaning was retained in various literary works down to about 1600, so that this is the sense in Shakespeare's *Henry VI, Part 3* (1593), where Richard says to Edward:

> Nay, if thou be that princely eagle's bird
> [i.e. the Duke of York's son],
> Show thy descent by gazing 'gainst the sun.

The sense of 'bird' to mean 'young woman', incidentally, arose as early as the thirteenth century, much earlier than the twentieth-century American 'chick' (although this itself meant 'child' equally early). It is thus odd to come across a reference to the Virgin Mary, in the long anonymous poem of the early fourteenth century known as the *Cursor Mundi*, as 'that blisful bird of grace'. See also **fowl** itself.

bitter (not sweet)

The sense development of this word was first 'biting', 'cutting', then 'cruel', 'harsh', then finally 'not sweet' (i.e. 'biting' to the taste or tongue). All these meanings are still current, so that a 'bitter' remark can be a 'biting' or 'cutting' one, a 'bitter' loss can be a 'cruel' one (and a 'bitter' person can be wounding), and the popular sense of the taste 'bitter' is used as a virtual opposite to 'sweet'. Most senses have existed from at least the twelfth century, although a 'bitter' wind or the like first occurs in Shakespeare's *As You Like It* (1600), where the second verse of Amiens' song begins:

> Freeze, freeze, thou bitter sky.

bivouac (camp without tents)

The word is of German origin, meaning literally a 'by-watch', and this was its original sense in English, to apply to an armed night watch. From this the modern sense arose of 'temporary camp without tents'. The original meaning is found only in dictionaries, the earliest being that of Edward Phillips published (in its sixth edition) in 1706, where 'bivouac' is defined as 'an extraordinary Guard perform'd by the whole Army, when [...] it [...] continues all night under Arms'. However, although the absence of tents was (and is) a characteristic of the bivouac proper, some such encampments did have tents, and indeed from the time of the First World War 'bivvy' came to be a soldier's slang word for a small tent.

blackguard (rogue, rascal)

The precise origin of the word is still unknown, although the term itself has changed its meaning somewhat over the years. In the sixteenth century, a 'blackguard' was a band of 'low' camp followers. A hundred years later, the word was used of a body of criminals or vagrants. Both these senses became obsolete, however, and the word came to apply to an individual 'rogue' rather than a group. Even so, the term occurs in sixteenth-century texts to mean, fairly innocuously, simply 'man dressed in black' or even 'bootblack', especially a 'shoeshine boy' (who admittedly might not be as innocent and honest as he seemed). In the early eighteenth century, Dean Swift has some lines about

> The little black-guard
> Who gets very hard
> His half-pence for cleaning your shoes.

blackleg (strikebreaker, 'scab')

The origin of the term is as mysterious as that of **blackguard** (see previous entry). Before it came to mean 'strikebreaker', however, 'blackleg' meant 'turf swindler', 'one who swindles in gambling'. This usage, now obsolete, was current in the eighteenth and early nineteenth century, and even the 'strikebreaker' sense has in recent years been transferred almost entirely from 'blackleg' to 'scab'.

blackmail (money or payment obtained by extortion or threat; general intimidation)
In the sixteenth century, 'blackmail' was the term used for payment ('tribute') extorted in Scotland and the English-Scottish Borderland by freebooting chiefs in return for protection. Only in the nineteenth century did the general sense of 'payment extorted by threat' appear. In more recent times, too, the term has not even necessarily involved money, but has usually implied a situation on the lines of 'You do that (or you stop doing that), or I will reveal what I know about you'.

blancmange (type of dessert made from cornflour and milk)
The blancmange is not what it was! Originally, in its prime, it was a semi-savoury dish, consisting of finely chopped or minced chicken or other meat, mixed with cream, rice, eggs, sugar, nuts and the like. This was in the fourteenth century. ('Medieval banquet' promoters, please copy.) The word comes from French, of course, where it literally means 'white food'. Chaucer mentions a blancmange of this kind in his *Canterbury Tales* (1386). The present entirely sweet dish seems to have evolved some time in the sixteenth century, perhaps as a result of being a recommended food for babies and young children.

blank (empty; expressionless)
It is not difficult to see that the word originated in French *blanc*, 'white', and this was the original meaning in English. The sense is now obsolete but was retained by some poets such as Milton and James Thomson as late as the seventeenth and eighteenth centuries (they both wrote of a 'blank' moon). The sense defined by Johnson in his *Dictionary* (1755) as 'empty of all marks' (of paper and the like) was current from the sixteenth century, and is in Shakespeare.

blatant (obvious)
The word was first used by Spenser in *The Faerie Queene* (1596), where it described the monster of a thousand tongues that was produced by Cerberus and Chimaera and that symbolized calumny:

Unto themselves they gotten had

A monster which the blatant beast men call,
A dreadful feend of gods and men ydrad [i.e. dreaded].

It is not quite clear how he derived or devised the word: perhaps it was based on a 'chattering' word such as modern 'bleat', 'blather' or the like. The original 'noisy' sense is now quite absent from the word, however, and 'blatant' today often means merely 'openly offensive', such as a 'blatant' lie, or a 'blatant' exaggeration.

blink (momentarily close the eyes)
In modern use, the word usually implies closing of the eyes, and therefore failing to see or notice. Shakespeare used the verb in the opposite sense, however, meaning 'take a peep', 'have a look', as in *A Midsummer Night's Dream* (1590), where in the 'Pyramus and Thisbe' scene in the last act, Pyramus says to Wall:

Thou wall, O wall! O sweet, and lovely wall!
Show me thy chink to blink through with mine eyne [i.e. eyes].

The noun had a similar sense, and perhaps still survives in such phrases as 'a blink of bright flame' and the Scottish 'blink' that means 'glance'. On the whole, however, 'blink' today means 'conceal' rather than 'reveal' when it concerns any kind of physical or mental 'brightness'. Compare **wink**.

blizzard (severe snowstorm)
The word is a surprisingly recent one, and when it originally appeared in America in the first half of the nineteenth century was used to mean 'sharp blow', 'knock'. By the middle of the century, however, the present sense was in use, and this is the prevalent one today. The origin of the word is unknown, although there is a strong suggestion (for both meanings) of 'blast' or some other 'blowing' word.

blouse (woman's garment resembling a shirt or smock)
As originally understood in English in the nineteenth century, a 'blouse' was a man's shirt or 'smock-frock' that answered to the

typical blue smock of the French workman. From about 1870, however, the garment was appropriated by women as a kind of fashionable 'tunic' (as many male garments have been), and it has remained in the female fashion world virtually ever since.

blubber (fat of whales)
The original meaning of the word was 'foam', 'bubble', with this sense recorded in the fourteenth century. The modern meaning of 'whale fat' developed only in the seventeenth century, when whaling had been established in earnest. However, the verb 'blubber', meaning 'weep copiously', has been in use also from the fourteenth century (originally in tales of heartbroken lovers).

bluff (rough and hearty)
In the seventeenth century, the word was used to describe an object that was nearly vertical or perpendicular, such as the bows of a ship or a coastline (hence the 'bluff' that is a cliff or headland). In the eighteenth century, the word came to be used of a person to mean 'blunt', or what Johnson in his *Dictionary* (1755) initially defined as 'Big, surly, blustering'. Perhaps as a result of the generally favourable nickname 'Bluff King Hal' given to Henry VIII, the overall meaning of 'bluff' was toned down to mean 'genially hearty', 'roughly good-natured', and this is the sense the word has today, where it is used. (The other 'bluff', meaning 'pretend to be stronger or cleverer' is not related to this one.)

blunt (not sharp; forthright in speech)
Both senses given here developed from the original sense of 'dull', 'stupid', as used in the twelfth century, and as found subsequently in Chaucer, Spenser and Shakespeare. The 'not sharp' sense arose in the fourteenth century, and the 'abrupt in speech' development followed in the late sixteenth, where Shakespeare, as often, was one of the first to use it.

boast (speak with excessive pride)
The original noun 'boast' in thirteenth-century English meant simply 'loud voice', 'outcry', as in the medieval text of *Kyng Alisaunder* (1300):

Now ariseth cry and boost
Among Alisaunders oost [i.e. host]
Of scorpiouns and addres.

Later, both noun and verb meant 'threat' ('threaten'), as in *The Historie and Life of James the Sext* (1582–8), which tells how he 'was boistit with toirtour unles he should tell'. This 'threat' sense continued in the Scottish use of the word until about the eighteenth century, although meantime at some stage in standard English the present meaning of 'speak too proudly' had developed.

bodice (part of dress above waist)
The garment (or part-garment) was originally called a 'pair of bodies' in the seventeenth century, when it was in effect a 'pair of stays'. However, 'bodies' was also the term for the upper part of a dress, and this is the sense that has remained today, where a 'bodice' is still in fashion, that is.

bodkin (type of blunt needle for drawing tape through a loop etc)
Bodkins are today about as fashionable as **bodices** (see previous entry), but the word itself has undergone a number of sense changes since it first appeared in the fourteenth century. Originally 'bodkin' was a kind of dagger, and this is the meaning of the word in Chaucer, Miles Coverdale's Bible (1535), and Shakespeare's *Hamlet* (1602), where it occurs in Hamlet's famous 'To be or not to be' speech:

When he himself might his quietus make
With a bare bodkin?

The next sense of 'bodkin' was to denote the small pointed instrument that was used for piercing holes in cloth and the like. This applied in the sixteenth and early seventeenth century. From the late sixteenth century, a 'bodkin' was the word for the long pin or pin-shaped ornament with which women fastened up their hair. Appropriately, the word occurs in Pope's *Rape of the Lock* (1714):

Then in a bodkin grac'd her mother's hairs,

and the most recent sense of the word, to mean a needle for drawing tape, also occurs in this same work, which is the earliest record we have of it:

Wedg'd whole ages in a bodkin's eye.

Bohemian (artistically unconventional)
Obviously, the basic (and earliest) sense of the word is the one that means 'native of Bohemia', and this occurs in Shakespeare's *Measure for Measure* (1603), for example. From the late seventeenth century, the word meant 'gypsy', based on the French word for 'gypsy' which was (and still is) *bohémien*, the theory being that gypsies were supposed to have arrived in western Europe from Bohemia. The most recent sense of 'social gypsy', or 'unconventional in manner or dress', especially of a writer or artist, appeared in the mid-nineteenth century, when the word was in fact introduced with this meaning by Thackeray in *Vanity Fair* (1848). In this work he describes the main character, Becky Sharp, as 'of a wild, roving nature, inherited from father and mother, who were both Bohemians, by taste and circumstances'. The term is now rather dated, especially since the emergence of equally colourful characters and lifestyles in the 'counterculture' movement of the 1960s, and indeed most true Bohemians of the original sort died out before the First World War.

boisterous (high-spirited and rowdy)
The original meaning of the word, when it first appeared in the sixteenth century, was 'stout', 'stiff' or 'bulky', and it was applied to such diverse objects as ship's cables and clothing. A text of 1586 even applies it to the human body:

About his boistrous necke full oft their daintie armes they cast

(William Warner, *Albion's England*). This sense was virtually obsolete by the end of the seventeenth century, and the 'rough' meaning prevailed. The origin of the word is unknown.

bolt (bar or rod used for fastening a door)
The original sense of the word, in Old English, was 'stout arrow', and a 'bolt' was the missile discharged from a crossbow, when it was also known as a 'quarrel'. As

such, it features in Chaucer and contemporary fourteenth-century writers, and also occurs in later historical novels, such as those by Scott ('Look that the cross-bowmen lack not bolts' is a remark made in *Ivanhoe*, 1819). This particular bolt is also the origin of the proverb 'A fool's bolt is soon shot' and indirectly of the still common phrase 'a bolt from the blue'. The present meaning of 'bolt' as the fastening for a door or other closure (e.g. that of a rifle breech) dates from about 1400, while the later 'nuts and bolts' sense emerged in the seventeenth century with the development of ship-building. All the current verbs 'bolt' ultimately derive from one or other of the two main senses, 'missile' and 'fastening', especially the former, which gave the different 'rapid movement' meanings, such as 'the horse bolted' and 'he bolted his food'.

bomb (explosive or incendiary device, typically one dropped from the air)
A 'bomb' (originally pronounced 'bum') began its life in the seventeenth century as a type of explosive shell fired from a mortar, and in his *Memoirs* (1687) Evelyn feelingly tells how 'I saw a trial of those devilish, murdering, mischief-doing engines called bombs, shot out of the mortar-piece on Blackheath'. This sense continued virtually down to the First World War, when bombs were up-dated and were first dropped from aircraft on a wide scale. (Originally bombs were 'thrown' from aircraft, as *The Times* reported in its issue for 9 October 1915: 'A German aeroplane flew over the outskirts of Paris early this morning and threw several bombs'). Subsequent bombs have become even more sophisticated and 'murdering', notably 'the' bomb or atom bomb.

bombardier (non-commissioned officer in the British artillery)
In the sixteenth century, a 'bombardier' was simply an artilleryman, who 'bombarded' with his 'bombard'. The rank of bombardier first appeared in the British army in the mid-nineteenth century, and in the United States the sense of 'bomb-aimer' in an aircraft for 'bombardier' first appeared after the First World War.

bombast (pretentious speech or writing)
The original sense of the word was 'cotton wool', especially as used for padding for clothes, and this usage was common in the sixteenth century. Almost simultaneously, the current sense of 'turgid talk' began to develop, and is first recorded in a text of 1589: 'To out-brave better pens with the swelling bumbast of a bragging blanke verse' (Thomas Nashe, quoted in Robert Greene's *Menaphon*). The word does not derive, as has been sometimes supposed, from the middle name of Paracelsus, who was really (and splendidly) Philippus Aureolus Theophrastus Bombastus von Hohenheim, but ultimately comes from Latin *bombyx*, 'silk'.

bonfire (large outdoor fire, usually one for burning rubbish)
In the fourteenth century, a 'bonfire' was what its name implies, a 'fire of bones', that is, a public fire where animal bones were burnt. Somewhat later, the word came to apply to a funeral pyre, or a fire on which heretics or banned books were burnt. But almost at the same time, a 'bonfire' could be a large ceremonial 'festival' fire, much as a 'Bonfire Night' one is now on 5 November, although even these would have been 'bone fires' in the proper sense in medieval times. In fact, the 'Guy Fawkes' bonfire interestingly combines just about all the different types of fire, since it is both a 'festival' fire and, commemoratively, a 'heretic' or at least a 'traitorous' one. At the same time it can be purely utilitarian, and burn up unwanted rubbish much as a regular garden bonfire can. This history of the word thus shows its true origin, which is therefore not from French *bon*, 'good', as Dr Johnson thought it was in his *Dictionary* (1755), and as some people still think it is.

bonkers (eccentric, mad, 'batty')
The slang word first emerged in the sense 'slightly tipsy' in the early twentieth century, and is so recorded in this sense in Eric Partridge's *A Dictionary of Forces' Slang* (1984), where he suggests it might have originated in a blow on the head, or 'bonk' on the 'bonce'. By the mid-twentieth century, however, the sense 'crazy' prevailed.

book (printed volume)
The very earliest sense of the word, in Old English, was simply 'written document', and this survives in some quite late usages, for example in Shakespeare's *Henry IV*, Part 1 (1596), where Mortimer says to Glendower of Lady Glendower:

> With all my heart I'll sit and hear her sing;
> By that time will our book, I think, be drawn.

In the Bible, too, the phrase 'the book of the purchase' in Jeremiah 32:12 (in the Authorized Version of 1611) was altered to 'the deed of the purchase' in the Revised Version of 1885, showing that 'book' was not the word as currently understood. But the modern meaning 'volume containing a literary or other work' also dates from Old English times, even though medieval books were not the sophisticated printed products we know today.

boon (blessing, benefit)
When the word began its career in the twelfth century, it meant 'prayer', 'request', so that a text of 1175 has the words 'Ah lauerd god, her ure bone', i.e. 'O Lord God, hear our prayer' (*Lambeth Homilies*). From this now obsolete use, the meaning 'thing prayed for', 'favour' developed, leading finally to the modern, more general sense. The word itself is of Old Norse origin, and is not related to French *bon*.

boor (coarse or ill-bred person)
In the fifteenth century, the word meant 'husbandman', from Dutch *boer* (as in the much later Boer War), and it comes in this sense in Shakespeare's *The Winter's Tale* (1611), where the Clown says to the Shepherd (in Act V): 'Let boors and franklins say it, I'll swear it' (i.e. 'Let peasants and yeomen say it'). From the sixteenth century, the word came to be applied specifically to a Dutch or German peasant, and at about the same time acquired its present derogatory meaning, much as 'peasant' itself has. (The 'Dutch colonist' sense of 'boer' came into popular use only with the Boer War, in the late nineteenth century.)

bore (tiresome thing or person)
In its earliest sense, some time in the eighteenth century, the word was used to mean 'annoyance', 'nuisance', so that the writer who said 'Conversation is a bore' (in *Antidote to Miseries of Human Life*, 1807) really meant 'It is annoying having to make conversation'. The sense 'tiresome thing' developed at about the same time, however, and the 'bore' who is a tiresome person followed in the nineteenth century, in time to be used by Dickens and Thackeray.

borough (town having special status)
In Old English, a 'borough' was basically a fortress (compare modern German *Burg*) or a fortified town, and this sense is preserved in many place-names that today end in '-borough' or '-bury' (where the 'fortress' was often a Roman castle). The modern meaning of 'borough' in the sense 'urban constituency' or (in Greater London) 'local government area', began to develop only in the sixteenth century, when the original 'fortress' concept was largely lost.

bounce (throw so as to rebound)
The original meaning of 'bounce' was 'beat', 'thump', and the sense occurs in a number of texts from the thirteenth century, including Spenser's *The Faerie Queene* (1596) which has the lines:

And wilfully him throwing on the gras
Did beat and bounse his head and brest
full sore.

The modern sense seems to have developed first only in the sixteenth century, with the earliest record of the word occurring in a text of 1519 and referring to a woman dancing:

She will bounce it, she will whip,
Yes, clean above the ground!

(*A New Interlude and a Mery of the Nature of the iiii. Elements*? by J. Rastell).

bounty (gift, gratuity)
As in the French equivalent (*bonté*), the original sense of the word was simply 'goodness', with this occurring in Chaucer and Caxton in the fourteenth and fifteenth centuries. The present meaning 'gratuitous payment' and the like first developed in the eighteenth century, with the famous 'Queen Anne's Bounty' for poor clergy established in 1704.

bower (arbour)
The poetic word originally meant simply 'dwelling' in Old English, as well as a more specialized 'lady's apartment'. The former is the sense in this early text: 'Bryng me to that bygly bylde [i.e. to that pleasant building], & let me se thy blisful bor' (*Early English Alliterative Poems in the West-Midland Dialect*, 1319). The modern sense emerged in the sixteenth century, with Shakespeare, as often, one of the first to provide a record of it (in *Henry IV* Part 1, only a few lines before the quotation given under **book** above).

boy (young male)
Before settling to its common modern sense in the fourteenth century, 'boy' was used in more specialized ways to mean not only 'male servant', but also 'fellow', 'knave', and thus had a 'lowly' connotation that the word later lost. The 'servant' sense appeared in Miles Coverdale's Bible of 1535, where I Samuel 2:13 is translated as: 'The prestes boye came, whyle the flesh was seething'. (In the Authorized Version of 1611, this is: 'Before they burnt the fat, the priest's servant came'.) In Shakespeare's *Henry V* (1599) however, the 'boys' ('there is none to guard it [the 'luggage'] but boys') are really camp followers. Of course, the same sense was revived much later for the 'boy' (often a grown man) who was a native servant in India or China in colonial days from the seventeenth century. The words for children of either sex have changed interestingly over the years, as can be seen in the various English translations of the Bible. In the Authorized Version (1611), for example, Zechariah 8:5 runs: 'And the streets of the city shall be full of boys and girls playing in the streets thereof'. In Wyclif's version of 1382, 'boys and girls' were 'infauntes and maydens', in his 1388 version they were 'yonge children and maidens', and in Coverdale's Bible of 1535 they were 'yonge boyes and damselles'. See also **girl**.

braid (plait, interweave)
Before the word settled to its present sense, which it also had in Old English, 'braid' was a verb used for a sudden jerky movement of one kind or another, such as brandishing a spear, dealing a blow, drawing a sword and the like. All these uses however, were virtually obsolete by about 1500.

brand (make of product, trade name)
The word also means 'piece of burning wood', of course, and this was the original Old English sense. The transition to 'trade mark' was made via the 'branding' that means 'placing a mark on' (whether cattle or criminals), and as late as the nineteenth century casks of wine and the like were literally 'branded' in many cases to have their contents indicated. Criminals and cattle, however, were usually 'branded' with a hot iron. (In 'brand new', by contrast, the reference is probably to newly forged steel rather than goods that have just been 'branded'.)

bravery (courage)
The earliest recorded sense of 'bravery' (in the sixteenth century) is as 'bravado', and an act of bravado was called 'a bravery'. By the end of the century, however, the present sense of courage had become widely established, and the 'bravado' sense became obsolete by about 1800, except for literary use. There was obviously a need for a word to express the attitude, however, and 'bravado' itself was enlisted for this purpose in about 1600 (from the Spanish), in time for Milton and Bunyan to use it in the seventeenth century.

bray (cry out, of a donkey)
In its original use, the word could apply to both men and almost any suitable animal, including horses, oxen and deer. Spenser uses the word in *The Faerie Queene* (1596), where the Giant 'loudly brayd with beastly yelling sound'. In his encyclopaedia *The Mirrour of the World* (1481), too, Caxton uses the verb to apply to an elephant: 'Thenne he begynneth for to braye, crye and waylle'. (Elephants now trumpet, while trumpets can 'bray'.) The contemptuous 'braying' of a human voice is a usage that developed only from the seventeenth century.

bread (food made of flour, usually sold in loaves)
In Old English, the word 'bread' meant simply 'piece', 'morsel', 'fragment', while actual bread, which certainly existed then, was known as '**loaf**' (see this word separately). By about 1200, however, the substance itself had come to be called 'bread', while 'loaf' was used for an individual baked article, as now. The sense development of 'bread' was thus: 'piece', 'piece of bread', 'bread'.

breath (air from the lungs)
The Old English meaning of the word was 'odour', 'smell'. This sense was obsolete by about 1400, however, as almost was another meaning of 'vapour' (although the latter was retained by some poets, such as Milton in *Paradise Lost*, 1667). This means that there must have been another word in Old English for what we now call 'breath', and that word was *ǣthm*, related indirectly to 'atmosphere' and directly to modern German *atmen*, 'to breathe'.

breeze (light wind)
In the sixteenth century, 'breeze' was used to apply specifically to a north or north-east wind, which in the tropics meant the trade wind. This sense is quite clear from various shipping logs and mariners' records, such as Sir John Hawkins' *Second Voyage Made to the Coast of Guinea and the Indies of Nova Spania* (1565), where he writes of 'the ordinary brise taking us, which is the north-east wind'. The word later came to be used of a cool wind blowing from the sea on tropical coasts, which on the Atlantic coast of tropical America would also have been a north or north-east wind, although subsequently a 'breeze' was a wind in any direction from the sea. (Even now, 'sea breeze' is a common association.) Finally, in the seventeenth century, the word came to have its present general meaning of 'light wind', and even came to be used as the designation of a wind force 2 to 6 on the Beaufort Scale (ranging from 'slight breeze' of force 2 to 'strong breeze' of force 6, via 'gentle breeze', 'moderate breeze' and 'fresh breeze' for forces 3 to 5, all of particular velocities).

bribe (corrupt by means of a gift or tempting offer)
The original meaning of 'bribe' in the fourteenth century was 'steal', so that a 'briber' was a thief and 'bribery' was theft. (The origin of the word seems to be in an Old French verb *briber*, 'to beg'.) Chaucer uses the verb in his *Canterbury Tales* ('The Cook's Tale') (1386):

> For ther is no thef withowten a lowke
>   [i.e. an accomplice],
> That helpeth him to wasten and to sowke
>   ['soak', 'milk']
> Of that he brybe kan, or borwe may.

This sense was obsolete by about the middle of the sixteenth century, however, and the present meaning prevailed, defined by Johnson in his *Dictionary* (1755) in its noun form as 'A reward given to pervert the judgment or corrupt the conduct'.

brisk (fresh, alert, quick)
In Marlowe and Shakespeare, in the sixteenth century, the sense of 'brisk' is 'smart', 'spruce', as in the latter's *Henry IV, Part 1* (1596), where Hotspur says of 'a certain lord, neat, and trimly dress'd' that:

>   he made me mad
> To see him shine so brisk and smell so
>   sweet.

However, Shakespeare also uses 'brisk' in its other, more familiar senses, and the 'smart', 'well-dressed' sense is not recorded much beyond 1600.

brittle (liable to break easily, fragile)
A sense 'transitory', 'impermanent' was current for 'brittle' for some time from the sixteenth to the eighteenth century, and frequently applied to abstract objects, as in Shakespeare's *Richard II* (1594), where the king, after his humiliating defeat by Bolingbroke, looks at his face in a mirror and exclaims:

> A brittle glory shineth in this face:
> As brittle as the glory is the face:
> (*Dashes the glass against the ground*).

broker (business agent or intermediary)
The original sense of 'broker' was 'pedlar', 'small trader', a shade of meaning that merged with the later 'secondhand dealer'

usage some time in the sixteenth century. Another obsolete sense of the word as 'go-between', 'matchmaker', 'pander', and this meaning is the one found in Shakespeare's *Two Gentlemen of Verona* (1591), where Lucetta brings Julia a note from Proteus, and Julia says of her:

> Now, by my modesty, a goodly broker!

This sense is not recorded later than the end of the same century.

brook (put up with, tolerate)
In Old English, 'brook' meant simply 'use', 'enjoy' (compare modern German *brauchen*). This sense was current down to the sixteenth century, and even later in literary use, such as Scott's historical novel *The Fair Maid of Perth* (1828), set in the late fourteenth century. The present sense dates from the sixteenth century, and almost from the first has the verb coupled with a negative (as in such a sentence as 'The matter brooks no delay', or 'He would brook no interference with his proposed action').

brothel ('bawdy-house', premises used by prostitutes)
The present word is actually short for 'brothel house', and 'brothel' itself originally meant 'worthless fellow' in the fourteenth century, and 'prostitute' in the fifteenth. The former occurs in Thomas More's *The Confutacyon of Tindales Answere* (1532), where he writes of 'the holy Lenton faste, whiche these brotheles so boldly take vpon them to breake', and the latter in the works (1535) of Bishop John Fisher, who asks 'Why doeth a common brothel take no shame of hir abhomination?' In his plays, Shakespeare uses both the full form ('brothel-house') and the current single word, both in the modern sense, although with the former referring to the inmates.

brown (colour between orange and black)
In Old English, 'brown' meant simply 'dark', 'dusky', a sense that was continued in poetry down to the nineteenth century, as in Tennyson's *To Maurice* (1854), which has the line:

> I watch the twilight falling brown.

This old sense also survives in the

expression 'a brown study', although this itself is not found before the sixteenth century. The modern colour 'brown' has been recorded from the thirteenth century.

bruise (injure without breaking the skin)
The original meaning of 'bruise' was much stronger, having the sense 'crush' or 'mangle', and interestingly the word was defined in these terms by Johnson in his *Dictionary* as late as 1755: 'To crush or mangle with the heavy blow of something not edged or pointed; to crush by any weight'. This sense appeared in a wide range of spellings ('brise', 'birse', 'briss', 'bruse' and the like) down to the end of the sixteenth century, and after this in an increasingly weaker use. Wyclif's Bible of 1382 says of Balaam's ass in Numbers 22:25 that it 'ioynede him silf to the wal, and briside the foot of the sitter'; the Authorized Version of 1611 tells how 'she thrust herself unto the wall, and crushed Balaam's foot against the wall'. Something of the former sense survives in the word 'bruiser' for a prize fighter or big 'tough guy', who is clearly more likely to 'mangle' than merely bruise!

brunt (main stress or force of a blow)
From the fourteenth to the seventeenth century, 'brunt' meant 'blow' itself, or even 'attack', as when in Malory's *Le Morte Darthur* (1470–85) we read that (in nice modern-looking English) 'Sir Gawaine gave him many sad brunts and many sad strokes'. The phrase 'bear the brunt' thus originally meant 'face the assault', 'receive the blow', and expressions such as 'the brunt of war' and 'the brunt of battle' also have a much more powerful and physical source than their use today.

brutal (inhuman, cruel, brutish)
Initially, the sense of 'brutal' from the fifteenth century was 'like a brute', i.e. 'animal', in such phrases as 'brutal beast', 'brutal creature', 'brutal slave'. The current sense began to emerge from the sixteenth century.

buccaneer (pirate, adventurer)
The literal sense of the word was originally 'one who cures flesh on a barbecue', from a French word itself based on a native West Indian word, and the name thus initially applied to a woodsman in the West Indies in the seventeenth century. From this, the word was transferred to pirates of the famous 'Spanish Main' whose culinary habits were similar. From this sense in turn the general meaning 'pirate' developed in the nineteenth century. See also **barbecue**.

buckram (type of stiffened cotton or linen fabric)
The modern word applies to coarse linen or cloth. Originally, however, 'buckram' was used of fine linen or cotton. The different sense can be found from contemporary records, such as one of 1550 that describes buckram as 'so thinne that a man mai see through it' (William Thomas, *Principle Rules of the Italian Grammer, with a Dictionarie*). The modern sense is first found in the fifteenth century.

budget (annual estimate made by the Chancellor of the Exchequer)
In the fifteenth century, 'budget' was a word for a pouch or wallet, taking its origin from Old French *bougette*, the diminutive of *bouge*, a leather bag. This sense existed down to about the eighteenth century, and as late as 1783 Dr Johnson is recorded (by Boswell) as having said, 'When I landed at Billingsgate I carried my budget myself to Cornhill'. From this, the meaning 'bundle', 'stock' developed, referring to the contents of the bag, as in a 'budget of papers', or figuratively as a 'budget of knowledge'. Finally, the present sense arose from the fact that the Chancellor, when presenting his statement, was said to 'open the budget'. The phrase is first recorded in 1733. A private individual's 'budget' in turn followed from this, although down to about the end of the nineteenth century the word was used mainly humorously. See also **bulge** (below).

bulb (rounded root of a plant)
In the sixteenth century, 'bulb' invariably meant 'onion'. A hundred years later, however, the word had acquired the present general sense it has today. The use of 'light bulb' first appeared in the mid-nineteenth

century, with the promotion of electricity as a lighting power.

bulge (protuberance, swelling)
This word is related in origin to '**budget**' (see above). It is not surprising, therefore, that its initial sense was the same: 'wallet', 'pouch'. In the seventeenth century the word came to be used of a ship's hull, where it has now been superseded by 'bilge'. The general sense of 'swelling' followed a century later, deriving from the verb ('protrude') which was in use somewhat earlier.

bulldozer (machine for pushing earth, clearing land, etc)
A bulldozer was originally a person in the nineteenth century, with the term applied to someone who 'bull-dozed', or (in America) intimidated blacks by violence. A passage in the *American Newspaper* explained the term and its alleged origin in an issue in 1876: 'If a negro is invited to join it [a society called 'The Stop'] and refuses, he is taken to the woods and whipped. This whipping is called a "bull-doze", or doze [i.e. dose] fit for a bull'. The word came to apply to the machine (also first in the United States) from the 1930s.

bullet (cartridge, lead missile fired from gun, pistol etc)
The original meaning of 'bullet' was 'cannonball', this deriving from the French *boulet*. Such a missile would have been of metal or stone, and a record of 1577 refers to a gun shooting 'a bollet of twentiepound weighte' (Robert Recorde, *The Whetstone of Witte*). The modern much smaller bullet followed soon after, however, at first often defined as a 'little bullet' or a 'musket bullet' to distinguish it.

bulletin (news report, account)
In the seventeenth century, 'bulletin' was used to mean 'note', 'warrant' or the like. The modern meaning began to emerge in the mid-eighteenth century, when it frequently meant a report on a sick person's health, and later, from about 1800, a war or battle report sent from abroad to be published at home. From the 1920s in Britain, with the rise of the BBC and broad-casting, the word was specially associated with a news broadcast or a weather forecast. After the Second World War, however, the word was more implied than explicit, and a broadcast 'news bulletin' was just 'the news', while a 'weather bulletin' was just 'the weather forecast' or even 'the weather'. However, the word still features on the radio pages of *Radio Times* in a general sense, to give the times of 'major bulletins', for example, and 'racing bulletins'.

bully (blustering person, especially one who is cruel to another, weaker one)
This interesting word has done a virtual about-turn since it first appeared in the sixteenth century, because it originally meant 'sweetheart', 'fine fellow'! This explains some otherwise rather baffling literary references, particularly in Shakespeare, where the word occurs several times in this sense (e.g. 'What sayst thou, bully Bottom?' in *A Midsummer Night's Dream*, 1590, and Pistol's 'I love the lovely bully' in *Henry V*, 1599). As late as 1754, too, Richardson has the word in the 'sweetheart' sense in *Sir Charles Grandison:* 'I have promised to be with the sweet Bully early in the morning of her important day'. On the whole, however, the term was increasingly used of men, and thus passed down to its present meaning via senses such as 'swash-buckler', 'hired ruffian'. The latter of these is now obsolete, as is the eighteenth-century usage to mean 'protector of prostitutes'. As Defoe wrote in *Jure Divino* (1706):

Mars the Celestial Bully they adore,
And Venus for an Everlasting Whore.

bunch (cluster or tight group of similar things)
In the fourteenth century, a 'bunch' was a hump or swelling, such as a camel's hump or a swelling on the human body. In his translation (1398) of Bartholomaeus Anglicus' *De proprietatibus rerum*, John de Trevisa declared that 'a camell of Arabia hathe two bonches in the backe', and other texts have the word in this sense down to at least the nineteenth century, although in an increasingly specialized use. The modern meaning arose in the sixteenth century, and a dictionary of English and Latin words

published in 1570 translates Latin *floretum* as the agreeably English 'bunche of flowers'.

bungalow (single-storey house)
The original 'bungalow' was a lightly built, even temporary, one-storey house in India, usually having a thatched roof. Such houses first existed in the seventeenth century for Englishmen and other Europeans in India. (Not for nothing does the name suggest 'Bengal' or 'Bangladesh', since 'bungalow' means 'house in the Bengal style' and 'Bangladesh' means 'Bengal country'.) Most 'bungalows' were thus in India until more or less the end of the nineteenth century, when the word began to apply to any single-storey house, including ones in Britain.

bunny (child's word for a rabbit)
Before 'bunny' meant 'rabbit' it was a term of endearment for a woman or child, with both senses arising in the seventeenth century. In a comedy of 1606 called *Wily Beguilde*, one of the characters addresses his 'Sweet Peg' as 'my honey, my bunny, my duck, my dear', a nice selection of pet names. Bunny rabbits, however, are first recorded in 1690 (and their remote descendants, bunny girls, in the 1960s). Both words derive from 'bun' in the sense 'rabbit's tail', although 'bun', too, appears in the 'dear' sense in a text of 1614 (where it is applied by a woman to a boy, 'her pretty bun').

bureau (office)
A bureau was originally, in the eighteenth century, a writing desk, defined by Dr Johnson in his *Dictionary* (1755) as 'A chest of drawers with a writing-board'. Local auction rooms and estate agents' showrooms still stock nineteenth-century bureaux for sale, or even earlier and more valuable ones. The sense 'office' developed at about the same time, especially for a government organization, although the word is now more common in this sense in the United States (where it is the 'B' of 'FBI', of course, and occurs in such titles as the 'National Bureau of Standards' and the 'Bureau of Prisons').

burial (interment)
From the thirteenth to the early seventeenth century, 'burial' meant 'place of burial' i.e. 'tomb', 'grave', hence the word's figurative use in this sense in Shakespeare's *The Merchant of Venice* (1596), where Salanio describes a ship in a stormy sea as:

Vailing [i.e. lowering] her high-top
lower than her ribs
To kiss her burial.

The modern meaning of the word has been current from the fifteenth century, and also appears in Shakespeare.

burly (strong and heavily-built)
In the thirteenth century, the word was a term of approval, meaning 'handsome', 'stately'. This then modified to 'noble' as a general epithet of things, such as 'burly spear' or a 'burly bed', and finally emerged in its present sense from the fourteenth century.

busby (type of tall fur hat worn by hussars)
Originally, a 'busby' was a large kind of bushy wig, as worn in the eighteenth century. (There are no grounds for supposing that the word comes from the name of Dr Busby, the headmaster of Westminster School who died in 1695.) From the nineteenth century the name was transferred to the hussars' distinctive hat, and also came to be used for the similar headdress worn by the Brigade of Guards, although the men themselves do not use the term in a technical or formal sense.

business (occupation, affair)
The earliest sense of the word, in Old English, was 'care', 'concern', and this survived long enough for Wyclif to use it in his translation of the Bible of 1382, where in Ezekiel 12:19 he has: 'Thei shulen eete her breed in bisynes' (Authorized Version of 1611: 'They shall eat their bread with carefulness'). In the thirteenth century, 'business' was used to mean 'diligence', 'industriousness', and this in turn was used in the Authorized Version in this sense in Romans 12:11: 'Not slothful in business' (Revised Version of 1881: 'In diligence not slothful'). The meaning 'occupation' developed in the fourteenth century, and 'affair' in the sixteenth.

buttery (storeroom for food and drink; room in a college where food is served)
A 'buttery' was originally a 'butlery', that is, a liquor and wine store. The sense soon changed to 'foodstore' in general, however (perhaps aided by the association with 'butter'), so that Johnson in his *Dictionary* of 1755 was able to define the word as 'the room where provisions are laid up'. In the first act of *The Taming of the Shrew* (1596), Shakespeare seems to be using the word in the 'winestore' sense when the Lord says:

Go, sirrah, take them to the buttery.

But there is no doubt the meaning had changed by the time Pepys used it in his *Diary* (1665), when he records pleasantly: 'Then down to the buttery, and eat a piece of cold venison pie'. The 'college' sense emerged only in the seventeenth century, and originally the 'residence' of undergraduates at Oxford and Cambridge colleges was recorded by the noting of their names in the buttery books.

buxom (plump and good-looking)
The word has changed its meaning several times over the years, originating in the twelfth century as 'obedient', 'compliant', and passing through 'flexible' and 'blithe' before acquiring its modern sense some time in the sixteenth century. The word literally means (to coin a word) 'bow-some', that is, 'pliant', 'able to bend', and this was the initial sense as used morally. Some older literary texts look strange with the word applied in obsolete senses, such as the 'buxom air' that featured in a number of seventeenth-century poems (meaning 'unresisting'). (Milton's *Paradise Lost* and Dryden's *Palamon and Arcite* both have it.)

by and by (soon, shortly)
In its earliest sense, in the fourteenth century, the phrase meant 'one by one' or 'on and on'. In the fifteenth century the meaning 'immediately' had developed, so that where Tindale's Bible of 1526 has 'By and by the fever left her' in Mark 1:31, the Authorized Version, nearly a hundred years later, has 'And immediately the fever left her'. The sense 'soon' arose in the sixteenth century, and it is so used by Shakespeare in *Henry IV*, Part 1 (1596) near the end of the

play, where the Prince of Wales, seeing Falstaff lying on the ground after the death of Hotspur, says:

Embowell'd will I see thee by and by:
Till then in blood by noble Percy lie.

(Whereupon Falstaff gets up with a stentorian 'Embowelled!')

bye, by (in phrase 'by the bye')
A 'bye' was formerly a word in the sixteenth century for something secondary or subsidiary, usually occurring in various phrases such as 'bye and main' (entirely) or 'upon the bye' (in a minor matter). The sole fixed expression 'by the bye' (or 'by the by') is all that remains, meaning first 'as a subsidiary matter' in the seventeenth century, and then, as now, 'by the way' in the eighteenth. This is the same 'bye' that today appears in cricket and other sports, since in cricket a 'bye' is not a proper stroke, nor even an individual run for the player, but a single point for the side as a whole.

cabaret (stage show at nightclub or restaurant)
When the word first emerged in English use, in the seventeenth century, it applied to a French tavern. In his *Diary* entry for 23 September 1662, Pepys commented that 'In most cabaretts in France they have writ upon the walls [. . .]*"Dieu te regarde"*'. The modern sense of the word appeared just before the First World War, and the cabaret itself flourished soon after it.

cabin (room on a ship)
In its original sense, the word could apply to a number of places, ranging from a hut to a cave and a tent to a den. The first of these is the meaning in Shakespeare's

Twelfth Night (1601), where Viola, disguised as the pageboy Cesario, says to Olivia (on behalf of Orsino):

Make me a willow cabin at your gate.

In the Bible (Authorized Version of 1611), it means 'cells' in Jeremiah 37:16: 'When Jeremiah was entered into the dungeon, and into the cabins'. The 'ship' sense developed fully from the sixteenth century, although in his Bible of 1382, Wyclif has 'thi litil cabans' in Ezekiel 27:6.

cabinet (cupboard; board of councillors or ministers)
The word is related to '**cabin**' (see previous entry), and in fact had this meaning originally, as well as 'cottage', 'dwelling', 'animal's den' and similar senses. Hence, in Shakespeare's *Venus and Adonis* (1592):

Lo! here the gentle lark, weary of rest,
From his moist cabinet mounts up on high.

The meaning then became 'small room', 'boudoir' for a while, so that the Douai Bible of 1609 has in Genesis 6:14 (regarding Noah's ark): 'Cabinets shalt thou make in the arke' (Authorized Version, two years later: 'Rooms shalt thou make in the ark'). The next sense development was 'room for exhibiting works of art', and from this, 'case or cupboard for valuables'. This last meaning is still current, but all the others are obsolete. All, however, *were* current in the sixteenth century. The 'body of councillors' sense came about in the seventeenth century, when the word was really short for 'Cabinet Council' (as distinct from the 'Privy Council'), and this is the government 'Cabinet' that exists today.

cad (ill-bred person, 'rotter')
The word has been through many shifts of meaning before arriving at today's sense, which in itself is usually felt as 'mannered'. In the eighteenth century, a 'cad' was the word for an unbooked passenger on a coach, whom the driver took on board in order to make a little extra 'on the side'. In Dickens and Thackeray in the nineteenth century, a 'cad' was the conductor of an omnibus (hence the 'numerous cads and drivers of short stages' mentioned in *Pickwick Papers*,

1837). He was also a confederate or accomplice, a 'mate', as in Thomas Hood's *Kilmansegg* (1839):

Not to forget that saucy lad
(Ostentation's favourite cad)
The page, who looked so splendidly clad.

Finally, although not exhaustively, he was the 'fellow of low vulgar manners and behaviour' (*Oxford English Dictionary*) that he much less formidably is today ('I say, Sir, you cad!').

caddie (golfer's attendant)
Most golfers today do their own caddying, but a 'caddie' was an assistant of various trades before he became associated almost exclusively with golf. In fact, in the seventeenth century, he was an army cadet (hence the origin of the word), and moreover a Scottish one, as can be seen in an extract from John Row's *The Historie of the Kirk of Scotland, 1558–1637* (1634–46) which tells of 'ane young gentleman latelie come from France, pransing [. . .]with his short skarlet cloake and his long caudie [i.e. cadet's] rapier'. In the eighteenth century, 'caddie' was the word for an errand boy or porter, again originally Scottish, as described in Edward Burt's *Letters from a Gentleman in the North of Scotland* (1730), where 'the Cawdys, a very useful Black-Guard' attend 'publick Places to go of Errands; and though they are Wretches, that in Rags lye upon the Stairs, and in the Streets at Night, yet are they often considerably trusted'. (See **blackguard** in this respect.) Certainly, golf itself has a long and venerable history in Scotland.

cadge (beg)
In the seventeenth century, 'cadge' meant 'carry', especially a pack. From this the 'begging' sense developed. The earliest sense of all, however, was probably 'fasten', dating from the fourteenth century.

calculator (machine performing mathematical calculations)
The meaning as given here is the popularly understood one today, yet originally a 'calculator' would simply have been a person who calculated. The first 'calculating machines' were developed in the early nine-

teenth century, with the electronic versions appearing in the mid-twentieth.

camisole (kind of short bodice worn by women)
As originally used, the word applied to a woman's jacket, as can be seen in nineteenth-century novels, for example. (Thackeray's *Vanity Fair* of 1848 describes Mrs O'Dowd as 'arrayed in curl-papers and a camisole', and Charlotte Brontë's *The Professor* of 1857 tells how the heroine 'seldom wore a gown – only a shabby cotton camisole'). The undergarment (as distinct from the over) seems to have evolved shortly after, and at any rate was advertised in 1866. (Later, the garment progressed and modernized to the camiknickers or 'camiknicks' of First World War vintage.)

canal (artificial waterway)
Some two hundred years before it acquired its present meaning in the seventeenth century, 'canal' meant 'pipe for carrying liquid'. This sense is now obsolete, although the word is still used of certain channels of the body, such as the 'alimentary canal', or the 'semicircular canals' of the ear.

candid (frank, honest)
The word was defined by Dr Johnson in his *Dictionary* (1755) as 'Free from malice; not desirous to find faults', which is not quite the sense it has today. This former usage is the one found in many texts before and after Johnson's time, however, as in Jane Austen's *Pride and Prejudice* (1797) where she writes: '. . .to be candid without ostentation or design – to take the good of every body's character and make it still better, and say nothing of the bad – belongs to you alone'. The same sense is found in the corresponding noun, 'candour', as in the lines from Pope's *Essay on Criticism* (1711):

'Tis not enough, Wit, Art, and Learning join;
In all you speak, let Truth and candor shine!

The 'frank' sense of 'candid' was also current in the seventeenth century, though, and in the end this was the meaning that prevailed, as 'frankness' did for 'candour'.

canister (small container)
The word came into English from Latin *canistrum*, with both words related to 'cane'. The original sense of 'canister' in the seventeenth century was thus 'basket' (which is what the Latin word means, and of which it was a direct translation). The meaning soon generalized, however, to apply to any type of box or tin, especially a metal one, and the initial 'basket' sense became obsolete fairly rapidly.

canvass (solicit support or votes)
The word is directly related to 'canvas', and the verb's original meaning was 'toss in a canvas sheet' (for pleasure or punishment), with this sense seen in Shakespeare's *Henry VI*, Part 1 (1591), where Gloucester says to Winchester:

I'll canvass thee in thy broad cardinal's hat,
If thou proceed in thy insolence.

From this, the sense 'criticize', 'pull to pieces' developed, and then a more general 'discuss' ('canvass a matter'). The precise reason for the transfer to the current meaning is not very clear, but no doubt the 'discussion' aspect had something to do with it, and in canvassing for support a good deal of discussion and mutual criticism may be involved. However, the meaning 'solicit votes before an election' developed quite late, only in the nineteenth century.

capable (able)
A former meaning 'susceptible' is found for 'capable' in many seventeenth-century texts, as in Shakespeare's *Henry IV*, Part 2 (1597), where Morton says:

You were advis'd his flesh was capable
Of wounds and scars.

Similarly in *Hamlet* (1602), where Hamlet says of the Ghost:

His form and cause conjoin'd, preaching to stones,
Would make them capable.

However, the current meaning of 'able', 'having the capacity' was also current at this time, and the earlier sense had become obsolete by about 1700.

capitulate (surrender)
The word is related to both Latin *caput*, 'head' and such English words as 'capital' and 'chapter'. It is therefore not too surprising to find that its original sense, in the sixteenth century, was 'specify under headings', 'make terms', as in Shakespeare's *Henry IV*, Part 1 (1596), when Henry says:

> Percy, Northumberland,
> The Archbishop's Grace of York,
>   Douglas, Mortimer,
> Capitulate against us and are up.

From this the modern sense developed, since when surrendering, terms will need to be agreed.

caption (heading, title)
The current use of the word is American in origin, arising in the eighteenth century. In the fourteenth century, the word meant much more literally 'capture', 'seizure', as well as 'arrest'. In the seventeenth century, too, the sense 'objection' developed, showing the additional link with 'captious'. This meaning may still not be quite obsolete. The earliest record we have of 'caption' in the sense of 'heading' comes in the writings of the American president James Madison, who helped to draft the US Constitution and Bill of Rights. He points out (1789): 'You will see in the caption of the address that we have pruned the ordinary stile of [various words]'. The transfer to this meaning probably came about through the use of the word in legal documents to mean 'note of taking'.

captivate (entrance)
As with '**caption**' (see previous entry), there is a literal idea of 'capturing' behind the word, which thus originally meant 'take captive'. Documents of the seventeenth and eighteenth centuries tell of prisoners or sailors who had been 'captivated' in battle. This sense then developed to mean 'capture the mind', 'subjugate', until the current meaning was the sole one left, defined splendidly by Johnson in his *Dictionary* (1755) as 'To overpower with excellence'.

carcase, carcass (dead body)
At one time, the word could apply to human corpses, as well as the bodies of dead animals, a usage which is rare today. However, a recent humorous use of the word has developed to refer to a human body that is far from dead (as 'Get your carcase out of here!'), with this special sense occurring from the nineteenth century.

career (course of employment, life's run)
The word is bound up with horsemanship, and its original meaning in the sixteenth century was both 'racecourse' and 'gallop at full speed'. A related meaning was 'frisk' of a horse, defined more accurately (or technically) in John Baret's superb *An Alvearie or Triple Dictionarie* (1573) as 'The short turning of a nimble horse, now this way, nowe that way', and this is the sense of 'career' in Shakespeare's *Henry V* (1599), where Nym comments: 'The king is a good king: but it must be as it may; he passes some humours and careers'. The modern sense of 'course of employment' is actually quite recent, arising only in the nineteenth century.

carol (festive hymn, especially one sung at Christmas)
Carols date from medieval times, although in the thirteenth century the word meant 'ring dance', in particular one accompanied by a song. Thus in his translation (1387) of Ranulf Higden's *Polychronicon*, a 'universal history', John de Trevisa tells how he saw a girl ('a mayden') '. . .daunsynge in a carrole among other maydouns', and the word continued in this sense until at least the eighteenth century. From the fourteenth century, however, 'carol' had come to be used of the song itself, and from this it was only a short step to the special Christmas carol that first properly emerged in about 1500. The *Privy Purse Expenses of Elizabeth of York*, published in 1830 but dating from about this time (1500 or earlier), record a payment made 'to Cornishe for setting of a carralle upon Cristmas day'.

carp (find fault, complain argumentatively)
In its earliest sense, in the thirteenth century, the word meant simply 'talk', 'speak', and even two hundred years later had modified to merely 'sing', 'recite', with no 'bad' sense at all. Minstrels of the time

were popular for their 'harping and carping', or harp-playing and reciting. The 'find fault' sense developed in the sixteenth century, when perhaps the verb had come to be influenced by Latin *carpere*, which literally meant 'pluck' but figuratively had the sense 'slander'.

carpet (floor covering)
Carpets were not always just on the floor, but were formerly table cloths and altar cloths and even bed coverings in the fifteenth-century use of the word. Even as late as 1702 an issue of the *London Gazette* advertised 'One green Cloth Carpet, with a small Fringe round it, for the Communion Table'. But the sense 'floor covering' was also well established by the fifteenth century, and this was the one that outlasted the others, so that other words were used for the other coverings.

carrel (partitioned area or cubicle in library etc)
The word is related to '**carol**', with the 'ring' sense being the link between the two, although originally, in the fifteenth century, a 'carrel' was a 'study' in a monastic cloister. Here are the monks of Durham at work in them, in a contemporary description of 1593: 'In every wyndowe three Pewes or Carrells, where evry one of the old monks had his carrell, severall by himselfe, that when they had dyned they dyd resorte to that place of Cloister, and there studyed upon there books, every one in his carrell all the after nonne [i.e. all the afternoon]'. Times changed, however, and the word became obsolete in this sense, apart from a historic revival in the eighteenth and nineteenth centuries. In the twentieth century, however, it made a comeback in a secular sense as the word for a cubicle in a library, with this use first noted in an issue of the *Library Journal* in 1919. Many public libraries now offer their readers both enclosed 'carrels' and open-top 'study desks'.

cartel (combination of commercial enterprises or political groups)
In the sixteenth century, a 'cartel' was a written challenge, a letter of defiance to someone, and the word occurs in this sense in Ben Jonson's *Every Man In His Humor* (1598): 'I should send him a chartel presently'. A hundred years later, the word was used to apply to a written agreement regarding the exchange of prisoners, with this sense current down to the nineteenth century. These original meanings all came into English from the identical French word, which itself came from Italian *cartello*, 'placard', 'challenge'. The modern sense of 'cartel' in English, however, derives from German *Kartell*, since it was in that country that such business agreements and political coalitions arose in the nineteenth century.

carton (plastic or cardboard container)
The word comes from the identical French word which means 'cardboard', although before 'carton' meant 'container' in English (only in the twentieth century), it was the term for the white disc in the bullseye of a target in the nineteenth century. So this is what was meant when sports-loving readers of the *Daily Telegraph* for 15 July 1864 learned that 'Captain Heaton, out of 27 shots' scored '26 bull's-eyes, of which 13 were cartons'. As containers, 'cartons' were used in the twentieth century for food and household goods – first cardboard ones for soap and cigarettes, then plastic ones for milk and other drinks.

cash (money)
The original meaning of the word was 'moneybox', 'cashbox', 'till', as it still is in related languages (French *caisse*, Italian *cassa*, Spanish *caja*, and even German *Kasse* and Russian *kassa*), and it is only in English that the word came to mean 'money' (in the sixteenth century, when the earlier sense was also in use).

cassock (long black garment worn by clergy)
The cassock was a soldier's or horseman's cloak before it was a priest's garment, and the word is used by Shakespeare in this sense. From the seventeenth century, however, the clerical dress sense prevailed, itself dating from the Restoration.

catalogue (ordered list)
Today, a catalogue is a systematic register or list of things, such as a book catalogue or

a sales catalogue. Originally, it was simply a list, with no thematic divisions, so that various texts of the fifteenth and sixteenth centuries spoke of a 'catalogue of the popes' or a 'catalogue of monasteries'. A book published in 1660 was called *Englands Glory, Or, an Exact Catalogue of the Lords of His Maiesties most Honourable Privy Councel*. Such 'catalogues' would not even have been in alphabetical order. The modern concept of 'catalogue' arose in the seventeenth century, and it is appropriate that the first record we have of the word in its present sense is in an entry in Pepys' *Diary*, when in 1667 he reports: 'Home, and to my chamber, and there finished my Catalogue of books'.

cataract (waterfall)
The earliest use of the word in English was to mean 'floodgates of heaven', with reference to Genesis 7:11 ('windows of heaven' in the Authorized Version of 1611) and 8:2 (the same). The concept was of sluicegates that held back the rain, with the English word translating a Hebrew word meaning literally 'lattices', 'windows', as in the text quoted here. The sense 'waterfall' emerged only in the sixteenth century, as did the use of 'cataract' to mean 'clouding of the lens of the eye', the latter apparently arising from a rendering of Latin *cataracta*, 'portcullis'.

catarrh (inflammation of the mucous membrane of the nose)
Originally, the word meant merely 'running nose', ultimately from a Greek word that literally means 'downflow'. A 'running' of this kind, as in a 'streaming cold', was thought to be caused by fluid flowing down from the brain. One remedy for the affliction is given in one of the earliest records we have of the word, in Sir Thomas Elliot's *The Castel of Helth* (1539), where he writes: 'Egges be good ageinst Catars, or stilling out of the hed into the stomake'. The current meaning of the word dates from somewhat later in the same sixteenth century.

catastrophe (sudden disaster)
The word originally had a literary sense in the sixteenth century, meaning the 'denouement' of a play, or as defined by Dr Johnson in his *Dictionary* (1755): 'The change or

revolution which produces the conclusion or final event of a dramatic piece'. A modified version of this sense was used by Shakespeare in *All's Well That Ends Well* (1601), where the King of France says to Bertram, of his recently dead father:

> Thus his good melancholy oft began,
> On the catastrophe and heel of pastime.

Here the word means more generally 'disastrous end'. The modern meaning arose only in the eighteenth century, in a much looser and less 'final' sense, and the nineteenth century saw the expected transition of such a powerful word from its serious sense to its melodramatic ('what a catastrophe!'). The original Greek word *katastrophē* meant literally 'overturning'.

catherine wheel (type of rotating firework)
In its original use, as in heraldry, the term described a wheel with projecting spikes of the kind on which St Catherine was said to have been martyred. The firework of the name appeared some time in the eighteenth century, and features in the works of Dickens.

cattle (livestock, especially cows, bulls and calves)
The word is directly related to 'capital' and 'chattels', and in fact its sense in the fourteenth and fifteenth centuries was simply 'property', 'wealth'. Over the years the sense gradually shifted to 'moveable property' and finally settled to mean, more specifically, 'livestock' (initially other animals besides cows and bulls). The sense 'property' is now obsolete except in the expression 'goods and chattels'. Down to the seventeenth century 'cattle' was fairly regularly spelt 'cattel' (showing the link with 'chattel' even more closely), and it was only at the beginning of the eighteenth century that the present spelling took over.

cavalcade (procession of riders or carriages)
In its original sixteenth-century meaning, 'cavalcade' meant simply 'ride', that is, a march or raid made on horseback. The modern sense arose some hundred years later, and is first found in Evelyn's *Memoirs*

of 1644, where he says that he was 'desirous of being present at the cavalcade of the new Pope' (this would have been Innocent X). The general meaning 'procession' arose at about the same time, and the word itself received an additional boost in a 'showbiz' sense in the 1930s with the production of Noel Coward's *Cavalcade* (1932). Interestingly, he commented on his choice of title in later years, in *Australia Visited* (1941), where he writes: 'I was fortunate to be able to adminster a little artificial respiration to the word: – "Cavalcade". Before I wrote the play of that name the word had fallen into disuse', adding that now there are 'Cavalcades of practically anything that can be cavalcaded'.

ceiling (plaster covering the top of a room)
Originally, 'ceiling' was the word for any kind of lining of a room, both the inside of the roof and the walls, with the real meaning being the action of lining or 'ceiling', as in this very early notice of payment made to a carver, who received £2. 14s for his work: 'Item, to the kervour that tuk in task the siling of the chapel, in part of payment, ij *lib.* xiiijs' (*Accounts of the Lord High Treasurer of Scotland*, 1473). Later, a 'ceiling' was a tapestry screen or curtain, and the modern sense came into being only in the sixteenth century, where it is first found in Miles Coverdale's Bible of 1535 to translate Song of Solomon 1:17: 'Yᵉ sylinges of oure house are of Cedre tre, & our balkes of Cypresse' (Authorized Version of 1611: 'The beams of our house are cedar, and our rafters of fir').

cellar (underground store for wine, coal, etc.)
In the thirteenth century, when the word is first recorded, it meant 'storeroom' in general, deriving from Late Latin *cellarium,* 'set of cells', 'storehouse for food'. In this way, it could refer to a granary, a buttery or a pantry, and the general use of the word with this meaning continued down to the sixteenth century, and in poetry later still. However, the 'underground store' sense was also current for the word at this time, and it is hard to say exactly when the meaning transferred – or even in some cases to determine which kind of 'cellar' is meant. But the general meaning certainly became obsolete,

and it was the modern sense that continued alone.

Celt (person who speaks a Celtic language such as Gaelic or Welsh)
Although applying to an ancient people who speak an ancient language, the actual word 'Celt' first emerged only in the seventeenth century, when moreover it was the name used for a Gaul, translating the Latin *Celtae.* From the early eighteenth century, the name was used as it is today, with the word first current in French, however, so that its earliest record is in the title of a French book of 1703: *Antiquité de la Nation et de la langue des Celtes,* by Paul Pezron. He applied the word to the Bretons, and the sense of the word was then taken up in Britain to be used of the other peoples such as the Welsh, Irish and Scots who spoke languages related to Breton.

chafe (irritate, warm by rubbing, fret)
The original, now obsolete sense of the word was 'warm' generally (compare modern French *chauffer*). The earliest written record we have of this is in Wyclif's Bible of 1382, where part of Isaiah 44:15 (in the Authorized Version: 'He will take thereof, and warm himself') is: 'He toc of hem, and is chaufed'. This use lasted for some three hundred years. The other senses of 'chafe' are still current, and for the three given above, appeared in English respectively in the fourteenth, fifteenth and sixteenth centuries.

chagrin (vexation, mental distress caused by failure or frustration)
This is obviously a French word in origin, and when it first entered English in the seventeenth century, it meant 'anxious care', 'melancholy'. Pope has it in this sense in *The Rape of the Lock* (1712), showing also how the word was pronounced formerly (in fact down to quite recent times):

Hear me, and touch Belinda with
    chagrin;—
That single act gives half the world the
    spleen.

The current sense first came into use in the early eighteenth century, and by coincidence the earliest record we have of it is also in Pope, in a letter to Lady Montague of 1716, where he writes that 'if there be any circumstance of chagrin in the occasion' he feels he must be part of it.

challenge (invitation to a contest, legal objection)
The first meaning of 'challenge', from the thirteenth century, was 'accusation', 'reproach', with this sense in use down to the seventeenth century. The 'challenge to a contest' came about from the fourteenth century, and the 'legal objection' sense was first recorded in the sixteenth century.

chandelier (branched light)
When the word was first imported into English from French in the seventeenth century, it was used as a technical term to apply to a wooden framework that protected sappers in trenches. However, this limited sense was also of limited duration, and in the eighteenth century the modern 'branched light' meaning came into use. The word was first recorded with this sense in the antiquarian William Stukeley's *Palaeographia Sacra, or Discourses on Sacred Subjects* (1736), where he mentions 'lamps, branches, or chandeliers (as we now modishly call them)'.

chaos (disorder, confusion)
A sadly debased and demeaned word! It originally meant 'abyss', 'chasm' (from the Greek), and in the Rheims or 'Rhemish' Bible of 1582 was the word used in Luke 16:26 to render what in the Authorized Version of 1611 is 'great gulf' ('Betweene us and you there is fixed a great chaos'). It was Shakespeare who first used the general modern sense of the word, where in *Troilus and Cressida* (1606) Ulysses says:

> Great Agamemnon,
> This chaos, when degree is suffocate,
> Follows the choking.

chap (fellow, 'bloke')
The word is an abbreviation of 'chapman', which meant first 'trader', 'dealer', then 'purchaser', 'customer', and it is the latter senses that 'chap' itself had in the sixteenth century. The current usage developed in the eighteenth century, and a shade of the earlier meaning still exists in the colloquial use of 'customer' to mean 'fellow', 'chap' ('He's a funny customer').

chapel (place of worship)
Here it is just interesting to record all the gradual changes of meaning, with all the senses still current, to a greater or lesser degree. In the thirteenth century, a 'chapel' was a place set aside for prayer in a large house; in the fourteenth it was the word for a separate part of a church with an altar of its own (today some large chapels, such as King's College Chapel, Cambridge, have their own 'chapels' in this sense); in the fifteenth century, a chapel was a place of worship that was dependent on a church; in the seventeenth the use of the word was extended to mean a nonconformist place of worship (that is, one that in most of Britain is not Anglican); finally, in the same century the word came to be used for an association of printers. (King's College Chapel, mentioned here, would have been the earliest sense above, since it was, and is, the place of worship of the college.) All these different senses developed from the original chapel in France where the cloak (Latin *cappella*) of St Martin of Tours was preserved.

chaperon, chaperone (woman who accompanies and 'minds' a younger woman)
In the fourteenth century, the word was used for a hood or cap, showing its origin in French and its relation to English 'cape' and 'cap'. Such hoods were first worn by noblemen, then from the sixteenth century, by ladies. The current sense of the word appeared in the eighteenth century, the concept being that a 'chaperon' protects her charge in the same way that a hood protects the face. The alternative spelling with 'e' seems to have arisen from the wish to make the word look feminine (i.e. grammatically, as many French words with this ending are).

char (do the work of a charwoman)
In Old English, 'char' or 'chare' meant 'turn', in various senses. From the fourteenth century, the meaning of the word narrowed to 'turn of work', and especially

applied to domestic or household jobs. It was from this word and this sense that, in turn, 'chore' developed to mean 'small job' in the nineteenth century. It is not clear why the vowel changed in this way.

chariot (carriage)
The word today has a rather 'grand' ring to it, with associations of state or ancient history. Its original sense in the fourteenth century, however, was simply 'cart', 'wagon'. This became obsolete in the sixteenth century, at the latest, and the 'stately' sense is first recorded in Chaucer, also in the fourteenth century, where in his translation (1374) of Boethius' *De consolatione philosophiae*, he writes: 'Whan phebus the sonne bygynneth to spreden his clereness with rosene chariettes'. In the eighteenth century the word came to apply to a light four-wheeled carriage with only back seats. Unlike the post chaise, however, it did not have a coach box. Pepys mentions this sort of vehicle in his *Diary*, in the entry for 29 May 1661: 'We had great sport to try who should drive fastest, Sir W. Butten's coach, or Sir W. Penn's chariot, they having four, and we two horses'.

charisma (magnetic appeal of a person, great charm and 'personality')
In the seventeenth century, the word had a strictly theological application, referring to the free gift of God's grace (when it was more usually 'charism'). The modern sense first appeared as recently as the 1940s, when initially (as often now) it related more to powers of leadership.

charm (attractive feature of somebody or something)
The word derives ultimately from Latin *carmen*, 'song', and its original sense in English was thus 'incantation', that is, the singing or reciting of a verse that was held to have magic power or some kind of occult influence, especially to cure or heal. Chaucer has the word with this meaning in his *Canterbury Tales* ('The Knight's Tale') (1386):

To othere woundes and to broken armes
Somme hadden salues [i.e. salves] and
    somme hadden charmes.

The modern sense emerged in the sixteenth century, with a kind of bridge between the two meanings in Shakespeare's *The Merry Wives of Windsor* (1598), where Mistress Quickly says to Falstaff: 'I never knew a woman so dote upon a man: surely, I think you have charms, la; yes, in truth'. (Falstaff replies: 'Not I, I assure thee: setting the attraction of my good parts aside, I have no other charms'.)

chart (mariner's map)
The word originally meant 'map' in general, as it still does in many other languages (French *carte*, Italian *carta*, German *Karte*, Russian *karta* and the like), and can be found, therefore, in many geographical and historical accounts of the sixteenth century. The more specialized sense to apply to a navigator's map arose only at the end of the seventeenth century, when it was originally usually qualified as a 'sea chart'. The general sense was then taken over by 'map'.

chary (cautious, careful)
In Old English, 'chary' meant 'sorrowful', showing the word's direct link with 'care'. For a time from the fourteenth century, too, it meant 'dear', 'precious', as seen in these lines from *The Famous Chronicle of King Edward the First* (1593) by the poet and playwright George Peele:

And henceforth see you call it Charing-
    cross;
For why, the chariest and the choicest
    queen,
That ever did delight my royal eyes
There dwells.

The present sense was generally in common use from the sixteenth century.

chassis (framework for the body of a car or other vehicle)
The obviously French word was used in the sense 'window frame', 'sash' (to which it is related) when first adopted in English in the seventeenth century, and is first recorded in Evelyn's work on gardening (still very readable and useful) *Kalendarium Hortense* (1664): 'Open all the Windows from ten in the Morning till three in the Afternoon: Then closing the Double-sheets, (or Chasses rather) continue a gentle Heat'. The

57

modern sense developed in the early twentieth century, with the phenomenal rise of motoring as an art and of the motorist as its exponent.

chat (easy conversation or talk)
In the fourteenth and fifteenth centuries, the word meant 'chatter', and in origin is in fact a shortening of this. This is therefore the sense in Shakespeare's *The Taming of the Shrew* (1596), when Petruchio says to Baptista and other friends:

> But what a fool am I to chat with you
> When I should bid good morrow to my bride,
> And seal the title with a lovely kiss!

(His bride is of course the 'shrew', Katharina, his 'Kate': notice, incidentally, the Shakespearean prototype of 'S.W.A.L.K.' in the last line.) The modern use of 'chat' took over in the sixteenth century.

cheap (inexpensive, not dear)
The adjective developed in the sixteenth century from the noun in the phrase 'good cheap', meaning 'good bargain', 'good trading' (compare French *bon marché*), since 'cheap' as a noun dates back to Old English times, when it meant 'barter', 'market', 'price'. (This sense still survives in London's Cheapside, where the City's main medieval food market was, and in the word 'chapman' to mean a trader [see **chap**]; 'cheap', too, appears in other place names such as Chepstow, 'market place', and the many places called Chipping [Campden, etc].) The adjective arose to serve as a much needed opposite for 'dear'.

cheat (deceive, swindle)
The word originally meant 'escheat' in the fourteenth century, that is, to revert (of land or property) to a feudal lord as a result of the owner breaking a feudal bond or because there are no legal heirs when he dies. Quite clearly, this is a legal term with no suggestion of deception. From the sixteenth century, however, the word acquired its 'bad' overtone, no doubt from the practice that developed of gaining land or property by a false claim, or by failing to honour an agreement. For a time, 'cheat'

was thieves' slang for a stolen object, and this is the sense in Shakespeare's *The Winter's Tale* (1611), where Autolycus, having sung his song ('When daffodils begin to peer') says: 'With die and drab I purchased this caparison, and my revenue is the silly cheat. Gallows and knock are too powerful on the highway'. The modern verb and noun (as a person) came to be popularly used from this time.

cheer (happiness; shout of approval or welcome)
The basic sense of the word was originally 'face', as it still is in some other languages (such as Spanish *cara*), and this meaning lasted from the thirteenth century down to Shakespeare, where it comes in his *A Midsummer Night's Dream* (1590), in which Oberon says of Helena:

> All fancy-sick she is, and pale of cheer.

The next sense to develop was that of 'mood', 'spirit', as in the old expressions 'What cheer?' and 'be of good cheer'. Similarly, the meaning 'fare', 'provisions' arose, with the popularity of this sense lasting down to the nineteenth century, at least among poets and historical writers (who were attracted by the idea of a 'table of good cheer', for example). The phrase 'to make good cheer' also became widely used in the sense 'feast and be merry'. The 'happy' meaning of 'cheer', whether noun or verb, has been in use since the fourteenth century, but the 'joyful shout' sense dates only from the eighteenth century, when it was obviously new enough for Defoe to write, in *Captain Singleton* (1720): 'We gave them a cheer, as the seamen call it'. The modern sense of 'cheers', meaning merely 'thank you' or 'see you soon' ('Got the time, mate?' 'Half four.' 'Cheers.') arose in the twentieth century, initially as a drinking toast.

chemist (person trained in chemistry; pharmacist)
Both 'chemist' and 'chemistry' originally meant respectively 'alchemist' and 'alchemy' in the sixteenth century, the latter being the medieval 'science' and philosophical doctrine that aimed to turn base metals into gold and to discover a universal cure for all diseases and even achieve

immortality. Chemistry as the modern science, and the chemist who practises it, emerged in the seventeenth century (initially in the spelling 'chymistry' and 'chymist', from the false etymological connection with Greek *chȳmos*, 'juice', since chemistry was held to be 'the infusory art', *he chȳmike techne*, although the actual origin is in Greek *chēmeiā*, 'art of transmutation'). The sense 'pharmacist', as in the modern 'chemist's shop', was the last to arrive, appearing in the eighteenth century.

chest (large box or trunk; thorax)
The anatomical sense of 'chest' appeared only as late as the sixteenth century, as an extension of the basic meaning 'trunk with its contents' that had existed since Old English times.

chime (peal or ring of bells)
In the thirteenth century, 'chime' was used to mean 'cymbal', to which word it may possibly be related. From the fifteenth century it was the term for the apparatus used to chime bells, and a hundred years later, for the bells themselves and the sound they produced. Modern door chimes first came into fashion in the 1930s, and many houses have the originals or their electronic descendants today.

chimney (flue for smoke)
When the word was first used in English in the fourteenth century, borrowed from the French, it meant 'fireplace', just as French *cheminée* still means today. Hence such historical or dialect phrases as 'sitting by the chimney', and the former 'chimney-piece' that is now the mantelpiece. The modern meaning was in use at about the same time, however, and continued after the 'fireplace' sense became obsolete in the eighteenth century (when even then it was dated).

chivalrous (courteous, polite)
In the fourteenth century, the word meant 'knightly', 'characteristic of a knight', as its resemblance to 'chevalier' suggests. This sense continued until about the sixteenth century, or as long as the medieval knights did, when it fell out of use. In the eighteenth century it was revived, however, to apply to

the 'Age of Chivalry', that is, to the historic age of these same knights regarded as an era of gallantry, nobleness, and other fine virtues. In this new sense, the word first appeared in Thomas Warton's *The History of English Poetry* (1774–81), where he wrote that 'to sing romantic and chivalrous adventures was a very different task'. The corresponding noun 'chivalry' underwent a similar history, meaning originally 'cavalry', 'knightliness', then falling into disuse, and finally being revived in the eighteenth century to mean 'knightly system of medieval times'.

chorus (refrain of a song)
In the sixteenth century, the word was first used to refer to the character in Shakespeare's plays and the works of other Elizabethan dramatists who spoke the prologue and commented on events in the play in the same way that the Greek chorus had done in Attic drama. (In the Greek plays, originally, the chorus was a group of singers or dancers, whereas in English drama the word was used of a single character.) From the seventeenth century, the word came to mean 'choir', especially the body of singers who appear in operas and other instrumental works. From this, the use of the word passed fairly naturally to the musical composition that the chorus sang, and finally the 'refrain' sense appeared in the eighteenth century, especially to denote the lines of a song where the audience joined in. Both 'chorus' and 'choir' are related words.

chronic (constant, bad)
The present use of the word in its popular sense ('what a chronic waste of time', 'I had a chronic headache') is not only a debasement but a distortion of the original meaning, which clearly derives from Greek *chronos*, 'time' and in its proper usage means 'long-lasting'. This literal sense is still preserved to apply to diseases, distinguishing a 'chronic' or lengthy one (such as a 'chronic' inflammation) from an 'acute' or 'short and sharp' one (such as 'acute' appendicitis). The transition from 'long-lasting' to 'bad' probably came about through the association of the word with illnesses and diseases ('chronic rheumaticks' and the like).

chubby (round-faced)
Before it acquired its present meaning, 'chubby' meant 'thickset', that is, applied to the whole of a person's body, not just his or her face. This was in the seventeenth century. The current sense developed about a hundred years later. The word literally means 'like a chub' (i.e. the plump round fish of this name).

chuckle (laugh softly to oneself)
In its original sense, the word was almost the opposite of what it is today, since it meant 'laugh vehemently' in the sixteenth century, and was actually defined in these very words by Johnson in his *Dictionary* of 1755. The 'subdued' sense emerged only after about 1800, perhaps since the ending '-le' was regarded as a diminutive, to refer to a small laugh (compare 'crack' and 'crackle', 'spark' and 'sparkle', 'prick' and 'prickle'), or even under the influence of 'cackle'.

circulate (pass round)
This is a verb whose originally narrow sense has become generalized. In the fifteenth century, 'circulate' was a chemical (or alchemical) term, meaning 'subject to repeated distillation'. The process took place in a closed vessel of some kind, in such a way that the vapour condensed at the top and then flowed back down into the liquid being 'circulated'. By the sixteenth century, a meaning 'encircle' had developed, mainly used in descriptive texts rather than fiction. Finally, the present use became popular from the seventeenth century, meaning 'move or pass round'. The 'party' sense ('Darling, I think we'd better circulate') dates from the 1920s.

civil (not ecclesiastical; not military; polite)
The word has acquired several meanings and shades of meaning in its use down the centuries, stemming from its basic sense 'relating to a citizen' in the fourteenth century. This was the meaning that developed into 'courteous', 'polite' in the seventeenth and eighteenth centuries (originally more as 'refined' in society). At the same time, the word came to be used as the opposite of 'ecclesiastical' in the sixteenth century, and as the opposite of 'military' in the seventeenth. 'Civil law', too, was a term that arose in the fourteenth century to apply to the law of Roman citizens, and subsequently to English citizens, where it was distinguished first from 'canon law' and later from 'common law'. The 'civil' of 'civil service' is the 'non-military' one, and the term first appeared in the eighteenth century. A 'civilian', incidentally, was originally a student or professor of civil law in the fourteenth century, and the word is found in this sense in texts as late as the nineteenth century. See also **civil list** (below).

civil list (money granted by parliament annually to the royal family)
Before it acquired its present sense (in the strict sense, from 1830, the year of the accession of William IV), the term denoted, more meaningfully, a *list* of the charges for the *civil* or administrative government of the country, with this sense dating from the eighteenth century. The present use of the term is really a misnomer, and Macaulay commented on it in his *History of England* (1855): 'The expenses of the royal household are now entirely separated from the expenses of the civil government; but by a whimsical perversion, the name of *Civil List* has remained attached to [. . .] the revenue [. . .] appropriated to the expenses of the Royal Household'. Perhaps a more appropriate term would be something like 'household grant' (on the lines of 'household cavalry').

claret (red wine from Bordeaux district)
The word originally qualified 'wine' in the fourteenth century, with the term based on Old French *vin claret*. This initially denoted a light red wine in English, then a red wine, and finally, as now generally understood, a red Bordeaux wine. The first of these was thus in contrast to the 'red wines' (as they were then called) and the 'white wines', with the 'claret wine' being yellowish or in between. This contrast was no longer made after about 1600, and the emergence of the specific 'Bordeaux' sense is quite recent, apparently only from the nineteenth century. The word 'claret' was used on its

own fairly regularly from the sixteenth century.

clarity (clearness)
In the sixteenth century, 'clarity' meant 'lustre', 'splendour', and this sense was very common throughout the seventeenth century, when writers would talk of the 'clarity' of the sun to refer to its brightness. The modern sense arose in this same century, so that for some time the two overlapped, with 'clarity' extending its senses, however, to a wide range of concrete and abstract objects, such as colour, the sky, intellect, and style. Something similar happened with the related word 'clarify', which originally meant 'illumine', 'light up', then later 'make clear'.

clerk (accountant)
In the eleventh century, when the word was first used in English (adopted from Ecclesiastical Latin *clericus*, 'cleric'), a 'clerk' was an ordained minister of the church – hence the link with modern 'clerical' in its two senses ('relating to clergy', 'relating to a clerk'). By the thirteenth century, the meaning 'scholar' had developed, since clerks, in their original sense, were noted for their learning and knowledge, at least by comparison with most other people. This is the sense of the word in Chaucer's 'The Clerk's Tale' in his *Canterbury Tales* (1386), described in the 'Prologue' as:

A Clerk ther was of Oxenford also,
That vn to logyk hadde longe ygo

(i.e. he had studied logic a long time ago). From the sixteenth century, a 'clerk' was also a lay officer of a church, such as a 'singing clerk' or a 'parish clerk', and it was at about the same time that the current meaning arose, again with the implication that a person who can keep accounts, look after correspondence and records and the like, must be something of a scholar. A 'clerk in holy orders' is still the official designation of an ordained minister in the Church of England, as it was in the Roman Catholic church before the Reformation. The British pronunciation 'clark' was in use from the fifteenth century, and is reflected more accurately in the common surname Clark(e).

cliché ('stereotyped expression' [Eric Partridge, *A Dictionary of Clichés*])
A 'cliché' was originally a stereotyped block as used in printing, in its initial form a cast made by letting a matrix fall face down on a surface of molten metal just as it was about to cool. The word is obviously French, and is the past participle of the verb *clicher*, 'to stereotype', which itself is said to represent the sound of the matrix falling onto the molten metal (*cliche!*) The English usage dates only from the mid-nineteenth century. The current meaning of the word to denote a hackneyed expression (such as 'a dark horse' or 'my lips are sealed') dates from the end of this same century.

climax (greatest moment, 'high point')
The word is actually Greek for 'ladder', and was first used in English in the sixteenth century as a term in rhetoric, to denote an ascending series of expressions, as in the following example from a work by the theologian Richard Burthogge (*An Argument for Infants Baptisme*, 1684): 'This is the Clymax; if Believers, then Christ's; if Christ's, then Abraham's Seed; if Abraham's Seed, then Heirs according to the Promise'. The sense then came to acquire its present meaning as if applying to the topmost point of such an ascending scale (with this use described by the *Oxford English Dictionary* as 'due to popular ignorance and misuse of the learned word'). The first such use (or misuse) was recorded in the late eighteenth century, and in the twentieth the word again took on a specialized use, but this time in ecology and physiology.

cling (adhere, hold fast)
In Old English, 'cling' meant 'coagulate', 'congeal', and also 'shrink', 'wither'. A relic of the first of these senses, now long obsolete, can be seen in 'cling together'. The second, also no longer in use, applied to the shrinking of animal tissues in a dead body, for example, or even a living one that was becoming thin and 'drawn'. The rather bafflingly named 'cling' peach is so called since it is really a 'clingstone' peach, that is, its flesh clings to the stone of the fruit. The modern 'adhere' sense dates from the thirteenth century, but as used of humans occurs first only in the seventeenth century,

in Shakespeare: near the opening of *Macbeth* (1605) the 'bleeding sergeant' gives his report of the battle between Macbeth's forces and those of the rebel Macdonald:

> Doubtful it stood;
> As two spent swimmers, that do cling together
> And choke their art.

clinic (place of medical treatment or advice)

The word comes from Latin *clinicus*, 'one on a sickbed', itself from Greek *klīnē*, 'bed', and the first sense of the word in English was as an adjective in the seventeenth century, meaning 'pertaining to a sickbed', 'bedridden'. At the same time, the noun 'clinic' meant 'bedridden person', and only at the end of the nineteenth century does the word come to have its modern sense, which was borrowed from French *clinique* or German *Klinik*. (Originally, too, the public 'clinic', as distinct from the private clinic that is a private hospital, was an institution attached to a general hospital or medical school, though now it is usually a hospital department dealing with particular diseases or disorders, such as a 'fracture clinic'; there is also now the institution that is a place for specialized treatment, such as a 'child guidance clinic'.)

clod (lump of earth)

In the fourteenth century, a 'clod' was a 'clot', as a modern blood clot. The present sense did not develop until about a hundred years later.

closure (conclusion; object that seals or closes)

The oldest sense of the word applies to any object that encloses or closes, such as originally a barrier or fence. This meaning is described by the *Oxford English Dictionary* as obsolete, but the modern cap or clip that is a 'closure' belongs here, although admittedly a fairly recent use of the word. What is obsolete, however, is the sense 'enclosure' which came in the fifteenth century, about a hundred years after the basic word was first recorded. This sort of 'closure' was used for the action of enclosing, shutting or confining, as of land or an estate. The

parliamentary sense of 'closure' arose in the late nineteenth century, and superseded the earlier word 'cloture', taken direct from the French (whereas the English 'closure' here was based directly on 'close').

cloud (mass of watery vapour in the sky)

Here's a surprise: in Old English, 'cloud' meant 'hill', 'rock', and the word is perhaps related to 'clod'. This sense lasted down to about the end of the thirteenth century, when the word transferred to its present meaning, no doubt initially with particular reference to cumulus clouds (the 'hilly' ones). In making this transfer, it thus ousted the earlier word for 'cloud', which was 'welkin' in Old English and 'sky' in Middle English. The old, original sense of 'cloud' can be found surviving in a few place-names round Britain, such as the villages of Clutton ('hill-settlement') in Cheshire and Avon and, even better, the hill called The Cloud on the Cheshire-Staffordshire border east of Congleton. See also **welkin** and **sky** themselves.

cloy (satiate)

The word is directly related to Latin *clavus* and French *clou*, both meaning 'nail', and in the fourteenth century the meaning of 'cloy' was just this, 'nail', and in particular 'prick a horse with a nail' (i.e. when shoeing it). The progression to the modern sense was made in the sixteenth century, the linking concept apparently being a 'plugging' or 'filling', and possibly even more a 'clogging', since 'clog' and 'cloy' are similar words. Any linguistic link between the two, however, has not been definitely proved.

clumsy (awkward)

The original sense of the word was 'benumbed', 'moving as if benumbed', with the word itself perhaps a dialect one. This use of it can be seen in a rather fine line from the second part of John Marston's tragedy, the *History of Antonio and Mellida* (1702):

> The rawish danke of clumsie winter ramps the fluent summers raine.

Marston's use of this word (among other 'wild outlandish terms') was ridiculed by Ben Jonson in *The Poetaster* (1701), where

Crispinus (in other words, Marston) is made to speak of 'clumsie chilblain'd judgment'. However, the two became friends again later. The meaning 'awkward' was in use at the same time as this, however, in the late sixteenth century, and was the one that prevailed.

coal (black mineral used for fuel)
In Old English, 'coal' was the word for a glowing piece of wood or a cinder, a sense it had down to the fifteenth century, and possibly even later if this is what it means in Shakespeare's *The Winter's Tale* (1611), where in the last act Leontes says to Paulina:

> Stars, stars!
> And all eyes else dead coals.

From the thirteenth century, 'coal' meant 'charcoal', and was used in this meaning down to the seventeenth century, so that Izaac Walton, advising how to cook a chub in *The Compleat Angler* (1653), says: 'Let him then be boiled gently over a Chafing-dish with wood coles'. The modern sense is also recorded from the same century, although the fuel was originally called 'seacoal', perhaps because it was obtained from coal seams that had been exposed by the erosion of the sea on the coastline.

coarse (unrefined, crude)
From the fourteenth century, 'coarse' meant 'ordinary', 'common', and down to the eighteenth century was regularly spelt 'course'. It originally applied to cloth or clothes, by contrast with cloth that was 'fine'. The modern sense developed from the sixteenth century in various usages, with that of 'coarse language' emerging in the seventeenth century. 'Coarse fishing' is a nineteenth-century usage, implying fish that have a rough skin by contrast with the 'game fish', or the salmon family.

coast (seashore)
The word's basic sense is 'side', 'flank', from Latin *costa*, 'rib' (French *côte*), and 'coast' meant simply 'region', 'direction' in the thirteenth and fourteenth centuries before it meant 'land beside the sea'. (Even here, also in the fourteenth century, the meaning was qualified as 'coast of the sea' before the word

came to be used on its own.) The usage continued for some time, and makes strange reading in some cases, such as the following reference to a cucumber: 'The coastes or sides be long, and greene at the beginning, & afterward yellow' (Henry Lyte's translation [1578] of Rembert Dodoens' *Cruydeboeck*). From the eighteenth century, the word was used in Canada and the United States to mean 'hillslope', especially an ice-covered one that could be slid down on a sled, and this is the sense in some Canadian and American stories subsequently, as in Louisa M. Alcott's children's story, *An Old-Fashioned Girl* (1870), where the line occurs: '"Let's run," said Polly, as they came into the path after the last coast'. It is this 'coast', too, that became the verb that means 'freewheel downhill', as on a bicycle without pedalling or in a car without the use of the engine.

coax (encourage, persuade by flattery, gentleness etc.)
In the sixteenth century, when the word first appeared, the meaning was 'fool', 'deceive'. The spelling then, too, was 'cokes', and the usual phrase was 'make a cokes of'. (Johnson called it 'a low word' in his *Dictionary* of 1755.) Another meaning at this time was 'pet', 'fondle', as in this stage direction from Mrs Aphra Behn's play *Sir Patient Fancy* (1678), based on Molière's *Le Malade imaginaire:* 'For my sake, dear, pardon him this one time [*cokesing him*]'. These two senses then became obsolete and only the 'wheedle' one survived.

cockney (native Londoner)
In the fourteenth century, 'cockney' was a word for a small, misshapen hen's egg, regarded as a 'cock's egg', showing the origin in Middle English *coken* (the genitive plural of *cok*, 'cock') and *ey*, 'egg'. The word also meant 'spoilt child', 'milksop', with such a pampered child also called a 'nestle-cock'. From this developed the sense of 'effeminate townsman', especially one who was regarded by sturdy country-dwellers as 'soft', and typically one from London. This final meaning, which became established in the sixteenth century, was the one that settled in the modern usage, although today

most 'cockneys' are regarded as 'tough nuts' rather than effeminate city dwellers.

cocksure (oversure, arrogant)
Before the word meant 'feeling quite sure' (subjectively) it meant 'quite sure' (objectively), with this latter sense recorded in the sixteenth century. Here it is in the earlier sense, in Foxe's *Book of Martyrs* (1563): 'Whoso dwelleth under that secret thing, and help of the Lord, shall be cock-sure for evermore'. The present shade of meaning developed from the seventeenth century. The precise origin of the word is uncertain. A suggestion of 'sure as a cock is to crow in the morning' has been made, but this hardly seems to fit the sense. Perhaps the 'cock' is the word that means 'tap', although even this is rather difficult to explain convincingly.

coffin (box for a corpse)
The word is directly related to 'coffer', and this was in effect the original meaning of 'coffin' in the fourteenth century, as 'box', 'chest' or even 'basket'. The modern, more specialized sense developed from the sixteenth century, however, and the former meaning became obsolete soon after.

coin (piece of money)
The word had two separate meanings, both related, in the fourteenth century. The first was 'corner', 'corner-stone', which has survived in modern 'coign' (as in 'coign of vantage'). The second was 'die', that is, a die for stamping money. The link between the two was that the die was in the form of a 'corner' or wedge. These senses then became obsolete, while a third meaning, that of the money itself, survived to be used as the standard word today. The old 'corner' sense of 'coin' is also represented today by 'quoin' as an architectural term for the solid angle of a building. It is interesting that most other languages have a word for 'coin' that in English is represented by the word 'money', such as French *monnaie*, Italian *moneta*, German *Münze* and Russian *moneta*. All these (and 'money', therefore) relate to 'Moneta', the epithet of the Greek goddess Juno (meaning 'warner') in whose temple at Rome the original mint

was housed (with 'mint' also related to this name).

coition (copulation)
Before the word settled to its present meaning, it had the sense 'conjunction' in the sixteenth century, pointing to its literal Latin origin of 'going together' (*co-*, 'together' and *ire*, 'to go'). This could be in the astronomical sense of 'conjunction' (as of the planets) or mean simply 'uniting', 'meeting', whether of people or objects. The modern sense is first recorded in the seventeenth century.

collier (coalminer)
Because 'coal' originally meant 'charcoal' (see **coal** itself), the first meaning of 'collier' was similarly 'charcoal burner'. This was in the fourteenth century. The present meaning appeared about two hundred years later.

comedy (amusing play)
The word came to have its present sense only in the seventeenth century. Originally, in the fourteenth century, a 'comedy' was a narrative poem with an agreeable ending, the so called 'happy ending'. This particular sense may have been influenced by the title of Dante's *La Divina Commedia*, said to have been itself so called by its author because 'in the conclusion, it is prosperous, pleasant, and desirable', while its style was 'lax and unpretending', since it was 'written in the vulgar tongue, which women and children speak'. This is not to overlook the word's ultimate origin in Greek *kōmos*, 'revel' and the related *kōmōidos*, 'comic actor', 'comic poet'. From the sixteenth century, a 'comedy' was a miracle play or an interlude, again with a 'happy ending'. From this in turn came the modern meaning. Literary scholars say that the work that marked the transition from miracle play to modern comedy was Nicholas Udall's *Ralph Roister Doister*, written about 1553 and probably first performed about this time by the boys of Westminster School, where Udall was headmaster.

comfort (well-being, ease)
The earliest sense of the word was 'encouragement', 'support', even 'refreshment'.

This was in the thirteenth century, when also the modern meaning of 'relief in distress' was first recorded. The sense 'content', 'satisfaction' appeared in the seventeenth century, and the 'material wellbeing' sense only in the nineteenth century. Shakespeare uses the word 'comfort' as a sort of interjection, as in *Richard II* (1593), where Richard says to Gaunt:

What comfort, man? How is't with aged Gaunt?

Similarly in the same play, where Aumerle says to Richard:

Comfort, my liege! why looks your Grace so pale?

and seven lines later:

Comfort, my liege! remember who you are.

This is 'comfort' in the modern verbal sense 'soothe', 'console', so is rather similar to 'cheer up' or 'don't worry', or 'it's all right'. It is perhaps a pity that the use of the word in this manner is now obsolete: it is sometimes difficult to find a suitable word to say to a person when you want to comfort them.

commando (military unit trained for making surprise raids into enemy territory)
The term arose to apply to army units in South Africa in the nineteenth century, both before and during the Boer War of 1899–1902. The word was also used there to mean a raid or an expedition. From its application to Boer soldiers, the word was adopted in Britain in the Second World War to be used of bodies of picked men trained to repel any invasion by the Germans. Later, 'commando' was used of 'shock troops' elsewhere, especially on the Continent. The original borrowing of the word by the Boers was from Dutch *commando*, 'command'.

commode (chest of drawers; special chair with seat covering a chamber pot)
The two senses given here are still current for this piece of furniture, although the former meaning arose in the eighteenth century and the latter in the nineteenth. Before either, however, the meaning of 'commode' was 'woman's tall headdress'. This was a device in fashion in the last part of the seventeenth century and first part of the eighteenth, consisting of a wire framework covered with silk or lace and occasionally having so called lappets (small hanging flaps) hanging over the wearer's shoulders. Unless one is aware of this early meaning, an encounter with 'commode' in literature of the period could be baffling, if not bizarre. An example might be these lines from Edward Ward's *Hudibras Redivivus* (1706):

Stiff Commodes in Triumph star'd
Above their Foreheads half a Yard.

A similar spectacle to modern eyes is conjured up by these rather later lines from Thomas Parnell's poem *Allegory on Man* (1717):

Nor with long streets and longer roads
Dangling behind her, like commodes.

The 'close-stool' sense of the word is a reminder how suitable the term is for a domestic installation that corresponds functionally and linguistically to the public 'convenience'.

commuter (person who travels regularly by public transport to work and back)
Given that the standard meaning of 'commute' is 'change', the present sense of the word seems rather off course. The history of the modern 'commuter' lies in the so called 'commutation tickets' that were held by Americans travelling regularly by public transport in the nineteenth century. A commutation ticket was, as it still is in the United States, what in Britain is called a 'season ticket', that is, a ticket valid for a particular period of time (such as a month) that is obtainable at a reduced rate for regular use over a fixed route. (The ticket is so called since it is an 'exchange' for the fare paid.) Naturally, holders of such tickets came to be called 'commuters', and the word crossed the Atlantic to Britain some time just after the Second World War, as did the related verb 'commute'. The original sense of this verb, as mentioned above, was thus 'exchange' rather than 'change', a use current in the seventeenth century.

65

compass (mariner's instrument; range, limits)

The two senses given here were the last to emerge for the word. This was in the seventeenth century. The mathematical instrument called 'compasses' was in use from the fourteenth century. The earliest senses of all for the word, however, were the now obsolete 'ingenuity' and 'area', both current in the thirteenth century, with 'circle' appearing a little later. The ultimate origin of the word is in Vulgar Latin *compassare*, 'to pace off' (from *com-*, 'with' and *passus*, 'pace'). This can be quite easily seen to be relevant for the older senses, including the obsolete ones, but hardly seems appropriate for the modern ship's compass. This latter sense is thought to have derived from Italian *compasso*, which was the word not only for the compass but for the circular compass box in which it was housed. (Hence perhaps 'box the compass' as the term for naming all the points of the compass in their correct order.)

compatible (able to exist together easily)

An early sense of the word when it first arose in the fifteenth century was 'sympathetic', that is, 'suffering with'. From this arose the more general meaning current today.

compendium (collection of games, implements etc. in a single case or box)

The word is obviously taken direct from Latin, and so literally means 'that which is weighed together' (from *com-*, 'with' and *pendere*, 'to weigh'). When the word was first used in English, in the sixteenth century, it meant 'abridgment', 'condensation', 'digest', that is, an abbreviated account of a larger work, and this is still used in some contexts today. One now obsolete sense, however, was the seventeenth- and eighteenth-century one of 'sparing', 'saving', especially referring to some action or object that saved labour or was economical (such as spelling words with a single letter where there should really be a double). The modern sense, as in the definition above, is peculiarly British. Compendiums (or compendia) of games first appeared at the end of the nineteenth century, and the 'compendium' that was (perhaps still is) a

packet of stationery for letter-writing first appeared, apparently, in the First World War, when it was supplied to soldiers. (A definition of 1923 describes it as comprising a 'pad of note, envelopes, and blotting'; H. A. Maddox, *Dictionary of Stationery*.) The word is thus not related to 'pen'!

complacent (satisfied with oneself)

In the seventeenth century, 'complacent' meant 'pleasing'. The sense was short-lived, however, and the present meaning took over in the eighteenth century, when it superseded the earlier word 'complacential'.

complexion (colour and texture of the skin, especially of the face)

The word literally means 'combination', from the Latin root (*complex-*) that also gave 'complex' (this itself deriving from *com-*, 'with' and a form of the verb *plectere*, 'to weave'). Originally, the word could refer to any general 'combining', but especially related to the four so called 'humours' of the body (blood, phlegm, choler or yellow bile, melancholy or black bile). From this, the sense came to denote the constitution of the body and also of the mind (a person's 'temperament'). All these meanings were current for some time from the fourteenth century, and the 'bodily constitution' sense is the one, for example, in Shakespeare's *Hamlet* (1602), as when Hamlet says, in the final scene: 'But yet methinks it is very sultry and hot for my complexion'. The modern sense of the word arose in the fifteenth century, and also comes in Shakespeare, in *The Merchant of Venice* (1596), where the Prince of Morocco's opening lines in the second act are:

Mislike me not for my complexion,
The shadow'd livery of the burnish'd
sun.

The use of the word in the expression 'that puts a new complexion on things' dates from the sixteenth century, and is a development of the facial sense.

complicate (make complex or difficult)

The word had a literal sense of 'intertwine' in the seventeenth century, as when Donne wrote in one of his poems (*Selections*, 1631) of:

Sin enwrapped and complicated in sin.

The English sense derives from Latin *complicare* (*com-*, 'with' and *plicare,* 'to fold'). Passing through the sense 'mix up with' at about the same time, the word came to acquire its present meaning only in the nineteenth century.

comply (agree to do what someone else wishes or orders)
The ultimate origin of the word is Latin *complere,* 'to complete' (these two words are more obviously related), and when it first came into use in English in the seventeenth century, it had two distinct senses of 'fulfil' and 'do the polite thing'. Both these meanings are now obsolete, but both are first recorded in Shakespeare. The former comes in *Othello* (1604), where Othello says:

Vouch with me, heaven, I therefore beg
  it not
To please the palate of my appetite,
Nor to comply with heat.

The latter occurs in *Hamlet* (1602), where, in the 'players' scene', Hamlet says: 'Your hands, come then; the appurtenance of welcome is fashion and ceremony: let me comply with you in this garb'.

compost (mixture of decayed vegetation, manure etc. used as a fertilizer)
A compost is a compound (the words are of the same origin), but the present 'compost' was originally a quite different 'compound'. In the fourteenth century it was a 'compote' (another related word), that is, a dish of fruit or spice preserved in wine, vinegar, sugar or the like. The 'prepared manure' compound emerged only in the sixteenth century. For a time in the seventeenth century, however, the now obsolete sense 'composition' was expressed by 'compost'.

compromise (agreement reached by concessions being made on both sides)
The original sense of 'compromise' was not quite the same as it is now, and in the fifteenth century the word indicated a joint agreement to abide by a decision that had been taken, in other words, it was more literally a 'joint promise'. The term is found mainly in contemporary legal documents.

The present sense first developed about a hundred years later.

computer (calculating machine)
This bald definition means much more now that it did when the word first appeared in the seventeenth century, meaning not only a machine that computed or calculated but a person who did. (As an occupation, a 'computer' could have been a person employed to make calculations in an observatory, for example, or in surveying.) The use of the word in anything like the modern sense arose at the end of the nineteenth century, and an article in the issue of the magazine *Engineering* for 22 January 1897 describes a 'computer' that was actually a kind of circular sliderule. The first electronic computer was one developed in the United States for the US Army in the 1940s.

conceit (arrogance, 'cheek')
This word is one of the more famous 'sense shifts'. In the fourteenth century, it meant 'conception', 'thought', and also 'personal opinion', with all three senses in use down to the eighteenth century. The phrase 'in my conceit' thus meant 'in my opinion', and when Rosalind says to Orlando, 'I know you are a gentleman of good conceit' in Shakespeare's *As You Like It* (1600), she means, 'I know you are a gentleman who will understand well'. From the fifteenth century, 'conceit' came to mean 'fancy', 'fanciful opinion', not necessarily in a selfish sense, as in Thomas Dekker and Thomas Middleton's joint play *The Roaring Girle* (1611):

Some haue a conceit their drink tasts
  better
In an outlandish cup then in our owne.

At about the same time, 'conceit' even meant a concrete 'fancy', a fancy article, as near the beginning of Shakespeare's *A Midsummer Night's Dream* (1590), where Egeus lists the many gifts Lysander has given to Hermia, Egeus' daughter:

With bracelets of thy hair, rings, gawds,
  conceits,
Knacks, trifles, nosegays, sweetmeats.

The modern sense seems to have developed as a short form of 'self-conceit'.

concoction (something devised or put together, often hastily)
The word literally means 'cooking together', although Latin *concoctio* was also the word for 'digestion', as it originally was in English when it was first used (as the noun of 'concoct') in the sixteenth century. The physiology of the day distinguished three such 'concoctions': the 'first concoction' was digestion in the stomach and intestines, the 'second concoction' was the process by which the chyme so formed changed, as they thought, into blood, and the 'third concoction' was secretion. The modern sense, whether a physical brew such as a soup or drink, or a mental one such as a story or plot, developed as late as the nineteenth century.

concrete (not abstract; building material)
The first sense here dates from the fourteenth century, and the latter from the nineteenth. The original sense, now obsolete, was 'composite', however, and this basic concept lies behind both meanings, since if a thing is 'concrete' (not abstract) it has a 'composition' of different qualities (a house can be not only big, but old, tall, red, etc, while honour, an abstract noun, can only be honourable). The modern building material, on the other hand is a 'concrete composition' of gravel or sand and cement.

concur (agree)
In its original literal sense, in the fifteenth century, 'concur' meant 'collide', 'converge', reflecting its Latin source meaning 'run together' (*con-*, 'with', 'together' and *currere*, 'run'). Thus, in his translation (1470) of Caesar's *Commentaries*, John Tiptoft, who was also Earl of Worcester, says that the ships of friend and foe 'were sore brosyd [i.e. bruised, see **bruise**] by reason of concurring'. The word could similarly be used of people coming together, whether in combat or to meet as friends. In the sixteenth century, too, streams and rivers could 'concur' or run together at a confluence, as could lines, times, church feasts and the like. This second sense may not be quite dead, especially in the 'happening simultaneously' sense. But mostly the current meaning is of agreement with another's opinion.

condole (express sympathy with)
Although the verb literally means 'suffer pain with' (Latin *con-*, 'with' and *dolere*, 'suffer pain', 'grieve'), the original use of the verb in English was simply 'sorrow greatly', with the 'with' either unexpressed or merely absent. For example, in Shakespeare's *A Midsummer Night's Dream* (1590) Bottom says, when the friends are planning their play ('Pyramus and Thisbe'): 'If I do it, let the audience look to their eyes; I will move storms, I will condole in some measure'. The sense 'grieve with' arose in the sixteenth century, and the modern 'express sympathy' in the seventeenth.

confines (limits, bordered area)
In the fourteenth century, 'confines' could often mean simply 'region' without much idea of a limit or of 'confinement'. In Shakespeare's *Richard III* (1594), Queen Margaret thus says:

Here in these confines slily have I lurk'd
To watch the waning of mine enemies.

Similarly, in *Julius Caesar* (1601), Antony, in his impassioned speech after the murder of Caesar, says that Caesar's spirit:

Shall in these confines with a monarch's voice
Cry 'Havoc!' and let slip the dogs of war.

The modern sense of the word came into use in the sixteenth century.

confiscate (remove as a penalty or punishment)
The word is related to 'fiscal', and in the sixteenth century meant 'appropriate to the public treasury', applying to confiscated private property (when the second syllable was stressed, not the first). The more general sense, now familiar to schoolchildren, arose in the nineteenth century.

confound (confuse)
For some time from the thirteenth century, 'confound' meant quite concretely 'overthrow', 'defeat', with an extension of this, applied to plans and schemes rather than people, developing at the same time and lasting long enough to appear in the British National Anthem, with the relevant lines

running as Henry Carey wrote them in 1740:

Confound their politicks,
Frustrate their knavish tricks,
On him our hopes are fix'd,
O save us all!

The current sense of 'throw into confusion' was not much later, although the word today is perhaps mostly used as a mild curse ('confound it!'), a use which is of similar vintage, but originally meant 'bring to perdition', with the milder sense developing after about 1700.

confrere (learned colleague)
The literal meaning of the word is 'co-brother', or perhaps better, 'co-friar', and this was the original sense from the fifteenth century. This early meaning came from Medieval Latin *confrater*, but the modern sense, as used from the seventeenth century, is a direct borrowing of the French.

conjecture (guess, hazarded opinion)
In the fourteenth century, the word was used to mean 'interpretation', especially of signs, omens, dreams and the like. In Thomas Langley's translation (1546) of Virgil's *De inventoribus rerum*, for example, he writes: 'A certaine prophet commaunded euery man to stande stil til he had taken a coniecture of the birde that flowe by'. The present sense developed from the sixteenth century, and has been used increasingly weakly since, so that it now means little more than 'think' ('I would conjecture we ought to turn left here').

conjurer (magician)
A conjurer was originally a person who conjured spirits. This was in the fourteenth century, where the earliest recording we have of the sense is in Wyclif's Bible of 1382, so that the 'vagabond Jews, exorcists' of Acts 19:13 in the Authorized Version of 1611 were 'Iewis exorcistis, or coniureris'. Similarly, in Shakespeare's *Comedy of Errors* (1590), in the last scene, Antiphonus says:

This pernicious slave [i.e. Pinch],
Forsooth, took on him as a conjurer.

The modern 'magician' meaning first emerged in the eighteenth century.

conkers (boys' 'duel' game played with chestnuts on a string)
The great game of conkers was originally played with snail shells, hence the association with 'conch'. The sport is first recorded only in the nineteenth century, and the switch to horse chestnuts appears to have been made some time in the 1880s.

conscription (compulsory enlistment in the armed forces)
In the fourteenth century, 'conscription' (which literally means 'enrolling' or 'writing with') meant simply 'enrolment', with no suggestion of compulsory enlistment. The modern sense arose after 1800 when the word was borrowed from the identical French, itself applying to the compulsory enlistment that was decreed by the law of the new French Republic on 5 September 1798. (The law declared that young men between the ages of twenty and twenty-five should be compulsorily made to enter military service.) From this in turn the noun 'conscript' developed.

consign (hand to another, assign)
Latin *consignare*, from which the word came, means 'attest with a sign', and the earliest sense of the English word is thus 'attest', 'confirm', 'ratify'. This fifteenth-century sense was followed a hundred years later by the meaning 'mark with a cross', especially of a person who is being christened or confirmed. The current sense is first recorded at about the same time, and is now the only one.

consort (1 associate with; 2 spouse, especially of a royal person)
The first sense here is now the most general, and originally the verb meant 'accompany', 'escort', since it developed from the second sense. The latter, in turn, originally meant 'partner', 'mate', i.e. not necessarily a marriage partner. This second meaning dates from the fifteenth century, the other from the sixteenth. Both are now obsolete. From the sixteenth century, 'consort' was also used to apply to a concert of music, or to the musicians themselves. This is still the same word, although it appears to have been influenced by 'concert'.

contest (competition, conflict)
The noun developed in the seventeenth century from the verb, which itself originally meant 'bear witness to' in the sixteenth century, thus serving as a reminder that the 'test' element in the word is related to 'testify' and 'testament'. Even the noun initially meant 'argument', 'wordy war', so that the phrase 'without contest' meant 'uncontestably', 'without doubt'.

continent (mainland, especially that of Europe)
To begin with the current sense: 'continent' was a borrowing into English from French *continent* or Italian *continente*, which in turn derived from the Latin phrase *terra continuens*, 'continuous land'. This was a seventeenth-century extension of a sixteenth-century usage that included the now obsolete 'container' and 'summary'. The first of these occurs in Shakespeare's *A Midsummer Night's Dream* (1590), where Titania speaks of 'contagious fogs' which:

Have every pelting river made so proud
That they have overborne their
continents.

The second comes in *The Merchant of Venice* (1596), where Bassanio, having opened the casket, says:

Here's the scroll,
The continent and summary of my
fortune.

contretemps (disagreement)
This obviously French word (literally 'against the time') was originally used as a fencing term in the seventeenth century, to denote an untimely thrust, one made at the wrong moment. From this, the word came to acquire its present sense of 'disagreement', basically implying that at the right time, there could have been agreement. This sense arose in the nineteenth century.

conundrum (puzzle)
This strange word (perhaps deriving from some distorted Latin word such as *quinombrum*) has something of a strange history. In the sixteenth century it meant 'capricious idea', 'whim', or what was formerly called a 'crotchet'. In fact both this last word and 'conundrum' itself occur in a line from Ben Jonson's play *Volpone* (1605): 'I must ha' my crotchets! And my conundrums!' From the seventeenth century, the word meant 'pun' (which after all is not quite the same as a conundrum, which may not involve any play on words), and was defined in more or less these terms by Johnson in his *Dictionary* (1755): '*Conundrum*, a low jest; a quibble; a mean conceit [see **conceit** itself]: a cant word'. Subsequently it became a riddle involving a pun, and finally the puzzling statement or question that it is today, with this sense in use from the eighteenth century.

convent (nunnery)
Originally, from the thirteenth century, the word was used to apply to a body of monks, friars or nuns that lived together, and so embraced 'monastery' and 'friary'. From the eighteenth century, however, the sense was restricted to a nunnery. The convent after which London's Covent Garden is named was originally a community of monks: the Abbey (or Convent) of St Peter at Westminster. The word itself is related to 'convene', and literally means a group of people who have 'come together' (Latin *convenire*, 'to assemble').

conversation (mutual talk)
The word has had some interesting and even unexpected sense developments over the years. In the fourteenth century, it meant simply 'living', 'way of life', and appears in this sense more than once in the Bible, for example Psalm 50:23: 'To him that ordereth his conversation aright will I shew the salvation of God', and Philippians 3:20: 'For our conversation is in heaven'. In the sixteenth century, 'conversation' (which literally means 'a turning together') came to have the sense of 'sexual intercourse', as in Shakespeare's *Richard III* (1594), where Gloucester, speaking of the beheaded traitor Hastings, says:

I mean his conversation with Shore's
wife.

This sense survived in the old legal term 'criminal conversation' (usually abbreviated to 'crim. con.', meaning adultery). The modern meaning of the word also dates from the sixteenth century, although a hundred years later another sense developed, now obsolete, of 'acquaintance', 'company', as in the opening scene of Dryden's comedy *Marriage-a-la-mode* (1673): 'A Gentleman, Sir, that understands the Grand mond so well, who has haunted the best Conversations'. An echo of this sense survives in the modern 'conversazione', as a meeting of people to discuss intellectual or cultural matters.

convict (condemned criminal)
In the sixteenth century, the word was used of any convicted person, so that a thief would be a 'convict' as much as a murderer. From the eighteenth century, the word was restricted to a condemned criminal serving a sentence of penal servitude, such as the ones deported to Botany Bay or the ones that sometimes escaped from Dartmoor.

convince (make a person believe by argument or reasoning)
In the sixteenth century, the sense of the word was 'overcome', 'conquer', whether in argument or not, so that an armed force could 'convince' an enemy or a person could be 'convinced' by being proved to be wrong in an argument. In these lines from Shakespeare's *Macbeth* (1605), the sense is really the former, when Lady Macbeth, in her 'screw your courage to the sticking-place' speech, says:

His [i.e. Duncan's] two chamberlains
Will I with wine and wassail so convince
That memory, the warder of the brain,
Shall be a fume.

At the same time, 'convince' was also used to mean 'convict' or 'prove', the former in the criminal sense, the latter in the sense 'demonstrate', 'show'. All these senses are now obsolete, and the current meaning dates from the seventeenth century.

coop (cage for hens; place of confinement)
The earliest meaning of the word, in the thirteenth century, was 'basket', with the origin in a Germanic word that itself came from Latin *cupa,* 'tun', 'barrel' (hence the occupation of the cooper, who made and repaired barrels). From this sense the word came to apply to a basket that was used for

putting over hens when they were brooding or being fattened up. In the fifteenth century the word meant any kind of hen cage or pen, and a hundred years later was used in general for a place where anyone or anything was confined, especially a cage or prison. Probably the word is now most frequently used in the phrase 'cooped up' rather than as a noun, however.

cope (manage, deal successfully with)
To 'cope' was to 'come to blows' in the fourteenth century, since that was the sense in the French *colper,* 'to strike' (now *couper,* 'to cut') from which it derived. The meaning lasted down to the sixteenth century, and in appropriately historical or 'stylish' literature even later, as when it comes in Pope's translation (1725) of Homer's *Odyssey,* where he has the line:

Swear to stand neutral, while we cope in fight.

The modern sense dates from the sixteenth century, the shift of meaning implying that a conflict had come to a successful conclusion.

coquette (flirt, 'pert miss')
The word could also apply to men, usually in the spelling 'coquet' (or as a 'male coquette'), when it first entered English from the French in the seventeenth century. Indeed, the origin of the French word is male itself, since *coquet* derives from *coq,* 'cock', the reference being to what the *Oxford English Dictionary* calls 'the strutting gait and amorous characteristics' of the bird. In his musical play, *The Beggar's Opera* (1728), John Gay has a line that refers to both: 'The coquets of both sexes are self-lovers, and that is a love no other what ever can dispossess'. (The play was said to have made Gay rich, and Rich, its producer, gay.) From about the end of the century, however, all coquettes were female, and the male coquette or coquet went out of fashion. (The word itself, though, left something of a legacy in the man who was 'cocky', or arrogantly smart.)

coroner (official who holds inquests in the case of a sudden death)
The word is fairly obviously based on

'crown', and actually derives from the Latin title *custos placitorum coronae*, 'guardian of the pleas of the crown', this applying to an official in Norman times. In English, in the fourteenth century, a 'coroner' was an officer who had the responsibility of protecting the rights of crown property. Sone hundred years later, the sense had narrowed to its current one, since holding an inquest had been one of the duties of the earlier official. A reference to this comes in an Old French order of 1292: 'Et si nul homme murge en prisoun, si volom nous, qe le Corouner voise veer le cors, et prenge bone enqueste de sa mort, coment il avera este mort' ['And if any man die in prison, we wish the Coroner to come to see the body and hold a good enquiry into the (man's) death, (and establish) how he had been killed'].

corpse (dead body)
As still in modern French *corps*, 'corpse' originally simply meant 'body' in English, and also 'person'. A dead body was thus called a 'dead corpse', as in the Bible in 2 Kings 19:35, for example: 'And when they arose early in the morning, behold, they were all dead corpses'. (Occasionally other adjectives would be used, as a 'lifeless corpse', or, in Shakespeare's *Henry VI*, Part 2 [1593], a 'breathless corpse'.) The sense of just 'corpse' to mean 'dead body' prevailed, however, from about the seventeenth century. See also **corset** (below).

corset (boned supporting undergarment worn by women)
The word, etymologically a 'little body' (French *corset*, diminutive of *cors*, 'body') was originally a laced bodice worn as an outer garment by women in the middle ages, and in fact also by men. This was in the fourteenth century. The present garment, where it is still worn (as 'stays'), evolved in the eighteenth century. As *The Times* reported in its issue for 24 June 1795: 'Corsettes about six inches long, and a slight buffon tucker of two inches high, are now the only defensive *paraphernalia* of our fashionable Belles'. Modern surgical corsets are of course worn by both men and women.

costume (dress, suit)
Not for nothing does 'costume' suggest 'custom', since the words are related, and in the eighteenth century the word meant 'manners and customs belonging to a particular time and place', this sense itself arising from historical art, which aimed to portray people and events realistically. The modern meaning of 'costume' came in the nineteenth century.

cot (baby's or small child's bed)
In the seventeenth century, a 'cot' was a kind of light bedstead, for anyone, child or not. The word is an Anglo-Indian one, and originally applied to the bedsteads used by travellers in India (the Hindi source word is *khāt*). In the eighteenth century the word was taken over by the navy to be used for a sailor's (more precisely an officer's) swinging bed, a more elegant version of a hammock. Finally, in the nineteenth century, the word acquired its current meaning.

countenance (face or its expression; moral support)
The word is related directly to 'contain', and in the thirteenth century meant 'conduct', as well as what Dr Johnson in his *Dictionary* (1755) describes as 'calmness of look, confidence of mien'. Both these imply a 'containing' of oneself, a composure. In the fourteenth century, the general sense 'appearance' developed, as in Shakespeare's *The Taming of the Shrew* (1596), where the 'Pedant', impersonating Vincentio, says: 'Lay hands on the villain: I believe, a' means to cozen somebody in this city under my countenance' (i.e. 'he intends to cheat someone by pretending to be me'). The 'face' or 'expression' sense of the word emerged also in the fourteenth century, and the more recent 'support' in the sixteenth.

counter (table in shop, bank etc)
In the fourteenth century, a 'counter', as its name suggests, was an object used in counting or in keeping accounts, i.e. like the 'counters' in some modern games or in marking cards. From this, the sense developed naturally to mean first, a desk where money was counted, then a money-changer's table, and finally a tradesman's

or shopkeeper's 'surface' where goods were served. The current sense arose from the fourteenth century.

courage (bravery)
The word is related to French *cœur* 'heart', and this was precisely the original sense in English in the thirteenth century, particularly the heart regarded as the seat of thought, mind, spirit and a person's nature. Shakespeare uses the word in this sense in his *Henry VI*, Part 3 (1593), when Queen Margaret says to Henry:

My lord, cheer up your spirits: our foes
are nigh,
And this soft courage makes your
followers faint.

In the fourteenth century, the present sense arose, but so did a now obsolete meaning 'intention', 'purpose', as in Shakespeare's less well known *Timon of Athens* (1607), where Sempronius, speaking to Timon's servant, says:

I'd such a courage to do him good.

cousin (son or daughter of a person's uncle or aunt)
In the thirteenth century, the word had its present sense already, but it could also simply mean 'relative', in particular a nephew or niece. This usage lasted for some time, down to at least the seventeenth century, which can make a relationship confusing in literature of the period. Thus in Wyclif's Bible of 1382, Daniel 13:29 reads like this: 'She came with fadir, and modir, and sonnys, and alle hir cosyns'. In his second translation appearing six years later, the last three words had been amended to 'alle kynesmen'. Sometimes, fortunately, the exact relationship is stated, as in Shakespeare's *Much Ado About Nothing* (1599), when Leonato meets Antonio and says: 'How now, brother! Where is my cousin, your son?' ('Brother' means what it says here.) Even more confusingly, for modern readers, the custom developed in the fifteenth century for one sovereign to address another as 'cousin', or for a nobleman to do so similarly. Here, for example, is James IV writing to Henry VIII in 1513: 'To the richt excellennt, richt hie, and michty Prince oure

derrest Brothir and Cousing the King of Ingland'. This usage, not unexpectedly, occurs more than once in Shakespeare, too, as in *All's Well That Ends Well* (1601), where the King of France says he has received a letter from 'our cousin Austria'.

crafty (cunning)
The development of this word is similar to that of **artful** (which see). In its original Old English sense, it meant simply 'strong' (compare modern German *Kraft*, 'strength'), 'skilful', so that two thirteenth-century texts mention a 'crafti weorc man' and a 'crefty clerke'. The noun 'craft', too, meant 'strength', 'skill' in similar fashion. The modern sense of 'crafty' developed from the thirteenth century, and the former use, which continued down to the sixteenth century, became obsolete.

crave (long for)
In Old English, 'crave' meant 'demand', as in these rhyming lines from *The Story of Genesis and Exodus* (1250):

Quatso thu wilt for hire crauen,
Aske it with skil and thus salt hauen

(That is: Whatever you want to demand for her, ask within reason and you shall have it.) From the twelfth century, the sense 'beg for' arose, and the current 'long for', 'desire keenly' developed a hundred years later.

crayfish (crustacean resembling a small lobster; spiny lobster)
In the fourteenth century, 'crayfish' was used of any crustacean generally except crabs, with a lobster usually called a 'sea crayfish'. A hundred years later, the sense was restricted to the particular crustacean familiar today (especially the genus *Astacus*), known in the United States as a 'crawfish'. From the eighteenth century, however, the name also applied to the so called 'spiny lobster' (of the genus *Palinurus*). The word derives from Old French *crevice* or *crevis*, and is nothing to do with 'fish'.

crazy (mad)
The popular sense of the word is the most recent, arising in the seventeenth century. The original meaning in the sixteenth century was 'unsound', 'liable to fall to

pieces', from the noun 'craze' that meant 'crack' in the fourteenth century. ('Crazy paving' is more from the 'mad' sense than this earlier usage.) For a while in the sixteenth century, the word could mean 'having poor health', and this sense occurs in Shakespeare's *Henry VI*, Part I (1591), where Talbot says to the dying Duke of Bedford:

> Come, my lord,
> We will bestow you in some better place,
> Fitter for sickness and for crazy age.

A similar development occurred for the verb and noun 'craze', with the latter's sense of 'mania', 'fad' coming only in the nineteenth century.

credence (belief)
In the fourteenth century, 'credence' meant 'trust', 'credit', hence the still current 'letters of credence' that authorize a diplomat to act for his government. (The term itself dates from the same century.) The modern meaning 'belief' was also known in the fourteenth century, although the small table by a church altar called a 'credence table' got its name only in the nineteenth century. It developed from the 'credence' that was the word used for testing food (especially in a royal household) in the fifteenth century, and the rather later 'credence' that actually was the table on which the dishes were placed.

credulity (undue readiness to believe)
When the word was first used in English in the fifteenth century, it meant simply 'belief', 'credence' (see previous entry). By the seventeenth century it had acquired its present shade of meaning, following an earlier similar development for its adjective 'credulous'. No doubt a special word was needed for this concept in an age when people's religious and scientific beliefs were rapidly changing.

cretin (idiot, fool)
Today the word is used either contemptuously or humorously. Originally, however, it applied to certain mentally retarded dwarfs who lived in some Alpine valleys in the eighteenth century. Many of them had grossly enlarged heads and goitres. The word actually means 'Christian' (from Swiss patois *crestin*), with this name given to the people to indicate that although savagely deformed physically and mentally, they were not 'brutes' or animals but human beings after all.

crew (ship's company)
In the fifteenth century, the word was used for the reinforcement of a military force, thus pointing to the origin in Old French *creue*, 'increase' (these two last words are also themselves related). By extension, the word then came to mean an armed company in the sixteenth century, and settled to denote a ship's company in the seventeenth.

crib (1 child's bed; 2 illegitimately used translation)
The two words *are* related, and are in fact from one and the same source. On the face of it, however, the connection seems remote. In Old English, 'crib' was the word for 'manger', a sense it still has. From this, it came to mean 'wicker basket' in the fourteenth century, a sense now obsolete, and 'cabin', 'hovel' in the sixteenth, now a rather rarish use. The meaning 'child's bed' followed in the next century, originally one with barred or latticed sides, like a manger or feeding trough for animals. (A combination of both senses occurs in the Christmas 'nativity scene' crib, a model manger with a representation of the infant Jesus in it, referring to the traditional Bible story.) From the 'basket' sense a thieves' jargon word 'crib' developed, meaning 'steal', 'pilfer', and from this eighteenth-century meaning a new noun 'crib' emerged to mean 'theft' generally, and 'secretly used translation' a hundred years later. The idea is of a text that has been 'stolen' in the same way as a plagiarism.

crisis (crucial or dangerous situation, emergency)
The identical Greek word from which the English derives means literally 'decision', in the sense 'crossroads', 'make or break time', 'moment on which the future depends'. The earliest use of 'crisis' in English arose in the fifteenth century to denote the turning point of a disease, strictly, one that would lead

either to recovery or to death. From the seventeenth century, the word came to have its current sense, meaning a similar situation in life or events generally. As often happens with 'powerful' words, its use is today often trivialized, to mean little more than a minor but annoying upset ('Sorry, there's been a crisis in the kitchen.').

crisp (firm but brittle)
The word is related to 'crepe', which is somewhat closer to its original Old English sense of 'curly', especially of hair. From this, a sense 'wrinkled', 'rippled' arose in the fourteenth century, and the modern meaning developed some two hundred years later. Today, hair can be both 'crisp' and curly at the same time, since the first word has now more the sense 'stiff' or 'frizzy'. The rather unexpected current sense may have arisen from or at least been influenced by the actual 'brittle' sound of 'crisp' as a spoken word.

critic (reviewer)
A critic can praise or damn, criticize or commend. In Shakespearean times, however, a critic always passed censure and disapproved, as in his *Love's Labour's Lost* (1588), where we have the first record of the word in English, where Berowne says:

I, that have been love's whip;
A very beadle to a humorous sigh;
A critic, nay, a night-watch constable.

The modern sense, as in 'art critic', 'literary critic' and so on, first arose in the seventeenth century. This sense is actually closer to the Greek origin of the word in *kritikos*, 'able to discern or judge'.

croon (sing sentimentally)
This word has denoted a number of noises and utterances before it finally took on its present meaning. In the fourteenth century it meant even 'bellow', 'roar', as a dialect word. This meant that even bulls 'crooned'. From the eighteenth century the word came to mean 'murmur' 'hum softly', perhaps originally as a sort of ridiculous opposite of the earlier sense. This use of 'croon' is still current, especially in Scotland, where a mother can 'croon' a lullaby to her baby. Finally, the modern meaning, 'sing a

popular song sentimentally into a closely held microphone', came into being just after the First World War, when one such song was 'Croon, Croon, Underneat' de Moon'. The crooner had arrived!

crosier, crozier (bishop's staff)
The word was originally, in the fourteenth century, the name of the person who carried an archbishop's cross (hence the surname Crozier). From this, the meaning naturally developed to the bearer of a bishop's staff, and finally to the staff itself, this no later than the fifteenth century.

crowd (dense mass of people)
The Old English meaning of the word, as a verb, was 'press on', 'push', in turn reflected in the old word 'press' for a crowd. From the fourteenth century, the verb meant 'press in a throng', as it still can, and from this in turn came the noun 'crowd' in the sixteenth century.

crucial (very important, decisive)
The word ultimately derives from Latin *crux, crucis*, 'cross', and 'crucial' thus meant initially 'cross-shaped' in the eighteenth century, with this use mainly an anatomical one, as a 'crucial incision' made by a surgeon. The modern meaning arose in the nineteenth century from the use by Francis Bacon of the Latin term *instantia crucis*, 'instance of the cross' in his philosophical treatise (all in Latin) *Novum Organum* (1620), which he explained as a metaphor for a *crux* or finger-post at a *bivium* or bifurcation in the road. The term thus denoted an instance when a choice would have to be made between two rival hypotheses, just as a person at a crossroads has to decide which way to go. Boyle and Newton extended the sense of the phrase in their *experimentum crucis*, or 'crucial experiment', which would decide conclusively, one way or the other, which scientific phenomena would produce the expected result. The current popular use of 'crucial' is very recent, and dates from after the Second World War.

crumpet (small round porous cake eaten toasted and buttered)
Crumpets have changed over the years. Seventeenth-century ones were thin griddle

75

cakes, often made of buckwheat meal. The modern sort materialized in the eighteenth century, and soon came to feature cosily in Victorian life and literature, as in Anthony Trollope's novel *The Warden* (1855), in which: 'There was dry toast and buttered toast, muffins and crumpets'. Oddly, there is even a crumpet (of a sort) in the Bible, at least in Wyclif's translation of 1382, where Exodus 29:23 runs: 'A cake of a loof, a crusted cake spreynd with oyle, a crompid cake, of the leepe of therf looues' (Authorized Version of 1611: 'And one loaf of bread, and one cake of oiled bread, and one wafer out of the basket of the unleavened bread'). This 'crumpet cake' is probably a 'curled cake', as it were a 'crimped cake' with curly edges, as griddle cakes often are. So it is hardly a crumpet in modern terms, but an interesting forerunner.

crux (decisive point)
The English word is the exact Latin one that produced **crucial** (which see). In the eighteenth century, especially as used by Sheridan and Swift, the word means 'conundrum', 'riddle'. From the nineteenth century a 'crux' was a difficulty that was hard to solve, especially an intellectual or philosophical one. From the second half of the same century, the word acquired its more general sense to mean 'decisive point'. Today, it is often used rather as 'crunch' is in this sense, and indeed the latter word is sometimes used by some speakers in place of it ('the crunch of the problem', heard on BBC Radio Solent, 9 October 1984).

crystal (transparent quartz or something resembling it)
This sense goes back to Old English, when also the word could mean simply 'ice'. It occurred as this in several biblical texts and translations, such as those of Wyclif (1382) and Miles Coverdale (1535). What they were doing was rendering Latin *crystallum* literally. The spelling of the word was always 'cristal' down to about the sixteenth century, when because of this Latin word, it changed to 'crystal'. In the same century a spelling 'chrystal' was also quite common, under the influence of such words as 'chrysolite'.

cubicle (individual compartment or small room in a dormitory, swimming pool etc)
The word, which derives from Latin *cubare*, 'to recline', 'lie in bed', originally meant just 'bedroom' in the fifteenth century. Caxton's translation (1483) of *The Golden Legend*, for example, has the line: 'I was delyueryd of a chyld in my cubycle'. The word became obsolete in the sixteenth century but was revived in the nineteenth century for use (as a term for a sleeping compartment) in the dormitories of English public schools.

cuff (band of cloth at bottom of sleeve)
A 'cuff' was originally a word for a glove or a mitten, as in William Langland's lovely alliterative poem *Piers Plowman* (1362), where Piers goes out to plough:

He caste on his clothes, i-clouted and i-hole,
His cokeres [i.e. leggings] and his coffus, for colde of his nayles.

The current sense developed from the sixteenth century, and in the sense 'handcuff' from the seventeenth century.

cul-de-sac (road or street with no exit, blind alley)
The clearly French word means literally 'bottom of the bag' and its first use in English, from the eighteenth century, was an anatomical one to denote a vessel or the like that had an opening at one end only, such as the caecum or 'blind gut'. The 'blind alley' sense came later, in the nineteenth century, when the phrase also began to be used figuratively for a 'no way out' idea or situation, or an inconclusive argument. All these senses also exist in the French language, where *cul* itself is a rather 'ruder' word than 'bottom' is (anatomically) in English.

cunning (wily, smart, devious)
Like both **artful** and **crafty** (which see) 'cunning' was originally a favourable word, meaning 'learned' in the thirteenth century, just as the corresponding noun did in the fourteenth. This is because Old English *cunnende* meant simply 'knowing', and is related (as 'cunning' itself is, therefore) to 'can'. Even in the fourteenth century, 'cunning' meant positively 'able', 'skilful',

and the word occurs in this sense as late as 1601 in Shakespeare's *Twelfth Night,* where Sir Andrew Aguecheek says to Sir Toby Belch: 'An [i.e. if] I thought he had been valiant and so cunning in fence I'd have seen him damned ere I challenged him'. The present 'crafty' or 'artful' sense came about in the sixteenth century.

cur (inferior dog, 'wretch')
A 'cur', or 'cur-dog' as it was formerly called, was not a mongrel or a low-bred dog as now, but a watchdog or shepherd's dog. The word was in use in the thirteenth century, but even in 1697 Dryden, in his translation of Virgil's *Georgics,* wrote of a shepherd and 'his trusty Cur'. The use of the word to mean 'worthless fellow' developed in the sixteenth century (the first record we have of it is in Shakespeare's *A Midsummer Night's Dream* of 1590), and the 'inferior dog' shade of meaning also dates from about this time.

curate (assistant to a parish priest)
As his name implies, a 'curate' originally had a 'cure' or 'care' of souls, so he was first and foremost a spiritual pastor. This sense dates from the fourteenth century and is now obsolete, although still found in the Book of Common Prayer (1545), where in the Prayer for the Clergy and People in Morning Prayer, God is asked to send down his grace 'upon our Bishops, and Curates, and all Congregations committed to their charge'. The current sense of 'assistant to the parish priest' dates from the sixteenth century. Compare **curator** (below)

curator (person in charge of a museum, zoo etc)
Like a **curate** (see previous entry), a 'curator' was originally a person who had a 'cure of souls', so that there was no distinction between the two words. This was in the fourteenth century, and in the fifteenth the word came to be used for the legal guardian of a child, a term still current in Scottish law. The modern meaning developed in the seventeenth century.

curious (strange, puzzling; keen to find out)
The word had two distinct meanings in the fourteenth century, now both obsolete. The first was 'careful', 'studious', the second was 'carefully made', 'skilfully wrought'. The former sense occurs, for example, in Robert Fabyan's *Chronicles* (1494), where he writes: 'He shold take hym vnto his cure, and be to hym as curyous as he wolde be vnto his owne chylde'. The latter meaning comes in the Bible, where Exodus 28:27 refers to 'the curious girdle of the ephod'. A more general extension of this second sense, also now obsolete, meant 'fine', 'excellent', as when Pepys observed in his *Diary* that on 24 September 1665 there was 'A very calm, curious morning', or when Stephen Primatt, in *The City and Country Purchaser and Builder* (1667) described 'Salisbury Plain, and divers other places of champion ground in England, which are very famous for curious air'. But the sense that also arose in the fourteenth century, and endured, was 'keen to know', 'eager to learn'. In the seventeenth century, yet one more now non-existent sense of the word was 'interesting', as in the then common phrase 'it is curious to observe'. The present 'strange' sense of 'curious' dates from the same time. The word itself is directly linked to the root 'cure' (meaning 'care') behind **curate** (which see, above).

curtsy, curtsey (act of respect made by women)
The word, which is simply an alteration of 'courtesy', formerly also applied to a similar 'act of obeisance' made by men and boys. Thus Robert Laneham, in his *Letter* of 1575 describing the festivities at Kenilworth, tells how: 'The minstrell made a pauz & a curtezy, for *Primus passus* [i.e. the 'first step' or first part of his story]', and Claudius Hollyband, in his *Campio di Fior, or else the Flourie Field of Foure Languages* (1583) tells a young man how to behave: 'Put of thy cappe boye [. . .] Make a fine curtesie, Bowe thy right knee [. . .] As it hath bene taught thee'. As late as 1774, too, the Earl of Chesterfield, in one of his letters, reported that 'At Vienna men always make courtesies, instead of bows, to the Emperor'. The gesture is now almost exclusively a female one, perhaps in most countries quite exclusively.

custard (sweet sauce made with milk and eggs or from a commercial preparation)
The word 'custard' is related to 'crust', and when the dish first arose in the fifteenth century it was a kind of open pie containing pieces of meat or fruit covered with broth or milk, thickened with eggs, sweetened, and seasoned with spices. In about 1600 the custard changed its contents and consistency somewhat to become a dish or sweet made of a mixture of baked eggs and milk, a version that perhaps still exists in some places. Finally, the modern 'sauce' appears to have emerged in the nineteenth century, when certainly the earliest kinds of custard powders were available.

customer (person who makes purchases in a shop, especially regularly)
In the fourteenth century, a 'customer' was the word for either a customary tenant or a collector of customs (i.e. a customs house officer). The current sense arose some hundred years later, so was well established by Shakespeare's day, and the colloquial use of the word to mean 'person' (who one has to 'deal' with, as 'an awkward customer') followed in the sixteenth century.

cute (attractive, delicately pretty)
The first sense of the word to arise, in the eighteenth century, was 'clever', a use still fairly common (a 'cute remark'). In the nineteenth century, the 'attractive' or 'pretty' sense followed in American usage, applying to both things and people. In the twentieth century, the word also came to be used in a derogatory way, to mean 'affectedly or tastelessly attractive', as a 'cute little boy' in an outrageously garish suit, or a 'cute' style of writing which is more 'twee' than attractive. The word is actually a form of 'acute'.

cyclone (violent storm, hurricane, tornado)
The word was invented in 1848 by the meteorologist Henry Piddington in his small book *The Horn-book for the Law of Storms for the Indian and China Seas*, where he suggested that 'cyclone', from the Greek *kuklos*, 'circle', should be a suitable term to apply to any storm where the wind takes a circular course. Later, the word came to apply specifically to a hurricane or tornado that was limited in diameter but destructive in violence. Although both a hurricane and a tornado are (or can be) whirlwinds, the wind as a whole structure pursues a more or less straight course, not a circular one.

daft (stupid, mad)
Something like **silly** (which see), 'daft' initially meant 'mild', 'meek' in the thirteenth century, until it actually came to mean 'silly' itself a hundred years later, whether applying to a person or an animal (such as a sheep). From this the 'crazy' or 'mad' sense developed in the sixteenth century. The transition from 'meek' to 'stupid' may have been assisted by influence of the Middle English word *daff*, meaning 'fool', 'simpleton'. ('Daff' as a verb meaning 'play the fool' is still current in Scottish use.) But otherwise the sense development seems to be much the same as 'silly', as mentioned.

dainty (delicate and pleasing)
This word has an interesting history. It is etymologically related to 'dignity', and its earliest use was as a noun in the thirteenth century, meaning 'honour', 'esteem', 'favour', so 'affection', 'love'. From this came shortly after a sense 'liking', 'pleasure', and finally, although not much later, a meaning of 'delightful thing', or even just 'delicacy', as in Psalm 141:4: 'Let me not eat of their dainties'. The use of 'dainty' as a noun is now rare, although not altogether obsolete. However, the adjective 'dainty' developed on similar lines, meaning first 'choice', then 'pleasing to the taste', 'of delicate beauty'. These last two senses are the current ones, dating from the fourteenth

century. The two first senses, which date from the same period, are obsolete, however, although Tindale used 'dainty' to mean 'excellent' in his translation of the Bible (1526), where his version of Revelation 18:14 runs (in part): 'All thynges which were deyntie and had in pryce', with this same word preserved in the Authorized Version of 1611 ('All things which were dainty and goodly'). The 'fastidious' sense of the word was the last to arrive, in the sixteenth century.

dally (spend time idly)
This verb really has three senses, all current, and they developed in this order: 'talk lightly' (from the fourteenth century), 'flirt' (fifteenth) and 'waste time', 'dawdle' (sixteenth). 'Dalliance', meaning 'flirting', 'trifling', has a similar background.

damage (loss, harm)
The original meaning of the word was 'detriment', that is, loss caused by hurt or injury rather than injury itself. This dates from the fourteenth century and is the sense in the Bible (Authorized Version of 1611), where in Daniel 6:2 reference is made to the appointment of 'three presidents' to protect Darius, so that 'the king should have no damage'. The current sense developed at the same time, with the 'money loss' sense following a century later.

damp (slightly wet)
The relation with the noun 'damp' meaning 'foul air', 'poisonous gas' (as in 'fire damp', 'choke damp') can be seen in some seventeenth-century uses of the adjective to mean 'noxious', as in Milton's *Comus* (1634):

Such are those thick and gloomy
    shadows damp
Oft seen in charnel vaults and
    sepulchres.

Even earlier than this, however, the word was used to mean 'dazed', and something of this sense survives in usages such as 'damp spirits', i.e. depressed ones. This was in the late sixteenth century, when the noun 'damp' could mean 'stupor' as well. The present meaning 'slightly wet' developed from the eighteenth century.

damsel (young woman)
A slight but subtle shift of meaning took place in this word from the thirteenth century to the fourteenth. Its original sense was 'young unmarried lady', which later became 'young unmarried woman', without any implication of her rank or standing. The word itself fell out of regular use from about the seventeenth century, except in a historical or playful sense (much as **'wench'** is used today), although Walter Scott and other nineteenth-century poets made much use of the sixteenth-century variant 'damosel' (or 'damozel') to apply to a woman in a 'genteel' or stately sense. In the 'young unmarried woman' sense mentioned here, 'damsel' could also be freely used to mean simply 'girl', so that in his translation of the Bible in 1535, Miles Coverdale rendered Zechariah 8:5 (Authorized Version: ' . . . boys and girls playing in the streets . . .') as 'Yonge boyes and damselles, playnge vpon the stretes'. See also **boy**.

danger (possibility of harm or unjury)
The word is rather unexpectedly related to Latin *dominus*, 'lord', of which it is an alteration, through French. This basic sense can therefore be seen in the original use of the word in English in the thirteenth century to mean 'dominion', 'power of a master', a usage that survived down to the sixteenth century, where it occurs in Shakespeare's *The Merchant of Venice* (1596), when Portia says to Antonio, referring to Shylock:

You stand within his danger, do you
    not?

From this sense developed two more, similarly obsolete: 'liability to punishment' and 'hesitation'. The former of these is used in the Bible, in Matthew 5:22, where in the Sermon on the Mount, Christ says: 'Whosoever is angry with his brother without a cause shall be in danger of the judgement'. It was this sense that led directly to the current one ('liability to injury'), which first emerged in the fourteenth century. The corresponding adjective 'dangerous' has a similar sense history, meaning originally 'difficult to deal with' and later 'reluctant to comply' before settling to its modern usage. The 'difficult to deal with' sense is seen rather nicely (and rather late) in this sentence from Barnaby Googe's translation (1577) of Heresbachius's *Foure Bookes of Husbandrie:* 'The Oate is not daungerous in the choyse of his grounde, but groweth lyke a good fellowe in every place'.

dank (unpleasantly or unhealthily damp)
The word simply meant 'wet', 'watery' in the fourteenth century, with no sense of harmfulness, and was used of such everyday things as dew, rain, clouds and the like. Only from the sixteenth century did the adjective acquire its present connotation.

daunt (discourage, dispirit)
This sense of the word developed from the fifteenth century. Earlier, the adjective had been used to mean 'overcome', 'conquer', as when Chaucer, in his translation (1391) of Boethius's *De consolatione philosophiae,* wrote that Hercules 'dawntede the proude Cantauris'. This original meaning is reflected in the modern 'tame', to which 'daunt' is indirectly related.

debauch (tempt from virtue or innocence, seduce)
The specific 'seducing' sense of the verb originally in English applied not to virtue or chastity but allegiance, such as luring soldiers away from their leader, or a wife from her husband (hence the modern meaning). Even this was as late as the sixteenth century, and the use can be seen in a sentence from Evelyn's *Memoirs* (1651), for example, when he writes about 'Mr. John Cosin, son of the Dean, debauched by the priests'. Even in the nineteenth century, the American explorer Zebulon M. Pike, in *An Account of Expeditions to the Sources of the Mississippi* (1810), wrote how the Spaniards 'were making such great exertions to debauch the minds of our savages'. The present use of the verb arose in the seventeenth century.

debit (statement of money owing)
The original meaning of the word, hardly surprisingly, was 'debt', with this use widespread from the fifteenth century, based on Latin *debitum,* 'debt' (itself formerly spelt 'det' or 'dette'). The modern meaning dates from the eighteenth century.

debonair (urbane, light-hearted)
The word comes from the Old French phrase *de bonne aire,* 'of good family', and this sense can be clearly seen in the original meaning of the word in English in the thirteenth century, which was 'gracious', 'courteous'. Even Chaucer uses the word in this sense ('Zepherus the deboneire wynde' in 1374), and the modern usage dates from about the same period.

decimate (destroy a large part or number of)
The literal and original sense of the word was 'put to death one person in ten' (not nine out of ten, as is sometimes supposed), from Latin *decimus,* 'tenth', this being the punishment for mutinous soldiers, for example. The reference is to the practice in the Roman army, but the procedure was obviously observed in Britain in more recent times, as shown, for example, in John Dymmok's *A Treatise of Ireland* (1600), which tells how a body of men 'were by a martiall courte condemned to dye, which sentence was yet mitigated by the Lord Lieutenants mercy, by which they were onely decimated by lott'. The modern use of the verb is fairly recent, as when Charlotte Brontë wrote in a letter of 1848 that 'typhus fever decimated the school periodically'.

deck ('floor' of a ship)
This is one of the earliest meanings of the word, but not quite the earliest, which is the most basic, 'covering'. This was in fact the primary sense, so meant 'roof' rather than 'floor', and even applied to the 'deck' of a ship, which was regarded as overhead rather than underfoot. The 'floor' meaning prevailed, however, and an interesting development occurred a hundred years or so later, in the sixteenth century, when Shakespeare used the word to mean 'pack of cards', a sense that now seems quite modern, or at least American. This usage, the first record we have of it in English, comes in *Henry VI*, Part 3 (1593), where Gloucester says of Warwick:

But, whiles he thought to steal the single ten,
The king was slily finger'd from the deck.

From the nineteenth century, 'deck' came

to be used for a floor of a bus or tram, and in the twentieth it was adopted as the word for the unit of a tape recorder ('tape deck'), as well as that of a record player ('record deck').

deduce (establish by deduction, draw as a conclusion)
In the fifteenth century, when the current sense was first recorded, the verb also meant 'bring', 'convey', showing its literal relation to Latin *deducere*, 'to lead away'. This usage persisted for some centuries, especially among the more academic writers, as for example in Bishop Edward Stillingfleet's *Origines Britannicae* (1685), where he writes that: 'The Romans began to deduce Colonies, to settle Magistrats and Jurisdictions here'. However, the present meaning 'draw as a conclusion' developed at about the same time, even though in the sixteenth century a meaning 'deduct' also flourished for a time, as in the same author's *Origines Sacrae* (1662), which includes this small calculation: '1117. which being deduced from 3940. the remainder is 2823'.

deer ('antlered ruminant')
In Old English, 'deer' (or rather *dēor*) was the general word for 'animal' (see **beast**, which replaced it in this sense, and **animal** itself). From about the twelfth century, however, the word acquired its present narrower sense to apply to a single species of animal. Some language scholars hold that all three words ('deer', 'beast', 'animal') have a basic meaning 'breathing creature' (compare Latin *anima*, 'breath' and English 'animate' in the sense 'alive').

defeat (conquer)
The current meaning of the verb came about only in the sixteenth century. Originally, in the fourteenth century, the sense was 'undo', 'ruin', as in this text of 1435, referring to Calais: 'Ye saide pouere Toune of Caleys, yat be ye continuance of ye saide Staple [i.e. market] hath hiderto been gretly maintened [. . . is] like to bee defaited and lost' (*Rolls of Parliament*, 1278–1503). This, too, is the sense in Shakespeare's *Othello* (1604), where Desdemona says to Iago, of Othello:

And his unkindness may defeat my life,
But never taint my love.

A later, sixteenth-century usage was to mean 'disappoint', 'defraud', as when Milton wrote in *Paradise Lost* (1667) of death being 'defeated of his seisure'. This is now an obsolete sense, and although the modern meaning developed at about the same time, it is not found in either Shakespeare or the Bible.

defer (submit in opinion to)
The basic meaning of this verb in the fifteenth century was simply 'submit' in general, that is, submit oneself or submit something, 'refer' it, as in this sentence of 1541 from the works of the Protestant martyr and chaplain to Henry VIII, Robert Barnes: 'This matter was deferred of [i.e. by] both partes to the sentence of the kyng'. A century later, 'defer' was also used to mean 'offer' or 'proffer' so that worship could be 'deferred' to God and obedience 'deferred' to one's sovereign. Both these usages are now obsolete, and the modern meaning finally crystallized in the seventeenth century.

deft (smart and skilful)
The word is actually an alteration of '**daft**' (which see), so its original sense is the same as that word, i.e. 'gentle', 'meek'. From this thirteenth-century meaning the fifteenth-century one of 'skilful' developed, with this in turn coming to mean 'neat', 'pretty' a hundred years later. This last is now only a dialect usage, but the sense shift is interesting since it parallels others such as **buxom**, **handsome** and **tidy** (which see), where a purely descriptive word has become a term of personal praise.

Shee came to London very neat and deft,
To seeke preferment,

wrote the satirist Samuel Rowlands in his *Good Newes and Bad Newes* (1622).

defy (resist, challenge)
As originally used, the verb meant 'renounce one's allegiance'. This was in the fourteenth century, and the usage continued for some time subsequently, as in Richard Grafton's *A Chronicle at Large and Meere History of the Affayres of England* (1568),

where he tells how the king sent ambassadors ' . . .to sommon him: and that if he would not be otherwise advised, then the king gave them full authoritie to defye him'. The present meaning of 'defy' dates from the fourteenth century.

deign (condescend)

In the thirteenth century, 'deign' meant 'think fit', a sense that persisted for some centuries later, so that it occurs in Shakespeare and Milton. In the former's *Henry VI*, Part 3 (1593), for example, King Edward says to the Mayor of York:

> For Edward will defend the town and thee,
> And all those friends that deign to follow me.

The current meaning 'condescend' dates much later, from the sixteenth century.

delete (obliterate, erase)

To 'delete' somebody or something was to destroy or annihilate them, showing the literal sense in Latin *delere*, 'to wipe out', 'destroy'. The word is recorded in this meaning from the seventeenth century, and even has the sense in Sir Francis Palgrave's *The History of Normandy and of England* (1851–64), where he says that Carthage was 'deleted', not 'destroyed'. The current use originated in the same period, however.

delicate (sensitive, fragile)

In the fourteenth century, 'delicate' was used to mean 'delightful', 'elegant', or simply 'nice'. Thus in his translation of the Bible (1382), Wyclif gave for part of Isaiah 58:13: 'If thou [. . .] clepist a delicat sabot' (in the Authorized Version of 1611: 'If thou [. . .] calleth the sabbath a delight'). The sense seemed reluctant to alter, and even survived as late as the seventeenth and eighteenth centuries, so that Ralph Thoresby in his *Diary* of 1677–1724 recorded how on 4 April 1683 he travelled 'to Bigglesworth [i.e. Biggleswade] where there is nothing observable but a delicate new Inn'. In the same period, 'delicate' also meant 'fastidious', 'dainty', which sense also persisted, as in this nice observation in *The Rules of Civility* (1673): 'Some people being so delicate, they will not eat after a man has

eat with his Spoon and not wiped it'. The present sense of 'sensitive' finally developed in the sixteenth century.

demagogue (political leader or agitator who plays on popular prejudices)

The current use of the word is in a derogatory sense. Originally, however, a 'demagogue' simply denoted a popular leader, as the Greek source indicates (literally 'people leader'). The 'bad' sense was introduced by Milton in his *Eikonoklastes* (1649): 'Setting aside the affrightment of this Goblin word; for the King by his leave cannot coine English as he could mony, to be current'. This established the word in its present disparaging sense.

demean (conduct oneself)

The current sense developed from the fourteenth century, but some hundred years earlier the word meant simply 'carry on', 'manage', as in Lord Berners' translation (1523–5) of the *Chronicles* of Froissart: 'So often they went bytwene the parties, and so sagely demeaned their busynesse'. The spelling of the corresponding noun, 'demeanour', may have been influenced by an early form of 'behaviour' such as *havour*.

demise (death)

It is worth remembering that the current popular sense of the word, as given here, is not the only one. In the sixteenth century, the word meant, as it still does, 'transfer of an estate', with this legal term coming into English from Old French *demettre*, 'to dismiss' (in origin the same word). In the seventeenth century, 'demise' came to mean 'transfer of sovereignty', especially in the phrase 'demise of the crown'. From this in turn the modern meaning developed, since the death of a sovereign would cause his reigning authority to be transferred.

demur (object, take exception)

Initially, in the thirteenth century, 'demur' meant 'linger', a sense that survived in sporadic use down to the seventeenth century, as in Thomas Nicolls' translation (1550) of Thucydides: 'Yet durst they not demoure nor abyde vpon the campe'. In the seventeenth century, when the current sense arose, 'demur' could also mean 'hesitate', as in *Evelina* (1778) by Fanny Burney (Madame d'Arblay): 'You are the first lady who ever made me even demur upon this subject'. This sense is really obsolete, although 'demur' is still sometimes popularly understood to mean this today.

demure (reserved, modest)
This word may be related to 'demur', and it has certainly been influenced by 'mature', or rather, by the French word *mûr*, 'ripe', that derived from Latin *maturus*. Hence the overtone of 'grave', 'serious' behind the adjective. Its original use, in the fourteenth century, was to mean 'calm', however, especially as applied to the sea. The meaning 'serious' followed in the fifteenth century, and a now obsolete sense 'affectedly grave' in the seventeenth, as when Thomas Gray, in his *Ode on the Death of a Favourite Cat* (1771), wrote of his 'pensive Selima' being 'Demurest of the tabby kind'.

denigrate (defame, blacken)
Formerly, 'denigrate' was used to mean 'blacken' in a literal sense, so that a lotion could be said to 'denigrate' greying hair, or soot 'denigrate' a chimney. This use was current from the seventeenth century to the nineteenth, although increasingly rarely.

denim (twilled cotton fabric used for making trousers, etc)
It is strange to find a reference to 'denims' in the early eighteenth century, but here they are, in Edward Hatton's *The Merchant's Magazine, or Trades-man's Treasury* (1701): 'Serge Denims, that cost 6*l*. each'. But these are lengths of cloth, not trousers, and the material is serge, moreover, not cotton, as today. The first two words of this extract also indicate the origin of the name in French *serge de Nîmes*, that is, serge that has come from the French town of Nîmes. The present sense of 'denim' to apply to twilled cotton arose in the United States in the nineteenth century.

denounce (condemn publicly, accuse)
When the word first entered English from French in the thirteenth century, the meaning was closer to 'announce', that is, was 'declare', 'proclaim' and the like. Thus in the text of *Melusine*, by Jean d'Arras,

translated in about 1500, the line occurs: 'Anthony & Regnald came to their fader & moder, and denounced to them these tydinges'. The sense 'declare to be evil', which is the current one, developed only in the seventeenth century.

dent (hollow made by a blow)
The original meaning of 'dent', in the thirteenth century, was 'blow', 'stroke' in general, with this deriving as an altered spelling of 'dint'. Thus, an early text *Richard Coer de Lion* (about 1325) tells of 'a dente amyd the schelde', that is, a blow in the middle of the shield. But it was not because shields and metal armour became 'dented' with such blows that the modern meaning developed. The influence was the verb 'indent' (compare modern 'indentation'), and the 'hollow' sense came about only in the sixteenth century.

depart (leave, go away)
The verb could in fact mean 'go away' as early as the thirteenth century, but it also had other senses, now obsolete. Among them were the literal 'divide into parts', 'distribute', and 'separate', 'rent asunder'. The second of these comes in Caxton's translation (1483) of the *Golden Legend:* 'Yf thou haue but lytyl, yet studye to gyue and to departe therof gladly'. The original phrase 'Till death us departe' [i.e. separate] in the Book of Common Prayer of 1549 was altered to 'till death us do part' in the version of 1662, since the earlier sense of 'depart' had become obsolete (and the phrase could even have been misunderstood to mean 'until death leaves us'). 'Depart' as a euphemism for 'die' was a development of the sixteenth century.

depend (result from, be subject to certain conditions)
As with many verbs of this type, the original sense was literal, 'hang from', making odd modern reading in some texts of the sixteenth century and later. In Alexander Barclay's *The Mirrour of Good Manners* (1510), for example, one can read of an old man 'with bearde like bristles depending on his chin', and in Spenser's *Shepheards Calender* (1579) comes the line:

As on your boughes the ysicles depend.

But apart from literary or poetic use, this sense is now obsolete, and the figurative meaning is the current one.

depict (portray)

This verb, which superseded the earlier 'depaint', meant 'represent in colours' in the seventeenth century, as in Thomas Fuller's *The Historie of the Holy Warre* (1639), where he writes of a history of the Bible 'as richly as curiously depicted in needle work'. The present meaning 'portray' followed a century later.

deport (carry away, send abroad by way of punishment; conduct oneself)

The earliest sense of the verb, in the fifteenth century, was 'bear with', 'refrain', as in Caxton's translation (1477) of *The Historie of Jason:* 'I me deporte from hensforth for to speke ony more of this mater', and in the same work: 'I shall deporte and tarye for this present tyme to speke of the faytes of Jason'. The sense 'comport oneself' came in the sixteenth century, and that of 'carry off' a century later.

derrick (hoisting apparatus)

The name of the device comes from the surname of a famous seventeenth-century hangman at Tyburn, in London, and it is thus logical that 'derrick' should initially have been used as a nickname for both a hangman and a gallows. This is therefore the meaning of the word in such works as Thomas Dekker's *The Belman of London* (1608), where the line comes: 'He rides circuit with the devil, and Derrick must be his host, and Tyborne the inn at which he will light'. The modern sense arose in the eighteenth century, and the word is still in current technical use for various types of cranes and other lifting and hoisting contrivances, such as the tower over an oil well that supports the boring machinery.

despot (absolute ruler, tyrant)

The word ultimately derives from Greek *despotēs*, 'lord', 'master', and in the sixteenth century, when first in use in English, did not have its present disparaging sense. However, these first usages applied to historic rulers, such as those of Greece, when it was the word to designate bishops

and emperors, for example. Dr Johnson, in his *Dictionary* of 1755, defined 'despot' as follows: 'An absolute prince; one that governs with unlimited authority. This word is not in use, except as applied to some Dacian prince; as the *despot* of Servia'. The modern sense is beginning to emerge here, but did not fully do so in its current 'hostile' connotation until the time of the French Revolution (1789), when the word was revived and seized on by such poets as Cowper and Southey. The latter thus used it in his early poem *Joan of Arc* (1795):

> When pouring o'er his legion slaves on Greece,
> The eastern despot bridged the Hellespont.

destitute (impoverished, lacking possessions)

The adjective derives from Latin *destitutus*, 'forsaken', and this was the original meaning in English in the fourteenth century. It was probably introduced by Wyclif in his translation of the Bible (1382) from the Latin Vulgate, so that his version of Revelation 18:17 ran: 'For in oon hour so many richessis ben destitute' (in the Latin, 'destitutae sunt'). (In the Authorized Version of 1611 the same sentence is: 'For in one hour so great riches is come to nought'.) This sense became obsolete, however, and the current meaning, 'having no possessions', arose in the eighteenth century. The connection with poverty seems to have been prompted by Miles Coverdale's translation of the Bible of 1535, where Psalm 102:17 appears as: 'He turneth him vnto the prayer of the poore destitute' (Authorized Version: 'He will regard the prayer of the destitute'). In Coverdale's version, 'destitute' really has its early sense of 'forlorn'.

detect (discover, find, reveal)

The modern sense came in the sixteenth century. A hundred years before, the verb had meant 'uncover', 'expose' in a much more literal way, so that a sinner would 'detect' his sins to a priest when confessing them, and a plot could be 'detected'. The current meaning is thus 'reveal the secrecy of', and this followed in the sixteenth century. 'Detectives' (originally 'detective police') first appeared in the nineteenth century, since their job was to reveal the secrets of crimes. Latin *detegere*, from which the word comes, means 'uncover', or in a sense 'take the lid off', since Latin *tectum* is 'roof' (related to English 'thatch').

determine (establish, fix)
The verb is related to 'terminate', and its original sense in the fourteenth century was 'bring to an end' or 'come to an end'. This is the meaning of the word in Shakespeare's *Coriolanus* (1607), where Coriolanus says:

Shall I be charg'd no further than this present?
Must all determine here?

The usage is still found today in law, where an estate, for example, can be 'determined' or brought to an end. Something of the concept still remains in the common use of the verb, since if you 'determine' something, a matter that was unresolved or uncertain is now finally decided, and so terminated.

detritus (product of disintegration or erosion)
The origin of the word is the Latin verb *deterere*, 'to rub away' (past participle passive *detritus*), and the initial meaning of 'detritus' in English, when it was adopted from French in the eighteenth century was 'wearing away by rubbing', that is, denoted the action, not the product. The current sense was soon acquired, however, and the earlier meaning rapidly became obsolete.

devious (not straightforward, cunning)
The literal meaning of the word is 'out of the way' (Latin *de via*), applying to a place that was remote or isolated because it lay off the main road. This was the sixteenth-century usage, with a figurative sense developing fairly rapidly to mean 'straying from the way', 'erring', so that in due course Longfellow could write in *Evangeline* (1847):

Like the sweet thoughts of love on a darkened and devious spirit,

and R.L. Stevenson, similarly, in *Underwoods* (1887):

The river of your life I trace
Up the sun-chequered devious bed
To the far-distant fountain-head.

The use of 'devious' to mean 'underhand', 'untrustworthy', as 'by devious means' and 'a devious person' dates from the nineteenth century, but became popular in the twentieth.

devolve (pass to, as an obligation or inheritance)
The literal sense of the verb is 'roll down', and this was how it was first used in the fifteenth century, often with reference to rivers and streams 'rolling down' to the sea, as in Matthew Prior's *Carmen Seculare* (1700):

His Thames,
With gentle course devolving fruitful Streams.

The current meaning emerged in the sixteenth century.

dial (clockface, graduated control on radio, etc)
The word derives somewhat deviously from Latin *dies*, 'day', and its prime sense has always been with measuring time. Originally, from the fifteenth century, 'dial' had the sense 'sundial', as in John Lydgate's *Troy Book* (1430):

For by the dyal the hour they gan to marke,

with the same meaning occurring in the Bible, both in Miles Coverdale's translation of 1535 and the Authorized Version of 1611, where the latter has, in 2 Kings 20:11: 'And he brought the shadow ten degrees backwards, by which time it had gone down in the dial of Ahaz'. From the sixteenth century, 'dial' came to be used of the face of a clock, and also of a clock or timepiece itself, especially at first, the so called 'clepsydra', or water clock. In Shakespeare's *As You Like It* (1600), the word means 'watch', as in the famous scene where Jaques tells how he has met 'a fool i' the forest' [i.e. Touchstone]:

And then he drew a dial from his poke [i.e. pocket],
And, looking on it with lack-lustre eye,
Says very wisely, 'It is ten o'clock'.

The more modern use of 'dial', referring to

85

measuring devices that are not clocks, dates from the eighteenth century.

diction (pronunciation of words, choice of words)
In the fifteenth century, 'diction' meant simply 'word', 'phrase', with the modern sense of 'choice of wording' first recorded in the fine Preface to Dryden's *Fables, Ancient and Modern* (1700), where he writes: 'The first beauty of an Epick poem consists in diction, that is, in the choice of words and harmony of numbers'. As applied to speech, and the manner of speaking and pronouncing words, 'diction' is first recorded in John Mason's *An Essay on Elocution* (1748): 'Elocution: By which they always meant, what we call, Diction; which consists in suiting Words to our Ideas, and the Stile to the Subject'. This is now the better known usage of the word.

diet (special regime of food and drink)
In the thirteenth century, 'diet' meant 'food' in general, and occurs in Chaucer's *Canterbury Tales* ('The Pardoner's Tale', which has gluttony and drunkenness as one of its main themes) (1386):

He wolde been the moore mesurable
Of his diete sittynge at his table.

However, although this use is now obsolete, it is Chaucer who also has 'diet' in its modern sense, in the same work ('The Nun's Priest's Tale'):

No deyntee morsel passed thurgh hir
throte [. . .]
Attempree [i.e. temperate, moderate]
diete was al hir phisik.

diffident (lacking in confidence)
A brief consideration of the word will reveal that its main element is the same as that of 'fidelity' and therefore 'faith'. The original sense in the fifteenth century was thus 'distrustful', 'having no faith in'. Donne in his *Sermons* (1631) writes of 'a fainting and diffident Spirit', and Milton, in *Paradise Lost* (1667), advises:

Be not diffident
Of Wisdom, she deserts thee not, if thou
Dismiss her not, when most thou needst
her nigh.

The current meaning ('lacking in confidence') dates from the eighteenth century.

diffuse (scattered, not concise)
In the fifteenth and sixteenth centuries, 'diffuse' was used to mean 'confused', 'indistinct', as in Caxton's translation from the French of *The Pylgremage of the Sowle* (1413), where he writes that he has not translated word for word 'because of some thynges that were diffuse and in some place ouer derk [i.e. unduly obscure]'. In its modern sense, as a virtual opposite of 'confined' and 'condensed', 'diffuse' dates from the eighteenth century.

dilettante (art lover, 'dabbler' in a branch of knowledge)
The word is a direct borrowing of the Italian, meaning 'lover', or literally 'delighter', and in Italian, as originally in English, the reference was exclusively to music and painting. The usage was on a parallel with 'amateur' (which also means 'lover', although from the French), and applied to someone who devoted himself to art for the love of it, rather than professionally. This was in the eighteenth century, and the word gradually came to acquire its more general sense of 'amateur' (a 'mere dilettante') after about 1800.

dime (American coin value one tenth of a dollar)
It is perhaps worth recording that 'dime' meant simply 'one tenth' before it came to be the name of the coin in the eighteenth century. (It was actually first issued in 1796.) In its earlier use, therefore, the word dates back to the fourteenth century, and particularly refers to the tithe of 'one tenth' that was paid to the church or a ruler. A late fourteenth-century text has an example of this sense: 'His purvyours toke, without preiere [i.e. petition] at a parliament, a poundage [. . .] and a fifteneth and a dyme eke [i.e. also]' (*Political Songs and Poems Relating to English History* (1399).

dimple (small hollow in the cheek or elsewhere on the body)
Before it meant 'hollow in the cheek', 'dimple' meant 'hollow in the ground', with this sense dating from the thirteenth

century. (The word is indirectly related to 'deep'.) A survival of this can be seen in some local English place names, such as Dimple north of Bolton, where the name really means more 'pit'. The 'dimple' of cheek and chin has been recorded from the fourteenth century, a little later.

dint (in phrase 'by dint of': 'by means of')
The word is now used in English only in the phrase quoted here. Originally, however, it meant 'blow', 'stroke', exactly the same as the 'dent' which developed from it, and this was the sense in Old English. The usage persisted in poetry down to as late as the nineteenth century, and appears, for example, in the writings of Dryden ('with dint of Sword') and Cowper ('From the dint Shield me of dart and spear'). The word could also mean more generally 'dealing of blows', 'force of attack', whether literally or figuratively, as in Shakespeare's *Julius Caesar* (1601), where Antony, in his passionate speech after the death of Caesar, says:

O! now you weep, and I perceive you
     feel
The dint of pity.

The sole surviving usage, in the phrase 'by dint of', dates from the seventeenth century, developing from such phrases as 'by dint of sword'. See also **dent**.

diplomatic (tactful and considerate)
In its proper sense, of course, 'diplomatic' means 'relating to diplomacy', i.e. to the management of international relations by negotiation. This was the meaning of the word in the late eighteenth century in English. Before this, however, although in the same century, 'diplomatic' meant 'relating to official documents', that is, to diplomas, as in this text of 1784: 'Diplomatic science, the knowledge of which will enable us to form a proper judgement of the age and authenticity of manuscripts, charters, records, and other monuments of antiquity' (Thomas Astle, *The Origin and Progress of Writing*). The current meaning of 'diplomatic', as 'tactful', 'skilful in negotiating', developing from the skills required in international negotiations by a diplomat, first arose in English in the eighteenth century.

directory (book of directions or names and addresses)
As first used in English in the fifteenth century, 'directory' was an adjective, as it still can be today, especially in the legal sense of 'directing what should be done'. From the sixteenth century, the noun emerged in the meaning 'book of directions', often in a moral sense, as in this title of 1770: 'The Directory of Conscience, a profytable Treatyse to such that be tymorous [. . .] in Conscyence'. The various senses were then extended to apply to a book of directions for public worship in the seventeenth century, a book of names and addresses in a locality in the eighteenth, and a telephone directory in the nineteenth.

disastrous (calamitous)
In the sixteenth century, 'disastrous' was used in its literal sense of 'ill-starred' (the 'bad' prefix 'dis-' plus the word ultimately derived from Latin *astrum*, 'star'). This is what the word means, therefore, in a text such as Bartholomew Young's translation (1586) of part of Guazzo's *Ciuile Conuersation:* 'If shee aford me but one sparkle of hope and favour, she doth it to no other ende, but to make mee more desastrous'. Poets of later years thus would write of wooers who were 'disastrous' in love, for example. The present meaning, 'calamitous', 'relating to a disaster', is first recorded at the beginning of the eighteenth century.

discomfort (state of being uncomfortable)
From the fourteenth century, 'discomfort' could also mean 'discouragement' or 'distress', as in Wyclif's translation of the Bible (1382), where he renders the first part of Matthew 24:15 as: 'The abhominacyioun of discomfort, that is seid of Danyel, the prophete' (Authorized Version of 1611: 'The abomination of desolation, spoken of by Daniel the prophet'), and the same sense occurs in Shakespeare's *Antony and Cleopatra* (1606), where Enobarbus says to Antony:

                    What mean you, sir,
To give them this discomfort? Look, they
     weep.

The modern meaning is a nineteenth-century one, with the original word used in a weakened sense.

discourse (formal conversation, formal speech or piece of writing)
When Chaucer used the word in the fourteenth century, its meaning was 'reasoning', or what Johnson was to define in his *Dictionary* four hundred years later as 'The act of the understanding, by which it passes from premises to consequences'. Subsequently, 'discourse' came to mean 'conversation', 'talk' in a general sense, as in Shakespeare's *Richard III* (1594), where Stanley, on the morning of the Battle of Bosworth Field, says to Richmond:

Farewell: the leisure and the fearful time
Cuts off the ceremonious vows of love
And ample interchange of sweet
  discourse.

The present use of the word arose at about the same time, in the sixteenth century.

discover (find out)
The earliest sense of the verb was 'disclose', i.e. 'make known', with this dating from the thirteenth century and used by Shakespeare in, for example, *Romeo and Juliet* (1592), where, after the killing of Mercutio, Benvolio says to Escalus (the Prince of Verona):

O noble prince! I can discover all
The unlucky manage [i.e. management]
  of this fatal brawl.

In the fourteenth century, 'discover' was used even more literally for a while to mean 'uncover', as in Reginald Pecock's *The Repressor of Over Much Blaming of the Clergy* (1449): 'The principal Crucifix of the chirche schal be Discovered and schewid baar and nakid to alle the peple of the Processioun'. This, too, is the meaning of the verb in the Bible, as in Jeremiah 13:22: 'For the greatness of thine iniquity are thy skirts discovered, and thy heels made bare'. The current meaning 'find out' developed only from the sixteenth century.

discuss (investigate by reasoning)
When the word was first used, in the fourteenth century, it had the simple sense 'investigate', as in this text of 1340 from Richard Rolle of Hampole's *The Pricke of Conscience:*

We may noght fle,
Until al our lyf examynd be,
And alle our dedys, bathe goode and ille,
Be discussed, after Goddes wille.

An old medical sense of 'discuss' from the sixteenth to the eighteenth centuries was 'dispel', 'disperse', so that Bonet's *Mercurius compitalitius*, translated in 1684, says that 'Of all edibles, Garlick discusses wind most', and Dr Johnson, in the periodical *The Rambler* that he issued for a couple of years in the mid-eighteenth century, writes of a pomade that has 'virtue to discuss pimples'. This sense is in fact that of the Latin verb, *discutere*, from which the English word derives. Meanwhile, the present standard meaning of 'discuss' had been in use from the fifteenth century, although originally not in the much weakened modern sense of simply 'talk about' ('Did you discuss the programme at all?').

disease (illness, serious medical condition)
Although the word has had its present sense almost from the first time that it was recorded, in the fourteenth century, it also meant 'uneasiness', 'annoyance' originally, as in Chaucer's *Canterbury Tales* (Prologue to 'The Nun's Priest's Tale') (1365):

It is a greet disese,
Where as men han been in greet welthe
  and ese,
To heeren of hire sodeyn fal.

(That is: It is very annoying, when men have been leading a very wealthy and easy life, to hear of their sudden downfall.) Later uses of 'disease' in this obsolete sense reflected a greater awareness of the word's literal meaning, 'dis-ease', and it was even written with a hyphen like this, as in Chapman's version of the *Odyssey* (1615):

Doth sleep thus seize
Thy powers, affected with so much
  dis-ease?

disgust (loathing, abhorrence)
Unusually, 'disgust' is a word that has progressed from a weaker sense to a stronger. Originally, when first used in the

sixteenth century, it meant not much more than 'dislike', 'distaste', the latter being its literal sense in Old French *desgout* (modern *dégoût*). In his famous French-English dictionary published in 1611, for example, Randle Cotgrave translated French *desappetit* as not more than 'a queasinesse, or disgust of stomacke'. However, in the same dictionary, he uses 'disgust' in something much like its modern sense, when he translated French *desaimer* as 'to fall into dislike, or disgust of'. The earlier, weaker sense was virtually obsolete by the nineteenth century.

dishevelled (unkempt, untidy)
The word is based on the prefix 'dis-' in the sense 'un-', 'not' and the Old French word for 'hair', *chevel* (modern *cheveux*). In the fifteenth century in English, therefore, the meaning of 'dishevelled' was 'wearing nothing on the head', while in the sixteenth century it was (as now) 'uncombed', 'with hair flowing free'. An example of the former usage can be seen in this sentence from *Merlin, or the Early History of King Arthur* (1450): 'She was discheueled and hadde the feirest heed that eny woman myght haue'. From the seventeenth century, the word was also used figuratively to mean 'disordered', a sense in which it hardly appears today: 'Religion is no dishevelled mass of aspiration, prayer, and faith' (Henry Drummond, *Natural Law in the Spiritual World*, 1883).

dishonest (not honest)
Earlier senses of the word were more subtle than today's, and in the fourteenth century 'dishonest' meant 'involving dishonour', 'dishonourable'. This usage was prolonged, as often the case, by poets, and occurs in the 'inglorious triumphs and dishonest scars' of Pope's early *Windsor-Forest* (1704–10), for example. In the fifteenth century the word was also used to mean 'unchaste', with this sense found in Shakespeare's *Henry V* (1599), when the Archbishop of Canterbury talks of the 'dishonest manners' of German women. The current meaning caught on from the seventeenth century.

dismal (dreary, gloomy, causing dismay)
The word is not actually related to 'dismay'

and in fact derives, somewhat unexpectedly, from Latin *dies mali*, 'evil days', with reference to certain days in the calendar that were unpropitious. This, therefore, is the earliest use of 'dismal' in English, in the thirteenth century, and the word occurs in Chaucer's *The Dethe of Blaunche* (1369):

I trowe hyt was in the dismalle,
That was the .x. woundes of Egipte.

(The days were also called the 'Egyptian days', because it was believed they were first calculated by Egyptian astrologers. Chaucer seems to have interpreted them as more the biblical 'ten plagues of Egypt', however.) 'Dismal' was thus originally used as a noun in English. Later, the word passed into an adjective, with 'days' added, hence the still fairly common association of 'dismal' with a 'time' word, such as 'dismal summer', 'dismal weather' and 'dismal day' itself (where the alliteration helps). The next sense of 'dismal' to develop was simply 'unlucky', with this found, for example, in Shakespeare's *Henry VI*, Part 3 (1593), where Edward, alluding to the recently dead Clifford, says:

Now death shall stop his dismal
  threatening sound,
And his ill-boding tongue no more shall
  speak.

From the sixteenth century, when the sense was at its strongest (meaning 'disastrous', 'terrible'), the word gradually weakened its usage, until it came to mean little more than 'depressing', as today.

dissolve (melt in liquid)
Whether 'dissolving' sugar in a cup of tea or 'dissolving' into tears, today's use of the word is much milder than originally. In the fourteenth century, when the current use is also recorded, the verb could also mean 'release from life', i.e. cause the 'dissolution' or death of someone, either referring to the disintegration of the body, or the 'dissolution' of body and soul. This sense seems to owe something to Wyclif's translation of the Bible of 1382, where in Philippians 1:23, his 'Hauying desyr for to be dissoloued' is what the Authorized Version of 1611 has as 'Having a desire to depart'.

disuse (cease to use)
The present sense arose in the fifteenth century. Some time before this, the verb meant 'misuse' or 'abuse', with Wyclif in one of his sermons (1380) writing of: 'A riche man that disuside his richesse in pride and in glotonye'. This use of 'disuse' was obsolete by about the end of the fifteenth century.

ditto (the same)
The obviously Italian word (Tuscan dialect, in fact) means literally 'said', much as in English legal 'the said man' and colloquial 'the said hostelry' (meaning 'the pub I just mentioned'). The standard Italian word is *detto*, and apart from uses similar to English 'said', as mentioned (for example, *il detto libro*, 'the said book'), the word was particularly applied to a month that had just been named in a business letter. For example: 'Sotto li 27 di settembre mi fu significato que sotto li 18 detto . . .' ('On the 27th of September I was notified that on the 18th of the said month . . .'). The use in English of 'ditto' was originally based on this, and applied only to a month just mentioned, as in the following: 'They, 27 ditto, brought in two Squaws, a Boy and a Girl' (Richard Henchman in William Hubbard, *A Narrative of the Troubles with the Indians in New-England*, 1677). This means '27 June' since the date 30 June has just been mentioned. After the initial use of 'ditto' in this specific sense in the seventeenth century, the usage was extended to refer to anything that had been mentioned in speech or (particularly) writing. Italian still uses *detto* only to refer to months, however.

divan (type of couch or bed)
The word traces back its origin ultimately to Persian *diwan*, 'account book', and the first use of 'divan' in English, in the sixteenth century, was to refer to a council of state in Turkey, in particular one presided over by the sultan (or in his absence by the grand vizier). The word thus occurs in this sense, as might be expected, in the contemporary accounts of travellers and explorers, such as *The Principal Navigations, Voiages and Discoueries of the English Nation* (1599) by Richard Hakluyt, where he writes of '. . .requesting the ambassador within an houre after to goe to the Douan of the Vizir'. From this basic meaning, 'divan' then came to be the word for the council chamber itself, and so passed to the long, low seat that was a distinctive feature of the chamber, described by Henry Maundrell, for example, in *A Journey from Aleppo to Jerusalem* (1703) as a 'sort of low stage [. . .] elevated about sixteen or eighteen inches or more above the floor, whereon the Turks eat, sleep, smoke, receive visits, say their prayers, etc.'. From this in turn, 'divan' came to acquire a new meaning in English to apply to an English (not Turkish) room that was a sort of equivalent, otherwise a smoking room with sofas (in Victorian times called 'lounges'), and this is what the word means in the novels of Dickens and Trollope, for example. Thus in *Dombey and Son* (1848), Dickens writes that: 'Mr. Toots had furnished a choice set of apartments: had established among them a sporting bower; and a divan which made him poorly', and at one point in Disraeli's novel *Endymion* (1880), Mr Trenchard says to Endymion: '"We are going to the divan. Do you smoke?"'. However, in *The Old Curiosity Shop* (1840), Dickens uses 'divan' in more or less its modern sense: 'The bed being soft and comfortable, Mr. Quilp determined to use it, both as a sleeping place by night and as a kind of Divan by day'. This is one of the earliest records we have of the term in its current sense.

divulge (reveal, make known)
Today, the word implies the revelation or disclosure of something secret. Originally, in the fifteenth century, the sense was merely 'publish abroad', as in Caxton's translation (1490) of Virgil's *Aeneid:* 'Fame of his ouurages [i.e. works] hath ben dyuulged'. From the seventeenth century the verb took on its present connotation to refer to the disclosing of a secret or confidential matter.

dock (area of harbour or port for a ship to berth, unload, etc.)
As understood today, a 'dock' is normally a specially constructed section in a port or harbour where ships can be accommodated. This sense of the word first developed in the fifteenth century. Before this, a 'dock' was

a natural hollow or creek where a ship could stay at low water, and although the usage dates from the fourteenth century, the word was described in these terms as late as 1627 in Captain John Smith's *The Seaman's Grammar:* 'A wet docke is any place where you may hale in a ship into the oze out of the tides way, where shee may docke her selfe'. 'Docker', incidentally, meant 'person who lives by the docks' in the eighteenth century, and only came to have its present sense ('dock worker') a century later. (A 'docker', in the former use, was moreover usually understood to be someone who lived in Plymouth Dock, now Devonport.)

doctrine (teaching)
For a while from the fourteenth century, when the present sense arose, 'doctrine' also meant 'lesson', 'instruction', as in the Bible, for example, where in Mark 4:2 Jesus 'taught them many things by parables, and said unto them in his doctrine, [etc.]'. (In the Revised Version of 1881, 'doctrine' was changed to 'teaching' here.) Compare the related word **document** (below), with both words ultimately deriving from Latin *docere*, 'to teach'.

document (official piece of writing)
When the word was first used in English, in the fifteenth century, it meant 'instruction' or 'evidence', whether written or not. The modern sense arose only in the eighteenth century, specifically applying to something written.

dog (hound)
The general Old English word for 'dog' was 'hound' (more properly *hund*), so that 'dog' itself was probably the name of a particular breed or race of powerful dog, although it is not certain which exactly this was. In the earliest texts, therefore, 'dog' or its equivalent will often have this specific sense. The word was adopted into several foreign languages from English, often with the word 'English' (in the foreign language) to denote this particular breed, and it is still so that the word 'dog' in a foreign language denotes a definite breed. Often it is a mastiff, as French *dogue anglais* and German *Dogge* (which can also be a St Bernard, Newfoundland, or Great Dane, as Russian *dog* is).

Spanish *dogo*, on the other hand, usually means 'bulldog'. The standard word for 'dog' in Germanic languages is still 'hound'-based, as Old English was (for example German *Hund*), while Romance languages take the generic word from Latin *canis* (as French *chien*, Italian *cane*, and the like). Even 'hound' and *canis* are remotely related, in the mists of time, but 'dog' is distinct from both words. See also **dogged** (below).

dogged (determined, tenacious)
The earliest usage of the word in English, in the fourteenth century, was to mean 'malicious', 'spiteful', and so on, in other words, anything that had the bad qualities of a dog. Contemporary texts thus tell of 'dogged deeds' (no doubt welcoming the alliteration), while later, poetic works refer to 'dogged fortune' and the 'dogged heart' that a person might have. From the fifteenth century, 'dogged' was simply the adjective for 'dog', so meant 'canine', and this is the sense of the word in Shakespeare's *King John* (1595), when the Bastard, speaking to Hubert, says (although admittedly in a figurative use):

Now for the bare-pick'd bone of majesty
Doth dogged war bristle his angry crest.

Finally, the 'stubborn' sense, not entirely a bad one, emerged in the eighteenth century.

doily (small decorative mat placed under cakes etc on a plate or stand)
As with many words for fabrics, 'doily' comes from a proper name, here that of a draper (perhaps in the spelling 'Doiley' or 'Doyley') who kept a shop in the Strand, London, in the late seventeenth century. Originally, 'doily' was thus the word for a woollen material used for summer wear (it was 'at once cheap and genteel'), and as such is first recorded in Dryden's comedy *The Kind Keeper; or Mr Limberham* (1678), which refers to 'some Doily Petticoats'. (See **petticoat** itself.) The 'mat' sense evolved in the eighteenth century, although the original 'doily' then was a napkin, and was usually called as such, as in Swift's *Journal to Stella* where on 23 April 1711 he records: 'After dinner we had coarse Doiley-napkins, fringed at each end, on the table to drink with'. The modern 'doily' as we know it (or

knew it, for it is an increasing and outmoded rarity) came about in the mid-nineteenth century. Probably the demise of the doily began with Betjeman's mockery of it and the people who use it, in his poem (originally written in response to a magazine competition) now included in *A Few Late Chrysanthemums* (1954):

Beg pardon, I'm soiling the doileys
With afternoon tea-cakes and scones.

dole (portion of food or money given to the poor, unemployment benefit)
Old English *dāl* meant simply 'part', 'portion', as its German offspring *Teil* does today, with modern English 'deal' related to both. From this, the meaning shifted to 'what is apportioned', 'lot', 'fate', a usage that lasted from the thirteenth to the nineteenth century (increasingly rarely), and which occurs in Shakespeare's *All's Well That Ends Well* (1601), where Bertram says to the King of France, referring to Helena:

When I consider
What great creation and what dole of honour
Flies where you bid it, I find that she, which late
Was in my nobler thoughts most base, is now
The praised of the king.

From the fourteenth century, 'dole' meant 'portion doled out', and from this in turn came the modern colloquial word to denote the government unemployment benefit (first recorded in this sense just after the First World War).

doll (child's toy baby)
The common sense of the word dates only from the seventeenth century. Before this, 'doll' meant 'mistress', hence the significance of the name of Doll Tearsheet in Shakespeare's *Henry IV, Part 2* (1597). There is also a Doll Common in Ben Jonson's *The Alchemist* (1610), where she is 'the Cheater's punk', as the *Oxford English Dictionary* describes her, curiously in modern terms (but see **punk**). The name is a pet form of Dorothy, as Moll is of Mary. From the nineteenth century 'doll' has come to be used to mean 'woman', initially one who

was 'pretty, but silly or frivolous' (*OED* again), but later, more generally, and more positively, as a woman that is 'very beautiful or attractive' (*Supplement to the OED)*, as in the title of Damon Runyon's story (later the famous musical) *Guys and Dolls* (1931).

dollop (shapeless lump)
The current use of the word dates only from the nineteenth century. In the sixteenth, 'dollop' meant 'tuft', 'clump', as a farming word, for example in Thomas Tusser's *Fiue Hundreth Pointes of Good Husbandrie* (1573): 'Of barlie the longest and greenest ye find, Leave standing by dallops'. This usage appears to be obsolete now, even in dialect speech.

dome (rounded roof)
The word derived from Latin *domus*, 'house', in the earliest sense in which it was used in English, having this very meaning. The usage was continued in some literary texts down to the eighteenth century at least, as in Swift's *Riddles* (1724):

Sad charnel-house! A dismal dome,
For which all mortals leave their home.

Later senses of the word derive directly from French *dôme*, and include the now obsolete seventeenth-century meaning 'cathedral' (as still in German *Dom*). From this, it is easy to see the transition to the rounded roof of a cathedral, and to a vaulted roof generally, with this last sense coming in the eighteenth century.

doodle (absentminded drawing or scrawl on paper)
The senses given here may not apply to one and the same word. If they do, however, then the earliest meaning of 'doodle' was the seventeenth-century one of 'fool', 'simpleton', with the origin in Low German *dudeltopf*, 'noodle', 'fool'. An extension of this was the Yankee or Union soldier in America in the eighteenth century, the 'Yankee Doodle' (and later, 'Yankee Doodle Dandy'). 'Doodle' or 'doodlebug' was the American nickname of the larva of the tiger beetle before it was the English nickname ('doodlebug') for the German V2 or 'flying bomb' in the Second World War. The sense of 'doodle' meaning 'aimless scrawl',

however, was first recorded before the War. It is this 'doodle', though, which may have developed from some other word, such as 'dawdle'. The thing itself is hardly the name of an animate object, as the other 'doodles' are, unless of course the word really relates to the 'mindless' person who draws one.

doubt (uncertainty)
Both noun and verb 'doubt' originally meant also 'fear' in the thirteenth-century English, with the sense preserved in Shakespeare's *Timon of Athens* (1607), where, after Timon's banquet, Apemantus says: 'Faith, for the worst is filthy; and would not hold taking, I doubt me [i.e. I fear]'. A similar use comes in Scott's *The Antiquary* (1816); 'But I doubt, I doubt, I have been beguiled', and even in modern talk 'doubt' can virtually mean 'fear', as when someone says 'I doubt we're too late' (i.e. I'm afraid we're too late). But this is really more a dialect usage, and is not widely found.

down (hill)
Why are 'downs' so called when they go 'up'? The answer is because 'down' (or *dūn*) was the Old English word for 'hill' (while 'hill' was originally a general word for any height, including a mountain). The Old English word had become obsolete in this sense, however, by about 1300, after which time it was used for an open expanse of high ground, especially in the plural, as the South Downs or Berkshire Downs (or any others) are today. The Downs in the Goodwin Sands, off the east coast of Kent, formerly a gathering place of ships, came to be so called in the fifteenth century, taking its name from the North Downs, to the east of which it lies. From the sixteenth century, 'down' also meant 'dune', that is, a sandhill by the sea. This sense is not common today, however. See also **wold**.

doyen (senior or oldest person in a group)
The word came into English from French, where it means 'dean', and the sense 'senior member' arose by association with the dean who is the head of a 'chapter' in a cathedral. The current meaning is more generally 'old pro', referring to someone who has been long 'in the business' (whatever it is) and who is usually revered or looked up to by others in his group. A feminine equivalent, 'doyenne', came into being in the twentieth century. The original 'doyen' in English, however, dates from the seventeenth century.

drab (dull)
In the sixteenth century, 'drab' was a word for a kind of cloth, and almost certainly came into English from French *drap*, 'cloth'. From this, the word came to acquire the common colour of such cloth, which was its natural undyed colour of dull brown or grey. Hence the fairly general meaning 'dull', whether of an object's colour (where it usually is brown or grey still, as 'drab' walls) or in a figurative sense, as a 'drab' day or someone's 'drab' existence.

draper (dealer in cloth or clothes)
Originally, a 'draper', in fourteenth-century English, was a dealer in cloth only, since the word derived from Old French *drapier,* itself from *drap*, 'cloth'. (Compare **drab**, above) From this the verb 'drape' developed, initially meaning 'make into cloth' in the fifteenth century, then 'cover with drapery' in the nineteenth, much later. This modern sense is first recorded in Tennyson's poem *The Princess* (1847), where the lady stood:

Like some sweet sculpture draped from
  head to foot.

'Drapery' itself was used in English when 'draper' itself was, although it, too, initially meant 'cloth', 'textile fabric', and the 'artistic arrangement' sense came only in the seventeenth century.

dreadful (terrible, awful)
Like the two words that define it here, 'dreadful' is today normally used in a greatly weakened sense of its original, which was the thirteenth-century 'full of dread' or 'inspiring dread'. This survived, especially in literary use, well down to the eighteenth century, as in Shakespeare's *Richard II* (1593), where before the tournament or 'royal fight' King Richard addresses the combatants:

With harsh-resounding trumpets'
  dreadful bray,
And grating shock of wrathful iron arms.

The word also occurs in this sense in some older church hymns, such as the line:

Robed in dreadful majesty

in Charles Wesley's 'Lo! He comes in clouds descending' (1758). The modern sense prevailed after about 1700, although 'dreadfully' appears to have something of its modern use in Shakespeare's *Hamlet* (1602), where Hamlet says to Rosencrantz and Guildenstern: 'I will not sort you with the rest of my servants, for, to speak to you like an honest man, I am most dreadfully attended'.

dreary (dismal, mournful, depressing)
In Old English, 'dreary' (which derived from *drēor*, 'gore') meant 'dire', 'grievous', 'sad', with the last of these, for example, found in Chaucer's *Canterbury Tales* ('The Clerk's Tale') (1386):

Al drere was his cheere [i.e. expression] and hys lookyng.

The current, weaker sense is first recorded in the seventeenth century.

dress (clothes)
The noun derives from the verb 'dress', which originally in English meant 'put right', 'set straight' in the fourteenth century, and later 'prepare', 'treat'. If soldiers were thus properly paraded or 'prepared', they would be wearing their uniforms, and this is the link between the old sense and the modern, with Shakespeare bridging the two, old and new, as he often did, in *Antony and Cleopatra* (1606), where Lepidus says to Mecaenas and Agrippa:

Till I shall see you in your soldier's dress,
Which will become [i.e. suit] you both, farewell.

dummy (silent person; imaginary card player; model or fake object)
The sense of the word developed as in the three meanings given here, with 'dummy' being a colloquial word for a literally dumb person in the sixteenth century. The card game 'dummy', a 'player' who does not speak (hardly surprisingly, since he is imaginary), first appeared in the eighteenth century, and the separate sense 'stupid person', 'dolt' in the same century. The 'fake' meaning followed in the nineteenth century, initially as a commercial object of some kind for displaying goods, such as a model figure with hair, clothes, and the like (a tailor's 'dummy'). The baby's 'dummy' (originally a 'dummy teat') came somewhat later, in the early twentieth century, and the ventriloquist's 'dummy' is also of the twentieth century. The word now has various technical applications, from printing to computing.

dunce (stupid person)
This word has an unexpectedly academic origin, in the name of John Duns Scotus, the fourteenth-century Scottish theologian and scholar (known as the 'Subtle Doctor'). Originally, therefore, a 'dunce' was a follower of Duns Scotus. Later, however, the theologian's works and theories were attacked by the humanists and reformers in the sixteenth century, and 'dunce' then became a term of contempt for anyone who still held Duns Scotus's 'hairsplitting' doctrines as against the bold 'new learning'. From this, the word naturally passed to mean 'dull and obstinate person who refuses to learn'. The new sense arose from references by Tindale, the great Bible translator and humanist (later to be burnt at the stake), to the 'Duns men' and the 'Dunces disciples', when speaking of them scornfully. (He asked his readers whether they did not remember how ' . . . the old barkyng curres, Dunces disciples & lyke draffe [i.e. draff, 'dregs'] called Scotistes, the children of darkenesse, raged in euery pulpit agaynst Greke Latin and Hebrue'.)

dust (to clean by dusting)
The verb has changed its meanings over the centuries. In the thirteenth century 'dust' meant 'rise like dust'. In the fifteenth, the sense was 'reduce to dust'. A century later, 'dust' meant both 'soil with dust' and (just the opposite) 'free from dust'. The modern meaning is actually a rather perverse one, if you think about it. However, although most of the earlier senses are now obsolete, it is still possible to 'dust' a cake with fine sugar, for example, and birds such as spar-

rows like 'dusting', or working dust into their feathers.

Dutch (belonging to Holland)
The word is related to German *deutsch*, 'German', and this was the original sense in English in the fourteenth century. Wyclif used 'Dutch' as early as 1380 to refer to the language ('wryten in Latin in Englyssche or in Frensche or Duchyssche'). From the sixteenth century the word came to apply to Netherlanders, who spoke a 'German' language (after all, in modern terms, a Germanic one), and who were the 'Germans' that the English had the most to do with.

dwell (live, inhabit)
In Old English, *dwellan* meant 'to go astray', and this was therefore the primary sense of the verb. Here is one of the earliest examples we have of the word, in King Alfred's ninth-century translation of Boethius' *De consolatione philosophiae:* 'Me thinkth thæt thu me dwelige' [i.e. It seems to me that you are leading me astray]. From this first sense, a meaning 'tarry', 'delay' arose, as in Chaucer's *Canterbury Tales* ('The Nun's Priest's Tale') (1386):

Thilke tale is al to longe for to telle,
And eek it is ny day, I may nat dwelle.

(That is: This tale is too long for me to tell, and since it is nearly day I must not linger.) The present meaning developed from the thirteenth century, with the additional sense 'spend time' ('I do not want to dwell on this') following in the fifteenth century.

eager (keen, enthusiastic)
The earliest sense of 'eager', in the thirteenth century, was 'ardent', 'fierce', whether of people or animals (Chaucer has 'eagre as is a Tygre' in 'The Clerk's Tale' [*Canterbury Tales,* 1386]), although the present meaning dates from only a little later, in the fourteenth century. One obsolete sense of 'eager' also current at that time was 'pungent', 'acid', with this surviving long enough for Shakespeare to use it in one of his *Sonnets* (1600):

Like as, to make our appetites more
    keen,
With eager compounds we our palate
    urge.

The word came into English from French, where *aigre* still means 'sharp', 'acid', and a legacy of this is preserved in modern English 'vinegar' (literally 'sour wine').

eccentric (strange, erratic)
The original sense of the word, as properly still, was 'not concentric', that is, not having the same centre (of two circles). This meaning appeared in English in the sixteenth century. The sense 'odd', 'irregular', came in the seventeenth century, as applied to both actions and the people who performed them.

economy (resourceful use of money, etc)
The word is based on Greek *oikos*, 'house', and in the sixteenth century, when the noun was first used in English, it meant specifically 'management of a house'. This sense is now usually qualified as 'domestic economy'. The common current meaning of 'economy' developed in the seventeenth century with, however, the phrase 'political economy' emerging only in the eighteenth century as a translation of French *économie politique*. Similarly, an 'economist' was originally the head of a household (in the sixteenth century), then a 'money manager' in general (in the eighteenth), and finally, in its current sense, a specialist in or student of economics or political economy (only in the nineteenth).

eerie (frightening through ghostly or supernatural influence)
The earliest meaning of the word, in the thirteenth century, was simply 'fearful', 'timid', for whatever reason, so that a person could have an 'eerie' heart or 'eerie'

95

courage. The modern sense 'uncanny', however, as an 'eerie' silence or an 'eerie' sound, arose only in the eighteenth century, mainly in the works of Scottish writers such as Burns and Hector Macneill (who wrote 'Night comes dark and eerie' in a poem of 1795).

elated (filled with high spirits and enthusiasm, euphoric)
The Latin verb from which the word derives is *efferre*, 'to carry up' (past participle passive *elatus*). In the sixteenth century, therefore, the English word was first used to mean 'elevated', 'lifted up', in a literal sense. In the seventeenth century, 'elated' came to get its modern meaning, although it could also mean 'encouraged', and was used thus in the verb 'elate' in general, as in this line from Pope's translation (1725) of the *Odyssey:*

Schemes of revenge his pondering breast
    elate.

election (selection by votes)
For some time from the thirteenth century, an 'election' was simply an act of electing or choosing, especially with regard to a person's conduct, as in this dictum from Jonathan Edwards' *A Careful and Strict Enquiry into the Modern Prevailing Notions of* [. . .] *Freedom of Will* (1754): 'A man has a Thing in his Power, if he has it in his Choice, or at his Election'. The popular sense of 'election' to apply to the voting in of a political party or the like dates only from the seventeenth century. In modern English, therefore, 'elect' and 'election' are not as closely related as 'select' and 'selection'. See also **elegant** (below).

elegant (gracefully refined, tastefully attractive)
In his *Dictionary* of 1755, Johnson nicely defined 'elegant' as 'pleasing by minuter beauties', which is the general sense the word has today. Its origin is in Latin *elegans*, related to *elegere*, 'to elect', so that the exact implication is 'choosing carefully'. The early sense of *elegans* in Latin was also 'fastidious', and this was for some time a use of the word in English, implying an unfavourable or unrefined use of ornament or style, taste*less*

rather that taste*ful*. In his translation (1509) of the *Ship of Fools*, Alexander Barclay thus wrote that it was:

Not for man to be so elegant,
To such toyes wanton women may
    encline.

Today, however, the adjective is used almost always in a complimentary way.

elide (omit a vowel or syllable when speaking)
In modern use, 'elide' has almost a technical sense, referring to a person's speech or pronunciation in which a vowel is omitted (as we all do in 'I'm', 'can't' and 'won't', for example). This use of the verb dates only from the eighteenth century, however, and the original meaning was 'annihilate', and so was closer to the Latin *elidere*, 'to crush out', from which the word derives. The usage was almost exclusively a legal one, though, and the sense was thus often 'annul', as in this text of 1754: 'The concurring testimony of the husband and wife [. . .] is sufficient to elide this legal presumption' (John Erskine, *Principles of the Law of Scotland*). This sense is rare in law today, however.

eliminate (get rid of, remove)
The literal sense of the word is 'put out of doors', from Latin *eliminare*, itself based on *limen*, 'threshold' (compare modern 'subliminal'). This is found in some sixteenth- and seventeenth-century texts, as in a letter from Archbishop Parker of 1568, where he writes concerning a way in which it might be possible 'to help eliminate out of his [i.e. God's] house' an offending member. Later use of 'eliminate' in such a literal sense is usually humorous, however, as in Thackeray's *Vanity Fair* (1848): 'From which [room], with the most engaging politeness, she eliminated poor Ferkin'.

elongate (extend, make longer)
In the sixteenth century, to 'elongate' was to 'remove', as in this text of 1540 regarding the siting of an outdoor privy: 'Let the common howse of esement be [. . .] elongatyd from the howse' (Andrew Boorde, *The Boke for to Lerne a Man to be Wyse in Buylding of his House*). From the seventeenth century,

the meaning was also 'depart', 'move away', in particular of a heavenly body in astronomy. These two uses are now obsolete, and the current meaning, first recorded in the sixteenth century, is the only one. The old sense in fact preserved more accurately the Latin source in *elongare*, which is based on *longe*, 'far off'. Later, the word was more understandably connected with 'long'.

elude (avoid by cunning, slip away secretly)
In the sixteenth century, 'elude' meant '*delude*', 'baffle'. 'The people had bene eluded and caused to doe great idolatrie', wrote Charles Wriothesley in 1538 in *A Chronicle of England in the Reigns of the Tudors*. The present meaning of the verb followed in the seventeenth century, and the earlier sense became obsolete. The literal meaning of 'elude' is 'play out', from Latin *eludere* (to which 'ludicrous' is related).

emblem (symbol, identifying figure or mark)
The origin of the word is in Latin *emblema*, 'inlaid work' (in turn from Greek *emballein*, literally 'to throw in'), and in English an 'emblem' was at first an allegorical picture in the sixteenth century. Thus the Anglican preacher Thomas Fuller, in his *The Holy State and the Profane State* (1642) wrote: 'I like that Embleme of Charity [. . .] a naked child, giving honey to a Bee without wings'. The present sense is first recorded in Shakespeare's *All's Well That Ends Well* (1601), where Parolles tells the King of France's Lords, as they leave for the Florentine War, of 'one Captain Spurio, with his cicatrice, an emblem of war, here on his sinister cheek'. See also **embolism** (below), from the same origin.

embolism (obstruction of a blood vessel by a clot of blood, bubble of air, etc)
This medical sense arose in the nineteenth century, and it is perhaps worth recalling that 'embolism' had a much earlier, although similarly technical usage. This was in the fourteenth century, when it was the term for a a day or days that had to be added or intercalated in a calendar to correct errors that had arisen from the

difference between the civil year of 365 days (366 in a leap year) and the solar year of 365 days 5 hours 48 minutes 48 seconds. Such an intercalation is now effected by the extra day of the leap year. 'Embolism' literally means 'something thrown in', from Greek *emballein* (see **emblem**, above).

emotion (strong feeling)
The word is a relatively modern one, and is found only rarely before the latter half of the seventeenth century. (Interestingly, Evelyn referred to it in 1665 as a French word that might be profitably adopted into English.) Where it does occur before this, it had meanings such as 'agitation', 'physical disturbance', so that Sir Geoffrey Fenton, in *The Historie of Guicciardini* (1579), wrote that there were 'great stirres and emocions in Lombardye', and in 1709 Addison wrote in *The Tatler* of 'Publick Emotions, occasion'd by the Want of Corn'. In the popular sense of today, 'emotion' arose only in the nineteenth century, when 'emotive' is also first recorded.

emu (fast-running Australian bird)
Today the 'emu' is properly the bird *Dromiceius novae-hollandiae* that is related to the ostrich, with this meaning established in the nineteenth century. The name occurs in texts before this, however, to apply to other birds, not always readily identifiable, but not the 'emu' as now known. In the seventeenth century it was used as the name for the cassowary ('the Cassoware or Emeu' in Henry More's *An Antidote Against Atheisme* of 1653). In the eighteenth century it was wrongly identified with the American ostrich (*Rhea americana*). However, the emu and the cassowary are related (although the former does not have the bony 'helmet' on its head that the latter has), and there can be some excuse for equating the two by giving them the same name.

enable (give power to, provide with means for doing)
Before the current sense developed in the sixteenth century, 'enable' meant 'invest with legal status' some hundred years earlier. Although now obsolete · in this meaning, 'enable' survived in the use until the eighteenth century, so that a letter from

the Jesuit scholar James Wadsworth in 1615 spoke of the reasons that had prompted Henry VIII to 'disinherite Queene Mary, and enable Queene Elizabeth'.

encroach (intrude, trespass)
When first used in English, in the fourteenth century, 'encroach' meant 'seize unlawfully', and the word is used in this sense in John Fitzherbert's *A Ryght Frutefull Mater: and hath to Name the Boke of Surueyeng* [i.e. surveying] (1523), where he explains that he has written the book so that the lords should not 'haue their landes lost nor imbeselde nor encroched by one from another'. (He uses 'imbeselde' [i.e. embezzled] in the earlier sense here of 'taken away'.) The current sense of 'encroach' dates from the sixteenth century.

encyclopaedia (reference work dealing with a wide range of knowledge)
The word's ultimate source (via Latin) is Greek *enkyklios paideia,* 'general education', i.e. literally 'all-round education', and this is something like the original meaning of the word in English in the sixteenth century, when it was used for a general course of instruction, or applied more generally to a 'circle of learning'. For example, in the introduction to his remarkable (and still readable) *Pseudoxia Epidemica* (better known as *Vulgar Errors*) (1646), Sir Thomas Browne refers to his work as an 'Encyclopaedie and round of knowledge', whereas it is not really an encyclopaedia in the accepted modern sense at all. (It does give the lie to many popular beliefs of the time, however, such as that snails have no eyes and that elephants have no joints, despite 'the gross and somewhat cylindrical composure of the legs'.) The present use of 'encyclopaedia' arrived in the seventeenth century, when the word appeared in the title of such works, for example that of the German philosopher Alsted (Alstedius), published in 1632. The *Encyclopaedia Britannica* firmly established the word when in turn it first appeared in 1768.

endear (make dear)
Before the word had its modern sense in the seventeenth century, it meant 'make dear' in the other use of 'dear', that is, 'make

more costly'. This rather handy usage did not last much longer than the sixteenth century, however.

enforce (compel, give greater force to)
The two current senses given here date from the fifteenth century. Before this, the verb had a number of other meanings, now all obsolete. One of the main ones was 'strengthen physically or morally', 'reinforce', as in Lord Berners' translation (1523) of Froissart's *Chronicles,* where he writes that: 'The frenche kynge enforced his great nauy that he had on the see'. Similarly, in his translation (1483) of the *Golden Legend,* Caxton wrote:

Yet was saynt barnabe a man enforced to suffre paynes.

Another meaning of 'enforce' was 'strive', whether used reflexively or not, as in Wyclif's Bible translation of 1382, where he renders I Kings 19:10 as follows: 'Saul enforside to fitche to gidre with a spere Dauid in the wal' (Authorized Version of 1611: 'And Saul sought to smite David even to the wall with the javelin'). And yet another sense was 'drive by force', such as sending a stone from a sling, as in Shakespeare's *Henry V* (1599), when Henry says, during the Battle of Agincourt:

And make them skirr away, as swift as stones
Enforced from the old Assyrian slings.

engine (mechanical appliance, machine)
Obviously, such developments as the steam and petrol 'engine' are quite recent. Originally, from the thirteenth century, 'engine' meant just 'contrivance', 'plot', 'snare', with this sense quickly passing to 'mechanical contrivance', as in Robert Manning de Brunne's *The Story of England* (1330), in which, talking of the stones of Stonehenge, he says that giants:

sette them on an hil ful hey [i.e. high] With engyns fulle quentely [i.e. cleverly].

From the fourteenth century, 'engine' could mean 'genius', as Chaucer wrote in the *Canterbury Tales* ('The Second Nun's Tale') (1386):

A man hath sapiences thre [i.e. three
wisdoms],
Memorie, engin, and intellect also.

engineer (designer or builder of engines,
person trained in engineering)
Originally, an 'engineer' was a person who
designed or constructed military engines.
This was in the fourteenth century. Later,
the title was that of a person who designed
and constructed military works in general
for attack or defence, the forerunner of the
modern member of the Royal Engineers (for
example) who is responsible for 'paving the
way' for vehicles by building bridges, roads
and the like. It was the medieval type of
'engineer' who became associated in Shakespeare's *Hamlet* (1602) with a famous
expression, and this was the one mentioned
by Hamlet after the death of Polonius:

For 'tis the sport to have the engineer
Hoist with his own petar.

(This is the origin of the phrase in the
language.) See also **engine** (above).

engross (occupy the attention exclusively)
The current sense arose in the seventeenth
century. When the verb was first used in
English, in the fourteenth century, it meant
'buy wholesale' (i.e. 'in gross'), the purpose
being to buy up as much of a stock as possible so as to have the monopoly of selling
it. From this, a sense 'get together'
developed in the sixteenth century, as in
Shakespeare's *Henry IV*, Part 1 (1596),
where the meaning is first recorded. This is
the scene where Henry, Prince of Wales,
says to his father the King:

Percy is but my factor, good my lord,
To engross up glorious deeds on my
behalf.

From this in turn came the modern sense.
However, in the fifteenth century, another
sense of 'engross' appeared, meaning 'write
in large letters'. This is still a term applied
to the drawing up of legal documents, or
in the preparation of a written or printed
document in general. The origin of this
meaning is not quite the same as with the
other senses, since the word derives from
Old French *en grosse*, in turn from Medieval
Latin *grossa*, 'large writing'.

enhance (improve, increase the quality or
desirability of)
When first used in the fourteenth century,
the word meant 'raise' literally, as in these
two lines from John Lydgate's translation
(1430) of Bochas' *Fall of Princes*:

Cruelly he gan enhaunce his honde [i.e.
hand]
With his sweorde to yeue [i.e. give] her
a wounde.

The modern meaning, as applied both to
'heightening' something and to raising a
price, dates from the fifteenth century.

enigma (puzzle, something hard to
understand)
In the sixteenth century, when the word was
first used, it applied specifically to a riddle
in verse, usually connotating something by
obscure references, so that the subject had
to guess what was meant by what he read
or heard. An early mention of such a device
comes in Shakespeare's *Love's Labour's Lost*
(1588), where Armado says to Costard:
'Some enigma, some riddle: come, thy
l'envoy; begin'. The current sense followed
some hundred years later.

enjoy (take pleasure in)
The original meaning of the word, in the
fourteenth century, was much closer to 'joy'
as it is still understood, so that the sense
was 'be joyful'. Wyclif's rendering in 1382
of Luke 1:14 in his Bible was thus: 'And
manye schulen enioye in his natyuite'
(Authorized Version of 1611: 'And many
shall rejoice at his birth'). The weaker sense
of 'enjoy' meaning little more than 'use' was
first recorded in the fifteenth century, when
the main sense also arose.

enlarge (make larger or bigger; elaborate)
The basic sense dates from the fourteenth
century. For some time from the fifteenth,
however, a meaning 'set free', 'set at large'
was current, as in Hume's *History of Great
Britain* (1761): 'No man, after being
enlarged by order of court, can be recom-
mitted for the same offence'.

enormous (very large)
Two obsolete senses were current for the
word from the sixteenth century, when the

present meaning also arose. One was 'abnormal', 'monstrous', as in Milton's *Paradise Lost* (1667):

> Nature here played at will
> Her Virgin Fancies, pouring forth more
>   sweet,
> Wilde above rule or Art; enormous bliss.

The other sense was 'irregular', 'outrageous', as in *The Two Noble Kinsmen* (1634) by (probably) Shakespeare and Fletcher, which has the line:

> Oh great corrector of enormous times.

The current use of 'enormous' to mean 'shocking', as an 'enormous' crime, is really a blend of this with the main meaning 'very large'.

ensure (guarantee, make certain)
When first used in the fourteenth century, 'ensure' often meant 'assure', so that 'I ensure you' meant 'I want to convince you that what I say is true'. The present sense dates only from the eighteenth century.

entail (involve as a consequence)
The first sense of the verb to be used in English was the legal one, still current, that means 'settle an estate so that it passes only to the owner's heirs'. This is first recorded in the fourteenth century. In the sixteenth century, 'entail' came to mean 'attach', both in a restricted legal sense and more generally, as simply 'tack on'. Bunyan uses it in *The Holy City* (1665), for example: 'His Name was always so entailed to that Doctrine'. This usage became obsolete in the eighteenth century. The current meaning thus emerged quite recently, in the nineteenth century, when it is first recorded in Southey's *Sir Thomas More* (1829): 'A conquest which brought with it no evil and entailed no regret'.

entertain (show hospitality to, keep in mind, divert)
The verb was first used in English in the fifteenth century, as a borrowing of French *entretenir*, and its initial meaning was 'maintain', similar to that of the French (literally 'hold among'). It is first recorded in this sense in Caxton's translation (1490) of Virgil's *Aeneid:* 'His swete wordes and

drawynge [i.e. persuading] atysen [i.e. entice] and entertayne her in a contynualle thoughte towarde hym'. This usage was current for some time down to about the nineteenth century, becoming more or less standard in such phrases as 'entertain correspondence' and 'entertain discourse'. The verb is now obsolete in this meaning, however, or at least highly mannered. A further obsolete sense of 'entertain' evolved in the sixteenth century, to mean 'keep in service' (of a person), 'hold the attention' (of someone), and this is what the word means in Shakespeare's *The Merry Wives of Windsor* (1598), when Mistress Ford is reacting to Falstaff's love letter: 'How shall I be revenged on him? I think, the best way were to entertain him with hope, till the wicked fire of lust have melted him in his own grease'. The popular meaning 'amuse' finally emerged only in the seventeenth century.

enthral (captivate)
For a while in the seventeenth and eighteenth centuries, 'enthral' was used in a literal sense, 'capture', 'hold in slavery', as in Abraham Cowley's *Pindarique Odes* (1656):

> Ingrateful Caesar who could Rome
>   enthrall.

The more common meaning 'captivate', however, which had arisen slightly earlier, was the one that prevailed.

enthusiasm (keen interest or pleasure in something)
The clearly Greek origin here means literally 'divinely inspired', with *theos*, 'god' at the heart of the word. When first used in English, in the seventeenth century, 'enthusiasm' thus meant 'possession by a god', 'poetic frenzy'. This is the sense in Philemon Holland's translation (1603) of Plutarch's *Morals*, for example: 'The Daemons use to make their prophets and prophetesses to be ravished with an Enthusiasme or divine fury'. In the Preface to his translation (1693) of Juvenal's *Satires*, too, Dryden spoke of poetry as 'a kind of enthusiasm, or extraordinary emotion of soul'. From about the same time, the word also came to mean 'misguided religious

emotion', and 'enthusiasm' is defined in these terms in Johnson's *Dictionary* (1755): 'A vain confidence of divine favour or communication'. The present popular meaning therefore became established only later, in the eighteenth century.

entreat (beg earnestly, plead)
When first used in English, in the fourteenth century, 'entreat' meant merely 'treat', as in Caxton's *The Cronicles of Englond* (1480), where he records at one point that: 'The other Capytayns were [. . .] entreated as men of warre ben acustomed'. Similarly, 'entreaty' meant 'treatment', whether of people or of a subject. The latter is the sense in the introduction to Sir Henry Billingsley's translation (1570) of Euclid's work on geometry: 'The maner of entreatie in this booke is diuers from the entreaty of the former bookes'. By about the end of the eighteenth century, however, both verb and noun were obsolete in this use.

entrepreneur (person who manages a business or enterprise to make a profit)
When first borrowed from French into English in the early nineteenth century, 'entrepreneur' (literally 'undertaker') was the word used for a person who directed or organized musical or other entertainments. The current meaning came somewhat later, in the mid-nineteenth century, and is first recorded in a letter of Carlyle dated 15 September 1852, where he refers to a gaming establishment 'built by one French gambling *entrepreneur*' (with the word underlined as he still felt it to be not fully anglicized). The word was more or less formally adopted after this as a term in political economy for a director of a business, although in recent times the sense has become rather wider to denote any 'speculating' businessman who manages his own enterprise, especially one undertaking a financial risk.

envisage (have a mental picture of some future event or action)
The literal meaning of the word, in its French sense, is 'look in the face', and when 'envisage' was first used in English, in the early nineteenth century, it meant 'look straight at', 'face'. The earliest record we

have of it in this sense is in Keats's *Hyperion* (1820), which has the lines:

To envisage circumstance, all calm,
That is the top of sovereignty.

The sense 'contemplate', 'have a mental picture of' followed in the mid-nineteenth century, although not often with the 'future' aspect in which the word is mostly used today (as in 'I don't envisage any answer before Friday').

epicure (person with refined tastes, especially in food and drink)
Today's sense of the word is far more 'civilized' than it was when first used in English in the sixteenth century. It then implied 'glutton', even 'womanizer', and this was what Shakespeare meant when in *Macbeth* (1605) he makes Macbeth say:

Then fly, false thanes,
And mingle with the English epicures.

In Medieval Latin, *epicurus* was the word for a person whose chief happiness was in the pleasures of the flesh (of both or all kinds), and this itself comes from the name of the Greek philosopher, Epicurus, who taught, among other things, that 'pleasure is the highest good'. (There is some doubt, however, that Epicurus himself followed his own teaching in the subsequent popular sense of the word.) Also in the sixteenth century, however, 'epicure' began to acquire its present usage, in a more refined sense. The corresponding adjective 'epicurean' underwent a similar change, with the earlier, 'gluttonous' sense clearly apparent in such works as Milton's *Of Reformation Touching Church Discipline in England* (1641), where he writes of his subjects' 'unctuous, and epicurean paunches'.

equator (the 'great circle' of the earth that divides it into two hemispheres)
This is the common understanding of the word. But the usage arose only in the seventeenth century, and the much earlier meaning of 'equator' was the astronomical (then astrological) one as the equivalent 'great circle' of the heavens, that is, the celestial equator. This term was in use from the fourteenth century, and lies behind the word itself, since when the sun was in the

equator, day and night were of equal length. (Its full Medieval Latin title was *circulus aequator diei et noctis*, 'circle equalising day and night'.) The link between the celestial and the terrestrial equator is more than a semantic one, since if the plane of the terrestrial equator is extended indefinitely, it will cut the celestial sphere (the 'dome' of the sky) as the actual celestial equator itself. Astronomers still use the word in this sense.

equerry (officer in charge of horses or attending member of royal family)
The word has become wrongly associated with Latin *equus*, 'horse', hence the modern spelling and pronunciation. The real link is with French *écurie* (or an earlier form of this), 'stable'. Thus the original meaning of 'equerry' in English, in the sixteenth century, was simply as 'stables', especially those of a prince or member of the royal family. From this, the sense was extended to apply to the officer in charge of such stables. The earliest spellings of the word in English were on the lines of 'equiry' or 'escuirie', showing the further link (a true one, this time) with English 'squire', which is itself a shortened form of 'esquire' and so of identical origin.

equivocation (use of words in double sense so as to mislead)
As originally used in English, an 'equivocation' was simply an ambiguous use of words, not necessarily one designed to mislead. Here is John Lydgate complaining about one such ambiguity (as many of his contemporary churchmen did) in his translation (1413) of *The Pylgremage of the Sowle:* 'Ye clepe [i.e. call] seculum the world here abouen, what mene ye by this equyocacion of that name?'. The modern meaning of 'equivocation' is first recorded in Shakespeare's *Macbeth* (1605), where Macbeth says:

I pull in resolution and begin
To doubt the equivocation of the fiend
That lies like truth; 'Fear not, till Birnam wood
Do come to Dunsinane'.

err (go astray, be mistaken)
The earliest use of 'err' was simply 'wander', 'roam', and the word is recorded

in this sense from the fourteenth century, as in Wyclif's Bible (1382), where he translates Genesis 37:15 as: 'A man fonde hym in the feelde errynge' (Authorized Version of 1611: 'And a certain man found him and, behold, he was wandering in the field'). At the same period, however, the modern sense was also current, as again in Wyclif, where Isaiah 53:6 is: 'Alle wee as shep erreden' (Authorized Version: 'All we like sheep have gone astray'). The other current sense, 'be mistaken', also dates from the fourteenth century.

errand (trip to take a message or do something for someone else)
In Old English, an 'errand' was either a message or a mission, with both these senses, now obsolete, in use down to at least the eighteenth century. Even as late as 1725, Defoe used the word to mean 'message' in *A New Voyage Round the World:* 'The second messenger came in, and delivered his part of the errand'. As 'mission', the word had a 'lofty' sense which it does not have today, although the earlier connotation is preserved in the phrase 'errand of mercy'. As applied simply to the journey, as 'errand' mostly is in current use, the sense dates from the seventeenth century.

erratic (irregular, eccentric)
The word is directly related to **err** (which see, above), and so originally meant 'wandering', 'vagrant' (initially 'wandering' in a technical sense, as the 'erratic star' that was actually a planet, and an 'erratic' pain, which was one such as rheumatism, that 'wandered' or changed its position). In the following quotation from Scott's *Old Mortality* (1816), the meaning is 'vagrant': 'No entreaty could induce him to alter his erratic way of life'. Thus from these former senses, in use from the fourteenth century, the modern meaning emerged only in the nineteenth century.

escapade (reckless adventure, exciting flouting of the rules)
In the seventeenth century, when the word was first used in English, it meant simply 'escape', or at most 'runaway flight', as in Scott's *Guy Mannering* (1815): 'His second escapade was made for the purpose of

visiting the field of Rullion-green'. It was Scott himself, however, who gave us the first recorded use of the word in its modern sense, to denote a genuinely 'flighty' escape, so that his *Waverley* (1814) mentions a 'youthful escapade, which might be easily atoned'. The former meaning is now generally obsolete.

estate (portion of land owned by a particular person)
There are several senses now of 'estate', with the one given here the most common and the most recent, developing only in the eighteenth century. All the earlier senses are still current, however, even if some are very limited or obsolescent, and their history runs as follows: 'state', 'condition' (from the thirteenth century); 'show', 'pomp' (fourteenth century); 'social or political class', as the 'Third Estate' formerly designating the Commons; 'interest in property', as 'real estate' (both fifteenth century), 'property', 'possessions' (sixteenth). The earliest sense here is now mainly associated with biblical phrases, such as 'man's estate', although Browning seems to have used the word in this basic meaning in his *Red Cotton Nightcap Country* (1873):

> I am forty-three years old,
> In prime of life, perfection of estate.

ether (inflammable liquid formerly used as a general anaesthetic)
Greek *aither* was the word for the more rarefied and 'diviner' upper air, and in English the word came to be used, mainly in a poetic sense, for the clear sky, as in Scott's romantic poem, *The Bridal of Triermain* (1813):

> The wizard song at distance died,
> As if in ether borne astray.

In the seventeenth century, 'ether' was the term used to denote scientifically (in contemporary terms) the rarefied element that was believed to fill the upper regions of space, a 'substance of great elasticity and subtilty' (*Oxford English Dictionary*). This particular concept was pursued seriously by many eminent scientists, from Newton in the seventeenth century, to Bertrand Russell in the twentieth, but has not been developed later than about the 1920s, so the sense itself is now similarly dated. The remaining current sense, for the fluid, dates from the mid-nineteenth century, although the word was also formerly used from about the beginning of the nineteenth century to denote any chemical compound that was formed by the reaction of ethyl alcohol and either an acid (other than sulphuric acid) or a salt, so that nitrous acid, for example, gave nitrous 'ether' (now called ethyl nitrite). This usage became obsolete from about the end of the century.

ethnic (pertaining to race)
Greek *ethnikos* meant not only 'national' but also 'gentile', and the latter was the sense of the word as first used in English from the fourteenth century, where 'gentile' itself meant 'pagan', 'heathen', 'not Jewish or Christian'. The use continued sporadically down to as recently as the nineteenth century, and the word is found, for example, in a poem by Thomas Moore (*Epistles*, 1804):

> All the charm that ethnic fancy gave
> To blessed arbours o'er the western wave.

The noun 'ethnic' had a similar sense and time span. In the sense 'pertaining to race', the word had two stages of development. The first was more general, meaning 'concerning a race, its history and characteristics', and developed in the mid-nineteenth century in such terms as 'ethnic considerations', and the 'ethnic peculiarities of childhood'. The second meaning, the current one, which has the sense 'having common racial characteristics, especially within a larger system', emerged only in the twentieth century, and was first proposed (in the phrase 'ethnic group') by Julian Huxley and Alfred Haddon in their book *We Europeans* (1935).

euphoria (state of optimism and cheerfulness, especially an excessive one)
The word was originally spelt 'euphory' and had a medical sense defined as 'well-being, or the perfect ease and comfort of healthy persons, especially when the sensation occurs in a sick person' (H. Power and L.W. Sedgwick, *Lexicon of Medicine and Allied*

Sciences, 1879–99). This in turn enlarged on an earlier definition in John Kersey's edition of 1706 of Edward Phillips' dictionary, *The New World of English Words,* which was: '*Euphoria,* the well bearing of the Operation of a Medicine, *i.e.* when the Patient finds himself eas'd or reliev'd by it'. The spelling with '-ia' has generally prevailed in the twentieth century, however, especially with the popular development of the sense, as typified in Auden's verse in *Homage to Clio* (1960):

Good Queen Victoria,
In a fit of euphoria,
Commanded Disraeli
To blow up the Old Bailey.

euthanasia (the deliberate killing of an incurably ill person, 'mercy killing')
The Greek word that is the source of the word means literally 'easy death', and this was the original meaning in English in the seventeenth century, as in Bishop Joseph Hall's *The Balme of Gilead* (1646): 'But let me prescribe and commend to thee, my sonne, this true spirituall meanes of thine happy Euthanasia'. The current sense followed in the eighteenth century, first recorded in a figurative use in Hume's *Essays Moral and Political* (1742), where he wrote that absolute monarchy was 'the easiest death, the true *Euthanasia* of the British constitution'.

evening (last part of the day, when night falls)
It may seem strange that 'evening' could ever have had any other meaning than its present one. In Old English, however, *æfnung* was really a verbal noun meaning 'closing of the day', from the verb (*æfnian*) that meant 'grow towards evening'. The sense was therefore restricted to the time of dusk and of sunset. This is the use of the word in Wyclif's Bible of 1382 when he translates Matthew 27:57: 'Whanne the euenyng was maad, there came a riche man fro Armathia' (Authorized Version of 1611: 'When the even was come, there came a rich man of Arimathaea'). The later version here uses the word ('even') that had the modern sense of 'evening' but that was superseded by it from about the end of the

fifteenth century, at any rate in regular use. 'Even' still continues to be a popular poetic word, however, and survives in some compound words, especially 'evensong' and 'eventide'.

exaggerate (claim that something is larger than it really is)
In the sixteenth century, when first used in English, the verb was closer in sense to the Latin root word *agger,* 'heap' from which it derives. It then meant 'accumulate', 'pile up', in both a literal and a figurative sense, as in the Puritan pamphleteer Philip Stubbes' denunciation of evil customs, *The Anatomie of Abuses* (1583): 'With their flipping and flapping up and down in the dirte they exaggerate a mountain of mire'. The present meaning developed from the seventeenth century.

excellent (very good, firstrate)
In the fourteenth century, 'excellent' meant 'exalted', 'supreme', 'excelling'. An example of the use is in *The Life and Martyrdom of Saint Katherine of Alexandria* (1430), where: 'The excellent beute [i.e. beauty] was so greet that [...] Adrian [...] fille doun before hem [i.e. them] wyth greet drede'. The word could be used in an unfavourable sense, too, as in Shakespeare's *Titus Andronicus* (1588), where Aaron, with his bag of gold, says:

This gold must coin a stratagem,
Which, cunningly effected, will beget
A very excellent piece of villainy.

The 'exalted' sense can be seen in the Bible, in Psalm 148:13: 'Let them praise the name of the Lord: for his name alone is excellent'. It was Shakespeare, as in many other instances, who introduced the modern sense of the word, so that in *Othello* (1604), after Iago has sung his 'drinking song', Cassio exclaims: ''Fore God, an excellent song'.

excise (tax on certain commodities)
In the fifteenth century, 'excise' was a word in general for any tax or toll. The current, narrower sense arose in 1643, in which year the impost was officially adopted in imitation of such taxation in Holland. The first record of the word thus refers to Holland, in Spenser's *A View of the Present*

State of Ireland (1596): 'All the townes of the Lowe-Countreyes doe cutt upon themselves an excise of all thinges towarde the mayntenaunce of the warre'. When the tax was first introduced in England, as mentioned, it was very unpopular. Hence Johnson's definition of it in his *Dictionary* (1755): '*Excise*, a hateful tax levied upon commodities, and adjudged not by the common judges of property, but wretches hired by those to whom excise is paid'.

excursion (pleasure trip)
The first meaning of the word, as used in English in the sixteenth century, was 'escape', thus fairly closely reflecting its literal Latin sense of 'running out' (from the verb *excurrere*). This could be an 'excursion' of a river, when it overflowed its banks, the 'excursion' of a building, when it had an extension added that 'ran out' from it, or the 'excursion' of a military force by way of a sortie or sally. This last use survives in the expression 'alarms and excursions'. The 'trip' sense came in the seventeenth century, originally as a mostly individual kind of journey or ramble from one's home or base, with the more 'organized' concept firmly established in the nineteenth century with the introduction of special 'excursions' at special prices by train.

exeat (permission given to a student to be absent)
An 'exeat' is very much a school and college word, deriving, academically enough, from the Latin for 'let him go out'. It has been in use in this sense since the eighteenth century. Earlier, however, it was a sixteenth-century play direction having the meaning 'exit', i.e. indicating when a player was to leave the stage. However, 'exit' itself replaced 'exeat' in this function, and the latter word transferred to the schools. (Similarly, 'exeunt' as a stage direction was 'exeant', when more than one actor was to leave.) See also **exit** (below).

exhibition (display, public showing; grant or scholarship awarded by a school or college)
The original sense of the word, as used in the fifteenth century, was 'maintenance', 'allowance', almost always in the financial

sense. This became obsolete generally, but survives in the special educational usage as described above (although only from the seventeenth century). Later, the more popular sense of 'exhibition' appeared in the seventeenth century, meaning first 'visible display' (usually of an emotion), as an 'exhibition' of hatred, and then 'public organized display' a century later. The word was fully established with the 'Great Exhibition' of 1851 in London. (The usage in such a phrase as 'to make an exhibition of oneself' dates from around this time, possibly significantly.)

exit (way out)
As mentioned under **exeat** (above), 'exit' was originally a direction for an actor to leave the stage (from the Latin for 'he goes out'). This sense was current from the sixteenth century. From this, the meaning progressed naturally to the leaving itself, and is appropriately first recorded as such in Shakespeare, where in *Love's Labour's Lost* (1588), in the final scene, Holofernes is acting the part of Judas and says to Moth (who is playing Hercules): 'Keep some state in thy exit, and vanish'. From there the word came to mean generally any 'issuing forth', as for a baby being born, or an escape of steam, but the now familiar 'way out', as in a public building or railway station, came only in the nineteenth century.

exorbitant (greatly exceeding what is acceptable)
The word literally implies a going 'out of orbit', and the original sense, in the fifteenth century, was something like this, since the meaning then was 'deviating from the true path', applying to remarks that were off the subject, for example, or a person who had 'gone astray' morally or legally. 'We must resist and crush every exorbitant thought which draws to sin', wrote the biblical scholar Joseph Mead in 1638. The modern sense developed from the seventeenth century, including the popular meaning 'very costly', 'too expensive'.

expect (look forward to, anticipate)
The word has been in use since the sixteenth century, when it also had the now obsolete sense of 'wait' or 'wait for'. The former is

found in the Bible, in Hebrews 10:13: 'From henceforth expecting till his enemies be made his footstool'. The latter can be found in *The Tatler* in 1710, when its founder, Richard Steele, reported: 'There was a great crowd in my Antichamber, who expected Audience'.

expletive (swearword)
The literal sense of the word is 'filled out', from Latin *explere*. 'Expletive', thus, was originally an adjective meaning 'serving to fill out'. This was in the seventeenth century, with the noun, meaning 'word or phrase used to fill out a line', also dating from this time. Oaths and swearwords can of course serve to 'fill out' what a person has to say, and this meaning finally came about in the nineteenth century.

explode (burst or detonate, 'go off' with a loud noise)
It may seem unlikely that 'explode' could ever have meant anything else. In the sixteenth century, however, it meant 'reject', as when the mathematician Thomas Tryon wrote in his *Miscellanea* (1696): 'Not that I wholly Explode Astrology; I believe that there is something in it'. In the seventeenth century, 'exploded' came to be used to mean 'discredited', as in the familiar 'exploded' myth. The current meaning thus dates from the eighteenth century. The literal sense of the word, in its Latin origin, is 'drive off the stage by clapping' (*explodere*), so that the verb is actually related to 'applaud'.

exploit (feat)
'Exploit' originally meant 'progress', 'success', 'speed' in the fourteenth century, as in these lines from John Gower's *Confessio amantis* (1390):

> The sail goth up, and forth they straught [i.e. made their way],
> But none esploit therof they caught.

From the fifteenth century, the meaning developed to 'attempt to control', 'attempt to capture', especially in a military or naval context, as in Shakespeare's *All's Well That Ends Well* (1601), where Parolles says to the First French Lord, with his soldiers in their ambush: 'I must give myself some hurts and

say I got them in exploit'. Finally, the current sense prevailed from the sixteenth century, and the earlier meanings became obsolete.

export (send goods to another country)
Before the verb acquired its current sense in the seventeenth century, it meant simply 'carry away', 'carry off', applying to both things and people, as in Donne's *Biathanatos* (1624), where he writes that Paulinus '...delivered himselfe as a slave to the Vandals, and was exported from Italy to Afrique'. Even as late as 1691, John Ray wrote in *The Wisdom of God Manifested in the Works of Creation* that 'The Arteries are known to export the Blood'.

exquisite (delicate and flawless, extremely sensitive)
The literal meaning of the word is 'sought out', from Latin *exquisitus* (from *exquirere*, 'to search out'). When the word was first used in English, in the fifteenth century, it meant 'ingenious', 'abstruse', mostly as applied to language or turns of phrase or ideas, and this is the sense in Shakespeare's *Twelfth Night* (1601), where Toby Belch asks Andrew Aguecheek: 'Thy exquisite reason, dear knight?', and Sir Andrew replies: 'I have no exquisite reason for't, but I have reason good enough'. The present meaning began to emerge in the sixteenth century, but the word could also have the sense then of 'accurate', 'exact', which it now no longer has, as in Sir Thomas Elyot's *The Castel of Helth* (1539), where he says: 'The meate that shall make syckenes, must not a lyttell excede the exquisite measure'. This use became obsolete from the eighteenth century.

extinct (no longer found alive, defunct)
The word is based on Latin *stinguere*, 'to quench', and the first meaning of 'extinct' in English in the fifteenth century was therefore 'burnt out'. This was followed a hundred years later by the current, more popular meaning.

extol (praise highly, exalt)
The verb literally means 'lift up', and this was the sense it had when first current in English in the fifteenth century. The use can

be seen, for example, in Thomas Sternhold and John Hopkins' *The Whole Boke of Psalmes* (1562), where they render the second half of Psalm 86:4 (Authorized Version of 1611: 'For unto thee, O Lord, do I lift up my soul') as, in their versified version:

Unto thee Lord I extoll,
And lift my soule and minde.

The present sense dates from the same period.

extravagant (exceeding proper bounds)
As originally used in the fourteenth century, 'extravagant' (from Latin, literally 'wandering outside') had a precise usage to apply to particular papal decrees that were not contained in recognized collections, that is, regarding them as 'stray' decrees. These were later added to the collections (known in canon law as 'decretals') but kept their epithet of 'extravagant' for purposes of identification. The term usually occurred in the form 'constitution extravagant'. In *Hamlet* (1602), Shakespeare used 'extravagant' in its literal sense of 'wandering outside', where Hamlet refers to his father's ghost as 'the extravagant and erring spirit'. The modern sense emerged in the sixteenth century.

fabric (structure; cloth)
All senses of 'fabric' are still current, and the sense development has been as follows: 'building' (from the fifteenth century); 'structure or framework of a building' (seventeenth century); 'textile or cloth' (eighteenth century). Similarly, 'fabricate' originally meant 'construct' in the fifteenth century, then 'invent so as to deceive' in the eighteenth century. The ultimate source is Latin *faber*, 'smith'.

facial (pertaining to the face)
In the seventeenth century, 'facial' occurred in one or two fixed expressions, such as 'facial sight' and 'facial vision' to mean 'face-to-face', and even this in a theological context. Thus the Earl of Manchester (Sir Henry Montagu), in his *Manchester al mondo; contemplatio mortis et immortalitatis* (1633), wrote that St Stephen 'had a faciall sight of his Saviour'. This rarefied sense became obsolete in the eighteenth century, and a hundred years later the word acquired its present meaning. The noun, meaning 'facial beauty treatment', followed in the United States in the early twentieth century.

fact (thing done, true thing, piece of information)
The origin of the word is in Latin *factum*, 'thing done', 'deed', and this was the primary sense in English from the sixteenth century, now surviving in such legal expressions as 'accessory after the fact', 'accessory before the fact'. All other current senses arose at this time, too, although it was only from the eighteenth century that 'facts', as a plural concept, came to mean 'circumstances of the case'.

faint (timid, weak and dizzy, feeble)
The word was first used in English in the thirteenth century, when it had the now obsolete senses of 'feigned', 'sluggish', with the former word close to the source in Old French *feint*, 'feigned', 'shirked'. The latter meaning applies in these lines from *Richard Coer de Lion* (1325):

'Rowes on faste! who that is feynt,
In evel water may he be dreynt!'.

The sense 'feeling as if about to lose consciousness' came in the fourteenth century, when 'faint' could also mean 'weak', 'sickly', as in Miles Coverdale's Bible of 1535, where he renders the second clause of Psalm 143:7 as: 'My sprete waxeth faynte' (Authorized Version of 1611: 'My spirit faileth'). Finally, in the sixteenth century, the word came to have its popular meaning of 'indistinct'.

fairy (tiny supernatural being popular in children's stories)
The 'proper' sense of the word, from an

etymological point of view, is 'fairy folk', 'fairyland', that is, as a collective noun. This is still the current meaning in French *féerie* (the earlier form of which gave the English word), with *fée*, corresponding to old-fashioned English 'fay', meaning a single individual. This collective sense was therefore the original one in English, and occurs from the fourteenth century in Chaucer and in such works as Sir John Maundeville's *The Buke of John Maundeuill* (1400), where he tells of 'a faire lady of Fairye'. From the end of this same century, however, the sense shifted to mean a single fairy, although with 'fay' also having a less popular currency as the equivalent. The English development thus differs from the French.

fancy (whim, inclination, creative ability in art, literature, etc.)
The 'whim' sense was the original one to appear in English, from the fifteenth century, when for a while (in the sixteenth) the particular whimsical reference was to love, as in the famous words from Shakespeare's *The Merchant of Venice* (1596), in the song beginning:

Tell me where is fancy bred,
Or in the heart, or in the head?

In the sixteenth century, too, 'fancy' was at first synonymous with 'imagination' in the 'inventive' sense. Later, the two were distinguished, so that 'fancy' was the 'inventive' kind of talent, as displayed in literature, for example, and 'imagination' was the more 'realistic' creativeness of mind. Or as Ruskin put it in *Modern Painters* (1843–50): 'The fancy sees the outside [. . .]. The imagination sees the heart and inner nature'.

fang (long tooth)
The word did not begin its English life as 'tooth' at all, but as a word meaning 'capture', 'catch' (compare modern German *Gefangener*, 'prisoner'). This was in the eleventh century, and the sense endured until almost the eighteenth in certain texts, such as Shakespeare's *As You Like It* (1600), when the Duke, addressing his Lords in the Forest of Arden, speaks of:

The icy fang
And churlish chiding of the winter's wind.

The 'tooth' sense arose only in the sixteenth century, especially applying to the 'fangs' of dogs and the tusks of an elephant (and later, from the nineteenth century, the poisonous 'teeth' of snakes). The reason behind the shift of sense is not quite clear, although the common link must be the 'catching' one.

fantastic (unreal, incredible, eccentric)
The initial sense of 'fantastic' was 'unreal' in that it meant 'non-existent', 'produced by the fantasy', as a 'fantastic' fable or a 'fantastic' creature (such as a mythological one). This usage was current in the fourteenth century. A century later, the adjective developed the meaning 'imaginative', 'having imagination', as a 'fantastic' writer or a 'fantastic' artist. Shakespeare's *Two Gentlemen of Verona* (1591) has the word in this sense, where Julia, planning to disguise herself as a page boy so that she can enter the service of her beloved Proteus, says (when Lucetta suggests she should cut her hair short):

No, girl; I'll knit it up in silken strings
With twenty odd-conceited true-love
  knots:
To be fantastic may become a youth
Of greater time than I shall show to be.

The modern meaning dates from the sixteenth century. See also **fancy** (above).

farce (light comedy)
The word has an interesting and somewhat learned origin. In the thirteenth century the term, in its Latin form of *farsa* or *farsia* (literally 'thing stuffed', 'padding'), was used for the various stock phrases inserted in church services between the Greek words *kyrie* ('Lord') and *eleison* ('have mercy'). For example, the wording might be 'Kyrie, *genitor ingenite, vera essentia*, eleison', with these Latin inserts meaning respectively 'unbegotten father' and 'true being'. The practice spread to other, longer prayers and readings, so that in France, for example, rhyming verses were inserted into the chanting of Latin texts, such as the epistle. Subsequently, the French word *farce*, which derived from the Latin and in turn gave the English, was used for the extempore interludes or 'gags' inserted in religious dramas, if only to brighten up what could otherwise

be a rather stolid and serious moralizing. Finally, 'farce' was the English word, from the sixteenth century, for a light, often short comedy. The sense 'mockery' followed in the seventeenth century, with the adjective 'farcical' based on 'comical' and 'tragical'.

fare (money for a journey on public transport; food)
In Old English, the basic meaning of the word was 'journey', with the Old English verb *faran,* 'to go' behind both this 'fare' and the one that means 'get on' ('How did you fare?'). From this origin, in the now obsolete sense, the meaning 'journey money' developed in the fifteenth century, extending in the sixteenth century to 'passenger' itself. Meanwhile the meaning 'food' had developed independently from the thirteenth century, with the semantic link being the idea of 'getting on' or 'keeping going' through feeding, or of food being the necessary condition to enable a journey to be made. 'Farewell' originally meant 'go happily', and was said, however oddly, to someone setting out. Later, its sense became the equivalent of 'goodbye'. (That is, it was initially said by the person who stayed behind, and latterly by either of two people on parting.)

farm (land and buildings devoted to growing crops or raising animals)
This apparently age-old and unchanging word has actually altered its sense considerably since it was first used in English in the thirteenth century. It was then the term for a fixed annual payment or rent, whether in money or some other way. This shows the word's derivation from Medieval Latin *firma,* 'fixed payment' (i.e. one that is 'firm'). The sense can be seen, in its verbal use, in Shakespeare's *Hamlet* (1602), when the Captain says to Hamlet:

We go to gain a little patch of ground
That hath in it no profit but the name.
To pay five ducats, five, I would not
    farm it.

These lines show that the 'rent' sense of 'farm' soon came to be associated exclusively with the land that was rented, and the word came to designate such land, as well as the house on it (the 'farm' house) from the sixteenth century. Similarly, a 'farmer' was originally a rent collector (from the fourteenth century), and only a land cultivator and stockbreeder in the modern sense in the sixteenth century.

fascinate (interest greatly, intrigue)
The word was first used in English in the sixteenth century, in all its senses, with the most literal of these, now obsolete, being 'cast a spell over', 'bewitch'. Hence the use of the word in contemporary literature, as in Ben Jonson's *Every Man in his Humour* (1598): 'I was fascinated by Jupiter: fascinated: but I will be unwitch'd, and reveng'd, by law'. The modern sense, implying a 'bewitching' of the senses, developed from this in the nineteenth century.

fast (quick, speedy)
The earliest and most basic meaning of 'fast', still current in some contexts, was the Old English one of 'firm', as Chaucer's ironic use in *Anelida and Arcite* (1374):

                Als fast
As in a tempest is a roten mast.

This original usage can still be seen in such expressions as 'fast asleep', 'hard and fast', the nautical 'make fast' (secure a ship), 'fast friends', and so on (not forgetting the 'fastness' that is a fortress). 'Fast' meant 'rapidly' (as the adverb) from the thirteenth century, and 'rapid' (from this adverb) in the sixteenth. The transition from one sense ('firmly', so not moving) to an apparently contradictory one ('rapidly', so moving with some speed), can be explained by the common link of 'steadfastness of purpose', 'determination' (compare the similar 'run hard'). The final sense of 'fast' to materialize was 'dissipated', 'promiscuous', from the eighteenth century. The idea here is of someone who 'lives too fast', who is immoderate, as in Dryden's *Character of a Good Parson* (1700):

Of sixty years he seemed; and well might last
To sixty more, but that he lived too fast.

fastidious (demanding great care, difficult to satisfy)
In the fifteenth century, when the word was

first used, the meaning was 'disdainful', 'scornful', as in Edward Young's vast poem *Night Thoughts* (1742–5):

> Proud youth! fastidious of the lower
>   world.

The current meaning, 'easily offended', 'hard to please', followed in the sixteenth century. The derivation of the word is from Latin *fastidium*, 'disgust'.

fathom (unit of length equal to six feet)
An approximate guide to the length of a fathom can be shown by the distance from one fingertip to the other of a man standing with outstretched arms. This is no anatomical coincidence, but an etymological derivation, since 'fathom' was the Old English word (more precisely *fæthm*) for this measurement. The original meaning of the word was thus 'embrace' (when used in the plural) or 'bosom', in the sense 'area between breast and arms' (when used in the singular). The usage did not continue later than Old English, i.e. not beyond the eleventh century. The modern meaning, also originating in Old English times, came to be applied more or less exclusively to the water depth measurement from the sixteenth century, and is found in Tindale's Bible translation of 1526, where in Acts 27:28 he has: 'The shipmen [. . .] sounded and founde it .xx. feddoms' (Authorized Version of 1611: 'The shipmen [. . .] sounded, and found it twenty fathoms').

fault (error, mistake, failing)
In the thirteenth century, 'fault' meant '*de*fault', that is, 'lack', especially in the phrases 'for fault of' (i.e. 'in default of') and 'without fault' (i.e. 'without fail', compare modern French *sans faute* in this sense). The first of these phrases, although now obsolete, was in regular use until as recently as the seventeenth century, and it comes in Shakespeare's *Henry IV*, Part 2 (1597), where Prince Henry says to Poins: 'Albeit I could tell to thee, – as to one it pleases me, for fault of a better, to call my friend, – I could be sad, and sad indeed too'. Most other general meanings of 'fault' date from the fourteenth century, although the geological 'fault' is a term of the eighteenth century.

favour (friendly regard)
The current sense is also the oldest one, dating from the fourteenth century. The word could mean 'attraction' then, too, with this sense used by poets down to the nineteenth century, as in Robert Greene and Thomas Lodge's *A Looking Glasse for London and Englande* (1594), which has the line:

> Now ope, ye folds, where queen of favour
>   sits.

This obsolete usage was followed in the fifteenth century by the sense 'appearance', 'expression', 'face', with this preserved by Tennyson in *Queen Mary* (1875):

> What makes thy favour like thy bloodless
>   head
> Fall'n on the block?

The 'token' sense of 'favour' (worn to show your allegiance to the person or cause that you favour), is first recorded in Shakespeare's *Love's Labour's Lost* (1588), where the Princess of France says to Rosaline:

> Hold, Rosaline, this favour shalt thou
>   wear,
> And then the king will court thee for his
>   dear.

fearful (causing fear, very bad)
Today's use of 'fearful' is mostly a debased and weakened one, as 'What a fearful racket!'. The word originally meant what it says, in the fourteenth century, 'causing fear', 'dreadful' (in the literal sense of the word). The sense was in use down to the seventeenth century (later, in poetic works), and occurs in the Bible, for example in Deuteronomy 28:58: 'That thou mayest fear this glorious and fearful name, THE LORD THY GOD!'. But like **awful, dreadful** and **terrible** (which see), the adjective began to lose its literal meaning from about the seventeenth century.

feature (part of the face, distinctive part of something)
The ultimate source of the word is in Latin *facere*, 'to do', and the earliest sense in English, in the fourteenth century, was simply as 'form', 'shape', often implying 'good form', 'good shape', with reference to proportion or beauty, as when Richard III,

in Shakespeare's play of the name (1594), says (when still the Duke of Gloucester):

I, that am curtail'd of this fair proportion,
Cheated of feature by dissembling nature.

At the same time, the word could refer to any part of the body, such as a limb, and this was how Edward Young used 'feature', for example, in *The Brothers* (1753):

Shall I stab
Her lovely image stampt on every feature?

The narrower sense of this, meaning 'lineament of the face', had also been current from the fourteenth century, however, and this is the standard meaning today to apply to the human figure. The much more general meaning, 'characteristic part', developed only from the seventeenth century, with a newspaper 'feature' first recorded in the nineteenth century and a 'feature' film (or just a 'feature') coming in the early twentieth.

fellow (comrade, colleague, university lecturer, 'bloke')
As can be seen from the incomplete listing here, 'fellow' has been a word to designate the equal, the 'high' and the 'lowly', so has been unusually versatile! All the above senses are still current, and developed in the order given. Originally, however, in the eleventh century, the word meant 'partner', 'associate', this being the closest to the basic concept of a 'fee layer', that is, someone who lays down money in a joint undertaking. This is the only sense of 'fellow' that is now strictly obsolete. A reference in *English Gilds* (1400) thus has this sense when it speaks of 'Ye alderman & his felas'. The other senses developed as follows: 'comrade', 'mate' in the thirteenth century; 'member of a company', 'companion' in the fourteenth (with 'good fellow' arising at this time for an agreeable companion); 'senior member of a university or college' in the fifteenth, but also then the 'familiar' sense for 'man', 'bloke'. The unexpected 'academic' use came about because 'fellow' was the word chosen to translate Latin *socius*, 'companion', 'colleague'. (Compare the common link between 'colleague' and 'college' itself.)

fence (barrier marking boundary or protecting an area)
'Fence' is actually a shortened form of 'defence', and this was the original meaning of the word in the fourteenth century, usually implying 'self-defence'. From this, the sense developed to 'fencing' (the art) in the sixteenth century, so that an experienced fencer could be a 'master of fence' or 'teacher of fence'. This usage can be found even as late as the nineteenth century in some writers (even Macaulay wrote of a man who had 'consummate skill in fence') and the word was used by Shakespeare, as was its modern equivalent, 'fencing'. The common meaning 'dividing wall' developed from the sixteenth century, the basic sense link being in the ability of such a wall or barrier to serve as a 'defence' of one's property. The more recent slang word 'fence', meaning 'receiver of stolen goods', came in the seventeenth century, with the noun deriving from the verb. Such goods need to be protected, and the act of receiving needs to be carried out under cover.

ferry (boat carrying passengers over a stretch of water)
The current sense, as given here, is a very recent one, with 'ferry' simply short for 'ferryboat'. Properly, a 'ferry' is a place where people can cross water by boat, and this usage dates from the twelfth century, with the word itself coming from Old English *ferian*, 'to carry', related to *faran*, 'to go' (see **fare**, above). The interesting thing about 'ferry' (the boat) is that the word existed in Shakespeare's day, but then fell out of use by about the end of the eighteenth century. The modern sense dates from only about the middle of the twentieth century, and between about 1800 and 1950, therefore, 'ferry' invariably meant 'crossing place', 'place where ferryboat operates'. Compare the difference between the following: 'The numbers indicate the position of the ferry on the map' (J. Ingles Ker, *Scotland for the Motorist*, 1927) and 'A driver is expected to hurry only if he is late for a ferry' (Russell Beach [ed.], *AA Touring Guide to Scotland*, 1981). In the earlier book, the boat is referred to as 'ferry-boat', 'steamer', 'vessel' or some similar word, with 'ferry' used only for the crossing. The

AA Road Book of Scotland (1960) uses the words in both senses on the same page 'At certain ferries on popular routes congestion occurs', 'Passengers are allowed to remain in their vehicles on ferries'.

festival (time of celebration, or the celebration itself)
From the fourteenth century, 'festival' was for some time an adjective, applied to a 'feast-day' of the church. Even when the word became used as a noun in its own right, in the sixteenth century, the occasion was still mostly a church one. Shakespeare uses the word in both ways. In *King John* (1595), it is an adjective, when King Philip says:

> This blessed day
> Ever in France shall be kept festival.

In *Henry VI*, Part 1 (1591), it is a noun, when Charles the Dauphin, speaking of Joan of Arc, says:

> Her ashes [. . .]
> Transported shall be at high festivals
> Before the kings and queens of France.

The sense 'programme of musical performances' followed in the nineteenth century (Mrs Gaskell mentions the Worcester Festival in a letter written in August 1857), and the word then came to be used for other cultural events, such as 'festivals' of music and drama. (By the 1980s almost every town of any size in Britain seemed to sport an annual 'festival' of one sort or another, from the internationally known Edinburgh Festival to the Lancaster Literature Festival.)

fey (whimsical)
The sense as given here is the most recent, in popular currency only since the Second World War. The original, Old English meaning was 'dying' or 'fated to die', which became obsolete in standard English from about the fifteenth century but continued in Scottish use, as in Burns's *The Battle of Sherra-Moor* (1790):

> Thro' they dash'd, and hew'd, and smash'd,
> Till fey men died awa, man.

From this, a meaning 'disordered in the mind like one about to die' developed in the nineteenth century, with this established as a general sense, 'having magical or unearthly qualities'. The current usage is almost an ironic one, so that a 'fey' look is one that is whimsically 'otherworldly' or affectedly 'knowing'. The word is not related to 'fay', the poetic word for 'fairy'.

fiasco (great or humiliating failure or 'flop')
In the nineteenth century, a 'fiasco' was a failure or breakdown in a musical or theatrical performance, a 'flop'. The sense soon became extended to any kind of failure, however, such as a breakdown in the organization of something (a programme or operational system), and this is now the usual meaning. The origin of the word is in some phrase involving Italian *fiasco*, 'bottle', as if a person involved in a fiasco has 'broken his bottle'.

fickle (inconstant, capricious)
The Old English sense of 'fickle' was 'false', 'treacherous', as in these lines from a medieval poem of 1325:

> This eortheli ioie, this worldly blis,
> Is but a fykel fantasy.

The modern meaning of 'constantly changing' followed from the thirteenth century.

filter (device or material for separating solids from liquids, fine particles from coarse, etc)
The word is directly related to 'felt', and indeed meant this in Old English, deriving from Old French *filtre* (modern *feutre*, 'felt'). In this passage, the reference is thus to a piece of felt: 'Than es he sette apon a blak filtre, with the whilk [i.e. which] thai lift him vppe and setez him in his trone' (Sir John Maundeville, *The Buke of John Maundeuill*, 1400). Felt was a material that could serve as a filter for some chemical substances, hence the shift in sense to this in the sixteenth century, with 'filter' soon applied to substances other than felt that could serve the purpose.

fine (payment exacted as penalty or punishment)
In the twelfth century, when the word was

first used in English, it meant simply 'end', 'conclusion', showing its origin in French *fin* with the same sense. This is still the meaning of the word in Shakespeare's *All's Well That Ends Well* (1601) where Helena says, quoting the very words of the play's title:

> All's well that ends well: still the fine's the crown;
> Whate'er the course, the end is the renown.

From this, the sense developed to mean 'settlement of a lawsuit', and then 'sum paid on settlement of a suit'. This was as early as the thirteenth century, with the English word corresponding with the Latin legal term *finis* (literally 'end') similarly used for money paid on the conclusion of a lawsuit. The noun 'finance' has a development on the same lines. In the fourteenth century it originally meant 'end', 'settlement', 'payment', then 'stock' or 'tax' in the fifteenth century, with the modern meaning of 'funds' (in the plural) and 'management of money' following in the eighteenth century. The original sense of 'fine' is still preserved in the now rarish or literary expression 'in fine', meaning 'in short', 'in conclusion'.

firm (business organization)
This word has the same basic origin that **farm** has (see above), since the root is in Latin *firma*. In sixteenth-century English, 'firm' as used here meant 'signature', since this was the 'sign' by which a person had con*firm*ed a deal. Here the word was not taken from the Latin direct, but from Spanish *firma*, which in turn came from the Latin (and which is still the standard word meaning 'signature' today). From this, 'firm' in English developed to mean first, the name or 'style' under which a business was carried on, then the business itself. The former usage can be seen, for example, in Maria Edgeworth's *Moral Tales* (1801): 'All we want to know, is the number of your note, and the firm of the house'.

fizzle (make feeble fizzing sound)
In the sixteenth century, to 'fizzle' was to break wind silently, as can be seen in Philemon Holland's translation (1601) of Pliny's *Natural History:* 'As for Onopordon, they say that if Asses eat thereof, they will fall a fizling and farting'. (Onopordon, meaning literally 'ass fart', was the Greek name for the plant known as pellitory, belonging to the nettle family. Holland uses 'ass' rather than 'donkey' since the latter word had not yet arrived in English.) The modern meaning of 'fizzle' originated in America in the nineteenth century, initially in the sense 'fail', 'be a fiasco'. 'Fizzle' does not come from 'fizz' since the latter word is first recorded later (in the seventeenth century).

flagrant (outrageous, deliberate)
'Flagrant' belongs to the family of words that includes 'conflagration', 'phlegm' and 'flame', and so means literally 'burning', 'blazing', as it did in English when first current in the fifteenth century. This was either in a literal sense, as a 'flagrant flame' or a 'flagrant brand', or figuratively to mean 'ardent', 'passionate'. From the eighteenth century the word had its present sense, as Johnson put it in his *Dictionary* (1755), 'flaming into notice'.

flamboyant (ornate, showy, ostentatious)
This word, which is itself rather flamboyant, was originally an architectural term in English, borrowed from French in the early nineteenth century to mean 'having waving curves that resemble flames'. (This style was in fashion in France in the fifteenth and sixteenth centuries.) The current sense developed more generally from the use of the word to denote a florid or brightly coloured object in the later nineteenth century, as in Longfellow's *The Golden Legend* (1851):

> See, too, the Rose, above the western portal
> Flamboyant with a thousand gorgeous colours.

flask (container or bottle with narrow neck)
In the fourteenth century, a 'flask' was a wooden or skin container for wine or other liquid. From the sixteenth century, it was a leather or metal container for gunpowder, as used by soldiers and sportsmen (a

'powder-flask'). From the seventeenth century, the word came to be used of the long-necked glass bottles in which wine and olive oil were exported from Italy (also often known as a 'Florence flask'), with a version of this developed subsequently for use in laboratories. The sense 'container for drink carried on the person' followed in the nineteenth century, as a forerunner of the 'hip flask'. Dickens mentions a 'pocket-flask of sherry' in *Great Expectations* (1861). 'Vacuum flasks' also made their appearance in the nineteenth century.

flaw (blemish, slight imperfection)
The original meaning of 'flaw', in the fourteenth century, was 'flake', such as a flake of snow or a flake (spark) of fire. In *Henry IV*, Part 2 (1597), Shakespeare has King Henry, speaking to his son the Duke of Clarence, describe his other son Henry, Prince of Wales, saying he is:

As humorous as winter, and as sudden
As flaws congealed in the spring of day.

(Here the 'flaws' are flakes of ice rather than of snow.) From the seventeenth century the two modern meanings 'crack', 'breach' and more generally 'blemish' developed.

fleeting (passing quickly away)
In Old English, 'fleeting' meant 'floating' (Old English *flēotan* was 'to float' and the two words are closely related). Of a fish, too, it could mean 'swimming'. From the thirteenth century, a new sense 'shifting', 'inconstant' arose. Finally, the modern meaning 'passing swiftly', 'transitory' emerged in the sixteenth century, mostly referring to life and time initially, as in one of Shakespeare's *Sonnets* (1600):

How like a winter hath my absence been
From thee, the pleasure of the fleeting year!

flicker (burn irregularly, of a light or fire)
The Old English meaning of the verb (*flicorian*) was 'flutter', 'hover', especially of a bird. This sense was in use by some right down to the nineteenth century, as in Charlotte Smith's *Letters of a Solitary Wanderer* (1799–1801), where she describes flying fish 'emerging from the waves on their wing-like

fins, and flickering along the surface of the water'. In the thirteenth century, 'flicker' meant also 'fondle', 'flirt'. Chaucer used it in this sense, as did Robert Burton in *The Anatomy of Melancholy* (1621), when he commented: 'It is most odious, when an old acherontic dizzard that hath one foot in his grave [. . .] shall flicker after a young wench'. From the fifteenth century, the present meaning 'quiver', 'vibrate' came to be current, as of leaves, flags or feathers 'flickering' in the wind. Finally, the wider meaning 'burn fitfully' evolved in the seventeenth century.

flighty (inconstant, skittish)
Although obviously coming direct from 'flight', the original meaning of 'flighty', when first used in the sixteenth century, was 'swift', 'rapid', and this is the sense of the word in Shakespeare's *Macbeth* (1605), when Macbeth says to Lennox, after the appearance of the Witches:

Time, thou anticipat'st my dread exploits;
Thy flighty purpose never is o'ertook
Unless the deed go with it.

All the other current senses were in use from the eighteenth century.

flippant (unduly or inappropriately light-hearted)
At first, in the seventeenth century, 'flippant' meant 'nimble' as well as 'glib', 'talkative'. The latter sense was used by Addison in his *Spectator* (1711) when he wrote (as only male chauvinists or mockers might today): 'An excellent Anatomist has promised me to dissect a Woman's Tongue, and to examine whether there may not be in it certain Juices, which render it so wonderfully voluble or flippant'. The modern sense then followed in the eighteenth century. The word seems to have derived from 'flip' with the ending '-ant' based on such heraldic terms as 'couchant', 'rampant' and 'trippant' (respectively 'lying with raised head', 'standing on the left hindleg' and 'with right foot raised', all from French).

flirt (coquette, woman who behaves amorously without serious intention)
Both the noun and the verb have more or

less parallel sense developments and histories. In the sixteenth century, when the current sense first became popular, a 'flirt' was also a smart stroke, a quick jerk, with this usage still active in the nineteenth century, as when Thomas Hughes in *Tom Brown at Oxford* (1861) (the not so well known sequel to the popular *Tom Brown's School Days*, 1857) describes a dog as giving 'a joyful squeak and flirt of his hind-quarters in the air'. The use in this sense may still not be quite obsolete. A human 'flirt', too, was more a 'flighty' woman than one who 'made eyes' or the like. Johnson's definition in his *Dictionary* (1755) was 'a pert young hussey'. William Whitehead, poet laureate, in his *Songs and Poems* (1774) wrote of:

Ye belles, and ye flirts, and ye pert little things,
Who trip in this frolicsome round.

This means that a modern 'flirt' emerged only in the eighteenth century, when the reference was usually, as now, to a woman, but could also be to a man.

florid (over-ornate, ruddy)
As originally used, in the seventeenth century, 'florid', as the very word suggests, meant just 'flowery', 'flourishing'. This is the sense in Milton's *Paradise Lost* (1667):

The ambient Aire wide interfus'd
Imbracing round this florid Earth.

However, all the modern meanings date from not much later, and have also been recorded in this same century. A 'florid' complexion was originally considered a healthy one, which is not necessarily the case today.

foil (frustrate, prevent)
The modern sense (as in the popular 'foiled again!') developed in the sixteenth century from the literal meaning in the thirteenth, which was 'tread underfoot' (as a *fuller* did when shrinking and thickening cloth). This developed in the sixteenth century to the sense 'overthrow', 'defeat', applied in particular to a wrestler who 'threw' his opponent and as it were 'trampled' on him. This usage is preserved in Shakespeare's *As You Like It* (1600), where the Second Lord says to Duke Frederick:

Your daughter and her cousin much commend
The parts and graces of the wrestler
That did but lately foil the sinewy Charles.

The modern sense dates from this time, and therefore is not, incidentally, a term taken from fencing, where 'foil' (the sword) is quite a different word.

fond (having a liking for or an affection for)
'Fond' can mean 'foolishly tender', and when the word was first used in English, in the fourteenth century, it meant simply 'foolish', 'silly'. This sense was current for some time, and comes in Shakespeare's *All's Well That Ends Well* (1601), in the Clown's song:

Was this fair face the cause, quoth she,
Why the Grecians sacked Troy?
Fond done, done fond,
Was this King Priam's joy?

The present meaning arose in the sixteenth century, when one now obsolete sense of 'fond' was 'eager' (followed by 'of'), as in Narcissus Luttrell's *A Brief Historical Relation of State Affairs* (1678–1714): 'Many persons have blamed duke Schonberg for not fighting the Irish army, which our men seem'd so fond of'. (Something of this meaning may perhaps be present in such modern phrases as 'I'm not too fond of that'). Compare **fondle** (below).

fondle (handle tenderly or lovingly)
The word derives from 'fondling', the term used in the early fifteenth century for a foolish person (see **fond** above), with this particular word coming to mean 'person who is fondly loved' in the seventeenth century, when 'fondle' itself came to acquire the sense 'pamper'. The current meaning therefore dates from later than this, in the eighteenth century.

footman (liveried servant who waits at table, opens doors, etc.)
In the thirteenth century, a 'footman' was a foot soldier. The usage continued a surprisingly long time, on a rather limited basis, and even appears in *The Times* of 22

April 1896: 'They were suddenly attacked by a body of 200 horsemen, supported by a large body of footmen'. From the fourteenth century, a 'footman' could also be simply a man walking on foot, a pedestrian, although this was perhaps more a dialect usage. The earliest record of the word in this sense that we have is in fact in Wyclif's Bible of 1382, where he renders Numbers 11:21 as: 'Six hundryd thousandes of foot men ben of this puple' (Authorized Version of 1611, preserving this: 'The people, among whom I am, are six hundred thousand footmen'). The current sense, in that footmen now exist in any quantity at all, evolved in the fifteenth century. Originally, though, they were not the 'flunkeys' as now known, but runners (on foot), who attended their master when he was out driving. (Later, they were servants who ran before their master's carriage, and as such were known properly as 'running footmen'.) The liveried manservant appeared in the eighteenth century.

foreman (spokesman for a jury, head of a gang of workmen)
The two current senses of the word are specialized developments of the original meaning in the fifteenth century, which was simply 'leader', either a man who was out in front, leading the way, or a man who simply walked in front of another ('before' him), as in Robert Barret's *The Theorike and Practike of Moderne Warres* (1598), where he describes how a soldier should march 'keeping the lower end of his pike on the one side of his foremans legge'. The usage as 'principal juror' and 'workmen's leader' came in the sixteenth century.

forestall (prevent by taking action beforehand)
In the fourteenth century, to 'forestall' was to obstruct a person, this sense developing from the noun 'forestall' meaning intercepting, 'waylaying on the highway' (as a legal term). At about the same period, the verb also acquired a more specialized sense to mean 'prevent sales by buying up goods beforehand', as in a fair or a market (quite literally 'preempting', therefore). From this narrower sense developed today's wider meaning of 'preventing by anticipating',

with this first recorded in the sixteenth century.

forfeit (loss of something as a penalty, trivial punishment in a game)
The origin of the word is in Old French *forfaire*, 'commit a crime', and in the thirteenth century in English a 'forfeit' was a minor crime, a 'misdeed'. From the fifteenth century, the sense of 'fine', 'penalty', arose. This is today still one of the current meanings, and another, that of 'trivial punishment for breaking a rule' followed in the seventeenth century, where it is first recorded in Shakespeare's *Measure for Measure* (1603), when in the final scene the Duke, disguised as a friar, says that:

> The strong statutes
> Stand like the forfeits in a barber's shop,
> As much in mock as mark.

(He is referring to the gambling that went on in the parlours of barbers' shops. Barbers were not only hairdressers but surgeons and dentists down to Shakespeare's day.)

forlorn (sad and lonely because abandoned, desolate and pitiable)
Originally, in the fourteenth century, a 'forlorn' person was someone who was morally 'lost' or ruined in some way. Some contemporary translations or versions of the Bible thus referred to the 'Forlorn Son', not the 'Prodigal Son'. The present sense developed from the sixteenth century, and was predictably put to good use by many poets, including Spenser, Milton, Dryden and Tennyson. (In the nineteenth century, it was Keats who was to write:

> Forlorn! the very word is like a bell
> To toll me back from thee to my sole self!)

foul (offensive to the senses)
One now obsolete sense of the word from the fourteenth century was 'ugly', applied to both people and things and serving as the opposite of 'fair'. The usage is first recorded in Chaucer's *Canterbury Tales* (Prologue to 'The Wife of Bath's Tale') (1386):

> And if that she be foul, thou seist that she
> Coveiteth every man that she may se.

The word also occurs more than once in Shakespeare, for example in *Othello* (1604), when Desdemona asks Iago what he thinks of her: 'What miserable praise hast thou for her that's foul and foolish?'. Iago replies, using the word in both senses:

There's none so foul and foolish
    thereunto
But does foul pranks which fair and wise
    ones do.

In the Bible, in Job 16:16 ('My face is foul with weeping'), the ugliness is more disfigurement caused by tears. The identity of meaning is still current in such synonyms as 'foul weather', 'ugly weather', 'foul mood', 'ugly mood'.

founder (go lame [of a horse], fill with water and sink [of a ship])
The original meaning of 'founder', in the thirteenth century, was 'smash in', as in these spirited lines from the fourteenth-century verse romance *Richard Coer de Lion*:

He gaff Richard a sory flatt,
That foundryd bacynet and hat.

(That is: He gave Richard a grievous blow that smashed in his basinet, or light steel helmet, and his 'hat', or the heavier helmet he wore over it.) In the fourteenth century, the sense developed to 'stumble and fall' (of a horse) and the now obsolete 'send to the bottom' (of a ship). The former of these is found in 'The Knight's Tale' in Chaucer's *Canterbury Tales* (1386):

For which his hors for feere gan to turne,
And leepe asyde, and foundred as he
    leep.

Finally, in the sixteenth century, the meaning 'fill with water and sink' arose to apply to a ship.

fowl (bird raised for its flesh, wild bird hunted as game)
Various categories of bird are today called 'fowl'. but in Old English, this was the standard word for '**bird**' (which see for its own usage). Hence the predominance of the word in literature down to at least the sixteenth century, for example in the Scottish poet John Barbour's poem *The Bruce* (1375), in which 'the kyng [. . .] slepit

as foul on twist' (i.e. slept like a bird on a twig), and in Shakespeare's *Much Ado About Nothing* (1599), where Claudio, in an aside to Don Pedro (and referring to Benedick, who overhears their conversation) says: 'Stalk on, stalk on; the fowl sits'. Even in 1719, Defoe wrote in *Robinson Crusoe* that his hero 'saw a great fowl, like a hawk, sit upon a tree'. The modern restricted sense 'domestic cock or hen' arose in the sixteenth century. The nearest survival of the original 'bird' sense is in 'wildfowl'.

franchise (legal immunity or privilege; right of voting)
This pure French word meant simply 'freedom' originally, in the thirteenth century. In the *Canterbury Tales* (1386), Chaucer wrote (in 'The Parson's Tale') that among the good things a man could enjoy were health, strength, 'beautee, gentrye [i.e. good breeding], fraunchise', meaning by the latter freedom rather than servitude or slavery. The sense 'legal immunity' arose in the fourteenth century, and, as a development of this, 'district over which such immunity extends', in the fifteenth century. It was in the eighteenth century that 'franchise' came to mean 'right to vote', with the full term really being 'elective franchise'. Compare **frank** (below).

frank (honest, open)
In its earliest use in English, in the thirteenth century, 'frank' has its French sense of 'free', often occurring in the phrase 'frank and free', as in John Tiptoft (the Earl of Worcester)'s translation (1470) of Caesar's *Commentaries*: 'He was frank & free borne in a free cytye', and in Lord Berners' *The Boke of Duke Huon of Burdeux* (1533): 'He and all his company shall deperte franke and free at there pleasure'. From the fifteenth century, 'frank' came to mean also 'generous' and 'superior'. The former of these senses can be seen in Caxton's *The Book of the Ordre of Chyualry* (1484), where he writes that 'the knyghte must be free and franke', i.e. generous with money. The latter sense, now obsolete, was frequently used of plants, fruit and so on, as in Henry Lyte's translation (1578) of Rembert Dodoens' *Cruydeboeck*: 'There be two sortes of Sage, the one is small and franke, and the other is great'.

This sense is still preserved, however, in 'frankincense', which is literally a 'superior incense'. The meaning 'candid', 'open', finally developed for 'frank' in the sixteenth century. See also **franchise** (above).

frantic (desperately anxious)
In the fourteenth century, when first current in English, 'frantic' meant 'insane'. The sense sometimes occurs later than the sixteenth century, as in Anna Jameson's *Legends of the Monastic Orders as Represented in the Fine Arts* (1850), where writing of St Francis of Assisi she says: 'His father, believing him frantic, shut him up and bound him in his chamber'. The 'frenzied' sense of 'frantic' (the two words are actually related) arose in the sixteenth century.

fray (wear away by rubbing)
In the fourteenth century, when first in use in English, 'fray' meant simply 'rub' showing its close ties with 'friction' and 'friable'. In the fifteenth century, it meant 'bruise', 'clash', with a particular usage of this arising in the sixteenth century to apply to deer rubbing their horns, as observed in George Turberville's *The Noble Arte of Venerie or Hunting* (1575):

The old harts do fray their heads upon
    the yong trees.

The modern meaning, 'rub away' is first recorded in the eighteenth century in Richard Steele's *Tatler* (1710): 'Four striped Muslin Night-Rails very little frayed'. (A 'night-rail' was a sort of dressing jacket or dressing gown worn by women when in 'undress'.)

freak (physically odd or deformed person or animal)
In the sixteenth century, when first occurring in standard English, 'freak' meant 'sudden change' (as the well known 'freak of fortune', originally recorded as 'fortunes freakes' in the many-authored *A Myrroure for Magistrates*, 1563). From this, the word came to mean 'capricious prank' in the seventeenth century, as in the agreeable *Quidnuncki's* (1724) by John Gay:

Thus, as in giddy freaks he bounces,
Crack goes the twig, and in he flounces!

From the eighteenth century, a 'freak' could be the 'freaky' (in modern terms) product of the imagination. Emerson commented in *English Traits* (1856) that: 'Strawberry Hill, of Horace Walpole, Fonthill Abbey, of Mr. Beckford, were freaks'. From the nineteenth century, 'freak' acquired its modern meaning of 'grotesquely formed person or animal', the full expression being 'freak of nature' and corresponding to Latin *lusus naturae*. In the twentieth century, a 'freak' was a drug addict, who 'freaked out' on drugs, with the sense expanding to include anyone who was 'addicted' to something, as a 'power freak' or a 'Jesus freak' (a passionate evangelical Christian). The word seems to have many possibilities for denoting anything or anyone individualistic or 'nonconformist'.

freelance (person, especially journalist, photographer, etc., who works independent of a single employer)
In the first half of the nineteenth century, the term 'free lance' (as such, two words) was used to apply historically to a military adventurer in medieval times. In *Ivanhoe* (1820), thus, Scott has a character say: 'I offered Richard the service of my Free Lances'. (Such a man would have had a 'lance' that was 'free' to be put to use for anyone at any time.) Later in the same century, a 'free lance' was the term for a politician of no fixed allegiance, or one regarded as such, who simply attacked and criticized whenever he felt the urge. Late in the nineteenth century, the modern sense emerged to mean someone who worked for himself and not an employer (but who at the same time was not 'self-employed' in the modern sense). In the twentieth century, the meaning settled to apply to a person who either worked on a broad basis for several 'employers' or agencies, or someone who worked first for one employer, then another, without any long-term commitment or contract.

freemason (member of secret fraternity)
As originally understood in the fourteenth century, a 'freemason' was a stonemason who was 'free' to work where he wanted since he was not a member of any regular guild. The modern sense arose in the seven-

teenth century, when societies of stone-masons started to admit as members other masons of other crafts, with such men known properly as 'accepted masons'. The full title of the fraternity is thus today the 'Free and Accepted Masons'.

frequent (occurring often)
It seems unlikely that the word could ever have had a different meaning. Yet when first current in English, in the sixteenth century, 'frequent' had a number of other senses, among them 'crowded', 'well-known' and 'addicted'. The first of these occurs, for example, in the *Discourse Concerninge the Spanish Fleet Invadinge Englande* (1590), which in an eighteenth-century translation has the sentence: 'There was generally made throughout the whole realm a most frequent assembly of all sorts of people'. The 'addicted' sense comes in Shakespeare's *The Winter's Tale* (1611), where Camillo says to Polixenes (referring to his son Florizel): 'I have missingly [i.e. with regret] noted he is of late much retired from court, and is less frequent to his princely exercises than formerly he hath appeared'. The current meaning developed from the seventeenth century.

fret (worry, irritate)
The verb is related, although not directly, to 'eat', and this is what the Old English *fretan* meant, mainly with reference to animals. (Compare modern German *fressen*, 'to devour', as used of animals, and *essen*, 'to eat', of humans.) From this, the sense developed to 'chafe', 'irritate' in the thirteenth century, and to 'chafe', 'worry' in the sixteenth. This sense of 'fret' is not related to that of 'fretwork', which derives from an Old French word for 'ferrule'.

friend ('one joined to another in mutual benevolence and intimacy' [Johnson])
In Old English, 'friend' meant 'lover', a sense exploited by Shakespeare in *Love's Labour's Lost* (1588), where Berowne says to Rosaline:

O! never will I trust to speeches penn'd,
Nor to the motion of a school-boy's
tongue,

Nor never come in visor to my friend,
Nor woo in rime, like a blind harper's
song.

Something of this sense survives in modern 'girlfriend' and 'boyfriend'. From the twelfth century, too, 'friend' was frequently used to mean 'relative', 'kinsman', so that the *Ordynarye of Cristen Men* (1502) tells of 'All the sones & doughters of Adam & of Eue the whiche were our fyrst frendes', and in Shakespeare's *Two Gentlemen of Verona* (1591) the Duke, speaking to Valentine of his daughter Silvia, says:

But she I mean is promis'd by her friends
Unto a youthful gentleman of worth.

Even today, someone can speak of his or her 'friends', meaning relatives. ('I'm going to stay the night with friends'.)

frippery (showy clothes)
In its original sixteenth-century sense, 'frippery' meant 'old clothes', 'cast-offs'. A hundred years later, the meaning had altered somewhat to 'gaudy finery', 'tawdry ornamentation', as in Goldsmith's *She Stoops to Conquer* (1773): 'She is as fond of gauze and French frippery as the best of them'. Finally, from the eighteenth century, the sense was extended to mean 'ostentatious speech or writing', as Thomas Gray wrote in a letter of 1764: 'I can stay with great patience for anything that comes from Voltaire. They tell me it is frippery, and blasphemy, and wit'. The first of these three meanings is now obsolete.

frontispiece (illustration facing title page of a book)
The earliest meaning of the word in English was the sixteenth-century architectural one, 'main face of a building', or what today would be called the 'façade'. The usage continued for some years, so that James Ferguson, for example, in *The Illustrated Handbook of Architecture* (1855), referred to the three-gabled front of the cathedral of Orvieto, Italy, as a 'frontispiece' that 'is not without considerable appropriateness and even beauty'. (The word is not actually related to 'piece' but derives from Latin *frontispicium*, literally 'view of the forehead'.) In the seventeenth century, 'frontispiece'

acquired its present meaning, although for a time the term could also denote simply the title page of a book, rather than the illustration facing it.

frump (dowdy woman or dreary old-fashioned person)
As originally used, in the seventeenth century, a 'frump' was a jeer or hoax. The first of these is the sense in Beaumont and Fletcher's *The Scornful Lady* (1610): 'Sweet Widow leave your frumps, and be edified'. The latter meaning comes in Sir William Davenant's comedy *The Man's the Master* (1668): 'These are a kind of witty frumps of mine like selling of bargains'. In the seventeenth century, 'frumps' could mean 'sulks', 'bad mood', as in Dryden's *An Evening's Love* (1668): 'Not to be behind hand with you in your Frumps, I give you back your Purse of Gold'. The modern sense is first recorded in the nineteenth century.

fry (recently hatched fishes, young of other animals)
In the fourteenth century, the word could apply to human offspring, as to a man's children or family, or even a single child, as in Shakespeare's *Macbeth* (1605), where the Murderer kills Lady Macbeth's young son:

What! you egg.
Young fry of treachery! [*Stabbing him*].

Similarly in Francis Quarles' *Sions Elegies* (1624):

The tender frie,
Whom childhood taught no language,
    but their crie
T'expresse their infant griefe.

The meaning 'young fishes', in particular young salmon, also dates from the fourteenth century, and in the fifteenth the word came to be used of other young creatures, including children (especially in such phrases as 'young fry', 'small fry', and the like).

fulfil (carry out)
In Old English, the word meant what it says, 'fill full', as in Wyclif's translation of Genesis 1:28 in his Bible of 1385: 'Growe ye and be ye multiplied and fulfille ye the erthe' (Authorized Version of 1611: 'Be

fruitful, and multiply, and replenish the earth'). This sense continued in poetic use down to the nineteenth century, if not the twentieth, as in a poem (1830) by Tennyson:

Her subtil, warm, and golden breath
Which mixing with the infant's blood
Fullfills him with beatitude.

From the thirteenth century the modern sense developed, with however a 'link' meaning, now obsolete, of 'furnish fully', 'supply to the full' in use for a time. Wyclif, again, uses the word in this sense in Matthew 15:33: 'Therfore wherof so many loouys to vs in desert, that we fulfille so grete a cumpanye of peple?' (Authorized Version: 'Whence should we have so much bread in the wilderness, as to fill so great a multitude?').

fulsome (abundant, offensive, unnecessarily effusive)
The earliest sense of 'fulsome' is recorded in the thirteenth century, when the word meant 'abundant', 'plentiful' (showing the literal origin in 'full-some'). The usage persisted until at least the sixteenth century, as in the translation (1583) by Arthur Golding of Calvin's *Sermons upon Deuteronomie*: 'Likewise of their firstfruites instede of making good fulsome sheaues and bundels vnto God, they gelded them [i.e. removed their husks], and made them verie thinne and lanke'. This sense appears to have become obsolete some time shortly after, and indeed the word is so designated by the *OED*. In Sir Arthur Helps' *Realmah* (1868), for example, he uses the phrase 'this fulsome world', but comments: 'I use fulsome in the original sense'. However, the word is now fairly frequently used to mean 'abundant' (as in 'fulsome detail') so appears to have undergone a recent revival. The other 'bad' senses of 'fulsome' all date from the fourteenth century, with however a now obsolete 'good' usage current also for a time to mean 'well-grown'. An example of this can be seen in the same Golding's translation (1565-7) of Ovid's *Metamorphoses:*

His leane, pale, hore, and withered corse
    grew fulsome, faire, and fresh.

fun (amusement, enjoyment)
In the seventeenth century, a 'fun' was a

hoax or practical joke, with the noun deriving from the verb that meant 'hoax'. An example of this sense occurs in Thomas D'Urfey's *Wit and Mirth; or Pills to Purge Melancholy* (1719):

> A Hackney Coachman he did hug her,
> And was not this a very good Fun?

The current meaning 'amusement', 'sport' followed in the eighteenth century, where it is first recorded, appropriately enough, in Swift:

> Tho' he talk'd much of virtue, his head always run
> Upon something or other she found better fun.
> (*Miscellanies in Prose and Verse*, 1727)

The adjective 'funny' followed only in the eighteenth century (as 'funny ha-ha') and nineteenth (as 'funny peculiar').

funicular (cable railway)
The derivation of the word is Latin *funiculus*, a diminutive of *funis*, 'rope'. 'Funicular' was thus originally a term used (first in 1661) for a hypothetical filament of rarefied matter stated to exist by the Jesuit Franciscus Linus (Francis Line), who proposed his theory in his book *De Corporum Inseparabilitate*. From the nineteenth century, the word came to be used in a much more down to earth way to mean 'pertaining to a rope', especially with regard to its tension. In the latter half of this same century, the sense came to apply to a 'funicular railway', with the word alone used as a noun for such a railway in the early twentieth century (recorded as such in Webster's *Dictionary* in 1909).

furniture (movable articles in a room such as table, chairs, cupboards etc.)
Most senses of 'furniture', including many technical ones, date from the sixteenth century, when one main meaning, now obsolete, was 'the act of furnishing'. This was current down to the seventeenth century, and occurs in Shakespeare's *Henry IV*, Part 1 (1596), where Prince Henry says to Falstaff:

> Jack, meet me to-morrow in the Temple-hall
> At two o'clock in the afternoon:

> There shalt thou know thy charge, and there receive
> Money and order for their furniture.

English is unique in using the word in the current common sense, and many European Languages use a word for 'furniture' that derives ultimately from Latin *mobilis*, 'mobile', 'movable', such as French *meubles*, Italian *mobili*, Spanish *muebles*, German *Möbel* and Russian *mebel'*.

furore (craze, outcry)
The Latin word *furor* was the earlier version of this noun, and was so used from the thirteenth century to mean 'fury', 'rage', 'anger'. Caxton included it in his translation (1477) *The historie of Jason*: 'Considerest thou not the strengthe and force of my body and the furour of my swerde?'. From the eighteenth century, the sense developed to 'great enthusiasm', 'craze', where it is first recorded in Swift, *A Discourse concerning the Mechanical Operation of the Spirit* (1704): 'He seldom was without some female Patients among them, for the furor'. In the late eighteenth century, the Italian form 'furore' came to be used in exactly the same meaning, while the now frequent sense of 'uproar', 'outcry' arose only in the middle of the twentieth century, where it is first recorded in a letter from Henry Miller dated 7 October 1946 ('A tremendous furore', referring to the scandal that arose when some French publishers brought out translations of some of his books).

fuzzy (resembling fuzz, tightly curled, indistinct)
The word first meant 'spongy' when originally used in English in the seventeenth century, as applied to moss or some types of grass. The sense 'covered with fuzz' as of linen, came in the eighteenth century, as did the meaning 'indistinct'. As applied to tightly curled hair, 'fuzzy' arose only in the nineteenth century, where, as in the other senses, it seems to have been originally a dialect word. It seems more likely that 'fuzz' came from 'fuzzy' rather than the other way round.

gale (strong wind)
The word has been consistently and regularly used with its current meaning since the sixteenth century. Somewhat perversely, however, a sense 'gentle breeze' arose in the eighteenth century, mainly in poetic or figurative use. The reason for this particular development is uncertain. It is typically found in James Thomson's *The Seasons* (*Spring*) (1728), where the first line, with its reference to 'gentle Spring! ethereal mildness', makes it clear that no strong wind is meant. Thus, in this work:

The stately-sailing swan
Gives out his snowy plumage to the gale,

and later:

Can fierce passions vex his breast,
While every gale is peace, and every
    grove
Is melody?

Somewhat earlier than this, the sense is also found in the better-known lines from Pope's *Pastorals* (1709):

Where'er you walk cool gales shall fan
    the glade;
Trees where you sit, shall crowd into a
    shade.

(This is actually earlier than the first recording of the usage in the *OED*, which is the Thomson one, above.)

gallant (courageous, nobly chivalrous, ostentatiously courteous to ladies)
The earliest usage of 'gallant' dates from the fifteenth century, when it meant 'splendid', 'gorgeous', and it is first recorded in John Lydgate's *The Assembly of Gods* (1420):

Then was there set the god Cupido,
All fresshe & galaunt & costlew in aray.

This sense was current (perhaps still is) for many hundreds of years, with the use found, for example, in an item in the *Daily News*

for 30 March 1897: 'The Lord Mayor of Dublin, accompanied by the High Sherriff and the Town Clerk, gallant in scarlet robes, ermine trimmed'. In the sixteenth century, the sense was extended to 'fine', 'stately', in particular as a term of approval or praise, and often of a ship, as in Shakespeare's *The Tempest* (1610), where, in the final scene, the Boatswain proudly refers to his 'royal, good, and gallant ship'. The word could also mean 'handsome', of a woman, as in Lyly's prose romance *Euphues* (1579): 'This gallant girle, more faire than fortunate, and yet more fortunate than faithful'. The 'chivalrously brave' meaning first appears, perhaps typically, in Shakespeare, where in *Henry IV*, Part 1 (1596), Sir Michael discusses with the Archbishop of York who will take part in the rebellion against the king from among the many 'gallant warriors, noble gentlemen'. From the seventeenth century the new meaning 'attentive to women' emerged. This is the 'gallant' that is still usually pronounced with the second syllable accented.

galosh (rubber or plastic overshoe to protect against rain etc.)
The word has been in use in English since the fourteenth century, and originally applied to a wooden shoe or clog, in its most basic form attached to the foot with a leather thong. Later, 'galosh' was the term for a shoe with a wooden sole and an upper of leather, or some other material. By the seventeenth century, however, 'galosh' had come to mean 'overshoe', and this is undoubtedly the sense when Pepys recorded in his *Diary* on 15 November 1665: 'My Lady Batten walking through the dirty lane with new spick and span white shoes, she dropped one of her galoshes in the dirt'. The specific sense 'rubber overshoe' finally appeared when the footwear itself did, in the nineteenth century.

game (wild animals hunted for sport or food)
The association between 'game' in the 'hunting' sense and 'game' meaning 'sport' is not always readily made. The two are one and the same word, however, with a shift of meaning. The sense development is thus: 'amusement', 'diversion' (in Old English),

'organised sport' (from the thirteenth century), 'hunting regarded as a sport' (also thirteenth), and finally 'wild animals pursued by hunting' (likewise thirteenth century). All these senses are still current except the one that calls hunting a 'game'. The obsolete usage occurs in Shakespeare's *Henry VI*, Part 3 (1593), where Gloucester says, speaking of his brother, King Edward:

I have advertis'd him by secret means,
That if about this hour he makes this
    way,
Under the colour of [i.e. under the
    pretext of] his usual game,
He shall here find his friends.

gang (group of people working together, both legitimately and criminally)
In the twelfth century, a 'gang' was simply a 'going' or 'journey', with such expressions as 'a day's gang' in common use to indicate the length of a journey, as in the *Cursor Mundi* of the early fourteenth century:

Thre dais gang, na mare ne less,
We must weind in to wildirness.

In the fifteenth century, 'gang' came to mean 'road' or 'way', although mainly in dialect usage. Meanwhile, a secondary dialect sense of the word had developed, from the fourteenth century, to mean 'set of articles' such as a 'gang' of shrouds on a ship, of horses, or of teeth. This is the meaning that developed into the now common 'company of people', especially workmen, thieves and the like, with this sense found from the seventeenth century. Pepys recorded in his *Diary* in 1668: 'Home to dinner with my gang of clerks'.

garbage (rubbish, worthless writing)
In the fifteenth century, when the word is first recorded in English, 'garbage' meant specifically 'offals', that is, those of an animal used for food. From the sixteenth century, the meaning generalized to become 'refuse', with this usage now more common in America than Britain (where the equivalent is 'rubbish'). From later in the same century, 'garbage' also came to apply to worthless writing. In Jane Porter's novel *Thaddeus of Warsaw* (1803): 'She flew with voracious appetite to sate herself on the garbage of any circulating library'.

garble (distort, confuse)
The word has travelled from a good sense to a bad. In the fifteenth century, to 'garble' was to sift something and take the pick of it. This usage, now obsolete, was current down to at least the eighteenth century, so that John Ozell, in his translation (1708) of Boileau's *Lutrin*, could write:

Each Glutton hunts, and garbles out
Nice Bits.

From the seventeenth century, the sense became 'select unfairly', which itself came to embrace any deliberate misrepresentation or 'mischievous' distortion of written matter such as correspondence, and so on. Hence the current sense of 'distorted' in a way that may well not be deliberate, as a 'garbled' message.

garret (attic room)
In the fourteenth century, 'garret' was the word for a turret or watchtower. It acquired its present sense from the fifteenth century as a development of this.

gasket (sealing device used at a joint to prevent escape of gas, liquid etc.)
The word is nothing to do with 'gas'! Its history and origin are unusual. When first current in English, in the seventeenth century, a 'gasket' was the word for the small rope that secures a furled sail on a ship. The origin is said to lie in a nautical adoption of French *garsette*, 'little girl', applied in a transferred sense to the thin rope. (A similar development may have occurred with the nautical word 'grommet' for a ring of twisted rope, with this perhaps coming from French *gromet*, 'boy', which also gave English 'gourmet'.) From the nineteenth century, 'gasket' acquired the meaning 'strip of plaited hemp used for caulking a joint', with the link between the two senses being the 'securing'. The modern 'gasket', as a ring of some soft material placed between metal surfaces, dates from the early twentieth century.

gaudy (bright and tasteless, of clothes, materials, colours, etc.)
As first used in English, 'gaudy' did not have a disparaging sense but meant 'brilliantly fine', 'showy'. This was in the

sixteenth century. But certainly the current connotation can be clearly seen to appear in Shakespeare's *Hamlet* (1602), where Polonius says to Laertes, advising him to be 'familiar, but by no means vulgar':

Costly thy habit as thy purse can buy,
But not express'd in fancy; rich, not
  gaudy.

From the seventeenth century, too, 'gaudy' could apply to immaterial things, such as a person's 'gaudy' speech or writing, or 'gaudy' promises or dreams. Some may still feel that today we live in a 'gaudy' world, where all is 'fair seeming shows'.

gaunt (painfully thin and bony)
In its earliest use, in the fifteenth century, 'gaunt' was a favourable word, meaning 'slim and slender'. 'Sodaynelye', wrote Latimer, in a sermon preached before Edward VI in 1549, 'she was gaunte agayne'. (He was talking of a woman after childbirth.) Philemon Holland, in his translation (1601) of Pliny's *Natural History*, passed on worldly wisdom on the art of staying slim: 'They who feed ouermuch, and desire to be gant and slender [. . .] ought to forbear drinking at meales'. However, the current, unfavourable sense had certainly become well known by Shakespeare's time, hence his punning use of the word in *Richard II* (1593), when he makes John of Gaunt say:

O! how that name befits my
  composition;
Old Gaunt indeed, and gaunt in being
  old.

gaze (look intently)
The verb has been in use in English since the fourteenth century, when originally it also implied looking with curiosity or wonder. It occurs in the following advice to a young waiter in medieval times: 'Be symple in cheer; caste not thi looke aside, Gase not about, turnynge thi sight oueral' (*Stans puer ad mensam*, 1430). Even Pepys, as late as 1667, uses the word in its 'wondering' sense in his *Diary*: 'I did make them all gaze to see themselves served so nobly'. In modern use, an accompanying adverb will frequently indicate the notion of wonder or lack of it, as 'He gazed curiously at the house', and 'She gazed idly at the passing crowds'.

gazetteer (geographical dictionary)
In the seventeenth century, a 'gazetteer' was a term for a journalist, one who wrote for a gazette. Of the French writer Samuel Sorbière, Evelyn wrote in his *Diary* in 1664: 'He styles himself Historiograph du Roy, the mighty meede [i.e. merit] of the co'monest Gazetiere, as that of Conseiller du Roy is of every trifling petifoger'. The word usually had unfavourable connotations, as reflected in Johnson's definition in his *Dictionary* (1755): '*Gazetteer*, it was lately a term of the utmost infamy, being usually applied to wretches who were hired to vindicate the court'. The transference from journalist to geographical dictionary emerged through the title of Laurence Echard's 'The Gazetteer's; or Newsman's Interpreter: Being a Geographical Index'. This was published (in its second edition) in 1693, with Echard commenting: 'The Title was given me by a very eminent Person, whom I forbear to name'. In Part II of the work, published in 1704, Echard referred to it simply as 'the Gazetteer'.

generous (giving freely and readily, ample)
The word derives, through French, from Latin *generosus*, 'noble', and this was the first sense of the adjective when it entered English in the sixteenth century. The first record we have of it is in Shakespeare's *Love's Labour's Lost* (1588), when Holofernes, amid much wordplay and banter, addresses Armado as 'most generous sir'. The word comes in the same 'noble-born' sense elsewhere in Shakespeare, and also, again in *Love's Labour's Lost*, in its secondary meaning of 'magnanimous', when Holofernes (again) says to Berowne: 'This is not generous, not gentle, not humble'. The 'giving freely' sense developed later, in the seventeenth century.

genial (good-natured and friendly)
Latin *genialis*, 'nuptial' is the origin of the word, which thus had the same meaning when first used in English in the sixteenth century. Spenser used it in *Epithalamion*

(1595) (hardly surprisingly since the whole poem was written to celebrate his marriage, with its Greek title literally meaning 'upon the bridal chamber'):

And thou, glad Genius! in whose gentle hand
The bridale bowre and geniall bed remain.

From the seventeenth century, 'genial' came to mean 'conducive to growing', as 'genial' warmth or 'genial' soil, with the sense later becoming more generally 'agreeable', 'pleasantly warm'. Finally the 'friendly' modern meaning appeared in the eighteenth century.

genius (person of high intelligence and inventiveness)
The clearly Latin word that produced the modern English one means literally 'attendant spirit', and is thus related directly to the other 'spirits', the 'genie' or 'jinn'. The Latin sense was also the first one in English, in the sixteenth century, and occurs, for example, in Shakespeare's *Macbeth* (1605), when Macbeth says:

My genius is rebuk'd, as it is said
Mark Antony's was by Caesar.

From this, in the same century, the word came to apply to a person's own 'spirit' or character, his or her innate aptitude, and also to a person himself regarded as possessing such a distinctive spirit. This is the sense in a letter written by Dr Johnson to Mrs Thrale in 1780: 'Every man has his genius', he wrote, ' . . .my genius is in extremes'. From this finally the modern meaning developed in the eighteenth century to apply to a 'brilliant' or highly intelligent person.

gentle (mild, kindly, soft)
The modern popular sense of the word is the most recent, evolving in the sixteenth century. Modern 'gentleman', however, still bears much of the original thirteenth-century meaning, which was 'well-born', 'noble'. The well-known 'verray parfit gentil knyght' of the *Prologue* to Chaucer's *Canterbury Tales* (1386) does not quite belong here, since 'gentle' in this phrase means 'having the character of a well-born person', that is,

the knight was not himself 'noble' but had been created a knight by the king, whom he then served in battle as a mounted horseman and well-armed soldier. In the fifteenth century, 'gentle' acquired the sense, now obsolete, of 'domesticated', 'tame', more or less as an opposite of 'wild'. The application was as much to trees and fruits as to animals, with the former sense used figuratively in Shakespeare's *The Winter's Tale* (1611), where Polixenes says to Perdita:

You see, sweet maid, we marry
A gentler scion to the wildest stock.

When the current meaning developed a hundred years later, 'gentle' could also be used to mean 'pliant', 'supple', which is not quite the 'soft' sense it has today. An example of the usage is in Edward Topsell's *The Historie of Foure-Footed Beastes* (1607), where he advises: 'Another charge of a Horse-keeper is to keep his Horses lips soft, tender, and gentle, so as he may more sensibly [i.e. readily] feel his bit'. This meaning became obsolete in the eighteenth century.

genuine (real, not spurious)
The word first became current in the sixteenth century, when it had the now obsolete meaning 'native', 'natural'. The sense can be seen in these lines from Michael Drayton's great topographical poem *Polyolbion* (1612):

A constant Mayden still she onely did remaine,
The last her genuine lawes which stoutly did retaine.

The present sense became current from the seventeenth century.

geology (science of the history and structure of the earth)
The first meaning of the term in English, in the eighteenth century, was to denote a science that dealt generally with the earth. Traditionally, it encompassed geography, hydrography (the study of seas and oceans), phytography (dealing with the classification of plants) and 'zoography' (approximating to a descriptive zoology). Even Johnson defined the word in general terms in his

Dictionary (1755): '*Geology*, the doctrine of the earth; the knowledge of the state and nature of the earth'. The modern sense owed much to the publication of James Hutton's 'Theory of the Earth', published in 1795, which was the first general geological study (in modern terms) to appear in English, with its author thus the first geologist proper. Hutton used the word 'geology' in the current sense in his book, and the meaning has remained in use since.

gestation (carrying of young in the womb)
Much as '**geology**' (see above) was first a general term, then later a specific one, 'gestation' also moved to its present meaning from a former, sixteenth-century sense of simply 'carrying' or 'being carried', deriving from Latin *gestus*, the past participle passive of *gerere*, 'to carry', 'to bear'. This early use could therefore apply to being carried on horseback, for example, or in a carriage, especially as a form of exercise. In *The Castel of Helth* (1539), Sir Thomas Elyot defined 'gestation' as, among other things, 'sytting in a chaire, whiche is caried on mens shulders with staves', or 'syttynge in a boate or barge, whiche is rowed', or 'rydying on a horse', and so on. All rather passive, except the last, but still regarded as 'exercise'. The word was used in this sense right down to the nineteenth century, which thus makes odd reading to modern eyes. 'Moderate gestation, and a temperate course of diet, will be found to answer the purpose of promoting convalescence', wrote the *Medical and Physical Journal*, in an issue of 1808. However, the modern sense had also been in use from the early seventeenth century, and is now the main meaning, together with the figurative usage, 'conception and development of a mental plan'.

gesture (motion or movement of the body or limbs to express an emotion, etc.)
The word has the same ultimate Latin source as '**gestation**' (see above), and its original meaning, in the fifteenth century, was thus 'bearing', 'carriage', with the whole phrase 'gesture of the body' usually understood. The sense can be found in the Book of Common Prayer (1549), in the 'Publick Baptism of Infants', where after the Gospel, the priest makes an 'Exhortation'

reminding those present that Christ 'by his outward gesture and deed' commanded children to be brought to him and 'declared his good will toward them'. Shakespeare has the usage, too, in *As You Like It* (1600), where Rosalind says to Orlando: 'If you do love Rosalind so near the heart as your gesture cries it out, when your brother marries Aliena, shall you marry her'. In the sixteenth and seventeenth centuries, 'gesture' could also mean 'posture', especially in prayer and worship. Sir Thomas Browne, in his *Pseudodoxia Epidemica* (better known as *Vulgar Errors*) (1646), wrote: 'As for their gesture of position, the men lay downe leaning on their left elbow'. The current sense also dates from the fifteenth century, in its more restricted meaning.

giblets (bird's internal edible organs such as heart, liver, etc)
In the fifteenth century, 'giblets' meant 'entrails' generally, in the sense 'garbage'. The current sense developed in the sixteenth century, and from the seventeenth to the nineteenth century the word could also simply means 'odds and ends', 'things of little value', as in these lines from a satirical poem (1658) by John Cleveland:

They fear the Giblets of his Train, they fear
Even his Dog, that four-leg'd Cavalier.

giddy (dizzy, frivolous)
In Old English, *gydig* meant 'mad', 'possessed', a sense that became obsolete in about the fourteenth century but reappeared in dialect use in the seventeenth century, especially to mean 'mad with fury'. The modern 'dizzy' sense first arose in the sixteenth century, when the word also came to mean 'flighty', or what Johnson called 'elated to thoughtlessness'. The 'intensive' use of 'giddy', as in 'it's the giddy limit' (and the famous 'my giddy aunt!') first came into currency at the end of the nineteenth century.

gingerbread (cake or biscuit flavoured with ginger)
In origin, the word has nothing to do with 'bread', but derives from the early form

(from French) *gingebras*, 'ginger paste'. In the thirteenth century, therefore, 'gingerbread' meant 'preserved ginger', and it was only in the fifteenth century that the modern usage appeared (almost as if the association with 'bread' led to the introduction of the cake itself). Such cakes were formerly coloured and gilded, hence the still current expression 'take the gilt off the gingerbread' for 'remove what is attractive', 'spoil the enjoyment'.

gingerly (cautiously, slowly and carefully)
Just as 'gingerbread' is nothing to do with 'bread' (see above), so 'gingerly' has no connection with 'ginger'. Its actual origin is Old French *gent*, 'well-born', 'dainty' (compare **gentle**), hence the initial sense in English, in the thirteenth century, of 'daintily', 'elegantly', even 'mincingly'. Here is the word in John Skelton's self-flattering poem *A Ryght Delectable Treatyse vpon a Goodly Garlande or Chapelet of Laurell* (1523):

> With,
> Gingirly, go gingerly! her tayle was made of hay,
> Go she neuer so gingirly, her honesty is gone away.

The modern meaning is first recorded in the early seventeenth century.

girl (female child)
Unlikely as it may seem, in the thirteenth century, 'girl' could mean a child of either sex, a 'youth' or a 'maiden', and because of this ambiguity, a boy was usually referred to as a 'knave girl'. The word was mostly used in the plural, to mean 'children', 'young people'. In the following lines from the *Prologue* to Chaucer's *Canterbury Tales* (1396), the reference is to young men:

> In daunger hadde he at his owne gyse
> The yonge girles of the diocyse,
> And knew hir counseil, and was al hir reed.

(That is: He [the Summoner, who summoned sinners to court before a church trial] had all the young fellows of the diocese in his power, and not only had all their confidences but advised them what to do.) The current sense of the word dates from only the sixteenth century.

glad (happy, joyful)
The Old English sense was not only 'full of joy', as 'glad' still means today, but 'bright', 'shining', as well as 'cheerful', 'merry', with both these meanings now obsolete. The latter use was still in vogue with nineteenth-century poets, such as in these lines from Wordsworth's *The Fountain* (1799):

> And often, glad no more,
> We wear a face of joy, because
> We have been glad of yore.

The usage 'full of brightness or beauty', especially as applied to inanimate objects, arose only in the seventeenth century, and is first recorded in Milton's *Paradise Lost* (1667):

> Glad Eevning and glad Morn crownd
> the fourth day.

glamour (charm, romantic attractiveness)
This is indeed a word to conjure with. It is an eighteenth-century Scottish word meaning 'magic', 'enchantment', and was introduced into the literary language by Scott. Its origin, however, is unexpectedly in 'grammar' (which to many long-suffering students has precious little glamour), and the Scottish word arose as a corrupt form of this. The sense development from 'grammar' to 'magic' arose because at the time of transferral of meaning, all learning (such as grammar) was becoming regarded with increasing suspicion, and was increasingly looked on as a sort of 'mumbo jumbo', which some of it undoubtedly was. Here is Burns playing on both senses, in his *Captain Grose's Peregrin* (1789):

> Ye gipsy-gang that deal in glamor,
> And you deep read in hell's black grammar,
> Warlocks and witches.

From this meaning, a second sense shift was made to 'romantic charm', more understandably since such attraction can be seen as a form of magic, a 'spell'. The word in this usage dates only from the nineteenth century. See also **grammar** itself.

glee (merriment)
This word had two main meanings in Old English, both now obsolete: 'play', 'sport',

and 'music', 'minstrelsy'. Here is the second sense in Chaucer's *An A.B.C.* (1366):

We han none other melody ne glee
Us to rejoyce in our adversitee.

From the twelfth century, the word acquired its present sense of 'merriment', 'rejoicing'. However, it seems to have fallen out of use from about the fifteenth century, and occurs neither in Shakespeare nor Milton, although the former does have (once) the word 'gleeful' in *Titus Andronicus* 1600), where Ramora says to Aaron:

My lovely Aaron, wherefore look'st thou sad,
When every thing doth make a gleeful boast?

Moreover, in Edward Phillips' dictionary of 1706 the word is marked as 'obsolete' and Johnson, in turn, in his *Dictionary* of 1755, says that 'glee' is 'not now used except in ludicrous writing, or with some mixture of irony and contempt'. However, the word comes in Goldsmith's *The Deserted Village* (1770):

Full well they laugh'd with counterfeited glee,

and occurs in Wordsworth, Macaulay and many other writers from then onwards, surviving fairly healthily today. The specialized musical use of 'glee' to mean 'unaccompanied partsong' dates only from the seventeenth century, which is also clearly an extension of the original basic meaning.

glimmer (give out a faint light)
The word has done a virtual turnabout. In the fourteenth century, it was used to mean 'shine brightly', for example in Lord Berners' *The History of Arthur of Little Britain* (1530): 'He sawe yᵉ bryght sonne glimmering on yᵉ faire chirches & hye steples'. Generally from the fifteenth century, however, the sense altered to the modern 'shine faintly', and Lord Berners' example here is the last record we have of the word in its former meaning. Shakespeare may have promoted the *noun* 'glimmer' by using it (in the modern sense) in *The Comedy of Errors* (1590), where, near the end of the play, Aegeon says:

Yet hath my night of life some memory,
My wasting lamps some fading glimmer left.

gloat (watch or think about something with satisfaction or relish)
In the sixteenth century, when first used in English, 'gloat' meant 'look askance at', 'give a sidelong glance at', as in these lines from George Gascoigne's *The Complaynt of Phylomene* (1576)

Ne could he loke a side,
But like the cruel catte
Which gloating casteth many a glance
Vpon the selly ratte.

From the seventeenth century, the word had emerged in a new sense as 'look at amorously', 'glance at admiringly', as in Nicholas Rowe's *The Tragedy of Jane Shore* (1714);

Teach every Grace to smile, in your behalf,
And her deluding Eyes to gloat for you.

The modern meaning finally emerged in the eighteenth century, with its implication of malicious pleasure or *Schadenfreude*. However, although quite commonly used in the seventeenth and eighteenth centuries, 'gloat' does not appear in Edward Phillips' dictionary of 1706, and Johnson, although including it in his own *Dictionary* of 1755, merely quotes the lines from Rowe, above, together with the comment: 'This word I conceive to be ignorantly written for *gloar* [meaning "stare"]'. In fact, the word seems to have been taken into English from some Scandinavian source, and could even be related to Old English *geolu*, 'yellow'.

go-kart, go-cart (type of low-set racing car with small wheels)
Originally, and always in the spelling 'go-cart', the word was the term in the seventeenth century for a light framework on castors or rollers designed to help a small child to learn to walk. Richard Steele commented in an issue of his *Spectator* in 1711 that: 'The Ladies now walk as if they were in a Go cart'. In the eighteenth century, the word came to apply to a hand-cart, so that Goldsmith in an essay in his periodical called *The Bee* (1759), wrote that: 'She [i.e. a character nicknamed Mrs

Roundabout] put me in mind of my Lord Bantam's sheep, which are obliged to have their monstrous tails trundled along in a go-cart'. In the nineteenth century, a 'go-cart' progressed to being a type of light open horse-drawn carriage. Thomas Hughes, best known for *Tom Brown's School Days*, mentions in *The Scouring of the White Horse* (1859) how about a dozen parties proceeded 'in all sorts of odd go-carts and other vehicles'. Finally, in the second half of the twentieth century, and with an altered commercial spelling as 'go-kart', the current meaning developed to apply to the miniature racing car, with 'kart' as a shorter form of this and 'karting' as the general term for the sport of racing in such cars. It is perhaps worth recalling that the basic meaning of 'go' in Old English was 'walk', and therefore that the first sense of 'go-cart', as the child's device, is the closest to the original concept.

gore (blood, especially when clotted)
In Old English, 'gore' (*gor*) meant 'dung', 'filth', not 'blood', with the latter sense emerging only in the sixteenth century. The transference of sense came through the linking idea of 'unpleasant effusion', 'matter flowing out of the body'. In poetic language, 'gore' was particularly exploited in the sense 'blood shed in battle or general carnage', as in Smollett's *Ode to Independence* (1760):

The Saxon prince in horror fled
From altars stained with human gore.

gore (wound or stab with a horn or tusk)
This word, not related to the 'gore' above, originally meant 'stab' generally from the fourteenth century, usually with a weapon of some kind. The verb comes in Miles Coverdale's translation of the Bible in 1535, where he renders Ezekiel 23:46: 'These shal stone them, and gorre them with their sweardes' (Authorized Version of 1611: 'And the company shall stone them with stones, and dispatch them with their swords'). This use became obsolete in the nineteenth century, when even then it was somewhat artificially preserved in historical novels such as those of Scott. The current usage, as applied to stabbing by an animal's horn, also dates from the sixteenth century.

gorge (ravine)
The sense of 'ravine' given here is probably the best known when the word is a noun, although of course the verb 'gorge' meaning 'fill one's stomach' is also in current popular use. The two are connected, and both derive from the original use of the word in English, in the fourteenth century, to mean 'throat', where the borrowing was direct from the French. From the fifteenth century, 'gorge' came to be used as the term for the crop of a hawk, and a hundred years later the sense was extended to mean 'contents of the stomach', hence the still current expression 'my gorge rises' (i.e. I am disgusted or sickened). In the seventeenth century, 'gorge' came to be used in military parlance for the neck of a bastion or other outwork in a fortification, and developing in turn from this, the meaning 'ravine' followed in the eighteenth century. Interestingly, the French word *gorge* that originally gave the English, and that is today the standard word for 'throat', has followed almost exactly the same sense developments, including the fortification and the ravine.

gossip (chatty talk, person who likes revealing petty secrets)
This word is one of the most unexpected 'sense-benders'. The Old English word that lies behind it (*godsibb*) meant 'godparent', with this meaning in use, if increasingly as a dialect term, down to the nineteenth century. It comes, for example, in Evelyn's *Diary* (1649), where he writes of a child's parents 'being so poore that they had provided no gossips' for its christening. A godfather or godmother was a familar figure to the family, and therefore it is hardly surprising that by the fourteenth century the sense had extended to mean 'well-known acquaintance' in general, with the original meaning (as it were, 'God sib') forgotten. This use can be found in even quite recent poetry, as in Keats's *Eve of St Agnes* (1820):

Ah, Gossip dear,
We're safe enough; here in this
arm-chair sit.

In *A Midsummer Night's Dream* (1590), Shakespeare used 'gossip' to apply in particular to a woman's female friends who had been invited to be present at a birth.

This is therefore what Puck meant when he said:

> And sometimes lurk I in a gossip's bowl,
> In very likeness of a roasted crab.

Shakespeare, too, was the first to use the word as a verb, where in *The Comedy of Errors* (1590), the Duke says (repeating the word in its noun form):

> With all my heart I'll gossip at this feast.

It was from this verbal use that 'gossip' came to mean 'talk idly' in the seventeenth century, and that the noun finally acquired, in turn, its own current meaning of 'tittle-tattle' in the nineteenth century.

gourmand (person devoted to excessive eating and drinking)
The disparaging use of 'gourmand', almost meaning 'glutton', has existed in English since the fifteenth century. In the eighteenth century, however, the word acquired a more favourable sense, closer to 'gourmet' (although not under the influence of it since this latter word was not used in English until a century later). This usage can be seen, for example, in a fairly trivial poem of 1839 by Winthrop M. Praed:

> You know that I was held by all
> The greatest epicure in Hall,
> And that the voice of Granta's sons
> Styled me the Gourmand of St. John's.

Charlotte Brontë, too, used the word favourably, with an appropriately feminine ending, in *Villette* (1853): 'Fifine was a frank gourmande; any body could win her heart through her palate'. This meaning appears to have been ousted, or even replaced, by 'gourmet', however, when it caught on in the nineteenth century, and 'gourmand' today has only its undesirable sense.

grammar (study of the sounds, forms and syntax of a language)
In its earliest use in English, in the fourteenth century, 'grammar' meant 'Latin', or at least the study of the Latin language. (The word came into English, via French, from Latin, where itself it had its origin in Greek *grammatikē tekhnē*, 'art of letters'.) This is because Latin was the only language that was taught grammatically. It was only from the seventeenth century that the term came to apply to other languages, including of course English, and that there was then a need to distinguish between 'Latin grammar' and any other. So 'Latin' is the meaning of 'grammar' in Caxton's translation (1485) of the *Life of Charles the Great*, where he says that Charles was 'Instructe in gramayre & other scyences'. Ben Jonson's book *The English Grammar* (1636) was thus the first to speak of a 'grammar' that was not Latin. Similarly, any 'grammar school' recorded in the sixteenth century or earlier would have been one for the teaching of Latin, such as the one that Shakespeare went to in Stratford on Avon, and the kind that is mentioned in his *Henry VI*, Part 2 (1593), when Cade says to Lord Say: 'Thou hast most traitorously corrupted the youth of the realm in erecting a grammar-school'. For a further development in the sense of 'grammar', see **glamour**.

grange (farmhouse or country house together with its outbuildings)
In its earliest and most basic sense, as borrowed into English in the thirteenth century from French, 'grange' meant 'granary', 'barn'. The sense was in fairly regular use to the fifteenth century, and in poetry after this, as in Milton's *Comus* (1634):

> When, for their teeming flocks and
>   granges full,
> In wanton dance they praise the
>   bounteous Pan.

From the fourteenth century, the word came to acquire two distinct meanings. The first, from the 'granary', was the name of the place where the harvest was gathered and stored in such barns, in other words a farm, usually with outbuildings. From about the seventeenth century, this in turn developed into a country house with farm buildings attached, the traditional residence of the 'gentleman farmer'. Hence 'Grange' as a frequent word in the names of some country houses, such as Badley Grange in Cheshire. The second meaning of 'grange' was as the word for an outlying farmhouse that belonged to a religious establishment, such as a monastery, or to a feudal lord. This is the sense of the word in Chaucer's *Canterbury Tales* ('The Miller's Tale') (1386):

He is wont for tymber for to go,
And dwellen at the grange a day or two.

Many such farms are today still called
'Grange Farm'.

grasp (seize or hold firmly with the hand)
In the fourteenth century, 'grasp' was
virtually synonymous with 'grope', and
implied the 'clutching' at something, as if
seeking for support, or of a blind person. In
Wyclif's Bible of 1382, Deuteronomy 28:29
is rendered: 'Thou shalt graasp in mydday,
as is woned a blynd man to graasp in derk-
nissis' (Authorized Version of 1611: 'And
thou shalt grope at noonday, as the blind
gropeth in darkness'). In Shakespeare's
Henry VI, Part 2 (1593), too, the word has
this sense, when Warwick, surveying Gloucester's dead body, says:

His hand abroad display'd, as one that
    grasp'd
And tugg'd for life, and was by strength
    subdu'd.

The sense became obsolete from the nineteenth century, and meanwhile the current
usage, found from the sixteenth century,
was the one to remain.

grass widow (woman whose husband is
away temporarily)
The term was first used in English in the
sixteenth century, when it applied to an
unmarried woman who was known to have
had intercourse with several men, in
modern terms, perhaps, an 'unmarried
mum'. The expression was even semi-
official, and the church register at Stoke-by-
Nayland, Suffolk recorded that on 31
January 1582 ' . . .was buri'd Marie the
daughtᵣ of Elizabeth London graswidow'.
From the nineteenth century the term had
its current sense, originally as referring to
the wives of husbands on government or
military service in India. The origin of the
expression seems to lie in the 'grass' that for
the first kind of woman had served as a
marriage 'bed'. The Anglo-Indian sense
may have simply regarded the 'grass' as
that of the Indian hills where such wives
languished while their husbands were away
on duty.

grate (iron frame to hold coal in fireplace)
In the fourteenth century, a 'grate' was a
general word for a grille or grating. Coverdale's Bible of 1535 tells how in 2 Kings
1:2: 'Ochosias fell thorow yᵉ grate in his
chamber at Samaria' (Authorized Version
of 1611: 'And Ahaziah fell down through a
lattice in his upper chamber that was in
Samaria'). Johnson, in his *Dictionary* of 1755,
defined the verb 'grill' as 'to boil on a grate
or gridiron', and as late as 1872, Orby
Shipley, in *A Glossary of Ecclesiastical Terms*,
defined 'grate' as 'an ornamental iron screen
around a monument'. This sense is now
obsolete, as is another that developed in the
sixteenth century, when 'grate' came to be
a word for a cage or prison. This explains
the use in Shakespeare's *The Merry Wives of
Windsor* (1598), where Falstaff suggests to
Pistol that he and Nym had 'looked through
the grate, like a geminy [i.e. pair] of
baboons'. The modern meaning, for the
frame in the fireplace, and also for the
fireplace itself (where such fireplaces still
exist), arose in the seventeenth century,
early enough to appear in the Bible of 1611
(in Exodus 27:4).

gravity (seriousness; force attracting
bodies to centre of the earth)
The earliest senses of 'gravity' in English
were figurative ones, with the word acting
as the noun corresponding to 'grave'. Some
of the senses are now obsolete, such as the
one that meant 'dignity' or 'authority'. This,
together with still current meanings such as
'seriousness' and 'sobriety of bearing', arose
in the sixteenth century. It was thus only in
the seventeenth century that the word came
to be used in the physical sense, first as
'physical weight', then as 'gravitational
attraction'.

gravy (savoury sauce made from juices of
cooked meat)
When 'gravy' first appeared on English
tables in the fourteenth century, it was a
dressing for white meat, fish, and vegetables
that seems to have consisted of a mixture of
broth, so called 'almond milk' (made of
sweet blanched almonds and water), spices,
and, often, wine or ale. Here is a contemporary recipe for making this sort of 'gravy':
'Oysters in Gravey. Schyl Oysters and seeth

hem in wyne and in hare own broth, cole the broth thrugh a cloth, take almandes blaunched, grynde hem and drawe hem up with the self broth & alye [i.e. mix] it with floer of Rys and do the oysters therinne, cast in powder of gynger, suger, macys [i.e. mace]' (*The Forme of Cury*, 1390). Modern 'gravy' first emerged in the sixteenth century.

grief (deep distress)
In the thirteenth century, when the word was first current, it could mean both 'hardship' and 'displeasure' (compare modern 'grievance'). In the fourteenth, the meaning was also 'hurt', 'injury' (compare 'come to grief'). When Bishop Shaxton wrote a letter to Cromwell in 1535 and said 'Yet perceive I right manifestly your grief towards me', the word meant 'anger'. All these senses are now obsolete, and the only surviving one, also dating from the fourteenth century, is 'great mental distress'. A similar sense development occurred for 'grieve' and 'grievance'.

grin (smile broadly to express amusement or pain)
The gesture can hardly have changed over the centuries, but the emotions it indicates have. In Old English, 'grinning' denoted either pain (as today) or anger (now expressed differently). Dogs and wolves were thus said to 'grin' to show their ferocity, and something of the sense still exists in a 'grinning' skull, for example, which expresses evil. The 'grin' of amusement developed only in the fifteenth century. Even here, however, there is still a connotation of unpleasantness, and a 'broad grin' is often a sly one.

gripe (cause internal pain)
The word is related to 'grip', 'grope' and 'grasp', and the last of these was its meaning in Old English. It was current for some considerable time, and occurs, for example, in Shakespeare's *Henry IV*, Part 1 (1596), when Worcester says to the King:

You took occasion to be quickly woo'd
To gripe the general sway into your
     hand.

When Cromwell, too, made a speech on 20

April 1657, he should not be misunderstood (in modern terms) when he said: 'I meant to gripe at the Government.' Even in the eighteenth century, Pope, in his version (1715–20) of the *Iliad* could write of:

The children, in whose arms are borne
(Too short to gripe them) the brown
     sheaves of corn.

In the sixteenth century, 'gripe' came to mean 'afflict', as in Shakespeare's *Henry VI*, Part 3 (1593), when Northumberland says:

I should not for my life but weep with
     him,
To see how inly sorrow gripes his soul.

From this, the transition to physical 'griping' was quite natural, and the word first occurs in this current sense in the seventeenth century, while the colloquial 'gripe' meaning 'complain' arose (originally in the United States) in the twentieth century.

grizzle (cry fretfully)
In the eighteenth century, to 'grizzle' was to grin mockingly, especially in local West Country usage, such as in *A Dialogue in the Devonshire Dialect, by A Lady* (actually Mrs Mary Palmer) (1837): 'The ould man grizzled: No sure, lovy, sed he, I ne'er had the leastest inkling for such a thing'. From the nineteenth century, the word acquired its present meaning. It is possible the verb may have derived from a reference to 'patient Grizel', or Griselda, who personified a meek and patient wife.

grocer (dealer in fruit, vegetables and other household foods)
A 'grocer' was originally a 'dealer in gross', that is, a merchant who sold or dealt in large quantities. This was in the fifteenth century, when the current sense also arose due to the fact that the Grocers' Company, founded in 1345, consisted of wholesale dealers in foreign products, especially spices, sugar, dried fruit and the like. From the eighteenth century, tea, coffee and cocoa were added to the distinctive products that a grocer sold, with wines and spirits included from the middle of the nineteenth century. The more specialist 'greengrocer' first appeared in the eighteenth century.

Originally the word was usually spelt 'grosser' but changed the double letter to 'c' under the influence of 'spicer'. (Compare modern French *épicier*, the standard word for 'grocer'.)

groom (person in charge of horses; bridegroom)
The word has really developed along three lines since the thirteenth century. Originally, a 'groom' was simply a word for 'boy'. In *The Lay of Havelock the Dane* (1300) a character thus says: 'Ich am now no grom; Ich am wel waxen [i.e. grown]' The usage continued until about the end of the fourteenth century, by which time the meaning had been extended to 'man', with this sense resurrected in pastoral poetry of the sixteenth and seventeenth century to mean 'shepherd'. Even Wordsworth employed the word to mean this, as in *The White Doe of Rylstone* (1815):

And, up among the moorlands, see
What sprinklings of blithe company!
Of lasses and of shepherd grooms.

Meanwhile, a secondary sense 'manservant' had developed in the thirteenth century, and this is the one that came to mean 'horse attendant' (from the seventeenth century), while also coming to designate, in the fifteenth century, an officer of the Royal Household, especially in the Lord Chamberlain's department. (Such officials usually had a special designation, as 'Groom of the Great Chamber' or 'Groom of the Crossbows'. Not all 'grooms' were men in this sense, as is clear from this reference in Evelyn's *The Life of Mrs. Godolphin*, 1685: 'The late Countess of Guilford, Groome of the Stoole [i.e. Stole] of the late Queens Mother'.) The third sense of 'groom' is of course the one that is short for 'bridegroom', and this abbreviated form is first recorded in Shakespeare's *Othello* (1604), when Iago says, after Montano has been wounded in a fight with Cassio:

Friends all but now, even now,
In quarter and in terms like bride and groom
Devesting them [i.e. undressing] for bed.

The word in this sense is nearly always paired with 'bride', although again Shakespeare, in *Cymbeline* (1611), pioneered its individual use, where Guiderius addresses Belarius:

Were you a woman, youth,
I should woo hard but be your groom.

grub (insect larva; food)
The earliest meaning of the word in English, in the fourteenth century, was 'short person', 'dwarfish man'. However, this soon became obsolete, and the meaning 'insect larva', that is first recorded only a little later, was the one to prevail. The transference to 'food' ('lovely grub') came about in the seventeenth century. The idea is that food can be as attractive to humans as grubs are to birds. The word came to be particularly associated with school stories and stories for boys in the nineteenth century: 'We had brought some grub with us and a bottle of grog' (Rolf Boldrewood, *Robbery Under Arms*, 1888).

gruff (rough and surly)
Before the word arose in its present sense in the seventeenth century, it was current in Scottish and commercial use some hundred years earlier to mean 'coarse-grained', as applied to chemicals, sugar, meal and the like. As applied to the voice, 'gruff' has been in use since the eighteenth century.

guess (hazard an answer or piece of information)
In the thirteenth century, to 'guess' was to take aim at something such as a battle target with a weapon. From this, the sense naturally passed to mean 'estimate an answer'. 'Estimate' itself has now taken on a more precise meaning, hence the colloquial modern 'guesstimate' to denote a combination of both, an estimate made without adequate information.

guilt (state of having done something wrong)
In Old English, 'guilt' (*gylt*) was the offence or crime itself. 'Forgyf us ure gyltas' is the way the *Anglo-Saxon Gospels* of the tenth century translate the first half of Matthew 6:12 ('Forgive us our debts' in the Authorized Version of 1611, or 'Forgive us our trespasses' in the better known Lord's

Prayer). From the twelfth century, 'guilt' came to mean 'responsibility for an event or action', or basically 'fault', while a hundred years later, the word was used to mean 'what one deserves', especially as a penalty. From both these now obsolete senses the current meaning 'fact' (later 'state') 'of having committed a crime' developed, the former in the fourteenth century, the latter in the sixteenth.

gum (firm flesh in which teeth are fixed)
The current sense developed only in the fourteenth century. In Old English, *gōma* was the word for the whole of the inside of the mouth or throat. Something of this meaning survived in Coverdale's translation of Psalm 22:15 in his English Bible of 1535: 'My tunge cleueth to my goomes' (Authorized Version of 1611: 'My tongue cleaveth to my jaws'). For some time the word was pronounced 'goom' (like 'loom').

gymkhana (children's horseriding contest or display)
The word is not connected with 'gym' but is a corruption of Hindi *gend-khāna*, literally 'racket court', 'ball house', and this was the origin of the nineteenth-century Anglo-Indian usage, when the word was defined in *Hobson-Jobson*, the famous Anglo-Indian dictionary of 1886 by Sir Henry Yule and Arthur C. Burnell, as: 'A place of public resort at a station, where the needful facilities for athletics and games of sorts are provided'. From this, the meaning developed to mean the athletics display itself, especially in such phrases as a 'gymkhana club' or a 'gymkhana meeting'. Naturally, horseracing and polo were early ingredients of such meetings, and this element survived in the European 'gymkhana', which seems to have evolved in its present form some time in the 1930s.

haggard (drawn or weary-looking)
In the sixteenth century, 'haggard' had a specific sense to apply to an untamed hawk, especially a female one caught in its adult plumage. The word thus described the bird, as 'untamed', and was the term for the hawk itself. Hence, in Shakespeare's *Much Ado About Nothing* (1599), Hero's comments to Ursula about Beatrice:

I know her spirits are as coy and wild
As haggerds of the rock.

From this, the word passed to mean 'wild-looking' as applied to a person, with this usage first recorded in the seventeenth century.

haggle (wrangle, bargain)
The present sense dates from the seventeenth century. In the sixteenth, when the word was first in use, it meant 'hack', 'mangle', 'mutilate by cutting', as in Shakespeare's *Henry V* (1599), where Exeter reports on the course of the battle at Agincourt:

Suffolk first died: and York, all haggled over,
Comes to him, where in gore he lay insteep'd.

'Haggling' in the 'wrangling' sense implies verbal 'hacking'.

handkerchief (piece of cloth for blowing the nose, wiping the face, etc.)
In the fifteenth century, the word was 'handcoverchief', showing that originally the cloth was a 'kerchief', or cloth for covering the head (Old French *cuevrechief*) that was carried in the *hand* (or pocket, when it was a 'pocket handkerchief'). It was also used for covering the neck, when it was a 'neck handkerchief', or simply a 'neckerchief'. The Geneva New Testament of 1557 translates Acts 19:12 as: 'From his body, were brought vnto the sycke, napkyns or

handkerchefs' (Authorized Version of 1611: 'So that from his body were brought unto the sick handkerchiefs or aprons'). The much handier and homelier 'hanky' emerged at the end of the nineteenth century.

handsome (good-looking, generous)
The modern word has lost the sense of the original meaning, which was, as the word suggests, 'hand-some', or more precisely, 'easy to handle'. This was in the fifteenth century, and the use can be seen in the first record we have of the word in *Torrent of Portugal* (1435):

Sir Torrent gaderid [i.e. gathered] good cobled stonys,
Good and handsom ffor the nonys [i.e. for the purpose].

From this now obsolete sense came another, simply 'handy', 'convenient', as in the following piece of advice to beekeepers from Barnaby Googe's translation (1577) of Heresback's *Foure Bookes of Husbandry*: 'Carry all your Coames into some handsome place, where you meane to make your Honie'. This was in the sixteenth century, when all the current senses also arose, including 'considerable', 'generous' (a 'handsome' gift) and the best-known meaning, defined nicely by Johnson in his *Dictionary* (1755) as 'beautiful with dignity'. This last had developed in time for Spenser and Shakespeare to use it.

hangar (large building housing aircraft)
When first used in English, in the nineteenth century, 'hangar' meant simply 'shed', although the reference was usually to one where carriages were kept. 'Mademoiselle', says a character in Thackeray's *Henry Esmond* (1852), 'may we take your coach to town? I saw it in the *hangar*'. The word is in italics since it was not yet felt to be fully anglicized from the French (where the word still means 'shed' today, as well as 'hangar'), and indeed was pronounced much as in French, similar to 'en gare', with a nasal 'n'. It was the French use of the word to mean 'place where aircraft are kept' that gave the first English use, too, in the early twentieth century, as when the *Daily Chronicle* reported on 31 October 1902 that:

'Mr. Santos Dumont [. . .] will construct a hangar in the Bois de Boulogne'. With the rapid rise of the aeroplane, and the coming of the First World War, the pronunciation was soon anglicized to rhyme with 'hanger'.

happy (enjoying pleasure or content, satisfied)
The earliest sense of 'happy' in English, in the fourteenth century, was that of enjoying 'hap' or good fortune, so really meant 'lucky' or even 'prosperous'. This use of the word can still be felt in such expressions as a 'happy' accident, a 'happy' escape, or the traditional birthday wish, 'Many happy returns'. The common 'contented' sense of 'happy' therefore arose somewhat later, in the sixteenth century'. In the Bible, 'happy' in John 13:17 ('If ye know these things, happy are ye if ye do them') has the now obsolete meaning 'blessed', still surviving in the phrase 'of happy memory', used of a deceased person.

harbinger (something that warns or foretells what is to come)
A 'harbinger' was originally a 'harbourer', a person who provided board and lodging. The word commonly existed in the form 'herberger', showing its link with modern French *auberge* and modern German *Herberge*, both meaning 'inn'. This sense was first recorded in the twelfth century. From the fourteenth century, the word was used of a person who went ahead of an army or royal party to obtain lodgings for them, a sort of medieval courier or travel agent. In the plural, the sense was that of an army's advance party that went ahead to prepare a camping ground. From this, the word came to acquire its modern meaning of 'forerunner', now almost entirely in figurative or literary use, as Milton's lovely lines from *On May Morning* (1630):

Now the bright morning star, day's harbinger,
Comes dancing from the east, and leads with her
The flowery May.

harbour (place of shelter for ships, port)
The popular sense is the most recent, evolving only in the sixteenth century. In

Old English use, 'harbour' meant 'shelter', 'lodging' (compare **harbinger,** above). From the thirteenth century, the sense modified a little to mean 'place of shelter', 'refuge'. (This is the 'harbour' that appears in the common English place-name Coldharbour, and Coldharbour Lane, since such a place would have had a shelter or refuge to protect wayfarers from the cold, much as a modern bus shelter does.) From this in turn came the modern sense as applied specifically to ships. Although close to 'haven' in form and meaning, incidentally, the two words are not related.

harebell (slender plant with blue bell-shaped flowers)
In the fourteenth century, 'harebell' was the name of the wild hyacinth, better known as the bluebell (*Endymion nonscriptus*). This is thus the flower that occurs in Shakespeare's *Cymbeline* (1611), when Arviragus, believing Imogen to be dead, mentions the flowers he will put on her grave:

> Thou shalt not lack
> The flower that's like thy face, pale
> primrose, nor
> The azur'd hare-bell, like thy veins.

It was only in the eighteenth century that 'harebell' became the name of *Campanula rotundifolia*, although in Scotland 'harebell' is still sometimes used of the bluebell.

hark back (return to earlier subject, recall past occasion or time)
The phrase was adopted in the nineteenth century from an earlier hunting term, applied to hounds when they 'harked back' or retraced their track to find a scent that had been lost. 'Hark' was used with an adverb (as 'Hark away!', 'Hark in!') by huntsmen when telling hounds which course to follow.

harlot (prostitute)
The word has not always applied exclusively to a female, nor always been quite so derogatory. When first current in the thirteenth century, a 'harlot' was a rascal or 'low fellow'. Chaucer used it in this sense in his *Canterbury Tales* ('The Reeve's Tale') (1385):

> Ye false harlot, quod the Millere, hast?

(so to say, 'What did you say you've done, you rascal?'). From the fourteenth century, the word could apply to a roving jester or juggler, or to someone who did something to raise a laugh, as well as simply meaning 'fellow', 'chap', as again in Chaucer in the same work (the *Prologue*), where the reference is to the Summoner (see **girl**):

> He was a gentil harlot and a kynde
> A bettre felawe sholde men noght fynde.

Finally, in the fifteenth century, the word came to have its present usage. It occurred frequently in sixteenth-century Bible translations, where it mostly replaced the 'whore' of Wyclif's translation of 1382, probably as it was regarded as a less offensive word.

harmony (combination of notes to make chords; agreement, concord)
In the fourteenth century, 'harmony' meant simply 'melody', 'music', and this is the sense of the word in Shakespeare's *The Tempest* (1610), where after the stage direction 'Solemn and strange music' Alonso says:

> What harmony is this? my good friends, hark!

The current meaning thus dates only from the sixteenth century.

harvest (crop of corn, gathering in of this crop in autumn)
In Old English, 'harvest' was the word for 'autumn' in general (compare modern German *Herbst*), and a mid-eleventh century text (*Byrhtferth's Handboc*) notes that 'tha feower timan' (the four seasons) were 'lengten [see **Lent**], sumor, hærfest, & winter'. The season and its name soon became associated with the gathering of crops, however, and the meaning in the modern sense became established in the sixteenth century, where it is first recorded in Tindale's Bible of 1526. (Tindale's rendering of part of Matthew 9:37 as 'The hervest is greate' superseded Wyclif's translation of 1388: 'There is myche ripe corne'.)

hassock (cushion for kneeling on or putting the feet on)
A 'hassock' was originally the word for a 'tussock', or a clump of matted grass or

other vegetation. This earlier sense goes back to Old English times, and can still be seen in the name of the Sussex town of Hassocks, where it was originally the name of a field. The transference from the outdoor 'hassock' to the indoor one came about in the sixteenth century, when hassocks were originally cushions filled with dried grass, straw or rushes.

haunt (visit as a ghost)
The sense development here is as follows: 'resort to habitually' in the thirteenth century, 'frequent the company of' in the fifteenth century, and 'visit as a ghost' in the sixteenth century. All these senses are still current, and the last of the three, perhaps not surprisingly, is first recorded in Shakespeare, where in *A Midsummer Night's Dream* (1590), during the 'Pyramus and Thisbe' scene, Quince exclaims: 'O monstrous! O strange! we are haunted'.

hazard (chance, accident, obstacle)
In its earliest recorded sense, 'hazard' was the word for a game of dice in the thirteenth century. This is the meaning in Shakespeare's *Henry V* (1599), when before the battle of Agincourt Lord Rambures says: 'Who will go to hazard with me for twenty prisoners?'. From the fourteenth century, the meaning developed to 'chance', 'venture', and the 'danger' sense followed a century later. The golfing 'hazard' came about in the nineteenth century, perhaps influenced by the earlier use of the term in billiards to mean a stroke that hit a ball into a pocket.

hazy (misty)
In the seventeenth century, 'hazy' could mean both 'foggy' and 'misty', with 'haze' itself a century later thus meaning both 'thick fog' and 'thin mist'. This was clearly a confusing state of affairs, and the 'misty' sense was the one that came to prevail in the nineteenth century. It was at the same time that 'hazy' also acquired its figurative sense of 'vague', 'uncertain'. The origin of the word is unknown.

headland (promontory)
The Old English sense of the word applied to the strip of land left at the ends of furrows or by the edge of a field, mainly as an area

where the plough could be conveniently turned. The meaning was transferred to the modern 'cape' or 'promontory' only in the sixteenth century.

hearse (funeral carriage)
The word derives from Old French *herse*, 'harrow', and in the fourteenth century was the name of the framework, resembling a harrow, that was designed to carry candles over a coffin, especially that of a famous person. From this, the meaning developed to denote the bier or coffin itself, and even the grave, as in Shakespeare's *Julius Caesar* (1601), when the First Citizen says, referring to the murdered Caesar: 'Stand from the hearse; stand from the body'. The current sense 'funeral carriage' followed in the seventeenth century.

heckle (harass a speaker with questions, interruptions, etc.)
This word has had an unusual history. It began life as 'hackle', the term for the long shining feathers on the neck of birds such as a domestic cock (hence the expression 'It made my hackles rise'). From this, in the fifteenth century, the meaning developed to the word for a comblike implement (called both 'hackle' and 'heckle') that was used for splitting fibres of flax or hemp. From this noun came the verb 'heckle' meaning to comb flax in this way. Hence the sense 'examine searchingly' and finally, in the nineteenth century, 'harass with questions'. Both 'heckle' and 'hackle' are indirectly related to 'hook'.

hectic (feverish, very busy, greatly excited or active)
The sense of this adjective has moved from the physical to the figurative. In the fourteenth century, 'hectic' (ultimately from Greek *hektikos*, 'habitual', in turn from *hexis*, 'habit', 'state of body or mind') was the term used to apply to a wasting disease such as consumption, one of whose main symptoms was flushed cheeks. From the seventeenth century the sense was extended to be used of a person who had this disease or of its characteristic flush. Hence the 'pretty, hectic girl of sixteen' (the narrator's sister) in Charles Kingsley's *Alton Locke* (1850),

and, in transferred use, the leaves in Shelley's *Ode to the West Wind* (1819) that were:

> Yellow, and black, and pale, and hectic red.

The current popular use of the word to mean 'frantic', 'feverishly active' developed only in the twentieth century, and is first recorded in Kipling: 'Didn't I say we never met in pup-pup-puris naturalibus, if I may so put it, without a remarkably hectic day ahead of us?' (*Traffics and Discoveries*, 1904).

henchman (trusted follower or supporter, especially in politics or crime)
In the fourteenth century, a 'henchman' (literally a 'horse attendant') was a squire or page of honour, who attended an important man such as a prince and walked or rode beside him in processions and the like. This sense was in regular use down to as late as the sixteenth century, and occurs in Shakespeare's *A Midsummer Night's Dream* (1590), where Oberon, King of the Fairies, says:

> I do but beg a little changeling boy,
> To be my henchman.

From the eighteenth century, the sense came to apply to the personal attendant of a Scottish Highland chief, i.e. his head 'ghillie'. This usage frequently occurs in the works of Scott, as may be expected. The meaning 'trusted follower' then developed in the United States in the nineteenth century, especially referring to a political supporter. From this in turn came the criminal 'henchman' or gang member. Occasionally a 'henchwoman' has appeared, too, as a kind of 'personal assistant'. (No doubt a 'henchperson' has also been recorded somewhere similarly.)

heyday (time of a person's greatest success or health, 'prime')
The rather unusual word originated as a spontaneous sixteenth-century exclamation denoting excitement, happiness, surprise or general exuberance, a sort of opposite of 'lackaday'. 'Hoyday, here is stuffe!' exclaims a character in Ben Jonson's *Every Man in his Humour* (1598), and similarly in Samuel Richardson's *Pamela* (1740): 'Hey-day, why so nimble, and whither so fast? said she'.

From this, in the same century, a noun emerged meaning 'state of excitement', as in Shakespeare's *Hamlet* (1602), when Hamlet says to the Queen:

> You cannot call it love, for at your age
> The hey-day in the blood is tame, it's humble.

Finally, in the eighteenth century, the modern meaning became established, first recorded in the works of Smollett and Sterne, respectively in *Peregrine Pickle* (1751) ('the heyday of his blood') and *A Sentimental Journey* (1768) ('I was interrupted in the heyday of this soliloquy, with a voice').

hierarchy (series of grades or ranks)
The word literally means 'holy rulers', with the 'hier-' as in 'hieroglyphics' ('sacred writing') and the '-archy' as in 'monarchy' ('sole ruler'). In the fourteenth century, 'hierarchy' was thus the ecclesiastical word for the three divisions of angels, each in turn divided into three orders. The so called 'celestial hierarchy' progressed (from the lowest to the highest): angels, archangels, principalities, powers, virtues, dominions, thrones, cherubim, seraphim. From this, the sense was extended to apply to the 'hierarchy' of priests or church rulers (e.g. deacons, priests and bishops). Finally, in the seventeenth century, the meaning was widened even further to include any 'power structure', with this new sense first recorded in Milton's *The Doctrine and Discipline of Divorce* (1643): 'There is a certain scale of duties, there is a certain Hierarchy of upper and lower commands'.

highland (upland)
In Old English, *hēahlond* was the word for a promontory or cape in general (both these words are of later origin, respectively from Latin and French). From the fifteenth century, however, 'highland' was used to apply specifically to the mountains of north and west Scotland, originally in the singular, but from the sixteenth century always in the plural (the 'Highlands'). Hence 'Highlander' for a native resident of these areas. By contrast, the 'Lowlands' evolved at about the same time to apply to the lower regions to the south and east of the 'Highlands'.

hike (long country walk made for pleasure, exercise or local interest)
To 'hike', now more common in American use than British, is to jerk or pull, to 'hoick', and this was the original meaning of the word in English in the eighteenth century. From the early nineteenth century, the sense developed to 'walk vigorously or laboriously', as if having to 'hoick' oneself along. Thus Samuel Wesley wrote in a letter of 1809: 'Adieu for the present, – we must Contrive one more Pull at Surry before I hyke over to Staffordshire'. This soon modified to mean 'walk for pleasure', with the corresponding noun 'hike' first recorded in 1865. The 'pull' sense also continued, with an extended meaning 'increase' also developing (from the twentieth century, specifically applied to prices). Hence twentieth-century 'hikers' and 'hiking' as well as 'hitchhiking'. 'Hike' was originally a dialect word.

hilarity (mirth, merriment, amusement)
The original sixteenth-century sense of the word was less boisterous, meaning more 'cheerfulness', 'calm joy'. Dr Johnson's biographer Boswell quotes him as saying (12 April 1776): 'No, Sir; wine gives not light, gay, ideal hilarity; but tumultuous, noisy, clamorous merriment'. The word acquired its present sense of 'fun and laughter' in the nineteenth century.

hinder (delay, impede)
In Old English, the verb (*hindrian*) meant 'injure', 'damage', hence in Miles Coverdale's Bible of 1535 his rendering of Luke 13:7 as: 'Cut it downe, why hyndreth it the grounde?' (Authorized Version of 1611: 'Cut it down: why cumbereth it the ground?'). The modern meaning emerged only from the fourteenth century, the connecting sense being 'obstruct', 'stop in action'.

hint (suggestion, insinuation)
The earliest record we have of the word is in two different senses, both in Shakespeare's *Othello* (1604), both, moreover, in a single speech by Othello (the one where he gives the 'story of my life' told to Desdemona). When he says:

It was my hint to speak; such was the process,

he uses the word in the now obsolete sense of 'opportunity', 'occasion'. But a few lines later, he uses the word in the modern sense:

If I had a friend that lov'd her,
I should but teach him how to tell my story,
And that would woo her. Upon this hint I spake.

Except in literary texts, the first sense fell out of use from the eighteenth century.

hip (exclamation used to begin a cheer)
The word was originally used in the eighteenth century to call to someone, or draw their attention, something like the modern 'hey!'. In the nineteenth century, this was adopted as the 'call' for a cheer, in the now familiar repeated manner of 'Hip hip hip, hooray!'. Thomas Hood included this in his whimsical poem *Sniffing a Birthday* (1845):

No flummery then from flowery lips,
No three times three and hip-hip-hips!

history (account or record of the past)
In its earliest sense in English, in the fifteenth century, 'history' meant 'story', that is, a narration or tale of events that were true or imaginary. The word is first recorded in Caxton's translation (1484) of *Aesop's Fables:* 'The carpenter told thystory to his felawes'. Later, 'history' came to apply to an account of true events only, and it was also in the fifteenth century that the word acquired its modern sense of 'study of the past', with this sense used by Shakespeare in *Cymbeline* (1611), where Iachimo muses:

To think that man, who knows
By history, report, or his own proof,
What woman is.

In the sixteenth century 'history' also came to be applied to the study of natural phenomena, such as those of a particular country or a particular species of animal. For example, the clergyman and natural history writer Edward Topsell wrote a book called 'The Historie of Serpents' (1608). But this sense of the word is now obsolete, except (as occurring in the last sentence) as 'natural history'. See also **story.**

hoarding (large board designed to carry advertisements)
As first used, in the nineteenth century, a 'hoarding' was a temporary fence made of boards, especially one round a building under construction or repair. Such fences were (and still are) used for displaying advertisements, and the name subsequently transferred to large boards that were specifically designed for these. In the second sense, the usage is a British one, with Americans calling such displays 'billboards'.

hobby (sparetime occupation or pastime)
In the fourteenth century, a 'hobby' was a type of small horse or a pony. The name was in use until at least the eighteenth century, with an announcement appearing in 1688 in the *London Gazette*, for example, that a 'black Welsh Hobby, near 13 hand' had been stolen. From this, the word passed to the well known 'hobby horse', the figure of a horse 'ridden' by a performer in a morris dance, as well as a similar figure used as a toy. Such a model was sometimes also called simply a 'hobby', as in Scott's *The Abbot* (1820): 'Prance, hobby – hiss, dragon, and halloo boys!'. It was the full form 'hobby horse', however, that came to have the modern sense in the seventeenth century, first recorded in Sir Matthew Hale's *Contemplations Moral and Divine* (1676-7): 'Almost every person hath some hobby horse or other wherein he prides himself'. Finally, in the nineteenth century, the shorter form 'hobby' became the established word for a private leisure activity. The word has had some success in other languages, such as French *le hobby*, German *das Hobby*, and Russian *khobbi*.

holiday (day free from work, time of celebration or relaxation)
This is a classic 'sense-change' word, originating in the earliest times as a 'holy day' or religious festival, and progressing to the modern meaning. In fact, the 'progression' is not clearcut, since most early 'holy days' were also 'holidays' in the modern sense, that is, they were days when people did not work and when they celebrated, even if the celebration was for religious reasons. It was probably not until the fourteenth century that it was possible to distinguish a 'holiday'

as a 'non-working day' pure and simple, or as a day that was not also a church festival. Paradoxically, the earliest record we have of the word in this sense is in a religious context with a non-religious usage:

Iesus went him for to plai
With childir on a halidai
(*Cursor Mundi*, early fourteenth century).

hollyhock (tall plant with large coarse leaves and showy flowers)
In the thirteenth century, 'hollyhock' was the name of the marshmallow (*Althaea officinalis*). From the sixteenth century, however, the name came to apply to the present plant (*Althaea rosea*). This had been introduced to England from China, and when it reached the country it was given the old name 'hollyhock' by William Turner in *The Names of Herbes in Greke, Latin, Englishe, Duche* [i.e. German] *and French* (1548), where he wrote: 'Malua hortensis is of two kindes. The one is called alone in greeke Malache in englishe Holyoke, and of thys sorte is the iagged mallowe'. (He went on to distinguish this from 'Althea and Hibiscis [. . .] in englishe marrishe Marrowe'.)

holocaust (widespread destruction and loss of life, especially by fire)
The word, from Greek, literally means 'burnt whole', and originally was used in the thirteenth century of a whole burnt offering as a religious sacrifice, with this first recorded in *The Story of Genesis and Exodus* (1250):

Ysaac was leid that auter on,
So men sulden holocaust don.

(That is: Isaac was laid on the altar so that a whole burnt offering could be made.) In his Bible translation of 1526, Tindale rendered Mark 12:33: 'A greater thynge then all holocaustes and sacrifises' (Authorized Version of 1611: 'More than all whole burnt offerings and sacrifices'). From the fifteenth century, 'holocaust' came to mean any large or complete sacrifice, often in a figurative sense, as a 'holocaust of love'. From the seventeenth century, however, the connotation of 'destruction by fire' was usually present, as in Milton's *Samson Agonistes* (1671):

Like that self-begotten bird
In the Arabian woods embost,
That no second knows nor third,
And lay erewhile a Holocaust.

After the Second World War, the word was adopted to apply to the mass murder of the Jews by the Nazis in the war.

homage (formal respect or recognition of a person, reverential tribute)
As a term in thirteenth-century feudal law, 'homage' was the public acknowledgment of allegiance made by a tenant or vassal to his king or lord, to whom he bound himself in service. He thus 'rendered homage' or 'made homage' (or if renouncing his allegiance in a similar ceremony, 'resigned homage'). In the fourteenth century, the word passed to its modern sense of 'allegiance' or reference to anyone or anything regarded as superior, as in Shakespeare's *The Comedy of Errors* (1590), where Antipholus of Syracuse says to Luciana:

Your weeping sister is no wife of mine,
Nor to her bed no homage do I owe.

honest (fair, upright, sincere and trustworthy)
The word has been in use in English since the thirteenth century, when it also had the sense, now obsolete, of 'comely', 'decent in appearance', as in Wyclif's Bible of 1388, where he renders Ruth 3:3 as: 'Be thou waischun and anoynted, and be thou clothid with onestere clothis' (Authorized Version of 1611: 'Wash thyself therefore, and anoint thee, and put thy raiment upon thee'). In the fourteenth century, too, 'honest' could also mean 'chaste', as in Shakespeare's *The Merry Wives of Windsor* (1598), where Mistress Page says:

We'll leave a proof, by that which we will do,
Wives may be merry, and yet honest too.

This usage is also obsolete, and is not the one in the well-known 'She was poor but she was honest', which simply means 'respectable', 'of good repute'.

hoodwink (deceive, delude, cheat)
The word had a literal sense when first used in the sixteenth century, and this was 'blind-fold', 'cover a person's eyes to prevent him or her from seeing'. The use continued sporadically until as late as the nineteenth century, when Washington Irving in *Astoria, or Enterprise Beyond the Rocky Mountains* (1836), wrote: 'One of the savages attempted to hoodwink him with his buffalo robe with one hand, and to stab him with the other'. The transfer to figurative use, as if 'pulling the wool over' someone's eyes, arose in the seventeenth century.

horoscope (type of astrological forecast or prediction)
When first used in the eleventh century, a 'horoscope' was an astrological term for a diagram of the planets and signs of the zodiac at a given moment, especially at a person's birth, which was interpreted to foretell his or her destiny. Chaucer dealt with horoscopes in *A Treatise on the Astrolabe* (1391). The modern concept of the word, however, to mean hardly more than 'prediction of the future', whether made by a professional astrologer on an individual basis or 'en masse' by a popular personality, developed from the nineteenth century. The *Pall Mall Gazette* of 7 July 1886 had a report on an 'able and gifted lady' who 'makes horoscopes, but only to order: price, 100 francs'.

horrid (horrible, nasty, unpleasant)
The sixteenth-century sense of 'horrid' was 'bristling', 'shaggy', as exactly in its Latin origin, *horridus* (from *horrere*, 'to tremble'). To twentieth-century eyes, some contemporary texts can thus make strange reading, as Spenser's 'haughtie Helmet, horrid all with gold' (*The Faerie Queene*, 1590), and Pope's:

Ye grots and caverns shagg'd with horrid thorn!
(*Eloisa to Abelard*, 1717)

In a letter of 1740, too, Thomas Gray wrote of the Apennines: 'They are not so horrid as the Alps, though pretty near as high'. The modern sense of 'horrible' is, as so often, first recorded in Shakespeare, in *Twelfth Night* (1601), when Sir Toby Belch says: 'I will meditate the while upon some horrid message for a challenge'. However, from the seventeenth century the word came to be current in its weakened sense to mean simply 'nasty', 'not nice', with this usage described by the *OED:* 'especially frequent as a feminine term of strong aversion'. Thus Princess Alice, Queen Victoria's second daughter, wrote (although much later) in her *Biographical Sketch and Letters* (1878): 'The horrid weather has kept me in these three days'. Perhaps this feminine 'horrid' to some extent equated with the male 'horrible', or still does ('a horrid boy', 'a horrible little man').

hospice (nursing home for the terminally ill)
In its first use in English, in the nineteenth century, a 'hospice' (from the French) was a kind of 'hostel', specifically a place of rest and entertainment for travellers or strangers run by a religious order, and particularly one belonging to the St Bernard or St Gotthard monks in the Swiss Alps. However, as is evident from a report in *The Times* of 18 December 1894, the word could also apply to a similar establishment for poor people in Britain: 'The hospice provides 20 beds, soup, bread, and coals to families, and penny dinners to sandwich-men'. From this in turn came the twentieth-century 'hospice' as a nursing home for the dying, with this sense first emerging in the 1970s (too late for inclusion in Volume II (H-N) (1976) of the *Supplement to the Oxford English Dictionary*). This current meaning reinforces the etymological connection of the word with 'hospital' as well as 'hostel'. (See **hospital** itself in this respect.)

hospital (institution for the care of the sick and injured)
In the thirteenth century, a 'hospital' was a hostel or hospice, that is a place where travellers, pilgrims and strangers could stay. (Hence the establishments of the Knights Hospitallers.) From the fifteenth century, a 'hospital' was a charitable institution or 'asylum' for the poor and the sick. The word still exists in this sense in such names as Greenwich Hospital (now the Royal Naval College) and (later) Chelsea Hospital, both in London, the former for old sailors, the latter for old soldiers. Finally the modern meaning was established in the sixteenth century, when also, however, 'hospital'

came to be the term for an institution for educating the young, as still in Christ's Hospital (founded in 1553), the public school. 'Hospital' is closely linked etymologically with 'hospice' (see above), and both words are linked with 'hostel' and 'hotel', which themselves are virtually one and the same word in origin.

host (large number, multitude)
In the thirteenth century, 'host' was the word for 'army', with this sense surviving in such biblical and religious phrases as 'hosts of heaven' and 'Lord God of Hosts', both occurring in Wyclif's English translation (1382) of the Bible. In the seventeenth century, the word acquired its modern sense of 'large number', as in 'a host of ideas', 'a whole host of books'.

hoyden (boisterous girl)
In the sixteenth century, a 'hoyden' was a boor or 'rude fellow', and so male. From the seventeenth century, the term was transferred to a similar female, a rude or ill-bred woman or girl, or what used to be called a 'romp'. Wycherley's *The Plain Dealer* (1674) has a reference to a 'Mrs Hoyden, that calls all people by their surnames'. This is obviously not the origin of the now rather mannered word, however, which may perhaps be related to 'heathen'. It is the sort of word one would expect to find in Shakespeare, but it does not occur in any of his works.

humane (kindly and considerate; liberal)
The word obviously derives from 'human', and until the end of the eighteenth century was simply an alternative spelling for this, in its standard sense of 'pertaining to human beings'. From about 1700, however, 'humane' became fixed in this spelling (and with its differentiated pronunciation 'hum*a*ne') to apply to the two meanings mentioned above: 1) befitting a member of the human race, so kind, considerate and compassionate; 2) relating to studies that refine or liberalize ('humane' studies). The first of these gave the title of the Royal Humane Society, which was founded in 1774 (originally as the 'Society for the Recovery of Persons apparently drowned'). The second relates to 'humanism', orig-

inally (as recorded by Coleridge in 1812) as the belief in the mere human nature of Christ, then (from about 1830) as the term for a devotion to human interests or the humanities, with the word itself actually deriving from the sixteenth-century 'humanist' who was a person devoted to 'the humanities', or literary studies that concentrated on the Latin and Greek classics.

humiliate (lower the dignity of, mortify)
In the sixteenth century, 'humiliate' meant simply 'humble' (mostly oneself), as in prayer, worship or veneration. Bishop John Fisher's *Godlie Treatisse Declaryng the Benefites of Prayer* (1560) thus states: 'For God his wyll is, that we should humiliate and deiect our selues in the sight of his maiestie'. The present meaning evolved from the eighteenth century, and the earlier sense became obsolete.

humour (sense of what is comic, witty or entertaining; mood)
This word is one of the best-known 'sense-changers' in English. It arose in the fourteenth century to mean 'fluid', 'moisture', both generally, and, in the physiology of the time, one of the four chief fluids (so called 'cardinal humours') that were believed to be contained in the body, these being blood, phlegm, choler (yellow bile) and melancholy (black bile). The former, general sense can be seen in Wyclif's Bible of 1382, where he has in Jeremiah 17:8: 'As a tree, that is ouer plauntide vp on watris, that at the humour sendith his rootes' (Authorized Version of 1611: 'As a tree planted by the waters, and that spreadeth out her roots by the river'). The second sense explains the meaning of 'humour' in, for example, Shakespeare's *Love's Labour's Lost* (1588), where the King of Navarre reads the 'letter from the magnificent Armado': 'So it is, besieged with sable-coloured melancholy, I did commend the black-oppressing humour to the most wholesome physic of thy health-giving air'. The four 'humours' of the body were held to determine a person's particular physical and mental qualities, and this led to the sense 'mental disposition' for 'humour' in the fifteenth century and to the more general 'mood', as today, in the sixteenth. All these senses occur in Shakespeare, in various plays. The development of 'humour' to mean 'faculty of expressing the comic' came too late for him, however, and arose only in the late seventeenth century. In the title of Ben Jonson's play 'Every Man in his Humour' (1598), the word has the sense 'liking', 'fancy', 'whim', as in the modern 'when the humour takes me'. This particular meaning was very common in the late sixteenth and early seventeenth century.

hurt (harm, injure, wound)
When the word was first used in English in the twelfth century, it also meant 'knock', 'strike' (compare modern French *heurter* in this sense). In Wyclif's Bible of 1400 he even used the word of a ship in translating Acts 27:41: 'Whanne we felden into a place of grauel [...] thei hurten the schippe' (Authorized Version of 1611: 'And falling into a place where two seas met, they ran the ship aground'). In his earlier translation of 1382 he used the word more regularly in this basic sense, as in John 11:9: 'If ony man shal wandre in the day, he hirtith not' (Authorized Version: 'If any man walk in the day, he stumbleth not'). This literal usage became obsolete from about the sixteenth century, however, and the current sense prevailed.

husband (married man)
In Old English, a *hūsbonda* was in a sense literally 'housebound', as the word suggests, since he was the 'master of the household', or 'bound' to the house and his family. He would have been married, of course, and had a wife, but it was his domestic position and obligation that lay behind the word that described him, not his marital status. From the thirteenth century, the word came to have its modern sense, although it also acquired the now obsolete meaning 'husbandman', 'tiller of the soil'. This was thus an extension of the duties of the male head of the household, now seen as a farmer and cultivator of land. From the fifteenth century, 'husband' was used to apply to a housekeeper or steward, as in a letter from Sir John Paston to his mother in 1475, where he writes: 'I purpose to leeffe alle heer, and come home to yow, and be yowr hosbonde and balyff'. In the sixteenth

century, as an extension of this, a 'husband' could be used of a man who managed affairs generally, and this is the sense in Defoe's *Robinson Crusoe* (1719) when Crusoe says: 'I had been so good a husband of my rum, that I had a great deal left' (This use still survives in the verb 'to husband' today.)

hussy (disreputable or immoral woman)
The word comes from 'housewife', and this is what it originally meant, with no derogatory sense, in the sixteenth century. On the contrary, it could even imply 'thrifty woman', as in Defoe's *Colonel Jack* (1722): 'Her being so good a hussy of what money I had left her'. From the seventeenth century, however, the word acquired its present opprobrious sense. As first used thus, 'hussy' was usually preceded by an adjective, such as 'light' (i.e. immoral, 'wanton') or 'little'. Such usage can be found, for example, in Swift's *Polite Conversation* (1738): 'No, Miss; you are very light; but I don't say, you are a light Hussy', and in a letter of 24 April 1775 by Madame d'Arblay (Fanny Burney), in which she tells how a certain gentleman 'patted my cheek, and genteely called me a little hussey'.

hutch (pen or coop for a small animal, such as a rabbit)
The fourteenth-century meaning of 'hutch' was 'chest', 'coffer', i.e. a container for storing things, such as clothes or money. It was only in the seventeenth century that the word came to apply to an animal's cage or pen, as well as a small cabin or hut where a human being could live or work. In Defoe's *Robinson Crusoe* (1719), the castaway records: 'I cannot express what a satisfaction it was to me to come into my old hutch'.

hypochondria (morbid concern about one's health)
In the sixteenth century, 'hypochondria' was a term for the upper abdomen, those organs under the ribs, such as the liver, gall bladder, spleen and so on, that were believed to be the source of melancholy and 'vapours'. In his *Select Discourses* (1652), the Platonist philosopher John Smith wrote that: 'If our spleen or hypochondria [. . .] send up such melancholic fumes into our heads as move us to sadness and timorous-

ness, we cannot justly call that vice'. From the seventeenth century the word acquired a developed sense 'morbid state of mind', 'melancholy for which there is no apparent cause', with this usage first recorded in Dryden's *An Evening's Love* (1668): 'I know what you would say, that it is melancholy; a tincture of the hypochondria you mean'. In its current pathological (or popular) sense, 'undue concern or anxiety about one's health', the word dates from the nineteenth century (or, in the form 'hypochondriasis', from the eighteenth).

icon, ikon (religious picture or image used as object of devotion in the Orthodox Church)
The origin of the word is Greek *eikōn*, 'image', 'likeness', and in the sixteenth century the first meaning in English was simply this, 'image' or 'picture', especially an illustration or 'cut' of an animal or plant in a natural history book. In 1710, for example, William Salmon published his 'Botanologia; an English Herbal', described by him as 'beautifully adorned with exquisite Icons or Figures of the most considerable Species'. The modern meaning of 'icon', as used by the Eastern Orthodox Church, arose only in the nineteenth century, when detailed travel accounts of life and customs in Russia and other eastern European countries were first widely published in English (such as Robert Pinkerton's *Russia* of 1833, or Sir Donald Mackenzie Wallace's book of the same title of 1877).

idiom (distinctive expression of a particular language, especially one that does not obey standard grammatical rules or have a literal meaning)

The kind of 'idiom' defined here is the one that is the most widely known. Yet the word also has other meanings, still current, that existed earlier than this. In the sixteenth century, 'idiom' came to be the term for the particular language of a country, its 'native tongue', as the 'English idiom' or the 'vernacular idiom'. At the same time, 'idiom' also meant the language or dialect used by a particular group or class of people. Thus John Davies, in his translation (1662) of *The Travels of Mandelslo from Persia into the East-Indies* wrote that the Chinese: 'when they speak, cannot understand one the other, by reason of the diversity of the Idioms and Dialects that is among the Inhabitants of several Provinces'. Also in the sixteenth century, 'idiom' could be the word to apply to the particular character of a language, its special manner of expression, as the 'French idiom' found in English culinary terms, or the 'grammatical idiom' common to French and Spanish. The modern sense of 'idiom', as defined above, evolved only in the seventeenth century, and the even more recent and general sense of 'characteristic style or form' (as jazz in the 'New Orleans idiom' or painting in the 'surrealist idiom') was a development of the twentieth century. This usage particularly applies to literary, artistic or musical styles.

ignore (refuse to notice, pay no attention to)
The modern French verb *ignorer* means 'not to know', and this was the original sense of the word in English (compare 'ignorance'). It was used frequently by the scientist Robert Boyle (who once compared 'the little that I know, and they [his students] ignore'), and some people believed that he imported it into English. Dr Johnson was one of them and wrote of the word in his *Dictionary* (1755): 'This word Boyle endeavoured to introduce, but it has not been received'. However, 'ignore' was in use before Boyle's time, and he was thus not the first to use it. The current meaning arose only in the nineteenth century.

ilk (sort, kind)
The definition of the word given here is not the correct usage, although it is the popular one (as in 'leftwingers and others of that ilk'). In Old English, and so properly, it meant 'same', and is in fact related to 'like'. The early fourteenth-century *Cursor Mundi* thus told how Adam's son, Seth, went 'To paradis that ilke day'. The word survives (apart from the popular sense) only in the phrase 'of that Ilk' in Scottish titles, as 'Stuart of that Ilk', meaning 'Stuart of Stuart', i.e. Stuart of the same name or family. The usage is traditionally connected with the heads of Highland clans.

illumination (lighting; decorative embellishment of medieval manuscript)
The first sense of 'illumination', in fourteenth-century English, was 'spiritual enlightenment', and the earliest English translation (1450) of *De imitatione Christi* ('The Imitation of Christ') contained 'A praier for illuminacion of mynde'. The second sense to develop, in the sixteenth century, was 'lighting up', as in the 'illumination of public streets' or the well-known 'Blackpool Illuminations'. The final sense, although applied to an activity that easily pre-dates it historically, was that of 'decoration of a manuscript', with this usage recorded first in the seventeenth century. The reason for its late appearance is that the related verb, 'illuminate', replaced the earlier 'enlumine' in the eighteenth century, and this former verb, now obsolete, was the contemporary one to be used of medieval manuscripts, and occurs in Chaucer, for example. Compare **illustration** (below).

illustration (drawing or picture accompanying a text or in a book)
The earliest use of 'illustration' in English was in the fourteenth century, when it had the same meaning as '**illumination**' (see above), that is, it meant 'enlightenment'. Its use continued for some time, and the word is found, for example in *The Pilgrimage of Perfection* (1526): 'The persone that receyueth suche illustracyon or lyght, is all quyet & restfull bothe in soule & body'. In the sixteenth century, the meaning had developed to 'example', 'elucidation', 'explanation', so that John Smith, in *The Mysterie of Rhetorique Unvail'd* (1657), wrote that 'antithesis' was 'the illustration of a thing by its opposite'. Finally, in the nineteenth century, the word came to have its

current sense, and one of the earliest records of it can be found in an advertisement in *The Quarterly Review* for February 1817: 'Westall's Illustrations to the Works of Walter Scott, Esq. In 8vo, beautifully engraved from the Paintings of R. Westall, R.A.'.

imagination (act of or capacity for forming a mental picture)
The present usage has been current since the word first entered English in the fourteenth century. Another sense of similar date, however, has now become obsolete. This was 'scheming', 'planning', 'devising', now familiar only from the Bible, as for example in Lamentations 3:60: 'Thou hast seen all their vengeance and all their imaginations against me'. So similarly with the corresponding verb, in the perhaps more familiar quotation from Psalm 2:1: 'Why do the heathen rage, and the people imagine a vain thing?'. 'Imagination' in this sense has been obsolete since the eighteenth century.

imbecile (idiot, mental defective)
As an adjective, 'imbecile' originally meant 'weak' generally in the sixteenth century. Thus a translation (1599) of Gabelhouez's *Boock of Physicke* states that in one condition a patient may 'drinck verye smalle, and imbecille wynes, and take heede of all manner of strong wynes what soever'. Only in the nineteenth century did the word come to mean 'mentally weak', 'idiotic', and the noun from this appeared at the same time. Until the nineteenth century, the adjective was usually rhymed with 'trestle', by confusion with 'embezzle'.

immaterial (unimportant)
The proper sense of the word, of course, is 'not consisting of matter', otherwise 'incorporeal', and this was its original meaning from the fourteenth century (although not commonly until the sixteenth). The current popular meaning 'unimportant' evolved in the seventeenth century, and was disapproved of by Dr Johnson, who wrote of it in his *Dictionary* (1755): 'This sense has crept into the conversation and writings of barbarians'.

immune (free, especially from infection or contagion)
From the fifteenth century, the word meant 'free', 'exempt' generally, much as it does now ('immune from taxation'). In the seventeenth century, however, this usage became obsolete, and the next sense to emerge was the nineteenth-century one (borrowed from French *immune*) meaning specifically 'safe from infection'. This was in about 1880, and some twenty years later, the word once again acquired (or reacquired) its general sense, so that the *Daily News* of 5 July 1900 was able to report on 'a man whose achievements should render him immune from all mud throwing'.

imp (little devil, mischievous child)
In Old English, an *impa* was a young shoot or sapling (from the verb *impian*, 'to graft', 'implant'). Hence Chaucer wrote in the *Canterbury Tales* ('The Monk's Prologue') (1386):

> Of fieble trees ther comen wrecched ympes.

From the fourteenth century, the sense was extended to mean 'offspring', 'child' (usually a boy), as in the epitaph (1584) to Lord Denbigh in the Beauchamp Chapel of St Mary's Church, Warwick, which reads: 'Heere resteth the body of the noble Impe Robert of Dvdley [. . .] sonne of Robert Erle of Leycester'. (This was Robert Dudley, the young son of Robert Dudley, Earl of Leicester, the courtier and favourite of Queen Elizabeth.) From the sixteenth century, the sense of 'imp' progressed (or retrogressed) to mean 'child of the devil', 'little demon', that is, an evil spirit, especially one of the kind that witches were said to be familiar with. Finally, from the seventeenth century, the word took on its modern sense of 'mischievous child', or 'little devil' of the human variety. In *Gulliver's Travels* (1727), Gulliver (through his author Swift) tells how he caught a young male Yahoo aged three, 'but the little imp fell a squalling, and scratching, and biting'.

impertinent (cheeky, insolent)
The literal sense is 'not pertinent', or 'irrelevant', and this was what the word meant in the fourteenth century. The usage comes

in Shakespeare's *The Tempest* (1610), where Prospero says to Miranda:

> Hear a little further,
> And then I'll bring thee to the present
> business
> Which now's upon us; without the which
> this story
> Were most impertinent.

From the sixteenth century, 'impertinent' meant also 'inappropriate', 'absurd', 'silly'. John Davies, in his translation (1662) of Olearius' *Voyages and Travels of the Ambassadors Sent [. . .] to the Great Duke of Muscovy*, wrote that: 'The opinion the Muscovites have of themselves and their abilities, is sottish, gross, and impertinent'. In the seventeenth century the modern sense evolved, so that Lady Mary Wortley Montagu, in a letter of 30 August 1716, could write to Mrs Thistlethwaite: 'It is publicly whispered, as a piece of impertinent pride in me, that I have hitherto been saucily civil to everybody'.

impinge (make an impression, encroach)
From the sixteenth century, 'impinge' has been used literally, although decreasingly so, in the sense 'strike', 'hit'. Thus Robert Burton, in *The Anatomy of Melancholy* (1621), wrote that: 'A ship that is void of a Pilot, must needs impinge upon the next rock or sands, and suffer shipwrack'. From the eighteenth century, however, the figurative use of the verb has been used increasingly frequently, and this is the popular usage of 'impinge' today.

imply (express indirectly)
In the fourteenth century, 'imply' could mean 'enfold' or 'involve' both literally and figuratively. Spenser used it in a literal sense, for example, in *The Faerie Queene* (1590–6):

> An hatefull Snake, the which his taile
> uptyes
> In many folds, and mortall sting
> implyes.

The current sense evolved in the sixteenth century. The word is ultimately from Latin *implicare*, 'to fold in', so is directly related to 'implicate'.

improve (enhance, raise to better or higher status, quality etc.)
In the sixteenth century, the verb meant 'turn to profit', either of money or land, so that a will recorded in the Bury St Edmunds Register in 1646, for example, contains the clause: 'Item I give vnto Frances Browne, my grandchilde, fifty pounds, to be payd into her father's hands [. . .] and to be improved by him for her vse, and to be payed to her at her age of sixteene years'. The use of the verb as applied to land was common in the seventeeth and eighteenth centuries in the American colonies, for example: 'Where lands lye in common unfenced, if one man shall improve his land by fencing in several, and another shall not, he who shall so improve shall secure his lands against other men's cattle' (*Massachusetts Colony Laws*, 1642). The general sense, 'enhance', 'raise in quality', finally developed in the seventeenth century, and these now obsolete specialized uses have blended with it. Etymologically, 'improve' is not related to 'prove' or 'approve', but derives from Old French *prou*, 'advantage', itself related to Latin *prodest*, 'it is of advantage'.

impudent (insolent, cheeky)
The word can be easily analysed into 'im-pudent' (so to speak), and so to mean 'lacking pudency', or more simply, 'immodest', and this was its original sense in the fourteenth century. The usage comes in Chaucer, and also in the Bible, in Ecclesiasticus 19:2:'He that cleaveth to harlots will become impudent'. The present-day sense emerged in the sixteenth century.

inane (silly)
The current sense of the word is a weaker usage that the original, which in the seventeenth century was 'empty' (from Latin *inanis*). 'Inane' was even used as a noun in this meaning, mostly with reference to the 'formless void' of infinity or space, as in Samuel Parker's *Six Philosophical Essays* (1700), where he wrote of atoms ' . . . dispers'd and dancing in the great Inane'. In the nineteenth century, 'inane' came to mean 'empty-headed', with this sense first recorded in Shelley's tragedy *The Cenci*

(1819), in 'some inane and vacant smile'. From this the current usage developed.

inborn (inherited, innate)
In Old English, 'inborn' (*inboren*) meant 'native', 'born in a particular place', a usage that continued sporadically from the seventeenth century when the long disused original word had been forgotten and was 're-created'. For example, Philemon Holland's translation (1609) of Marcellinus' *Roman Historie* mentions hills that ' . . .were passable for none but the inborne inhabitants that knew the wayes verie well'. The modern usage of 'inborn' dates from the sixteenth century.

inclement (rainy, stormy, bad)
Today the word is used only of weather. Originally, when the current sense also arose in the seventeenth century, 'inclement' could also mean literally 'not clement', 'showing no clemency', and the use is illustrated punningly by John Molle in his translation (1621) of Camerarius' *Living Librarie* when he says (echoing the pun in the Latin original): 'Pope Clement the fift, was inclement and cruell'. It seems to have been Milton who introduced the modern sense, or at any rate influenced its development, from his line in *Paradise Lost* (1667):

> Th' inclement Seasons, Rain, Ice, Hail and Snow.

income (money earned, salary)
In the thirteenth century, 'income' meant literally what it says, 'arrival', 'coming in'. The use is first recorded in the fourteenth-century *Cursor Mundi*:

> At the income of the firth monet [i.e. first month]
> Ioseph him went to nazareth.

Shakespeare uses the word in the same sense in *The Rape of Lucrece* (1593):

> Pain pays the income of each precious thing.

From the sixteenth century, 'income' came to mean 'fee paid on entering', 'admission fee'. The usage could be literal or figurative, as in a sermon by the Puritan preacher

William Bridge written in 1646: 'There are no In-com's, no Incom's to be paid at our coming in to Jesus Christ'. The modern meaning developed from the seventeenth century, with 'income tax' first recorded in 1799.

incomprehensible (not understandable, unintelligible)
As first used in English in the fourteenth century, 'incomprehensible' meant 'unable to be understood', 'passing all understanding', so therefore 'limitless', 'boundless'. The sense was chiefly associated with theological use, as especially in the Athanasian Creed (in the Book of Common Prayer), which defines the Trinity in terms of: 'The Father uncreate, the Son uncreate: and the Holy Ghost uncreate. The Father incomprehensible, the Son incomprehensible: and the Holy Ghost incomprehensible. The Father eternal, the Son eternal; and the Holy Ghost eternal'. The modern sense was first current in the seventeenth century.

indent (make an official order)
The literal sense of the word is 'make a toothlike notch in', and this is the origin of the 'indenture', or official deed or document detailing an agreement between two parties, since in the fourteenth century, and for some time after, corresponding documents were identically 'indented' or notched in the different copies, showing that they agreed. The original procedure was as follows: the copies were written on one piece of parchment or paper, and then cut in two in a wavy or jagged line, so that when brought together again at any time, the two edges exactly tallied and showed that they were parts of one and the same original document. (Hence the expression 'pair of indentures'.) From this, to 'indent' came to mean 'draw up a contract', 'make a requisition' in subsequent years. The special typographical sense 'indent', meaning 'set in from the margin', developed in the seventeenth century.

indifferent (not interested; mediocre, not very good)
The original fourteenth-century meaning of the word was 'neutral', 'impartial', 'disin-

terested', so that one could have an 'indifferent' judge or 'indifferent' justice (i.e. fair and even-handed). Both current senses 'immaterial' and 'neither good nor bad' evolved in the sixteenth century, although the euphemistic use to mean 'not very good' (as 'indifferent' health or an 'indifferent' performance) arose about a hundred years later.

indiscreet (not discreet, injudicious)
In the fifteenth century, 'indiscreet' meant 'lacking discernment', as in Chapman's translation (1611) of Homer's *Iliad:*

O Priam! thou are always pleased with indiscreet advice.

Current usage dates from the sixteenth century, and is first recorded in Shakespeare's *Love's Labour's Lost* (1588), where Sir Nathaniel says it would ill become him 'to be vain, indiscreet, or a fool'.

indisposed (slightly unwell; not inclined)
Before it acquired its current euphemistic usage to mean 'slightly unwell' (sometimes resorted to by actresses and female performers, who do not wish to be more specific), the word had a number of now obsolete senses. In the fifteenth century, 'indisposed' could mean 'not in order', 'not fitted', or 'ill-disposed'. The first of these occurs, for example, in the *Orologium sapientiae or the Seven Poyntes of Trewe Wisdom* (1425): 'I have so litil fors taken of indisposed deth'. (This is the earliest record we have of the word. The sentence means: 'I have done so little to prepare for a sudden death', that is, one that is 'out of order'.) The 'slightly unwell' sense occurred early enough for a character in Massinger's play *The Duke of Milan* (1623) to escape an interview by saying:

If I am sought for,
Say I am indisposed.

The meaning 'not inclined' arose in the seventeenth century.

individual (single, separate)
Although not in common use, 'individual' was sometimes employed in the sense 'indivisible' from the fifteenth century, and was even contrasted with its opposite, 'dividual',

as in the following extract from Martin Fotherby's *Atheomastix* (1619): 'Some make their god of Atomes, and indiuidual moates [i.e. particles]: some of diuidual numbers; as Epicurus, and Pythagoras'. The modern sense became established from the seventeenth century.

industry (diligence; manufacturing concern)
In the fifteenth century, 'industry' meant 'skill', 'dexterity', with this sense first recorded in Caxton's translation (1477) *The Historie of Jason:* 'I shal deliuere to him the industrie and teche him how he shal wynne the flees of golde'. Similarly, 'industrious' meant 'skilful' before it acquired its present sense, which dates from the sixteenth century, as do the current meanings of 'industry'. However, 'industriously' meant 'intentionally' for a while from the seventeenth century, with this usage first recorded in Shakespeare's *The Winter's Tale* (1611), where Camillo says to Leontes:

If industriously
I played the fool, it was my negligence,
Not weighing well the end.

For this use, the derivation was taken from the Latin phrase *de industria*, 'of set purpose', 'deliberately' (found in Terence and Cicero), rather than Latin *industria*, 'diligence', which gave the other modern English words.

infant (young child, baby)
When first used in English in the fourteenth century, 'infant' could apply to a child of any age, not simply a young one, as now. Examples of the sense can be found in various translations of the Bible. In Wyclif's version of 1382, for instance, he renders Zechariah 8:5 as: 'And streetis of the citee shuln be fulfilled with infauntis and maydens, pleyinge in the stretis of it' (Authorized Version of 1611: 'And the streets of the city shall be filled with boys and girls playing in the streets thereof'). In the Rhemish New Testament (1582), however, Luke 18:15 appears as: 'They brought vnto him infants that he might touche them' (Authorized Version virtually the same), showing that the meaning had become restricted in the current sense. The

use of 'infant', to mean 'minor' in the legal sense, developed out of Anglo-Norman in the sixteenth century. The origin of the word is Latin *infans*, 'unable to speak'.

infest (swarm in, live on parasitically)
The fifteenth-century sense of 'infest' was 'attack', 'harass', with this use persisting even until the nineteenth century, so that Walter Landor, in one of his *Imaginary Conversations* (1824–9), has a character say: 'I am infested and persecuted and worried to death by duns [i.e. creditors]'. The modern meaning dates from the seventeenth century.

infirm (feeble through age or sickness)
The earliest sense of 'infirm', in the fourteenth century, was 'weak', 'unsound', as applied to a structure, for example, or the rays of the sun. In *The Religion of Protestants A Safe Way to Salvation* (1638), William Chillingworth wrote: 'A building cannot be stable, if any of the necessary pillars thereof be infirme and instable'. The current meaning dates from the time of Shakespeare, and indeed is first recorded in his *King Lear* (1605), where the word comes more than once, as when Lear, speaking of himself, says to the Fool:

A poor, infirm, weak, and despis'd old man.

From 'infirm' the adjective, the noun 'infirmary' developed in the seventeenth century to apply to a hospital, and many old or famous hospitals are still called 'Infirmary' today, such as the Royal Infirmary, Edinburgh and the Radcliffe Infirmary, Oxford.

influence (power to achieve some effect or result)
The word literally means 'in-flowing', and in the fourteenth century was an astrological term applied to the supposed 'in-flowing' or streaming from the stars or the heavens of an ethereal fluid, held to affect the lives of men on earth. The sense is first recorded in Chaucer, but also occurs, for example, in Caxton's translation (1483) *Caton:* 'The synne whyche I haue doon ageynst myn owne wylle and by the influence of the planette on which I am borne'. Similarly,

the word comes in the Bible (Job 38:31: 'Canst thou bind the sweet influences of Pleiades, or loose the bands of Orion?') and in Shakespeare's *Hamlet* (1602), where Horatio speaks of the death of Julius Caesar, when:

The moist star
Upon whose influence Neptune's empire stands
Was sick almost to doomsday with eclipse.

In the fifteenth century, 'influence' came to mean 'infusion of power' especially of a divine or spiritual kind, as the 'pure influence flowing from the glory of the Almighty' in the Bible (Wisdom of Solomon, 7:25). Finally, the modern meaning of 'influence' arose in the sixteenth century, where Shakespeare, as in many other cases, was among the first to introduce and exploit it. Thus in *Love's Labour's Lost* (1588), near the end of the play, Rosaline says:

Why, that's the way to choke a gibing spirit,
Whose influence is begot of that loose grace
Which shallow laughing hearers give to fools.

ingenious (original, inventive, resourceful)
In the fifteenth century, 'ingenious' meant 'very clever', 'talented', with this now obsolete sense occurring, for example, in Shakespeare's *Richard III* (1594), where Gloucester says of York:

O! 'tis a parlous boy;
Bold, quick, ingenious, forward, capable.

The modern use arose in the sixteenth century, while at the same time 'ingenious' began to be used for '**ingenuous**' (which see, below). Thus William Beveridge, Bishop of St Asaph, in a sermon published in 1680 spoke of an 'ingenious confession', and, in the 'well-born' sense of 'ingenuous', Joseph Washington, in his translation (1692) *A Defence of the People of England by John Milton,* wrote: 'All manner of Slavery is scandalous and disgraceful to a freeborn ingenious Person.'. This erroneous use is still current today, and for similar confusion of 'ingenuous' and 'ingenious', see below.

ingenuous (frank and candid, innocent in a childlike or gullible way)
The current sense 'frank', 'open' (as an 'ingenuous' smile or an 'ingenuous' confession) dates from the sixteenth century, when also the now obsolete sense 'noble-minded' arose. This even came to mean 'free-born', 'high-class', deriving direct from the Latin word *ingenuus*, as when Charles Merivale, in *A History of the Romans under the Empire* (1850–62) wrote that Augustus allowed Roman citizens to intermarry with freedwomen ' . . .because the females of ingenuous birth were not numerous enough to mate them'. Perhaps the use of the word in the context of Roman history is defensible, considering its Latin origin, but it is still misleading. The modern popular usage of 'ingenuous' to mean 'innocent', 'naive' arose in the seventeenth century. And, just as 'ingenious' came to be wrongly used for 'ingenuous', so the opposite happened, with several quite well known writers using 'ingenuous' when they meant 'ingenious', especially in the seventeenth century when the two words first became widely current. Even Shakespeare gets it wrong in *Love's Labour's Lost* (1588), in the scene where Holofernes (who admittedly is a pompous schoolmaster) says: 'If their sons be ingenuous, they shall want no instruction'. The noun 'ingenuity' underwent a similar development to 'ingenuous', even meaning 'ingenuousness' itself for a while until, in the seventeenth century, it settled to its current sense of 'cleverness in contriving'.

inmate (person living in an institution of some kind; fellow resident)
In the sixteenth century, 'inmate' was more or less a legal term for a lodger or subtenant, and an Act of 1589 declared: 'There shall not be any Inmate or more Famylies or Housholdes than one, dwellinge or inhabitinge in anye one Cottage'. The current sense developed from about the same time, however, with the 'institutional' connotation (the 'inmate' of a prison or mental hospital, for example) arising in the nineteenth century. The derivation of the word

is not from 'in' but from 'inn', from the idea of such a person living in a lodging house. See **inn** itself (below).

inn (small hotel, public house)
In Old English, an 'inn' was simply a dwelling-place, somewhere where a person lived, his or her 'house'. In John de Trevisa's translation (1387) of Ranulf Higden's *Polychronicon*, he thus wrote: 'In the side of the hille was the yn of Lazarus, of Martha, and of Marie Mawdeleyn; that toun hight [i.e. was called] Bethania'. The current meaning, both 'hotel' and 'lodging-house' (for law or university students), dates from the fourteenth century. This use survives in London's 'Inns of Chancery' and 'Inns of Court' as buildings with historic legal ties, and there was a 'New Inn Hall' in Oxford until the nineteenth century (when it was merged with Balliol College).

inoculate (vaccinate)
The origin of the word lies in the Latin verb *inoculare*, 'to implant', 'engraft' (in turn from *oculus*, 'eye', 'bud'), and this horticultural usage was the first to develop in English, in the fifteenth century. The prodigious correspondent Mrs Mary Delany recorded in one of her many letters (1752): 'I have just inoculated two orange-tress of my own raising'. The medical sense evolved in the eighteenth century (originally in the noun 'inoculation') with, at first, specific application to smallpox. 'Vaccination' was at first called 'vaccine inoculation' (meaning inoculation of the cowpox virus).

insight (power of discernment, penetration by understanding)
As first used in the twelfth century, 'insight' meant 'inner sight', that is, a vision or understanding *in* the mind (as distinct from the current concept of a 'sight' *into* something). The earliest record of the word in English is in the long poem called *The Ormulum*, written in the early thirteenth century by a monk named either Orm or Ormin. (As the extract following shows, the monk had his own special kind of spelling.) 'He ghifethth himm [. . .] innsihht tunderstanndenn all thatt mann maghgh unnderstanndenn'. This sense became obsolete in

the seventeenth century, and the modern meaning was first recorded in the sixteenth.

insolent (impudent, showing disrespect)
When first current in English in the fourteenth century, 'insolent' meant 'haughty' 'arrogant'. The word occurs in poetry as late as the nineteenth century, for example in Shelley's 'lyrical drama' *Hellas* (1821):

> One star with insolent and victorious light
> Hovers above its fall.

The present sense of 'insolent' dates from the sixteenth century.

install (place in office, establish)
The verb really means what it says, and its earliest sense, current from the sixteenth century, thus was 'place in office by seating in a stall or official seat', with particular reference to a canon in the choirstall of a cathedral, or to a Knight of the Garter or a Knight of the Bath in the stall of the chapel of his particular order. Edward Hall's *Chronicle* (1548) tells how, 'to be had in the more reputacion', Cardinal Wolsey 'determined to be installed or inthronised at Yorke'. By the eighteenth century, however, 'install' had come to mean 'instate', 'place in office' generally. The sense 'fix in position' (as when 'installing' a fireplace or a telephone) arose in the nineteenth century and was a borrowing from the French verb *installer*.

instantly (immediately)
In the fifteenth century, 'instantly' meant either 'urgently' or 'just now'. In his translation (1477) *The Historie of Jason*, thus, Caxton wrote: 'When he had required them instantly and admonested them to doo well he dide doo marche them ayenst their enemyes'. In the Bible, too, Luke 7:4 has: 'And when they came to Jesus, they besought him instantly'. The 'just now' use of 'instantly' survived until as late as the seventeenth century, when in William Lithgow's *The Totall Discourse of the Rare Adventures and Painfull Peregrinations of long Nineteene Yeares Trawayles* (1632), the intrepid Scottish traveller tells how on arriving at Messina, he met two Englishmen 'who instantly were both come from Malta'. The

current meaning of the adverb dates from the sixteenth century.

insulate (detach from contact, influence, etc.)
Latin *insula* means 'island', and when first used in English in the sixteenth century, 'insulate' meant 'turn into an island'. The great antiquarian tourist John Leland, in his *Itinerary* (1552), describes how: 'The Ryver of Avon so windeth aboute Oundale Toune [i.e. Oundle] that it almost insulatithe it, savyng a little by West North West'. (The river at Oundle is in fact the Nene.) Both the modern general sense of 'insulate' and the electrical and heating one date from the eighteenth century. The closely related 'isolate' has the same 'island' origin.

insult (treat with scorn or abuse, cause offence)
As first current in the sixteenth century, to 'insult' was to triumph over someone, or boast over them. Fynes Moryson, in *An Itinerary* (1617), commented: 'Nothing is more frequent, then for little girles to insult over their brothers much bigger than they, reproving their doings'. Pepys, too, in the entry of 16 June 1666 in his *Diary*, noted that: 'The Dutch do mightily insult of their victory, and they have great reason'. The present common meaning of 'insult' dates from the seventeenth century.

intercede (intervene on behalf of someone else)
The word literally means 'go between', and this was what it meant (more precisely 'come between') when first in use in the sixteenth century. Thomas Granger, in *Syntagma Logicum, or the divine Logike* (1620), thus observed: 'When one thing mooveth, and another is moved, motion intercedeth', and Robert Cary, in *Palaeologia chronica; or a Chronological Account of ancient Time* (1677), mentions that between two particular events 'there do intercede 51 Years'. The modern sense developed from the seventeenth century. Compare **intervene** (below).

interfere (meddle, impede, intervene unnecessarily)
This common verb, seemingly so innocent, has a highly specialized original sense. It

literally means 'strike each other', ultimately from Latin *inter-*, 'each other' and *ferire*, 'to strike', and in the sixteenth century it was the word used to describe the action of a horse when it struck the inside of one of its fetlocks with the hoof of the opposite foot, so knocking one leg against the other. It is necessary to know this in order to understand such extracts as the following properly:

> My horse to weare greate breeches is
> now asynde [i.e. assigned]:
> Why? to keep him from enterferyng
> behynde
> (John Heywood, *A Dialogue Conteynyng
> Prouerbes and Epigrammes*, 1562)

From the seventeeth century, the sense was extended to apply to any things that collided, clashed or struck each other, both literally and figuratively. In Thomas Scott's sermons *The High-waies of God and the King* (1620), for example, he speaks of someone 'with eyes staring [and] teeth grating and interfering', and as late as 1762, in his *History of Great Britain*, Hume wrote that: 'The two republics were not inflamed by any national antipathy, and their interests very little interfered'. The current sense dates from the sixteenth century, while the specific connotation 'intervene', 'interpose' (as when 'interfering' in a domestic quarrel) arose some hundred years later.

interlude (interval, intermission)
The word is older than it might perhaps appear. In the fourteenth century, an 'interlude' (literally 'between-play') was a light or humorous dramatic performance or piece of mimicry inserted in a longer, and more solemn mystery play, where it served as contrasting material and also as a sort of medieval 'commercial break'. Later, in the seventeenth and eighteenth centuries, the term was used for a popular stage play, such as a comedy or farce. Also from the seventeenth century, however, an 'interlude' was simply an interval in the performance of a play, whether simply a break between the acts or an organized entertainment of some kind. This is the sort of interlude that Dryden was referring to in *The Cock and the Fox* (1700):

> Dreams are but interludes which fancy
> makes;
> When monarch reason sleeps, this mimic
> wakes.

Finally, 'interlude' came to mean no more than 'intervening period of time', with this sense developing in the eighteenth century.

internecine (mutually destructive)
This word is a red herring, since its first half is not the usual 'between' *inter-* at all. It comes from Latin *internecare*, where the basic word is *necare*, 'to kill' and the *inter-* is an 'intensive' prefix, giving an overall sense of 'kill down to the last man', 'destroy'. In its proper sense, therefore, 'internecine' means 'accompanied by great killing', and this interpretation was the one made by Butler to translate Latin *internecinum bellum* in his *Hudibras* (1663):

> Th' Ægyptians worshipp'd Dogs, and for
> Their Faith made internecine war.

(In the 1674 edition, he changed 'internecine' to 'fierce and zealous'.) However, perhaps understandably, Johnson misinterpreted the meaning of 'internecine' in his *Dictionary* (1755) as 'endeavouring mutual destruction', taking the 'inter-' to mean 'each other' as it often does, and that is the sense the word now has.

intervene (fall between, in time; interfere by force)
Like '**interfere**' (which compare, above), 'intervene' originally meant 'come between' when first used in the sixteenth century. Even as late as 1839, De Quincey used the now obsolete meaning in *Recollections of the Lakes and the Lake Poets*, when he wrote of woodlands 'that meander through the valley, intervening the different estates with natural sylvan marches'. It was in the seventeenth century that the present senses emerged.

intrigue (secret plot)
The word dates from the seventeenth century in English use, when it could also mean simply 'intricacy', 'something complex or mazelike'. Thus in *Charles II's Escape from Worcester* (1660), one can read how: 'His majesty was had to his lodging,

and the intrigues of it shewn him'. This usage was virtually obsolete by the end of the century, however, and the modern sense was the one that lasted.

intuition (immediate insight, instinctive knowledge)
When first current in the fifteenth century (although rarely in this sense before the seventeenth), 'intuition' meant 'contemplation', 'view'. The preacher Jeremy Taylor thus wrote, in *The Great Exemplar of Sanctity and Holy Life* (1649), that 'disciples must not onely abstain from the act of unlawfull concubinate, but from the impurer intuition of a wife of another man'. A similar obsolete use of the word, in the sixteenth century, was to mean 'regard', 'reference', so that 'with intuition to' meant 'with reference to', and 'in intuition to' meant 'in respect of'. The current popular sense has been in use since the eighteenth century.

inveigle (win by enticing, flattery or deceit)
At first, in the fifteenth century, 'inveigle' meant 'deceive', 'beguile', so that Latimer, in a sermon of 1552, wrote that the devil 'intendeth to inveigle even very kings, and to make them negligent in their business and office'. The present use of the verb dates from the sixteenth century, shortly before the earlier sense became obsolete.

invent (devise for the first time, imagine)
The Latin source of the verb is *invenire*, 'to come upon' (from *venire*, 'to come'), and this was the original sense of 'invent' in English in the fifteenth century. It was current down to at least the seventeenth century, and occurs in Spenser's *The Fairie Queene* (1590–6), for example, when Florimell, seeking her beloved Marinell:

vowed never to returne againe
Till him alive or dead she did invent.

This literal meaning, equating to 'find', explains the name of the church festival known as the 'Invention of the Cross' (3 May), celebrating the supposed finding of the Cross by Helena, mother of the Emperor Constantine, in AD 326. The modern

meaning of 'invent' developed in the sixteenth century.

investment (money paid out to earn interest or gain profit)
To 'invest' is literally to 'clothe' (compare 'investiture', 'vestment' and even 'vest'), so an 'investment' was originally a 'clothing' in the sixteenth century, with this sense first recorded in Shakespeare's *Henry IV*, Part 2 (1597), when Westmoreland, speaking of (and actually addressing) the Archbishop of York, says:

Whose learning and good letters peace
  hath tutor'd,
Whose white investments figure
  innocence.

From this, the word passed to meaning 'investiture' (in the sense of both 'conferring of an office' and 'endowment' generally), and to its modern usage, both these in the seventeenth century. (The modern sense, although first recorded in 1615, however, is not in Johnson's *Dictionary* of 1755.) The transfer of sense from 'clothing' to 'depositing money' is explained by the fact that a financial 'investment' is intended to give the money a new 'form', with the concept derived from Italian *investire*, 'to clothe', 'invest money'.

involve (engage, include)
Latin *involvere*, which lies behind the word, means literally 'to roll in', and this is reflected in the original sense in English, in the fourteenth century, which was 'wrap round'. *The Revelation to the Monk of Evesham* (1482) thus records how: 'Ther brake vppe a flame of fier that inuoluyd hem' (i.e. the flame enveloped them). As is often the case, the literal usage was sustained (or revived) by poets in much later times, so that Elizabeth Barrett Browning used the word in the same way in her verse romance *Aurora Leigh* (1857):

                                    I saw
Fog only, the great tawny weltering fog,
Involve the passive city.

The modern usage dates from the seventeenth century.

irk (make weary, irritate, annoy)
In the thirteenth century, 'irk' meant not 'make weary', as now, but 'grow weary', 'feel disgusted', 'be loath to'. In *The Story of England* (1330) by Robert Mannyng of Brunne (Bourne in Lincolnshire), we therefore read:

> So manye ther were in chaumbre & halle,
> Men schuld yrke to telle them alle.

So also in Richard Grenewey's translation (1598) of the *Annals* of Tacitus: 'Euery souldier irked with the remembrance of his labours'. The current usage first developed in the fifteenth century.

item (also; piece of information, individual object)
The first sense of 'item' to appear in English, in the fourteenth century, was the one meaning 'also', formerly (and perhaps sometimes still) used when making a list or inventory, when 'itemising', in fact. One of the most famous such lists in literature is the one in Shakespeare's *Twelfth Night* (1601), where Olivia relates the 'divers schedules' of her beauty to Viola (who is disguised as the youth Cesario): 'It shall be inventoried [. . .] as *Item*, Two lips, indifferent red; *Item*, Two grey eyes, with lids to them; *Item*, One neck, one chin, and so forth'. ('Item' itself derives from Latin *ita*, 'just so'.) In the sixteenth century, 'item' became a noun to mean both 'maxim' and 'enumerated article'. The first of these senses is now obsolete, but occurs, for example, in Bunyan's *Pilgrim's Progress* (1684), where one of the characters: ' . . .has Need of an Itum, to caution him to take heed, every Moment of the Day'. The modern meaning, 'piece of news', dates only from the nineteenth century.

jangle (ring a bell discordantly)
The earliest sense of the verb, as recorded from the thirteenth century, is 'chatter', 'babble'. Robert Mannyng of Brunne in *The Story of England* (1330) has the lines:

> Thenne come Saxoyns, men of Angle,
> Als they couthe [i.e. as they could] on ther speche iangle.

The word could even apply to birds, as in *The Squyr of Low Degre* (1400):

> The iay iangled them amonge,
> The larke began that mery songe.

From this the sense developed to 'speak harshly', 'grumble', as in Wyclif's Bible of 1382, where he translates Exodus 17:2 as: 'The which ianglynge agens Moyses, seith, gif to us water, that we drynken' (Authorized Version of 1611: 'Wherefore the people did chide with Moses, and said, Give us water that we may drink'). This usage is now virtually obsolete, although it survived until the nineteenth century. The sense 'make a discordant noise' dates from the fifteenth century, but as applied specifically to the ringing of a bell (or something similar) is first recorded in Shakespeare's *Hamlet* (1604), where Ophelia says:

> Now see that noble and most sovereign reason,
> Like sweet bells jangled, out of tune and harsh.

jape (joke, jest)
This now rather dated or mannered word ('I say, what a jolly jape!') arose in the fourteenth century when, as a verb, it had three distinct senses. The first was 'trick', 'fool', 'deceive', as in Chaucer's *Canterbury Tales* ('The Knight's Tale') (1386):

> Thus hath he iaped thee ful many a yer,
> And thou hast maked hym thy chief squier.

The second sense was 'have sexual intercourse with': 'He had rather that any man should gape his owne wif then kisse Jane Slaiter mowthe', one can read, in the *Durham Depositions* (1530–91), while the following lines occur in George Gascoigne's *To Bartholomew Withipoll* (1572):

First in thy jorney iape not overmuch.
What laughest thou Bat bycause I write
so plaine? [. . .]
Methinks plaine dealing biddeth me to
cast
Thys bone at first amid my doggrell
rime.

The third sense is the current one. It fell out of use from the sixteenth century for a while, because of its association with the second sense above. However, it was revived in the nineteenth century by Scott, Lamb and others. Here it is as used by Caxton before it was abandoned, in his translation (1483) of *Le Livre du Chevalier de la Tour Landry* (as 'The Knight of the Tower's book of teaching for his daughters'): 'There was a grete noyse and the men and wymmen iaped togeder eche with other'.

jargon (special language used by a group, meaningless talk)
In Chaucer's day, in the fourteenth century, 'jargon' was used for the twittering or chattering of birds. Chaucer himself has the word in his *Canterbury Tales* ('The Merchant's Tale') (1386):

He was al coltissh ful of ragerye [i.e. wantonness],
And ful of Iargon as a flekked pye [i.e. as a magpie].

This sense became obsolete in the fifteenth century, but was revived in the nineteenth, sometimes with a suggestion of the modern meaning 'confused language', 'lingo' or even of the 'specialized language' sense, as in Longfellow's *The Return of Spring* (1830):

With beast and bird the forest rings,
Each in his jargon cries or sings.

The usage of 'jargon' to mean 'meaningless talk' also dates from the fourteenth century, while the 'specialised language' sense, as the 'jargon' of stockbrokers or the world of rock music, first arose in the seventeenth century.

jaunt (short pleasure trip)
The modern noun derives from the verb, which itself originally meant 'ride a horse up and down' in the sixteenth century. It can be seen in these lines from Barnaby Googe's translation (1570) of Kirchmeyer's *The Popish Kingdom or Reigne of Antichrist:*

Then followeth Saint Stephens day,
whereon doth euery man
His horses iaunt and course abrode, as
swiftly as he can.

This now obsolete sense was accompanied by another at about the same period, which was 'trot or trudge about', 'run to and fro', as found in Shakespeare's *Romeo and Juliet* (1592), where the Nurse says to Juliet:

Beshrew your heart for sending me
about,
To catch my death with jauncing up and
down.

The current meaning developed in the seventeenth century. The origin of the word is unknown. It is not related to '**jaunty**' (see next entry), which derives from French *gentil*, 'gentle'.

jaunty (sprightly, 'perky', rakish)
The word arose in the seventeenth century from earlier 'jentee' or 'juntee' or some similar spelling, which itself derives from French *gentil* (see previous entry). Two now obsolete senses of 'jaunty' were thus 'genteel' (as applied to people) and 'elegant' (as applied to things). 'They look upon a Jantee air and Mien to be excellent Virtues', wrote Thomas Gordon in *Another Cordial for Low Spirits* (1752), and 'A true jauntee manner of dressing is, to be sure, a vast advantage', opined Thomas Hull in *The History of Sir William Harrington* (1771). Both these senses fell out of use from the nineteenth century.

jeopardy (risk, liability to loss or some other fate)
The origin of the word lies in French *jeu parti*, literally 'divided game', hence implying an even chance or uncertainty in something. The expression was first used in English in the fourteenth century, when it especially applied to a chess problem, and was in fact the technical term for this down

to about 1500. In Chaucer's *The Dethe of Blaunche* (1369), we thus find the lines:

But god wold I had ones or twyes
Y-kond and knowe the Ieupardyes
That kowde the Greke Pictagoras,
I shulde haue pleyde the bet at ches.

(That is: If only to God I had been able once or twice to solve the chess problems that the Greek Pythagoras could solve, I should have played better at chess.) In the same period, 'jeopardy' came also to mean 'device', 'trick' generally, as in Robert Henryson's translation (1480) of Aesop's *Fables:*

In his minde hee kest [i.e. planned]
The juperties, the wayis and the wile,
By what meanes hee might this Cocke
    beguyle.

From this the meaning developed to its present sense. This happened early enough, however, for it to occur in Chaucer, as in his *Troilus and Criseyde* (1374):

For Troye is brought in swich a Iupartye
That it to save is now no remedye.

In his *Dictionary* of 1755, Dr Johnson declared that 'jeopardy' was 'a word not now in use'. He was mistaken, however, since literary evidence shows that it was in regular use throughout the eighteenth century.

jest (joke, quip)
The word derives, through French, from Latin *gesta*, 'doings', 'exploits', and in the thirteenth century in English 'jest' thus meant 'deed', especially a noteworthy or 'noble' one. As such, it was usually spelt 'gest' and was almost always used in the plural. As a parallel meaning, 'gest' (in the singular) was also used for a story or romance in rhyme ('in gest' meant 'in verse'), with this sense later coming to mean simply 'story' of any kind. In the (verse) Prologue to his (prose) 'Tale of Melibeus' in the *Canterbury Tales* (1386), Chaucer wrote:

Lat se wher thou kanst tellen aught in
    geeste
Or telle in prose somwhat at the leeste.

(For the 'deed' sense of 'gest' or 'jest', compare the well known Old French epic

poems called the *Chansons de geste*.) From this original meaning, 'jest' came to apply to any diverting or idle tale in the fifteenth century, and in turn passed to its present sense some hundred years or so later. It occurs in almost all its modern usages in Shakespeare, therefore, from 'taunt' and 'fun' to 'joking' and 'merriment' (as Yorick, who was a 'fellow of infinite jest').

jet (spurt out in a stream)
In the sixteenth century, when the word was first in use in English, the meaning of 'jet' was 'project', 'protrude', 'stick out', in other words 'jut' (which itself is an altered spelling of 'jet'). Thus George Sandys in his *Travels* (1615) wrote how some houses he saw abroad were 'jetting over aloft like the poopes of ships, to shadow the streets', and *Observations both Historical and Moral upon the Burning of London, September 1666* (1667) recorded that magistrates had allowed builders to 'incroach upon the streets, and to jet the tops of their houses, so as from one side of the street to touch the other'. The modern sense of 'jet' arose in the seventeenth century.

jewel (precious stone, especially one used as an ornament)
The original thirteenth-century sense of 'jewel' was for the ornament itself, whether made of precious stone or of a precious metal such as gold or silver. In John Gower's *Confessio amantis* (1390) one finds the lines:

Of gold he leide Sommes grete
And of jeueals a strong beyete [i.e.
    acquisition].

The word could be used in a figurative sense, too, from the fourteenth century, as it still can (like 'treasure' and 'gem'). The modern meaning, applying to just the stone in the ornament, developed in the sixteenth century.

jilt (reject a lover peremptorily or unfeelingly)
The word first emerged in English in the seventeenth century, when as a noun it meant 'loose woman', 'harlot', with the earliest record of it in Wycherley's *Love in a Wood* (1672). Here, in the list of characters

(the 'Dramatis Personae'), Mrs Crossbite is described as 'an old cheating Jilt, and Bawd to her Daughter'. The verb 'jilt', which was first recorded twelve years earlier, in *No Droll but a Rational Account* (1660), initially had the wider sense of 'deceive', 'cheat', as can be seen from its use in this work: 'Treacherous tell-tales, that frequent clubs and Coffee-houses, whose chief business was to jilt others into discourse'. Still in the verbal sense, 'jilt' was described in Thomas Blount's *Glossographia* (1674) (a dictionary of 'hard words') as 'a new canting word, signifying to deceive and defeat ones expectation, more especially in the point of Amours'. This seems to mark the transition point from the general to the specific. The noun in its modern sense (now rarely used) arose at about the same time as its original 'harlot' sense, i.e. in the seventeenth century, although the meaning seems to have become established by the time Johnson published his *Dictionary* of 1755, since he defines 'jilt' there as 'a woman who gives her lover hopes, and deceives him'. It is a pity that the word arose too late for Shakespeare to have exploited it, as he almost certainly would have done.

jockey (professional rider in horseraces)
The word began its currency in English by simply being a pet form of 'John' or 'Jock', with the usage evolving as a Scottish one designed to refer to a person contemptuously. This was in the sixteenth century, and the name comes in Shakespeare's *Richard III* (1594), where Richard reads out the lines on the scroll found on Norfolk's tent on the day of the battle of Bosworth:

Jockey of Norfolk, be not too bold,
For Dickon thy master is bought and
    sold.

(Shakespeare was here reproducing the lines written on Norfolk's gate by a friend in an attempt to persuade him not to support the king in battle:

Jack of Norffolke be not to bolde,
For Dykon thy maister is bought and
    solde.

The Duke of Norfolk was John Howard.) 'Jockey' then came to mean 'lad', 'fellow', 'boy', with this usage found as late as the nineteenth century in Dickens's *Dombey and Son* (1848): '"You're Dombey's jockey, a'nt you?" said the first man. "I'm in Dombey's House, Mr Clark", returned the boy'. In the seventeenth century, 'jockey' came to mean 'horsedealer' before it meant 'horserider', with the earlier sense, now obsolete, found in Pepys' *Diary* entry for 4 December 1668, for example: 'I, and W. Hewer, and a friend of his, a jockey, did go about to see several pairs of horses, for my coach'. This meaning of the word fell out of use from the nineteenth century, and the 'rider' sense, first found in Evelyn's *Diary* entry for 22 July 1670, was the one that prevailed.

jolly (high-spirited, jovial, very pleasant)
The oldest sense of this word, as recorded in the fourteenth century, is still current to mean 'lively', 'jovial', 'merry'. However, other senses have come and gone since. Among them are 'gallant', 'confident' and 'amorous'. The first of these is found, for example, in Spenser's *The Faerie Queene* (1590):

Full jolly knight he seemd, and faire did
    sitt,
As one for knightly giusts and fierce
    encounters fitt.

The second, which invariably had a derogatory usage, occurs in Caxton's *The Game and Playe of the Chesse* (1474), translated from the French, where he describes a character as 'a Iolye man without Iustyse and cruel'. The third meaning also comes in Caxton, in his translation (1483) of the *Golden Legend*: 'He sholde send to her all the yonge men that were Ioly for to enforce and to make her do theyr wyll'. All three senses were obsolete from the seventeenth century, and the modern meaning 'very pleasant' developed in the sixteenth.

journal (periodical)
In the fourteenth century, a 'journal' was a so called 'diurnal', that is, a church service book containing the special prayers (Canonical Offices) for the different hours of the day. The two words are of one and the same origin, with 'journal' the French form and 'diurnal' closer to the Latin (*diurnus*, 'of the day'). In the sixteenth century, 'journal' came to mean 'daily

record', as it still can, as well as 'itinerary', a now obsolete sense. The latter was a publication giving information for travellers on the daily stages of a route, in other words of a **journey** (see the next entry below). The meaning 'daily newspaper' developed in the eighteenth century, and extended to other periodicals, not necessarily daily ones. Today, too, 'Journal' forms part of the name of a number of local newspapers and professional publications, such as the 'Grantham Journal' and 'Salisbury Journal' for the former, and 'Trade Marks Journal' and 'British Medical Journal' for the latter.

journey (travel from one place to another)
The earliest senses of the word are closely connected with 'day' (French *jour*), so that in the thirteenth century a 'journey' was a day's travel (the original sense of French *journée*) and in the fourteenth it was a day's work (hence 'journeyman' as a term for a person who is employed by the day for his work). In medieval times, a 'journey' in the 'travel' sense was usually reckoned to be about twenty miles, although of course this varied depending on the transport. A long voyage would thus be measured in so many 'journeys', as in these lines from the earliest record we have of the use, *The Story of Genesis and Exodus* (1250):

Fro Bersabe [ie. Beersheba] iurnes two
Was that land that he bed him to.

In the following lines from the fourteenth-century *Cursor Mundi*, 'journey' means 'spell of work' (almost 'shift'):

Fra that time nedis hat thai,
Do tua iornays apon a day.

(That is: From then on they had to do two spells of work a day.) Today, it is the 'travel' usage of 'journey' that has prevailed.

juggler (special kind of entertainer or conjuror)
Before he became the specialist in the art of multiple throwing and catching, the 'juggler' was a more wide-ranging jester or magician in the twelfth century. (The ultimate origin of the word is Latin *jocularis*, 'buffoon', to which English 'jocular' and 'joke' are also related.) In the following lines

from the fourteenth-century *Cursor Mundi*, the 'jugglers' are magicians:

Than cald the king his enchaunturs,
The craftes of his iogulurs,
Dun thai kest a wand ilkan,
And thai wex dragons son onan.

(That is, the 'jugglers' each waved a wand and the other performers duly turned into dragons.) The present meaning developed from the eighteenth century.

junket (type of sweet milk dessert; feast or festive occasion)
It might be thought that the feast came first and the dessert developed from it. In fact it is the other way round. The chronology of 'junket' is as follows. In the fourteenth century, the word was the term for a basket for fish, especially one made of rushes. In the fifteenth century, the sense developed to mean a dish prepared with cream, especially one that was originally laid in or on rushes. In the sixteenth century the term spread from the dish to any dainty dish or confection, and hence to a feast, which comprised several such 'dainty dishes' (including 'junket' itself!). The original basket (for catching or carrying fish) featured in Wyclif's Bible of 1382, where the basket in which the baby Moses was laid (Exodus 2:3) was a 'ionket of resshen' (Authorized Version of 1611, 'ark of bulrushes'). The following reference to the dessert shows that originally it was a sort of cream cheese: 'Be ware of cow creme & [. . .] Iouncat, for these wyll make your souerayne seke but he ete harde chese' (*Bahees Book*, 1475). The general meaning 'delicacy' is now obsolete, but it was current to the seventeenth century, as for example in this tasty extract from William Adlington's version (1566) of Apuleius' *The Golden Ass*: 'Bread pasties, tartes, custardes and other delicate ionckettes dipped in honie'. From the nineteenth century, in American use, a 'junket' came to be the term for a trip made by an official at public expense.

keen (sharp, intense, enthusiastic)
In Old English, 'keen' (*cēne*) meant both 'wise' and 'brave'. An example of the latter sense comes in Chaucer's *Canterbury Tales* ('The Monk's Tale') (1386), where we read that Cenobia:

> So worthy was in Armes and so keene
> That no wight [i.e. living being] passed
> hire in hardynesse.

These senses are now obsolete, but all the other meanings of 'keen' developed over the centuries, with the meaning 'penetrating' (as a 'keen' mind) appearing in the eighteenth century and 'keen on', meaning 'attracted to' evolving in the twentieth (as applied to amorous aims).

kill (put to death)
The word may seem age-old, but it evolved in its present sense in the fourteenth century out of the Old English meaning 'strike', 'beat'. A fourteenth-century alliterative poem in the West Midland dialect has the gruesome words in this sense: 'We kylle of thyn heued' (i.e. we strike off your head), and it is easy to see how this could develop to the modern sense, with 'kill' first meaning 'put to death with a weapon', then 'put to death' in general.

kind (benevolent, sympathetic and compassionate)
In Old English, *cynd* meant 'natural', 'native', showing the relation of the word with 'kin' and with the other 'kind' that means 'class', 'group', 'sort'. An example of the sense can be seen in this couplet from the early fourteenth-century popular verse romance *Sir Beues of Hamtoun* ('Bevis of Hampton'):

> Kinde hit is, wimman te be
> Schamfaste and ful of corteisie.

(That is: It is natural for women to be modest and full of courtesy.) In the thir-teenth century, the meaning developed to 'well-born', with this now obsolete sense persisting down to at least the seventeenth century, as in Stephen Gosson's *The Schoole of Abuse* (1579), where he states: 'The kindest Mastife, when he is clapped on the back, fighteth best'. The common popular sense 'benevolent' arose in the fourteenth century.

knave (rogue; jack, in playing cards)
In Old English, 'knave' was the standard word for 'boy', 'male servant' (compare modern German *Knabe*, 'boy'). The *Scottish Legends* (1375) show the basic 'boy' sense:

> Grant ws grace a barne to hafe,
> Othire a madyne or a knaf.

(That is: Give us grace to have a child, either a girl or a boy.) In the 'servant' sense, the word comes in the *Ancren riwle* (1225), the devotional manual for nuns (the 'Rules for Anchoresses', as it were), which mentions 'the kokes knaue, thet wassheth the disshes ithe kuchene'. From the latter, the meaning passed fairly readily to 'worth-less fellow' in the thirteenth century, and to the 'jack' of a pack or cards in the sixteenth century, where it is the lowest court card and represents a soldier or servant. Compare **knight** (below).

knight (rank of merit or man holding it)
In days of Old English, a 'knight' was a boy or a youth (compare modern German *Knecht*, 'servant', 'farmhand'). The biblical words 'There is a lad here' in John 6:9 (in the 'Feeding of the five thousand') are rendered in the *Lindisfarne Gospels* of 950 as 'Is cnæht an her'. This same translation renders part of Luke 12:45 as 'Onginneth [. . .] slaa tha cnæhtas & thiuwas' (Autho-rized Version of 1611: 'Shall begin to beat the menservants and maidens'), showing the progression of the word to mean 'servant'. These senses became obsolete by the thirteenth century at the latest, when the modern sense of 'soldier of rank' emerged. The current meaning 'man of nonhereditary rank below a baronet', that is, the 'knight' who is so appointed by the sovereign (and who is thus entitled to be called 'Sir'), finally arose in the sixteenth century. A man of this rank was regarded

as being of a status corresponding to that of the medieval knight, the nobleman who had been promoted (usually) from first 'page' then 'squire' by the sovereign.

knit (form a fabric with the use of special needles or a machine)
'Knit' is related to 'knot', and in Old English 'tie with a knot' was the meaning of the word. The usage is preserved in the Bible, where Acts 10:11 has 'a great sheet knit at the four corners' (in Tindale's Bible of 1526 this was 'a greate shete knytte at the iiij. corners'), and in Shakespeare's *King John* (1595), where the young prince Arthur says to Hubert, who has come to put out his eyes:

Have you the heart? When your head
     did but ache,
I knit my handkercher about your
     brows.

The sense became virtually obsolete from the eighteenth century.

knuckle (bone at a finger-joint)
In the fourteenth century, a 'knuckle' could be any bone-joint, such as the knee or elbow, and only in the fifteenth century did the narrower sense develop. The original usage survived in some poetic works, such as Arthur Golding's translation (1565) of Ovid's *Metamorphoses*, where the 'knuckles' are knees:

With wearie knockles in thy brim she
     kneeled sadly downe.

lace (figured fabric of fine thread)
In the thirteenth century, 'lace' was the word both for a string or cord for tying something (as it is still in 'shoelaces'), and

for a noose or snare. The latter sense, now obsolete, was often used figuratively, as the 'lace of death' or the 'laces of the devil'. The modern meaning 'ornamental braid', 'figured fabric' developed in the sixteenth century, since such a fabric is made from several threads (of cotton, silk or whatever) all 'laced' closely together.

lack (not have, be without)
In the twelfth century, 'lack' as a verb meant 'be absent', 'not be available', that is, a person or thing would 'lack' rather than a person 'lacking' something. This usage is preserved in the Bible, where Genesis 18:28 begins: 'Peradventure there shall lack five of the fifty righteous'. (It is fair to say, too, that modern English can still use 'be lacking' in this sense, as in 'There's only one thing lacking'.) Also in the thirteenth century, 'lack' could mean 'blame', the concept here being that if you blame someone or something you find him or it 'lacking'. An example of the sense comes in the *Babees Book* ('Babies' Book') of 1475:

Ne drynk behynde no mannes bakke,
For yf thou do, thow art to lakke.

The modern meaning of 'lack' dates from the fourteenth century, while the earlier senses became obsolete from the eighteenth.

lad (youth, boy)
Like '**boy**' itself, (which compare, above), 'lad' meant 'servant' before it acquired its more general sense of 'youth'. The first meaning was current in the thirteenth century, with the implication that the 'servant' was of lowly birth, or a 'varlet', and with the word frequently contrasted with 'lord'. (The latter usage survives in the Scottish proverb, 'Lay up like a laird, and seek like a lad'.) Thus Coverdale's Bible of 1535 has 'the prestes lad' in I Samuel 2:15 where the 1611 Authorized Version has 'the priest's servant'. The modern meaning 'youth', 'boy', dates from the sixteenth century.

lady (woman of superior social position)
The common use of the word, as defined here (and as popularly contrasted with 'lord' or 'gentleman'), arose only in the nineteenth century. Originally, in the thir-

teenth century, a 'lady' was the mistress of the household, by contrast with the **husband** (which see) who was the master. By a similar contrast, 'lady' also meant 'wife'. The first of these senses can be found in Wyclif's Bible of 1382, where his rendering of Proverbs 30:23 has: 'Bi an hand womman, whan she were eir of hir ladi' (Authorized Version of 1611: 'And an hand-maid that is heir to her mistress'). The latter sense, 'wife', is found in Caxton's translation (1483) of *Le Livre du Chevalier de la Tour Landry*, for example, where he mentions 'A grete lady, that was lady to a baron'. This usage was common in polite society in the eighteenth and first half of the nineteenth century in English, so that Jane Austen, in *Sense and Sensibility* (1797–1811), wrote that: 'By a former marriage, Mr. Dashwood had one son; by his present lady, three daughters', and the issue of the *Liverpool Mercury* for 11 June 1841, for instance, announced that: 'On Thursday, the 3d instant, the lady of Thomas William Phillips, Esq. [gave birth to] a daughter'. In more recent times, the use of 'lady' to mean 'wife', however, has been more 'proletarian', as in 'your good lady', 'the lady wife' and the like. The title 'Lady', still in use, also dates from the thirteenth century, and led to the nineteenth-century connotation of 'woman of refinement', as in George Eliot's *Silas Marner* (1861): 'She had the essential attributes of a lady – high veracity, delicate honour in her dealings, deference to others, and refined personal habits'. The word has travelled a long way from the original Old English *hlǣfdīge* that meant literally 'bread kneader'!

lair (animal's resting place)
The word is related to 'lie', and in Old English meant 'lying down', 'bed' and even 'grave', 'tomb'. The 'bed' sense was current until at least the eighteenth century, and can be found, for example, in Henry Hutton's *Follie's Anatomie* (1619)

Robin has for tobaccho sold his chaire,
Reserving nothing but a stoole for 's lare.

The meaning 'grave' existed even longer in Scotland, and in 1890 a notice in Stromness Churchyard read: 'The Committee appointed by the Heritors to take charge of

the new Burial Ground have had before them alternative plans for placing of lairs'. The sense 'animal's bed' arose in the fifteenth century.

large (big, great)
When first current in English, in the twelfth century (when it was adopted from French), 'large' meant 'liberal', 'generous'. The use in this sense lasted until at least the eighteenth century, and is found, for example, in Shakespeare's *Henry VI*, Part 2 (1593), where Gloucester speaks of:

The poor King Reignier, whose large style
Agrees not with the leanness of his purse.

'Large' could also mean 'ample', 'abundant', with this sense found as late as 1667 in Milton's *Paradise Lost:*

And we have yet large day, for scarce the Sun
Hath finisht half his journey.

In the fourteenth century, 'large' came to mean 'broad' (the sense of modern French *large*), and often occurred in the phrase 'long and large', as in these lines from one of William Dunbar's *Poems* (1500–20):

Ane croce that was baith large and lang,
To beir thai gaif that blessit Lord.

(That is: They gave a cross that was both broad and long to the Blessed Lord to carry.) The present common meaning 'great', 'big' developed from the fifteenth century.

larva (insect in its grub state)
The word itself is Latin for 'spectre', 'ghost', 'mask', and this was what 'larva' meant in English in the seventeenth century, in an admittedly restricted currency. The Presbyterian preacher Richard Baxter, in his *Plain Scripture-Proof of Infants' Church Membership and Baptism* (1651), wrote: 'I live almost perpetually in my bed or chair or pulpit; as Calvin said of Cassander; such a *larva* I am that am here called up'. The transition from this sense to the insect arose from the fact that when in its larval state the perfect insect (the 'imago') cannot be recognized, and so is a 'mask', or in disguised form. The first use of the term in this sense comes in

John Ray's *The Wisdom of God Manifested in the Works of the Creation* (1691), where he writes: 'We exclude both these from the degree of *Species,* making them to be the same Insect under a different *Larva* or Habit'. This usage was then formally adopted by Linnaeus for the insect's particular stage of development.

lavatory (toilet)
The root of the word is Latin *lavare*, 'to wash', and the earliest sense of 'lavatory' in English was that of 'vessel for washing', i.e. anything from a washbasin to a bath. Clearly, early texts with this usage read curiously today. Thus, in Wyclif's Bible of 1382, Exodus 30:18 is rendered: 'And thow shalt make a brasun lauatory with his foot to wasshe with' (Authorized Version of 1611: 'Thou shalt also make a laver of brass, and his foot also of brass, to wash withal'). In ecclesiastical use, in particular, a 'lavatory' was a piscina (a basin by the altar in a church where water can be poured after use for ceremonial washing) or a lavabo (a similar vessel where the priest can ritually wash his hands). This explains the sense behind the words in Longfellow's prose romance *Hyperion* (1839): 'On a lavatory, below, sat a cherub'. In early figurative uses, too, the word looks incongruous or even blasphemous to modern eyes, as in the morality play *Mankind* (1475); 'By hys gloryus passyone, that blyssyde lauatorye'. The present meaning of 'lavatory' evolved in the seventeenth century, being first a room for washing the hands, then a similar apartment with a water closet, then finally, in the twentieth century, the 'loo' itself. Compare the etymological evolution of **toilet**.

lawn (area of regularly mown grass)
A 'lawn' was originally a 'laund' in the fourteenth century, with this word related to 'land'. A 'laund' was a glade or pasture, and the 'lawn' that evolved from it in the sixteenth century was thus at first an open space or glade between woods. This is therefore the sense of the word in the following lines from Robert Greene's *Farewell to Folly* (1591):

Her stature and her shape was passing tall,

Diana-like, when longst the Lawnes she goes.

Even in Wordsworth's *The Waggoner* (1805) the sense is the same:

Thence look thou forth o'er wood and lawn,
Hoar with the frost-like dews of dawn!

The modern meaning of 'lawn' arose in the eighteenth century, although there was something of a transitionary sense first, as can be seen in this definition from Philip Miller's *The Gardener's Dictionary* (1733): '*Lawn* is a great Plain in a Park, or a spacious Plain adjoining to a noble Seat [...] As to the situation of a Lawn, it will be best in the Front of the house, and to lie open to the neighbouring Country and not pent up with Trees'.

ledger (accounts book)
In the fifteenth century, a 'ledger' was a book, such as a register, that permanently *lay* in the same place, hence its name. A hundred years later, the sense had already passed to the accounts book, so that Pepys could write in his *Diary* entry for 7 January 1662: 'So to my office all the morning, signing the Treasurer's ledger'.

legend (semi-historical or mythical tale; inscription, caption)
When first in use in English, in the fourteenth century, a 'legend' was specifically the story of a saint's life, or a collection of such stories. One of the best known in literature is the so called 'Golden Legend', a medieval collection of saints' lives having as one of its sources the *Legenda Aurea* of Jacobus de Voragine (Jacopo de' Varazze), the thirteenth-century archbishop of Genoa. (A translation of this was made in English by Caxton in 1483. His colophon or 'tail-piece' read: 'Thus endeth the legende named in latyn *legenda aurea*, that is to saye in englysshe the golden legende'.) In the fifteenth century, a 'legend' was a book of readings or 'lessons' for use in church services, consisting of passages from the Bible and the lives of the saints. The modern meanings of the word, as 'semi-historical story' and 'inscription', both arose in the seventeenth century. All senses are suitable

for a word that derives from Latin *legenda*, literally 'things to be read'.

Lent (period of forty days before Easter observed as a time of fasting and penitence by many Christian churches)
'Lent' comes at a time of year when the days are noticeably beginning to 'lengthen' in spring. The two words are related, and 'lent' was originally the actual word for 'spring' in English in the eleventh century, occurring either in this shorter spelling or in the longer 'lenten' that is closer to the Old English (*lencten*). A poem of 1310 contains the attractive line:

Lenten ys come with love to toune,

and John de Trevisa's translation (1387) of Ranulf Higden's *Polychronicon* explains: 'The evenes of the day and of the nyght is ones in the Lente, and efte in hervest [i.e. again in autumn; see **harvest**]'. 'Spring' finally replaced 'lent' as the name of the season in the sixteenth century, although the church sense of 'Lent' had been current from the thirteenth century.

let (allow; offer or give for lease or rent)
Almost all current senses of 'let' date from Old English times, when it could also mean 'leave behind', 'allow to remain', however. This now obsolete usage was current down to the seventeenth century, and occurs in Shakespeare's *The Winter's Tale* (1611), when Hermione says to Polixenes:

When at Bohemia
You take my lord, I'll give him my
commission
To let him there a month behind the gest
[i.e. period of staying]
Prefix'd for's parting.

Also down to the seventeenth century, 'let' could mean 'omit to do', as in Shakespeare's *The Rape of Lucrece* (1593):

When Collatine unwisely did not let
To praise the clear unmatched red and
white.

'Let' is related to 'lassitude', and probably the basic concept behind all senses of the verb, both obsolete and current, was originally 'let go through weariness'.

lewd (coarse, suggestive, lustful)
This word ranks among the most dramatic sense shifts in the English language. In Old English, it meant 'lay', 'not clerical', a sense that lasted until about the sixteenth century. This could apply to men who were not priests or members of a religious order, or to things that were not holy, as in Wyclif's Bible of 1382, where I Samuel 21:4 reads: 'I haue not leeuyd loouyes at hoond, but oonli hooli breed' (Authorized Version of 1611: 'There is no common bread under mine hand, but there is hallowed bread'). Since the laity were relatively 'unread' or illiterate, by comparison with the clergy, the next sense of 'lewd' to develop, in the thirteenth century, was 'unlearned', 'unlettered'. This usage was also current to the sixteenth century, and is found, for example, in John Bellenden's translation (1536) of Boethius' Latin *History and Chronicles of Scotland*, where he explains: 'I have maid this translation mair for pleseir of lawit men, than any vane curius clerkis'. In fact in this period two current expressions were 'learned and lewed' or 'lewed and clerks' to express the contrasting 'literate and illiterate', 'lettered and unlettered'. From this, the sense passed in the fourteenth century to 'low', 'ignorant', 'vulgar' and hence the modern 'coarse', 'lascivious', with 'lewdness' being an alleged typical characteristic of the untaught. The sense 'ignorant' is now obsolete, but was in use down to the seventeenth century, and is found, for instance, in Roger Ascham's *The Scholemaster, or Plaine and Perfite Way of Teachyng Children the Latin Tong* (1568), where he writes of 'the small discretion of many leude Scholemasters'. The present-day meaning thus arose early enough to be used by Chaucer and to come in the Bible ('certain lewd fellows of the baser sort', in Acts 17:5).

liaison (cooperation, close consultation and communication)
The word is pure French (from *lier*, 'to bind'), and first arose in English in the seventeenth century to be a culinary term for a kind of thickening for sauces, mainly consisting of egg yolks. In the nineteenth century, the sense extended to a different sort of 'mixing', that of an illegitimate or secret romance. Finally, in the twentieth

century, the word acquired its military usage of 'cooperation of forces', with special 'liaison officers' appointed to effect this. (Their operation brought about the jargonistic verb 'liaise', first recorded in the 1920s.) The word has thus had a variety of different applications in a relatively short time in its transition from sauces to the services.

libel (harming of a person's good reputation by a printed statement)
The word is related to 'library' in that it derives from Latin *libellus*, 'little book' (a diminutive of *liber*, 'book'). The fourteenth-century sense of 'libel' was 'little book', 'document'. Wyclif used it in his Bible translation of 1382, where in Numbers 5:23 he has: 'And the preest shal wryte in a libel thes cursid thingis' (Authorized Version of 1611: 'And the priest shall write these curses in a book'). In the fourteenth century, 'libel' came to be used for the formal plea or declaration of a plaintiff. Miles Coverdale used this sense in his Bible translation of 1535, with Job 31:35 reading: 'Let him that is my contrary party, sue me with a lybell' (Authorized Version: 'That mine adversary had written a book', which one cannot help feeling is less effective). In the sixteenth century, 'libel' acquired the meaning, now obsolete, of 'published pamphlet', 'publicly circulated leaflet', especially one that defamed a particular person. Shakespeare uses the word in this sense in *Richard III* (1594), when in the opening speech of the play ('Now is the winter of our discontent') the future king says:

Plots have I laid, inductions dangerous,
By drunken prophecies, libels, and
  dreams,
To set my brother Clarence and the king
In deadly hate the one against the other.

Finally, in the seventeenth century, the term came to have its modern usage.

libertine (man who leads a dissolute life)
In its first sense in English, a 'libertine' was a freedman, that is, a liberated Roman slave. The earliest record we have of the use is in Wyclif's Bible of 1382, where he has in Acts 6:9: 'Summe risen of the synagoge, that was clepid of Libertyns' (Authorized

Version of 1611: 'Then there arose certain of the synagogue, which is called the synagogue of the Libertines'). No further record of the word in this sense is found until the sixteenth century, when the modern meaning is also first documented, both as 'freethinker' and as 'licentious man'. The overall concept is of someone who has been liberated from a 'strict' way of life so is free to 'kick over the traces' and exceed the conventional bounds of morality and conformity.

lieutenant (military rank of junior army or navy officer)
Like many military ranks, the word is directly French in origin, and means literally 'place holder' (*lieu tenant*). In the earliest use of the word, in the fourteenth century, a 'lieutenant' was thus an officer who took the place of another, and acted as his 'vice' or deputy. This was not necessarily a military position, as is shown, for example, in John de Trevisa's translation (1387) of Ranulf Higden's *Polychronicon*: 'Hubert archebisshop of Caunterbury was leeftenaunt of the pope and of the kyng of Engelond'. The military usage followed in the sixteenth century, when a 'lieutenant' was originally regarded as an officer who was deputizing for a captain. (In the British forces now he is next in rank below a captain in the army, but next below a squadron leader in the air force and next below a lieutenant commander in the navy.)

lights (lungs of a slaughtered animal)
In the twelfth century, the word meant 'lungs' generally. (Both words are related, and the lungs are so named for their light weight.) From about the fifteenth century, the sense was narrowed to apply to the lungs of slaughtered animals, especially those of sheep, pigs and bullocks, formerly used as pet food.

lilt (sing or speak with fluctuating pitch or intonation)
Today a 'lilting' voice is just as likely to be a speaking one as a singing one. In the fourteenth century, however, to 'lilt' was not only to lift up the voice in song but to sound a note on an instrument such as the pipes. Even in the eighteenth century, to 'lilt up'

was to 'tune up', as in these lines by the Scottish poet Allan Ramsay:

Lilt up your pipes, and rise aboon
Your *Trivia* and your moorland tune.

Except in Scottish dialect usage, 'lilt' is now restricted to the singing or speaking voice, especially one that is musical and rhythmic.

linger (stay behind, be slow)
To 'linger' was simply to 'dwell' in the thirteenth century, as in the following lines (about Adam) from the fourteenth-century *Cursor Mundi:*

And leuer was sithen to lenger in hell
Than langer in this liue to duell.

(That is, he would then rather have lived in hell than stayed any longer in that place.) The current meaning of 'linger' dates from the sixteenth century.

lingerie (women's underwear and nightwear)
The word entered English direct from French in the nineteenth century, when it was the term for 'linen articles collectively', especially those in a woman's wardrobe or 'trousseau'. ('Lingerie' and 'linen' are closely related words, and French *linge* is 'linen'.) *The Court Magazine* (1835) announced that: 'It is expected that lingerie will be this season in very great request, both in morning and half-dress', and the *Illustrated London News* of 21 November 1885 had a picture of 'A happy bride supplied with "a handsome lingerie"'. Today, however, the word simply means 'women's underwear', even when at its skimpiest and certainly not made of linen. This recent sense development is not noted by the *Supplement* to the *OED,* although Volume II (H-N) appeared in 1976, when the current usage was already well established.

list (column of written words or names)
The earliest sense of the noun 'list' in English was 'border', 'edge', 'strip', as current in Old English and as still in use in certain specialized contexts, such as the 'list' that is a band or strip of material or a 'selvage'. From this, the word acquired the meaning 'boundary' in the fourteenth century, with the plural form used for the

'lists' that bounded the area where tilting matches or tournaments were held (hence 'in the lists' or 'enter the lists' in a transferred sense to indicate participation in some sort of contest). The basic Germanic word was adopted by Romance languages, such as French and Italian, and it is from French that the word was readopted into English, where it is first recorded in its modern common meaning in Shakespeare's *Hamlet* (1602). Here, in the first scene, Horatio tells how Fortinbras:

Hath in the skirts of Norway here and there
Shark'd up a list of lawless resolutes.

This usage is a reminder that in the earliest applications of the modern sense, 'list' related to a catalogue of names of soldiers serving in a particular army. This special use survives in such military expressions as 'the active list', 'the retired list' and the publications such as 'The Army List' and 'The Navy List' that give the names of all officers in the army and navy respectively.

literature (literary work)
In the fourteenth century, 'literature' meant merely 'polite learning', implying a knowledge of 'letters' or books. The sense was in use down to the nineteenth century, and is the only one given by Johnson, for example, in his *Dictionary* of 1755. Certainly Johnson himself always used the word in this way, as in *The Lives of the English Poets* (1779–81), where he wrote of Milton: 'His literature was unquestionably great. He read all the languages which are considered either as learned or polite'. Even George Borrow, in *Wild Wales* (1862), wrote that the 'boots' at an inn where he stayed was 'a fellow without either wit or literature'. The modern meaning of 'literature' in English is thus very recent by linguistic standards, as it is in French, and it is first recorded in Sir Humphrey Davy's *Elements of Chemical Philosophy* (1812): 'Their literature, their works of art offer models that have never been excelled'.

lithe (pliant, gracefully supple)
In Old English, 'lithe' meant 'gentle', 'mild', whether of people and their manner or of things. The *Prose Psalter* of 1325 thus

rendered the modern 'The Lord is good to all' of Psalm 145:9 as: 'Our Lord is lithe to alle', and *The Romaunt of the Rose* (1400) has the lines:

> The savour soft and lythe
> Strook to myn herte without more.

(That is, the soft, gentle scent immediately struck me.) These now obsolete senses were superseded by the current meaning, which arose in the fifteenth century.

litter (rubbish or waste materials left strewn about)
The sense progression with this word, from Old English to modern usage, is from 'bed' to 'bad', so to speak. 'Litter' is related to both English 'lie' and French *lit*, and in its earliest sense it actually meant 'bed'. The first record of the word used thus is in the fourteenth-century *Cursor Mundi*, where these two lines will strike a chord with Bible readers:

> Quen he had made me hale and fere,
> 'Rise vp,' he said, 'wit thi litere'.

In the fourteenth century, 'litter' came to mean a portable couch (one carried on people's shoulders or on the backs of animals, the forerunner of the modern stretcher), and in the fifteenth century the sense was extended to be used for 'bedding' generally. It was at this time, too, that 'litter' transferred from the bedding to what lay on it, in particular the newly born young of an animal. Finally, in the eighteenth century, the word was used to designate any disorderly accumulation of things left lying about, and especially rubbish. All these senses are still current with the exception of the basic 'bed', although the 'portable couch' is now a thing of the past.

lively (alert and energetic, 'merry and bright')
In Old English, the word meant simply 'living', 'alive', with the sense continuing in sporadic use down to the seventeenth century, so that it occurs in Shakespeare's *Titus Andronicus* (1588), where Titus says of Lavinia:

> Had I but seen thy picture in this plight
> It would have madded me: what shall I
> do
> Now I behold thy lively body so?

By the thirteenth century, 'lively' had come to mean 'vigorous', 'active', with the connotation 'animated' developing in the fourteenth century and 'merry' in the fifteenth.

loaf (shaped mass of bread)
In its earliest sense, 'loaf' was simply '**bread**' itself (see this other word separately), and Old English *hlāf* lies behind modern '**lady**' (see this also). The word could be used figuratively, too, so that the *Lindisfarne Gospels* of 950 render the modern biblical 'I am that bread of life' (John 6:48) as 'Ic am hlaf lifes'. The sense soon gave way to the modern meaning, however, and is not recorded later than the twelfth century. (Some non-Germanic languages have adopted a form of 'loaf' as their standard word for 'bread', such as Russian *khleb* and Finnish *leipä*.) The usage of 'loaf' to apply to sugar arose in the fourteenth century.

loam (kind of crumbly fertile soil)
In Old English, 'loam' was just 'earth' or 'clay', hence the sense in Mowbray's words in Shakespeare's *Richard II* (1593) when he says:

> Men are but gilded loam or painted clay.

In the fifteenth century, 'loam' came to mean 'mixture of moistened clay', as still used for plastering, for example, and the current sense of 'fertile soil' ('clay loam' or 'sandy loam') followed in the seventeenth century.

loan (thing lent)
The word came into English from Old Norse *lān*, and in its earliest use meant 'gift', 'grant', in particular one made by a superior, and often in the sense of something given by God. This usage did not last much beyond the fourteenth century, by which time the modern meaning had developed. Chaucer used the word in both senses in his *Canterbury Tales* (1386): 'God be thanked of his loone' in 'The Summoner's Tale', and in 'The Shipman's Tale':

> No wight [i.e. person] in al this world
> wiste of this loone.

loath, loth (reluctant)

The word is most common today in such expressions as 'nothing loath' and 'I would be loath to do that'. In its earliest sense, in Old English, 'loath' meant 'hostile', 'hateful', showing the word's direct relation with modern 'loathe' and 'loathsome'. It occurs with this meaning in *The Story of Genesis and Exodus* (1250):

> And nithful neddre, loth and lither,
> Sal gliden on hise brest nether.

(That is: And malicious snakes, hateful and wicked, shall glide down onto his breast.) The modern use of 'loath' (or 'loth') dates from the fourteenth century.

lobby (entrance hall, anteroom)

The word was first recorded in English in Thomas Becon's *The Relikes of Rome* (1553): 'Our Recluses neuer come out of their lobbeis, sincke or swimme the people'. From this, it would appear that the original 'lobby' was a monastic term for a cloister of some kind. A few years later, Shakespeare used the word to mean 'passage' or 'corridor' in his *Henry VI*, Part 2 (1593), when Suffolk says to Walter Whitmore, who has seized him:

> How in our voiding lobby hast thou
>   stood
> And duly waited for my coming forth?

(A 'voiding lobby' here means a lobby into which people pass as they vacate or 'void' a room.) From this, the term came to apply specifically, in the seventeenth century, to the 'lobby' in the House of Commons, the anteroom into which members go to vote during a division. From this in turn the word passed to the people who vote in a particular lobby or, more generally, who support a particular interest or cause. These latest developments of the sense arose respectively in the nineteenth and twentieth centuries.

locket (small case worn round the neck and containing a small memento)

The word is related to 'lock', although not the lock of hair that a locket traditionally contains! In the fourteenth century, a 'locket' was the iron crossbar of a window. In the sixteenth century the word came to denote the metal plate or band on a scabbard. By the seventeenth century, a 'locket' had evolved as the term for either a patterned group of jewels, or a catch or spring to fasten ('lock') an ornament. Except for the scabbard, all these senses are now obsolete, and the current meaning, which also arose in the seventeenth century, is thus virtually the sole one. The origin of the word is French *loquet*, 'latch'.

lode (vein of ore)

The word is related to both 'lead' (in the sense 'conduct') and 'load', and is in fact a spelling variant of the latter. In Old English, 'lode' (*lād*) meant 'way', 'journey', as in these lines from *Sir Tristrem* (1320):

> He toke his lod unlight,
> His penis with him he bare.

(That is: He made his heavy [literally 'unlight'] way, and carried his money ['pennies'] with him.) By the fourteenth century, the word had come to form the 'lodestar', or 'guiding star' (in particular, the Pole Star), and in the sixteenth century, a 'lodestone', the 'guiding stone' that was actually a piece of magnetite used by sailors as a magnet and thus served as a basic compass by pointing to the north. The sense 'vein of ore' arose in the seventeenth century.

loft (room or space under a sloping roof)

In Old English, 'loft' meant 'air', 'sky' (compare modern German *Luft*, 'air' and English 'aloft'). The *Trinity College Homilies* (1200), in describing God's creation of the world, say: 'He maketh the fisses in the sa, the fueles [i.e. birds] on the lofte'. In the thirteenth century, 'loft' acquired the sense 'upper room', 'attic', that it has today, while in the sixteenth century the meaning was extended to denote a gallery or floor, such as an 'organ loft' in a cathedral or the upper floor of a barn.

lollipop ('sweet on a stick')

The word was first used in English in the eighteenth century. In the plural, it meant 'sweets' generally. In the singular, it usually denoted a particular kind of sweet, an easily dissolvable one made of treacle or sugar (a sort of soft toffee). The present type of 'lollipop', the round flat sweet on a stick, is a development of the twentieth century, and it is this variety that in due course produced the 'lollipop man' and 'lollipop lady' who stop traffic with their lollipop-like sign and see schoolchildren safely over the road.

lord (noble rank or its bearer, 'peer of the realm', ruler)
The present form of the word is a much reduced and distorted version of the Old English original, which was *hlāford* (and even earlier *hlāfweard*), meaning literally 'loaf ward', 'keeper of the bread' (compare modern English 'breadwinner'). This expressed the basic relation of a head of the household to those who ate his bread, and thus the primary and earliest sense of 'lord' was 'master', 'ruler' and even '**husband**' (which also see). The fourteenth-century *Cursor Mundi* states that whoever hits his thane (servant) with a stick:

If he [the thane] liue ouer a dai or tuin,
The lauerd sal vnderli na pain.

(That is, if he lives on for one or two days, the master shall undergo no penalty.) The rank of 'lord' arose in the fourteenth century, and the designation for a peer followed a hundred years later. For a similar word, see **lady**.

lot (large amount)
In Old English, *hlot* meant 'portion', 'choice', and this was thus the earliest sense, as the modern 'drawing lots' and 'it was my lot to be the one chosen'. In the sixteenth century, 'lot' came to denote a prize in a lottery, and in the seventeenth, a plot of land. In the eighteenth century the sense 'set of articles' developed, such as 'lot no. 8' (or whatever) at an auction sale, and finally 'large amount' in the nineteenth. The use of 'lot' in 'an interesting lot of people' or 'a lazy lot' (of people) is midway between the 'large amount' and the 'set of articles', and really dates from the eighteenth century similarly. The singular use of the word in such phrases as 'he's a bad lot', however, arose only in the nineteenth century. The 'lottery prize' sense is now obsolete.

lotion (liquid preparation for cosmetic or external medicinal use)

This sense of the word has been in use since it first entered English from French in the fourteenth century. It is worth recording, however, that for a while from the sixteenth century, 'lotion' could mean 'washing', usually for medical reasons. Thus in the translation of Gabelhouez's *Boock of Physicke* that appeared in 1599, this recommendation appeared: 'Everye weeke twice washe his head, and after the lotion of the same, strawe [i.e. sprinkle] agayne of this poulder [powder] in the sores'. This usage became obsolete in the eighteenth century.

lovely (attractive, beautiful)
The word has had this sense since the thirteenth century, where it is first recorded in the *Cursor Mundi* in its modern meaning ('Thai spitted on his luueli face'). 'Lovely' could also mean both 'loving' and 'lovable', and both these senses were current from the eleventh century. The former, for example, comes in Chaucer's *Anelida and Arcite* (1374):

For sheo to him so lovely was and trewe,

and the latter in the 1450 translation of *De imitatione Christi*: 'Louely fader, it is worthy that this houre thi seruaunte suffre somwhat for the'. The former sense came to mean 'amorous', too, in the fifteenth century, with this usage found in Shakespeare's poem *The Passionate Pilgrim* (1599):

Sweet Cytherea, sitting by a brook
With young Adonis, lovely, fresh, and
   green,
Did court the lad with many a lovely
   look.

(Shakespeare was here playing on the two senses of the word, the first being the modern one, the second the now obsolete one.) The 'loving' sense of 'lovely' fell out of use in the eighteenth century, and the 'lovable' one in the nineteenth.

lozenge (medicated sweet)
In the fourteenth century, a 'lozenge' was a diamond-shaped figure, a 'rhomb', as it still is properly today. The meaning 'medicated tablet' arose in the sixteenth century, when such tablets were originally diamond-shaped. The heraldic use of the word dates from the original currency of the term.

lucid (clear, plain)
The word was adopted by English from the French in the sixteenth century. When first recorded, however, it meant 'shining', as in Spenser's *Mother Hubberds Tale* (1591):

> With azure wings he cleav'd
> The liquid clowdes, and lucid
> firmament.

The more common current sense arose in the seventeenth century.

ludicrous (ridiculous)
The present meaning arose only in the eighteenth century. A hundred years earlier 'ludicrous' had other, now obsolete senses, such as 'jocular' and 'frivolous'. The first of these occurs as late as the eighteenth century in Johnson's *The Lives of the English Poets* (1779–81), where he declares that Pope's *The Rape of the Lock* is 'universally allowed to be the most attractive of all ludicrous compositions'. The latter sense comes in an advertisement of 1827 for Burton's *The Anatomy of Melancholy*, which says that 'the ludicrous Sterne has interwoven many parts of it into his own popular performance' ('it' here being Burton's work). The basic origin of the word is Latin *ludicrus*, 'playful'.

lusty (healthy and vigorous, strong and 'beefy')
In the thirteenth century, when first current in English, 'lusty' meant 'joyful' or 'pleasing'. The first of these senses occurs in Chaucer's *Canterbury Tales* ('The Knight's Tale') (1386):

> And from his courser, with a lusty herte,
> Into a groue ful hastily he sterte [i.e. leapt].

The second can be found in John Gower's lyrical *Confessio amantis* (1390):

> Now be the lusti somer floures,
> Now be the stormy wynter shoures.

Both meanings became obsolete in the eighteenth century, and the only sense now left is the one that arose in the fourteenth century.

luxury (great comfort and ease)
The earliest sense of this word, now obsolete, was 'lasciviousness'. This was in the fourteenth century, although the usage was still current in the eighteenth century, as evidenced in *A Complete History of Algiers* (1728–9) by the historical writer J. Morgan (no one is sure what his first name was): 'To say nothing of the Luxury and Debaucheries which reigned in the Camps, which he describes as the filthiest of Brothels'. The modern meaning arose in the seventeenth century, and a similar sense development occurred for the adjective 'luxurious'.

machine (mechanical device or engine)
In the sixteenth century, 'machine' meant 'structure', 'fabric', either figuratively, as the 'machine' of society or even of the world, or literally, as the 'machine' of an architectural monument or of some kind of carriage. In the following example, from a translation (1682) of Boileau's *Le Lutrin*, it is a pulpit:

> Behind this Machine, cover'd as with a skreen,
> The Sneaking Chanter scarce could then be seen.

In this quotation, from Charlotte Smith's novel *Celestina* (1791), it is an elaborate bonnet box: 'Her new laylock bonnet [. . .] for the safety of which she was so solicitous that she would have taken the great machine in which it was contained into the coach, had it not been opposed by the coachman'. From this now obsolete usage, 'machine' progressed in the eighteenth century to its current senses, including 'military engine', 'wheeled vehicle', 'mechanical device' and so on.

madonna (picture, statue or other representation of the Virgin Mary)
The word is Italian for 'my lady', and this

was its usage in English in the sixteenth century before it became exclusively adopted as a title of the Virgin Mary. The sense comes in Shakespeare's *Twelfth Night* (1601), for example, where the Clown says to Olivia: 'Good madonna, why mournest thou?'. The word was also used to mean an Italian lady, as in John Fletcher's *The Fair Maid of the Inn* (1625): 'A dancer [. . .] that by teaching great Madonnas to foot it, has miraculously purchast a ribanded wastcote'. This usage, however, is not recorded later than the seventeenth century. The first use of 'Madonna' as a title for the Virgin occurs (more than once) in Evelyn's *Diary* (1700), where he refers, for instance, to 'A faire Madona of Pietro Perugino, painted on the wall'.

magazine (periodical; cartridge holder in a gun; weapon store)
The three senses given here are enough to show that the word has had a varied history over the years. Its first meaning in English, in the sixteenth century, was 'storehouse', specifically a weapons store. This sense is still not obsolete. In the seventeenth century, 'magazine' came to mean 'storehouse of information', especially in the titles of 'factual' books, such as Samuel Sturmy's 'The Mariners Magazine' (1669) or George Shelley's 'The Penman's Magazine: or, a New Copy-book, of the English, French and Italian Hands' (1705). From this now obsolete usage, the word passed to its present meaning as 'periodical', being first recorded in this sense in the title of 'The Gentleman's Magazine: or, Monthly Intelligencer', published in 1731 (and appearing regularly until 1914). The 'cartridge chamber' sense first arose in the eighteenth century as a development of the 'weapons store' meaning. The word as a whole derives, through French, from Arabic *makhāzin*, the plural of *makhzan*, 'storehouse'.

maid (female servant)
The word was in use in the twelfth century in English, when it was simply a shortening of 'maiden', which itself could mean 'girl', 'young woman' as well as 'female servant'. The use of 'maiden' for 'servant' became finally obsolete in the seventeenth century, however (when even 'maiden of honour'

became 'maid of honour') and 'maid' had meantime been established in this specialized sense from the fourteenth century. For a while, from the fourteenth century to about 1700, 'maid' could also be applied to a man to mean 'male virgin', and Shakespeare plays on the sense in *Twelfth Night* (1601), when in the final scene Sebastian says to Olivia:

You are betroth'd both to a maid and a man.

(He means that she is betrothed to himself, whom she had mistaken for Cesario, who was actually Viola disguised as a page when, earlier, Olivia had fallen for 'him'!) The loss of the final '-en' from 'maiden' to form 'maid' is similar to the formation of 'eve' from 'even'.

main (chief)
In dialect use in thirteenth-century English, 'main' meant 'large in size', a sense preserved by Milton in *Paradise Lost* (1667):

Themselves invaded next, and on thir heads
Main Promontories flung.

In the fourteenth century, the meaning 'strong', 'mighty' developed, with this surviving in the phrase 'by main force'. At the same time, the dialect use extended to 'great in number' or 'great in degree', with particular application to warfare, so that 'main battle' became a standard expression for a pitched battle, as distinct from mere skirmishing. This now obsolete sense can be seen, for example, in John Marston's *The History of Antonio and Mellida* (1600):

Huge troups of barbed steeds,
Maine squares of pikes, millions of harguebush [i.e. arquebuses].

The current sense of 'main' then followed in the fifteenth century. The word has acquired a number of special usages, such as the 'main drain' (first recorded in the eighteenth century), from which the noun 'the main' or 'the mains' developed, now applying to gas and electricity services as well as water. The phrase 'in the main' arose in the sixteenth century, apparently from 'the main chance', originally a throw of dice in a game of chance.

171

malice (deliberate desire to harm)
In the thirteenth century, 'malice' meant simply 'badness', from the identical French word and meaning. The word is first recorded in the *Cursor Mundi:*

> Mikel malice was first in man
> Bot neuer forwit sua mikel as than.

(That is: There was much badness first in man, but never before as much as then.) By the fourteenth century, the meaning had become more precise as 'harmfulness', 'power to harm'. This is the sense in Shakespeare's *King John* (1595), where King Philip says:

> Our cannons' malice vainly shall be spent
> Against the invulnerable clouds of heaven.

The usage became obsolete in the seventeenth century, and the current meaning, which had first arisen in the thirteenth century, was the one to prevail. The specifically legal sense of 'malice', however (the premeditated evil intent to commit a crime, especially murder), arose in the sixteenth century, and became familiar from the legal phrase 'malice aforethought'.

man (adult male, human being)
Both the meanings given here were current in Old English, although the more prominent sense was 'human being', so that the distinctive words for 'man' and 'woman' were *wer* and *wīf*, or *wǣthman* and *wīfman*, that is, literally 'man human being' and 'woman human being', with the latter word giving 'woman' itself.

This 'human being' sense of 'man' persisted long in the language, and even in the eighteenth century, it obviously did not seem ambiguous to Hume to write, in his *Political Discourses* (1752): 'There is in all men, both male and female, a desire and power of generation more active than is ever universally exerted'. In recent use, the general meaning 'person' usually occurred when 'man' was in the plural, and preceded by some such word as 'all', 'many'. But even so the word was still seen or felt to have a more 'male' connotation than an equal division of the sexes, with 'men' embracing 'women' (as the hoary old pun went), so

that many people now avoid the word altogether and instead say 'people' or 'everybody' or 'everyone' instead (as I have just done in this sentence).

manage (cope successfully, succeed in handling)
The verb was first used in English only in the sixteenth century, and in many cases down to the eighteenth century was spelt 'menage'. This belies the original sense of the word, which was 'handle a horse', as well as 'conduct' something or 'control' somebody generally. The 'horse' sense occurs, for example, in Spenser's *The Faerie Queene* (1590):

> A goodly person, and could menage faire
> His stubborne steed with curbed canon bitt,

and also in Thomas Hoy's *Agathocles* (1683):

> An Hard-mouth'd Beast, for slacken'd Raines unfitt,
> And must be menag'd with the Spur and Bitt.

The development of this to 'cope successfully' came in the eighteenth century, with the spelling regularized as today, but also with the 'French' spelling 'menage' (associated with *menager*, 'to use sparingly') adopted in the seventeenth century for the separate noun 'housekeeping', while at the same time the noun 'manage', which meant 'place where a horse is handled', 'riding school', was similarly assimilated to the French spelling 'manege', which is the standard one today for such an establishment (and more especially an area for schooling a horse in dressage). Some quotations of the eighteenth century show a confusion between 'manage', 'menage' and 'manege', so will not be reproduced here!

manhandle (handle using human force)
The earliest sense of the word, in the fifteenth century, was 'wield a tool', and it was only in the nineteenth century that the present meaning evolved, with the additional usage 'handle roughly', also arising at this time, perhaps influenced by the dialect word 'manangle', an altered spelling of 'mangle'.

manicure (treatment of the hand and fingernails)
The word came into English from French in the late nineteenth century. At first (in 1880) it meant 'manicurist'. Soon, however, (from 1887) it settled to mean the treatment itself, although the earlier meaning is still not obsolete. (Compare the two meanings of 'pedicure'.)

manipulation (manual management; artful control to one's own advantage)
The earliest sense of the word, in the eighteenth century, was a specific one relating to the handling of chemical apparatus. 'It is only by an exact similarity in all the essential points of Manipulation', wrote Richard Kirwan in *Elements of Mineralogy* (1784), 'that results exactly similar can be expected'. In the nineteenth century, the meaning 'manual control or management' arose, including the surgical sense of 'manipulation' to indicate examination of a part of the body. The current 'devious influence' sense was beginning to emerge, too, when in Harriet Beecher Stowe's *Uncle Tom's Cabin* (1852) one reads: 'In the zeal of her manipulations, the young disciple had contrived to snatch a pair of gloves and a ribbon, which she had adroitly slipped into her sleeves'. The application to financial manoeuvring to gain advantage followed later in the same century, with 'market manipulation' recorded first in 1908.

manor (large house formerly owned by a lord)
This word and 'mansion' have virtually exchanged senses over the centuries. In the thirteenth century, a 'manor' was in fact a 'mansion', that is, a country residence, the principle house of an estate. A survival of this sense can be found in the names of some country houses as 'Blank Manor', such as 'Avebury Manor', Wiltshire (built 1550) and 'Sedgebrook Manor', Lincolnshire (built about 1632). Locally, such houses are often called simply 'the Manor'. In the fourteenth century, 'manor' as a concept was extended to mean a lord's mansion with the estate belonging to it, and in the sixteenth century, a 'manor' was a unit of territory consisting of such an estate under a lord. Compare **mansion**.

mansion (house of the lord of a manor; grand residence)
In its earliest sense, as current in the fourteenth century, a 'mansion' was simply a dwelling or living place, or even the act of dwelling or living, as preserved in Shakespeare's *Timon of Athens* (1607), where Timon says:

Timon hath made his everlasting mansion
Upon the beached verge of the salt flood.

By the sixteenth century, a 'mansion' had come to be a term for a manor house, with the use of the word soon extended to mean any large or grand residence, whether actually called 'Mansion' (or 'Manor') or not. The same is true of a 'mansion house', although this came to be the title of the official residence of a church official (originally) and specifically that of the Lord Mayor of London (from the mid-eighteenth century, when the Mansion House was built). In the nineteenth century, the word, with its now 'grand' connotations, was adopted for the large blocks of flats that were erected in Victorian London. Such buildings were hardly sumptuous, as the real 'mansions' had been, with the result that the word was to some extent 'demoted', as instanced by a report in the *Daily Chronicle* of 17 June 1901: 'The inhabitants of Cornwall Mansions, finding that the word is now applied to less than ultra-select blocks of residences, have petitioned the Kensington Council to change the name of Cornwall-place'. (They were unsuccessful, and Cornwall Mansions are still here, next to the Royal Albert Hall, together with several other 'Mansions'.) Compare **manor** (above).

manufacture (process of making articles or products)
'Manufacture' implies 'made by hand' (Latin *manu factum*), and when first current in the sixteenth century, the word meant 'object made by manual labour'. From this, the sense progressed to 'making of articles either by physical labour or by machinery' in the seventeenth century, with a now obsolete meaning 'manual work' also developing, so that the *Boston Record* reported in 1660 that no person must

'. . .occupy any manufacture or science, till hee hath compleated 21 years of age'. Today, too, 'manufacture' nearly always implies the production of goods on a large scale, which was not in the original senses.

manure (animal dung used as fertilizer)
The noun developed in the sixteenth century out of the fourteenth-century verb 'manure' which meant 'cultivate', 'till', and this in turn evolved from the original meaning, in the same century, that was 'occupy', 'administer', 'manage', especially as applied to land or property. This first sense shows the close relation between 'manure' and 'manoeuvre', both deriving from the French, and with the former being an adaptation of the latter word. Early spellings of 'manure' are thus closer to 'manoeuvre' in this meaning, as in the 1430 *Rolls of Parliament:* 'The saide tenauntz and lond holders dar not inhabite, maynour nor occupye the saide Toun'. Later spellings were the same as currently, which makes for odd reading unless one appreciates the different sense, so that Sir Thomas Smith, in *The Common-wealth of England and Maner of Government thereof* (1577) readily wrote that the Commonwealth was 'gouerned, administered and manured by three sortes of persons'.

marathon (long-distance race)
The word properly applies, as it originally did when first recorded in 1896, to the long-distance race of the Olympic Games, which were revived (in Athens) in that year. Various extended senses of the word developed in the twentieth century, to apply to different feats of endurance (the *Daily Chronicle* of 5 November 1908 reported a 'Murphy Marathon' as a potato-peeling contest), and especially ones of long duration, such as a 'marathon sitting' of the House of Commons or a 'marathon' court case. One consequence of this was the use of the '-thon' element to denote some lengthy activity or contest, with the first part of the word denoting what was involved. Examples are 'talkathon', 'walkathon', 'movie-thon' and 'telethon', the last being a long television programme, with guest celebrities, that is designed to raise money for charity.

maroon (brownish-red colour; distress rocket)
French *marron* means 'chestnut', and this word was adopted by English in the sixteenth century to denote the sweet (edible) chestnut. This sense soon fell out of use. In the eighteenth century, a secondary sense of French *marron* was borrowed by English for the name of the dark reddish-brown colour, which properly in French is *couleur marron*, 'chestnut colour'. In the same century, and again from French, 'maroon' was used to name a type of firework, that 'popped' like an exploding chestnut when being roasted. Later, in the nineteenth century, a 'maroon' was an explosive rocket used as a distress signal, and in the First World War the word came to mean an air-raid warning, with the devices themselves used at the end of the war to celebrate victory. (The *Daily Mirror* of 12 November 1918 reported that in London: 'Bells burst into joyful chimes, maroons were exploded, bands paraded the streets, and London gave itself up wholeheartedly to rejoicing'.)

martyr (person put to death for adherence to a cause)
The word is an old one (in Old English it was *martir*), and originally denoted a person who *voluntarily* underwent death, and in particular for the Christian faith. Thus Wyclif, the Bible translator, wrote in 1388 that: 'Of Seint Steven men bene certayne by holy writte that he is a gloriouse martire'. However, by the sixteenth century, the word had come to be used of anyone who had lost his or her life (or been tortured) for any cause, and not necessarily voluntarily. Possibly this new sense was reinforced by the execution of 'King Charles the Martyr' in 1649 (his nickname was recorded by Evelyn in 1672), since he would hardly have volunteered to submit to execution. As with many 'severe' words, too, the sense of 'martyr' has now been weakened to mean little more than 'sufferer', 'victim of tedious circumstances'. Even in 1847, Frances Anne Kemble (better known as Fanny Kemble, the actress and writer), wrote in her *Records of Later Life* (published in 1882): 'She is a martyr to dyspepsia and bad cooking'.

match (slender piece of wood with special head for igniting)
The sense has developed along with the object. In the fourteenth century, a 'match' was a wick (compare modern French *mèche* in this sense), that is, the wick of a candle or lamp. Thus, an English translation (1422) of the Latin *Secreta secretorum* advised as follows: 'Yf the mecche be ouer depe y-sette in the oyle, hit shall anoone be y-queynte'. (That is, if the wick is set too low in the oil, it will go straight out.) From the sixteenth century, the word came to apply to the various successive forerunners of the modern match, such as lengths of inflammable cord, wood and so on. The present 'match' dates recognizably from about 1830 (when it had to be prepared in a rather complex process of dipping and drying before being ignited by contact with a special chemical).

mawkish (feebly sentimental, maudlin)
The word derives from 'mawk', an old word for a maggot, therefore it is not so surprising to find that its original sense in English, in the seventeenth century, was 'nauseating', 'sick-making', as well as 'nauseated', 'having no appetite'. Thus, Swift wrote in *The Progress of Marriage* (1745):

The dean who us'd to dine at one,
Is maukish, and his stomach gone.

In the eighteenth century, the current sense evolved, and the earlier meaning became obsolete.

meat (animal flesh as food)
In Old English, *mete* was 'food' in general, especially solid food as contrasted with drink (hence the still current expression 'meat and drink'). The usage of the word in this sense lasted for some time, so that Thomas Norton was able to write in *The Ordinall of Alchimy* (1477) that 'Without Liquor no Meate is good', and Dr Johnson, in *A Journey to the Western Islands of Scotland* (1775), relates how his guides told him that: 'The horses could not travel all day without rest or meat'. The modern meaning of 'meat' became current only in the fourteenth century. The apparent preservation of the old 'non-flesh' sense in 'mincemeat'

is misleading, since mincemeat originally contained meat.

medal (coin-shaped piece of metal with inscription, issued as an award etc.)
Originally, in the sixteenth century, a 'medal' was a metal disc used as a charm or trinket, not as a commemorative award or prize, as it is today. This is therefore the meaning of the word in Shakespeare's *The Winter's Tale* (1611), where Leontes says to Camillo, referring to Polixenes and his supposed relationship with his wife, Hermione:

Why, he that wears her like her medal, hanging
About his neck.

This sense of 'medal' became obsolete in the seventeenth century, and the current meaning dates from about that time.

medley (mixture)
The word is related to 'mêlée', and in the fourteenth century meant explicitly 'combat' or 'conflict', in particular hand-to-hand fighting between two parties of combatants. Thus Malory, in *Le Morte Darthur* (1470–85), recorded how: 'Lucas and Gwynas & bryaunte & Bellyas of Flaundrys held strong medle ayenst vj kynges' (i.e. four held their own against six). In the fifteenth century, 'medley' came to mean 'combination', 'mixture', at first in an acceptable sense, but later (from the seventeenth century) disparagingly, as when Pepys recorded in his *Diary* entry for 18 January 1669: 'To the Duke of York's playhouse and there saw "The Witts", a medley of things'. However, also in the seventeenth century, a 'medley' came to denote a musical mixture or 'pot-pourri', and in this sense soon lost its connotation of disapproval. With the arrival of the 'medley relay' in sport, in particular in swimming events and athletics, the word has now virtually lost any sense of 'conflict' or discord.

meek (submissive, long-suffering)
The original meaning of 'meek' in the twelfth century was 'gentle', 'kind', a usage that persisted until at least the seventeenth century and that survives in Shakespeare's

Julius Caesar (1601), when Antony, after the death of Caesar, says:

> O! pardon me, thou bleeding piece of earth,
> That I am meek and gentle with these butchers.

The sense of 'meek' in the Bible, however, as familiarly in 'Blessed are the meek', is the modern one, where the word represents the Christian virtue of pious humility and submission. It seems likely, though, that Charles Wesley, in his well-known hymn (1742) 'Gentle Jesus, meek and mild', was aiming to recreate the original sense, as were other writers, such as Blake, in repeating or echoing the phrase. The specifically 'submissive' sense of 'meek' thus dates from the fourteenth century.

melancholy (depression, dejection, sadly pensive mood or state)
The origin of the word lies in the Greek for 'black bile', and when first used in English in the fourteenth century, 'melancholy' described the physical and mental condition of supposedly having too much 'black bile', that is, an excess of one of the four chief **'humours'** (see this word) of the body. As first understood, the symptoms of the condition showed themselves in undue sullenness and a tendency to sudden unexplained bursts of anger. Later, the state was seen to be one of depression and sadness, a feeling of 'gloom and doom'. The 'sullen' connotation can be found in Shakespeare's use of the word in *King John* (1595), where King John says to Hubert:

> Or if that surly spirit, melancholy,
> Had bak'd thy blood and made it heavy-thick.

The 'sad' sense of 'melancholy', however, is first recorded as early as in Chaucer's *Troilus and Criseyde* (1374):

> Bycause he wolde soone dye,
> He ne eet ne dronk, for his malencolye.

The Elizabethan poets made quite a cult of 'melancholy' as a mental and emotional attitude of refinement, and the concept features widely in Ben Jonson's *Every Man in his Humour* (1598), for example ('I will be more proud and melancholie, and gentle-

man-like than I haue beene, I doe ensure you'), and this usage persisted for some time, so that 'melancholy pleasures', for instance, were not thought of as absurd or self-contradictory.

melodrama (play in which plot and action are more important than character or motive)
The word came into English from French, with its ultimate Greek source meaning 'song play'. When the melodrama was first imported to England in the early nineteenth century, it had the characteristics of the French *mélodrame*, which was a kind of sensational play interspersed with songs. Of the many English melodramas of this 'early' period, among the best known were Douglas Jerrold's *Black-Ey'd Susan* (1829) and the classic *Maria Marten; or, The Murder in the Red Barn* (1830). Later, the English melodrama lost its essential musical ingredient, and became a sensational drama with a violent and mostly crude appeal to the emotions. Among this 'late' type some of the best known English melodramas were Mary E. Braddon's *Lady Audley's Secret* (1863) and *The Bells* (1874), based on Mrs Henry Wood's novel *East Lynne* (1861). This is thus the current concept of 'melodrama', with its vividly contrasted hero or heroine and villain, and its general 'blood and thunder' (if not 'thud and blunder') content. With the coming of the cinema, however, the melodrama itself became a thing of the past from about the 1920s.

melody (tune)
The word has had three distinct senses over the years, all still current. The oldest, from the thirteenth century, is 'sweet music', 'music that is delightful to listen to'. Shakespeare's works would not have been complete without it, and 'melody' in this sense comes, for example, in *A Midsummer Night's Dream* (1590), in the Fairies' Song ('Philomel, with melody'). Poets from Milton onward, too, made much of the sense and sound of one of the most evocative words in English, such as James Thomson in *The Seasons* (*Spring*, 1728):

> Lend me your song, ye nightingales; oh pour

The mazy-running soul of melody
Into my varied verse.

The second sense to emerge was the seventeenth-century one of 'tune', 'air', and this is the meaning of 'melody' in Keats's *Ode on a Grecian Urn* (1819):

Heard melodies are sweet, but those
    unheard
Are sweeter.

The final meaning of the word was the technical musical term used for 'the arrangement of single notes in expressive succession' (*OED*), as distinguished from 'harmony'. This usage arose in the eighteenth century.

memento (object serving as a memorial, reminder or souvenir)
The word is Latin for 'remember' (grammatically the imperative of the verb *meminisse*, 'to remember'), and its initial use in English was to designate one or other of two prayers in the Mass in the fifteenth century that began with this word. (The two prayers commemorated, respectively, the living and the departed.) From the sixteenth century, 'memento' came to mean 'reminder' or 'warning' generally, so that you would give or send a person a 'memento' to do something, much as today one business colleague can pass another a 'memo'. From the eighteenth century, 'memento' acquired its current sense, where it was first recorded in Cuthbert Shaw's *A Monody to the Memory of a Young Lady* (1768):

Where'er I turn my eyes,
Some sad memento of my loss appears.

memoir (type of autobiographical account)
As originally used, in the sixteenth century, a 'memoir' was a note or record, or more of a memorandum. This sense became obsolete in the eighteenth century. From the seventeenth century, in its plural use, the word came to have its present sense, meaning both 'record of events' (as told by a particular person) or 'record of transactions', such as the 'Memoirs read before the Anthropological Society of London' (1865). The first of these meanings is the more general now, and occurs in the titles

of a number of autobiographies, such as Siegfried Sassoon's two books 'Memoirs of a Fox-Hunting Man' (1928) and 'Memoirs of an Infantry Officer' (1930).

memorize (commit to memory, learn by heart)
In the sixteenth century, 'memorize' meant 'cause to be remembered', as in Shakespeare's *Macbeth* (1605), when the wounded Sergeant says:

Except they meant to bathe in reeking
    wounds,
Or memorize another Golgotha.

The present meaning dates only from the nineteenth century, when the first sense became obsolete.

menial (lowly, degrading)
In the fourteenth century, 'menial' merely meant 'domestic', without any sense of 'servile'. This was thus the word chosen by Wyclif to translate Latin *domesticam* in his English Bible translation of 1338, so that Romans 16:5 has: 'Grete ye wel her meyneal chirche' (Authorized Version of 1611: 'Greet the church that is in their house'). From the seventeenth century, 'menial' became applied to servants and their work, since such work was of a domestic nature, and from this in turn 'menial' took on its generally disparaging modern sense (as a 'menial' task). The word itself is actually related to 'mansion', and is nothing to do with 'mean', as is sometimes supposed.

mere (simply as it is and nothing more)
The earliest meaning of 'mere', in the fifteenth century, was 'done without the help of anyone else', especially in a legal sense. Thus if a person did something 'of his mere motion', he alone did it, without the assistance of anyone else. In the sixteenth century, 'mere' came to have two virtually opposite senses, the first of which is now obsolete. These were, respectively, 'as it is in the fullest sense of the word', 'nothing less than', and (the current sense) 'simply as it is', 'nothing more than'. The first sense thus really meant 'absolute', 'perfect', and this is the usage in Richard Hooker's *Of the Lawes of Ecclesiastical Politie* (1594), when he wrote: 'Our God is One,

or rather very Oneness, and meer Unity'. Or, in a more down to earth way, in Defoe's *Robinson Crusoe* (1719), when Crusoe says that he ' . . .became, in a little time, a mere pastry-cook, into the bargain', meaning that he was a perfect one. This sense fell out of use in the eighteenth century, and 'mere' now has the other, 'restricting' meaning.

meretricious (showily but falsely attractive)
Latin *meretrix* means 'prostitute', and when the word was first current in English in the seventeenth century, it frequently related specifically to prostitutes. Thus Bacon wrote in *The New Atlantis* (1626): 'The Delight in Meretricious Embracements (wher sinne is turned into Art) maketh Marriage a dull thing', and Henry More, in *An Exposition of the Seven Epistles of the Seven Churches* (1669), said of Jezebel that she '. . . for all her paintings and fine meretricious pranking herself up, [. . .] was to be thrown out at the window'. The literal usage became obsolete in the nineteenth century and only the figurative sense prevailed.

merge (combine, unite, blend, or cause to do this)
As first current in the seventeenth century, 'merge' meant 'immerse', 'plunge', more figuratively than literally, so that the Puritan pamphleteer William Prynne, in *The Unbishoping of Timothy and Titus* (1636), wrote of his subjects that they ' . . .merge themselves in pleasures, idlenesse, or secular affaires'. However, in the nineteenth century, some poets used the literal meaning, such as J.M. Neale in a hymn of 1866:

All his spite the Tempter urges;
Casts in fire, in water merges,

(where the last three words, in the Latin original from which he was translating, represent *aquis mergit*). The current meaning thus dates from the eighteenth century, with the first business or company 'merger' recorded (in America) in the nineteenth century.

merry (happy, high-spirited, slightly drunk)
In Old English, 'merry' (*myrge*) did not have its present sense, but meant simply 'pleasant', 'agreeable', and this is the proper meaning of 'Merry England', now usually misunderstood as something like 'Good Old Rollicking, Frolicking England'. (The phrase itself is first recorded in the *Cursor Mundi* of the early fourteenth century:

Brut that berne bolde of hand,
First conquerour of meri ingland.

The first three words here mean 'Brut the warrior', referring to Brut or Brutus the Trojan, the legendary first king of Britain.) A similar sense applied to music or sounds that were 'merry', such as birdsong, and to the weather when it was fine or the wind when it was favourable. This last sense, for example, comes in Shakespeare's *The Comedy of Errors* (1590), when Dromio of Syracuse reports to his master Antipholus:

The ship is in her trim; the merry wind
Blows fair from land.

In the fourteenth century, 'merry' acquired much of its present meaning, although it was at first more 'agreeably lively' than 'amusing', and at first applied to the particular pastimes and customs associated with medieval England, such as feasting and sport. Otherwise the usage applied to people and their characters, and it is here that 'Robin Hood and his Merry Men' belong, with this phrase first recorded (in the spelling of its day) in 1510. The 'amusing' aspect of 'merry' followed in the fifteenth century, originally applied to a saying, and the 'slightly drunk' sense was first noted in the sixteenth century. A later usage of the word to mean 'pleasantly amused' is now obsolete. It was first recorded in Shakespeare's *Timon of Athens* (1607), when Lucius says to Servilius:

I know his lordship is but merry with me.

One of the most popular modern uses of 'merry', to wish someone the 'compliments of the season' (as 'Merry Christmas'), appeared near the end of the sixteenth century, so is not purely Dickensian, as is sometimes thought.

meteor ('shooting star')
In the fifteenth century, 'meteor' was used

to apply to any natural phenomenon of the atmosphere, so that 'aerial meteors' (or 'airy meteors') were winds, 'aqueous meteors' (or 'watery meteors') were precipitation of some kind, such as rain, snow, hail or dew, 'luminous meteors' were such phenomena as the aurora, rainbows, haloes and the like, and 'igneous meteors' (or 'fiery meteors') were lightning and. . . meteors proper, which exclusive sense the word came to acquire from the sixteenth century, where it is first recorded, as such 'pioneering' words often are, in Shakespeare. It comes in *Richard II* (1593), where the Captain says to Salisbury:

The bay-trees in our country are all wither'd
And meteors fright the fixed stars of heaven.

(Some seventeenth-century works use 'meteor' to denote a comet, but this misuse was shortlived.)

meticulous (extremely or excessively careful)
The ultimate Latin root word from which 'meticulous' derives is *metus*, 'fear', and this is reflected in its original currency, in the sixteenth century, when it meant 'timid'. Even as late as 1674, Zachary Cawdry's *Catholicon* has the word in this sense: 'They strive not so much to ingage Meticulous Scrupulous Women and Mechanicks'. This usage became obsolete thereafter, and the current meaning dates only from the nineteenth century.

microphone (device for converting sounds and electrical signals for transmission or recording)
In the seventeenth century, a 'microphone' was an instrument for amplifying or intensifying sounds, defined in the *Philosophical Transactions of the Royal Society* for 1683 as a 'magnifying ear Instrument'. In 1878, the word was adopted for the device invented by Professor David Hughes 'by means of which the telephone is made to reproduce faint sounds with more than their original intensity' (*OED*). In other words, Hughes's instrument was a telephonic transmitter, and for some time after this 'microphone' became synonymous with 'transmitter' until the familiar 'broadcasting' microphones, as

separate instruments, emerged in the twentieth century.

middling (of medium size or quality, mediocre)
The current sense dates from the sixteenth century. A hundred years earlier, 'middling' meant 'intermediate', 'midway between two extremes', as in Ben Jonson's 'A certaine midling thing, betweene a foole and a madman' (*Bartholomew Fayre*, 1614). This usage became obsolete in the eighteenth century.

midriff (middle part of human torso or garment that covers it)
The word is an Old English one (*midhrif*), literally meaning 'mid belly', and from the eleventh century to the twentieth 'midriff' was exclusively used of the diaphragm, the body partition of muscle and connective tissue that separates the chest and abdomen (technically, the thoracic and abdominal cavities). Hence the expression 'tickle the midriff', said of something that provokes laughter. From this 'internal' sense, however, 'midriff' came to mean the mid-portion of the torso, or the garment covering (or revealing) it. This sense shift occurred only in the 1930s and was the result of innovation in fashions. The meaning 'diaphragm' is still current, however, even if it is the newer sense that has stolen the popularity.

mild (not strong, gentle)
In Old English, 'mild' meant 'gentle', 'not rough', as now, although it could also mean 'gracious', 'kind', especially as applied to a superior, such as a king. In John de Trevisa's translation (1398) of Ranulf Higden's *Polychronicon*, written in Latin prose, he talks of: 'Theobald the mylde, eorle of Campania' (translating Latin *pius* as 'mild'), and Milton used the word in this sense in *Paradise Lost* (1667):

Remember with what mild
And gracious temper he both heard and judg'd
Without wrauth or reviling.

This sense, too, was specially applied to God, Christ and the Virgin Mary, to be combined with '**meek**' (which see) in more recent times in an attempt to recreate the original meaning. In the thirteenth century, 'mild' could mean 'tame', a usage that no longer exists, although it persisted to the nineteenth century. In his *Natural History* (1774), Goldsmith thus wrote of an elephant: 'Mild, peaceful, and brave, it never abuses its power or its strength'. The additional sense of 'not strong' was acquired by 'mild' in the fifteenth century, and it is this usage that applies to the weather or the climate ('mild morning').

mildew (whitish growth on plants; growth of fungi on paper, leather, etc.)
The Old English meaning of the word was 'honeydew' (compare Latin *mel*, French *miel*, 'honey'), that is, the sugary substance deposited on plants by aphids or, less often, by fungus. This usage was current from the eleventh century to the seventeenth. The modern meaning arose in the fourteenth century.

minion (servile attendant, petty official)
There has been a sort of 'role reversal' here. The word came into English, in the sixteenth century, from French *mignon*, which means 'darling'. The original sense was thus 'lover', 'lady-love'. The connotation soon changed from favourable to unfavourable, however, and the word was used disapprovingly of a mistress or 'paramour', with this usage already occurring in Spenser's *The Faerie Queene* (1590):

A mincing mineon,
Who in her loosenesse tooke exceeding ioy.

At the same time, 'minion' meant 'favourite', whether a close friend, a favourite child, a favoured servant, a loved animal, or, more generally, a popular 'idol' or 'hero' (or 'heroine'). Thus in George Pettie's translation (1581) of Guazzo's *Ciuile Conuersation*, the word is used of a child: 'I cannot abide the folly of some fathers who make some one of their children their darling and minion'. And in William Somerville's poem *The Chace* (1735), it refers to an animal:

That pamper'd Steed, his Master's Joy,
His Minion, and his daily Care.

This sense particularly applied, however, to the favourite of a king or queen, or other royal personage, and although at first intended flatteringly, the later usage was contemptuous, like that of the 'lover'. Hence Swift, in *Gulliver's Travels* (1726), had Gulliver say: 'I had no Occasion of bribing, flattering, or pimping, to procure the Favour of any great Man, or of his Minion'. From this in turn 'minion' came to mean 'hussy' on the one hand and 'abject servant' on the other, with this connotation well established by the early seventeenth century. The sense as a whole has thus gone from good to bad, or from 'worshipped' to 'despised'. For something like the converse of this, see the next entry.

minister (church official, high officer of state)
Whereas '**minion**' (see above) fell in sense from favoured to unfavoured, 'minister' has done almost the reverse, and progressed from lowly to superior. In the thirteenth century, a 'minister' was a servant, a subordinate, one who ministered. The sense can be seen in Henry Bradshaw's *The Life of Saint Werburge of Chester* (1513):

The mynysters were redy theyr offyce to fulfyll
To take vp the tables at theyr lordes wyll.

From the fourteenth century, 'minister' was the word for an official of the church who both 'ministered' to his flock and their needs and held a sacred office, in particular that of a clergyman (who is still designated as 'minister' in the Church of England Book of Common Prayer). Such a 'minister' was therefore both 'subservient' to his people and to God, yet superior to his flock in the office he held, and in the status he had in the church. The term 'minister of religion', too, is still current to serve as the official designation of the man who is otherwise a 'clergyman' (in the Church of England) or a 'minister' (in other Protestant denominations). This therefore serves as a sort of 'halfway house' to the 'elevated' minister who is the 'minister of state', with the sense evolving in the seventeenth century. He now more *ad*ministers than simply ministers, but he still serves people, government and country, despite his superior status, so the title is not quite such a misnomer as it seems.

mint (place where money is coined)
In Old English, 'mint' (*mynet*) was the word for a coin itself, deriving ultimately from Latin *moneta* that also gave 'money'. The modern meaning developed in the fifteenth century. See also **coin**.

miscarry (suffer a miscarriage [of a foetus]; go wrong)
The verb has three distinct senses, the first of which is now obsolete. In the fourteenth century, to 'miscarry' was to perish or be destroyed, as applied to a person who had been killed, for example, or a ship that had sunk or been wrecked. The usage was current down to the eighteenth century, so that in 1668, Sir William Temple, in a letter to Charles II, wrote that: 'If we had miscarried, your Majesty had lost an honest diligent Captain and sixteen poor Seamen'. The second sense, 'suffer a miscarriage', arose in the sixteenth century, and the third, 'go wrong', in the seventeenth, where it is first recorded in Shakespeare's *Coriolanus* (1607), when Junius Brutus says to Sicinius Velutus, speaking of Cominius:

> For what miscarries
> Shall be the general's fault.

mischief (playful annoyance, injury or damage)
The thirteenth-century meaning of 'mischief' was 'misfortune', 'distress', as in Chaucer's *Canterbury Tales* (1386), where in the Prologue we learn of the Parson:

> He ne lafte nat, for reyn ne thonder,
> In sikness ne in meschief, to visyte
> The ferrest in his parisshe.

(That is, he never neglected, in rain or thunder, sickness or distress, to visit the furthest in his parish.) This sense became obsolete in the seventeenth century. The further sense development of 'mischief' was: 'harm', 'injury' in the fourteenth century, 'cause of harm' in the sixteenth, and 'petty or playful annoyance' in the eighteenth.

misericord (ledge on seat of choirstall on which, when it is raised, person can support himself when standing)
This is a rarish word, and a specialized one, but it has undergone some interesting sense changes. In the fourteenth century, a 'misericord' (literally a 'pitiful heart') simply meant 'mercy', 'pity'. The usage survived as an exclamation, borrowed from the French, as late as the eighteenth century, meaning 'Mercy on us!' (or something similar). Thus a character in Vanbrugh's play *The Confederacy* (1705) exclaims: 'Misericorde! what do I see!'. In the fifteenth century, the word was adopted for the name of a dagger for giving the 'coup de grâce', or 'mercy stroke', to a gravely wounded person, or even oneself, in battle when there was no hope of recovery. (The dagger was also called a 'dagger of mercy'.) Finally, in the sixteenth century, the word acquired its present meaning, to denote the seat-ledge that provided support to a standing worshipper in the choirstalls of a church or monastery. The derivation is not a punning one, alluding to a kind of 'mercy seat', but is taken from another use of 'misericord' as a term for an apartment in a monastery where some relaxation of the normally strict rules was permitted, in particular the place where monks ate when they were allowed a special diet for reasons of infirmity or old age. It would have been such monks that would most have needed physical support while standing throughout the lengthy services.

mistake (make an error or slip, be or go wrong)
In the thirteenth century, to 'mistake' was to transgress, to err, as in Chaucer's *The Romaunt of the Rose* (1366):

> Ladyes, I preye ensample taketh,
> Ye that ayeins [i.e. against] your love
> mistaketh.

In the fourteenth century, 'mistake' acquired its most literal sense, to mean 'take wrongly', i.e. to 'mis-take'. Wyclif used it in his Bible translation of 1382, where Deuteronomy 5:11 runs: 'Thow shalt not mystaak the name of the Lord thi God idillich' (Authorized Version of 1611: 'Thou shalt not take the name of the Lord thy God in vain'). Both these usages are now obsolete. The next sense to emerge was the fifteenth-century one of 'misunderstand', still current, and in the following century 'mistake' finally came to be used in its present popular sense of 'go wrong'.

moan (low groan of pain or grief)
The earliest sense of 'moan', in the thirteenth century, was 'complaint', 'lament'. It occurs, for example, in John de Trevisa's translation (1398) of *De proprietatibus rerum*, by Bartholomaeus Anglicus: 'The kite seketh his meete wepynge wyth voys of pleynynge and of moon'. The word was particularly favoured in this sense by nineteenth century romantic poets such as Keats and Tennyson, with the latter including it, for instance in *The Miller's Daughter* (1832):

And oft I heard the tender dove
In firry woodlands making moan.

The current meaning of 'moan', referring to the low sound of grief or other emotion, arose only in the seventeenth century, and first occurs in Milton's sonnet *On the late Massacre in Piedmont* (1673):

Avenge O Lord thy slaughter'd
Saints,[. . .]
                    Their moans
The Vales redoubl'd to the Hills.

mode (fashion, manner)
As currently used, 'mode' has a wide range of technical and specialized senses, ranging from physics to music, philosophy to statistics. Its earliest usage, in the fourteenth century, was in the meaning 'tune', 'melody', and the first record we have of it is in Chaucer's translation (1374) of Boethius' Latin work, *De consolatione philosophiae*, where the sentence occurs: 'Musyce: A damysel of oure hows that syngeth now lyhtere moedes or probasyons now heuyere'. (The second half of this translated the Latin *nunc leviores, nunc graviores modos*, i.e. 'now lighter, now heavier modes'. Chaucer explains 'modes' as 'probations', so to speak 'demonstrations' or 'trials'.) The next sense of 'mode' to develop was the sixteenth-century one of 'mood' (in grammar and logic). Both these usages are now obsolete, with 'mode' now replaced by the actual word 'mood' in the two technical senses.

The musical 'mode' above related solely to the so called diatonic scales of music in Ancient Greece, each of which had a name (such as the Dorian Mode, Lydian Mode, and so on). In the seventeenth century, a new use of 'mode' in a musical sense arose to apply to the medieval type of church music in which plainsong was composed. Here, the 'modes' were scales derived from, and named after, the Greek ones, although essentially different from them. The philosophical 'mode' also evolved in the seventeenth century. All these 'modes' are based on Latin *modus*, 'measure', 'manner', 'method', 'tune'. The last English 'mode' to arrive was the fashion one, also in the seventeenth century, but adopted from French *mode*, not Latin.

modern (present-day, up-to-date, recent)
The word came into English in the sixteenth century, when it was taken (through French) from Late Latin *modernus*, itself based on Latin *modo*, 'just now'. It has had its current sense ever since, but it also had two now obsolete meanings. The first of these was 'existing now', so that a formal Scottish document of 1555 refers to 'our maist gracious quene moderne', and a charter of 1752 of the Society of Antiquaries of London states that 'Martin Folkes, Esquire' has been nominated 'to be the first and modern President of the said Society'. The other defunct usage of 'modern' is one found frequently in Shakespeare, where it means 'ordinary', 'everyday'. In *As You Like It* (1600), for example, it can be found in Jaques's famous 'All the world's a stage' speech, where the 'justice' or judge is described as:

Full of wise saws and modern instances.

Both senses were out of use by the end of the eighteenth century

moist (damp, slightly wet)
The word has been in use in English since the fourteenth century, when it also had two meanings, now obsolete, of 'new', 'fresh', and 'liquid', 'watery'. The first of these is found only in Chaucer, when in *The Canterbury Tales* (1386) the Prologue to 'The Pardoner's Tale' mentions 'A draughte of moyste and corny Ale' and in the Prologue

to the work as a whole, the 'worthy woman from beside Bath city' (as she is translated in a modern version) has her dress described:

Hir hosen weren of fyn scarlet reed
fful streite yteid and shoes ful moyste
    and newe.

The 'liquid' sense of 'moist' was longer lived, and although also found in Chaucer is equally found in Shakespeare, in *Henry IV*, Part 2 (1597). Here, Prince Henry says to his father, when rebuked by him for appearing too eager to succeed him:

O! pardon me, my liege; but for my tears
The moist impediments unto my speech,
I had forestall'd this dear and deep
    rebuke.

This usage is not recorded later than the seventeenth century.

mole (dark-coloured spot or mark on the skin)
In Old English use, a 'mole' was a discoloured spot on cloth or linen (compare 'iron mould', which is the same word). The 'mole' on the human skin was a sense that developed from the fourteenth century. Knowledge of the earlier meaning is desirable to understand the following correctly (which does not thus relate to the animal!): 'One yron mole defaceth the whole peece of Lawne' (Lyly, *Euphues*, 1579).

molest (attack, injure, harmfully meddle with)
The derivation of the verb lies in Latin *molestare*, 'to annoy', and this was the original sense of 'molest' in English, in the fourteenth century. It is first recorded in Chaucer's *Troilus and Criseyde* (1374):

But how this cas doth Troilus moleste,
That may non erthely mannes tonge seye.

The usage was still current in the seventeenth and eighteenth centuries in poetical works, as in Abraham Cowley's *Several Discourses by way of Essays in Verse and Prose* (1667):

These are the small uneasie things
Which about Greatness still are found,
And rather it Molest than Wound.

The modern sense developed from the fifteenth century, and the earlier usage became obsolete by about 1750.

monument (commemorative structure such as a statue, memorial)
In its earliest use, in the thirteenth century, a 'monument' was a burial place. This sense is found in both Shakespeare and the Bible. In *Romeo and Juliet* (1592) the word comes in Juliet's pleading lines to her mother:

Delay this marriage for a month, a week;
Or, if you do not, make the bridal bed
In that dim monument where Tybalt
    lies.

In the Bible, the sense occurs in Isaiah 65:4: 'Which remain among the graves, and lodge in the monuments'. By the fifteenth century, 'monument' had come to mean 'written document', especially a legal one (where, however, some writers may have confused it with 'muniment'). The 'proper' title of 'Foxe's Book of Martyrs' (1563) was thus 'Acts and Monuments of these latter and perillous Dayes'. The modern meaning finally evolved in the sixteenth century. (With regard to the earliest sense mentioned above, it is worth noting that Welsh *mynwent* is still the current word for 'churchyard', 'graveyard'.)

mood (frame of mind)
In Old English use, 'mood' meant 'mind' itself down to about 1400, as well as 'pride'. The former sense comes in *An Old English Miscellany*, of the twelfth and thirteenth centuries, where the reference is to the biblical 'Woman of Samaria' (see John 4:10):

Wymmon, if thu vnderstode
Hwo hit is that drynke byd,
Thu woldest beon of other mode.

In the twelfth century, 'mood' came to mean specifically 'anger', a sense occurring in Shakespeare's *Two Gentlemen of Verona* (1591), where the Second Outlaw says to the First:

And I from Mantua, for a gentleman,
Who, in my mood, I stabb'd unto the
    heart.

Something close to the sense, too, comes as late as 1855 in Tennyson's *Maud:*

> What! am I raging alone as my father raged in his mood?

But the regular usage of this meaning is now certainly obsolete. The main sense, 'frame of mind', is an old one, and dates from the same Old English period as the other meanings mentioned above. 'Moody', too, underwent a similar series of usages and sense changes ('brave', 'proud', 'angry'), with its modern meaning of 'temperamental' first recorded in Shakespeare's poem *The Rape of Lucrece* (1593), where it occurs more than once:

> And moody Pluto winks while Orpheus plays,

and, nearer the end:

> Unmask, dear dear, this moody heaviness.

morale (mental and emotional pitch, 'spirit')
When first adopted from the French in the eighteenth century, 'morale' was used in English to mean 'morals'. Lord Chesterfield, in a letter to his son of 6 January 1752, wrote: 'If you would know their *morale,* read Pascal's *Lettres Provinciales*'. (He was talking about the Jesuits.) Again, Julia Pardoe, in *The Beauties of the Bosphorus* (1839), wrote: 'Here the Frank traveller may see more of the habits and morale of the Turkish women than he can hope to do elsewhere'. This sense then became obsolete, and the current meaning dates from the nineteenth century, when it was specifically applied to the 'community spirit' or esprit de corps of troops. The actual French word in this sense is not *morale* but *moral* (while *morale* means 'morality').

moron (stupid or slow-witted person)
As first used, the word had a very precise sense, and 'moron' (from Latin *morus* or Greek *moros,* 'stupid') was officially adopted in 1910 by the American Association for the Study of the Feeble-minded to describe an adult with a mental age of eight to twelve. By the 1920s, however, the word had become generally adopted to mean simply a 'dim' person or a foolish one, soon finding its way into popular conversation and fiction.

mortar (bowl-shaped vessel in which substances are pounded with a pestle; type of artillery gun; kind of building material)
There has been a rather unexpected transference of sense here. The vessel came first in the thirteenth century, with the building material dating from about the same time. (Building 'mortar' was originally prepared in a 'mortar'.) In the seventeenth century, the 'gun' sense arose. This was properly called a 'mortar-piece' and was so named from its early shape resembling that of the vessel. All three meanings are still current, even though the preparation of substances with a pestle and mortar is now rare. (Perhaps 'chefs de cuisine' still use it most.)

mortuary (place where dead bodies are kept before burial or cremation)
In the fourteenth century, a 'mortuary' was a gift claimed by a parson from the estate of a parishioner who had died. A will made in 1469 stipulated: 'I will that the parson of Brympton [in Somerset] have for me to his mortuarie a donne hors of mine'. This custom seems to have been observed in some English parishes as recently as the early nineteenth century. In the fifteenth century, 'mortuary' came to mean simply 'funeral'. Thus in *Selimus, Emperour of the Turkes* (1594), perhaps written by the dramatist Robert Greene, come the lines:

> When thus they see me with religious pompe,
> To celebrate his tomb-blacke mortarie.

Both these senses are now obsolete, and the modern meaning dates only from the nineteenth century (first recorded in the *Morning Star* of 1 June 1865).

moth (night-flying insect resembling a butterfly)
Until the sixteenth century, 'moth' meant specifically 'clothes moth', and in the word's earliest use, from the tenth century, the reference seems to have been to the larva rather than the insect itself, since it is frequently alternated with 'clothes worm' (or the equivalent). The use of 'moth' to

mean the night-flying insect, as distinguished from a butterfly, dates really only from the eighteenth century. In Ephraim Chambers's *Cyclopaedia Supplement* (1753) an article on the various species of the insect first defines them as: 'those butterflies which fly by night, and which the French thence call *papilions nocturnes*, and we vulgarly *moths*'. However, in his *Dictionary* of 1755, Johnson defines 'moth' as: 'a small winged insect that eats cloths and hangings', thereby recording only the former sense (and preserving the fiction that it is the moths that eat the clothes, whereas it is actually their larvae).

mound (small hill of earth or stones, whether artificial or natural)
The word looks as if it is a long established one, and probably related to 'mount' or 'mountain'. But in fact it is neither (its origin is still unknown), and it was first recorded in English in the sixteenth century, originally in the sense 'hedge', 'fence'. This usage was current until the eighteenth century, and is found in Dryden's translation (1597) of Virgil's *Pastorals*:

Nor Cold shall hinder me, with Horns and Hounds,
To thrid the Thickets, or to leap the Mounds.

The word could also mean 'embankment' in the sixteenth century, especially one built for defence, and this is the sense Johnson gives 'mound' in his *Dictionary* (1755): 'Anything raised to fortify or defend; usually a bank of earth and stone'. But this is not the modern meaning of the word, which was first recorded in the eighteenth century in Pope's version (1725-6) of Homer's *Odyssey*:

Now all the sons of warlike Greece surround
Thy destin'd tomb, and cast a mighty mound.

From this sense of 'tumulus', the meaning developed finally in the nineteenth century to a natural hillock or 'mount', and here the first recording is in Scott's *The Lady of the Lake* (1810):

The shaggy mounds no longer stood
Emerging from entangled wood.

much (great in quantity or extent, to a great degree, great amount)
The only use of 'much' as an adjective today is to denote quantity or extent, as 'not much money', or 'with much pleasure'. Originally, however, in the thirteenth century, 'much' could mean 'great', 'large' generally, with a 'much man' even being a common way of denoting an adult, or at any rate a relatively mature person, as in this quotation (where the word comes twice) from the prose romance *Merlin or the Early History of King Arthur* (1450): 'Antor [i.e. Arthur], that hadde this childe norisshed till he was a moche man of xv yere of age, he hadde hym trewly norisshed, so that he was faire and moche'. This sense became obsolete from the sixteenth century, but survives in some English place names, such as Much Wenlock (which was also known as More Wenlock in the seventeenth century), Much Hadham and Much Hoole, which are on a parallel with places called 'Great' (such as Great Yarmouth) and 'Magna' (such as Chew Magna). The other sense of 'much' in different parts of speech developed in the fourteenth century (as 'much warmer' in the adverbial sense, and 'much of the time', as a noun).

muddle (confuse)
The word dates from the seventeenth century, when for a while it meant 'wallow in mud' (the two words are related), as in these lines by Swift, written in 1745:

He never muddles in the Dirt
Nor scowers the Street without a Shirt.

The meaning became obsolete in the nineteenth century.

mummy (dead body embalmed for burial in the manner of the ancient Egyptians)
The current meaning dates only from the seventeenth century. In the fourteenth century, 'mummy' was used for a medicinal preparation made from mummies, or for any similar liquid or gum used medicinally. It is partly to this that Shakespeare was referring in *The Merry Wives of Windsor* (1598), when Falstaff says, talking of death by drowning: 'A death that I abhor, for the water swells a man, and what a thing should I have been when I had been swelled! I

should have been a mountain of mummy'. In the sixteenth century, 'mummy' was the word, therefore, for any general curative preparation, or 'sovereign remedy', as in Thomas Timme's translation (1605) of Duchesne's *Practise of Chymicall and Hermeticall Physicke* (with 'mummy' misprinted or misspelled): 'This worke is very admirable; by which the true numie, the uniuersal medicine, and the true balsam conseruing and restoring nature, is made'. Both these meanings became obsolete in the eighteenth century.

museum (building or institution preserving and displaying objects of value)
Despite the association of museums with antiquity and (etymologically) the Muses of Greek mythology, the word itself came into English only in the seventeenth century, originally actually *as* a 'home for the Muses', or a building dedicated to learning and the arts. As such, it was often a sort of 'scholar's study' in a private residence, as illustrated by this letter of 1645 written by the Welsh scholar James Howell: 'To my Honoured Friend and Fa. Mr. Ben Johnson. I thank you for the last *regalo* [i.e. entertainment] you gave me at your Musaeum, and for the good company'. The modern understanding of the word dates from a statement in the *Philosophical Transactions of the Royal Society* for 1683 referring to 'Mr. Ashmole's Musaeum at Oxford'. (This was the year the Ashmolean Museum, as it is now known, was founded.)

must (has to)
In Old English, 'must' was originally the past tense of 'mote', basically meaning 'may', so therefore had the sense 'was able to' or 'was permitted to'. Hence in *Arthur* (1400), where a latish use of the word occurs:

Mordred fly toward Londoun,
He must not come in the toun.

(That is, he was not able to enter the town.) This usage became obsolete in the fifteenth century, while the modern use of 'must' dates from the fourteenth century, when it almost always applies to the present or immediate future, unless used in reported

speech in the past (as in 'He said he must go').

namely (that is to say)
In the twelfth century, 'namely' meant 'especially', 'above all', and in use was usually preceded by 'and'. The *Lay folks mass book* (1375) has these lines:

I thonk God of his godnesse,
And nomely now of this messe.

The sense was still current (although increasingly rarely) in the eighteenth century, as in Edward Topsell's *The Historie of Serpents* (1608): 'I finde some difference about the nature of this living creature, and namely whether it be a Serpent or a Fish'. The current meaning of 'namely' arose in the fifteenth century.

nanny (child's nurse; child's name for grandmother)
Both senses are probably of 'baby talk' origin, with 'nanny' having a female connotation (as in 'nanny-goat', where the derivation is probably in the first name Nanny, a pet form of Anne). Children originally called their nurses 'nanny' in the late eighteenth century, and the word is first recorded in a letter of 1795 from the youthful Lady Newdigate, who reported: 'Nanny Ashcroft got me ye most delightful & perfect Warm Sea Bath last night [. . .] after wch I ate my Bason of Milk & went to Bed'. Some time in the early twentieth century, or possibly the late nineteenth, 'nanny' (as well as 'nan' and 'nanna') also became a child's pet name for his or her grandmother, where it was (and even today still is) a more 'lowly' equivalent to the standard 'granny'. As nurses went out, however, or became more 'exclusive', so grandmothers came in to take

their place, and to a large extent supersede them in the role of childcarers. This factor may have reinforced the establishment of 'nanny' as a homely name for a grandmother and have linked the sense of the word with its earlier sole meaning of 'nurse'. It cannot be definitely proved that this actually *is* one and the same word, however, and more research is needed in this domestic area. The *Supplement* to the *OED* does not give the 'grandmother' sense of the word, only that of the nurse.

native (person born in a place or living there)
In its earliest meaning, in the fifteenth century, a 'native' was the word for a person who was born a slave or bondman (a 'thrall'). This sense is obviously now historic, and became obsolete from the seventeenth century in its everyday use. In the sixteenth century, 'native' became an astrological term for a person born under a particular sign or planet. Hence the use of the word by Scott in *Guy Mannering* (1815): 'Mars having dignity in the cusp of the twelfth house, threatened captivity or sudden and violent death to the native.' It was also in this century that the more familiar meaning 'person born in a particular place' evolved, and a hundred years later the sense was extended to apply to a person *living* in a particular place, but not necessarily born there. The astrological sense is still current in the jargon of horoscopists.

naughty (badly behaved, wicked, harmlessly mischievous)
This word is a sense shift classic. Its relationship with 'naught' and so 'nought' is made more apparent when it is known that its original sense, in fourteenth-century English, was 'poor', 'needy', i.e. having little or nothing. The word occurs in Langland's *Piers Plowman* (1377), which talks of 'alle maner of men' [. . .] 'that nedy ben and naughty'. At the same time, 'naughty' also came to mean 'bad', in the sense 'inferior in quality', and this was used by several writers down to at least the seventeenth century, when it was still quite common. Thus, rather bizarrely to twentieth-century eyes, we read Tindale writing (1526): 'As

this is a naughty argument, so is the other', Robert Burton, in *The Anatomy of Melancholy* (1620), saying: 'Thou wilt not have bad coin, bad soil, a naughty tree', and even in 1683, Joseph Moxon, in *Mechanick Exercises, or the Doctrine of Handy-Works,* advising on printing procedures: 'The Compositer will bow the Letter, and pop it into a Waste Box in the Case, where he puts all naughty letters'. The Burton quotation above is a reminder, too, that 'naughty' could equally apply to food or drink that was 'bad', as in the well-known biblical verse in Jeremiah 24:2: 'One basket had very good figs, even like the figs that are first ripe: and the other basket had very naughty figs, which could not be eaten, they were so bad'. It seems strange that as late as 1896 it was possible to write, as Arthur D. Coleridge did, in *Eton in the Forties,* that a particular type of cherry was ' . . . fraudulent, sour, and naughty throughout'. From the sixteenth century, 'naughty' was applied generally to mean 'morally bad', with contemporary literature again reading incongruously, as even in Shakespeare, where in *Measure for Measure* (1603), Elbow, speaking to Esaclus, and talking of his wife, says: 'I say, sir, I will detest myself also, as well as she, that this house, if it be not a bawd's house, it is pity of her life, for it is a naughty house'. Better known than this, however, is Portia's line in *The Merchant of Venice* (1595):

So shines a good deed in a naughty world.

The 'morally bad' sense became more and more trivial, especially in its application to children (from the seventeenth century), so that today this is the sole use of the word remaining. (Although even now, 'naughty' of children can be quite strongly disapproving, and certainly much more than it would be used of an adult.)

nerve (band of tissue conveying sensation etc. in the body)
The sense of 'nerve' given here was the second to evolve, in the seventeenth century. The first meaning, in the previous century, was that of 'sinew', 'tendon', still current in such expressions as 'strain every nerve' but hardly otherwise. Eighteenth- and nineteenth-century poets conserved the original

meaning, however, so that Shelley could write, in *Julian and Maddalo* (1818):

> Like some maniac monk, I had torn out
> The nerves of manhood by their bleeding
> root.

net (free from deductions, not gross)
The word came into English in the fourteenth century from French *net*, 'neat', so is closely related to the latter. And this was more or less the original meaning of 'net' which could be used in senses ranging from 'trim', 'smart' (of dress) to 'clean', 'bright'. It could even mean 'neat' itself, as in John Cleveland's *Elegy on Ben Jonson* (1637), which has the lines:

> When thou in Company wert met,
> Thy Meat took Notes, and thy Discourse
> was Net.

The 'clean' sense occurs in the Douai Bible of 1609, where Proverbs 5:3 is rendered: 'The lippes of an harlot are as a hony combe distilling, and her throte netter then oyle' (Authorized Version of 1611: 'For the lips of a strange woman drop as an honeycomb, and her mouth is smoother than oil'). The present meaning of 'net' developed in the sixteenth century.

newfangled (modern in an unnecessarily complicated way)
In the fifteenth century, 'newfangled' meant 'fond of novelty', a sense rarely used today. Bishop John Alcock, in *Sermo pro episcopo puerorum* (1496), wrote: 'Boyes of fyfty [*sic*] yere of age are as newe fangled as ony yonge men be', and Trollope, in *The Last Chronicle of Barset* (1867), wrote: 'When his time came to be made a bishop, he was not sufficiently new-fangled; and so he got passed by'. The current popular sense of 'newfangled' dates from the sixteenth century.

news (report or information given on recent events etc.)
When the word was first used in English, in the fourteenth century, it meant 'novelties'. This usage did not last long, and one of the last records we have of it is in Thomas Stapleton's *A Fortresse of the Faith* (1565), where he writes of the differences ' . . . betwene the auncient faith of England and the vpstert newes of protestants'. The modern meaning of 'news' arose in the fifteenth century, although the word was not in common use until after about 1500.

nice (pleasant, agreeable; delicately discriminating)
In Old French, which gave the word to English in the thirteenth century, *nice* meant 'silly', 'simple', and in turn was based on Latin *nescius,* 'ignorant'. Quite clearly, there has been a noticeable sense shift since then! In fact there have been almost as many meanings as any English word has had, with many still current but the early senses now obsolete. First, then, the meaning was the same as the French, with a shade of 'foolish' to the basic 'stupid'. Usage was fairly common in this sense in the fourteenth and fifteenth centuries, and in John de Trevisa's translation (1387) of Ranulf Higden's *Polychronicon*, for example, we read: 'He made the lady so mad [i.e. infatuated] and so nyce that sche worshipped hym as the grettest prophete of God Almyghty'. In the fourteenth century, 'nice' meant 'wanton', even 'lascivious'. This sense occurs, for instance, in Chaucer's *The Romaunt of the Rose* (1366):

> Nyce she was, but she ne mente
> Noone harme ne slight in hir entente,
> But oonely lust & jolyte.

The meaning is also found in Shakespeare's *Love's Labour's Lost* (1588), when Moth, Armado's pert page, says to his master: 'These are compliments, these are humours, these betray nice wenches'. The same sense, although relating to conduct rather than people, comes in Antony and Cleopatra (1606), where Antony says:

> For when my hours
> Were nice and lucky, men did ransom
> lives
> Of me for jests.

In the fifteenth century, 'nice' acquired the sense 'coy', 'shy'. This could be used of people literally or things figuratively, as in Milton's *Comus* (1634):

> Ere the blabbing eastern scout,
> The nice Morn on th'Indian steep
> From her cabin'd loop-hole peep,

or in Dryden's last rhymed tragedy, *Aureng-Zebe* (1676):

Virtue is nice to take what's not her own.

All these meanings are now obsolete, and it was in the sixteenth century that the 'fastidious' or 'minute and subtle' sense of 'nice' emerged (as in a 'nice' distinction, meaning a fine one), while the popular general 'pleasant', 'agreeable' sense finally evolved from the eighteenth century. The precise reason for this particular sense development from 'stupid' to 'agreeable' is not easy to explain. By the sixteenth and seventeenth centuries, too, so many meanings were current, including the now obsolete ones, that it is often difficult or even impossible to tell with any certainty exactly which sense a particular writer intended. Even today, ambiguity can arise in such a phrase as 'a nice sense of fun' (agreeable or discriminating, or perhaps ironic?). It is almost certainly a coincidence that the popular modern catch phrase 'naughty but nice' contains two English adjectives that have altered their meanings almost more than any others.

niece (person's brother's or sister's daughter)
Down to about 1600, from its adoption into English from French in the thirteenth century, 'niece' often meant 'grand-daughter', or even some more remote female descendant. In some texts, it is impossible to say for certain exactly which relationship is meant, whether 'granddaughter' or 'niece' in the modern sense. In a few cases, a later version of a passage will make the situation clear. Thus in John de Trevisa's translation (1387) of Ranulf Higden's *Polychronicon,* he tells of the death of 'Hilda, abbesse of Whitby', who was 'kyng Edwyn his nese'. Granddaughter or niece? From the later edition of 1432-50 we learn that she was in fact the 'doghter of the doghter of kynge Edwinus', with these words substituted for the earlier ones. A similar ambiguity does not seem to have arisen over 'nephew'.

nightmare (frightening dream)
The word has had its current sense only since the sixteenth century. Earlier, from the thirteenth century, a 'nightmare' was an

evil female spirit that created such dreams by settling on a sleeper (it was believed) and causing a sense of weight or oppression. This particular meaning is found in fairly recent poets, such as Shelley and Tennyson, with the latter writing, for example, how:

King Arthur panted hard
Like one that feels a nightmare on his bed
(*The Morte d'Arthur,* 1842).

The use of 'nightmare' to mean 'object of terror', 'frightening situation' dates only from the nineteenth century.

nipper (youngster)
In the sixteenth century, a 'nipper' was a thief, a person who 'nipped' (or 'pinched'). In the nineteenth century, a 'nipper' was a costermonger's boy assistant, so called not because he stole, but because he had to be smart or 'nippy'. From this second sense, the word came to be a term for any small boy. So there has been not so much a change of sense here as a use of two distinct meanings of one and the same verb. Even so, there is a connection between the thief and the boy, since both have to be smart and move fast.

noise (loud or harsh sound)
It may seem unlikely that 'noise' could ever have had any other sense, and it is true that the modern meaning is also the oldest, first recorded in the thirteenth century. However, 'noise' has also had other meanings, now all obsolete, and the earliest of them, of the same period as the current sense, was 'loud outcry'. Today, this survives only in the expression 'hold your noise', but it was earlier in common use until about the eighteenth century. This is the sense of 'noise', therefore, in Shakespeare's *The Comedy of Errors* (1590), when Antipholus of Ephesus is trying to get into his own house and is denied entry by his wife Adriana, who says from inside ('within'):

Who is that at the door that keeps all this noise?

'Noise' could also mean 'rumour' at this time, so that there could be a 'noise' of a defeat in battle or of someone's death. In the fourteenth century, 'noise' could even mean 'pleasant sound', in a precise contrast to its present sense. One of the best known instances of this comes in the Book of Common Prayer, where Psalm 47:5 begins: 'God is gone up with a merry noise' (in the Bible, this is 'God is gone up with a shout'). Finally, in the sixteenth century, 'noise' came to mean 'band of musicians'. In John Lyly's *Mother Bombie* (1594) come the lines:

> Then I wish'd for a noyse
> Of crack-halter Boyes [i.e. rogues]
> On those hempen strings to be twanging.

These later meanings are now obsolete, and 'noise' simply means 'disagreeable sound'.

nondescript (dull, without obvious interest or originality)

The word began its life as a seventeenth-century natural history term meaning 'not hitherto described', as applied to a particular species or the like. The *Philosophical Transactions of the Royal Society* of 1772 tell of a 'fine non-descript owl' that fed on hares, and Henry M. Brackenridge, in his *Views of Louisiana* (1812), told how 'Mr. Bradbury has discovered nearly one hundred and fifty non-descript plants', meaning ones that had not been previously officially recorded and categorized. (Such species, where they exist, are now termed 'undescribed'.) The modern, general meaning of 'nondescript' dates only from the nineteenth century.

noon (midday)

It seems impossible that 'noon' could ever have meant anything other than 'midday'. Yet the ultimate origin of the word is Latin *nona hora*, 'ninth hour', that is, the ninth hour from sunrise, which is clearly three o'clock, not twelve midday. So what has happened? The answer is that 'noon' originally *was* three o'clock in the afternoon, with this old sense reflected in Wyclif's Bible of 1382, where in Mark 15:33, relating to the account of the Crucifixion, he has: 'Derknessis ben maad [. . .] til in to the nynthe our, that is, noon' (Authorized Version of 1611: 'There was darkness [. . .] until the ninth hour'). This 'name' for three o'clock was adopted early in the office of 'nones', that is, one of the seven set services held at certain times prescribed by the church. (These were the so called 'canonical hours', with the other six offices as follows: *matins* at night [later at dawn], *laud* at dawn [later, after matins], *prime* at six a.m., *terce* at nine a.m., *sext* at twelve midday, *vespers* in the late afternoon, after *nones* at three, *compline* before retiring at night.) From the twelfth century, however, 'noon' gradually transferred from three o'clcok to midday, mainly due to the midday meal being served then, at a time that was felt to be a more natural 'halfway' break in the day. Later, the office of 'nones' was itself frequently said earlier, which reinforced the transfer of the name. Finally, from the thirteenth century, 'noon' became established as the alternative term for 'midday' or twelve o'clock. The only other language where a similar 'time shift' occurred is Dutch, where 'noon' is now *noen*. Most other languages use a word or term corresponding to 'midday' (as French *midi*, German *Mittag*, Russian *polden'* and so on). Not that one really needs three different ways of expressing '12.0', as English has!

normal (usual, standard)

The current popular meaning of 'normal' arose only in the nineteenth century. Before that, from the seventeenth century, it meant (as it still can) 'rectangular', 'perpendicular', mainly in technical uses, such as mathematics and astronomy. The sense was adopted into English from French, which in turn based the word on Latin *norma*, 'carpenter's square', 'pattern', 'rule'.

nostalgia (wistful longing for the past)

When first current in the eighteenth century, 'nostalgia' meant 'home sickness', especially as experienced by Englishmen abroad. This was not a 'wistful longing' but quite a serious medical condition, resulting in severe depression and 'melancholy'. The malaise seems to have arisen during the American War of Independence, when many Britons were certainly miles from home, and James Thacher, in *A Military Journal during the American War* (1775-83), records: ' . . .many perplexing instances of indisposition, [. . .] called by Dr. Cullen *nostalgia* or home sickness'. The modern, more general and less acute sense of 'nostalgia' arose only after the First World

War, and is first recorded in D.H. Lawrence's *The Lost Girl* (1920): 'The terror, the agony, the nostalgia of the heathen past was a constant torture to her mediumistic soul'.

nosy (unduly inquisitive, prying)
The present use of 'nosy' evolved in the nineteenth century. Before that, from the eighteenth century, 'nosy' meant simply 'having a large nose', with the word used as a nickname. Thomas Pownall ('Governor Pownall') commented in the journal *Archaeologia* in 1788 on: ' . . .an admirable caricatura of a musician, what the vulgar of this day would call *Nosey,* playing on a violin'. In the mid-nineteenth century, too, 'Old Nosey' was a nickname for the Duke of Wellington, since 'like many other persons of character, Wellington had a very big nose' (Eric Partridge, *A Dictionary of Slang and Unconventional English,* 1951). After 'nosy' (or 'nosey') acquired its 'inquisitive' sense in the latter half of the nineteenth century, 'Nosey Parker' followed it (led by the nose, as it were) in the early twentieth, where he is first recorded on a set of picture postcards dated 1907 ('The adventures of Nosey Parker').

nourish (supply with nourishment, foster)
In the thirteenth century, when the sense 'foster' was first current, 'nourish' also meant 'bring up', 'nurture', as well as (physically) 'suckle', 'nurse'. The former meaning, now as obsolete as the latter, occurs in Wyclif's Bible translation of 1382, where in I Timothy 5:10 he has: 'If she norische sones, if she resseyue pore men to herbore' (Authorized Version of 1611: 'If she have brought up children, if she have lodged strangers'). The 'suckle' sense can be found, for example, in *Merlin or the Early History of King Arthur* (1450): 'Therfore was the moder suffred to norishe it tell it was x monthes of age', as well as again in Wyclif's Bible: 'Forsoth wo to wymmen with childe and noryschinge in tho dayes' (Authorized Version: 'And woe unto them that are with child, and to them that give suck in those days!') (Matthew 24:19). The most familiar sense of 'nourish', 'sustain with nourishment', arose in the fourteenth century.

novel (book containing a sustained tale or story)
The earliest sense of 'novel', in the fifteenth century, was 'novelty', with the plural use ('novels') meaning 'news'. (See **news** itself for an identical development.) The first use of the word in anything like its modern meaning occurs in the sixteenth century, when 'novel' (or more usually 'novels') was applied to such tales or short stories as were contained in Boccaccio's *Decameron* or Margaret of Navarre's *Heptameron.* Robert Burton, in *The Anatomy of Melancholy* (1621), refers to the former of these works as 'Bocace Nouells', and in his *Memoirs* (1674) Evelyn writes of 'Marguerite of Valois [. . .] whose novels are equal to thos of the witty Boccaccio'. The modern 'novel', as the 'prose narrative', emerged as a meaning in the seventeenth century, when it was at first contrasted with a 'romance' since it was shorter than this and bore a more realistic relation to life. (In a letter written in 1774, Lord Chesterfield declared that: 'A Novel is a kind of abbreviation of a Romance'.) The first recorded use of 'novel' in its current sense, however, comes in Milton's *The Doctrine and Discipline of Divorce* (1643): 'This is no mere amatorious novel'. Similarly, a 'novelist' was an introducer of novelties in the sixteenth century before he or she became a writer of novels in the eighteenth.

nude (naked, unclothed)
Somewhat unexpectedly, the word had a figurative sense before it acquired its literal one in the seventeenth century (and even then it was rare until the nineteenth). The reason lies in the historic development of 'the nude' as an art form (with this particular expression current in the eighteenth century) and of an increasing need to find a word apart from 'naked' to apply to the human figure in a 'decent' manner. ('Naked', moreover, tended to imply the whole body, and 'nude' was a suitable word for use of parts of the body, such as 'nude' shoulders, with an additional connotation of the artistic.) Thus when Ouida, in her novel *Moths* (1880), wrote: 'He was so used to seeing pretty nude feet at Trouville', she was using a word that was more 'artistic', therefore more stylish and connotative, than 'bare', while 'naked' would have been

absurd. The earliest senses of 'nude' date from the sixteenth century, and had both a legal usage and a general. In law, for example, a 'nude promise' was one that had not been formally recorded, and a 'nude executor' was merely a nominal one. (As defined by Henry Swinburne in *A Briefe Treatise of Testaments and Last Willes* [1590]: 'If the testator giue his goods to one person, and make another executor: this executor is called Nude executor, for that he reapeth no commoditie by the testament'.) The early general sense of 'nude' meant 'bare', that is, 'mere', so that Edward Waterhouse, in *A Short Narrative of the Late Dreadful Fire in London* (1667), wrote of 'a bare accident and a nude casualty'. The word as a noun meaning 'nude figure in painting' is first recorded in Edward Hatton's *New View of London*, published anonymously in 1708: 'A *Nude* or *Nudity*, is a naked Figure painted or sculpted, without Drapery (or Cloathing)'.

nuzzle (nudge with the nose, nestle)
In the fifteenth century, to 'nuzzle' was to grovel, the concept being that of bringing the nose down to the ground. The usage was rare but was recorded in 1425 as used by St Elizabeth of Spalbeck: 'Sche noseles downe forwarde and wonderly crokes her body'. The sense 'push with the nose' arose in the sixteenth century, and 'nestle' a hundred years later.

obnoxious (offensive, highly unpleasant)
Latin *obnoxius*, which gave the word, meant 'exposed to harm', and this was the original meaning of 'obnoxious' in English, in the sixteenth century. Robert Burton, in *The Anatomy of Melancholy* (1621), wrote that 'the finest wits [. . .] are before other obnoxious to it [i.e. melancholy]', and in 1712 Addison wrote in the *Spectator*: 'We are obnoxious to so many Accidents'. In fact, down to about the end of the eighteenth century, this was the main sense of the word. It also meant 'subject to authority', however, so that John Cleveland, in *The Rustick Rampant* (1658), could write that 'Kings are only the Tenants of Heaven, obnoxious to God alone'. This sense became obsolete in the eighteenth century. The current meaning of 'obnoxious' dates from the seventeenth century, and came to develop its sense because of association with 'noxious', so that for a time it actually meant 'harmful', as 'noxious' does. John Woodall, in *The Surgions Mate* (1617), advised that: 'Cold aire in time of sweating is obnoxious and dangerous'. This sense fell out of use by the end of the century.

obsequious (compliant in a servile way)
In the fifteenth century, when the word was first current, 'obsequious' meant merely 'readily compliant', without the association of servility that it acquired a hundred years later. This is the sense in Shakespeare's *The Merry Wives of Windsor* (1598), when Falstaff says to Mistress Ford: 'I see you are obsequious in your love', and similarly in Milton's *Paradise Lost* (1667):

Light issues forth, and at the other dore
Obsequious darkness enters.

This usage was virtually obsolete by the end of the nineteenth century.

occult (pertaining to the supernatural)
When first current in English, in the sixteenth century, 'occult' meant simply 'hidden', 'secret', with no special reference to the supernatural or mystic. Thus John Maplet, in *A Greene Forest or a Naturall Historie* (1567), wrote that metals were ' . . . nothing else but the earths hid and occult Plants', and the naturalist John Ray, in *Observations made in a Journey through Part of the Low-Countries, Germany, Italy and France* (1673), commented that in Milan: 'These suffrages are all occult, that is, given by putting of balls into balloting boxes'. The adjective could also mean 'mysterious', 'not easily comprehensible', that is, as it were, 'hidden from the mind', and it is this sense that in turn led to the current meaning,

which dates from the seventeenth century, and at first related to such medieval sciences as magic, alchemy, astrology and theosophy.

offend (break a moral law, wound a person's feelings)
Latin *offendere* means 'strike against', and in the fourteenth century, in English, 'offend' could mean 'stumble' (literally) as well as 'do wrong'. In his English Bible translation of 1382, Wyclif uses the word in both its senses. It occurs literally in Zechariah 12:8: 'He that shal offende of hem in that day' (Authorized Version of 1611: 'He that is feeble among them at that day'), and in Romans 11:11: 'Wher thei offendiden so that thei schulden fallen doun?' (Authorized Version: 'Have they stumbled that they should fall?'). In James 3:2, however, he uses the word of 'moral stumbling': 'Alle we offenden in many thingis' (Authorized Version: 'For in many things we offend all'). The literal usage is now long obsolete, as is the further sense 'attack', 'physically wound'. This is first found in Chaucer, as in *The Legend of Good Women* (1385):

Whan a flye offendith him or biteth
He with his tayle awey the fle smytheth.

This sense is not recorded after the eighteenth century, and the current meaning 'wound a person's feelings' arose in the fourteenth century when the 'do wrong' sense did.

officious (over-zealous in carrying out one's duties)
In the sixteenth century, 'officious' meant both 'eager to please' and 'dutiful', each in a non-critical sense. The second of these now obsolete meanings comes in Shakespeare's *Titus Andronicus* (1588), at the point where Titus, having cut the throats of Chiron and Demetrius, says:

Come, come, be every one officious
To make this banquet.

The modern meaning followed in the next century, when 'officious' could also have the sense 'official', a usage that lasted down to the nineteenth century, when it is found, for example, in the writings of Newman, who when speaking of the sermons of seven-teenth-century Protestants, declared them to be often 'mere repertories of miscellaneous and officious learning' (*Discourses on the Scope and Nature of University Education*, 1852). The diplomatic sense of 'officious' to mean 'unofficial', as distinct from 'official' (for example, 'officious talks'), evolved only in the nineteenth century.

orchard (area of fruit trees)
Before the word acquired its specialized sense, dominantly from the fourteenth century, 'orchard' meant 'garden' more generally, with or without fruit trees, herbs and so on, and it was one of the standard translations of Latin *hortus*. For example, John de Trevisa, in his translation (1387) of Ranulf Higden's *Polychronicon*, rendered Latin *in quo horto captus fuit* as 'in that orch-eyerde [Crist] was i-take', and Wyclif, in his Bible translation of a year later, had for Isaiah 1:30: 'Whanne ye schulen be [. . .] as an orchard with out watir' (Authorized Version of 1611: 'For ye shall be [. . .] as a garden that hath no water'). This meaning then became obsolete.

orchestra (group of instrumental musicians)
'He passed directly from the Stage by the Orchestra, to take up his place among the Knights'. This extract from Philemon Holland's translation (1606) of Suetonius' *Historie of Twelve Caesars* is too early to relate to the modern symphony orchestra, or to any group of musical performers, since the modern 'orchestra' only evolved from the eighteenth century. Most earlier uses of the word will thus refer, as here, to the semi-circular area for the chorus in an ancient Greek theatre, with this sense current in English from the seventeenth century. Even later references to an 'orchestra' may not necessarily mean the players themselves but the part of the theatre where they sat (compare the modern 'orchestra stalls'). So this is the meaning, therefore, in Maria Edgeworth's *Harrington* (1817), when she writes: 'The impatient sticks in the pit, and shrill catcalls in the gallery, had begun to contend with the music in the orchestra'. The sense is still not obsolete to be used of the special space in front of the stage where players perform in a modern theatre.

ordeal (trying experience, 'hard time')
In Old English, an *ordāl* was a term applied to a special type of trial or virtual torture, in which a suspected criminal was subjected to some physical feat of endurance, usually an unpleasant and dangerous one, such as plunging his hand into boiling water, carrying heated metal, walking barefoot and blindfolded between red hot ploughshares, and the like. The result of this was regarded as the verdict of God: if he survived, God permitted it; if he suffered or even died, God willed it. This procedure, also found in other Germanic countries, survived in England almost down to Chaucer's day, and certainly after the Norman Conquest. The current meaning of the word, in its weakened and more general sense, dates only from the seventeenth century.

organ (musical instrument commonly found in churches; instrument or means of function)
There are three distinct senses of 'organ', of which the two current ones are defined here. The forerunner of the modern church organ dates from as early as the eighth century, when the instrument is mentioned in Latin texts. However, no record of it in Old English writings has been found, and the earliest mention we have of an organ is in Chaucer's *Canterbury Tales* (1386), where in 'The Nun's Priest's Tale' one finds the lines:

His voys was murier than the murie organ,
On Messedayes that in the chirche gon.

(Compare the 'merry organ' of modern Christmas carols.) So this is the first rather late reference to the musical instrument. Mentions of an 'organ' in the Bible are almost certainly *not* the familiar 'pipe and pedal' instrument, and specialist knowledge or opinion is required as to the precise instrument meant. Some of the references have not been retained in the modern Authorized Version. For example, in Wyclif's English Bible of 1388, he renders Psalm 137:2 as: 'In salewis in the myddil therof; we hangiden vp oure orguns' (Authorized Version of 1611: 'We hanged our harps upon the willows in the midst thereof'). Similarly, the instrument mentioned in Genesis 4:21 is not the modern one ('And his brother's name was Jubal: he was the father of all such as handle the harp and organ'). The sense 'part or member of an animal or plant performing a particular function' dates from the fifteenth century, and the 'body of persons' meaning (as 'organ of local government') developed in the sixteenth century. Finally, the 'journal' sense, as 'the official organ of the Conservative Party', evolved in the eighteenth century.

orientate (adjust position or bearing, establish a direction)
The verb developed in the nineteenth century from the earlier 'orient', which in the eighteenth century meant, quite literally, 'place so as to face the east', and in particular to build a church with its main length running east and west. The idea of finding this one specific bearing then became generalized to establishing *any* bearing or position. Even some nineteenth-century uses of 'orientate', however, have the original meaning that 'orient' had, as in Richard Jefferies' novel *Green Ferne Farm* (1880): ' "Don't disturb the skeleton!" cried Felix, anxious to make scientific notes [. . .] whether the grave was "orientated" '.

ounce (snow leopard)
From the thirteenth century down to the eighteenth, the name of this animal applied to the lynx, not as now the snow leopard (or, as formerly known, mountain panther). In fact, 'ounce' and 'lynx' are really one and the same word, since Latin *lynx* gave French *lonce* which in turn produced English 'ounce', with the *l* of the French word taken to be the word for 'the' (as if it was really *l'once*). 'Lynx', therefore, is the meaning of the word in Shakespeare's *A Midsummer Night's Dream* (1590), for example, when Oberon squeezes the love-in-idleness onto Titania's eyelids:

Be it ounce, or cat, or bear,
Pard, or boar with bristled hair,
In thy eye that shall appear
When thou wak'st, it is thy dear.

outing (excursion, trip)
The pleasant homely word originally meant 'expedition' in the fourteenth century, and

'expulsion' in the fifteenth (that is, 'ousting' rather than 'outing' in the modern sense), so that Archbishop Laud wrote in 1639: 'Salvation need not be feared by any dutiful child, nor outing from the church'. The current meaning developed in the nineteenth century, and is first recorded in John Clare's *The Village Minstrel* (1821):

The long rural string of merry games
That at such outings maketh much ado.

ovation (enthusiastic applause)
In the sixteenth century, 'ovation' in English was used only of the Roman 'lesser triumph' (as distinct from the triumph proper), when the ceremonies were not so imposing since the feat had not been judged worthy of the full acclaim. Sir Thomas North, in his translation (1579-80) of Plutarch's *Lives*, wrote: 'At the second Triumph called the Ovation, he onely sacrificed a Mutton, which the Romans call in their tongue *Ovem*, and therefore it was called Ovation'. (Although the word has nothing to do with the sheep, but comes from Latin *ovare*, 'to exult'.) A century later, 'ovation' came to mean 'exultation', a usage popular with some poets down to the nineteenth century, from the *Poems* (1649) of Richard Lovelace:

When his fair Murdresse shall not gain
one groan,
And he expire ev'n in Ovation,

to Henry Hart Milman's heroic poem *Samor* (1818):

And bounds in wild ovation down the
vale.

Both these meanings are now obsolete, and the current sense of 'ovation' can be found from the nineteenth century only.

overtone (secondary or suggested sense of a word or statement)
The word began its career in the mid-nineteenth century as a technical musical term for a higher tone (a 'harmonic') produced when a lower (the 'fundamental') is sounded. (The effect can be the most easily heard when a bell is struck.) By the end of the century, however, the second, more common sense of 'overtone' had evolved to

apply to the 'resonance' of meaning of a particular word or phrase in literature, especially poetry. Thus 'azure' has overtones of 'haze', and 'April' of 'apricot', 'primula' and 'rill'. In his *Ode to a Nightingale* (1819), Keats commented on another word with overtones:

Forlorn! the very word is like a bell
To toll me back from thee to my sole
self!

In the twentieth century, this rather specialized sense broadened to be used of any general connotation or implication in thought, style, behaviour or the like, as when saying 'His remarks have overtones of snobbishness'. The word first came into English as a borrowing, or translation, of the German musical term *Oberton*, itself a shortened form of *Oberpartialton*, 'upper partial tone'.

overture (opening of associations or an acquaintance; introductory orchestral piece)
In the fourteenth century, 'overture' meant 'opening', 'aperture' generally and literally. Thus the fifteenth-century translation of *Secreta secretorum* mentions that human beings 'haue throgh al the body the ouertures large, that clerkys callyth Pores', and as late as the eighteenth century, Pope, in a letter to the Duke of Buckingham, described the kitchen at Stanton Harcourt as 'one vast Vault to the Top of the House; where one overture serves to let out the smoak and let in the light'. The usage became obsolete shortly after this. The sense 'opening of negotiations' dates from the fifteenth century, but the musical 'overture' only from the seventeenth, in particular with reference to the piece played before an opera. (This kind of overture was extensively developed by the French composer Lully for his operas and ballets.)

owe (be under obligation to give or repay)
In Old English, to 'owe' was to 'own', with this sense in use down to about the end of the seventeenth century. Chapman, in his version (1611) of Homer's *Iliad*, wrote of:

The horse
The Gods bred, and Adrastus ow'd,

and even as late as 1664 Pepys mentions in his *Diary* some storehouses that were 'of no great profit to him that oweth them'. The common meaning of 'owe', however, arose early, in the twelfth century, with some of the figurative uses following later. (The sense 'acknowledge one's indebtedness', as 'he owes his life to her', arose in the sixteenth century.)

packet boat (passenger boat carrying mail and cargo and regular route)
The 'packets' carried by a packet boat were not originally simply the mail, as now. In the sixteenth century, the 'packet boat' (or 'post bark' or 'post boat', as it was also called) was the boat that carried the 'packet' of state letters and despatches. The *Report of the Secret Committee on the Post Office* (1598-9) records the allowance for the crossing from Holyhead to Ireland: 'as well for serving the packett by lande as for entertaining a bark to carie over and to returne the packet, at x li. the moneth'. The current usage of the word, where it still exists, dates from approximately the seventeenth century.

pageant (colourful display or spectacle with historic tableaux of local or topical interest)
The word is indeed itself a historic one, and dates from the fourteenth century, when it originally was the term for a scene acted on a stage, in particular a scene from a mystery play. The *Coventry Leet Book: or Mayor's Register* of 1457 records how Queen Margaret saw 'alle the pagentes pleyde save domesday, which myght not be pleyde for lak of day [i.e. daylight]'. In the fifteenth century, the word came to be used for the stage on which such scenes were acted, this originally being the movable 'carriage' with stage machinery, so that a record of 1500 relating to the York mystery plays notes that 'the cartwryghts' were ordered 'to make iiij new wheles to the pagiaunt'. In the sixteenth century, the sense was transferred to a tableau or series of tableaux displayed to the public from a fixed stage or moving cart, rather in the manner of an early 'float'. This was not quite the modern use of the term, since the subjects of such displays were classical, allegorical and the like, and not connected with local history. A description of such 'pageants' displayed to celebrate the coronation of Queen Anne in 1533 mentions 'a rightly costly pageant of Apollo with the Nine Muses among the mountains', and 'a sumptuous and costly pageant in manner of a castle wherein was fashioned a heavenly roof and under it upon a green was a root of stock whereout sprang a multitude of white and red roses', etc. (Edward Arber, ed. *An English Garner*, 1877-96). Then, in the nineteenth century, there followed something like the modern 'pageant', as a fine, showy spectacle, but the 'local history' element was still not an essential ingredient until late in the century.

page boy (boy or young man employed in hotel etc. to deliver messages and the like)
Back in the thirteenth century, a 'page' was simply a general word for 'boy' or 'lad'. John Barbour's *The Bruce* (1375) thus records:

He had A Sone, A litill Knave,
That wes than bot a litill page.

The word could even apply to a baby, as Chaucer's *Canterbury Tales* (1386) show, in 'The Reeve's Tale':

A child that was of half yeer age
In Cradel it lay and was a propre page.

Even as late as the sixteenth century (although no later), 'page' was still in use in the basic sense, as when Richard Stanyhurst, in his translation (1582) of Virgil's *Aeneid*, wrote: 'My father vnwelthy mee sent, then a prettye page, hither'. In the fourteenth century, 'page' acquired three new meanings: 'youth being trained for knighthood', 'male person of low standing', 'boy servant or attendant' (the last being one in a large household). The third of these is closest to the modern sense, and such employees were often designated by their special work, such as 'page of the kitchen' or 'page of the stable'. (Compare similar but later uses of 'boy', as 'cabin boy', 'stable boy', 'shop boy' and so on.) Finally, the modern meaning, or something like it, emerged in the eighteenth century, with the sense first recorded in Cowper's poem *Truth* (1718):

> She yet allows herself that boy behind;
> [. . .]
> His predecessor's coat advanced to wear,
> Which future pages yet are doomed to share.

The small page boys who serve as train bearers at weddings arose, or are recorded, no earlier than the nineteenth century.

pamper (overindulge, treat with extreme care or luxury)
The original sense of the word, in the fourteenth century, was 'cram with food', 'feed luxuriously', so that to 'pamper up' meant 'feed up'. The usage was current down to at least the eighteenth century, so that Dr Johnson, in a letter to Mrs Thrale of 16 July 1775, recorded: 'After dinner I went to Snowhill; there I was pampered, and had an uneasy night'. The modern meaning arose in the sixteenth century.

pandemonium (chaos, uproar, tumult)
The word literally means, from the Greek, 'all devils', and first occurred as *Pandaemonium*, the name devised for the capital city of Hell by Milton in his *Paradise Lost* (1667):

> A solemn Council forthwith to be held
> At Pandaemonium, the high Capital
> Of Satan and his Peers.

The name became the synonym for any 'haunt of great wickedness' from then on, later acquiring a more generalized (and weakened) meaning 'place of uproar', 'scene of disorder'. (The *Daily News* of 29 November 1897 recorded that: 'On Saturday pandemonium again reigned in the Reichsrath'.)

pander (cater for a person's weaknesses or vices)
The verb evolved from the noun, which originally, in the sixteenth century, was a term for a go-between in a secret love affair. (The word itself comes ultimately from Pandarus, the procurer in Greek mythology, with his name used first by Boccaccio then by Chaucer for the man who procured for Troilus the love of Criseyde, or Griseida. Hence, in Shakespeare's *Troilus and Cressida* [1606], Pandarus's words to Troilus and Cressida: 'If ever you prove false one to another, since I have taken such pains to bring you together, let all pitiful goers-between be called to the world's end after my name; call them all Pandars; let all constant men be Troiluses, all false women Cressids, and all brokers-between Pandars'.) An example of the early sense generally in English can be found in Spenser's *Mother Hubbard* (1591):

> Ne, them to pleasure, would he sometimes scorne
> A pandares coate (so basely was he borne).

The current meaning developed in the seventeenth century, with the noun first recorded in Shakespeare (as above). The spelling with '-er' is due to the influence of other 'agent' words such as 'lover', 'reader' (falsely suggesting a verb 'to pand').

pane (piece of glass in a window, panel)
In the thirteenth century, a 'pane' was a piece of cloth, or part of a garment, as in *Merlin or the Early History of King Arthur* (1450): 'Thei kneled to sir Gawein, and folded the panes of her [i.e. their] mantels'. In this inventory from *The Paston Letters* (1422-1509), the 'pane' is a counterpane: 'Item, ij blankettys, j payre of schettys. Item, j rede pane furryd withe connyngs [i.e. rabbit furs]'. The 'window' pane emerged in the fifteenth century, when windows began to be regularly glazed, and the sense 'panel' (as in the wainscoting) was current from the sixteenth century. However, an earlier use of the word to mean 'section', 'side' was known from the fourteenth century, although today this sense is limited to technical meanings (such as one of the sides of a nut or bolt head, or a

division of a sheet of postage stamps). Compare **panel** (below).

panel (flat piece of wood etc. in a frame; group of people)
Like **pane** (which compare, above), 'panel' started off its career in the language to mean 'piece of cloth'. This was in the thirteenth century, when the particular cloth so designated was one placed under a horse's saddle to prevent its back from being chafed. These two lines from the fourteenth-century verse romance *Ywain and Gawain* (translated from the French) mention it:

> Luke thou fil wele thi panele,
> And in thi sadel set the wele.

(That is: See that you place the panel fully under the saddle, and sit properly in the saddle.) In the fourteenth century, 'panel' came to be the word for a piece of parchment attached to a writ on which names of jurymen appeared, hence the list itself, and hence (ultimately) a list of any people carrying out a particular job or assignment, such as the twentieth-century 'panel' of doctors and the members of a discussion group or quiz contest (in radio and television 'panel' games). In the fifteenth century, 'panel' evolved as the word for a section of fence, and from this, a hundred years later, came the use of 'panel' for the 'pane' of a door and the like. Further developments were the eighteenth-century 'panel' that was a type of board used for painting, and the nineteenth-century photograph size (as in a 'panel portrait'). The word has had a long, lively and productive history, from the saddle cloth to the 'panels' of a parachute in the twentieth century, and there seems no end to the technical uses of the term, many of which are associated with the 'instrument panel' of the nineteenth century (e.g. 'control panel', 'power panel').

panorama (unobstructed view of landscape; comprehensive consideration of events, views etc.)
This, like **pandemonium** (which see), is an invented word, containing Greek elements meaning 'all viewing'. The deviser of the term was the eighteenth-century portrait painter and art teacher Robert Barker, who in about 1789 so named his invention of a picture of a landscape or other scene made and constructed so that it appeared to unfold round a viewer as he stood in the centre of a cylindrical display (with the painting running round the inside of this), or so that it literally unfolded in front of him, appearing section by section. (Barker patented his device in 1787, and originally called it 'La nature à coup d'oeil', i.e. 'nature at a glance'.) In the nineteenth century, this handy word acquired a figurative use for any 'continuously passing' scene or train of thoughts, and was taken up by writers of surveys or studies of various subjects. (Soon books appeared with titles like 'The Political Panorama' [1801], 'The Panorama of Youth' [1806] and 'The Panorama of Science and Art' [1812].) Hence the title of one of the BBC's longest-running documentary programmes, first appearing in 1953 and still broadcast regularly over thirty years later.

pantechnicon (furniture van)
Like **panorama** (see above), 'pantechnicon' is an invented word, based on the Greek elements meaning (somewhat loosely) 'all the arts' (Greek *tekhnē* is 'art', 'craft', 'skill' and the root of English 'technical'). The word was devised in 1830 as the name of a building in London (in Motcomb Street, Belgrave Square) that was designed as a bazaar or market for all kinds of artistic work. But the enterprise was not a commercial success, and within a few years the building had become a large warehouse for storing furniture. Hence the vans that transported articles of furniture to and from it were known as 'pantechnicon vans', later simply 'pantechnicons'. (The building itself was destroyed by fire later in the century.) The word is used only infrequently now, with the vehicle today called a 'removal van'.

parameter (measurable or quantifiable limit or boundary)
The word arose in the seventeenth century as a strictly mathematical term, meaning 'third proportional to a diameter and its conjugate', and in particular came to be used for the so called 'principal parameter' or 'parameter of the curve', meaning, as applied to a conic section, the focal chord

perpendicular to the axis. Later, in the nineteenth century, this sense was widened in mathematics to apply to any arbitrary constant whose value shows it to be a member of a particular system, such as a family of curves. Other technical usages followed in the twentieth century, for example in electronics, statistics, and computing. The most marked sense change, however, was to the general 'parameter' that means simply 'boundary' or 'limit'. This usage became common in the media from the 1960s, in such phrases as 'economic parameters', 'political parameters' and 'parameters of power'.

paramour (illicit lover, mistress)
The word is now a dated or affected (or 'poetically charged') one. Its sense has varied, though, and deteriorated over the years. It originated as French *par amour*, 'by love', and was first used in English adverbially in this sense, in the thirteenth century. As such, it could even sometimes be simply a polite phrase meaning 'of your kindness', 'if you please' and the like. Here is an example of its use at that time:

'Felawe', a saide, 'par amur:
Whar mai ich finde themperur?'
(*The Romance of Sir Beues of Hamtoun*)

At the same time, the common phrase 'to love par amour' almost always meant 'be in love with', 'love by way of sexual love', as in 'The Knight's Tale' in Chaucer's *Canterbury Tales* (1386):

I telle thee outrely ffor paramour
I loued hire first er thow.

(That is, in modern terms: I tell you frankly, I slept with her before you did.) In this usage, the adverbial 'paramour' seems almost to have been understood as a noun, and as the grammatical object of the verb 'love', with the result that the word actually became a noun, meaning either 'love' (i.e. sexual love) or 'lover', 'sweetheart'. In the first of these senses it was usually distinguished from standard 'love', as in Chaucer's work again ('The Cook's Tale'):

He was as ful of love & paramour
As is the hyve ful of hony sweete.

In the second usage, the word had no derogatory sense, and indeed was as 'pure' as 'sweetheart' mostly is or was. An example of its usage can be seen in the fifteenth-century *The Knight of Curtesy and the Fair Lady of Faguell*:

His paramour she thought to be,
Hym for to love wyth herte and minde,
Nat in vyce but in chastyte.

'Paramour' even came to be a term of religious address for the Virgin Mary (as used by men) or for Christ (by women), and a fifteenth-century carol has Christ addressing Mary thus:

To his moder then gan he say, [. . .]
My swete moder, myn paramour,

But, equally, it is in Chaucer (Prologue to 'The Wife of Bath's Tale') that the usage 'illicit lover' is found:

My fourthe housbonde was a reuelour
[i.e. a reveller]
This is to seyn he hadde a paramour.

And despite the courtly 'lady love' of the knight, the 'paramour' who figures in poetry from the sixteenth century, it was the 'bad' sense that prevailed, except where the word was artificially preserved by poets.

paraphernalia (awkward accessories or procedures)
The Greek words that produced the word in English, first in the seventeenth century, mean literally 'beside the dowry', and the original meaning of the term was for those articles of property that the law allowed a married woman to retain as her own. Thus, until the law was abolished in the nineteenth century, this meant things such as clothes, jewels, personal toiletries and the like. From the eighteenth century, the sense was extended, however, to mean 'belongings', 'accessories' and so on in general, and this is the meaning of the word today, with a figurative use often found (as in the 'paraphernalia' of applying for a job or a licence of some kind, with all its 'trappings').

parcel (package; plot of land)
The oldest sense of the word, dating from the fourteenth century, was simply 'part', 'portion', 'particle'. This now survives only in the expression 'part and parcel'. The

'portion of land' sense evolved in the fifteenth century, and a hundred years later 'parcel' acquired a further meaning as 'small party of people'. This is first recorded in Shakespeare's *Love's Labour's Lost* (1588), where Moth sings:

A holy parcel of the fairest dames
That ever turn'd their backs to mortal
    views!

The modern 'parcel' as a package began to emerge in the seventeenth century, when the *Oxford Almanack* (1692) records: 'For the carriage of the greatest parcel, (all being to be esteemed parcels under one quarter of an hundred weight,) one shilling'. Shakespeare's use became obsolete in the nineteenth century, except where still used as 'lot', 'pack' ('I'm not going to be spoken to like that by a parcel of shop assistants!').

park (enclosed area of lawns, flower beds, sports facilities etc. open to the public; area designated for leaving vehicles)
At first, in the thirteenth century, a 'park' was a tract of land held by the king and used for hunting. (Unlike a 'forest' or a 'chase' it was enclosed.) This gradually led to the public 'park' of today, although it is difficult to say precisely when the one became the other. Certainly by the seventeenth century 'park' was used in its modern meaning, as recorded in his *Diary* entry of 15 May 1663 by Pepys: 'I walked in the Parke, discoursing with the keeper of the Pell Mell'. At the same time, in the eighteenth century, many country houses acquired 'parks' or planned estates, rather in the manner of the royal hunting 'parks', with these being used both for recreation or keeping animals such as sheep, deer or cattle. They were not open to the public, however (although many are today, if only to raise an income for the upkeep of the house and its grounds). Some such 'parks' actually gave their names to the houses they surrounded, such as Osterley Park, London. Also in the seventeenth century, 'park' came to be the military term for the enclosed area where artillery, horses, stores and the like were kept in an encampment, and it is from this that the modern 'car park' evolved in the twentieth century, with the word even used for a building for the first time in its history (a 'multistorey carpark' or an 'underground carpark'). From an open area containing the beasts of the chase, a 'park' has thus come to designate an enclosed structure for housing the 'steeds' of businessmen and women and shoppers, who are engaged in a 'chase' of their own elsewhere.

passenger (person travelling in a vehicle)
In the fourteenth century, a 'passenger' was a traveller or wayfarer in general, and often, in fact, one on foot. (The word, after all, means simply someone who is 'passing' or making a 'passage' somewhere.) Scott used the word in the 'pedestrian' sense as late as the nineteenth century, in *The Fair Maid of Perth* (1828): 'She avoided the High Street [. . .] and reached the wynd by the narrow lanes. [. . .] Even these comparatively lonely passages were now astir with passengers'. The 'vehicle' passenger arose in the sixteenth century, with the word usually having the implication that the vehicle is a public, fare-paying one, whether going by road, rail, sea or air. (One notable exception to this, however, is the seat next to the driver in a private car, the 'passenger' seat.) The first sense of 'passenger' is now obsolete, except in the still sometimes used expression, 'foot passenger', meaning a traveller who makes a short part of a longer journey on foot (as between a harbour jetty and a railway station).

passion (strong feeling, especially of sexual love; outbreak of anger)
The earliest 'passion' was recorded in English in the twelfth century, and was the suffering of pain, and in particular the sufferings of Christ (as which today it is usually spelt with a capital letter). This is therefore the meaning in the Bible in Acts 1:3, where the word was retained from Wyclif's translation of 1382 down to later versions of the sixteenth and seventeenth centuries (in the Authorized Version of 1611: 'To whom also he shewed himself alive after his passion'). In the fourteenth century, the sense expanded from physical suffering to mental, and entered the emotional fields of strongly experienced hope, fear, love, hate, joy, ambition, desire, grief and much else that can be keenly felt. In the sixteenth century, there was a kind

of polarization of meaning into 'angry outburst' on the one hand, and 'amorous feeling' on the other, with the latter sense of 'passion' acquiring a more specifically sexual connotation in the seventeenth century. Finally, and also in the seventeenth century, 'passion' gained its inevitably weakened sense (after so much strength) as merely 'great liking for' (as a 'passion' for riding or growing azaleas).

pastel (paste made of powdered pigment or a drawing made with it; light shade of colour)
The artistic 'pastel' evolved in the seventeenth century, and is first mentioned in Evelyn's *Sculptura* (1662): 'Rubbing in the shades with pastills and dry compositions'. Such a type of drawing produced pictures in light or pale colours, and in the late nineteenth century the word was adopted as a fashion term for light-coloured dress materials, so that the *Daily News* of 21 October 1899 reported: 'The soft, wraith-like tints [...] are now in fashion again. The modern name for them is "pastels", [...] for these soft, half-faded tones bear the same relation to real colours as pastels do to oil-paintings'. In the twentieth century, this use of 'pastel' was extended to textiles and interior decorating generally, and anything from curtains to car upholstery can now be in 'pastel shades'.

pastiche (literary or artistic work imitating the style of some previous work)
The present word gradually replaced the earlier 'pasticcio' (Italian for 'pie'), which was first used in English in the eighteenth century to mean a work of art compiled from pieces or fragments of some earlier work. For example, an opera could be a medley of extracts from previous operas, or a painting could be concocted from fragments or details of different earlier paintings by different artists. In some cases, such works attempted to recreate the style of the originals, in others they were simply a 'pot-pourri' or even a frank hotchpotch. (The aim must have been purely commercial in many cases, since an opera of this type would contain a selection of 'old favourites' designed to attract the public.) Later, when 'pastiche' began to supersede 'pasticcio' in

the nineteenth century, the sense altered to denote a work that was much more consciously in the style of an earlier work, but at the same time more creatively so, so that it was almost a parody. The 'pastiche' has thus on the whole looked up since its debut as a 'pasticcio'.

pasty (small pie containing meat and vegetables or fruit)
The original thirteenth-century 'pasty' was almost always a venison pie, and even when fish 'pasties' evolved in the sixteenth century (or possibly earlier), the content was still just meat (or fish). From the nineteenth century, and under the influence of the 'Cornish pasty', such pies also came to contain vegetables, and the 'pasty' in general became almost exclusively associated with this county dish. Also, fruit 'pasties' or turnovers appeared in the nineteenth century, so that today, a 'pasty' is not the clearcut thing it once was in Chaucer's day.

pavilion (building on sports ground where players can change and relax)
Back in the thirteenth century, a 'pavilion' was a large peaked tent, especially a stately one for a royal or other 'grand' personage. The use of the word in this sense is still not perhaps quite dead, and occurs, for example, in the Bible, where in I Kings 20:12 one reads that: 'Benhadad heard this message, as he was drinking, he and the kings in the pavilions'. In the seventeenth century, the modern sports pavilion began to emerge, initially as a light building or shelter in a park, a sort of superior kiosk or summerhouse. The cricket 'pavilion' seems to have gained its individuality at least as early as the eighteenth century, and *The Times* of 1 June 1799 reported that a military ceremony was held at Lord's cricket ground, with a presentation of colours to the corps, and that after the ceremony was over, the titled guests 'partook of a cold collation provided for them in the pavillion'.

pay (give money in return for services or goods)
The earliest sense of 'pay', in the twelfth century, was 'pacify', 'please', thus relating quite closely to the verb's ultimate origin in

Latin *pacare*, 'to pacify' (in turn related to *pax*, 'peace'). In the *Cursor Mundi* of the fourteenth century, therefore, this is the sense in the lines:

Wel he wend wit this tithing
For to pai dauid the king.

The usage was obsolete by the end of the fifteenth century, and the modern meaning of 'pay', which had developed from the thirteenth century, became the predominant one.

pearmain (variety of apple)
It seems strange that a name like this should be used of an apple, not a pear. Yet originally it *did* apply to a pear! This was not because the word itself is related to 'pear', however, since the name ultimately derives from 'Parma', the town in Italy. Even so, in the fifteenth century, a 'pearmain' was a pear, and may have been the crisp, cooking variety that is now known as a 'warden'. The apple 'pearmain' took over the name from the sixteenth century, with the variety having several subvarieties such as the 'winter pearmain', 'summer pearmain' 'russet pearmain' and so on. Presumably the original pear was imported, or was believed to come, from Parma (as Parmesan cheese did).

peculiar (strange)
The first sense of the word to be current in English, in the fifteenth century, was not the modern one of 'odd', 'strange', but that of 'belonging to a particular person or thing' (as in a custom that is 'peculiar' to a particular country). In the sixteenth century, 'peculiar' came to mean 'individual', 'particular', and this is the sense in Shakespeare's *Hamlet* (1602), where Rosencrantz says to Claudius:

The single and peculiar life is bound
With all the strength and armour of the
mind
To keep itself from noyance.

The modern meaning followed only in the seventeenth century, the concept being of something or someone that was 'individual' in an abnormal or unexpected way.

pedant (person who attaches much

importance to book learning and who is pedantic)
The current sense dates from the sixteenth century. A contemporary usage of 'pedant', however, meant simply 'schoolmaster', at least in Shakespeare's *Love's Labour's Lost* (1588), where no contemptuous connotation is implied in Berowne's 'love' speech:

A domineering pedant o'er the boy
Than whom no mortal so magnificent!

In fact, 'pedant' was used much as 'pedagogue' down to the end of the seventeenth century, while the disparaging sense of the word dates from only a little later than the Shakespearean use quoted here.

peevish (fretful, moody, petulant)
In its earliest use, 'peevish' meant 'silly', 'foolish', with this sense found in the fourteenth century. The first record of the word, whose origin is still unknown, is found in a characteristically colourful alliterative line in Langland's *Piers Plowman* (1393):

And bad hym 'go pisse with his plouh,
peyuesshe shrewe!'

In the fifteenth century, the word came to mean 'spiteful', 'malignant', so that Richard Grafton, in *A Chronicle at Large and Meere History of the Affayres of England* (1568), wrote: 'In derision of the king, they made certaine peeuishe and mocking rymes which I passe ouer'. A further sense followed in the sixteenth century, when 'peevish' could also mean 'perverse', 'obstinate' (not quite its modern meaning, which also dates from this time). An example of its usage comes in Shakespeare's *Two Gentlemen of Verona* (1591), when Thurio says of Silvia:

Why, this it is to be a peevish girl,
That flies her fortune when it follows
her.

This, and the two earlier senses, are now all obsolete.

penknife (pocket knife)
The knife is so called since it was originally used for making or mending quill pens. This, therefore, was what the word meant in the fifteenth century. However, a knife is a knife, and the penknife could be used for cutting objects other than quill pens, as

recorded, for example, in the Bible: 'When Jehudi had read three or four leaves, he cut it [i.e. the roll in which Baruch had written Jeremiah's prophecy] with the penknife, and cast it into the fire' (Jeremiah 36:23). The modern penknife with folding blade had developed by the nineteenth century, when the pen itself had long passed the quill stage.

penthouse (rooftop luxury apartment)
The word has been influenced by 'house' but does not derive from it. A 'penthouse' is thus really an 'appendage', as it were, or a structure of some kind attached to or literally 'hanging on' ('appending') another. In its earliest sense, in the fourteenth century, it was therefore a subsidiary structure such as a shed or barn, attached to the wall of another, larger building. (This sense still sometimes applies today.) The first record we have of the word is in the *English Metrical Homilies* of 1325, where the structure is mentioned in a biblical nativity setting:

Thar was na herberie
To Josep and his spouse Marie,
Bot a pendize that was wawles,
Als oft in borwis tounes es.

(That is: There was no lodging place for Joseph and his wife Mary but a wall-less penthouse, as often found in fortified towns ['borough towns'].) By the fifteenth century, the word had come to be used of an 'annexe' in general, and not necessarily one with a sloping roof, as the original 'penthouse' had. In Chester, for example, the 'Pentice' was a largish building formerly attached to St Peter's Church, where it was used for sheriffs' courts and banquets. (It was pulled down in the early nineteenth century.) In other words, the original lowly 'lean-to' shed was moving decidedly upwards in use, size and status. Finally, in the twentieth century, the 'penthouse' moved about as high as it could go, in all senses, when it became the term for a luxury flat on the roof of a tall building. Such apartments were first designated after the First World War (one is mentioned as being under construction in the April 1921 issue of *Country Life*).

perforce (of necessity)
This now mannered or dated word orig-inally meant 'forcibly' in the fourteenth century, when it was first current in English. The usage lasted until the seventeenth century, so that the explorer Captain John Smith, in *The Generall Historie of Virginia, New-England and the Summer Isles* (1624), wrote: 'The Salvages assayed to carry him away perforce'. The current use of the word arose in the sixteenth century.

perplex (baffle by being complicated, puzzle)
In the sixteenth century, 'perplex' meant not so much 'puzzle', 'baffle' as 'make uncertain', 'trouble with doubt'. The usage is first recorded in Shakespeare's *King John* (1595), when King Philip says to Pandulph:

I am perplex'd, and know not what to say.

Pandulph replies:

What canst thou say but will perplex thee more,
If thou stand excommunicate and curs'd?

The modern meaning developed in the seventeenth century.

peruse (read)
As currently used, 'peruse' means almost 'read through casually', with the verb generally having a humorous overtone. In the fifteenth century, the meaning was both 'use up' (now obsolete) and 'examine or revise carefully', which still survives as the 'serious' sense of the word. The general meaning 'read through', and the corresponding noun 'perusal', dates from the sixteenth century, and it may well be that the modern humorous usage derives from the affectation for the word that several writers had from Shakespeare onward. Certainly, nineteenth-century sailors used 'peruse' (as a noun) to mean simply 'look round' ('Let's go and have a bit of a peruse'), and this would have helped to 'demote' the otherwise serious sense.

pest (harmful plant or animal; annoying person)
The two senses given here evolved in the seventeenth century, with the original meaning of 'pest', a hundred years earlier,

being 'pestilence', 'plague'. In Scotland, in the sixteenth and seventeenth centuries, 'the pest' was the common term for bubonic plague. This usage became obsolete in the nineteenth century.

petrol (motor fuel)
When first current in English, in the sixteenth century, 'petrol' meant generally 'petroleum', and thus served as a doublet for this word, which also entered English use then. Near the end of the nineteenth century, however, 'petrol' was adopted as the word for the refined petroleum that is the fuel as we know it today. This new sense was borrowed from French *essence de pétrole*, literally 'essence of petroleum', so that in modern French, *essence* is now 'petrol', and *pétrole* is 'petroleum'.

petticoat (woman's undergarment)
The origin of the word lies in Old French *pety cote*, literally 'little coat', and in the fifteenth century, when sometimes written in two words in English, a 'petticoat' was a small coat worn by men under a doublet. John Russell's *The Boke of Nurture* (1460) contains the following recommendations: 'Se that youre souerayne haue clene shurt & breche, A petycote, a dublett, a longe coote'. At the same time, a 'petticoat', as a female garment, was also a kind of skirt, and Sir Philip Sidney, in *The Countesse of Pembrokes Arcadia* (1586), tells how he saw: 'Sixe maides, all in one liuerie of scarlet peticotes, which were tucked vp almost to their knees'. By the sixteenth century, the garment was still an outer one, when it was a skirt (bottom half of costume) as distinct from a bodice (top half). In his *Diary* entry for 18 May 1662, Pepys approved of one he saw: 'She was in her new suit of black sarcenet [i.e. soft thin silk] and yellow petticoate very pretty'. Equally, however, a 'petticoat' was also an underskirt of calico, flannel, or some other material, and it seems likely that this is the garment mentioned in Shakespeare's *The Taming of the Shrew* (1596), where Bianca says to Katharina (her sister, the 'Shrew'):

Unbind my hands, I'll pull them off myself,
Yea all my raiment, to my petticoat.

If this is indeed the garment as described,

it is the first record we have of it, and therefore the forerunner of the modern 'petticoat'.

petulant (pettish, peevish)
Before acquiring its modern sense in the eighteenth century, 'petulant' had two earlier meanings, now both obsolete. The earliest sense, in the sixteenth century, was 'lascivious', 'wanton'. The usage is first recorded in John Marston's *The scourge of villanie* (1598):

Deride me not, though I seeme petulant
To fall into your chops.

In the seventeenth century, 'petulant' meant 'pert', 'cheeky', and Dryden, in *A Discourse Concerning the Origine and Progress of Satire* (1693), wrote of 'the petulant scribblers of this age'. The modern meaning is first recorded in Johnson's *Dictionary* (1755) to define 'peevish' ('petulant, waspish, easily offended').

philander (flirt, have several love affairs)
The word was originally a noun, or more precisely a name, itself deriving from the Greek for 'man loving' and implying a woman who loves her husband. However, the name was presumably taken to mean not 'man loving' but 'loving man', since it became the stock 'lover' name in certain early plays and stories. Thus in Ariosto's *Orlando Furioso* (1532), Filandro was the young man loved (and subsequently ruined) by the oversexed Gabrina, and in Fletcher and Massinger (or Beaumont and Fletcher)'s *The Laws of Candy* (1647) one of the characters is 'Philander Prince of Cyprus, passionately in love with Erota'. But above all, the name seems to have been particularly coupled with that of Phillis, especially in a ballad of 1682 entitled 'The faithful Lovers Downfal: or, The Death of Fair Phillis Who Killed her self for loss of her Philander', with lines from this running, for example:

Philander, ah Philander! still the bleeding Phillis cries,
She wept awhile, And she forc't a Smile, then clos'd her eyes and dyes.

'Philander' was thus a nickname for a lover, especially a 'passionate' one, as in Charles

Pigott's *The Female Jockey Club* (1794): 'Those philanders of former times once led Captivity Captive, too happy to be bound in her fetters'. And in the eighteenth century the noun became used as a verb meaning (not so passionately), 'flirt'. In his *Autobiography* (1805), Alexander Carlyle, the Scottish minister, recorded how he spent one day: ' . . .between disputing with my landlord, and walking about and philandering with the ladies'.

philology (science of language)
When first current as a term in English, in the seventeenth century, 'philology' was used for the study of literature, in a general sense, including grammar, literary criticism and so on. It could even mean simply 'polite learning'. In the eighteenth century, this usage acquired a narrower sense to mean 'study of language', 'linguistics', with the earlier meaning becoming finally obsolete in the nineteenth century.

photogenic (looking attractive when photographed)
In the first half of the nineteenth century, 'photogenic' was the same as 'photographic', and 'photogenic drawing' was the term chosen by the photographic pioneer William Fox Talbot for photography itself, or for a photograph. Thus the title of a paper of Fox Talbot's appearing in 1839 in the *Proceedings of the Royal Society* was: 'Some account of the Art of Photogenic Drawing, or the Process by which Natural Objects may be made to delineate themselves without the aid of the Artist's Pencil'. (A rarer contemporary meaning of the word in the sense 'sensitive to light' is still current for certain medical conditions, such as 'photogenic epilepsy'.) The modern popular meaning, 'photographing attractively', evolved in the United States in the 1920s, especially in connection with the cinema. In recent use, the word is often little more than a synonym for 'good-looking', or at most as a synonym for 'handsome' (of a male) or 'pretty as a picture' (of a female).

physics (science that deals with matter and energy)
When first current in English, in the sixteenth century, 'physics' meant 'natural science', meaning that of the whole natural world, organic and inorganic. This was gradually narrowed down so that by the eighteenth century the term applied to inorganic nature (that is, without the world of animals and plants studied by biology), and finally chemistry was also excluded, likewise in the eighteenth century.

picket (person posted by a trade union at a workplace during a strike to prevent workers from breaking the strike)
The key word here, in the development of the senses, is 'post'. Originally, in the seventeenth century, 'picket' was the word, as it still is, for a pointed stake. In the eighteenth century, the term came to be applied to a detachment of troops, the reference being initially to the stakes to which the troops tied their horses. The trade union 'picket' developed from this in turn in the nineteenth century. This current sense is first recorded in *The Times* of 22 August 1867: 'The pickets kept their places from early morning till night; they reviled the workmen who went in and out; they forced women to call upon the police for protection; they threatened that those who took work [. . .] should have none when the Union was triumphant'.

picnic (outdoor meal)
Originally, when picnics first became fashionable in the mid-eighteenth century, an essential feature of the meal was that each participant contributed to it. The concept of such a meal or party as a whole seems to have been imported to Britain from France or Germany, and the first record available of a picnic is one held in Germany in 1748. In that year, Lord Chesterfield wrote to his son, who was in Germany (possibly in Berlin): 'I like the description of your *Picnic;* where, I take it for granted, that your cards are only to break the formality of a circle'. The transition from this sort of 'picnic' (which was not an outdoor one), to the 'alfresco' sort now existing, came in the nineteenth century, when first, the meal was held out of doors, and second, the tradition of each person contributing was no longer a requirement. Even so, as late as 1868, Robert Latham, in *A Dictionary of the English Language* (which

was based on an already revised edition of Johnson's *Dictionary*), defined 'picnic' as: 'open air party, in which a meal, to which each guest contributes a portion of the viands, is the essential characteristic'.

piety (devotion to religious worship and duties)
In the thirteenth century, 'piety' meant 'pity', and was not fully distinguished from this sense until the sixteenth century. Even as late as 1606, when Philemon Holland made his translation of Suetonius' *Historie of Twelve Caesars*, he felt there would be no ambiguity in writing: 'Of your gracious Piety (which I know I shall hardly obtaine)'. In the sixteenth century, 'piety' came to apply to filial or similar duties ('filial piety', as now), and only a century later did the word acquire its religious meaning. Compare **pity** itself.

pilgrim (traveller to religious centre)
In its earliest use, in the twelfth century, 'pilgrim' was simply a word for any kind of traveller or wayfarer, merely a 'wanderer' or 'sojourner'. (In its ultimate derivation, the word can be traced from Latin *per ager*, 'through the field', 'through the country'.) Wyclif used the word (in a non-religious sense) in his Bible translation of 1382, where he rendered Hebrews 11:13 as: 'For thei ben pilgrymes, and herborid men vpon the erthe', and I Peter 2:11 as: 'I beseche you, as comelynges and pilgrimes'. (The Authorized Version of 1611 keeps this in the respective passages: 'They were strangers and pilgrims on the earth': 'I beseech you as strangers and pilgrims'.) From the thirteenth century, 'pilgrim' acquired its religious use, occurring in one of the earliest and best known texts in this sense in the Prologue to Chaucer's *Canterbury Tales* (1386):

Pilgrimes were they alle
That toward Caunterbury wolden ryde.

The 'traveller' sense of the word was popular with poets of the eighteenth and nineteenth centuries, and cannot be said to be fully obsolete as such.

pineapple (large tropical fruit with yellow flesh)

Neither 'pine' nor 'apple' in the modern sense, of course. But originally, in the fourteenth century, 'pineapple' was the word for a pinecone, since the cone is the fruit of the pine and 'apple' had the former general meaning 'fruit'. In the seventeenth century, the name was adopted for the fruit as we know it today (called in many other languages *ananas*), with the transfer of name made because of the resemblance of the pineapple to a large pinecone. By about 1700 the 'pinecone' sense of the word was virtually obsolete.

pip (seed in core of apple or pear, segment of orange, etc.)
The word is short for 'pippin', the variety of apple, and this was its sense when first current in the sixteenth century. It seems to have originated, in this meaning, in the cries of Irish costermongers, and at any rate the first records we have of it relate to this usage. The transfer of sense from apple to seed evolved in the eighteenth century. However, 'pippin' itself had also meant 'pip' continuously from the thirteenth century, and this must have influenced the shift of sense, even though it is documented as deriving from the apple. (Additionally, there may have been an influence of the other sense of 'pip' to mean 'spot on playing card or dice'. Perhaps the pips in a fruit were seen as resembling these other 'pips' in their contrasting colours, i.e. dark against light.)

piquant (appetising, agreeably provocative)
The first sense that 'piquant' had, in the sixteenth century, was 'piercing', 'cutting', even 'severe' or 'bitter', this being closer to the original French word meaning 'stinging' (*piquer*, 'to prick', 'sting'). In his translation (1549) of Erasmus's *Moriae encomium* (as *The praise of folie*), Sir Thomas Chaloner wrote: 'Who is he so blunt and restiue, that could not with theyr pickant spurres be quickened?'. The more agreeable modern and toned down sense developed in the seventeenth century, and by the end of the nineteenth century the earlier meaning had become almost obsolete.

pittance (meagre allowance)
The word is related to both '**piety**' and '**pity**' (see these as separate entries), and in the thirteenth century a 'pittance' was a pious donation made to a religious house so that extra food, wine and the like could be provided on particular festivals, or to commemorate a benefactor's death. (The latter would be 'worth a mass'.) Here is a record of such a pittance from a will deposited in Bury St Edmunds in 1463: 'To eche monk [. . .] xij *d.* and a petaunce amonges them, eche man a french loof and a quart wyn'. This meaning developed in the fourteenth century to mean a small allowance of some kind, originally of food. From this in turn, in the sixteenth century, 'pittance' came to mean 'meagre wage or allowance'. The implication seems to have been that what was originally quite generously given was later pruned back for reasons of economy or lack of interest in a declining tradition. A simple innate meanness may also have been at work!

pity (compassion)
The modern meaning of 'pity' is also the oldest, dating from the thirteenth century, when the word could also mean 'mildness', 'tenderness', which is not quite what it means today. In the fourteenth century, however, 'pity' came to mean 'piety' (in its present sense), as in one of John Lydgate's *Minor Poems* (1430):

God the endew withe a croune of glory;
And withe septre of clennes and pitee.

(That is: May God endow you with a crown of glory and with a sceptre of purity and piety.) This sense fell out of use shortly after. See also **piety** (above).

placebo (medicine that works by its psychological effect alone)
The word is Latin for 'I shall please', and this is the first word of the antiphon (response) to the first psalm sung in the vespers for the dead in the Roman Catholic church (*Placebo Domino in regione vivorum*, 'I shall please the Lord in the land of the living'). This then became the name of the service itself in the thirteenth century. In the nineteenth century, the word was adopted for the medicine that was purely palliative and given to 'please' a patient who felt the need of it. Both meanings, in their different ways, are still current.

plaintive (mournful, melancholy)
The word suggests 'complaining', and this is in fact what it originally meant in the fourteenth century. So in John Lane's *Tom Tel Troth's Message, and his Pen's Complaint* (1600) one has the lines:

Thus men by women, women wrongde by men,
Giue matter still vnto my plaintife pen.

This meaning became obsolete in the eighteenth century, while the current sense developed from the sixteenth.

planet (heavenly body revolving round the sun)
In old astronomy, in the twelfth century, a 'planet' was the word for any heavenly body that appeared to move among the fixed stars. Astronomers of the day thus held that the seven planets, in the accepted order of their distance from the Earth, were: the Moon, Mercury, Venus, the Sun, Mars, Jupiter and Saturn. Even in texts down to the seventeenth century, references to 'the seven planets' would have implied these seven bodies. The current understanding dates from the same century, and the earliest record we have of the 'new order' is found in the title of Bishop John Wilkins' 'A Discovrse concerning a New Planet. Tending to prove, That 'tis probable our Earth is one of the Planets' (1640). Modern astronomy then moved fairly fast to establish the new definition of 'planet', and named them, now in order of distance from the Sun, as: Mercury, Venus, the Earth, Mars, Jupiter and Saturn, later adding, when they were discovered, Uranus (in 1781), Neptune (1846) and Pluto (1930). The change in sense of the word was of course caused by the realization in the sixteenth century, largely as a result of the work and theories of Copernicus, that these bodies revolved round the Sun, not the Earth, and that the Earth itself revolved round the Sun.

plasma (liquid part of blood)
The popular understanding of the word, as

defined here, is neither the oldest sense nor the only one. The derivation lies in Late Latin *plasma*, 'mould', 'image' (itself from Greek *plassein*, 'to mould'), and when first current in the eighteenth century 'plasma' meant simply 'form'. Even in the nineteenth century, in his *Imaginary Conversations of Literary Men and Statesmen* (1824–9), Walter Savage Landor, in the volume giving the dialogues of Southey and Porson, wrote: 'A great portion of his compositions is not poetry, but only the plasma or matrix of poetry'. However, this use of the word soon became obsolete, and 'plasma' has acquired the following mainly technical (scientific) senses in the century as shown: 'green variety of quartz' (eighteenth), 'colourless liquid part of blood' (nineteenth), 'ionised gas' (twentieth, more precisely: 1928).

plausible (possible, valid but suspect)
The current meaning dates from the sixteenth century, when the word also had two or three other senses, now obsolete. Among them were 'laudable', 'deserving applause', and 'acceptable', 'agreeable'. The first of these, for example, is used by Gabriel Harvey in his *Foure Letters* (1592): 'The plausible examples of diuers such vertuous Romanes, and sundry excellent Greekes'. The second occurs in John Stow's *The Annales of England* (1592): 'This change was very plawsible or well pleasing to the Nobility and Gentrye'. Both these meanings fell out of use by about the end of the eighteenth century, although they were widely current in the sixteenth and seventeenth.

plethora (excess, superfluity)
The modern sense became current in the seventeenth century. The original meaning, however, was a special medical one dating from the sixteenth century, when 'plethora' (in Greek literally 'fullness') was the term for an abnormal condition in which there was believed to be too much blood in the body (or, as later modified, too many red corpuscles in the blood). This, therefore, was what Sheridan meant in *The School for Scandal* (1777), when he makes Joseph Surface say to Lady Teazle: 'Your character at present is like a person in a plethora, absolutely dying from too much health'. The word is no longer in technical use.

pluck (courage, 'grit', firm resolve)
The verb 'pluck', in the literal sense of 'pull off', 'pick off' (as of feathers), first became current in English in the fourteenth century. The noun followed a century later to mean 'act of plucking'. In the seventeenth century, 'pluck' came to be used for an animal's heart, liver and lungs, as used for food, with the usage referring to the fact that these were 'plucked' from the carcass. From this in turn, and originally as a slang word used by boxers, the modern sense 'courage' evolved, since someone who had 'pluck' had 'heart' or 'guts'. The word has since come to be regarded as a typically 'British' one, even if done to death in school stories and tales of fortitude in battle and the like.

plumber (person who installs and repairs water piping and fittings)
In the fourteenth century, a 'plumber' was, as his name literally suggests, a worker in lead (compare French *plomb*, 'lead'). Even as late as the seventeenth century this basic sense was current, and can be found, for instance, in Ben Jonson's comedy *The Alchemist* (1610):

And, early in the morning, will I send
To all the plumbers, and the pewterers,
And buy their tin, and lead vp.

The modern understanding and use of the word became established in the nineteenth century, or perhaps even the late eighteenth. (Modern plumbers, too, frequently work in materials other than lead!)

poison (deadly substance in liquid or solid form)
'Poison' literally means 'potion' (the two words are of one and the same origin), and in the thirteenth century, when the word came into English from French, there was no sense of 'poisonous' to it. In the following line from Langland's *Piers Plowman* (1377) the meaning is 'specially prepared drink':

And poysoun on a pole thei put vp to his lippes.

The same sense occurs as late as the sixteenth century in Lyly's *Euphues* (1579): 'Yᵉ Phisition by minglyng bitter poysons with sweete lyquor, bringeth health to the body'. But also in the thirteenth century, 'poison' could be used for a 'potion' or medicine that had been 'doctored', or had a deadly or dangerous drug added, and from this the meaning generally spread to its current sense, with this dating from the fourteenth century.

Pole (native of Poland)
In the sixteenth century, 'Pole' was the name of the country itself. Hence, in Sir Thomas Elyot's *The Castel of Helth* (1539): 'In any other countrey than England, Scotland, Ireland, & Poyle', and even in James Fraser's *Chronicles of the Frasers* (1700): 'After the peace he went up to Pole with other Scotsshmen'. The present name, which developed by association with (but not directly from) English 'land', dates also from the sixteenth century, while 'Pole' passed to its modern meaning of 'native of Poland' in the seventeenth century. (Before this, Poles were called either 'Polacks' or 'Polanders'. The former occurs in Shakespeare's *Hamlet*, 1602.)

police (government administration dealing with public order)
In the sixteenth century, when the word was usually pronounced with the stress on the first syllable (rhyming with 'Hollis'), 'police' meant either 'policy' (in the sense 'prudent procedure') or 'civilization'. The latter sense can be found as late as the eighteenth century in Burke's *A Letter to a Member of the National Assembly* (1791), where he is writing about the Turks: 'A barbarous nation, with a barbarous neglect of police, fatal to the human race'. The modern meaning dates from the eighteenth century, when the word originally related to the civil administrations of other countries, in particular France and Scotland. In the latter country Commissioners of Police, named after the French equivalents (*commissaires de police*), were established by Queen Anne on 13 December 1714, and the London police force, known for some time as the 'New Police', was established in 1829 by Sir Robert Peel. This is therefore the final 'arrival' of the word in its current sense.

policy (course of action, overall plan)
The word dates from the fourteenth century, when it originally meant 'government', 'administration'. This is the sense in Shakespeare's *Henry V* (1599), when in the opening scene the Archbishop of Canterbury says of the king:

Turn him to any cause of policy,
The Gordian knot of it he will unloose.

The meaning fell out of use in the eighteenth century, and the modern senses date from the fifteenth century. (The 'policy' that is the insurance document is a different word, and has not altered its meaning since the sixteenth century.)

polite (courteous, well-mannered)
This adjective is related to 'polish', and when first current in English, in the fifteenth century, actually meant 'polished' or 'burnished' in a literal sense (taken from Latin *politus*, the past participle passive of *polire*, 'to polish'). Even as late as the seventeenth century, Evelyn refers to potter's earth as 'exceeding polite and smooth' (*Terra*, 1675), and Ralph Cudworth, in *The True Intellectual System of the Universe* (1678), writes of 'Polite Bodies, as Looking-Glasses'. This sense then became obsolete. Meanwhile, in the sixteenth century, 'polite' had progressed to meaning 'polished' in the figurative sense, as applied to a person's tastes, culture or manners, or a combination of these. In her poem, *To the Archbishop of Canterbury* (1664), Katherine Philips thus writes:

Majestic sweetness, temper'd and
refin'd,
In a Polite, and comprehensive Mind.

In his preface to *A Dissertation upon the Epistles of Phalaris* (1697), too, Richard Bentley writes how: 'All the Lovers of Polite Learning [...] give me thanks'. It is the 'manners' aspect of the word that prevailed, however, although perhaps one can still talk of 'polite letters', meaning refined writing, and be understood.

poll (casting or counting of votes)
The current sense of the word, as in 'going to the polls' on an election day, arose only in the seventeenth century. The source of

the word is its literal meaning 'head', and this was the sense of 'poll' for some time from the thirteenth century. In the *Laud Troy Book* (1400), for example, the word comes in these lines:

Thei stroke to-gedir with so gret myght,
That bothe vpon here pol lyght.

(That is, they [two knights on horseback] fought together so vigorously that they both landed on their heads.) Much later, in *The Indicator* (in 1820), Leigh Hunt wrote of '. . .receiving the full summer showers with an uncovered poll'. Clearly, a good way of counting people is by a 'counting of heads', and the first record we have of 'poll' used in this sense comes in Shakespeare's *Coriolanus* (1607), when Coriolanus says:

We are the greater poll, and in true fear
They gave us our demands.

This usage soon passed, in the same century, to the present meaning 'counting of votes at an election'.

polytechnic (college offering advanced courses at or below degree level)
The British 'polytechnic' has existed in three forms since it first materialized in the nineteenth century. The original was the so called 'Polytechnic Institution' in London. This opened in 1831 to exhibit objects connected with the industrial arts ('polytechnic' means literally 'many arts') and had a laboratory and a lecture theatre. It closed in 1881, but then reopened as a technical school. (This was the establishment that became known as the 'London Polytechnic' or 'Regent Street Polytechnic', catering mainly for working-class students.) Other such establishments opened elsewhere (there were twelve in London by 1904) and continued to operate on much the same lines, offering a blend of general and technical (industrial) courses. From 1965, the role of polytechnics changed to what they are today, regional centres of higher education. The term thus has three possible senses, depending which type of establishment is meant. Many polytechnics have merged with other establishments, such as colleges of education, and the Regent Street Polytechnic itself merged with the Holborn College of Law, Language and

Commerce to become the Polytechnic of Central London (but still based at the old address, 309 Regent Street).

population (inhabitants of a place)
The earliest sense of the word, in the sixteenth century, was simply 'inhabited place', 'place that is populated'. Thomas Nicholas, in his translation (1578) of Cortez' *Conquest of the West India*, wrote: 'They received their advise that neere at hand were great populations, and soone after he came to Zimpanzinco'. Similarly, in his *Pilgrimage* (1613), Samuel Purchas wrote of a country that 'hath in it, by estimation, threescore thousand Populations, or inhabited places'. This sense then became obsolete, and the modern meaning dates from the seventeenth century.

pornography (depiction of the erotic in art or literature)
Greek *pornē* means 'prostitute', so the term literally means 'writing on prostitutes'. When the word was first used in English in the nineteenth century, it had this sense for a time, and indeed in Robley Dunglison's *Medical Lexicon* (1857), this is the definition of the word ('*Pornography*, a description of prostitutes or prostitution, as a matter of public hygiene'). The sense was soon extended to erotic art and literature generally, but especially in Greece and Rome. Even the revised edition (1864) of Webster's *Dictionary* defines the word as: 'licentious painting employed to decorate the walls of rooms sacred to bacchanalian orgies, examples of which exist in Pompeii', and as late as 1896, the Scottish scholar John Mackail, writing about Plautus's *Casina* and *Truculentus* in his *Latin Literature*, said that the works were 'studies in pornography which only the unflagging animal spirits of the poet can redeem from being disgusting'. Doubtless the classical origin of the word itself implied a special link with the classical world, whose eroticism was at least widely known and acknowledged, even if not explicitly dealt with or reproduced. However, contemporary eroticism was already being branded as 'pornographic' at this time (*Harper's Magazine* of November 1890 mentions 'Parisian artistic pornographers'), so the transition from just prosti-

tutes to general impurity or obscenity was complete by the turn of the twentieth century.

porridge (food made by boiling oatmeal in milk or water)
Originally, 'porridge' was actually 'pottage' (the first word being an alteration of the second), that is, a soup made by stewing meat, vegetables, herbs and so on together, and often thickening it with barley. This sense was current from the sixteenth century to the eighteenth, and even in Johnson's *Dictionary* of 1755 'porridge' is defined as 'food made by boiling meat in water; broth'. Porridge as we know it, and the Scots traditionally make it, dates from the seventeenth century.

portly (stout and fat)
In its original sense, in the sixteenth century (when the current meaning also arose), 'portly' was quite a complimentary term, meaning 'of dignified bearing', 'imposing' (the word relates to 'port' in the now obsolete sense 'carriage', 'bearing'). Even in the nineteenth century the word still had the sense, at any rate as it occurs in William Ballantine's *Some Experiences of a Barrister's Life* (1882): 'He was a man of portly presence, a good scholar, I believe, and much respected'. The modern meaning is first explicitly recorded in Shakespeare's *The Merry Wives of Windsor* (1598), where Falstaff (who else?) tells how Mistress Page had cast her eye over him: 'Sometimes the beam of her view gilded my foot, sometimes my portly belly'.

posse (body of men who can be called to arms by a sheriff)
The word is short for the medieval Latin term *posse comitatus*, literally 'force of the county', with this borrowed in America from English law in the seventeenth century. At about the same time, the word was adopted by a number of writers to mean 'force' or 'band' generally. Thus, in a letter of 14 September 1728 to the publisher of the *Dublin Weekly Journal*, Swift writes: 'With these two single considerations I outbalanced the whole posse of articles that weighed just now against me'. Similarly, Stevenson in *Across the Plains* (1879–88) tells

how at one stage he ran and ' . . .beheld a posse of silent people escorting a cart'. This usage is still not obsolete, but the word is now not often employed in the sense.

post (mail)
The 'post' of today has its historic beginnings in the 'post' of the sixteenth century. Then, the word was a term for the men with horses who were stationed or 'posted' along a route to carry the royal 'packet' or other letters from one stage to another. A document of 1506, when the word was first recorded, gives the names and 'stages' of individual 'posts' between London and Exeter, beginning: 'To Gilbert Burgh one post lying at Bagshote, Thomas Anesley an other post lying at Basyngstoke' (and so on, with a further seven 'posts' to Exeter). The men named here would have had the job of riding with all speed to the next 'post' mentioned. At the same time, the word came to be applied to any rider or courier who bore letters or despatches, whether on a fixed route (as usually) or not. Towards the end of the same century, 'post' was also in use for a horse, vehicle or boat that carried letters, and this new sense is first recorded in Shakespeare's *Henry IV*, Part 2, where Falstaff says: 'I have speeded hither with the very extremest inch of possibility; I have foundered nine score and odd posts'. (He means that, with his great weight, he has caused several posthorses to founder or collapse.) Finally, in the seventeenth century, 'post' came to mean not the person or vehicle that carried the mail but the mail itself, or more precisely, a single despatch of mail. In the seventeenth century, too, the word expanded in the broadest sense to mean the agency that organized the despatch of mail, in other words the post office (or 'letter office' as it was originally called). Pepys could thus write in his *Diary*, on 14 March 1663: 'So to write by the post, and so home to supper'.

potpourri (musical or literary medley)
One early sense of the word to be used in English, still not quite obsolete, was 'mixture of dried flowers or herbs kept for their perfume'. This is rather surprising in view of the French origin, which is *pot pourri*, literally 'rotten pot'. But this refers to an

even earlier sense, also found in English, which was 'meat stew', otherwise 'hotch-potch'. (The French expression in turn translated Spanish *olla podrida*, for a similar stew, with the 'rottenness' referring not to the meat but to the confusingly mingled smells of several kinds of meat cooking together.) So the 'potpourri' in English dates first from the seventeenth century, when it appeared in Randal Cotgrave's *A Dictionarie of the French and English Tongues* (1611), and was defined as follows: '*Pot pourri*, a pot porride; a Spanish dish of many seuerall meates boyled, or stued together'. In the eighteenth century, the sense 'petal perfume mixture' evolved, and finally, in the nineteenth century, the 'musical medley' meaning emerged. (According to Grove's *Dictionary of Music and Musicians* [1878–89], the term was devised by the pianist and composer J.B. Cramer [died 1858] for 'a kind of drawing-room composition consisting of a string of well-known airs'. Both kinds of 'potpourri' still smack of the drawing room even today, but cannot be said to be defunct.)

pounce (seize suddenly, leap on)
The first sense of the verb in English, in the seventeenth century, was 'seize like a bird of prey', with this usage in turn coming from the noun 'pounce' which was a technical term for one of the three front claws of a hawk, as opposed to its 'talon' at the rear of the foot. Pope used the word in this meaning in his translation (1726) of Homer's *Odyssey*:

Each fav'rite fowl he pounc'd with
    deathful sway,

as did the poet John Clare in *The Village Minstrel* (1821):

And like a hawk from covert sprung
It pounc'd my peace away.

The more general sense 'seize suddenly' developed in the eighteenth century, when the verb was followed by 'on', 'upon' or 'at'.

prank (playful act, practical joke)
When first current in English, in the sixteenth century, a 'prank' was a trick, and quite often a wicked or malicious one, certainly no laughing matter, as the modern

version is (or is intended to be). Thomas More, in *The Confutacyon of Tindales Answere* (1532), wrote: 'Now hath it bene an old prank of heretykes, to vse that fashyon of malycyouse corruptynge the bookes of the holye scrypture'. In *Hamlet* (1602), too, Shakespeare makes Polonius say to the Queen, regarding Hamlet's threatening behaviour:

Tell him his pranks have been too broad
    to bear with.

This usage became obsolete in the eighteenth century, however, and the modern 'prank' is the milder, less malicious one.

precipice (vertical steep rock or mountain)
The origin of the word lies ultimately in Latin *praeceps*, 'headlong', and when first used in English, in the sixteenth century, 'precipice' actually meant 'headlong fall', either literally or figuratively. In *Every Man in his Humour* (1598), Ben Jonson writes of:

Precedents, which are strong,
And swift, to rape youth to their
    precipice.

But this usage lapsed in the seventeenth century when the literal sense took over.

precision (exactness, precision)
The current sense evolved in the eighteenth century. A hundred years earlier, however, 'precision' meant 'cutting short', closely following the literal sense of the Latin origin in *praecidere*. The currency was narrow in this meaning, however, and almost entirely found in philosophical writing, such as Gilbert Watts' translation (1640) of Bacon's *Advancement of Learning*, where he writes, learnedly enough: 'We call Prenotion a Precision of endless investigation'. This sense became obsolete hardly more than a hundred years later.

preposterous (outrageous, ridiculous)
This impressive word, itself a little preposterous (in the popular sense), derives from a Latin source that literally means 'with the hindside in front', i.e. from a word composed of *prae-*, 'in front' and *posterus*, 'hinder', 'following' (as in 'posterior'). The original meaning of 'preposterous' in

English, therefore, in the sixteenth century, was 'reversed', 'inverted in position', or otherwise 'putting the cart before the horse'. In Michael Hawke's *Killing is Murder and No Murder* (1657), for example, he writes: 'Though the Monster lurk in Cacus cave, yet notwithstanding his preposterous steps will be discovered'. This usage became obsolete in the nineteenth century, however, and the present meaning of the word, which also dates from the sixteenth century, was the one to prevail.

presently (soon, in due course)
This straightforward everyday word has had four different senses apart from the current one, as defined above. In the fourteenth century, it meant 'so as to be present', 'on the spot', 'personally'. In 1380, when the sense was first recorded, Wyclif wrote: 'Yif a man be presently nygh his sheep, & fayle not to fede hem [i.e. them] & to defende hem [. . .] his bodily presense is skileful [i.e. proper] to hym to dwelle vpon these sheep'. In the fifteenth century, 'presently' came to mean 'at present', 'now', a sense it still has in America and Scotland. This usage is found quite recently in British or Southern English, and indeed seems to be on the increase at the present time (or presently). For example, the *Leeds Mercury* of 4 July 1901 reported a case involving 'a young man belonging to Rotherham and presently staying with his parents at Bridlington', and in the colour supplement of the *Daily Telegraph* of 24 January 1969 an article spoke of a Northern Ireland Protestant who was 'presently chairman of the Derry Labour Party'. (Somewhat earlier, a BBC weather forecaster was heard to announce, on 20 May 1963, that 'warm air is presently moving north-east'.) For about two hundred years from the sixteenth century, 'presently' was also used in the sense 'just now', 'recently'. Thus John Gerard, in *The Herball, or General Historie of Plants* (1597), advises of certain plants: 'Neuer cast any colde water vpon them presently taken out of a well'. Meanwhile, 'presently' was also frequently used to mean 'at once', 'immediately', as in Shakespeare's *Two Gentlemen of Verona* (1591), when Proteus says to Julia (who is disguised as a boy):

Go presently, and take this ring with thee.

This meaning became obsolete in the nineteenth century. The modern, weakened sense of 'presently' developed gradually from the sixteenth century, and prevailed over the 'at present' sense when it mostly fell from popular use in the seventeenth century, even though, as mentioned, it never quite died out and is now reemerging.

press (newspapers and magazines, or the people who write and publish them)
The sense of the word has developed over the centuries as follows (century of origin in brackets): 'crowd', 'throng' (thirteenth), 'instrument used for pressing or compressing' (fourteenth), 'machine for printing' and 'place where printing is done' (sixteenth), 'matter that has been printed' (eighteenth). All these meanings are still current, although the use of 'press' for 'crowd' is not common and even perhaps archaic. It was the great influence of printing that brought the printing 'press' to the fore, above all other machines, and caused the word to be used not just for the machine, but the matter printed and the people who printed it, with 'the press' encompassing the whole medium.

prestige (high standing, superiority in the eyes of others)
The original sense of 'prestige', now obsolete, arose in the seventeenth century as 'illusion', 'conjuring trick'. (Compare the pompous 'prestidigitator' as a word for a conjuror, also the more down to earth 'hey presto' adopted by him.) Thus the Scottish *Justiciary Record* of 1661 reports: 'The Dittay [i.e. indictment] does not condescend upon the Sorcery and prestiges whereby the Pannell did effectuat the particulars lybelled'. This sense fell out of use in the eighteenth century, and the current meaning (which after all relates to a kind of 'magic' glamour) became popular from the nineteenth century.

pretend (feign, represent oneself falsely)
From the fourteenth century, the sense of 'pretend' has gradually shifted from 'claim to be (with good grounds)' to 'claim to be

(with little or no grounds)'. The exact point of transition from the old meaning to the new is hard to pinpoint, but was probably in the sixteenth century. On the other hand, 'pretender', in the sense 'claimant', was certainly current until the eighteenth century (the age of the historic Old Pretender and Young Pretender, the Scottish Stuarts who claimed the British throne). The earlier sense is undoubtedly no longer current, however.

pretty (attractive, beautiful in a delicate or superficial way)
The only sense of the word in Old English (*prættig*) was 'crafty', 'wily', and in eleventh-century translation from the Latin, 'pretty' is used to render such words as *versipellis* ('sly'), *sagax* ('keen'), *astutus* ('artful') and *callidus* ('crafty'). In the fourteenth century, 'pretty' had lost its derogatory sense to mean simply 'clever', 'ingenious', as well as 'fine', 'brave'. The first of these could apply to both people and things, so that Holin-shed's *Chronicles* of the sixteenth century tell of 'Andrew White a good humanician, a pretie philosopher', and Bishop John Jewel's *A Defence of the Apologie* (1567) declares that: 'When the right Key of Knowledge was lost and gone, it was time to deuise some other prety pick-locks to worke the feat'. The 'fine' or 'brave' meaning virtually corresponded to modern 'nice'. Hence Pepys, writing his *Diary* entry for 11 May 1660, mentions 'Dr. Clerke, who I found to be a very pretty man and very knowing', and as late as 1886, a character in Stevenson's *Kidnapped* says: 'A pretty lad like you should get to Cramond [. . .] in two days of walk'. A survival of this sense, which is otherwise archaic if not obsolete, is a remark such as 'He's a pretty fellow', corre-sponding to 'He's a nice one' or 'He's a fine one'. The modern use of 'pretty' thus dates from the fifteenth century, when it could originally apply to men as well as women. For a similar sense development, compare **artful**, **crafty**, **cunning**, **fine** and **nice**.

prevalent (widespread, occurring commonly)
In the sixteenth century, 'prevalent' meant 'having great power', 'influential'. 'Love is more prevalent in obtaining what you desire than fear', wrote William King, in his trans-lation (1711) of Naude's *Political Consider-ations upon Refin'd Politicks*. Even in the seven-teenth century, it could mean 'predomi-nant', as when Hume wrote, in his *History of Great Britain* (1761): 'The Puritans, though then prevalent, did not think proper to dispute this great constitutional point'. Both these senses became obsolete or at least rare by the nineteenth century, and it is the current meaning, which also dates from the sixteenth century, that prevailed. (However, the related verb, as occurring in the last sentence, still has the sense 'predominate', whereas the adjective does not.)

prevaricate (act or speak evasively, 'dodge', hedge)
The original meaning of this verb in English, in the sixteenth century, was 'deviate from the right course', 'go astray', 'transgress'. The Rhemish New Testament (1582) has in Acts 1:25: 'Shew [. . .] whom thou hast chosen, to take the place of this ministerie and Apostleship, from the which Iudas hath prevaricated'. In the Authorized Version of 1611, this reads: 'Shew [whom] thou hast chosen, that he may take part of this ministry and apostleship, from which Judas by transgression fell'. The current sense developed in the seventeenth century, the concept being that of 'deviating' from a straightforward course by evading it.

prevent (stop, keep from happening)
This verb is a notorious sense-shifter in the language. It originally meant 'act in antici-pation' in the fifteenth century, and can be found in the Bible and Shakespeare, as well as generally in literature. Psalm 119:148 has a typical example of it: 'Mine eyes prevent the night watches, that I might meditate in thy word'. In *Julius Caesar* (1601), too, Brutus says to Cassius:

> I know not how,
> But I do find it cowardly and vile,
> For fear of what might fall, so to prevent
> The time of life.

Probably even more familiar instances are the related usages of 'prevent' to mean 'go before with spiritual guidance', found from the sixteenth century. Set against the modern meaning of the verb, these perhaps seem the strangest, with two occurring in the Prayer Book: 'Prevent us, O Lord, in all our doings' (Collect at end of Communion Service) and 'Lord, we pray thee that thy grace may always prevent and follow us' (Collect for the 17th Sunday after Trinity). The modern sense finally emerged in the seventeenth century.

prime (first in importance or quality)
In the fourteenth century, 'prime' meant 'first in time', a now obsolete sense. The usage was found as late as the eighteenth century, so that John Mortimer, in *The Whole Art of Husbandry* (1707), could write: 'If the prime Swarm be broken, the second will both cast and swarm the sooner'. The second sense to evolve was the mathematical one ('prime' number), which followed in the sixteenth century. The final meaning, and the current one, that of 'first in quality or importance', followed in the seventeenth century, when it is first recorded in Shakespeare's *The Tempest* (1610), with Ferdinand asking Miranda:

> My prime request,
> Which I do last pronounce, is, – O you
>   wonder! –
> If you be maid or no?

(She replies:

>   No wonder, sir;
> But certainly a maid.)

probable (likely, apparently true)
The first sense of 'probable' in English, in the fourteenth century, was 'commending itself', 'worthy to be believed'. In his *England in the Reign of Henry the Eighth* (1538) Thomas Starkey writes: 'I can not wel tel what I schal say, your resonys are so probabyl'. The current meaning dates from the seventeenth century, when it is first recorded in Shakespeare's *Antony and Cleopatra* (1606), with Caesar saying to his train, in the final speech of the play (and in response to the First Guard's theory that Cleopatra had died by being stung by an asp):

>   Most probable,
> That so she died; for her physician tells
>   me
> She hath pursu'd conclusions infinite
> Of easy ways to die.

problem (matter requiring solution or resolution, difficulty)
In its earliest recorded sense, in the fourteenth century, a 'problem' was a difficult question or even a riddle or puzzle. The sense comes in Wyclif's English Bible of 1382, where in Judges 14:15 he has: 'Faage to thi man, and meue hym, that he shewe to thee what bitokeneth the probleme'. In the Authorized Version of 1611, this is: 'Entice thy husband, that he may declare unto us the riddle'. (This is the famous riddle: 'What is sweeter than honey? and what is stronger than a lion?'.) The modern meanings of 'problem', including the mathematical one, evolved from the sixteenth century, with the specific chess 'problem' arriving in the nineteenth.

prodigious (amazing, enormous)
From the sixteenth century to the eighteenth, 'prodigious' often literally meant 'of the nature of a prodigy', with this word in turn having its original meaning 'omen', 'portent'. Hence the sense of the words in Oberon's song at the end of Shakespeare's *A Midsummer Night's Dream* (1590):

> Never mole, hare-lip nor scar,
> Nor mark prodigious, such as are
> Despised in nativity,
> Shall upon their children be.

The modern meaning of the adjective evolved from the sixteenth century, first in the sense 'amazing' (as a 'prodigious' effect), then in the common usage 'enormous', 'extraordinarily large' (as a 'prodigious' appetite). 'Prodigy' acquired its now usual 'child genius' sense only in the seventeenth century, first recorded in Evelyn's sad *Diary* entry for 27 January 1658: 'Died my deare son Richard, [. . .] 5 yeares and 3 days old onely, but at that tender age a prodigy for witt and understanding'.

programme (outline of forthcoming event or entertainment)
The original sense of 'programme' in English was the Scottish one of the seventeenth century, when the word meant 'public notice'. Scott uses it in his novels with this meaning, so that in *The Antiquary* (1816) one can read: 'Will three shillings

transport me to Queensferry, agreeably to thy treacherous program?' and in *St. Ronan's Well* (1824): 'The transactions of the morning were [. . .] announced [. . .] by the following program'. The spelling (not 'programme') is noteworthy here, and was regularly used by Scott, as well as some other writers such as Carlyle and the philosopher Sir William Hamilton. It is still the chief American spelling, and is now the standard British one when applied to computers (mostly from the early 1960s). (In fact, the spelling 'program' may perhaps one day become general in the English-speaking world, on a line with 'anagram', 'diagram', 'telegram' and so on.) The present-day meaning of the word dates from the nineteenth century, with the familiar radio and television 'programme' evolving naturally in the twentieth century when the two media themselves evolved.

promiscuous (indulging in casual sexual relationships)
The proper sense of the word, still just about current, is 'consisting of mixed members', 'confusedly mingled', 'indiscriminate', with this meaning in use from the seventeenth century. The adjective was thus applied, for example, to a 'promiscuous' crowd or a 'promiscuous' massacre. Something of the modern sense seems to be emerging in Scott's *Old Mortality* (1816), where he writes of: 'the profane custom of promiscuous dancing – that is, of men and women dancing together in the same party', although the predominant meaning here is still 'indiscriminate'. The current use of the word thus evolved only in the twentieth century, with the first record of the sense in Andrew Lang's *A History of Scotland from the Roman Occupation* (1900–7), where he writes of people who were ' . . .still polyandrous or promiscuous in the relation of the sexes'.

propaganda (dissemination of information or ideas with the aim of promoting or defaming)
The word has its origin in the ecclesiastical *Congregatio de propaganda fide*, or 'congregation for propagating the faith', the organization established in 1622 by Pope Gregory XV as a committee of cardinals of the Roman Catholic church that was responsible for foreign missions. From this, 'propaganda' came to mean the promotion of any particular doctrine or practice, with the English currency of the word, however, dating only from the nineteenth century. It is interesting that it is only in English that the word has acquired its defamatory sense, so that in European languages, including Russian, the word simply means 'dissemination of ideas, teachings, views, knowledge etc'. The 'bad' sense seems to have emerged on the political scene in the United States.

proper (appropriate, correct, genteel)
The earliest sense of 'proper' in English was the same as the modern French *propre*, meaning 'own', 'belonging to oneself'. Like the French, too, the word was preceded by a possessive adjective such as 'my', 'his' and so on. Sir John Maundeville, in *The Voiage and Travaile of Sir John Maundeville Knight* (1400) tells how one person was killed 'with his own propre Swerd', and in Shakespeare's *The Tempest* (1610), Ariel says:

And even with such-like valour men
   hang and drown
Their proper selves.

This usage developed from French in the thirteenth century and was virtually obsolete by the nineteenth, except in certain scientific senses, such as 'proper motion' in astronomy and, in the twentieth century, 'proper time', 'proper mass' and so on in physics. The second sense of 'proper' to develop in English was the still current one of 'correct', 'accurate', dating from the fourteenth century. The word also acquired its meaning 'fine', 'good' at this time, a usage that is now debased, as in 'a proper little minx'. Originally, though, it had a quite acceptable sense, as in the Bible: 'Moses, when he was born, was hid three months of his parents, because they saw he was a proper child' (Hebrews 11:23). Finally, the 'appropriate' or 'right' sense evolved in the fifteenth century, and occurs in these lines from Cowper's poem *Pairing Time Anticipated* (1795):

Choose not alone a proper mate,
But proper time to marry.

prophet (person who predicts)

The original sense of 'prophet' in English, in the twelfth century, was to designate a person who was an inspired revealer of God's will. This is the 'prophet' who is mentioned many times in the Bible, for example in Exodus 7:1 ('Aaron thy brother shall be thy prophet'), I Kings 18:19 ('the prophets of Baal four hundred and fifty, and the prophets of the groves four hundred'), Acts 13:1 ('certain prophets and teachers'), Titus 1:12 ('One of themselves, even a prophet of their own'), and so on, including the most quoted one in Matthew 13:57 ('A prophet is not without honour, save in his own country'). The modern meaning of the word, as applied to someone who can (so he believes) predict the future, dates from the thirteenth century, and is not found in the Bible. It occurs, however in Shakespeare's *King Lear* (1610), where in the final scene, Regan says:

Jesters do oft prove prophets.

propriety (fitness, decorum, decency)

This word, that so confusingly looks like 'property', actually meant that when it was first current, in the fifteenth century. 'When men give', wrote John Flavel, in *The Fountain of Life Opened* (1672), 'they transfer Propriety to another'. This usage became obsolete by about the end of the eighteenth century, and the current meaning dates from the seventeenth century in the sense 'fitness', 'suitability', and from the eighteenth when the sense is 'decency' (when it often occurs in the plural, as 'the proprieties').

proscenium (area of stage)

The word has two senses, depending if one is talking about the ancient Roman and Greek theatre or the modern European one. In the Greek or Roman theatre, the 'proscenium' was the whole area of the stage between the background and the **orchestra** (see this word separately). In the modern theatre, it is the space between the curtain and the front of the stage (or orchestra pit), or put another way, the area in front of the so called 'proscenium arch', which is the arch through which the audience sees the stage. The first sense has been current in

English since the seventeenth century; the second, since the nineteenth. The word literally means 'before the scene', with Greek *skēnē* being the word for the building that formed the background of the stage.

prove (try, test, show to be true)

The senses developed in the order shown here. First, in the twelfth century, 'prove' meant 'test', 'try'. This usage is found in the Bible, but is otherwise obsolete, except in technical senses. In the Bible, thus, the verb has the sense 'test' in the following: 'And this he said to prove him: for he himself knew what he would do' (John 6:6), and 'Prove all things; hold fast that which is good' (I Thessalonians 5:21). In technical usage, one can still 'prove' a new weapon or a new car model. The meaning 'establish', 'show to be true' followed from the thirteenth century, whether used as a term in logic ('evince the truth of a proposition not admitted to be true, from other propositions the truth of which is established') or generally.

publish (make known generally, issue a printed work)

The second sense developed in the sixteenth century from the first, which itself dates from the fourteenth century. All the following expressions relate to the first meaning: 'publish a will' (execute it properly in front of witnesses), 'publish a libel' (communicate it to one or more people), 'publish the banns of marriage' (announce in public the names of those intending to marry). The second sense does actually come in the Bible, although not in the main text but in the translators' preface in the Authorized Version of 1611, where, addressing King James, they speak of the 'vehement and perpetuated desire' that they have 'of accomplishing and publishing of this work'.

pudding (sweet or savoury dish)

The word has various senses and shades of usage, depending on the type of dish involved. The oldest 'pudding' in English, however, is the forerunner of the haggis, that is, the animal's stomach or other organ stuffed with meat, seasoning and the like, otherwise basically a sausage. This sort of 'pudding' dates from the thirteenth century. Modern types of this sort are 'black pudding' (made from suet and pigs' blood) and 'white pudding' (made from minced pork and fat). The modern sweet or savoury pudding made with flour (or rice or tapioca, for example), including the whole traditional range of 'plum pudding', 'Christmas pudding', 'rice pudding', 'suet pudding', 'Yorkshire pudding' and the like, dates only from the sixteenth century.

pug (breed of small dog)
This versatile word has had a whole host of meanings over the centuries. In the sixteenth century, for example, it was both a term of endearment and a word for a prostitute. The first of these comes in John Marston's play *Antonios Revenge* (1600), where one of the ladies says: 'I have had foure husbands my selfe. The first, I called, sweet duck: the second, deare heart: the third, prettie pugge'. The second occurs (and is first recorded) in a letter of 24 September 1601 written by Lord Cecil to James I (James VI of Scotland), in which he advised the king that if he were to ' . . . remember the Lo. Admyrall and the Lord Threasurer with a couple of Pugges or some *vscough baugh* [i.e whisky] or some such toyes, it would shew that you do not neglect them, whoe, I protest, are to you wonderfull kynde' (*The Secret Correspondence of Sir Robert Cecil with James VI, King of Scotland*, 1612). 'Pug' was also in the sixteenth century a term for a bargeman (especially the so called 'Western Pugs' who navigated barges down the Thames to London), and apparently also for a ship's boy, to judge by the following extract from William Phillip's translation (1598) from the Dutch of Lindschoten's *Discours of Voyages into y* Easte and West Indies:* 'The officers and most of the sailers were on land, none but pugs and slaues being in the ships: for [. . .] wheresoeuer they anker, presently [i.e. immediately] they goe all on land, and let the shippe lie with a boy or two in it'. (The original Dutch word translated as 'pugs' here was *putgers*.) In the seventeenth century, 'pug' came to be the word for a demon or imp, a 'sprite', and also the nickname for a monkey or ape, as which it could be used of children (as 'monkey' still can).

Finally, in the eighteenth century, the word acquired its best known meaning as the breed of dog with the tightly curled tail and wrinkled face. This was originally known as a 'pug dog', with the name probably deriving from one of the earlier senses given here (possibly the term of endearment rather than the imp or monkey). The dog in turn gave the expression 'pug nose' for a broad, flat (or apparently flattened) nose. The origin of the word in general is uncertain, but may relate to 'puck', especially in view of the 'sprite' sense.

punk (young person who expresses his or her rejection of society by outlandishly distinctive clothes, hairstyles and music, the latter known as 'punk rock')
The definition given here is the current and predominant one, referring to the youth movement of the 1970s and 1980s in Britain. It seems certain, however, that the word will acquire further senses, at any rate to judge by its versatility in the past. On the whole, whatever its sense, it has had a connotation of 'badness' or 'rottenness' (literally in one instance), although this has not prevented its enthusiastic adoption by the people who have been so designated. The various senses, in chronological order, are given below, with an appropriate example of usage for each. It should be stressed, however, that several dictionaries enter one or more of the meanings separately, and sometimes imply that not all 'punks' are interrelated, either in etymology or meaning. There seems a consistent enough sense development overall, however, to justify a single basic origin. Centuries or decades are given in brackets.

1 'prostitute' (sixteenth): 'My lord, she may be a punk; for many of them are neither maid, widow, nor wife' (Lucio to Vincentio, the Duke, about Mariana, in Shakespeare's *Measure for Measure*, 1603).

2 'rotten wood', 'fungus growing on wood', 'touchwood' (eighteenth): 'Caleb worked on the hollow log [. . .]. With the hatchet he cleared out all the punk and splinters inside' (Ernest Thompson Seton, *Two Little Savages*, 1903).

3 'something worthless', 'nonsense',

'rubbish' (nineteenth): 'We [. . .] men stuff ourselves up with the idea that they're romantic and unemotional. All punk, my son' (Dorothy Sayers, *Unnatural Murder*, 1927).

4 'passive male homosexual', 'tramp's young companion' (1900s): 'The involuntary homosexuals tend to be good-looking young men [. . .] forced into becoming jailhouse "punks" by older men serving long sentences' (*New Yorker*, 24 October 1977).

5 'worthless person', 'young criminal' (1910s): 'Two young punks got off a train carrying a lush [i.e. drunk] between them' (William Burroughs, *Junkie*, 1953).

6 'boy or novice in show business, especially the circus' (1920s): '*Punk*, a boy or any young man not yet professionally dry behind the ears' (*American Speech*, volume 17, 1942).

7 'punk rocker' (as defined above) (1970s): 'Johnny Rotten and the Sex Pistols are punks. They sing "Anarchy in the UK" ' (*Sunday Times*, 28 November 1976).

The origin of the word is unknown, although some suggest sense 2 may be an alteration of 'spunk' (in the meaning 'tinder').

puny (smallsized or feeble)
The original sense of the word, in the sixteenth century, was 'junior', so that a junior judge was called a 'puny judge' (or 'puny justice'). This sense is still current in legal jargon, but with the spelling 'puisne' (from the identical French word meaning 'born after', from *puis*, 'afterwards' and *né*, 'born'; a person 'born after' another is clearly junior to him). This meaning soon developed to 'raw', 'inexperienced', as in Shakespeare's *Henry VI, Part 1* (1591), where after the death of the two Talbots, father and son, the Bastard of Orleans says:

How the young whelp of Talbot's,
    raging-wood [i.e. raving mad]
Did flesh his puny sword in Frenchmen's
    blood!

Still in the sixteenth century, the present

meaning also developed, and like the last meaning above, is first recorded in Shakespeare, this time in *Othello* (1604), where Othello says:

I am not valiant neither,
But every puny whipster [i.e. novice]
    gets my sword.

pupil (school or privately taught student, person receiving tuition or instruction)
In the fourteenth century, 'pupil' was a legal term for an orphan who was a minor and therefore a ward. This sense is first recorded in Wyclif's English Bible translation of 1382, where James 1:27 includes the Christian duty: 'To visite pupilles, and widewes in her tribulacioun'. (The word was explained in the Bible as meaning 'that is, fadirles or modirles, or bothe'. The corresponding passage in the Authorized Version of 1611 runs: 'To visit the fatherless and widows in their affliction'.) This usage is still current in Scots law for a boy under fourteen or a girl under twelve who is under the care of a guardian. The more familiar sense of 'pupil' arose in the sixteenth century.

puppy (young dog)
The word meant 'lap dog' or 'toy dog' before it meant 'young dog'. This earlier sense was first current in the fifteenth century. William Horman's *Vulgaria* (1519) tells how: 'Lytel popies, that serueth for ladies, weere [i.e. wear] sumtyme bellis, sumtyme colers ful of prickis for theyr defence'. The sense 'young dog' is first recorded in Shakespeare's *Two Gentlemen of Verona* (1591), where the servant Launce, who actually has a dog (called Crab) says: 'One that I brought up of a puppy; one that I saved from drowning, when three or four of his blind brothers and sisters went to it'. (He is not talking about Crab but about the 'little jewel' of a dog that Proteus had bought for Silvia and that Launce had lost.) Shakespeare also has our first record of the child's word 'puppy dog', which occurs in *King John* (1595), where Philip the Bastard says, after the First Citizen's stirring speech about Blanch of Spain and Lewis the Dauphin:

Here's a large mouth, indeed,
That spits forth death and mountains,

rocks and seas,
Talks as familiarly of roaring lions
As maids of thirteen do of puppy-dogs.

purchase (buy)
In the thirteenth century, the sense of 'purchase' was either 'contrive', 'devise' or 'procure', 'get'. The first of these occurs, for example, in Caxton's translation (1481) of *Godeffroy of Boloyne:* 'Wel they apperceyued certaynly that themperour pourchassed for them alle the euyl [i.e. evil] that he myght'. The second sense is also found in Caxton, this time in his translation (1489) of *The Foure Sonnes of Aymon:* 'None ought not to complayne my deth, sith that I have purchaced it myself'. The current meaning of 'buy' dates from the fourteenth century.

purple (colour midway between red and blue)
Originally, the Old English word (*purpure*) meant 'crimson', or some other shade of red. Later, it settled to its present colour, with almost an equal blend of red and blue. The former shade was that of the dress of emperors and kings, hence in the Bible, in John 19:2 'And they put on him a purple robe'. The modern meaning dates from the fourteenth century. The name of the colour was very popular with poets from the sixteenth century to apply to blood, in particular in the sense 'bloody', 'blood-stained'. Blood is properly red, of course, but the poets were echoing the 'crimson' meaning of 'purple' in the earlier sense (the 'royal' one). In *The Faerie Queene* (1590), Spenser even calls blood 'red' in one line and 'purple' in the next:

> The red blood flowed fresh
> That underneath his feet soone made a
> purple plesh [i.e. pool].

pyjamas (nightwear consisting of matching jacket and trousers)
The word derives from Hindi *pājāma,* itself from Persian *pā,* 'leg' and *jāma,* 'garment'. 'Pyjamas' are thus properly trousers, and in origin the loose baggy ones of silk or cotton, tied round the waist, as worn by Muslims. These were adopted by Europeans, with a jacket added, as a sleeping garment in the nineteenth century. The English word is first recorded in the eighteenth, however, when it refers to the Indian garment, although the *OED*, in its entry for 'pyjama', states that it is 'in England often in trade use inaccurately applied to a sleeping suit of loose trousers and jacket'. (In the *Supplement* of 1982 it rightly states that this definition 'is now the prevailing sense'.) Before 'pyjamas', people simply wore 'shirts' in bed (later qualified as 'night shirts'), and the expression 'in one's shirt' was common down to the nineteenth century to mean 'in one's nightwear'. In the twentieth century, 'pyjamas' even became a daytime garment again in the fashion world, when they were worn as beachwear (otherwise 'beach pyjamas').

quaint (unusual but attractive)
The modern meaning of the word has developed only from the eighteenth century. When it first became current in English, in the thirteenth century, 'quaint' meant not only 'skilled' and 'elegant' but even 'proud', 'fastidious'. The first of these senses is preserved in Shakespeare's *Henry VI*, Part 2 (1593) as well as in *The Taming of the Shrew* (1596). In the former play, Suffolk says to Salisbury:

> But you, my lord, were glad to be
> employ'd,
> To show how quaint an orator you are,

and in the later play, Tranio refers to:

> The quaint musician, amorous Licio.

The second sense, that of 'elegant', occurs in the *Lay Folk's Catechism* of 1357: 'Ne worshipe not men for here fayre clothes, ne for here quaynte schappis that sum men usen'. (That is: Do not worship people for their fine clothes, nor for the elegant fashions that some people follow.) In *The Merry Wives of Windsor* (1598), too, Fenton says that Anne Page, if dressed as the Fairy Queen, will look 'quaint in green'. In the fourteenth century, the sense of 'quaint' developed further as 'strange', 'unfamiliar', and this usage can be seen in Milton's ode *On the Morning of Christ's Nativity* (1629), where he has the lines:

> A drear, and dying sound
> Affrights the Flamins at the service
> quaint.

This then progressed to the modern meaning, which is first recorded in Southey's poem *Joan of Arc* (1795):

> He for the wintry hour
> Knew many a merry ballad and quaint
> tale.

quell (subdue, overwhelm completely)
In Old English, the verb (*cwellan*) meant 'kill', with this sense found in *The Romance of William of Palerne* (1350), a long alliterative poem:

> Briddes & smale bestes with his bow he
> quelles.

In the fourteenth century, the sense became 'suppress', 'extinguish', a usage that is still current (as in 'quelling' someone's fears), and finally, in the sixteenth century, the best known meaning 'crush', 'overwhelm' evolved.

queue (line of people waiting for something)
French *queue* means 'tail', and this was the first sense of the word in English, when it came to be used in the sixteenth century, although only in the heraldic meaning. (When a lion on a coat of arms has two tails it is said to be *queue fourchée*, literally 'fork-tailed'.) In the eighteenth century, 'queue' came to be a fashion term for a long plait of hair, in particular the 'pigtail' that hung down behind from a man's hair or from his wig. This sense is still not obsolete, even though the reference may now probably be to the hairstyle of the Japanese or Indians, rather than the British. The British 'queue' of people, however, often taken to be a long-standing tradition, was adopted from the

French in the nineteenth century. It is therefore a *French* characteristic in the first place, and many nineteenth-century references to a 'queue' are specifically to one in France, whether of carriages or of theatregoers. Even so, foreign commentators on Britain maintain that the phenomenon suits the national character exactly. ('Queueing is the national pastime of an otherwise dispassionate race. The English are rather shy about it, and deny that they adore it', George Mikes, *How to be an Alien*, 1946.)

quick (rapid, lively)
'The quick and the dead'. The familiar phrase is a reminder that 'quick' formerly had quite a different sense from the current one. Old English *cwic* meant simply 'alive', 'living', and although this direct sense is now obsolete, the basic meaning of the word can still be detected in a 'quickset' hedge (one grown from live cuttings) and the 'quick' that is the sensitive flesh under the nails. By the thirteenth century, however, the modern meaning had already emerged, although the special sense meaning 'fast to learn' ('she is very quick at school') followed only in the fifteenth century.

quilt (thick, warm cover for a bed)
Originally, quilts were forms of bedding for lying *on*, not *under*, as now, with this sense derived from the original Latin *culcita*, 'mattress'. The word was first current in English in the thirteenth century, but the 'mattress' sense persisted in some cases down to the seventeenth century, as in Locke's *Some Thoughts Concerning Education* (1693), where he recommends: 'Let his Bed be hard, and rather Quilts than Feathers' (i.e. with a padded mattress rather than one filled with feathers). However, the 'cover' sense of the word was certainly fully established by the nineteenth century, so that unhappy maidens in Victorian novels could muffle their sorrow in them ('She threw herself on her knees by her bed side, and hid her face in the quilt', Mrs Harriet Smythies, *The Bride Elect*, 1852).

quintessence (most perfect example or nature of a thing)
As originally conceived, the 'quintessence' (literally 'fifth essence') of old philosophy

was the substance of which the heavenly bodies were composed, and which was latently present in everything. It was therefore one of the major tasks of alchemy to attempt to extract it by means of distillation. This usage was common in English from the fifteenth century. A hundred years later, however, the modern meaning was already current and was the one to prevail when the medieval understanding was abandoned in the seventeenth century (or eighteenth, at the latest).

quite (fully, absolutely; fairly, rather)
This word is notoriously tricky for foreign learners of English, who find it difficult to decide which sense to use, or which is meant. 'I was quite alone' means that I was absolutely alone, but 'I am quite tired' means that I am fairly tired, not very. And if she is 'quite ill', is she very ill or only slightly indisposed? The original meaning of 'quite' in English was the 'absolutely' one, which dates from the fourteenth century. As John Skelton wrote in his charming poem *Phyllyp Sparowe* (1529):

Comfort had he none
For she was quyte gone.

And as Robert K. Douglas wrote in his *Non-Christian Religious Systems* (1879): 'A man should be quite certain what he knows and what he does not know'. Quite. Yet it was in the nineteenth century that the now common sense of 'fairly' for 'quite' arose. It developed out of a special usage of the word, from the eighteenth century, that meant 'actually', 'really', implying that what the writer or speaker said was really so. For example, Fielding, in *Tom Jones* (1749), wrote that a certain widow was 'quite charmed with her new lodger', meaning that she really was charmed (not simply satisfied), and in one of his essays (1848), the astronomer Sir John Herschel wrote that: 'A ship sailing northwards passes quite suddenly from cold into hot water', meaning that the change really was sudden, not gradual, as one might expect. So when Thoreau, in his narrative account *Walden* (1854), wrote: 'Perhaps I have owed to this employment and to hunting, when quite young, my closest acquaintance with Nature', which did he mean, 'surprisingly young' (as in the earlier sense) or 'fairly young' (as in the new sense)? It is not always so easy! What has actually happened is that the earlier use of 'quite' (meaning 'really') has come to be associated with certain adjectives, such as 'different', 'separate', 'right', 'wrong', 'sure' and so on, while with other, less 'definite' adjectives the modern sense is the commoner. But it is still quite difficult to determine on occasions, and one needs to be quite certain which of the two senses is meant.

quiz (test of knowledge, usually for entertainment or in informal instruction)
The earliest sense of the unusual word in English was the eighteenth-century one of 'eccentric person', especially 'person who mocks or ridicules'. The meaning is now obsolete, but as late as 1845 Charlotte Brontë could write in *The Professor*: 'He was not odd – no quiz'. In the nineteenth century, 'quiz' came to mean 'practical joke' or 'hoax'. Scott used the word frequently in this sense, and in a letter of 14 April 1810 wrote: 'I am impatient to know if the whole be not one grand blunder or quiz', while an entry in his *Journal* for 11 February 1826 runs: 'I should have thought the thing a quiz, but that the novel was real'. It was in the same century that the now familiar meaning 'set of questions' evolved. The earliest record we have of it is in a letter of 26 December 1867 written by the American psychologist and philosopher William James, in which he says: 'Occasional review articles, etc., perhaps giving "quizzes" in anatomy and physiology [. . .] may help'. The genesis of the modern 'quiz' was thus American, and it is similarly in the American *Scribner's Magazine* that the first reference to the radio 'quiz' is recorded, with the issue of February 1942 having a feature headed 'Quiz by the Quiz kids'. The origin of the word (which suggests Latin *quis*, 'who') is still unknown, despite several more or less plausible attempts to explain it.

quote (cite the words of another)
The word dates from the fourteenth century, when to 'quote' was to mark a book with numbers (as for chapters) or with references to other works. (The ultimate source of the verb is Latin *quot*, 'how many'.) John de

Trevisa, in his translation (1387) of Ranulf Higden's *Polychronicon*, writes: 'Stevene the archbisschop [. . .] coted the Bible at Parys, and marked the chapitres'. The next sense to emerge was the one of 'cite', 'refer to' in the sixteenth century, that is, by giving a reference to a book by saying which chapter, page and so on is meant. A figurative use of this comes in Shakespeare's *Love's Labour's Lost* (1588), when Boyet says of King Ferdinand:

> His face's own margent did quote such
> amazes,
> That all eyes saw his eyes enchanted
> with gazes.

Finally, the modern meaning ('repeat words from another source') developed in the seventeenth century. (However, the meaning 'repeat the spoken words of another as an authority', as in the familiar 'Don't quote me on this', was a development only of the 1950s.) 'Quotation' has had a similar sense evolution, from 'numbering' in the fifteenth century to 'marginal reference' in the sixteenth and 'citing of a passage' in the seventeenth. The stock market 'quotation' or price statement followed in the nineteenth century, and it is in this same century that the first use of 'quote' to mean 'quotation' is also recorded. The 'stocks and shares' 'quotes', however, came about only in the 1950s. The *Daily Mail* of 8 June 1959 had a paragraph headed '"Quotes" for readers', continuing: 'The following list of prices is a selection from readers' requests for quotation of some of their shares which do not fluctuate sufficiently to be quoted daily'.

rabbit (small long-eared animal related to the hare)
As originally used in English, in the four-

teenth century, 'rabbit' applied only to the young of the animal, with the adult rabbit being, called a 'cony'. (This last word does not mean 'rabbit' where it occurs in the Bible, however, but refers to the hyrax, and in particular the Syrian rock hyrax. In the case of Coney Island, New York, however, it is almost certainly the real rabbit that is meant.) So in his translation (1398) of the *De proprietatibus rerum* of Bartholomaeus Anglicus, John de Trevisa wrote: 'Conynges [. . .] bringeth forthe many rabettes & multiplieth ful swithe [i.e. very rapidly]'. Even as recently as the seventeenth century, Edward Topsell, in *The Historie of Foure-Footed Beastes* (1607), wrote: 'If two males be out to one female, they fight fiercely; but they will not hurt the rabbets'. It cannot have been long after this, however, that the word was extended to include the adult animal.

race (contest in running or moving rapidly)
The earliest meaning of 'race', in the thirteenth century, was 'onward movement', 'rush'. The word is first recorded in the *Cursor Mundi*:

> Sun and mon, and water and stern,
> That rinnes nu wit ras sa yern.

(That is: Sun and moon, water and stars, that run now with movement so rapid.) In the fourteenth century, 'race' came to mean 'running', 'a run', especially in the phrase 'in a race' or 'with a race', and the 'race' that is a strong current of water dates from the same time (with special versions of this, such as a 'millrace' following later). Finally, in the sixteenth century, the word acquired its modern meaning, early enough for it to appear in the Bible, as: 'Know ye not that they which run in a race run all, but one receiveth the prize?' (I Corinthians 9:24).

radical (basic, fundamental, extreme)
The ultimate source of the word is the Latin for 'root', *radix*, genitive *radicis*, and in the fourteenth century, 'radical' meant specifically 'pertaining to a root', and more precisely was used of the moisture occurring naturally in animals and plants as a 'vital fluid'. From the thirteenth century, the word was thus current in such expressions

as 'radical moisture', 'radical **humour**' (see the latter word) and 'radical sap'. From the sixteenth century, 'radical' came to be used of other roots, such as those in mathematics and linguistics. Finally, the much more general meaning 'thorough', 'fundamental' evolved from the seventeenth century, with the phrase 'radical reform' first recorded a hundred years later. The word became a noun at this time, too, with the sense of 'radical' meaning 'advocator of radical reform' dating from the nineteenth century. (Scott, in a letter to *The Times* of 16 October 1819, wrote: 'Radical is a word in very bad odour here, being used to denote a set of blackguards'.)

raid (military foray or attack)
The word is first recorded in the fifteenth century, when it meant 'military foray made on horseback'. It was a Scottish form of 'road' (compare 'laird' and 'lord'), and thus related to English 'inroads'. Andrew Wyntour, in *The Orygynale Cronykil of Scotland* (1425), recorded:

Schyr Andrew syne [i.e. then] wyth
  stalwart hand
Made syndry radis in Ingland.

This sense fell out of use in the sixteenth century, but was revived by Scott in the nineteenth and then became established in its general meaning, as now. Scott reintroduced 'raid' in *The Lay of the Last Minstrel* (1805):

In raids he spilt but seldom blood,

and used it again in the Introduction to *Rob Roy* (1818) ('A war which opened the low country to the raids of the clan Gregor').

random (arbitrary, haphazard, done at will or casually)
The adjective followed some time after the noun, which now is regularly used only in the phrase 'at random'. In the fourteenth century, 'random' meant 'great speed', 'violence', implying force and impetuosity. In Caxton's translation (1477) *The Historie of Jason*, we can thus read how the ship '...hurtlyd again the ground in suche a random and force that hit was all to broken'. At this stage, common phrases with the word were 'in random' or 'on random' or

'with great random'. The phrase 'at random' (or 'at the random') followed in the fifteenth century, when it properly related to hawking and the tournament, later meaning 'at speed', 'with force' more generally. Thus by the sixteenth century 'random' was commonly used with verbs of moving, striking, throwing, speaking, thinking and taking, to mean, as now, 'haphazard', 'without aiming'. Only in the seventeenth century did the adjective arise separately. Technically, a 'random shot' in shooting a missile is or was one that was fired at any range other than point blank. Later, it was simply understood to be a haphazard or unaimed shot.

rank (luxuriant or vigorous in growth, offensive, foul, flagrant)
The word had two basic meanings in Old English, now both obsolete. One was 'proud' and the other 'full-grown'. The first of these evolved to mean 'stout and strong' in the twelfth century, and 'swift' or 'violent' in the thirteenth, when the senses became obsolete. The second was the 'productive' one as far as modern English is concerned, since it progressed to meaning 'luxuriant', 'vigorous in growth' in the thirteenth century, 'gross' or 'coarse' in the fourteenth, and finally 'offensive in smell', 'rancid' and 'downright' (as 'rank disobedience') in the sixteenth. Neither of the Old English meanings were current much beyond the fifteenth century.

ransack (search with the aim of stealing, plunder)
Originally, in the thirteenth century, 'ransack' meant simply 'search', without any idea of robbing. One could thus 'ransack' a person or a place in order to make an examination, in particular to look for something that had been stolen (so the exact opposite of the modern sense). Jehan Palsgrave, in *Lesclarcissement de la langue françoyse* (1530), writes: 'He hath ransaked all the chystes I have for his beades'. The modern meaning arose in the fourteenth century, when searching for stolen property became searching to steal property, a deterioration in sense and moral purpose.

rape (force a woman to have sexual intercourse)
There is an interesting comparison to be seen here with the related word **'rapture'** (see below). 'Rape' has always retained its 'bad' sense. 'Rapture', on the other hand, progressed from 'bad' to 'good'. Yet both ultimately originate from Latin *rapere*, 'to seize'. In the case of 'rape', the first meaning in English, in the fourteenth century, was 'seize', 'kidnap', and in particular 'seize a woman by force'. This is the sense in Shakespeare's *Titus Andronicus* (1588), in the interchange between Saturninus and Bassanius:

> *Saturninus.* Traitor, if Rome have law or we have power,
> Thou and thy faction shall repent this rape.
> *Bassianus.* Rape call you it, my lord, to seize my own,
> My true-betrothed love and now my wife?

The modern meaning 'violation of a woman' emerged in the fifteenth century, also occurring in Shakespeare (and also in this same play). Care is needed in distinguishing between these two senses in a number of literary and artistic works where the word occurs. In 'The Rape of the Sabines', for example, whether in Plutarch's original account, or Rubens' great painting, the reference is to a capturing or kidnapping of women of the Sabine tribe. In Pope's 'Rape of the Lock' the allusion is obviously to a capture (of a lock of hair). But in Shakespeare's own poem 'The Rape of Lucrece' (1594), the reference is to a rape in the modern sense, that of Lucretia, a famous Roman lady, by Sextus, the son of Tarquinius Superbus, the legendary king of Rome.

rapture (delight, ecstasy, passionate pleasure)
As mentioned above (under **rape**), 'rapture' is a word that has enhanced its meaning over the years. But the transition from 'carrying off by force' and 'rape' to 'state of ecstasy' was very rapid, and occurred within the seventeenth century. As so often, Shakespeare is in the forefront of the different usages. In his *Pericles* (1608), the sense is 'seizing and carrying off', when Pericles says:

> And spite of all the rapture of the sea,
> This jewel holds his binding on my arm.

Yet in the almost contemporary *Coriolanus* (1607), the meaning is 'passionate excitement', when Brutus says:

> Your prattling nurse
> Into a rapture lets her baby cry
> While she chats him.

This is not quite the modern sense, but it approaches it. The modern meaning proper is first recorded in Milton's *On the Morning of Christ's Nativity* (1629), where he writes of 'such musick sweet':

> As all their souls in blisfull rapture took.

The senses of 'seizing and carrying off' (whether plunder or a woman) and 'rape' were both obsolete by the eighteenth century.

rascal (rogue, mischievous person or animal)
In the fourteenth century, when the word first entered the language, the sense was 'rabble', 'camp followers' as a collective noun. A parallel meaning, however, was (again collectively) 'young deer', often with reference to the inferior ones in a herd. This sense is found as late as the seventeenth century in John Norden's *The Surveyors Dialogue* (1607): 'What Deere hath the Lord of this Mannor in his Parke, red and fallow; how many of Antler, and how many rascall'. In the fifteenth century, 'rascal', in a singular sense, acquired the meaning 'one of the rabble', 'man of low birth', and a century later the modern sense evolved as 'rogue', 'scamp'. It is interesting, though, that the word applied equally to men and animals, as it still does today, so that a 'little rascal' can be either a naughty child or a disobedient pet.

read (look at and understand what is written or printed)
Can this common word ever have had another meaning? The verb is an old one, and dates from Old English times. But it could also mean, as a basic sense, 'think', 'guess', 'make out the meaning of', without any involvement of written matter. This concept is preserved in some quite late texts,

as in Nicholas Breton's *Pasquils Fooles-cappe* (1600):

> Let him be sure that better wits doe reede
> Such Madhead fellowes are but Fooles indeede.

The 'interpret' sense of the verb still survives in the palmist who 'reads palms'. The modern meaning involving writing has also existed from the earliest times, however, so there has been no 'sense shift' proper, simply a dual meaning and usage.

recipe (instructions for preparing a dish)
The word is Latin for 'take!' (as an imperative), and this was its original use in English in the fourteenth century, in the directions to surgeons and cooks. Thus the translation (1400) of Lanfrank's *Science of Cirurgie* contains the direction at one point: 'Recipe litargium [i.e. litharge of gold or litharge of silver] as myche as thou wolt', and a culinary direction in the *Babees Book* (1475) begins: 'Recipe brede gratyd, & eggis'. The transference of the word to the directions or instructions themselves followed in the sixteenth century for a medical prescription and in the eighteenth century for a cooking recommendation. The medical sense has now been superseded by the use of 'prescription' itself, but for a long time a letter 'R' (often as 'Ŗ') headed medical prescriptions as a reminder of the original word. The use of 'recipe' to mean 'formula', 'means' in a general sense (as a 'recipe for success') dates from the seventeenth century.

recoil (spring back)
The word is not related to 'coil', despite the associations with guns and spring-loaded breeches. The verb was adopted in English from French *reculer* in the thirteenth century, and originally had the sense of the French, that is, first 'drive back' then 'retreat', 'retire'. The latter usage can be seen, for example, in Lord Berners' *The Boke of Duke Huon of Burdeux* 1533): 'When Huon sawe them he sayd to his men "syrs, it is good that we recule to our cyte"'. Even in the much later translation (1640) of Saulnier's *Love and Armes of the Greeke Princes; or the Romant of Romants*, the sense is still preserved: 'Doest thou not know that

worthy Knights must never recuile for any consideration of danger whatsoever'. The sense 'spring back' finally evolved in the sixteenth century, and the earlier meanings became entirely obsolete by the nineteenth century.

recuperate (recover one's health; regain losses)
The verb first became current in English in the sixteenth century, when its initial meaning was 'recover' in general, whether health, losses, a position or some other thing. In the following, from Dekker and Chettle's comedy *Patient Grissil* (1603), the meaning is 'recover the use': 'My opinion is, I shall never recuperate the legitimate office of this member, my arm'. In the sixteenth century, 'recuperate' came to mean 'restore the health of'. This sense survived until the nineteenth century, when it occurs, for example, in Thomas Nichols' *Forty Years in American Life* (1864), in which it is asked why certain sisters were not sent: ' ... to recuperate themselves in healthier conditions'. The modern meaning, 'recover one's health', evolved also from the nineteenth century, as did the more general sense, 'recover one's losses'. This is not obsolete, but is more frequently used than it might otherwise be through its false association with 'recoup', which is close in meaning but is actually another verb.

reduce (decrease, diminish)
The verb literally means 'lead back' (Latin *reducere*), and this was its sense when first current in English, in the fourteenth century. As Bishop John Fisher wrote in the sixteenth century: 'So must yͤ heretickes be reduced vnto yͤ wayes of yͤ churche' (*English Works*, 1635). In the fifteenth century, the sense moderated to 'restore' (of a condition), or 'bring down' (of an enemy or the like). The first of these is found in Shakespeare's *Henry V* (1599), when the Duke of Burgundy says to the gathered company, speaking of the evils of the past:

> Which to reduce into our former favour
> You are assembled.

The second sense was very common in the sixteenth and seventeenth centuries, when one side or the other aimed to 'reduce' armies, countries, troops, rulers and castles. Just one example of many can be seen in William Coxe's *Account of the Russian Discoveries between Asia and America* (1780): 'A body of troops whom he sent before him to reduce the fortress found it quite deserted'. This sense then passed to 'bring down in status', as 'reduced to walking' and in the name of the charitable organization 'Society for the Assistance of Ladies in Reduced Circumstances', where the meaning shades into 'diminished', as 'reduce' usually indicates today. The current sense thus dates from this time.

refund (pay back)
Latin *refundere*, which gave the English word in the fourteenth century, means literally 'pour back', and that was thus the first sense of 'refund'. The meaning was current until as recently as the eighteenth century, and is found, for instance in *The Government of the Tongue* (1674) ('by the author of The Whole Duty of Man', ascribed to Richard Allestree): 'One may as easily perswade the thirsty earth to refund the water she has suckt into her veins'. The modern usage, 'pay back', developed from the sixteenth century.

regiment (body of troops)
In the fourteenth century, 'regiment' had the sense 'rule', 'government', or 'control' more generally. The first of these was very common in the hundred years or so from the mid-sixteenth century, and occurs, for example, in Abraham Fleming's *A Panoplie of Epistles* (1576): 'What place is there in all the world, not subject to the regiment and power of this citie?'. The modern usage arose in the sixteenth century, when however 'regiment' could also mean 'regimen of health'. All senses apart from the military one are now obsolete, however.

regular (steady, uniform, arranged according to plan)
In the fourteenth century, the adjective meant specifically 'subject to a religious rule', and for some time was the standard opposite of 'secular'. The usage is still current in ecclesiastical parlance in such expressions as 'canons regular' (ones who live under a monastic rule, usually an Augu-stinian one). The modern meaning of 'regular' developed from the sixteenth century, subsequently acquiring several technical uses, as the 'regular army', 'regular verbs' in grammar, 'regular flowers' in botany, and so on, at different dates.

relay (type of race run in stages; electrical transmission system; broadcast)
The three senses defined here are the most recent ones, virtually all arising in the twentieth century. (The 'relay race' is first recorded in 1898.) Back in the fifteenth century, a 'relay' was a set of fresh hounds (and also sometimes horses) posted to resume the chase in a deerhunt when a previous set had been tired out. Hence the sense in William Somerville's poem *The Chace* (1735):

Press'd by the fresh Relay, no Pause allow'd,
Breathless and faint, he faulters in his Pace.

In the seventeenth century, the meaning was extended to apply to a set of fresh horses available to take over on a particular route, and from this in turn, 'relay' in the nineteenth century came to be used of humans working in a relief gang. Finally, the word came to be used in the 'take over' or 'pass on' senses defined above, with additionally 'relays' of motor vehicles emerging in the Second World War. The origin of the whole concept is not in 'lay again' but more 'leave again', since the derivation is in Old French *relaier*, which had this meaning.

relent (become less strict, forgive)
As originally used in the fourteenth century, 'relent' meant 'melt', 'dissolve', with both a literal and a figurative sense. 'Behold how Yse to Water doth relent', wrote George Ripley, in *The Compound of Alchymy* (1471), while the earlier *Lamentatyon of Mary Magdaleyne* (1475) (by some attributed to Chaucer) has the lines

Myne herte alas relenteth all in paine,
Whiche will braste [i.e. burst] both senewe and vaine.

This meaning became obsolete in the eighteenth century, and the current sense dates from the sixteenth century.

reluctant (unwilling)
The word is a fairly recent one in English, first becoming current in the seventeenth century, when it meant 'struggling', 'resisting', as in Milton's *Paradise Lost* (1667):

> Down he fell
> A monstrous Serpent on his Belly prone,
> Reluctant, but in vaine,

and in Pope's translation (1726) of Homer's *Odyssey*:

> A while, reluctant to her pleasing force,
> Suspend the restful hour with sweet discourse.

The modern meaning, 'unwilling' arose in the eighteenth century, and the original sense fell out of use in the nineteenth.

rely (depend on, trust)
The source of the word is French *relier*, 'bind together', and that was virtually the original English sense when the verb was first current in the fourteenth century. Its main meaning was 'assemble', both with or without a grammatical object (i.e. gather people together, or simply gather). The usage can be seen in these two lines from Caxton's translation (1481) of *Godeffroy of Boloyne*:

> Rogier relyed his lytil felawship
> And cam deffendyng hym toward the toun.

Substitute 'rallied' for 'relied' here and the old and new words will match in both meaning and derivation. The modern sense of 'rely' finally evolved in the sixteenth century, with the earlier meanings becoming obsolete shortly after.

repercussion (undesirable consequence)
The word literally means 'striking back', 'reverberation', and in its earliest uses in English, in the sixteenth century, the senses were all literal, relating to physical impacts such as water driven back from land, or the reverberation or echo of a sound. A particular usage of 'repercussion' was found in medicine, where it was a term for various ways of repelling fluids or swellings from the body, employing different remedies. In science, too, 'repercussion' was used for the reflecting of lights, rays and the like. Michael Drayton's poem *The Owle* (1604) gives one example of the way the word was used:

> That (with the Repercussion of the Aire)
> Shooke the great Eagle sitting in his Chaire.

The sense 'blow given in return' then followed in the seventeenth century, with this subsequently becoming figurative rather than literal. But at first the 'return act' was not an unpleasant one, simply a response to what one had done. Thus Dr Johnson wrote in the journal *The Rambler* in 1751: 'Tenderness once excited will be hourly increased by the [. . .] repercussion of communicated pleasure'. It was therefore only in the twentieth century that the 'repercussion' of an act became an undesirable one, with the usage increasingly in the plural, as in 'There'll be repercussions as a result of this'.

repertory (type of theatre company presenting different plays at one theatre)
The original meaning of the word in the sixteenth century was 'index', 'list', as well as 'storehouse', 'repository'. The first sense lasted until the eighteenth century, when in 1761 it appeared in the title of Andrew Ducarel's 'A Proposal for Publishing a general Repertory of the Endowments of Vicarages'. The second usage is still current, and promoted the next sense to develop, in the nineteenth century, which was that of 'stock of dramatic or musical works' (that is, 'repertoire'). This in turn produced the modern meaning, as in 'repertory theatre', a development in the history of the theatre that greatly interested Bernard Shaw. (In *Our Theatres in the Nineties* [1897] he wrote: 'What we want in order to get the best work is a repertory theatre with alternative casts'.)

reprieve (postpone or remit a prisoner's punishment)
Surprisingly enough, the word originally meant 'send back to prison', when it was first used in English in the sixteenth century. Yet perhaps not so surprisingly when the origin of the verb is considered,

since it derives from Old French *repris*, the past participle of *reprendre*, 'to take again', 'taken back' (with which even 'prison' itself is etymologically related). We thus read in Robert Fabyan's *The Newe Cronycles of Englande and of Fraunce* (1494): 'They were repryed, and sent vnto the Toure of London, where they remayned longe after'. The modern meaning evolved in the sixteenth century. The development of the apparent about-turn of sense seems to progress as follows: 'send back to prison', 'remand', 'remand without trial', 'postpone trial', 'postpone or delay execution', 'remit execution', 'remit any prison punishment'. In short, a lengthy remand or even imprisonment, originally without trial, could lead to a remission of the sentence when no good cause could be found for continuing it. This negative concept then became a positive one.

resolve (solve, settle)
In the fourteenth century, to 'resolve' was to 'dissolve' or 'melt'. Wyclif used the word in this sense in his translation (1388) of the Bible into English, where in Job 28:2 he has: 'A stoon resolued, ethir meltid, bi heete, is turned in to money' (Authorized Version of 1611: 'Brass is molten out of the stone'). Similarly, in Richard Eden's translation (1555) *The Decades of the Newe World or West India*, one can read: 'Cleopatra resolued a peearle in vineger & drunke it.' In the fifteenth century, a new sense 'soften', 'slacken' evolved, often in a medical context, as: 'Oyle of Rue is hot, resolving pain' (John Partridge, *The Treasurie of Commodious Conceites and Hidden Secrets*, 1573). A late use of the 'slacken' sense (more exactly 'weaken' here) occurs in Nicholas Rowe's *The Tragedy of Lady Jane Gray* (1715):

Every moving accent that she breathes
Resolves my courage, slackens my tough
   nerves.

The modern meaning finally became established from the sixteenth century, when also the noun 'resolve' (as 'courage') is first recorded (in Shakespeare's *Romeo and Juliet*, 1592).

restive (refractory, fidgety, restless)
Today, the word is used as if it really means 'not wishing to rest'. Originally, it meant just the opposite, 'wishing to rest', otherwise 'not wishing to move', 'inactive'. This was in the sixteenth century, when the adjective was first current. A character in Ben Jonson's play *Newes from the New World* (1621) thus says that someone: ' . . .went to Edenburgh o' foot, and came backe; marry he has been restive [. . .] ever since for we have had nothing from him'. Even as late as 1833, Charles Lamb wrote in a letter: 'Of my old friends, I have lived to see two knighted, one made a judge, another in a fair way to it. Why am I restive?'. In the seventeenth century, 'restive' particularly came to be used of horses that refused to move or go where they were directed. Thomas Hobbes, in his translation (1675) of Homer's *Iliad*, has the lines:

The horses us'd thereto will you obey;
To me, it may be, they will restive stand.

A stubborn horse will not simply stand still, of course, but will become awkward and impatient, or refractory, and it is from this concept that the modern meaning developed little more than a hundred years later, at the same time transferring from horses to humans. Hence the overlap with 'restless', which had evolved in this sense somewhat earlier.

retriever (type of gun dog)
In the fifteenth century, a retriever's main job was to 'retrieve' in the literal sense (from Old French *retrover*, modern *retrouver*), that is, find game that had been lost and flush it up again (as with partridges, for example). Hence the otherwise rather obscure lines by Francis Quarles in his poem *Sions Elegies* (1624):

Meanewhile, the treason of the quick
   Retriuers,
Discouers nouell dangers, and deliuers
   Her to a second feare

It was only in the nineteenth century that the sense changed to its present usage, so that retrievers now find and recover dead or wounded game. The meaning altered more from a change in the use of the dogs rather than from any natural linguistic or semantic development.

reverie (daydream, wistful musing)
This word has changed its sense quite dramatically since it first entered English (from French) in the fourteenth century. Then, it meant 'wild delight', 'riotous behaviour', in fact 'rave-up' (which word is related to it, as also, although less directly, are 'revel' and 'rebel'). The first recorded 'reverie' is in Chaucer's *The Romaunt of the Rose* (1366):

> The swetnesse of her melodye
> Made al myne herte in reuerye.

Twenty years later, in *The Canterbury Tales* ('The Reeve's Tale') the 'reverie' was rather more wanton:

> And oonly for hire myrthe and reuerye
> Vp on the wardeyn bisily they crye.

(That is: Just for their mirth and wild enjoyment, they [two college students] go and riotously shout after the warden [of their college].) The modern, much calmer meaning of 'reverie' evolved in the seventeenth century, largely as a result of the readoption of the word from French *rêverie*, with the original French verb *rever*, 'to rebel' having modified to *rêver*, 'to dream'.

ribald (coarse, lewd, crude)
The word began its life in English as a noun, with the adjective evolving only in the sixteenth century. Three hundred years earlier, a 'ribald' was a kind of lower class retainer in the household of a king, prince or baron, and as such was generally regarded as a 'menial' or 'worthless' person, and also a licentious and scurrilous one. (The term particularly applied to such servants in French households in the fourteenth and fifteenth centuries, when they were also employed as irregular troops in the army.) Hence, in Spenser's *The Faerie Queene* (1590):

> When that lewd rybauld, with vyle lust
>   advaunst,
>   Laid first his filthie hands on virgin
>   cleene.

Once the adjective emerged, it was applied equally to humans and their conduct, and also, rather unexpectedly, to birds, as in Shakespeare's *Troilus and Cressida* (1606),

where Troilus, about to leave Cressida in the early morning, says to her:

> O Cressida! but that the busy day,
> Wak'd by the lark, hath rous'd the ribald
>   crows,
> And dreaming night will hide our joys
>   no longer,
> I would not from thee.

ridge (long stretch of high ground, narrow raised strip)
In old English, 'ridge' (*hrycg*) was the standard word for 'back' as part of the body, whether of humans or animals. Thus Malory's *Le Morte Darthur* (1470–85) tells how the dragon: ' . . . smote the bore on the rydge whiche was x foote large fro the hede to the taylle'. The word was transferred in the eleventh century, possibly earlier, to natural objects such as long low hills and the crests of waves, and it was at about this time that 'back' began to oust 'ridge' as the word for the part of the body.

rigmarole (tiresome procedure)
The word first became current in English in the eighteenth century, when it was used of rambling or disjointed talk, or any meaningless harangue. Mrs Mary Delany uses the word more than once in her *Autobiography and Correspondence* (1779–88), writing at one point: 'At first she could not tell me what to make of such a *rig-my-role*', and later: 'How I have run on! Burn this rig-me-role instantly, I entreat your ladyship'. This use is still current. In the mid-twentieth century, however, a new sense developed, transferring from tiresome words to tiresome deeds or duties. This usage is first recorded in *The Times* of 24 June 1955; 'The Government set up [. . .] the whole rigmarole of scheduling, listing, and building preservation orders'.

rink (arena for ice skating)
When first used in English, in the fourteenth century, a 'rink' was an area alloted to a contest in general, whether a race, a combat or a joust. The usage was exclusively Scottish, however, which explains how in the eighteenth century the term came to apply in particular to a stretch of ice where the sport of curling was played. From this,

the word became a general designation for a prepared stretch of ice where people could skate. Later, the term was adopted by other sports such as (obviously) ice hockey and (less obviously) bowls. The word is actually related to 'rank'.

road (open way for traffic)
The word may seem so basic that it can hardly have had any other meaning. Yet in Old English, as *rād*, its sense was 'riding', that is, the act of riding on horseback, whether simply to make a journey or to make war on an enemy by riding against him. An example comes in the fourteenth-century *Cursor Mundi*:

Thir kinges rides forth thair rade,
The stern alwais tham forwit glade.

(That is: These kings rode forth on their journey, the star always shining before them.) The use of 'road' to mean 'riding' has been recorded down to the seventeenth century, when it occurs in Shakespeare. In *Henry VIII* (1613), Griffith, telling Queen Katharine how Cardinal Wolsey died, recounts:

At last, with easy roads, he came to Leicester.

The 'riding into battle' sense came to give 'road' the meaning '**raid**' (which see, above), so that the two words are closely related, as both are to 'inroads' (which literally implies 'riding inland'). This usage developed early, also in Old English. In the fourteenth century, the word came to be used as 'roadstead', in the sense 'sheltered stretch of water for ships'. The basic meaning is still here, since a roadstead is a place where ships can 'ride' at anchor. (Indeed, a former expression for a ship riding at anchor was to say that it was 'at road'.) Finally, it was only in the sixteenth century that the word acquired today's familiar meaning, and in this sense it was first recorded in Shakespeare's *Henry IV, Part 1* (1596), when one carrier says to another in the innyard at Rochester: 'I think this be the most villanous house in all London road for fleas'. But surely there were roads before the sixteenth century? There certainly were, but the former word for them was simply 'way' (hence 'highway'

and the word 'Way' still used in the names of Roman roads, such as the Icknield Way, where it translates Latin *via*).

romance (love affair, love story)
In the thirteenth century, 'romance' was a term for a tale of adventure told in verse, and especially having medieval legends as its subject. It was so called as it was written or told in French, the vernacular tongue spoken by settlers from Rome, as distinct from literary Latin. (Hence also the use of 'Romance' as the term for languages such as French that developed in the vernacular from Latin.) In French itself, such a tale was called a *roman*, with this word giving the name of one of the most famous medieval 'romances', the thirteenth-century 'Roman de la rose', subsequently translated into English (perhaps partly by Chaucer) as 'The Romaunt of the Rose'. (The French word *roman* today is the standard word for 'novel'.) Such early English 'romances' were of course full of tales of chivalry and of 'romantic' heroes and heroines, and it is easy to see the source of the modern meanings. The 'romance' itself as a literary genre developed in the sixteenth and seventeenth centuries into a prose work, or in particular into the Spanish historical ballad. (The French word for this was also *romance*.) The nature and content of all these tales and songs, with their emphasis on love, eventually led to 'romance' itself coming to mean 'love affair', 'love story'. The development is very recent, however, and arose in English only in the twentieth century, where it is first recorded in Bernard Shaw's *Overruled* (1916): 'I felt my youth slipping away without ever having had a romance in my life; for marriage is all very well but it isnt romance. Theres nothing wrong in it, you see'.

rosary (string of beads used by Roman Catholics in counting prayers)
Properly, and originally, a 'rosary' is what it says, a garden of roses. This meaning has been current in English since the fifteenth century. The word itself came to be used as the title of various books of devotion, in particular that of the Virgin Mary, called 'The Rosary of Our Lady'. This was in the sixteenth century, when other such books of

the name also appeared. (One of 1533 had the title: 'The Mystik sweet Rosary of the faythful soule: garnished rownde aboute [. . .] with fresh fragraunt flowers', and there were others of St Bridget, the Seven Dolours and so on.) From this usage, the sense soon passed naturally to the set of beads used for counting the various prescribed prayers or devotions, with the small beads representing 'Hail Marys' (or 'Aves') and the larger, less frequent ones 'Our Fathers' ('Paternosters') and 'Glorias'. The metaphorical use of flowers to represent a collection of written texts is not unique to the rosary: compare **anthology** and the various selections called 'A Garland of. . .' (something or other) or 'A Posy of. . .' (poems or verses or whatever). A more exact parallel with the concept of the 'rosary', however, is the thirteenth-century collection of lyrics by the Persian poet Sa'di, called 'The Rose Garden' (or 'Golistan').

rota (list of people for duties, roster)
The word looks an old one, deriving from Latin *rota*, 'wheel'. This is indeed its origin, but the first English 'rota' can be dated quite precisely from 1659, when it was the name of a political club founded by James Harrington with the aim of advocating the rotation of ministers in government office. (In 1660 Harrington published a work entitled: 'The Censure of the Rota upon Mr. Milton's Book, entitled, The Ready and Easie way to Establish a Free Commonwealth'.) Within a few years, the word had become adopted generally to mean a rotation of duties, although the sense 'list of persons and their duties', or 'roster', did not appear until the nineteenth century, when it was first recorded in Hughes's *Tom Brown's School Days* (1857) ('the senior fag who kept the rota').

ruse (dodge, trick)
The ultimate derivation of the word is Latin *rursus*, 'back', and in the fifteenth century in English a 'ruse' was a detour or a doubling or turning in a track, especially one made by a hunted animal to avoid the hounds. As *The Master of Game* (1410) records: 'Somtyme he goth away with hem and then he maketh a ruse in some side [i.e. in some direction]'. The current meaning 'dodge' arose somewhat later, in the seventeenth century. Until the fifteenth century there was a verb 'to ruse' used in the hunting sense.

rush (move with force or speed)
The original sense of the word, in the fourteenth century, was 'force out of place,' 'drive back', with no implied speed or eagerness. So in John Barbour's *The Bruce* (1375) come the narrative lines:

> In the stour so hardyly
> He ruschyt with hys chewalry,
> That he ruschyt his fayis ilkane.

(That is: He retaliated so courageously with his horses in the battle that he drove back each of his foes.) The 'speedy' sense of 'rush' soon appeared, however (Wyclif's Bible of 1382 has it), and this additional connotation seems to have evolved from the very sound of the word, rather as today 'whoosh' implies speed. (Compare, too, modern German *rauschen*, which although meaning 'rush' is not related to the English verb.)

sabbatical (periodic paid leave of absence from a university teaching post in order to research or rest)
The word properly means 'pertaining to the Sabbath', hence 'pertaining to every seventh year', since this, like the Sabbath itself (the seventh day of the week), was prescribed by Mosaic law to be a year of rest, when the land remained uncultivated and all slaves were set free. The sense was adopted by English in the sixteenth century (in the biblical understanding), and in the nineteenth as a similar year of respite and refreshment for an academic (originally in the United States, and every seventh year, as in Jewish practice). At Wellesley College,

the women's college in Massachusetts, the head of a nominated department was awarded a 'Sabbatical Grant' every seven years for: 'A year's leave of absence, to be passed in Europe, and with it, her half-yearly salary' (E.N. Horsford, *Scheme adopted by the Trustees, Wellesley College*, 1886). The term became a noun on its own in the twentieth century.

sad (sorrowful, unhappy)
The Old English sense of the word was 'sated', 'jaded', 'weary', reflecting the connection of 'sad', although indirectly, with both 'sated' and 'satisfied'. An example of the usage can be seen in the following lines from the fourteenth-century *Cursor Mundi*:

Thof that thou euer vpon him se,
Of him sadd sal thou neuer be.

(That is: Although you will always look at it, you will never be weary of it.) By the fourteenth century, 'sad' had come to have its present meaning of 'sorrowful' as well as certain other senses that are now obsolete, such as 'grave' and 'steadfast'. In the following lines from Chaucer's *Canterbury Tales* ('The Man of Law's Tale') (1386), the sense is 'sober-living', 'trustworthy':

In Surrye whilom [i.e. once] dwelte a
compaignye
Of chapmen riche and therto sadde and
trewe.

The sense of 'sad' to mean 'deplorable' (as 'a sad decline in good behaviour') followed rather later, in the seventeenth century, which was also when the specialized meaning 'heavy' (of bread that has not risen, for example) emerged.

sagacious (very wise, discerning)
The word ultimately derives from Latin *sagire*, 'to perceive keenly', and when first current in English, in the seventeenth century, was especially used to apply to a keen sense of smell, as of hounds on the scent. In *The Historie of Fourefooted Beastes* (1607), where it is first recorded, Edward Topsell used the adjective of bees: 'The Bees seeke out their King if he loose himselfe, and by a most sagacious smelling-sence, neuer cease till he be found out.' Just over a

hundred years later, Pope used it in a more common context, in his *Essay on Man* (1732):

And hound sagacious on the tainted
green.

However, the current meaning of the word also evolved in the seventeenth century, and the earlier usage became obsolete shortly after Pope's inclusion of it above.

sake (as in 'for my sake', 'for God's sake')
The noun is now used only after 'for', as in the phrases mentioned here. Originally in Old English, it was a word meaning 'strife', 'dispute', 'guilt' (*sacu*), itself related to modern 'seek'. A common phrase in medieval times was thus 'without sake', meaning 'without cause', 'without any reason', which is the sense in the following lines from the *Early English Psalter* (1300):

Alle to me witherwendand,
With-outen sake or any skil.

(That is: Everyone opposing me without cause or any reason. Here the phrase translates Latin *sine causa*. See also **skill**.) The only surviving use of 'sake' after 'for' ('for the sake of X' or 'for X's sake') followed in the thirteenth century.

sample (specimen)
When first in use in English, in the thirteenth century, 'sample' meant more 'example', 'warning', especially as a fact or story used to illustrate what could happen. Not surprisingly, many such 'samples' were stories from the Bible, whether narratives from the Old Testament, or parables from the New. This usage was current down to the sixteenth century, when it became obsolete. In the fifteenth century, however, the present meaning first developed, although at first it was not so much a commercial 'sample', as today, but a small quantity of something. The first record (even sample) of the sense is found in an extract of 1428 in the *Miscellany* of the Surtees Society (which collected old Northumbrian texts): 'Of ye whilk [i.e. which] plaster and lyme a sample is redy in ye chambre to shew'.

sampler (exercise in embroidery worked by a young person learning to sew)

In the thirteenth century, a 'sampler' was merely an 'example' or 'pattern', that is, an original or 'master copy' for others to follow. Wyclif used the word to translate Exodus 25:40 in his English Bible of 1382: 'Bihold and do after the sawmplere, that to thee is shewid in the hil' (Authorized Version of 1611: 'And look that thou make them after the pattern, which was shewed thee in the mount'). In fact, many 'samplers' were biblical or religious ones of this kind down to the seventeenth century, when the sense became obsolete. This doubtless influenced the nature of the modern embroidered 'sampler', which is first recorded in the sixteenth century. Edward Topsell's *The Historie of Serpents* (1608) ingeniously contrives to combine both senses: 'Arachne first invented [. . .] working with the needle, which this mayd of Lydia first learned from the Spiders, taking her first Samplers and patterns from them for imitation'.

sanity (soundness of mind)
Latin *sanus,* which gave English 'sane', meant 'healthy', 'sound' as applied to either body or mind (as commemorated in the Latin tag *mens sana in corpore sano,* 'a healthy mind in a healthy body', the ambitious adage of the nineteenth-century English public school). Therefore 'sane' itself meant both 'sound in mind'and 'healthy in body' when the word was first current in English, in the seventeenth century, with the latter sense becoming obsolete in the nineteenth century. 'Sanity', from Latin *sanitas,* predates this, however, and when in use in the fifteenth century meant only 'bodily health'. It was then Shakespeare who is first recorded as using the 'mental soundness', in *Hamlet* (1602), where Polonius says of Hamlet: 'A happiness that often madness hits on, which reason and sanity could not so prosperously be delivered of'. Meanwhile, the usage as 'bodily health' became obsolete in the nineteenth century.

sash (band of cloth worn round the waist or across the body diagonally)
Arabic *shāsh,* that gave the word, means 'muslin', 'turban', and it was in the latter sense that 'sash' was first used in English, in the sixteenth century. Hence the observation of George Sandys in his *Travels* (1615): 'All of them weare on the heads white Shashes and Turbants, the badge of their religion'. This meaning became obsolete in the eighteenth century, while the current sense is recorded from a hundred years before this.

satellite (natural or artificial body in space orbiting a greater body)
The earliest recorded usage of the word is in the sixteenth century, when it denoted an attendant on a person of high rank or importance. It cannot have been in common use, however, since texts containing it are not numerous and it is not in Johnson's *Dictionary* of 1755. It was used much more frequently from the eighteenth century, in fact, although today the sense has been very much put in the shade by more modern 'satellites'. As a word for a heavenly body, such as the Moon, or the equivalent bodies that revolve round other planets, the meaning evolved in the seventeenth century, or more precisely in 1611, when the German astronomer Kepler used the word as a rendering of Latin *satelles,* 'attendant', to apply to the satellites of Jupiter. (These had just been discovered by Galileo, who called them *Sidera Medicaea,* 'Medicean stars', in honour of his patron Cosimo de' Medici.) Artificial 'satellites' followed in the twentieth century, of course, with the first record of such a vehicle found in the issue of *Discovery* for October 1936, where an article referred to: ' . . .the scheme for building a metal outpost satellite and propelling it in a fixed orbit 600 miles above the earth's surface'. This clearly predates the first actual satellite to be launched into space (usually regarded as the Russian 'sputnik' launched on 4 October 1957). Purely in the realms of science fiction or fantasy, Jules Verne had envisaged just such a 'satellite' in his novel *Les Cinq Cents Millions de la bégum* (1879), usually translated as 'The Begum's Fortune' or 'The Begum's Millions'. The sense of 'satellite' to apply to a country that is politically dependent on another also dates from the nineteenth century, at first in a figurative sense of the astronomical body, but later, in the twentieth century, as an individually distinguished concept.

saturate (soak right through)
In the sixteenth century, to 'saturate' was to satisfy or satiate (all three words are related), so that you could 'saturate a hunger' or 'saturate an ambition'. The *London Gazette* wrote in 1683 of 'Cruel Persons whose Blood-thirsty minds nothing could Saturate, but the Sacrifice of two Princes at once'. This then passed the following century into a scientific sense to denote a chemical method of making one substance combine with (or dissolve) the maximum quantity of another, such as an alkali 'saturating' an acid. From this in turn the modern meaning evolved in the eighteenth century.

saucer (small round dish holding a cup)
The modern 'saucer' has lost its original connection with sauce! In the fourteenth century, the word was used for either a metal receptacle holding condiments at a meal, or a dish or deep plate that similarly held sauce or salt. In the contemporary verse romance *Richard Coer de Lion* we can thus read the instructions:

Now, styward, I warne the,
Bye us vessel gret plenté,
Dysschys, cuppys, and sawsers.

The sense was extended in the seventeenth century to a dish to hold other things, in particular one holding blood in blood-letting, or placed under a flowerpot, with the modern teacup 'saucer' following in the eighteenth century.

saunter (stroll, walk in a leisurely way)
In the fifteenth century, 'saunter' meant 'muse', 'daydream', as in the following lines from Sir William Forrest's *The Pleasaunt Poesye of Princelye Practise* (1548)

When straungers greate yowre presence hathe none
take of yowre nobles youe compenye too keepe:
doo not your selfe sitt santeringe alone:
as wone that weare in studye most deepe.

(This was the author's advice to Edward VI, then aged ten.) In the seventeenth century, 'saunter' came to mean 'wander aimlessly', a now obsolete sense, with the present meaning following in the eighteenth century.

savage (fierce, extremely angry)
The ultimate source of the word is in Latin *silva*, 'wood', 'forest', and the original sense of 'savage' in English, in the thirteenth century, was fairly close to this, meaning 'natural', 'in a state of nature', especially as applied to wild animals. The meaning is preserved in Shakespeare's *The Merchant of Venice* (1596), where Lorenzo says to Jessica, speaking of wild horses:

You shall perceive them make a mutual stand,
Their savage eyes turn'd to a modest gaze
By the sweet power of music.

It was only some time after this that the meaning progressed (or narrowed) to 'fierce'. But it was also Shakespeare who brings us the first record of a further sense of 'savage' as used of people, with the meaning 'uncivilised'. In *Love's Labour's Lost* (1588), thus, it is Berowne who speaks of a 'rude and savage man of Inde', and the word was happily adopted by many poets thereafter, usually romantically, as in Gray's 'Pindaric Ode' *The Progress of Poesy* (1754):

She [i.e. the muse] deigns to hear the savage youth repeat,
In loose numbers, wildly sweet,
Their feather-cinctur'd chiefs and dusky loves,

and Tennyson in *Locksley Hall* (1842):

I will take some savage woman, she shall rear my dusky race.

The sense of 'savage' today has become much more generalized in this usage, and is related more to abstract nouns, such as 'savage pleasure', 'savage heart'.

scales (instrument for weighing)
Today, a single 'scale' is understood as a weighing pan, where such pans still exist (although 'scale' is also increasingly used for the whole instrument). Originally, in the thirteenth century, a 'scale' was a drinking bowl (hence, incidentally, the drinking toast 'skoal!' and the commercial name of a brand of lager). The meaning 'balance pan' emerged early, however, in the fourteenth

century, and the 'drinking cup' sense gradually became disused. This account also confirms that the modern weighing machine is not so called because it has a 'scale' on which the weight can be read off, as is sometimes thought. (The false association may have encouraged the use of the word in the singular, however, coupled with the fact that most modern machines do not have separate weighing pans or 'scales' proper.)

scamp (rogue, rascal)
In the eighteenth century, a 'scamp' was usually specifically understood to mean a highway robber or even the robbery itself. Grose's *A Classical Dictionary of the Vulgar Tongue* (1785) defines the word thus: '*Scamp*, a highwayman; royal scamp, a highwayman who robs civilly; royal foot scamp, footpads who behave in like manner'. The second sense occurs in the *Life of Miss Davies* (1786): 'He resolved to go upon the scamp'. The more general meaning 'rascal', 'layabout' followed in the nineteenth century.

scavenger (person who collects or salvages refuse or discarded material)
The word was originally 'scavager', and this was the title of the officer who took 'scavage', that is, a toll levied by the mayor or sheriff of a town on goods offered for sale by travelling merchants. This sense dates from the fifteenth century, when 'scavage' is itself first recorded. Later, the 'scavager' was given the additional duty of keeping the streets clean, and at the same time the word itself was altered to 'scavenger' in the same way that 'messenger', 'passenger' and similar words had evolved and acquired an 'n'. (Messengers, after all, carry 'messages', and passengers make a 'passage'.) The duties of a 'scavenger' lasted in many towns down to at least the eighteenth century, possibly even the nineteenth, although the sense had become more generalized by the sixteenth century to mean 'refuse collector', 'one who works to remove public evils'. The modern concept of 'scavenging' as a kind of hobby or pastime dates only from the twentieth century, and it was in the United States that 'scavenger hunts' were first organized in the 1940s. (The object is to set out and collect certain designated objects from a local area. The sport became popular in Britain somewhat later: 'The outdoors scavenger hunt is a good exercise after overeating', *The Times*, 24 December 1977.)

schedule (timetable, programme)
In the fourteenth century, a 'schedule' was simply a ticket or brief note. The *Plumpton Correspondence* of 1460 to 1562, published by the Camden Society, has the following in a letter of 1465: 'Scribled in hast with mine owne hand [. . .] the 21 of June, which day your dayly Bedewoman [. . .] desired that by this rude sedule, she may humblie be recommended to your [. . .] mastership'. By the fifteenth century, a 'schedule' was an explanatory slip accompanying a document of some kind, and a hundred years later had acquired something like its modern sense, to mean 'classified statement', 'list'. As an extended sense of this, 'schedule' in turn came to mean 'programme', 'timetable' in the nineteenth century, where the usage was mainly American, as it mostly still is (with the pronunciation 'skedule', also). The various dreaded British income tax 'schedules' (A, B, C, D and so on) originally evolved in an act of 1803, with the designated 'schedules' referring (in the fifteenth-century sense mentioned above) to those actually accompanying the act.

scheme (plan, design)
A 'scheme' was a figure of rhetoric in the sixteenth century, denoting a recognized way of deviating from the ordinary use and order of words for the purposes of special effect. Among such devices would be the use of metaphor, hyperbole, apostrophe (addressing a personified thing, as 'O Freedom!'), and so on. Today the devices themselves are usually collectively referred to as 'figures of speech', and the use of 'scheme' in this sense became obsolete in the seventeenth century, when the modern meaning of the word evolved.

science (study of the laws and phenomena of the natural world)
The word dates from the fourteenth century, when its most general meaning was simply 'knowledge'. The sense was in use down to the eighteenth century in the language of 'learned' writers and poets, and it is what Shakespeare meant in *All's Well That Ends*

Well (1601), for example, when he makes the King of France say:

> Plutus himself,
> That knows the tinct and multiplying medicine,
> Hath not in nature's mystery more science
> Than I have in this ring.

Similarly, the sense is that used by Pope in his translation (1725) of Homer's *Odyssey*:

> For lo! my words no fancy'd woes relate:
> I speak from science, and the voice is Fate.

However, 'science' could also mean 'specialized branch of learning' at this time, even though in its medieval usage the so called 'seven liberal sciences' were often equated with the 'seven liberal arts'. (These were themselves divided into the 'trivium', comprising grammar, logic and rhetoric, and the 'quadrivium', consisting of arithmetic, music, geometry and astronomy.) 'Science', or 'the sciences' as understood today, emerged really only in the eighteenth century in anything like the modern meaning, since it was then that people began classifying the different branches (such as 'biological science', 'mathematical science' and also 'exact science', 'descriptive science' and so on). The most common understanding of 'science' now, however, is of what is properly called 'natural science', that is, such disciplines as physics, chemistry and biology that deal with the natural world, its phenomena and life. This concept evolved in popular usage only in the nineteenth century.

scold (reprimand severely or in anger)
Originally, in the thirteenth century, a 'scold' (as a noun) was a woman who used coarse language, with the sense modifying later to apply to a more generally abusive woman. This usage was still quite common down to the eighteenth century, and is not entirely obsolete even now. The verb 'scold' dates roughly from the fourteenth century, and originally meant 'quarrel noisily', as still in Shakespeare's *The Taming of the Shrew* (1596), where Tranio says to his master Lucentio, of Katharina (the 'Shrew' of the title):

> Mark'd you not how her
> [i.e. Bianca's] sister
> Began to scold and raise up such a storm
> That mortal ears might hardly endure the din?

By the nineteenth century, however, 'scolding' had become a more one-sided business, involving a reprimand or reproof, as in Charlotte Brontë's *Jane Eyre* (1847): 'I just put my two arms round her, and said, "Come, Bessie! don't scold" '.

score (record of points in a game)
The word has had several sense shifts over the centuries, with all the meanings still current. At first, in the fourteenth century, 'score' meant 'set of twenty' with this sense doubtless coming from the practice of making a 'score' or notch on a piece of wood when counting. (This would have been used when counting sheep: the shepherd counted aloud or mentally to twenty, then put one notch on his stick before starting the next set of twenty. The verb 'score' meaning 'notch', 'cut', was already in use at this time.) From this, the meaning progressed to the tally itself as the 'score', and later, in the sixteenth century, to the amount of a bill or reckoning, especially that of an innkeeper (the 'slate' of its day). This usage is nicely illustrated in Shakespeare's *The Taming of the Shrew* (1596), where in the first act of the play (the 'Induction'), Sly says: 'Ask Marian Hacket, the fat ale-wife of Wincot, if she know me not: if she say I am not fourteen pence on the score for sheer ale, score me up for the lyingest knave in Christendom'. In the seventeenth century, the further sense 'account', 'reason' evolved, and this is the one that today gives the expression 'on that score'. Finally, in the eighteenth century, the word acquired two more meanings, first the record of the points won in a game, and second the music 'score'. (The latter is said to be so called since the related staves for the different instruments were connected by a 'score' or line marking off the bars.) The modern usage of 'score' in such expressions as 'know the score' or 'what's the score?' developed in the twentieth century from the 'score' of a game.

237

scuttle (container for coal)

This word is not related to the 'scuttle' that is an opening in a ship's deck. The coal 'scuttle' developed in the nineteenth century from what was originally an old English word for a dish or 'trencher'. This in turn, admittedly rather strangely, came to have the sense 'corn basket' in the fourteenth century, and a hundred years later 'scuttle' was the term for any basket with a widish mouth. It was more precisely from this, then, that the coal holder emerged in recent times.

season (one of the four distinctive periods of the year)

Originally, in the thirteenth century, 'season' simply meant 'time', 'period', although by implication this was often a special or appropriate one, such as a 'season' for planting or harvesting. The Bible preserves this sense in Acts 14:17: 'He did good, and gave us rain from heaven, and fruitful seasons'. The use of the word in this way is still common, of course. The particular association with spring, summer, autumn or winter came only in the fourteenth century, when one of these four words would usually be accompanied by 'season', and the modern meaning is implicit in the 'Prologue' to Chaucer's *Canterbury Tales* (1386):

After the sondry seasons of the year,
So changed he his mete and his soper.

(That is: He varied his dinner and supper according to the season.)

secretary (person who handles correspondence; club officer keeping records; government minister)

The sense of 'secretary' did not arise in the order given here, since this is the 'order of popularity' as far as the word is commonly understood. In the fourteenth century, a 'secretary', as the word implies, was a confidant, someone to whom secrets could be entrusted. This usage is found even down to the nineteenth century, when it occurs in Scott's *Guy Mannering* (1815): 'My good woman, [. . .] a faithful secretary to her sex's foibles'. The 'correspondence handler' then emerged in the fifteenth century, although originally such a

'secretary' would have been the man who conducted the correspondence of a king. An example of the sense can be seen in the following item from the *Manners and Household Expenses of England in the Thirteenth and Fifteenth Centuries*, relating to 1465: 'My mastyre paid to the Kinges secretory, for makenge of a lettre fro the Kynge into Wales, for my Lord, vj. s. viij. d. (i.e. six shillings and eightpence, or one noble, as a third of a pound]'. The government 'secretary' who heads a state department evolved in the sixteenth century as a translation of the French *secrétaire d'état*, 'secretary of state', while the 'secretary' who is the correspondence and records officer of a club or society followed in the eighteenth century, as did the 'company secretary'. It was only in the nineteenth century, however, that the 'office secretary' really emerged (then usually called 'office clerk' or, more generally, 'office girl' rather than 'secretary').

secure (safe, dependable)

When first current in English, in the sixteenth century, 'secure' meant 'carefree' 'not anxious', even 'over-confident'. The word was often contrasted with 'safe', as in Francis Quarles's *Enchyridion* (1640): 'When the Devil brings thee Oyle, bring thou Vinegar. The way to be safe, is never to bee secure'. Even in the nineteenth century, this usage is found in Macaulay's *History of England* (1859): 'They were secure where they ought to have been wary, timorous where they might well have been secure'. The modern meaning of 'secure' also dates from the sixteenth century, however, and is found in both the Bible and Shakespeare, the former in the Rhemish New Testament of 1582, where Matthew 28:14 has: 'And if the President shal heare of this, we wil persuade him, and make you secure' (Authorized Version of 1611: 'And if this come to the governor's ears, we will persuade him, and secure you'). (The earlier text is closer to the Latin Vulgate, reading: *et securos vos faciemus*, 'and will make you secure'.)

sedition (incitement to rebel)

As originally used in English, in the fourteenth century, 'sedition' meant 'violent party strife', especially when rioting and general disorder were involved. Wyclif used the word in his Bible translation of 1382, to render Mark 15:7: 'Barabas, that was boundan with sleeris of men, and that hadde don manslaughtre in seducioun, that is, debaat in cytee' (Authorized Version of 1611: 'Barabbas, which lay bound with them that had made insurrection with him, who had committed murder in the insurrection'). This sense then passed into 'mutiny' itself, in the sixteenth century, and finally, in its ever weakening usage, to its current meaning of 'incitement to rebellion' in the nineteenth century.

seedy (rather unwell, 'off colour')
Literally, of course, 'seedy' means 'full of seeds', and this was the basic meaning of the word in the sixteenth century, as it still can be of a plant or crop with many seeds. However, when a plant runs to seed, it looks shabby or 'ill', and this was the next sense to evolve for the adjective, in the eighteenth century, as applied to anything that looked 'run down', such as a 'seedy' coat or a 'seedy' little railway station. But when used of people at this time, it simply meant 'unkempt', 'shabby-looking', and it was not until the nineteenth century that the meaning settled to 'ill-looking', 'unwell'. Dickens used the word in both senses.

seethe (be in a state of emotional agitation)
The word is related to 'sodden', and in Old English meant simply 'boil'. Wyclif used the verb in his Bible translations of both 1382 and 1388 to render the first half of Genesis 25:29, with his second version running: 'Jacob sethide potage' (Authorized Version of 1611: 'Jacob sod pottage'). This meaning is now obsolete, but is found in texts right down to the nineteenth century, where Macaulay uses it in his *History of England* (1849): 'A poor man whose loyalty was suspected [. . .] was compelled to ransom his own life by seething the remains of his friends in pitch'. In the sixteenth century, 'seethe' developed the meaning 'soak', 'steep', which is where 'sodden' most obviously belongs in modern terms (it is actually the past participle of 'seethe', as an alternative to 'seethed'). A century later the

figurative sense 'be inwardly agitated' emerged, with this current meaning first recorded in Shakespeare's *Troilus and Cressida* (1606), although admittedly of things rather than people. Pandarus says to a servant: 'I come to speak with Paris from the Prince Troilus: I will make a complimental assault upon him, for my business seethes'. (The servant replies: 'Sodden business: there's a stewed phrase, indeed'.)

seminary (educational establishment; institution for training priests)
As so often, the word first had its literal sense in English, which in the fifteenth century was 'seed plot', 'seed bed' (from which young plants were transplanted). In Evelyn's translation (1658) *The French Gardener* he thus advises: 'Then taking your grafted trees out of the seminary, you shall transplant them into this nursery'. This sense became obsolete in the nineteenth century. Meanwhile, from the sixteenth century, 'seminary' had become established in a transferred (or perhaps one should say transplanted) sense to designate a place of education as well as an establishment in the Roman Catholic Church for training young priests, especially future missionaries. In the educational usage, 'Seminary for Young Ladies' was common in the nineteenth century as the title of several private schools for girls. The term became something of a joke, however, and died a fairly rapid death after Gilbert and Sullivan's *Mikado* (1885) mocked the institution musically with its trio of:

Three little maids, who, all unwary,
Come from a ladies' seminary,
Freed from its genius tutelary —
Three little maids from school!

sensible (showing good sense)
The adjective has three main current meanings, which evolved at different times in its history. First, in the fourteenth century, 'sensible' meant 'perceptible by the senses'. Today, the usage is more scientific than general, as the 'sensible horizon' in astronomy, and 'sensible heat' (as opposed to latent heat) in physics. But it is still possible to talk of a 'sensible chill in the air' in a rather stilted way, and certainly the word

came fairly readily to Shakespeare in *Macbeth* (1605), when Macbeth, in his famous 'Is this a dagger I see before me' speech, says:

Art thou not, fatal vision, sensible
To feeling as to sight?

In the fifteenth century, 'sensible' acquired the meaning 'conscious', 'aware', as in the advice given by Bacon in one of his *Essays* (1625): 'Be not too sensible, or too remembring, of thy Place, in Conuersation', and as in one of Lamb's *Essays of Elia* ('Grace before Meat') (1821): 'We may be gratefully sensible of the deliciousness of some kinds of food beyond others'. The most common meaning, however, 'showing good sense', arose only in the sixteenth century. 'My loveliest, my most sensible of girls', wrote Goldsmith in *The Vicar of Wakefield* (1766), yet only eleven years earlier Johnson, in his *Dictionary*, had stigmatized the adjective and the meaning as used only 'in low conversation'.

sentence (complete expression of a thought in speech or writing; court decision)
In the thirteenth century, 'sentence' meant simply 'sense', 'meaning'. The usage can be nicely seen in Chaucer's *Canterbury Tales* (1386), where in 'The Nun's Priest's Tale' he deliberately mistranslates a Latin proverb:

Mulier est hominis confusio:
Madame, the sentence of this latyn is,
Woman is mannes Ioye [i.e. joy] and al
his blis.

In the fourteenth century, the sense 'judgment', 'decision' evolved, as the 'sentence' of a court, while 'sentence' could also at this time be a term for a saying or maxim. The now obsolete usage also comes in Chaucer, this time in 'The Man of Law's Tale':

Herke what is the sentence of the wise:
Bet is to dyen than haue Indigence.

(That is: It is better to die than be indigent or poor. Compare the saying, 'Better to die a beggar than live a beggar'.) Finally, the word gained its modern meaning in the fifteenth century, so that a 'sentence' came to be a thought expressed in words, as in

this one. (Although grammarians and linguists are still arguing as to what exactly comprises this sort of 'sentence'. It was long regarded that a grammatical sentence should always contain a verb. Now not so.)

sentiment (mental attitude or emotion, romantic or nostalgic feeling)
The basic meaning of the word is 'feeling', 'sensation', and this was what it meant when reintroduced from French, in the seventeenth century (having earlier been recorded, in the spelling 'sentement', in the fourteenth century). Thus Robert Sharrock, in *The History of the Propagation and Improvement of Vegetables* (1660), writes of 'the approach or sentiment of the coole and fresh aire'. The current meaning 'mental attitude' also dates from the seventeenth century, but the more specialized sense, 'refined sensibility', evolved in the eighteenth century, and owes its origin to Sterne's *Sentimental Journey* (1768), where he says: "Tis the monarch of a people so civilized and courteous, and so renown'd for sentiment and fine feelings, that I have to reason with'. Interestingly, the French word *sentimental* was adopted from English in the identical word that was used to translate the title of Sterne's book. Sterne is said to have used the English adjective 'sentimental' in a letter of 1739. Certainly it was very popular in the mid-eighteenth century.

sequin (small spangle for decorating a dress or other garment)
The original 'sequin', in the seventeenth century, was the name of an Italian gold coin (in Italian, *zecchino*, literally 'little mint'). In the nineteenth century, this name was adopted for the ornaments that were then in fashion, from the fancied resemblance of the spangles to the coins. The *Daily News* of 3 June 1882 reported: 'Never before, probably, have dress trimmings been more artistic than they are now. Sequins are the newest'.

sergeant (noncommissioned officer in the army and air force)
The English 'sergeant' began his career in the twelfth century simply as a 'servant', since that is what the word basically means (with the 'v' of 'servant' in Romance langu-

ages altered to 'g'). Hence in the fourteenth-century *Cursor Mundi*:

He [i.e. Abram] did to-geder samen his men,
Thre hundret aght sariants and ten.

(See Genesis 14:14.) In the thirteenth century, 'sergeant' (frequently spelt 'serjeant', as still in some special titles) came to be the word for a common soldier, as well as a rank, and its bearer, next below a knight and apparently approximating to 'esquire'. The designation was also first used at this time for an officer appointed to arrest offenders, the one who became called 'sergeant at arms' (also regularly 'serjeant at arms' until quite recently). Originally this was an armed officer who attended the king as well as carrying out his other duties. Later, the title became that of the official in each of the Houses of Parliament who enforced order and also had the power to arrest offenders. In the fifteenth century, 'sergeant' was used as the title of an officer of the Corporation of London (especially the one known as 'sergeant at mace'), and finally in the sixteenth century the word gained its best known sense as a military rank, although probably at first having a higher status than today's noncommissioned officer. (He was originally called 'sergeant of a band'.) Even this does not exhaust the various uses and senses of 'sergeant' that have come into being from the days of the 'servant' to the twentieth-century 'sarge'.

sexton (church officer employed to look after church property)
The word is related to 'sacristan', and when first current in English, in the fourteenth century, it was the title of an officer whose duties were closer to that of today's sacristan, that is, the 'sexton' looked after the vestments and sacred vessels in a religious house, cathedral or the like. From the sixteenth century, however, his duties became much more basic, and the name became particularly associated with the man who rang the church bell and dug the graves. In this role he was commemorated, if not exactly immortalized, in Hood's punning lines from *Faithless Sally Brown* (1826):

His death, which happen'd in his berth,
  At forty-odd befell:
They went and told the sexton, and
  The sexton toll'd the bell.

shambles (scene of chaos or disorder)
As originally current in English, in the fifteenth century, the 'shambles' was a meat market, with the word the plural of 'shamble', a special kind of table or stall on which meat was placed for sale. From this sense, the word passed fairly naturally the following century to mean 'slaughterhouse'. And it was also in the sixteenth century that this sense in turn was transferred to mean 'scene of carnage'. Hence the modern 'shambles'. Around Britain traces of the original meat market remain in some towns where there is still a building or street called 'The Shambles' today (such as at York, Nottingham, Chesterfield, Chippenham and Devizes).

shampoo (wash the hair; clean a carpet)
The original sense of the verb 'shampoo' (itself from Hindi *cāpo*, imperative of the verb *cāpnā*, 'to press', 'to shampoo') was 'massage the limbs', this meaning being current in English from the eighteenth century (later, as applied to part of the routine of a Turkish bath, before it became obsolete in the twentieth century). Hence, in James Forbes' *Oriental Memoirs* (1814–15), this description (where 'she' is the subject's wife): 'She first champoes her husband, and fans him to repose; she then champoes the horse'. Hence, too, the meaning of the word in Dickens' *Dombey and Son* (1848), where we are told: 'Miss Pankey was shampooed every morning'. And even as late as 1898, the meaning was still related to massaging rather than hair washing: 'In Tahiti, too, a traveller, on entering a house, is always given a mat to lie on, and his weary limbs are shampooed whilst food is prepared for him' (Jean A. Owen, *Hawaii*). However, as a noun, 'shampoo' had also come to denote the familiar liquid hair washing preparation by the mid-nineteenth century, and the verb evolved almost simultaneously. Later, in the twentieth century, 'shampoo' came to denote a similar washing or detergent preparation for cleaning a carpet or some other surface.

shears (cutting or trimming instrument similar to a large pair of scissors)
The word is an old one, and in Old English actually was the normal word for 'scissors'. In Chaucer's *Canterbury Tales* (1386), thus, we can read in the Prologue to 'The Wife of Bath's Tale':

> How Sampson loste his heres,
> Slepynge, his lemman kitte it with hir
> sheres.

(That is: While Samson was asleep, his lover cut his hair with her scissors.) By about the fifteenth century, however, something like the modern shears began to emerge with the increasing need to cut cloth and shear sheep. Even so, as late as 1623, in *Brittain's Ida* (said to be written by Spenser but now attributed to Giles Fletcher), we find the line:

> His Nimph-like face ne're felt the nimble
> sheeres.

'Scissors' (originally spelt without the 'c') dates from the fourteenth century.

sheer (thin and fine, pure; precipitous)
In the sixteenth century, 'sheer' meant 'bright', 'shining', whether applied to light or water. Hence such place-names as Sheerness ('bright headland') in Kent, and towns and villages called Sherborne ('bright stream'), and also the sense of the word in Dante Gabriel Rossetti's poem *My Sister's Sleep* (1871):

> Without, there was a cold moon up,
> Of winter radiance sheer and thin.

But the meaning 'fine' as applied to fabrics (later familiar in 'sheer silk stockings') also dates from the sixteenth century, as does the sense 'utter' ('sheer bliss'). The rather unexpected meaning 'precipitous', 'vertical', as of a 'sheer cliff' or a 'sheer drop' arose only in the eighteenth century, however, and is first recorded in Wordsworth's poem *Hart-Leap Well* (1800):

> And climbing up the hill – (it was at
> least
> Four roods of sheer ascent).

sheet (bed linen, piece of paper, broad expanse)

The senses of the word developed in the order given here, although the Old English meaning was first basically 'broad piece of linen' before it became the 'sheet' of a bed in the thirteenth century. Both the other senses evolved in the sixteenth century. All meanings except the early Old English one are still current.

sherbet (sweet powder used for making fizzy drinks)
Through Turkish and Persian, the word is ultimately of Arabic origin, with its source in *sharbah*, 'drink'. When the word first became current in English, in the seventeenth century, it referred only to an oriental cold drink made of sweetened water and fruit juice, often cooled with snow. This not particularly exotic beverage, therefore, is the one referred to in Byron's poem *The Bride of Abydos* (1813), in lines similarly undistinguished:

> A cup too on the board was set
> That did not seem to hold sherbet.

However, it was in the nineteenth century that the familiar powder form of 'sherbet' evolved, and this is the prevailing sense today, although the word can also be used of a type of water ice, likewise of nineteenth-century vintage.

sherry (type of fortified wine)
Originally, in the sixteenth century, 'sherry' was the term for a still white wine made near the Spanish town of Xeres (now Jerez de la Frontera), near Cadiz. Hence the actual English word, and thus its meaning in the following interchange from Ben Jonson's play *Bartholomew Fayre* (1614): '*Bartholomew Cokes*. Sack? You said but e'en now it should be Sherry. *Puppet Jonas*. Why so it is; sherry, sherry, sherry'. Less than a hundred years later, however, the name came to apply to other Spanish wines of this type, and in succeeding centuries to 'sherries' from other parts of the world, such as 'Californian sherry', 'South African sherry' and even 'British sherry'. The wine featuring as 'sack' in many of Shakespeare's plays (and much loved by Falstaff) was a related dry white wine, but not 'sherry' itself. The nearest he gets to that is in *Henry IV*, Part 2 (1597), where Falstaff praises the

wine: 'A good sherris-sack hath a two-fold operation in it'.

shift (move, alter)
In old English, 'shift' meant merely 'arrange', a now obsolete sense, and it was not until the thirteenth century that the meaning 'change' emerged, with the further sense 'alter' (as of 'shifting' a position) arising a century later. However, as a noun, 'shift' did not evolve until the sixteenth century, when it meant 'expedient', 'subterfuge', with the meaning 'change of position' following only in the eighteenth century. The garment 'shift' belongs to the sixteenth century, though, and is thus an earlier specialized sense of 'change' since it was an undergarment worn by both men and women that was frequently changed. The women's garment was originally called a 'smock', but this was felt to be a somewhat 'indelicate' word, so was replaced by 'shift' in the seventeenth century, with the later 'chemise' mostly ousting the 'shift' in the nineteenth century for the same reason. And even though 'chemise' has now in turn been mainly superseded by 'slip', the 'shift' still exists as a term for a type of loosely fitting dress.

show (point out, make to be seen)
In its original Old English, the verb meant 'see', 'look at', 'examine'. The sense is not recorded later than about 1300, but occurs, for example, in the *Anglo-Saxon Gospels* (1000), where the familiar words from Luke 12:27, 'Consider the lilies how they grow', appear as: 'Sceawiath tha lilian hu hi wexath'. The modern meaning of 'show', however, arose in the twelfth century. It is difficult to see why there was a sense turnabout from 'see' to 'cause to be seen', especially as related verbs in other Germanic languages have kept the original sense; German *schauen*, for example, is 'see', 'look at', 'view'.

shrewd (cunning, astute)
Today, the word has a good sense, and to be 'shrewd' is to be sagacious and clever. Originally, however, the senses were all bad. In the fourteenth century, 'shrewd' meant 'wicked' as well as 'hurtful' or 'dangerous'. The latter meaning is used by

Shakespeare in *Richard II* (1593), when he makes Richard talk of men who 'lift shrewd steel against our golden crown'. In the sixteenth century, too, the adjective could mean 'naughty' of children, as again used by Shakespeare, this time in *Love's Labour's Lost* (1588), when Rosaline, referring to the powers of Cupid, says to Katherine:

> For he hath been five thousand years a
> boy,

and Katharine replies:

> Ay, and a shrewd unhappy gallows [i.e. rogue] too.

Despite this and other derogatory usages, it was also in the sixteenth century that the present favourable sense began to emerge, with the word as a whole thus doing a sort of reverse of '**artful**' (which see), progressing from bad to good.

shroud (burial garment)
The word has not always had its present gloomy, funereal associations. In Old English, it meant simply 'garment', and in the plural 'clothes'. 'Lo, here a shrowde for a shrewe', runs a line in a York mystery play of 1440, and as late as 1638, George Sandys, in one of his poetic paraphrases of books of the Old Testament (at this point, of Job 38:9), wrote without any apparent ambiguity:

> Swadled, as new-borne, in sable shrouds.

The modern meaning 'burial garment', 'winding sheet' developed only in the sixteenth century, and shortly after, the original sense became obsolete.

shunt (move a train from one line to another, divert)
In the thirteenth century, 'shunt' meant 'swerve', 'shrink away', 'hang back'. Its use can be seen in the strange sixteenth-century *Song of John Nobody*:

> Then I drew me down into a dale,
> wheras the dumb deer
> Did shiver for a shower, but I shunted
> from a freyke.

(That is: I avoided being a brave warrior.) This is the last recorded instance of the sense, which then became obsolete. In the eighteenth century, a dialect meaning of 'shunt' emerged, as 'shove', and clearly it was directly from this that the modern sense evolved a century later. The transference to figurative and extended senses happened almost immediately, such as 'shunting' money from one business to another, or diverting an electric current by 'shunting' it.

silly (foolish, unwise)

This adjective is well known for its remarkable sense shift over the centuries. It was originally spelt 'seely', and in the thirteenth century meant both 'happy' and 'blessed', 'holy'. The first of these senses occurs, for instance, in Thomas Usk's allegory *The Testament of Love* (1387–8): 'Then, say I, thou art blisful and fortunat sely, if thou knowe thy goodes that thou hast yet beloved'. In a response of a church primer of 1400, the meaning is 'blessed': 'Cely art thou, hooli virgyne marie, and worthiest al maner preisyng'. At the same time, 'seely' could mean 'innocent', 'helpless', in the sense of 'pitiable', and had a usage in expressing compassion for people and animals. Both meanings were still current in the seventeenth century, as in Richard Carew's *The Survey of Cornwall* (1602): 'The seely Gentlewomen, without regard of sexe or shame, were stripped from their apparrell to their verie smockes'. (For this last word, see **shift**.) In the Douai Bible of 1609, too, the second half of Isaiah 10:30 is rendered: 'Attend Laisa, seelie poore Anathoth' (Authorized Version of 1611: 'Cause it to be heard unto Laish, O poor Anathoth'). (The original Latin adjective was *paupercula*, 'poor little'.) A final sense of 'seely', likewise dating from the thirteenth century, was 'insignificant', 'poor', 'trifling'. An example of this can be found, for instance, in Shakespeare's *The Rape of Lucrece* (1593), where, near the end of the long poem, we read of Brutus that:

He with the Romans was esteemed so
As silly-jeering idiots are with kings,
For sportive words and uttering
    foolish things.

The regular spelling 'silly' arose in the fifteenth century, when the middle vowel sound changed from a long 'ee' to a short 'i'. It is in this familiar form that some contemporary texts have the most incongruous look, from the point of view of the modern meaning. Arthur Golding's translation (1587) of de Mornay's *Woorke concerning the Trewnesse of the Christian Religion*, for example, contains the statement that Christ: ' . . . leaueth neither children nor kinsfolk behind him to vphold his silly kingdome' [i.e. his feeble one], and the same sense comes more recently in the poem *Sighs & Grones* found in George Herbert's collection of poems *The Temple* (1633), which has the words:

Thou onely art
The mightie God, but I a sillie worm.

In Shakespeare's *Two Gentlemen of Verona* (1591), the sense is more 'helpless', 'defenceless', when Valentine says to one of the Outlaws:

I take your offer and will live with you,
Provided that you do no outrages
On silly women, or poor passengers.

If there is a link between these usages and the modern meaning 'stupid', it is perhaps to be found in such more or less stock expressions as 'silly sheep' or even 'silly old man' (or 'you silly thing'), where the sense of foolishness is to some extent blended with compassion. Otherwise, it can be generally stated that the modern understanding of the word really developed from the sixteenth century, and there is no doubt that Shakespeare was using the adjective in the present-day way when in *A Midsummer Night's Dream* (1590) he allows Hippolyta to comment on the performance of 'Pyramus and Thisbe' by Bottom and his friends: 'This is the silliest stuff that ever I heard'.

singsong (session of group singing)

When first current in English, in the seventeenth century, a 'singsong' was not a singing session but a jingling or monotonous ballad, a poem that had more musical than poetical content. Thus, in the Prologue to his *Satires of Dr. Donne Versified* (1735), Pope wrote that he had never:

. . . daggled thro' the town,
To fetch and carry sing-song up and
    down,

and Madame d'Arblay (Fanny Burney) in a letter of 19 November 1775 said she recommended 'the sing-song and prettiness of Waller and Cowley'. The modern meaning followed in the eighteenth century, and the 'singsong' that is a monotonous 'up and down' tone of voice came in the nineteenth.

sire (father of a horse)
The original use of 'sire' was the familiar but now obsolete form of address or 'lordly' title. The vocative use was especially common when addressing a king, with 'Sire' now replaced by 'Your Majesty'. Thus, in the fourteenth-century verse romance *King Alisaunder* (about Alexander the Great) come the lines:

A knyght com sone rennyng,
And saide, 'Sire, up on hast!'.

(That is: A knight soon came running and said, 'Your Majesty, make haste!') 'Sire' was also the early form of 'Sir' as 'Sire John' or 'Sire William'. In the thirteenth century, 'sire' became a word for a father, and this usage gained popularity in subsequent years with a number of poets, from Milton onwards. So Dryden, in his translation (1697) of Virgil's *Georgics,* has the lines:

Nor be with harmful Parsimony won
To follow what our homely Sires have
    done,

Cowper, in *his* translation (1791) of Homer's *Iliad,* has the line:

The sceptre of his sires he took,

and Scott, in *The Lord of the Isles* (1814), wrote:

In distant ages, sire to son
Shall tell thy tale of freedom won.

There are almost certainly several poets since who have used the word in this way. It was in the sixteenth century, however, that 'sire' came to acquire its only standard sense today, as the male parent of a horse, presumably to match the already existing 'dam' as the word for the female parent.

siren (warning or other signal in the form of a horn, hooter or the like)
This is only the best known sense, of course.

Over the years, three separate meanings for 'siren' have been recorded at intervals of approximately two hundred years. First, in the fourteenth century, the word gained English use as the name of the mythological female monsters whose voices lured sailors to their destruction (as notably in Homer's *Odyssey*). John de Trevisa refers to them in his translation (1387) of Ranulf Higden's *Polychronicon:* 'The thre Sirenes, that were half maydens, half foules, and hadde wynges and clawes'. (In fact in many early texts the word was used as if it meant 'mermaid', although the two sea creatures are of differing origins and mermaids do not properly belong to classical mythology. In any case, they were 'half woman, half fish', not as described by de Trevisa.) From the sixteenth century, 'siren' was the word used to apply to a woman who sang sweetly or alluringly, or who simply enticed, as the mythological maidens did. This usage is first recorded in Shakespeare's *Comedy of Errors* (1590), where Antipholus of Syracuse addresses Luciana in rhyme:

O! train me not, sweet mermaid, with
    thy note,
  To drown me in thy sister flood of
    tears:
Sing, siren, for thyself, and I will dote:
  Spread o'er the silver waves thy
    golden hairs.

The modern mechanical siren, forerunner of the factory hooter and air raid siren, came into being in 1819, when the French engineer Charles Cagniard de la Tour devised an acoustical instrument which could produce musical tones and count the vibrations in a particular note. (In 1820, the *Annual Register* reported of this 'Syren, a new Acoustical Instrument': 'In consequence of this property of being sonorous in the water the instrument has been called the Syren'.) The siren on steamships that gave warnings of fog and the like followed later in the same century, and electric sirens were developed in the twentieth.

skirt (women's garment worn from the waist; margin, edge)
It might be thought that the 'margin' or 'edge' sense of the word came first, to denote what was perhaps originally the 'edge' or

'border' of a dress or robe. But this is not the case, and the garment was called by this term as early as the thirteenth century, although at first it was not a separate piece of clothing but the lower half of a dress. Its earliest mention comes in the *Cursor Mundi:*

Sco lift hir skirt wiv-vten scurn,
And bar-fote wode sco that burn.

(That is: She lifted her skirt without any bashfulness and waded barefoot over the stream.) The meaning 'border', 'edge' emerged only in the fifteenth century. The Old English word *scyrte* actually meant 'shirt', rather than 'skirt', as did the Old Norse *skyrta* that directly gave the latter word. The shift of sense (sense of 'shift', as it were) has not been satisfactorily explained.

sky ('vault of heaven')
The Old Norse word *skȳ* that gave the English word meant 'cloud', and this was the original meaning in English also for some time from the thirteenth century. (Compare **welkin,** which also meant 'cloud' before it meant 'sky', as in the extract below.) Here is the word in the earliest record we have of it, the *Bestiary* of 1220:

Up he teth [i.e. goes],
til that he the heuene seth [sees],
thurgh skies sexe and seuene
til he cumeth to heuene.

And here is 'sky' again, two hundred years later, in John Lydgate's *Reson and Sensuallyte* (that is, the 'upper' reasoning of the mind and the 'lower' nature of the senses) (1407):

As sterris in the frosty nyght,
Whanne walkne [i.e. welkin] is most
    bryght,
With-oute cloude or any skye.

The usage did not last beyond the sixteenth century, even in poetry, and the modern meaning of the word, which dates from only a little later (in the *Cursor Mundi*) was the one to predominate.

slang (colloquial language)
As first used, in the eighteenth century, 'slang' meant 'jargon', 'cant', from which it is now properly distinguished. This meant not only 'coarse' vocabulary but specialized words of a particular group or profession.

Jeremy Bentham, in his *Rationale of Judicial Evidence* (1802–12), wrote about 'scraps of written lawyer's slang', and George Eliot, in *Middlemarch* (1872), makes the interesting observation: 'Correct English is the slang of prigs who write history and essays. And the strongest slang of all is the slang of poets'. Today, we would call this 'jargon' or at least 'idiom'. The present sense of 'slang', as 'nonstandard' (some say) colloquial language, arose in the nineteenth century, when in 1818 John Keble wrote of his students at Oxford: 'Two of the best come to me as a peculiar grinder (I must have a little slang)' (Sir John T. Coleridge, *Memoir of John Keble,* 1869).

sleuth (detective)
In the twelfth century, 'sleuth' meant 'trail', 'track'. Here is the word (misspelt) in two lines from the fourteenth-century *Cursor Mundi:*

In that way sal thou find forsoth
Thi moders and mine our bather slogh
    [correctly, 'sloth'].

(That is: On that road you will indeed find the trail of both your mother and mine). In the fifteenth century, 'sleuth' came to be used as a shortening of 'sleuthhound', that is, a species of bloodhound that was used for tracking down game or tracing the trail of fugitives, especially in Scotland. Finally, the word became adopted in the nineteenth century for a detective, who carried out the duties of a 'sleuthhound' at a more sophisticated level.

slipshod (untidy, careless, slovenly)
The literal meaning of the word is 'wearing slippers', or 'wearing shoes that slip because they are too big', and this was the sense of 'slipshod' in the sixteenth century. The word comes in a translation (1682) of Boileau's *Le Lutrin:*

Another durst not stay to tye his shooes,
But slip-sho'd hobbl'd, lest he Breakfast
    loose [i.e. lose].

The transference to the present-day meaning came about in the eighteenth century.

slug (shell-less mollusc resembling a snail)
It seems remarkable that the word in its present popular sense emerged only in the eighteenth century. Originally, in the fifteenth century, a 'slug' was simply another way of saying a 'sluggard'. Here it is in Sir Edward Hoby's *A Curry-Combe for a Coxe-Combe* (1615): 'Hee that is lumpish at his meales, will proue but a slug in his more serious affaires'. And even in the nineteenth century, in William Tennant's poem, *Anster Fair* (1812):

> For who like arrant slugs can keep their heads
> In contact with their pillows now unstirr'd?

In the sixteenth century, the sense progressed to apply to a slow-moving ship, a sailing vessel that moved sluggishly through the water. The *Philosophical Transactions of the Royal Society* reported in 1687 on such ships: 'They will certainly be Sluggs, not near so good Sailers as Ships made of Timber fell'd later in the Year'. Finally, as mentioned, the term passed to the slimy mollusc. But there were obviously slugs before the eighteenth century: what were they called then? The answer is simple, they were. . . snails!

sly (cunning, furtive)
As originally used and understood in the twelfth century, 'sly' meant 'skilled', 'clever' (compare **artful, crafty** and **cunning,** for example), and the adjective was quite often coupled with a synonym, such as 'wise and sly' or 'quaint and sly' (with '**quaint**', which see, here meaning 'skilled' also). In the following lines from Bishop Grosseteste's *Castel off Loue* (1320), 'sly' is coupled with 'crafty' itself:

> So slye and crafty they shull byn alle,
> That they shull do all thyng that in here hert doth falle.

But the modern 'bad' sense of the word appears early, and was the one to prevail, so that the 'clever' meaning, apart from one or two poetic usages, was virtually extinct by the end of the fifteenth century.

smoulder (burn and smoke without flame)
Originally, in the fourteenth century, to

'smoulder' was to 'smother'. Caxton's translation (1489) *The Book of Fayttes of Armes and of Chyualrye* has the sentence: 'The hete of the soone was so brennynge hoot [i.e. burning hot] that almost hyt smoldred the rommayns'. The modern meaning then evolved in the sixteenth century. However, for some reason the verb then fell out of use, except as the poetic word 'smouldering', until it was revived by Scott in the nineteenth century. It occurs in *The Lady of the Lake* (1810), which tells of a feud that still 'Smoulders in Roderick's breast', and also, in a similar figurative use, in *The Lord of the Isles* (1814):

> He wak'd a spark, that, long suppress'd,
> Had smoulder'd in Lord Ronald's breast.

After this, the verb resumed its literal sense. It is interesting that in his *Dictionary* of 1755, Johnson, referring to the only form 'smouldering' then current, commented on it: 'This word seems a participle; but I know not whether the verb *smoulder* be in use'.

smug (self-satisfied, complacent)
As originally used in the sixteenth century, 'smug' was a more complimentary adjective than it is now, meaning 'trim and neat', 'smooth', 'sleek'. It could apply to both males and females, or to their faces, or to objects. In *His Farewell to Militarie Profession* (1581), Barnaby Rich wrote that: 'The Duke [. . .] perceiuyng him to be a proper smogue yong man, gaue hym entertainment', while John Lyly's *Midas* (1592) has two apparently complimentary lines telling of:

> Cross-gartred Swaines, & Dairie girles,
> With faces smug, and round as Pearles.

Surely, too, in Shakespeare's *Henry IV*, Part 1 (1596), Hotspur uses the word in a favourable sense when he says:

> I'll have the current in this place damm'd up,
> And here the smug and silver Trent shall run
> In a new channel, fair and evenly.

The sense seems to have deteriorated after about the mid-seventeenth century, down to which time it was quite normal to speak of an attractive girl, for example, as a 'good smug lass'.

snack (light refreshment)
The now rather attractive word began its life in English in the fifteenth century as a dialect term for a dog bite! Even as late as 1896 the sense is still found in some texts: 'The bitch overtook the hare and gave a snack at its hinder parts' (Adam Lilburn, *The Borderer*). From this, the meaning progressed in the seventeenth century to 'share', 'portion', or even 'drop of something to drink'. The latter sense also occurs in some nineteenth-century writings, as in Kingsley's *The Saint's Tragedy* (1848):

And take his snack of brandy for
    digestion.

Finally, the present meaning appeared in the eighteenth century.

snob ('superior' or 'stuck-up' person)
In the eighteenth century, 'snob' had two somewhat specialized senses. It was a dialect term for a shoemaker or cobbler on the one hand, and a university slang word (at Cambridge) for a townsman. As late as 1880 the November number of *Fraser's Magazine* wrote, with regard to the shoemaker: 'Even among the snobs the custom of the trade is against giving credit', while the *Saturday Review* of September 1865 declared: 'Happily the annals of Oxford present no instance of a "snob" murdered in the streets'. From this, the sense expanded to denote a 'lower class' person generally, one who had no pretensions to rank or refinement. This usage evolved in the nineteenth century. As the *Lincoln Herald* of 22 July 1831 reported: 'The nobs have lost their dirty seats – the honest snobs have got 'em'. It was Thackeray, however, who gave the word prominence and its present-day veneer of false superiority or pretentiousness to 'class'. He used the word, for example, in *The Irish Sketch-Book* (1843), where he writes of a snob displaying his character by 'swaggering and showing off in his coarse dull stupid way'. But it was in his collection of papers entitled *The Snobs of England, by One of Themselves*, published in *Punch* in 1846–7, that he properly established the term in its current meaning. (His

papers were republished in 1848 as *The Book of Snobs*.) By 'positive' snobs, he writes, he means 'such persons as are Snobs everywhere [. . .] being by nature endowed with Snobbishness', and 'He who meanly admires mean things is a Snob'. Despite such lavish promotion of the word, its ultimate origin is still unknown.

socket (hole or opening made or intended to hold something inserted into it)
The word is not a 'little sock' in origin, as if the object inserted were a 'foot', but is actually a 'little ploughshare', as a diminutive of Old French *soc* having this meaning. In English, a 'socket' was at first, in the thirteenth century, a term for the head of a spear or lance that resembled the tip of a ploughshare. In *Arthur and Merlin* (1330), we thus read how:

Gaheriet mett the douke Fannel
With a launce, the soket of stiel,

and the sense can be found as late as the sixteenth century in the following gory extract from William Stewart's verse translation (1535) of Boethius' Latin history of Scotland (under the title *The Buik of the Croniclis of Scotland*):

Than with the speir [. . .]
He hit the king richt in at the e [i.e. eye],
The scharpe sokkat syne [then] throw
    his heid is gone.

The modern meaning of 'socket' dates from the fifteenth century, and the old sense became obsolete shortly after.

sole (only, exclusive)
As current in the fourteenth century, 'sole' in English meant specifically 'single', 'unmarried'. The sense is first recorded in Chaucer's *Canterbury Tales* (1386), where in 'The Merchant's Tale' he speaks of an widowed woman being:

Soul as the turtil that lost hath hir make
    [i.e. mate].

William Lambarde's *A Perambulation of Kent* (1576), too, tells how: 'King Edward the Confessor (being otherwise of himself disposed to haue liued sole) tooke unto his wife Edgitha'. But the word was used more frequently of women than men, and still survives (just) in the legal term 'feme sole' for a single woman (whether unmarried, divorced or widowed, or one separated from her husband and owning her own property). In the fifteenth century, the meaning was extended to 'solitary', 'alone', a now obsolete usage. 'Whan the kynge hath goon so ferre that alle his men he lost, than he is sole', wrote Caxton in *The Game and the Playe of the Chesse* (1474), and in *Manfred* (1817) Byron has the line:

I should be sole in this sweet solitude.

But the other meaning that emerged in the fifteenth century, that of 'one and only', is still current, as is the sense of 'exclusive' that followed a hundred years later (as in 'for your sole use').

solicit (approach with a request)
The verb has a number of now obsolete meanings. In the fifteenth century, when it first became current in English, 'solicit' could mean both 'disturb' and 'manage' (in the sense of running a business and the like). The first of these comes in the earliest English translation (1450) of *De imitatione Christi:* 'If it were so with me, mannys drede shuld not so solicite me, ner the dartes of wordes shuld not meve me [i.e. perturb me]'. The same sense is given to the word in Edward Young's verse tragedy *The Revenge* (1721):

How good in you, my lord, whom
     nations cares
Solicit, and a world in arms obeys!

The second sense can be found, for example, in Clarendon's *History* (1647): 'A Committee was come from the Parliament in Ireland, to solicite Matters concerning that Kingdom'. A further, related meaning at this time, also now obsolete, was 'urge', 'plead'. An example of this comes in Shakespeare's *Twelfth Night* (1601), where Olivia says to Viola (the latter disguised as Cesario):

But, would you undertake another suit,
I had rather hear you to solicit that
Than music from the spheres.

The original sense 'disturb' just mentioned went on to give a meaning 'entreat', 'petition' in the sixteenth century. This usage is not really obsolete, but is somewhat stilted, or at least formal (as 'soliciting the government for funds'). It is, however, the sense that in the eighteenth century produced the meaning 'importune for sex', which is still current. The sense of 'manage', in its turn, progressed to giving a meaning 'sue for' in the sixteenth century (as in 'soliciting a favour' or 'soliciting an interview'), and it is this sense development that led to the modern 'solicitor' who acts as a legal agent.

soluble (able to be dissolved; solvable)
The original meaning of the word, in the fourteenth century, was a medical one, 'not suffering from constipation'. 'Dry figges and old make the bodye soluble', wrote Sir Thomas Elyot in *The Castel of Helth* (1539). This sense, though a handy opposite of 'constipated' ('Take Solvit regularly to stay soluble'), became obsolete in the nineteenth century. The two current meanings 'able to be dissolved' and 'solvable' (as in a 'soluble' problem) evolved respectively in the fifteenth and eighteenth centuries.

sonata (musical composition for one or two instruments in three or four movements)
The term was originally used, in the seventeenth century, to denote an instrumental work, by contrast with a 'cantata', which was a musical work for voices. This usage soon became obsolete, however, and the sense settled to the definition above, with the word mainly applied, however, to a work for piano or violin. Like 'symphony', 'concerto' and to a lesser extent 'quartet', 'sonata' frequently features in the nickname of a musical work, such as Purcell's 'Golden Sonata', Beethoven's 'Kreutzer Sonata' and 'Moonlight Sonata', and Mozart's 'Trumpet Sonata' (for piano, not trumpet).

soothe (calm, comfort, allay)
The word is related to 'soothsayer', the predictor of the future, and in Old English 'soothe' meant 'prove to be true' (compare the archaic expression 'in sooth' or the word 'forsooth'). This meaning was recorded as recently as the sixteenth century (although no later), in Nicholas Trotte's introduction (1588) to Thomas Hughes' *The Misfortunes of Arthur:*

They hold the grounds which time & vse
hath sooth'd
(Though shallow sense conceiue them as
deceits).

In the sixteenth century, 'soothe' gained a number of additional senses, such as 'declare to be true', 'flatter by agreeing', 'gloss over' and 'encourage'. All of these are now obsolete, and the two modern meanings, 'calm' and 'allay', emerged respectively in the seventeenth and eighteenth centuries.

soppy (wet, soggy; sloppily sentimental)
The literal sense of the word is 'full of sops', and this is the first recorded meaning found in English, in the seventeenth century, in Randle Cotgrave's *A Dictionarie of the French and English Tongues* (1611), where he defines the French *offeux* as: 'Soppie; or full of lumpes, or gobbets'. The current meanings of 'soppy', however, as defined above, both date respectively from the nineteenth and twentieth centuries. The former comes in Dickens' *David Copperfield* (1850), where the reference is to Yarmouth: 'It looked rather spongey and soppy, I thought, as I carried my eye over the great dull waste'.

spanner (implement for turning a nut)
In the seventeenth century, a 'spanner' was a tool for winding up the spring in a wheel-lock gun. The word was imported from German, where the verb *spannen* means 'strain', 'stretch', 'tighten'. In the eighteenth century, this sense was extended to an implement that could turn or tighten any nut or bolt-head.

spar (box using light or merely gesturing blows, as in training)
In the fifteenth century, to 'spar' was to strike out or spring out rapidly, either with the feet or a weapon. The word was particularly used of cocks in a 'sparring' contest, when they strike out or fight with their feet or spurs. From this, the sense passed in the eighteenth century to similar movements or gestures made by boxers. Johnson defined the verb in his *Dictionary* (1755) as: 'to fight with prelusive strokes'.

specious (false, deceptively attractive, superficially genuine)

The word has gone from a good sense to a bad over the years. Its ultimate origin lies in Latin *speciosus*, 'beautiful', 'plausible', and in the fourteenth century this was more or less what 'specious' meant. The sense was current down to at least the nineteenth century, and applied to people and things, and in particular to birds and flowers. 'Specyous & beautyfull is he aboue all the chylder of men', says *The Pilgrimage of Perfection* (1526), and the Rhemish New Testament (1582) tells in Acts 3:10 how the lame man that was later healed was: 'He which sate for almes at the Specious gate of the temple' (Authorized Version of 1611: 'He which sat for alms at the Beautiful gate of the temple'). As for the birds and the bees, the *Philosophical Transactions of the Royal Society* noted in 1688 that: 'There be other sorts of Goldfinches variegated with red, orange and yellow Feathers, very specious and beautiful', and in his contribution to the *Memoir and Correspondence of Sir J.E. Smith* (1832), Samuel Goodenough, Bishop of Carlisle, reports on: 'Bees, several new ones, one very specious indeed'. The modern sense of the word arose in the seventeenth century.

spencer (man's short fitted jacket or coat; woman's knitted vest)
The family name has produced several items or styles of clothing. The earliest 'spencer' was the eighteenth-century wig so named. Here it is in a couple of lines from a contemporary popular song, taken from *Satirical Songs and Poems on Costume from the 13th to the 19th Century*, published by the Percy Society in 1849:

At us the fribbles may strut and look big,
In their spencers, bobs, and ramelies.

('Fribbles' are frivolous fellows; 'bobs' and 'ramelies' are also types of wig, the latter named after Ramillies in Belgium, where the Duke of Marlborough won his victory in 1706.) This 'spencer' was probably named after Charles Spencer, the third Earl of Sunderland (1674–1722), who wore such a wig. The second 'spencer' to appear was the short double-breasted overcoat worn by men in the late eighteenth century and early nineteenth. Dickens features one in *Bleak House* (1853): 'A very respectable old gentleman, [. . .] dressed in a black spencer and gaiters and a broad-brimmed hat'. This garment was named after George John Spencer, second Earl Spencer (1758–1834), well known for wearing this type of coat. Next came the nineteenth-century 'spencers', including the close-fitting jacket or bodice worn by women and children in the early part of the century (and later revived in a modified form), a man's coat (as defined above), and a form of life-belt. The women's garment also appears in Dickens, this time in *Sketches by Boz* (1835–7), where one can read how: 'There was considerable talking among the females in the spencers'. This 'spencer' was an evolution of the man's overcoat, so was named after the same Spencer, as was the shorter man's jacket or coat. The garment was worn by Stevenson on his travels, as he records in *Travels with a Donkey in the Cevennes* (1879): 'My travelling wear of country velveteen, pilot-coat, and knitted spencer'. The life-belt seems to have been named after its inventor, a Mr Knight Spencer, who lived in the early nineteenth century. It is described in an issue of the *Philological Magazine* for 1803, in an article entitled: 'Account of the Marine Spencer for the Preservation of Lives in Cases of Shipwreck'. (Yet another 'spencer' was the American repeating rifle, the 'Spencer carbine', named after its inventor, Christopher Miner Spencer.) Of all these, the man's coat still certainly exists, and there may well be some women still wearing the 'spencer' that was originally a top garment and is now a nether one.

spick and span (trim and neat and tidy)
The phrase is really short for 'spick and span new', and 'brand new' was what it originally meant in the seventeenth century. In his *Diary* entry for 15 November 1665, Pepys mentions: 'My Lady Batten walking through the dirty lane with new spick and span white shoes', and in a letter written in 1793, Cowper relates: 'I have built one summer-house already, with the boards of my old study, and am building another spick and span, as they say'. The modern meaning of the phrase arose in the nineteenth century.

spill (cause a liquid to overflow or drop)
Old English *spillan* meant 'kill', 'destroy', 'ruin', and the verb was widely current from the fourteenth to the sixteenth century. Thus in Robert Manning of Brunne's *The Story of England* (1330) come the lines:

> Androcheus saw his felon wille,
> That the kyng thoughte hym to spille,

and John Skelton's poem *Now Synge We* (1529) has a paraphrase of Christ's words:

> Thus was I spylt,
> Man, for thy gylte,
> And not for myne.

Even in the nineteenth century the sense was still in use, as in William Morris's poem *The Earthly Paradise* (1868-70):

> Then if mine old line he must spill
> There let God save him if He will.

From this, the sense developed specifically to 'spill blood' in the twelfth century and to its modern common meaning two hundred years later.

spinster (unmarried woman)
As the word suggests even today, its original meaning was 'spinning woman', 'female spinner'. The sense is first recorded in Langland's *Piers Plowman* (1362):

> And my wyf at Westmunstre that
> wollene cloth made,
> Spak to the spinsters for to spinne hit
> softe.

In his translation (1600) of Leo's *Geographical Historie of Africa*, John Pory wrote: 'Their women are excellent spinsters, whereby they are saide to gaine more than the men of the towne', and even in the twentieth century, it was possible to read of a certain young lady that 'she would be a famous spinster and needlewoman' (*Contemporary Review*, 31 July, 1910). This particular designation was frequently added to the names of women, in order to give their occupation, for example in a record of 1380: 'Alicia Moris Spynnestere', and in later times: 'Joan Lambe, widow of London, spynster' (1564), 'Elizabeth Harris of London, Spinster' (*London Gazette*, 1711), and rather more artificially, in Goldsmith's *She Stoops to Conquer* (1773): 'Constantia

Neville, spinster, of no place at all'. For whatever reason, many 'spinsters' (in this literal sense) never married, which explains the transference of the word to its modern usage, and from the seventeenth century it has been the legal designation of an unmarried woman. Popularly, too, the word has applied from the same date to an 'old maid', who probably never will marry. 'Providence is wonderfully kind to plain little spinsters with a knack of making themselves useful', wrote Miss Mary Braddon (actually Mrs Maxwell) in her novel *Mount Royal* (1882).

spire (steeple)
In Old English, the word meant 'stalk', 'stem', with this sense still in poetic use in the nineteenth century, as in Shelley's *Alastor* (1815):

> Tall spires of windlestrae [i.e. withered grass]
> Threw their thin shadows down the rugged slope.

In the thirteenth century 'spire' came to mean 'reeds', 'rushes', and was the word used by Wyclif in his Bible translation of 1382 to render Exodus 2:3, where the 'daughter of Levi': 'puttide hym [i.e. Moses] forth in a place of spier of the brenke of the flood' (Authorized Version of 1611: 'laid it in the flags by the river's brink'). In the fourteenth century, 'spire' progressed to mean 'shoot', 'sprout' (today more often in the spelling 'spear'), and finally acquired its 'steeple' sense by analogy in the sixteenth century, when it is first recorded in Thomas Lodge's *Wits Miserie and Worlds Madnesse* (1596): 'His beard is cut like the spier of Grantham steeple'.

split (divide forcibly, tear apart, separate)
In its earliest usage, in the sixteenth century, the verb refers exclusively to a ship breaking up on rocks. The sense soon extended to general use however. The first records we have of both uses are in Shakespeare. In *The Comedy of Errors* (1590), Aegeon says:

> Our helpful ship was splitted in the midst,

and in *Henry VI*, Part 3 (1593), the wounded Clifford says, as his last lines before fainting:

> Come, York and Richard, Warwick and the rest;
> I stabb'd your fathers' bosoms, split my breast.

spring (first season of the year)
The original English word for the season was 'lent' (see **Lent**), and this was replaced by 'spring' only in the sixteenth century. It is first recorded in *Tottel's Miscellany* (1547), by Henry Howard, Earl (by courtesy only) of Surrey: 'Description of Spring, wherin eche thing renewes, saue onelie the louer'. The earlier use of the word was thus to describe a time 'wherein eche thing renewes', that is, when things rise or begin, like young plants, and the source (in more senses than one) of the original Old English word is the sense 'place of rising', 'place where stream begins', with this basic use of 'spring' still current, of course. The device known as a 'spring' (typically, a length of coiled metal) also derives from this origin, since it 'rises with strength', as a stream does, as young plants do, and even as the season does generally. However, the sense arose earlier than the season, in the fifteenth century.

sprite (kind of playful graceful fairy)
The word is simply a variation of 'spirit', and early records of 'sprite' show it to mean 'spirit' in a number of different senses. Here it is, for example, used to express a familiar proverb in the fourteenth-century *Cursor Mundi* (for the origin, see Matthew 26:41):

> Thof the spreit ai redi be
> The flesche be fus to plight [i.e. ready to sin].

Both Tindale and Coverdale, too, used 'sprite' in their respective Bible translations of 1526 and 1535, with the word today appearing as 'spirit'. Even poets of much more recent times use 'sprite' in the 'spirit' sense, as in Gray's ode *The Descent of Odin* (1761):

> Who thus afflicts my troubled sprite?

However, the word is also recorded in the meaning 'fairy' from the fifteenth century, and this is the sense in which 'sprite' is understood today, if it is used at all.

stable (building housing horses)
Formerly, a 'stable' also housed cattle (compare modern French *étable*, 'cowshed', 'cattle stall'), and even in the Bible the word is used for a building not intended specifically for horses: 'And I will make Rabbah a stable for camels' (Ezekiel 25:5). However, the sense soon settled in English from the thirteenth century to its present association with horses only.

stage (period, step; raised platform; platform where play is acted in a theatre)
In its earliest senses in English, in the thirteenth century, 'stage' meant either 'storey', 'floor' (compare modern French *étage* as the standard word for this) or 'station', 'position', especially with regard to an ascending series. The meaning 'storey' was used by Wyclif in his Bible translation of 1382 to render Acts 20:9 'He ledd by sleep fel down fro the thridde stage' (Authorized Version of 1611: 'He sunk down with sleep, and fell down from the third loft'). The present meaning of 'raised platform' developed in the fourteenth century from the second of these, and in turn gave the acting 'stage' in the fifteenth century, in plenty of time for Shakespeare to let Jaques make his famous 'All the world's a stage' speech in *As You Like It* (1600).

stair (step on a staircase)
In Old English, 'stair' meant a whole flight of steps, not simply a single one. This sense is found in literature down to the present day, and there are still some Scots who talk of going 'up the stair' or 'down the stair' where most people would now say 'upstairs' or 'downstairs'. The first narrowing of the sense was to apply it to a single flight of steps, as noted by Johnson in his *Dictionary* of 1755: 'Stair was anciently used for the whole order of steps; but *stair* now, if it be used at all, signifies, as in Milton, only one flight of steps'. Finally, from the sixteenth century (fourteenth, when used in the plural), 'stair' came to apply to a single step.

stale (of drink: 'flat' and tasteless; of food: old, musty-smelling and hard)
As originally applied in the fourteenth century to wine, ale, mead and the like, 'stale' meant 'old and strong', since it implied that the liquor had stood long enough to clear. Hence the adjective had a favourable association, and 'good and stale' was a frequent term of approval for strong drink, and 'stale beer' was similarly recommendatory down to the eighteenth century. 'I daily live in a very comfortable Affluence of Wine, Stale Beer, Hungary Water [i.e. oil of rosemary distilled with alcohol], Beef, Books, and Marrow-Bones', declared Addison in 1709 in the *Tatler*. The modern meaning of 'stale' thus emerged only in the sixteenth century, as applied equally to food, drink, immaterial things (such as news and jokes) and people. Only the last of these is no longer current. A 'stale' person was someone past his or her prime, especially an 'old maid' who is unlikely to marry. In Thomas J. Hogg's *The Life of Shelley* (1858), he relates: 'I found only two stale women; a stale middle-aged woman who acted as waiter and chambermaid, and an older and still staler woman, the landlady'.

stark (absolute, sheer; barren, desolate)
The original Old English sense of 'stark' (*stearc*) was both 'hard', 'unyielding' and 'violent', 'severe'. 'The hungre was so grete, & the cold so stark', wrote Robert Manning of Brunne, in *The Story of England* (1330), and as late as the nineteenth century, Tennyson wrote in his drama *Harold* (1876):

> For he is only debonair to those
> That follow where he leads, but stark as death
> To those that cross him.

These senses are now obsolete, and the current meanings evolved only from the fourteenth century. 'Stark naked' dates from the sixteenth century, but it is an alteration of 'start naked', which is recorded as early as the thirteenth century (deriving from 'start', the old word for 'tail').

starve (die of hunger)
Old English *steorfan*, which gave the modern word, meant 'die' generally (compare modern German *sterben*). In *Troilus and Criseyde* (1374), Chaucer thus wrote how Christ:

Vpon a cros oure soules for to beye
First starf, and ros, and sit yn heuene a-
boue.

This sense became obsolete in the eighteenth century, however, and the modern
meaning, first recorded in the sixteenth
century, was the one that prevailed.

stationer (shopkeeper who sells stationery,
books, periodicals etc.)
The original 'stationers' of the fourteenth
century were those booksellers who had a
regular 'station' or shop at a university,
unlike most booksellers, who were itinerant
vendors (in modern terms, 'travelling
salesmen'). The *Rolls of Parliament* for
1393–4 thus refer to ones at Cambridge as:
'Stationers & Bokebynders del dit Univ-
ersite'. From the sixteenth century, too,
'stationer' came to be a term for a bookseller
who was also a publisher, with this sense
current until the eighteenth century. Meanwhile, the 'stationer' as understood today
had become established from the seventeenth century, when shopkeepers first
began to specialize in selling the 'stock in
trade' of a bookseller (paper, pens, ink and
the like) which the bookseller had formerly
sold himself. Because of this, a new term
was needed for the writing materials that he
sold, and this emerged in the eighteenth
century as (fairly obviously) 'stationery'.

steed (horse, especially one used for
riding)
In Old English, 'steed' was the standard
word for 'stallion'. In about the twelfth
century the word came to apply in
particular to a highly spirited horse (which
a stallion or stud horse would often be
anyway), and especially one that was used
as a battle horse or that was ridden in tournaments and pageants. (The word at this
time for an 'ordinary' riding horse was
'palfrey'.) From the early seventeenth
century, however, 'steed' was simply a word
for a riding horse in general, moreoever, one
with poetic or 'grand' overtones. But this
last sense development had not yet occurred
in Shakespeare's day, so that any 'steeds'
he mentions are ones ridden in battles or
tournaments, such as the one referred to by
the Duke of York in *Richard II* (1593), and
ridden by Bolingbroke:

Mounted upon a hot and fiery steed.

(In *Richard III*, however, the defeated king
did not offer to give his kingdom for a
'steed': he simply wanted a horse, *any*
horse.) The word retains today its poetic
or humorously pompous connotation ('my
trusty steed' may even not be a real horse
at all, but simply a bicycle).

steeplechase (horserace over jumps, as
distinct from a 'flat' race)
Originally, in the eighteenth century, a
'steeplechase' was a horserace across
country (and so across hedges, ditches and
the like) towards the steeple of a church,
which made a convenient landmark as a
winning post. In the nineteenth century, the
term came to apply to an artificially laid
out course, and the race run on it, with the
obstacles of the cross-country race becoming
the 'fences' or 'jumps' of the planned course.
The nearest modern equivalent to the original 'steeplechase' is thus the so called
'point-to-point'. A local Leicestershire
legend claims that the original steeple is the
one specially built on Lubenham Manor,
near Market Harborough, so that members
of the district hunt had a landmark to make
for when chasing across country.

stickler (person who is fussy or insists on
correct observance etc.)
In the sixteenth century, a 'stickler' was an
umpire or the settler of a dispute, literally
someone who 'stickled'. The word could
apply in a sporting sense or even a religious
one, as in Sir Thomas Chaloner's translation (1549) of Erasmus's *Moriae encomium*
('In Praise of Folly'): 'Hereby it appeared
that Jesus was the stickler or moderator'.
Similarly Dryden, in *The Death of Oliver
Cromwell* (1659), wrote:

Our former Chiefs, like Sticklers of the
War,
First sought t'inflame the Parties, then
to poise.

And even Shakespeare had a form of the
word in *Troilus and Cressida* (1606), when
near the end of the play, Achilles says of the
setting sun:

The dragon wing of night o'erspreads
the earth,

And, stickler-like, the armies separates.

This sense became obsolete in the nineteenth century, though, and the present meaning, in its weakened usage, dates from the seventeenth century.

story (tale, account, entertaining narrative)
The word is directly related to 'history', and indeed derives from a shortened form of the Old French *estorie* (modern *histoire*). So in the thirteenth century, a 'story' was a historical account, in speech or writing, and at first almost always that of a biblical event or the legend of a saint, the former as an episode of history from the Old Testament. The word is used in this sense by Chaucer in the Prologue to the *Canterbury Tales* (1386), where we are told of the Pardoner (who sold 'pardons' and indulgences):

He was in chirche a noble ecclesiaste,
Wel koude he rede a lesson or a storie
But alderbest he song an Offertorie.

In the fourteenth century, the meaning of 'story' developed to 'recital of events' and 'entertaining narrative', that is, its modern meaning, with the particular usage 'account' ('that's his story') first recorded in Shakespeare's *All's Well That Ends Well* (1601), where the King, questioning Diana about a ring, says:

The story then goes false you threw it
him
Out of a casement.

(She replies: 'I have spoke the truth'.)
Compare **history**.

stout (fat, corpulent)
In the fourteenth century, the word meant both 'proud', 'fierce' and 'strong', the latter applying to a person's body or build (as it still can). The first meaning here is still not quite dead, if one considers such expressions as a 'stout heart', or a 'stout denial'. The sense 'fat', however, followed only in the nineteenth century, when it has come to be used mainly of men (as typically a 'stout old gentleman').

stow (put away in store or in a special container)

The modern usage is mainly associated with ships and the navy, with sailors 'stowing' hammocks and a cargo being 'stowed' in the hold. But in Old English 'stow' simply meant 'place', 'put in position', without any particular idea of putting away or storing. The sense was still in use in the sixteenth century, as in Thomas Phaer's translation (1558) of Virgil's *Aeneid:*

And captiue children stode, and
tremblyng wifes in long aray
Were stowed about and wept.

Shakespeare has it, too, in his poem *The Rape of Lucrece* (1593):

Till sable night, mother of Dread and
Fear,
Upon the world dim darkness doth
display,
And in her vaulty prison stows the
Day.

The sense then became obsolete. The noun 'stow', simply meaning 'place', can still be found, however, in several English place-names, such as the many towns and villages called just 'Stow' (or 'Stowe') or ending in the word, such as 'Chepstow' (literally 'market place'; see **cheap**). Even 'Bristol' is really 'Bridgestow', or 'bridge place'.

strange (unusual)
The earliest sense of the word in English, in the thirteenth century, was 'foreign', 'alien' (compare modern French *étranger*, 'foreigner'). So this was what John de Trevisa meant when in his translation (1387) of Ranulf Higden's *Polychronicon* he wrote: 'The Flemmynges that woneth in the weste side of Wales haueth i-left her straunge speche and speketh Saxonliche i-now'. Even the seventeenth-century down-to-earth *Rates of Marchandizes* (1642 uses the word regularly when setting forth the rules and regulations for customs purposes ('That if any English transport Coales in strange Bottoms to pay Strangers Custome', etc.) But the usage became obsolete shortly after this, and the modern meaning was the one that lasted. It arose soon after the narrower sense just mentioned, and is also first recorded in the thirteenth century. A similar development happened with 'stranger', which first meant 'foreigner', then 'unknown person' (in the

fourteenth century), and then finally 'newcomer' (in the fifteenth).

stride (walk with long steps)
The original meaning of 'stride' in Old English was really 'straddle', that is, stand or walk with legs apart. This usage has been recorded down to the seventeenth century. As Barnaby Googe wrote, in his translation (1577) of Heresbach's *Foure Bookes of Husbandry:* 'If wee assaye to take vp a thing from the ground, stryding, and not with our legges together, wee take it vp with more ease and strength'. Spenser uses the sense, too, in *The Faerie Queene* (1590):

The gate was open, but therein did wait
A sturdy villein, striding stiffe and bold.

(That is, he was standing there, not walking.) The modern usage of 'stride' evolved in the twelfth century.

strut (walk with an erect body and a stiff gait)
In the fourteenth century, 'strut' meant 'bulge', 'swell', as well as 'stand out'. A typical use might be to refer to a cow's full udders, as in Drayton's *Polyolbion* (1612), where he describes 'the daintie Clouer':

That makes each Vdder strout
abundantly with milke.

In Herrick's collection of poems *Hesperides* (1648), the sense is more 'pack full', 'cram tight':

                    And let
Thy servant, not thy own self, sweat,
To strut thy barnes with sheafs of
    Wheat.

In Chaucer's *Canterbury Tales* ('The Miller's Tale') (1386) 'strut' means 'stand out', 'protrude':

Crul [i.e. curly] was his heer, and as the
    gold it shoon,
And strouted as a Fanne, large and
    brode.

The modern sense of the verb emerged only in the sixteenth century, when it also meant 'swagger' for a time.

style (manner, fashion, mode)
The word literally means 'stylus', that is,

the former sharp-pointed instrument used for drawing letters on a wax tablet, and this is the earliest meaning of 'style' in the thirteenth century. It could also mean 'written work' as a result of this, with the sense found as late as the sixteenth century, as in Spenser's *The Shepheards Calender* (1579):

Well couth [i.e. could] he tune his pipe,
    and frame his style.

These uses are now of course obsolete, but they are the genesis of the many modern meanings of 'style', which developed in the following order: 'manner of talking or arguing' (fourteenth century), 'distinctive fashion' (fifteenth), 'way of expressing dates' (e.g. 'New Style', 'Old Style') (sixteenth), 'distinctive design or execution in art or architecture' (eighteenth).

success (good fortune, achievement of a goal)
The present meaning dates from the sixteenth century, when the word could also be used in the sense 'result' or 'outcome', whether good or bad. This needs to be borne in mind when literature of the period is read or studied. When the word is qualified with an adjective, the meaning is clear, as in Norton and Sackville's *Gorboduc* (1561):

One sort that saw the dangerous
    successe
Of stubborne standing in rebellious
    warre.

But in Daniel Neal's *The History of the Puritans* (1732–8), the sense can be 'favourable outcome' or 'unfavourable outcome' when he writes: 'The success of this war will fall within the compass of the next year'. As applied to a person's fortune, however, 'success' was almost always qualified as 'good' or 'bad' (or 'ill'), which explains the apparently self-contradictory usage in passages such as the following, from Southey's *History of the Peninsular War* (1823–32): 'With so little accuracy do the French relate the circumstances of their ill success'. Both these uses of 'success' are now obsolete, and the word almost invariably means 'desired outcome', 'favourable result'.

suggestion (proposal of an idea)
In the fourteenth century, when the word

first entered English from French, its meaning was 'prompting to evil', even 'temptation by the devil'. This usage was current to the seventeenth century, and can be found in Shakespeare's *King John* (1595), in Pandulph's words to King Philip:

> And better conquest never canst thou
>   make
> Than arm thy constant and thy nobler
>   parts
> Against these giddy loose suggestions.

Throughout this same period, too, 'false suggestion' was a common term for a false or trumped up charge or statement. However, the modern meaning also arose in the fourteenth century, and is now the one that predominates.

supersede (take the place of someone or something else, succeed)
In its original sense, in the fifteenth century, to 'supersede' was to 'postpone'. In the *Acta Dominorum Concilii* ('Acts of the Lords Auditors of Causes and Complaints') (1466–94), where the sense is first recorded, a ruling reads: 'He sall supercede the payment of the said v^c frankis'. In the sixteenth century, 'supersede' could mean both 'render superfluous' and 'refrain from'. The first sense is found in a letter of 11 February 1684 from John Ray to the botanist Sir Hans Sloane: 'It is not my intention to supersede the use of any approved botanic authors'. The latter meaning comes in Edward Topsell's *The Historie of Foure-Footed Beastes* (1607), when he writes: 'I superseed any further discourse heereof, till we come to the declaration of the greater beast'. All three senses are now obsolete, and the modern usage of the verb dates from only the seventeenth century. (Latin *supersedere*, from which it ultimately comes, means both 'be superior to' and 'refrain from', or literally, 'to sit over'.)

supervise (oversee, superintend)
The first record we have of the word in English, in the sixteenth century, is in Shakespeare's *Love's Labour's Lost* (1588), where it means merely 'survey', 'look over'. As usual in this play, the pompous classical word is one used by the verbose schoolmaster Holofernes, who referring to a song Sir Nathaniel has just sung, says: 'Let me supervise the canzonet'. He means simply 'Let me see the song', 'Let me read the words'. This usage was current down to the eighteenth century, when Bishop Ken has the word in his poem *Preparatives for Death* (1711):

> All my Omissions supervise,
> And to what Guilt they all arise
> To my own self my Vileness shew.

(His hymns were ten times better than his turgid verse.) The present-day meaning of 'supervise' thus dates from the seventeenth century.

suppose (imagine, be inclined to think)
In its earliest sense, in the fourteenth century, 'suppose' was more directly 'believe', 'think', and this usage can be found down to the eighteenth century. The modern meaning thus makes texts of this period seem vaguer than they really are, as when in Malory's *Le Morte Darthur* (1470–85) we read this interchange: 'It semeth [. . .] said kynge Arthur that ye knowe his name, and fro whens he is come [. . .] I suppose I doo so said Launcelot or els I wold not haue yeuen hym thordre of knyghthode'. (He means, I believe I do.) Shakespeare, too, uses the word more than once in this sense in *Henry VI*, Part 1 (1591), as when Richard Plantagenet says:

> Let him that is a true-born gentleman,
> [. . .]
> If he suppose that I have pleaded truth,
> From off this brier pluck a white rose
>   with me.

Even the Bible has it, in II Corinthians 11:5: 'For I suppose I was not a whit behind the very chiefest apostles'. But the sense 'assume', which is still current, also dates from the fourteenth century, even though the modified meaning, 'be inclined to think', 'entertain as an idea' evolved somewhat later, in the seventeenth century (as in 'Where do you suppose he is?').

surly (ill-humoured, bad-tempered)
This word has taken a dive from lofty to base. It originally meant 'lordly', 'majestic' in the sixteenth century. In Shakespeare's *Julius Caesar* (1601), although used adverb-

ially, 'surly' has this sense when Casca recounts:

Against the Capitol I met a lion,
Who glar'd upon me, and went surly by.

However, the word soon acquired an overtone of 'haughty' or 'arrogant', and this led to the current meaning, which arose in the seventeenth century. Its origin, even so, lies in 'sir', showing its 'masterful' meaning when first current.

surround (encircle, go round)
When first current in English, in the fifteenth century, 'surround' meant 'overflow', 'flood'. Holinshed's *Chronicles* of 1587 thus detail how a certain enclosed pool was 'surrounded at euerie high water' and a court case of 1631 tells of: ' . . .one complaining against another for letting downe a sea wall soe that not onely his but diverse other men's grounds were surrounded'. How did this meaning come about, when the word is so obviously derived from 'round'? The answer is that it is not, and its true origin is in Old French *suronder*, in turn from Late Latin *superundare*, 'overflow' (as it were, 'super-inundate'). However, the word came to be associated with 'round', and this is the sense it acquired in the seventeenth century.

swain (shepherd, lover)

Who is Silvia? what is she,
That all our swains commend her?

This, by Schubert out of Shakespeare (*Two Gentlemen of Verona*, 1591), is the popular image of a 'swain', romantically rustic. Yet in the twelfth century, when the word was first current in English, it meant merely 'young man attending a knight', and a little later simply 'male servant'. In the fourteenth century the meaning was generalized even further to just 'man', 'boy', so that in a York mystery play of 1440 the child Jesus is referred to as 'that litill swayne', and in Spenser's *The Shepheards Calender* (1579) Cupid is called 'a naked Swayne'. There is of course a hint of romance in this, but it was only in the sixteenth century that the word acquired its popular meanings, both 'country labourer' (and in particular, 'shepherd') and 'country lover'. The latter

was to become the idealized wooer of pastoral poetry in the years that followed, such as Dryden's translation (1697) of Virgil's *Pastorals*, where he declaims:

To the dear Mistress of my Love-sick Mind,
Her Swain a pretty Present has design'd.

(The romance may be originally Roman, but the sentiment is typically seventeenth century.) If the word is still current, it is therefore in this sense, with all the earlier ones obsolete. But it also survives in the former understanding in 'boatswain' and 'coxswain', who are both literally 'boat servants' (*cok* was a word for a small boat).

swap, swop (exchange)
The somewhat schoolboy-smacking verb originally meant 'strike', 'hit' in the fourteenth century, as well as more specifically 'strike hands on making a bargain'. The general sense can be found, for example, in the alliterative romance *Destruction of Troy* (1400):

With a swinge of his sworde [he] swappit hym in the fase,

and as late as 1600 in Edward Fairfax's translation of Tasso's *Godfrey of Bulloigne*:

And then Alarcos head she swapt off cleene.

The word could also refer to a kiss (a 'smacker'), as in Nicholas Breton's *A Floorish vpon Fancie* (1577–82):

To [. . .] swap ech slut vpon the lippes, that in the darke he meetes.

The narrower sense of 'swap', relating to striking a bargain, can be found, for instance, in Robert Greene's *The Black Bookes Messenger* ('Laying open the Life and Death of Ned Browne, one of the most notable Cutpurses, Crosbiters, and Connycatchers [i.e. 'mug-catcher', or thief], that euer liued in England') (1592): 'Wee like two good Horse-corsers, made a choppe and change, and swapt vp a Rogish bargaine, and so he married my wife and I his'. From this, the sense passed in the sixteenth century to the modern semi-slang usage. It seems likely that, as suggested by the Greene extract, the bargaining term was particularly popular among horse dealers, and that this is the immediate source of the schoolboy 'bargain'. The word itself is almost certainly of imitative origin, representing the hearty slap of the hand (or the 'smacking' of the kiss).

sweepstake (contest in which all the stakes go to the winner)
In the fifteenth century, 'sweepstake' was the word for the person who won all the stakes in a game, not the prize itself. He had thus 'swept the stakes'. 'He that will exploit wonderments, and karrie all before him, like a sweepe-stake', wrote Gabriel Harvey, in *Pierces Supererogation* (1593). The word was particularly fashionable as a ship name from the fifteenth century to the seventeenth, since it suggested a good 'prize' to those who were prepared to gamble on the outcome of a sea battle. (A ballad of 1650 was entitled: 'The Seaman's only Delight: Shewing the brave Fight betwen the George-Aloe, the Sweepstakes and certain French Men at Sea'.) For a time from the sixteenth century, too, 'sweepstake' could mean generally 'total removal', otherwise a 'clean sweep'. The word usually occurred in the phrase 'to make sweepstake', as in Miles Coverdale's *An Exhortacion to the Careinge of Chrystes Crosse* (1550): 'If the pope and his prelates were charitable, they woulde, I trowe, make swepe stake at once wyth purgatorye'. Finally, in the eighteenth century, the word came to have its present meaning.

swing (move backwards and forwards)
The word had two senses in Old English, both now obsolete. The first was 'scourge', 'flog', as in the *Assumption of Our Lady* (1330):

With oute gult thei me swongen,
And to a piler thei me bounden.

The second sense was 'rush', 'move impetuously', as in Nicholas Udall's comedy *Ralph Roister Doister* (1553):

Tibet Talkapace. Well Trupenie neuer but flinging.
Annot Alyface. And frisking?
Tom Trupenie. Well Tibet and Annot, still swingyng and whiskyng?

The next sense to appear was 'flourish', 'brandish', in the fourteenth century. This is still current, of course, as is the main meaning defined above, which finally emerged in the sixteenth century: 'Moche lyke the pastyme that boyes vse in the churche when their master is awaye, to swinge and totter in a belrope' (Roger Ascham, *Toxophilus, the Schole of Shootinge*, 1545).

switch (device for altering direction or current; riding whip)
The word has four main senses, all still current, with the first being the sixteenth-century 'riding whip', recorded in Shakespeare's *Romeo and Juliet* (1592):

Mercutio. Come between us, good Benvolio; my wit faints.
Romeo. Switch and spurs, switch and spurs; or I'll cry a match.

The sense then developed to 'thin flexible shoot' in the seventeenth century, as again in Shakespeare, this time in *Henry VIII* (1613), where the Porter says, reacting to the noise and tumult inside the palace: 'Is this a place to roar in? Fetch me a dozen crab-tree staves, and strong ones: these are but switches to 'em. I'll scratch your heads: you must be seeing christenings!'. The mechanical device, such as the familar light 'switch', then followed in the eighteenth century, and in the nineteenth century came the 'long bunch of hair' meaning (transferred from the riding whip), referring usually to the tress of false hair sometimes added by women to their natural hair. '"If I couldn't afford any other clothes, I might wear a switch, too!" hissed the Amazonian queen' (Bret Harte, *The Man on the Beach*, 1878).

swoop (descend suddenly)
In the sixteenth century, 'swoop' meant more 'sweep', that is, it described the action of sweeping along with trailing garments or the like. The sense is nicely illustrated in Thomas Drant's *A Medicinable Morall* (a version of Horace's *Satires*) (1566):

He swings and swoupes from streete to streete,
with gowne that sweepes the grounde.

This use became obsolete in the eighteenth

century. Meanwhile, a century earlier, 'swoop' had acquired a second sense of 'pounce on', which is closer to the modern meaning but is not exactly what the word denotes today, since it is not possible to 'swoop' something. Thomas Otway's comedy *Friendship in Fashion* (1678) has an example: 'Thou shalt every morning swoop the Exchange in triumph to see what gaudy bauble thou canst first grow fond of'. This sense fell out of use in the nineteenth century, with the modern meaning evolving in the eighteenth.

symbol (something that represents something else)
As first used in English, in the fifteenth century, 'symbol' applied to the summary of Christian belief that is now called the Apostles' Creed. (The word itself comes, through Latin, from Greek *symbolon*, 'token', 'mark of identity', from *symballein*, literally 'to throw together', 'compare'. The concept is that of verifying one half of an identity token by comparing it with the other half. Christians were thus 'verified' or identified as being different from heathens.) Caxton referred to this summary as 'the credo and symbole of the fayth' (*The Arte and Crafte to Knowe Well to Dye*, his translation of 1490). The popular meaning of the word, however, as defined above, evolved in the sixteenth century, where it is first recorded in Spenser's *The Faerie Queene* (1590):

> That, as a sacred Symbole, it [i.e. a bloodstain] may dwell
> In her sonnes flesh.

The usage of 'symbol' to refer to a written character, such as a mathematical 'symbol', followed in the seventeenth century.

symphony (orchestral work, usually in four movements)
The word began its English career rather vaguely in the thirteenth century, when it simply referred to various musical instruments when played together. Wyclif used it in his Bible translation of 1382 to render what must be one of the most musical verses (in content) in the whole book, Daniel 3:7: 'Anoon as alle peplis harden the sown of trumpe, pype, and harpe, sambuke, and sautrie, synphonie, and al kynde of musikis'

(Authorized Version of 1611: 'When all the people heard the sound of the cornet, flute, harp, sackbut, psaltery, and all kinds of musick'). (Notice that the 'synphonie' has been omitted as adding little to the overall complement.) In the fifteenth century, 'symphony' came to acquire the sense 'harmony', at first mainly a musical one, but later used generally, as in Jeremy Taylor's *Liberty of Prophesying* (1646): 'The Jewes pretend that the Christians have corrupted many places, on purpose to make symphony between both the Testaments'. Both these usages of the word are now obsolete, but something like the modern meaning first appeared in the seventeenth century, with the specific reference of 'symphony' to a piece played by a group of instruments. Pepys recorded in his *Diary* for 19 May 1661: 'Captain Cooke, Mr. Gibbons, and others of the King's musicians were come to present my Lord with some songs and symphonys, which were performed very finely'. The full modern meaning, however, did not emerge until a century later, with the development of the genre itself, from Bach's sons onwards.

tabloid (smaller size newspaper, usually with popular content and appeal)
The 'tab*loid*' began life as a 'tab*let*'! The word was originally a trade mark for a make of medicinal tablets registered by the manufacturers, Burroughs, Wellcome & Co, on 14 March 1884. The word was adopted by the media of the day as a novel term for 'compressed' or summarized news that was presented in a popular format, just as the medicinal tablet was itself made of compressed or concentrated substances and was widely popularized. As early as 1901, the media were using the term 'tabloid jour-

nalism' (*Westminster Gazette*, 1 January), and despite complaints by the company that their patented name was thus being misused, their appeal was overturned in the courts two years later. Mr Justice Byrne's verdict was:

> The word Tabloid has become so well-known [...] in consequence of the use of it by the Plaintiff firm in connection with their compressed drugs that I think it has acquired a secondary sense in which it has been used and may legitimately be used so long as it does not interfere with their trade rights. I think the word has been so applied generally with reference to the notion of a compressed form or dose of anything.

(*Reports of Patent and Trade Mark Cases*, 20 November – 14 December, 1903). But this was not quite yet 'tabloid' newspapers in the modern sense, and papers of this type first emerged in Britain after the First World War. According to the *Encyclopaedia Britannica* for 1926: 'The introduction of tabloids may be explained [...] by the passing remark of Lord Northcliffe, "If some American does not start one I shall have to come over to do it"'. The original trade name was formed by substituting the familiar scientific ending '-oid' for the ending of 'tablet'. It is now no longer in use.

tact (sense of thoughtfulness or propriety, doing 'the right thing at the right time')
In the seventeenth century, when the word was first used in English, it had its literal meaning of 'sense of touch' (compare 'tactile'). This therefore explains the meaning in such texts as the following, from Alexander Ross's *Arcana microcosmi* (1651): 'Of all the creatures, the sense of tact is most exquisite in man'. This usage became obsolete in the nineteenth century. The modern meaning evolved some hundred years earlier than this, as a direct borrowing of French *tact*, itself first used in the new sense by Voltaire in 1796.

talent (mental or physical 'gift' or aptitude)
In its earliest usage in English, in the thirteenth century, 'talent' meant 'inclination', 'disposition', which was the meaning of Latin *talentum*. The sense was current down to the fifteenth century, and occurs, for example, in Caxton's translation (1485): *Thystorye of the Knyght Parys and the Fayr Vyenne*: 'Grete talent and desyre she had to knowe hym'. In the fourteenth century, 'talent' was adopted (again from Latin *talentum*) as the word to render the sum of money known in Greek as *talanton* (literally 'balance', 'weight'). Wyclif used the word in his Bible translation of 1382 to render the parable of the talents in Matthew 25:14–30 (it is still there in the Authorized Version of 1611), and it is from this usage that the modern meaning 'mental ability', 'intellectual gift' developed in the fifteenth century.

tall (high, lofty)
Strange as it may seem, the meaning of this common word evolved only in the sixteenth century. Before that, some two hundred years earlier, 'tall' had several different meanings, almost all of which are now obsolete. Two of the chief ones were 'handsome', 'elegant', 'good-looking', and 'brave', 'valiant'. The first of these was current until the seventeenth century, and occurs in Marlowe's tragedy *The Jew of Malta* (1592): 'That such a base slave as he should be saluted by such a tall man as I am, from such a beautiful dame as you'. The second sense comes, for instance, in Meredith Hanmer's *The Historie of Ireland* (1604): 'Both sides lost many a tall man'. The usage became obsolete in this meaning in the nineteenth century, although something of the concept remains in the expression 'walk tall'. As usual, Shakespeare was one of the pioneers of the new sixteenth-century meaning, and in *Love's Labour's Lost* (1588) Costard asks the Princess of France: 'Which is the greatest lady, the highest?'. She replies: 'The thickest, and the tallest'.

tambourine (type of small drum with only one 'head' and loose metallic discs)
The word occurs in some sixteenth-century literature where its precise sense is not clear. It is obviously not a 'tambourine' in the modern meaning, however. Two notorious instances are in Spenser's *The Shepheards Calender* (1579) and Ben Jonson's *The Sad Shepherd* (1637). The former has the lines:

I sawe Calliope wyth Muses moe
[i.e. more] [. . .]
Theyr yuory [ivory] Luyts and
Tamburins forgoe.

The latter has the line:

Though all the Bels, Pipes, Tabors,
Timburines ring.

After this, the word lapsed into a sort of limbo, and is found neither in Johnson's *Dictionary* of 1755 nor two other leading English dictionaries of this period, Nathan Bailey's of 1721 and John Ash's also of 1755. The first certain use of 'tambourine' in its modern sense is thus in the *Geographical Magazine* in 1782, where it is described as: 'a hoop covered with parchment, and furnished with small pieces of metal hanging to the edges of it'.

tamper (meddle, interfere with)
In the sixteenth century, 'tamper' meant 'work in clay', 'temper in clay' (i.e. mix it with water and knead it to a homogeneous consistency). The origin of the word is thus actually in 'temper', and the spelling perhaps evolved to reflect an 'artisan' pronunciation of 'temper'. An example of the usage can even be found in verse, as in the following lines from Thomas Tusser's *Fiue Hundreth Pointes of Good Husbandrie* (1573):

A fork and a hooke, to be tampring in claie,
A lath hammer, trowel, a hod, or a traie.

The modern use of 'tamper' evolved in its disparaging sense in the seventeenth century (although in the spelling 'temper' also in the sixteenth).

tangle (intertwine in disorder, entangle)
As first current, in the fourteenth century, to 'tangle' someone was to involve him or her in an awkward, complex or embarrassing situation, as illustrated in these lines from Norton and Sackville's *Gorboduc* (1561):

O happie wight [i.e. being], that suffres not the snare
Of murderous minde to tangle him in bloode.

This sense became obsolete in the seventeenth century, and the current meaning developed about a hundred years before this.

taper (long waxed wick for lighting candles etc.)
From the earliest times down to the nineteenth century, 'taper' simply meant 'candle' itself, deriving from the identical Old English word. In early usage, it was in particular a slender type of candle used for devotional or penitential purposes, as in the following extract from *The Brut, or the Chronicles of England* (1460): 'She was enioyned to open penaunce, forto go thrugh Chepe [i.e. Cheapside, London], bering a tapere in hir hand'. The present meaning evolved when the thing itself did (in the nineteenth century).

target (object to be aimed at)
As it historically evolved, a 'target' was originally a kind of light round shield of the fourteenth century, what was also called a 'buckler'. Edward Hall's *Chronicle* of 1548 thus lists: 'The kynges banner and courser, his coate of armes, his sworde, his target, and his helme'. In the eighteenth century, a 'target' was the word used to designate a shield-shaped target marked with rings for archery practice, and that is the genesis of the modern 'target' in its very wide sense of anything that is a goal or objective, in love or war or anything else.

tariff (list of prices, menu)
The word arose in the sixteenth century (from the Arabic) to denote both an arithmetical table and a schedule of duties on imported goods. (The first of these senses is now obsolete.) In the eighteenth century, the sense was extended to apply to a general list of charges or prices, with the British usage as 'menu' following in the nineteenth century.

tawdry (cheap and showy)
The word originated in the phrase 'tawdry lace' in the seventeenth century. This was a term for cheap and pretentious 'finery' and itself derived from the sixteenth-century 'tawdrie lace' or 'Seynt Audries lace' which was a kind of silk necktie sold at a fair held

in commemoration of St Audrey, otherwise Etheldreda ('noble strength'). She was the daughter of Anna, king of East Anglia, who died in 679 of a tumour of the neck caused by the plague. (She saw this affliction as a divine retribution for her former fondness for wearing necklaces.) 'Tawdry laces' were fashionable throughout the sixteenth century and early part of the seventeenth and one is mentioned in Shakespeare's *The Winter's Tale* (1611), where Mopsa says to Autolycus: 'Come, you promised me a tawdry lace and a pair of sweet gloves'. The adjective 'tawdry' evolved alongside the 'tawdry lace', and is also first recorded in the seventeenth century.

team (group of people working or playing together)
The basic Old English sense of the word was 'brood', whether of people or animals. This implies a number of related beings, a 'family'. Thus the *Metrical Chronicle* (1297) of Robert of Gloucester tells of 'foure gode sones' growing up in a family:

Adelbold & adelbright, adelred and alfred,
This was a stalwarde tem.

For animals, too, we still talk of a 'team' of horses or dogs working together, and some dialects use the word for a litter of pigs or a brood of ducks, for example. Although the literal 'human family' sense became obsolete in the fifteenth century, the modern meaning superseded it, in a more general usage, a hundred years later. The sense was not so much a transference from the 'family' meaning as from that of animals working together. Compare the related **teem** (below).

tease (annoy, irritate by persistent 'hassle')
The common meaning as defined here arose only in the seventeenth century. It was a transference of sense from the Old English 'tease' which was the action of separating threads or fibres ('teasing' flax or wool, for example). The concept overall, of both senses, is that of 'worrying' at something over a period of time. The old meaning of 'tease' is still current, either in technical processes or in simply 'teasing out' a lock of hair by combing or brushing it, for example.

teem (be abundant)
The root of the word is Old English *tēman*, 'bear', 'bring forth', which also lies behind '**team**' (which see, above). The earliest meaning of 'teem' was therefore literally this, and the sense is found in literature down to as late as the eighteenth century. It comes, for example, in Shakespeare's *Henry V* (1599), in the Duke of Burgundy's 'duty' speech to the English and French kings at Troyes:

Nothing teems
But hateful docks, rough thistles, kecksies, burs.

The same understanding lies behind his use of the word in *Othello* (1604), where Othello, having struck Desdemona, says to her:

If that the earth could teem with woman's tears,
Each drop she falls would prove a crocodile.

The modern meaning of 'teem' arose in the sixteenth century, and particularly became associated with crowds and pouring rain.

temperament (person's natural 'mood' or disposition of character)
In the fifteenth century, 'temperament' referred to a suitable mixture of elements in a compound, in particular as they occur in the body (such as heat or blood), and in the seventeenth century the use of the word emerged to apply specifically to the combination of the four so-called '**humours**' that existed (see this word). A person might therefore be said to have a 'sanguine temperament' or a 'choleric temperament' or a 'melancholic temperament'. The modern use of the word dates only from the nineteenth century, where it is first recorded in Byron's *Don Juan* (1821):

He was a man of a strange temperament.

Compare **temperature** (below).

temperature (state of being hot or cold)
In the sixteenth century, 'temperature' meant the same as '**temperament**' (see above) as well as 'mixture' generally. Thus in Bacon's *Advancement of Learning* (1605) he states: 'As touching the manners of learned men [. . .] no doubt there be amongst them,

as in other professions, of all temperatures'. We owe the modern usage of the word to Boyle, who in 1670 wrote a work entitled: 'Of the Temperature of the Submarine Regions as to Heat and Cold'. This is the first recorded instance of the current meaning, which is now the predominant one.

tennis (sport played with racket and balls on a court)
Some people are surprised to find the game mentioned in Shakespeare, for example ('Tennis-balls, my liege', *Henry V*, 1599), but tennis dates from much earlier than this. It was not the same game as today, of course, but was what is now called 'real tennis' (that is, 'royal' tennis), played with rackets in a walled court. The first record we have of it is in 1400, in John Gower's *In Praise of Peace:*

Of the Tenetz to winne or lese a chace,
Mai no lif wite er that the bal be ronne.

(That is, in modern terms, the result of a rally will not be known until the ball is missed by one of the two players. In real tennis a 'chase' is the second impact of the ball on the floor of a ball which a player's opponent has not returned for some reason.) The modern sense of 'tennis' thus applies exclusively to what is strictly 'lawn tennis', which itself arose as a game (as a development of an outdoor version of 'real tennis') in about 1874. In August 1888 the *St. James' Gazette*, referring to the simple word 'tennis', lamented: 'It is melancholy to see a word which has held its own for centuries gradually losing its connotation. Such a word is "tennis", by which nine persons out of ten to-day would understand the game of recent invention played on an unconfined court'. The game and the new meaning flourished simultaneously from then on, with the word appearing in a whole range of literature, both factual and entertaining. One example of the latter can be found, for instance, in the novel *The Younger Set* (1908) by the American author R.W. Chambers: 'Eileen [...] strolled houseward across the lawn, switching the shaven sod with her tennis bat'.

terrible (arousing terror; great; bad)
Like '**awful**' (which see), 'terrible' has now lost its original fifteenth-century sense of 'arousing terror'. So the writer who told in 1565 of 'the marvelloussest and terriblest storm' was using the word in its proper sense (this fine phrase quoted from Sir James Picton's *Selections from the Liverpool Municipal Archives and Records, 1207–1835*, 1883–6). But the present popular usage dates from only a century later, and is now the almost sole meaning of the word to express something large ('a terrible amount of trouble'), unpleasant ('a terrible smell') or bad ('a terrible game').

terse (concise, curt)
The word dates from the seventeenth century, when it meant 'smoothed', 'polished', either in the sense 'neat and trim' or 'polite', 'refined'. Ben Jonson wrote in *The Poetaster* (1601) of a street that was 'polite and terse', and Robert Burton in *The Anatomy of Melancholy* (1621) describes a 'polite and terse Academicke'. This sense was obsolete by the nineteenth century, and the present meaning dates from the eighteenth. In recent times, however, there has been an increasing tendency for the word to mean not so much 'concise' (a 'terse' statement) but 'abrupt', 'curt'. This usage is not recorded in the *OED* and is a twentieth-century development. Overall, therefore, the word has plummeted from 'polite' to 'rude'!

texture (nature, character or structure of something)
The word is directly related to 'textile' and in the fifteenth century meant 'weaving'. The earliest record of the word comes in Osbern Bokenham's *Lyvys of Seyntys* (1447):

Mynerve hyr self wych hath the sovereynte
Of gay texture, as declayryth Ovyde.

'Texture' could also mean 'what is woven', 'product of the weaver's art', and is used in this sense as late as the nineteenth century by Browning in *Red Cotton Night-Cap Country* (1873):

When the dyer dyes
A texture, can the red dye prime the white?

But otherwise the literal uses are now

obsolete, and the general sense, as defined above, evolved in the seventeenth century.

thews (muscles, sinews)
This is now a rare or highly stylized word, but it has had an interesting sense development over its long history. In Old English, *thēaw* meant 'conduct', 'usage', 'custom', and in the plural soon acquired the sense 'personal qualities'. Wyclif used the word in his Bible translation of 1382 for I Corinthians 15:33: 'Forsoth yuele spechis corumpen goode thewis' (Authorized Version of 1611: 'Evil communications corrupt good manners'). In the sixteenth century, the meaning progressed to be used not simply of manners or qualities, but of bodily powers and physical abilities, and Shakespeare used 'thews' to refer in general to any physical parts or features of the body that indicated strength. Thus in *Julius Caesar* (1601) Cassius says to Casca:

> For Romans now
> Have thews and limbs like to their
>   ancestors,

and in *Hamlet* (1602) Laertes tells Ophelia:

> For nature, crescent, does not grow alone
> In thews and bulk.

The modern meaning, specifically associated with muscles and sinews (which latter word even suggests 'thews'), developed from Scott's interpretation of Shakespeare's sense as 'muscular development'. Hence in *Rob Roy* (1818) he writes: 'My fellow-traveller, to judge by his thewes and sinews, was a man who might have set danger at defiance'.

thrift (economy, saving)
The sense development here can be summed up by considering the directly related word 'thrive'. 'Thrift' can imply little money and a need for economy. 'Thriving', on the other hand, suggests prosperity. How can the two be reconciled? Originally, in the thirteenth century, 'thrift' did actually mean 'thriving condition', with this sense soon passing to 'prosperity', 'good fortune'. The meaning was preserved in some writing down to the seventeenth century, and is found, for example, in Bunyan's *A Treatise of the Fear of God* (1679): 'Every grace is nourished by

the Word, and without it there is no thrift in the soul'. The usage then became obsolete. Meanwhile, in the fourteenth century, the sense had developed from 'prosperity' to 'gains' and so to 'savings', and from this now obsolete meaning the current sense of 'economical management' arose in the sixteenth century. In other words, the shift altered from the ends (the wealth) to the means (the economy needed to gain wealth).

thrill (excite greatly)
The verb properly means 'pierce', 'bore a hole', and this was its original sense in the thirteenth century, whether literally or figuratively. The earliest record we have of the word is in the fourteenth-century *Cursor Mundi*, relating to a medical condition:

> The fester [i.e. fistula] thrild his bodi thurgh.

The usage is found as late as the seventeenth century, in *Merry Drollery* ('a collection of jovial poems, merry songs, with drolleries') (1661), where a sword is described (how drolly is best left as a matter of taste) as:

> Thrilling, and drilling,
> And killing, and spilling.

The sense then fell out of use. Meanwhile, as he frequently did, Shakespeare had seized on the word in the sixteenth century to make it mean 'greatly excite', 'affect with emotion', and thus gave it the modern meaning. The sense shift is first recorded in *Romeo and Juliet* (1592), where Juliet, bidding farewell to Lady Capulet before she drinks the poison, says:

> I have a faint cold fear thrills through my veins.

Shakespeare used the verb in many other plays similarly, including *King John* (1595), *Henry IV*, Part 1 (1596) and *King Lear* (1605). But that was not the end: the verb even acquired another, now obsolete meaning in the seventeenth century, which was 'hurl a weapon' (so that it pierces). An example of this use comes in Thomas Heywood's *Troia Britanica* (1609):

> He thrild a Iavelin at the Dardans [i.e. Trojan's] brest.

And the final sense to emerge was the one that means 'quiver', especially as applied to sounds or light. This followed in the eighteenth century, when it was well exploited by poets and romantic writers generally. There is a good example in Hardy's *The Return of the Native* (1878): 'The great valley of purple heath thrilling silently in the sun'.

thud (fall or strike with a heavy blow)
The word is of Scottish origin, and when first current in English, in the sixteenth century, applied not so much to a blow or heavy sound as a blast or gust of wind. The usage is first recorded in Gavin Douglas's translation (1513) of Virgil's *Aeneid*, where he describes a blast of wind that came 'thud-dand doun' on the Aegean Sea, and the sense was current down to at least the eighteenth century. It was in this century that the modern meaning began to appear, although it was not generally established until about 1850, mainly through the works of writers who used the word for 'local colour'. Typical examples are in Emily Brontë's *Wuthering Heights* (1847) and George Eliot's *Adam Bede* (1859). In the former the word backs up a vigorous denial: '"Noa", said Joseph, giving a thud with his prop on the floor'. In the latter, the reference is to feet: 'Lisbeth heard the "thud" of a running foot-step on the turf'.

thug (tough, aggressive person; brutal criminal)
The original 'Thugs' (with a capital 'T') were members of an association of professional robbers and murderers in parts of central and northern India. Their organization has a religious basis, since the bodies of their murdered victims, or the possessions of those they robbed, were regarded as sacrifices to the god Kali. The system operated from the sixteenth century down to the nineteenth, when it was gradually suppressed. (The origin of the name is the Hindi word for 'thief'.) Thus many contexts relating to the term in the nineteenth century may properly be a reference to this association, as one is, for example, in the *Daily News* of 22 September 1897, which reported that: 'When the Prince of Wales was in India, a Thug criminal showed him how victims were strangled'. (Thus did the future Edward VII gain experience of the lifestyle of some of his mother's less orthodox subjects.) The sense of the word was transferred to any violent criminal in the same century. By coincidence, the word is curiously suitable in English to apply to its aggressive subject, and fits in well with such terms as 'ugly' (especially 'plug-ugly'), 'thump', 'slug' (in the sense 'hit hard'), 'drug' and, later, 'mug'.

ticket (slip or card confirming payment for admission, a journey, etc.)
Most senses of the word, since it was first current in English in the sixteenth century, are still in use. The earliest sense was 'written notice', 'label' (as a price 'ticket'). At the same time, 'ticket' could also mean 'voucher', 'promise to pay'. This is now obsolete, although the expression 'on tick' meaning 'on credit' survives as a reminder of the sense ('tick' here is a shortening of 'ticket'). The common 'ticket' that admits you to a public place or a journey on public transport followed in the seventeenth century. The election 'ticket', meaning the list of candidates, came next, in American usage, in the eighteenth century. Finally, the expression 'that's the ticket', arrived in the nineteenth century to set a seal of approval on the whole thing.

tickle (excite or amuse agreeably by touching or appealing in some way)
The original sense of the verb, in the fourteenth century, was 'be thrilled', 'be affected by an agreeable tingling sensation'. This usage, now obsolete, applied to the whole person as well as to parts of it, such as the lungs, the blood, the heart and so on. The sense is found down to the eighteenth century, and occurs, for instance, in Holinshed's *Chronicles* (1577–87): 'How the spirits and livelie bloud tickle our arteries and small veines, in beholding you the light of this realme', while a poem (1647) of Henry More has the lines:

This pretty sport doth make my heart to tickle
With laughter.

The modern meaning also arose in the fourteenth century, where it is first recorded in the Prologue to 'The Wife of Bath's Tale' in Chaucer's *Canterbury Tales* (1386):

It tikleth me aboute myn herte roote.

The 'physical' sense of tickling by touching followed somewhat later.

tide (ebb and flow of the sea; period of time)
The latter sense defined here is in fact the earliest to be current in English, and was found in Old English. It still survives in many compound words denoting 'seasons', such as 'springtide', 'eventide', 'Eastertide' and so on. At first, 'tide' meant 'portion of time' on its own, as well as 'point in time'. The *Destruction of Troy* (1400) thus has the line:

And thou tary in this towne, or any tide lenge,

and John Skelton, in his rollicking poem *The Tunning of Elynour Rumming* (1527), also had the word for an expression where we would now use 'time':

Such a lewde sorte
To Elynour resorte
From tyde to tyde.

The 'tide' of the sea was a sense that arose from the fourteenth century, and this is the source of the Shakespearean 'tide in the affairs of men'. However, 'tide and time', where the two words are really synonymous (both meaning 'time'), dates from the thirteenth century. Compare **tidy** (below).

tidy (neat, orderly)
The earliest meaning of 'tidy' in English, in the thirteenth century, was 'good', 'of good appearance', 'plump', with the sense still found in dialect use in the nineteenth century and possibly surviving even today. Thomas Tusser uses the word in his agreeable *Fiue Hundreth Pointes of Good Husbandrie* (1573):

If weather be faire, and tidie thy graine,
Make speedily carrege, for feare of a raine.

In Shakespeare's *Henry IV*, Part 2 (1597), also, the 'plump' sense occurs in Doll Tearsheet's loving scolding of Falstaff: 'Thou whoreson little tidy Bartholomew boar-pig,

when wilt thou leave fighting?'. However, from the fourteenth century, 'tidy' is also recorded to mean 'timely', and this must have been the initial basic sense, with the two words corresponding as '**tide**' and 'time' did (see previous entry). The modern meaning, 'neat', 'orderly', does not emerge until the eighteenth century, followed by the sense 'fairly large' (as in a 'tidy' sum) in the nineteenth.

tight (solid, taut; close-fitting; drunk)
In the fourteenth century, 'tight' had its original sense of 'dense'. In the *Torrent of Portugal* (1435) we thus read:

Hys squyer Rod all nyght
In a wod, that wase full tyght.

The sense 'impervious', 'closely constructed' (as in 'airtight') arose in the sixteenth century, and the meaning 'close-fitting' (as in 'tight' shoes) in the eighteenth. 'Tight' meaning 'drunk' followed in the nineteenth century, as did 'tight' in the sense 'close-fisted', 'stingy'. Only the earliest sense here is now obsolete.

tinsel (type of cheap glittering or sparkling ornament used for show)
In the sixteenth century, 'tinsel' was the term for the threads of silver and gold that were intertwined or interwoven in a rich cloth such as satin or silk to give an added effect of lustre and brilliance. The word did not thus have the 'cheap' connotation it has today. So Philip Stubbes' *The Anatomie of Abuses* (1583) describes how: 'Euery place was hanged with cloth of gold, cloth of siluer, tinsell, arrace, tapestrie'. From the seventeenth century, however, the sense became downgraded (later, this may have been additionally influenced by 'tinny'), and 'tinsel' now has its 'tawdry' meaning.

tippler (regular drinker)
In the fourteenth century, a 'tippler' was a seller of drink, a 'tapster', not a consumer of it. The sense was current down to the seventeenth century, when it is found in a parliamentary ordinance of 1642 concerning the proper observance of 'the Lord's Day' by: 'Every keeper of any Taverne, Inne, Cooks shop, Tobacco-house, Ale-house, or any other Tipler or Victualier'. The usage

then became obsolete, while the current meaning developed from the sixteenth century.

tissue (woven fabric; mesh or network; substance of the body; paper handkerchief)
The current senses of the word are fairly basic. In the fourteenth century, however, 'tissue' was the term for a kind of rich cloth, especially one that was interwoven with gold and silver. The *Calendar of Documents relating to Scotland* (1108 onwards) thus records in 1501: 'A gown of tawny cloth of gold of tisshue', and even as late as 1710 Celia Fiennes tells in her *Diary* ('Through England on a Side Saddle in the Time of William and Mary') of: 'Good bed Chambers and well furnished velvet damaske and tissue'. This meaning became obsolete, however, shortly after. Other senses developed in the following order: 'woven fabric' in the sixteenth century, 'fabric' generally in the eighteenth, 'body substance' (as 'muscle tissue') in the nineteenth, and 'paper handkerchief' in the twentieth (as a shortening of 'paper tissue', not 'tissue paper').

tobacconist (seller of tobacco)
The present meaning arose in the seventeenth century. A hundred years earlier, 'tobacconist' meant 'tobacco smoker', as can be seen in Ben Jonson's *Every Man Out Of His Humour* (1599): 'It pleases the world (as I am her excellent Tabacconist) to give me the style of Signior Whiffe'. This usage became obsolete in the eighteenth century, with the current meaning developing in the seventeenth.

toil (hard work, great labour)
In the thirteenth century, when the word was first in use in English, it meant 'verbal strife', 'argument'. The sense was used down to the nineteenth century in such phrases as 'toils of battle', 'toils of war', especially by poets. For example, Philip Francis, in his translation (1746) of Horace's *Epistles,* has the lines:

Like Gladiators, who with bloodless
   Toils
Prolong the Combat, and engage with
   Foils.

The present meaning of 'toil' developed in the sixteenth century from the verb 'toil' as used in the sense 'labour arduously', 'struggle', which was current two hundred years earlier (and which itself evolved from the 'verbal wrangling' sense).

toilet (lavatory)
The ultimate origin of this word is French *toile,* 'cloth', of which *toilette* is a diminutive. When the word was first imported into English in the sixteenth century, therefore, its meaning was 'cloth wrapper for clothes', a sense that also existed in the French. In the seventeenth century, however, English 'toilet' developed in the much more common French usage to mean both 'cloth worn over the shoulders when hairdressing' and 'cloth for a dressing table'. The former sense was recorded in John Phillips' translation (1684) of Plutarch's *Morals,* where the relevant extract also happens to retell a hoary but agreeable anecdote: 'Pleasant [. . .] was the answer of Archelaus to the barber, who, after he had cast the linen toilet about his shoulders, put this question to him, How shall I trim your majesty? In silence, quoth the King'. The second sense also soon led to a further related meaning, so that 'toilet' was not just a cover for a dressing table, but also the articles on the dressing table themselves. This usage is first recorded in Evelyn's *Diary* entry for 9 June 1662, where he recounts: 'The great looking-glasse and toilet of beaten and massive gold was given by the Queene Mother'. The next stage of sense development was in the following century, when the word was extended to mean 'act of dressing', that is, the activity that involved the 'toilet' that stood on the dressing table. The word also meant the table by now, and this led to the common expression 'at her toilet' of a woman dressing. A typical example comes in Washington Irving's *Bracebridge Hall* (1822): 'She actually spent an hour longer at her toilette, and made her appearance with her hair uncommonly frizzed and powdered'. Since dressing was clearly an important and demanding activity, it was only natural that it should have not just a table devoted to it, but a separate room, and in the nineteenth century that was the next meaning of 'toilet' to emerge. The room

had facilities not only for dressing but also for washing, and so also for bathing and 'natural functions'. So something like the modern toilet had arrived, with the development of both sense and object more American than British, and with the word soon distinctively applied not so much to the dressing room but to the bathroom or the lavatory itself. (Hence the common American euphemism of 'bathroom' for the place.) The whole sense development is in many ways similar to that of '**lavatory**' (which see), especially with regard to the connection with washing.

tomboy (girl who behaves like a conventionally 'boyish' boy)
The word seems a misnomer at first sight – why not 'tomgirl'? In fact the original sense meant 'boisterous boy', first recorded in Nicholas Udall's *Ralph Roister Doister* (1553):

> Is all your delite and joy
> In whiskyng and ramping abroade like
> a Tom boy?

This sense became obsolete almost by the end of the century, by which time the word had come to mean first, 'bold woman' and second, as now, 'boisterous girl'. The former meaning fell out of use in the eighteenth century, but can be found in Shakespeare's *Cymbeline* (1611), where Iachimo tells Imogen that she is like a lady

> To be partner'd
> With tom-boys hir'd with that self-exhibition
> Which your own coffers yield!

The 'tom' of the word is the familiar name 'Thomas' (in its pet form) usually denoting a male (as in 'tomcat' and 'tomfool'), and in 'tomboy' it also originally had this sense, as indicated. The 'gender' concept has now been obscured because of the sense change, however.

tome (large heavy or weighty book)
In the sixteenth century, when the current sense also arose, 'tome' originally meant 'volume', that is, one book in a series. The ultimate source of the word is Greek *tomos*, 'slice', 'piece', which identically gives surgical terms ending in '-tomy' where a cutting or 'slicing' is carried out (as an 'appendectomy' in a removal of the appendix). A literary work could thus consist of a 'first tome', 'second tome' and so on. In English, this sense became obsolete in the eighteenth century, but many other languages still use a form of 'tome' to mean 'volume' (for example French *tome*, Spanish *tomo*, Russian *tom*). The current sense of the word is first recorded in a book title of 1573, stating that the volume contained 'the whole workes' of Tyndall, Frith and Barnes 'collected and compiled in one Tome together'. The transference of sense was thus really from 'three separate tomes' to 'one single tome containing three sets of works'. The word today often has a semi-frivolous or absurdly self-deprecatory usage ('my little tome'). Compare **volume.**

tonic (something such as a medicine that invigorates and 'tones up')
The noun evolved in the eighteenth century from the adjective 'tonic' that originally meant 'pertaining to tone', 'relating to tension' in the seventeenth century (a sense that it still properly has in medical usage, as a 'tonic' spasm). The present noun is thus a shortening of 'tonic medicine' or 'tonic mixture', a medicine that is designed to improve or restore the general 'tone' of the body. The general use of 'tonic' to apply to anything that invigorates or 'braces' followed in the nineteenth century.

topic (subject, matter, theme)
The word originates as the Greek title, *ta topika*, of a treatise by Aristotle, this meaning literally 'matters concerning commonplaces' (from *topos*, 'place', 'commonplace'). Aristotle's work was (and still often is) translated as 'Topics', with the word serving in general to refer to any 'commonplaces' or general maxims. At the same time, the adjective 'topic' soon arose to relate to such a maxim. This was all in the sixteenth century. Thomas Nash, in *Nashes Lenten Stuffe* (1599), wrote: 'Had I my topickes by me in stead of my learned counsell to assist me, I might haps marshall my termes in better aray'. In the seventeenth century, 'topic' came to mean 'consideration', 'argument', a sense it no longer has. The usage was found as late as

the nineteenth century, however, and comes in Scott's *The Betrothed* (1825): 'Interrupting those tears to suggest topics of hope and comfort, which carried no consolation to her own bosom'. (That is, the 'topics' would have been arguments or 'cases' made in favour of hope or of comfort.) Finally, the present meaning evolved in the eighteenth century, so that a 'topic' is simply a 'subject'.

tout (solicit for custom or votes)
The original sense of 'tout' in English, in the fourteenth century, was 'peer', 'peep', 'look out'. The verb is found in the fifteenth-century *Alliterative Romance of Alexander:*

The kyng in his caban with his knightis he ligis [i.e. lies],
Tutand out of his tents.

In the seventeenth century, when this first meaning became obsolete, 'tout' acquired the sense 'watch', 'spy on', with this soon coming to apply to the 'tracking' of a race-horse or its trainer for betting purposes. The *Saturday Review* of 2 April 1870 argued that since: ' . . .the Prince of Wales is touted, Mr. Gladstone is touted, their minutest actions are minutely watched and regularly reported; why should not we be allowed to procure similar information about race-horses?'. This sense is still current, and in the eighteenth century it produced the wider meaning of 'solicit custom'.

toy (plaything)
The earliest usage of the word, in the four-teenth century, applied to amorous play or 'dallying'. There is only one record, however, in Robert Manning of Brunne's *Handlyng Synne* (1303), after which no further evidence of the word appears until the sixteenth century, when it had several senses. The sole quotation is as follows:

Whedyr hyt be yn a womman handlyng,
Or yn any other lusty thing; [. . .]
Amendeth ghow, pur charyte,
And maketh nat a-mys the toye,
That the fende of ghou haue Ioye.

(That is: Whether it be in the caressing of a woman or any other pleasant thing, correct me, pure love of God, and do not let me use dalliance wrongly, so that the devil has the pleasure.) Then, two hundred years later, the word resurfaced in the senses 'antic', 'trick' and 'trifling object' or (as now mainly) 'plaything'. Only the first of these is obsolete. It is first recorded in Henry Medwall's *A Goodly Interlude of Nature* (1500):

Though I say yt a praty [i.e. smart] boy [. . .]
He maketh me laugh wyth many a toy,
The vrchyn ys so mad.

This meaning was not in use later than the eighteenth century. Finally, the word came to have its modern sense in the sixteenth century.

trace (mark, sign of something left)
In the thirteenth century, 'trace' meant 'path', 'course', showing the word's close relationship with 'track' and 'tract'. The usage was current down to the eighteenth century, and is found, for example, in Spenser's *The Faerie Queene* (1596):

Now I begin
To tread an endlesse trace, withouten guyde.

A hundred years later, a further sense of 'trail of footprints' evolved, maintaining the link with 'track'. This became obsolete only in the nineteenth century, but occurs in Scott's *The Lady of the Lake* (1810), where the reference is to the track or trail left by a stag:

Two dogs of black Saint Hubert's breed [. . .]
Fast on his flying traces came.

Finally, the modern meaning 'small mark of something left' emerged in the seventeenth century. Compare **trade** (below).

trade (commerce, regular buying and selling)
Like '**trace**' (above), 'trade' began its life by meaning 'course', 'way', 'track', although it was first current in English in the fourteenth century, a little later. Its origin is not the same as 'trace', however, since it is related to 'tread', not 'track'. The sense of 'course' was therefore basically that of 'well trodden track'. The usage became obsolete in the sixteenth century, but can be found in the

fourteenth-century *Romance of Guy of Warwick:*

> Than loked he aboute vnder the wode
> shawe [i.e. in the wood]:
> The trade of horse he there sighe [saw].

The modern meaning of 'trade' followed in the sixteenth century. It was not this sense that gave 'trade wind', however, but the earlier 'course' meaning. This came to be used in the phrase 'to blow trade', meaning 'blow in a regular direction' (as if on a steady 'track'), and the 'trade winds' are so called since their direction is always constant.

travel (journey)
The word is directly related to 'travail' and so to French *travailler*, 'to work'. The sense history began in the thirteenth century, when 'travel' meant 'labour', both in the meaning of 'toil' and that of 'suffer the pains of childbirth'. However, for both these meanings the spelling was consistently 'travail' (or some form of it) down to the time when the two usages became obsolete, or at any rate archaic, in recent years. At the same time, the spelling 'travel' was used for the 'journey' sense, which also dates from the thirteenth century. The common link between the three meanings is their joint source in Latin *tripalium*, 'instrument of torture', itself literally meaning 'three stakes' (*tri-*, 'three' and *palus*, 'stake', as English 'pale' and 'pole'). Hard labour, giving birth and making a journey were thus a form of 'torture'. It is interesting that English has kept the 'journey' sense of the basic verb, whereas French has kept *voyager* for 'travel'.

treacle (type of syrup produced in refining sugar)
The word has had an unexpected sense development. In the fourteenth century, its meaning was 'salve', 'antidote', that is, a substance which could relieve or cure poisonous bites, the effect of poisons generally, and various malignant diseases. Its ultimate origin thus lies in Greek *thēriake*, 'antidote', itself based on *thērion*, 'wild animal'. (The English 'treacle' added an 'l' here in the same way as in 'principle', from French *principe*, and 'syllable', from Old

French *sillabe*.). The 'antidote' meaning was current down to as recently as the eighteenth century, with one of the best known examples of its use giving the so called 'Treacle Bible', that is, an early translation where Jeremiah 8:22 has 'treacle' instead of the Authorized Version's 'balm'. This can be found in Miles Coverdale's translation of 1535 ('There is no more Triacle at Galaad') as well as other versions. In the fifteenth century, 'treacle' appeared in various names of plants that were believed to have effective medicinal properties, such as 'churl's treacle' (garlic), 'English treacle' (germander) and 'countryman's treacle' (garlic or rue). These names are alas now all obsolete. Also no longer current in the next sense of 'treacle' to arrive in the sixteenth century, which was 'sovereign remedy', 'antidote for anything'. Richard Bradley's *Family Dictionary* of 1725 uses the word in this sense to say of garlic: 'To eat Garlick fasting is the Treacle of the Country People in the time of a Plague'. Finally, the word gained its modern meaning in the seventeenth century. The cause of this apparently unlikely sense development seems to be that sugar was formerly the 'vehicle' for the medicinal substance that was the antidote, as a sort of 'jam' round the medicine.

tremor (shaking of the body or of the earth during an earthquake)
The original meaning of 'tremor', in the fourteenth century, was 'terror', and this is first recorded in Chaucer's *Troilus and Criseyde* (1374):

> Swich a tremor fele a-boute his herte
> That of the feer his body sholde quake.

This usage is not found later than the fifteenth century, however, and the modern meaning dates from the seventeenth century, when the original Latin word that had given the first sense (*tremor*, 'tremble') was reintroduced.

trend (tendency, general direction)
The Old English meaning of 'trend' was 'revolve', 'roll' (compare modern 'trundle'), and this prevailed until the sixteenth century, when the modern sense of 'take a particular direction' evolved. An example of

the original usage can be seen in the following distraught lines from the four-teenth-century *Romance of Guy of Warwick:*

He went and trent his bed opon,
So man that is wo bigon.

(That is: He went and rolled on his bed, like a man beset by woe.) The noun 'trend', which is now more common than the verb, followed in the eighteenth century. The original 'rolling' sense is preserved in one or two English place-names, such as the Devon village of Trentishoe, near Lynton, whose name means 'circle height', and the suburb of Taunton, Somerset, called Trull, which is all that is left of Old English *trendel*, 'ring', 'circle'.

tribute (expression of gratitude or praise)
The original fourteenth-century sense of the word was 'tax paid to a superior', from Latin *tributum* in this meaning (itself from *tribuere*, 'to allot'). Such a tax in English usage could have been one paid by a prince to another as a sign of peace, for example, or one paid by way of rent or homage to a king by his subject. The word occurs in Shakespeare's *The Tempest* (1610) in this sense, when Prospero, the Duke of Milan, is talking about his brother Antonio, who also claims the dukedom:

Confederates, —
So dry he was for sway, – wi' the king
of Naples
To give him annual tribute, do him
homage.

This usage is now current only historically. The present general meaning of the word dates from the sixteenth century. Similarly, 'tributary' originally meant 'paying tribute' (the tax), and it was Shakespeare who is first recorded as applying the adjective to rivers (in *Cymbeline,* a year later than *The Tempest*).

trivial (unimportant, ordinary)
The first use of 'trivial' in English was in the fifteenth century, relating to the so called 'trivium' that in medieval times was the name of the lower division of the seven liberal arts, comprising grammar, rhetoric and logic (see **science** for the others). This sense in turn came from the *trivium* that

was the 'crossroads', or more exactly, 'place where three roads meet' (*tri-*, 'three' and *via*, 'way'), since the liberal arts mentioned were the 'common' or 'everyday' ones, spoken of in the street and at the crossroads. This particular concept was then trans-ferred to English 'trivial' itself in the sixteenth century, and although the sense is now obsolete, it is preserved in a line of John Keble's hymn 'New Every Morning' (1827):

The trivial round, the common task.

Also in the sixteenth century, the sense of 'unimportant' developed, with this first recorded in Shakespeare's *Henry VI,* Part 2 (1593), where the Duke of Suffolk is discussing the proposed murder of the Duke of Gloucester with Cardinal Beaufort and the Duke of York:

And yet we have but trivial argument,
More than mistrust, that shows him
worthy death.

This is now the prevailing meaning of the adjective.

truant (pupil staying away from school without permission)
In the thirteenth century, when the word was first current in English, it implied 'bogus beggar', 'idle rogue' and similar associated senses, although it was often simply a term of abuse. In his translation (1489) of *The Foure Sonnes of Aymon,* Caxton makes a character say: 'Now shall I be a goode trewaunt, for I can well ask brede whan me nedeth', and in Shakespeare's *Much Ado About Nothing* (1599), Don Pedro declares of Benedick: 'Hang him, truant! there's no true drop of blood in him, to be truly touched with love.' The current meaning arose in the fifteenth century, with the word also used of any idle or lazy person. The expression 'play truant' dates from the sixteenth century.

truncheon (policeman's club)
The original meaning of the word, in the thirteenth century, was 'fragment', especially a piece broken off from a spear or lance. This sense was preserved by poets down to the nineteenth century, and is

found, for instance, in Spenser's *The Faerie Queene* (1596):

Therewith asunder in the midst it brast [i.e. burst],
And in his hand nought but the troncheon left.

The modern sense, which can also apply to a staff of office or 'baton', dates from the sixteenth century. The word itself is related to 'trunk'.

tunnel (passageway under the ground)
In the fifteenth century, a 'tunnel' was a kind of tubular net for catching birds, deriving its name from Old French *tonne,* 'tun', 'cask' (modern French *tonneau*). This had a pipelike passage with a wide opening, and narrowed towards the end. In the sixteenth century, 'tunnel' came to be applied to a shaft or flue, as well as a pipe or tube in general. The word could also mean 'funnel'. Finally, in the eighteenth century 'tunnel' acquired a much 'larger' sense to denote a passage excavated under the ground. The earliest 'tunnels' were those that took canals underground for the purposes of carrying coal, and similar excavations were made in the mines themselves. Later, in the nineteenth century, the word became more closely associated with railways.

tycoon (wealthy and powerful businessman, magnate)
As originally used in English, in the nineteenth century, 'tycoon' was in effect a descriptive title for the shogun of Japan, that is for the military governor (or one of them) that ruled there until the revolution of 1867. This title, meaning literally 'great ruler', was one used to 'explain' the shogun to foreigners, with 'shogun' itself meaning 'general'. In the twentieth century, 'tycoon' was adopted for a successful businessman, first current in this sense in the United States.

tyre (inflatable or solid rubber covering for a wheel to run on)
The word probably derives from a shortening of 'attire', in the sense of something with which the wheel is equipped or 'clothed'. In the fifteenth century, when the spelling was either as now or 'tire' (as it still is in North America), the term was used for the curved pieces of iron plate (themselves individually called 'strakes') that were laid end to end or overlapping round the rim of a wheel. The usage was simply as 'tire', not 'a tire', with the word serving as a collective singular. Thus Philemon Holland, in his translation (1601) of Pliny's *Natural History,* wrote of iron: '. . .such as will not serue one white for stroke [i.e. strake] and naile to bind cart-wheels withall, which tire indeed would be made of the other that is gentle and pliable'. In the eighteenth century, the sense came to be applied to the continuous rim of a wheel, also made of iron or steel. Finally, with the arrival of the pneumatic tyre in the nineteenth century, the sense was transferred to the rubber covering.

umbrage (displeasure, feeling of resentment)
The derivation of the word is in French *ombrage,* 'shade', and this was the original meaning of 'umbrage' in English, in the fifteenth century. In Bishop Gavin Douglas's translation (1513) of Virgil's *Aeneid,* one finds the lines:

All the bewty of the fructuus feyld
Was wyth the erthis vmbrage clene
ourheild [i.e. covered over].

The sense soon developed to be specifically used of the shade of trees, and is so recorded right down to the nineteenth century, as in Charlotte Brontë's *Shirley* (1849): 'Often [. . .] she would spend a sunny afternoon in lying stirless on the turf, at the foot of some tree of friendly umbrage'. In the seventeenth century, 'umbrage' acquired the more general transferred sense of 'semblance', 'inkling', as of something that was a 'shadow' of its real self. Shakespeare uses the word in the first of these meanings in *Hamlet* (1604), where Hamlet says to Osric, of Laertes: 'His semblable is his mirror; and who else would trace him, his umbrage, nothing more'. It was also in the seventeenth century that the expressions 'give umbrage to' and 'take umbrage' evolved, in the present-day sense, with these modelled on the equivalent French phrases, *donner ombrage à*, 'make suspicious', and *prendre ombrage de*, 'take offence at'. The latter is now much the more common usage in English, and all the earlier senses of 'umbrage' are now obsolete.

uncanny (weird, mysterious, strangely coincidental)
The word is Scottish in origin (as 'canny' more obviously is), and in the sixteenth century meant 'malicious'. In James Dalrymple's translation (1596) of Bishop Leslie's *Historie of Scotland*, the usage can be seen in the following: 'Sum now, uncannie sawers [i.e. sowers], sew sum causes of contentiou betuene the Chancellor and the Gouernour'. In the seventeenth century, a meaning of 'careless', 'unreliable' developed, this in turn coming to mean 'not safe to deal with' a century later. This last sense implies that the person who is 'uncanny' is believed to have supernatural powers or associations. Scott used the word in this way, as in *Guy Mannering* (1815): 'I wish she binna uncanny! her words dinna seem to come in God's name, or like other folk's'. Finally, the modern meaning evolved in the nineteenth century, and was particularly common from about 1850. All except the earliest sense above are still current, even if as local or dialect words.

uncouth (rough, boorish, gross)
The word is an old one, and can be traced back to Old English *uncūth*, 'not known', 'not familiar', 'unusual'. (The second part of the word relates indirectly to Scottish 'ken'.) These different shades of meaning were mostly current down to at least the seventeenth century, as in Ben Jonson's *Sejanus his Fall* (1603):

It is no uncouth thing
To see fresh buildings from old ruines
spring.

From this, the present meaning evolved in the sixteenth century, the concept being that what is unfamiliar is strange and 'outlandish' or unpleasant. In the twentieth century, a semi-facetious usage of 'couth' developed as a deliberate opposite of 'uncouth', so that the *Guardian* wrote on 28 March 1963: 'Modern idiom and slang is used with reckless abandon and the couth and uncouth punch each other about the ears with unrelenting monotony'. The original Old English 'couth' actually meant 'known', as can be easily deduced from the above.

undergo (experience, suffer)
In Old English, to 'undergo' had its literal sense of to 'go under', especially with the idea of undermining or weakening. An example of the usage comes in the *Early English Psalter* (1300):

Ris vp, lauerd; forcome him swa,
And als-swa him underga.

(That is: Rise up, Lord; overcome him so, and thus work under him [to destroy him].) In the following, from the translation (1540) of Polydore Vergil's *English History*, the sense is part literally 'go under' and part 'undermine': 'Howbeit, hoping eyther to winne it by assault, or compell it to yeelde, they undergoe the wall'. The modern meaning 'submit to' dates from the thirteenth century, and the earlier senses were finally obsolete by the seventeenth century.

undertaker (funeral director)
The original sense of 'undertaker' was 'person who undertakes a task', 'helper', with this usage found from the fourteenth century. Wyclif used the word in his English Bible translation of 1382 to render Psalm 3:4: 'Thou, forsothe, Lord, art myn vndirtakere' (Authorized Version of 1611: 'But thou, O Lord, art a shield for me'). From the seventeenth century, the word came to be used of a contractor, any person who undertook to carry out work for another, and among such contractors were those who made the arrangements for funerals. This finally became the dominant meaning when the more general 'undertaker' became obsolete, or at least rare, in the nineteenth century.

untidy (in disorder)
Just as '**tidy**' (which see) originally meant 'timely', so 'untidy' formerly had the sense 'untimely' in the thirteenth century, as well as 'unseemly'. The latter meaning occurs in these lines from Langland's *Piers Plowman* (1377):

> With his vntydy tales he tened
> [i.e. annoyed] ful ofte
> Conscience and his compaignye.

This usage is barely recorded after the fifteenth century, by which time the present meaning had become established.

untruth (lie, falsehood)
'Untruth' is literally the condition of not being true or faithful, and this sense in Old English was the one that predominated until the fifteenth century. An example of the usage can be seen in the following from *A Myrrour for Magistrates* (1559):

> I through flattery abused his wanton
> youth,
> And his fonde trust augmented my
> vntruth.

The modern meaning evolved from the fifteenth century, however, when it was frequently contrasted with 'truth'.

unwieldy (awkward, difficult to handle)
When first current, in the fourteenth century, 'unwieldy' meant 'feeble', 'impotent', so was frequently found as an adjective for a sick or aged person. This sense is found in use down to the seventeenth century, and occurs, for example, in Reginald Scot's *The Discoverie of Witchcraft* (1584), where he refers to 'a toothless, old, impotent, and unweldie woman'. In Dryden's translation (1685) of Horace's *Odes*, too, come the lines:

> E're with'ring time the taste destroyes,
> With sickness and unwieldy years!

The modern meaning arose in the sixteenth century. The rather unexpected sense development seems to have been prompted by the fact that many old or ill people are (or were) corpulent, and moved with difficulty. Being 'unwieldy', after all, implies a lack of litheness and suppleness.

upset (disturb, overturn, trouble)
The verb has done something of a volte-face over the centuries. Originally, and literally, it meant 'set up', that is, to raise or erect something, as when building or constructing. This sense is found from the fourteenth century, and can be seen, for instance, in the following line from Robert Manning of Brunne's *Chronicle of England* (1330):

> Now is he in the see with saile on mast
> vpsette.

(Meaning that the sail has now been set up, not that it has fallen down!) This usage was current down to at least the seventeenth century, while the present-day meaning is recorded only two hundred years later. Its initial application was almost always to vehicles, horses, ships and so on being overturned or capsizing.

upshot (result, consequence)
The literal meaning of the word is 'final shot', and an 'upshot' was the term for the last shot in an archery contest. The royal accounts of Henry VIII record that his privy purse made this payment in 1531 to an archer for such a winning shot: 'Item [paid] to the same Coton for one up shotte that he wanne of the kinges grace, vj s. viij d. [i.e. six shillings and eightpence, or one noble]'. The present meaning emerged in the seventeenth century, and, typically, is first recorded in Shakespeare, where in *Hamlet* (1604), almost at the end of the play, and after the death of Hamlet (the 'upshot'), Horatio says:

> So shall you hear [. . .]
> Of deaths put on by cunning and forc'd
> cause,
> And, in this upshot, purposes mistook.

The sense developed from the phrase 'in the upshot', meaning 'at last'.

urbane (polite, civil, smooth-mannered)
In the sixteenth century, when first current, 'urbane' meant simply 'urban', as in Richard Carew's translation (1607) of Estienne's *World of Wonders*: 'They see greater cunning and dexteritie, and a more ciuill and urbane kind of life'. Even Wordsworth uses the word in this sense, so that in his

long poem (which might have been much longer if completed) *The Excursion* (1814), he tells of:

A poor brotherhood who walk the earth,
[. . .]
Raising [. . .] savage life
To rustic, and the rustic to urbane.

The modern meaning arose in the seventeenth century, from the concept that a town or city dweller would have greater refinement and better manners than a rustic resident. (Compare 'civic' and 'civil', and see also **humane** for a similar shift of meaning and pronunciation from an earlier word without 'e'.)

urchin (mischievous or scruffy child, 'brat')
The original meaning of 'urchin' in the thirteenth century was. . . 'hedgehog'! (Compare the 'sea urchin' with its spiny shell, often sold at seaside resorts as a quaint souvenir. Compare also the related modern French word for the animal, *hérisson*.) The word is found in Caxton's *The Cronicles of Englond* (1480):

Till that his body
Stykked as full of arewes as an vrchone
is full of prikkes.

The word was in dialect use as late as the nineteenth century, and may still be so in the north of England. The transference of sense to a small mischievous child in the sixteenth century may have had something to do with the use of 'urchin' also to mean 'goblin', 'elf', from the popular belief that these fairy creatures sometimes assumed the form of a hedgehog. The word was also a dialect term for a deformed person, especially a small hunchback or dwarf. As applied to ragged children, 'urchin' was particularly popular from the last quarter of the eighteenth century. Even so, the poet Cowper thought it necessary to explain what he meant when he wrote to Mrs Throckmorton, in a letter of 10 May 1790: 'He sent an urchin (I do not mean a hedgehog, [. . .] but a boy, commonly so called)'.

urinal (place or receptacle where men can urinate)

'There ye shall know, by the Urinal of his eyes, and the water standing therein, what convulsion-fits his soul suffers' (Sir George Mackenzie, *The Religious Stoic,* 1685). Quite clearly, there has been something of a sea change here! When first current in English, in the thirteenth century, 'urinal' was the word for a glass vessel used to hold urine for inspection, mainly to ascertain the state of the body for medical purposes, as is still done today. The quotation above is thus a figurative use of this. Because of the common practice, the word was adopted by alchemists as a term for a vessel for containing chemical (or alchemical) solutions, not urine at all. Chaucer mentions them in the *Canterbury Tales* ('The Canon's Yeoman's Tale', which is all about alchemists) (1386):

Sondry vessels maad of erthe and glas,
Oure vrynals and our descensories [i.e.
vessels used for distillation 'by
descent'].

In the fifteenth century, a 'urinal' was the word for a chamber pot, hence the sense in Milton's *An Apology against a Pamphlet* [. . .] *against Smectymnuus* (1641), where he talks of certain politicians who are: ' . . . lyable to a night-walking cudgeller, or the emptying of a Urinall'. The modern meaning finally developed in the nineteenth century, in time for Bernard Shaw to mention them in *Candida* (1898) ('a vast district [. . .] well served with ugly iron urinals').

vagary (capricious or whimsical act or notion)
The current meaning developed in the seventeenth century. A hundred years earlier, 'vagary' had a number of other senses, now all obsolete. The word derives

from Latin *vagari*, 'to wander' (compare 'vagrant'), and the original senses are all directly related to this. The most literal was 'ramble', 'wandering walk'. The sense could apply to creatures other than man, as in Samuel Purchas's *A Theatre of Politicall Flying-Insects* (1657): 'A hot Sun-shine [. . .] will quickly prompt them out of their Hives to take a short vagary'. (Despite the title, these really are bees, not politicians. The Samuel Purchas here, incidentally, is not the better known author of the same name who wrote *Purchas his Pilgrimage,* and who died in 1626.) 'Vagary' could also mean 'wandering in speech', which is obviously closer to the modern sense, and a further meaning was 'prank', 'frolic', also approaching the current usage. Milton has the latter sense in *Paradise Lost* (1667):

> Strait they chang'd their minds,
> Flew off, and into strange vagaries fell,
> As they would dance.

(This text is a reminder that the word was regularly stressed on the second syllable until quite recently).

valour (courage, prowess)
The initial meaning of the word, in the fourteenth century, was 'value', 'worth', referring to a person's qualities or rank. In *Libeaus Desconus* (1350) (better, *Li Beaus Desconnus,* otherwise 'The Handsome Stranger', a verse romance), come the lines:

> He was a noble dysour
> [i.e. dicer, gambler],
> Wyth ladyes of valour,
> A mery man of mouthe.

This sense became obsolete in the sixteenth century, and the current meaning, developing from the adjective 'valorous' in the same century, is the one that prevailed.

various (different, assorted)
As originally used, in the sixteenth century, 'various' meant 'variable', 'changing'. This sense was preserved by Sheridan as late as the eighteenth century in *The Rivals* (1775), where the Epilogue contains the lines:

> The servile suitors watch her various face,
> She smiles preferment, or she frowns
> disgrace.

The modern meaning (with a plural noun) was first recorded in Milton's *Comus* (1634):

> All the Sea-girt Isles
> That like to rich and various gemms
> inlay
> The unadorned boosom of the Deep.

vegetable (plant grown for food)
The word began its linguistic career as an adjective, in the fourteenth century. It then meant 'having the life of a plant', a sense that became obsolete in the seventeenth century. The next meaning to appear, still as an adjective, was the sixteenth century one 'pertaining to plants', as the modern 'vegetable kingdom' which is the same as the plant kingdom. In the same century, 'vegetable' first became a noun, meaning merely 'plant', that is, 'tree or herb that can vegetate or grow actively' (from Latin *vegetare,* 'to animate', 'enliven'). This is the widest sense of 'plant', as for example in a letter of the poet Gray written in 1737: 'Both vale and hill are covered with most venerable beeches, and other very reverend vegetables'. Finally, the specific sense as defined above evolved in the eighteenth century.

verge (edge, margin, border, brink)
This word has had something of a tortuous evolution over the years. Its ultimate derivation is Latin *virga,* 'rod'. The earliest record of it in English is as 'penis', a sense that was reintroduced in the eighteenth century, from French *verge,* to refer to the male organ of a mollusc or crustacean. In the fifteenth century, 'verge', like its Latin origin, was used to mean 'rod of office' (compare modern 'verger', the church or cathedral official who acts as usher and carried a verge or wand of office). At about the same time, the expression 'within the verge' became current to denote the land subject to the Lord High Steward, referring to his wand of office. By a transference of meaning, 'verge' thus came to mean the boundary of this land, and hence the modern meaning of 'border', 'edge' and the like. Where the roadside is grassy and soggy, local councils sometimes put up notices 'Soft verges'. One wonders what French visitors to Britain must make of this,

since in French, unlike English, *verge* still has all the old meanings mentioned above.

very (most, extremely)
The word derives from Old French *verai* (modern *vrai*), 'true', and this was the original sense in English, in the thirteenth century. Today, this usage conjures up the Bible ('verily, verily'), the Prayer Book ('Very God of Very God') and medieval tales ('in very sooth' and Chaucer's famous 'verray parfit gentil knight'). There is some justification for this, and certainly 'very' occurs in early English translations of the Bible, although often replaced in the Authorized Version of 1611. Thus Tindale's version (1526) has for Mark 11:32: 'All men counted Ihon, that he was a veri prophett' (Authorized Version: 'All men counted John, that he was a prophet indeed'), and Coverdale, nine years later, translates John 6:55 as: 'For my flesh is yᵉ very meate, and my bloude is yᵉ very drynke' (1611: 'For my flesh is meat indeed, and my blood is drink indeed'). The Chaucer phrase includes a more modern use of 'very', however (as 'the very reverse'), although the basic idea of 'true' is there. The modern usage of 'very' meaning 'extremely', however, only really emerged in the fifteenth century, when it accompanied an adjective or adverb, not a noun. One of the earliest records we have of 'very' in this usage is where it is frequently found still today, in the 'sign-off' of a letter, and one of the *Paston Letters* of 1448 concludes: 'Vere hartely your, Molyns'. ('Hartely' here means 'sincerely', even 'affectionately', not 'heartily'.)

vest (undergarment for the top half of the body)
The word is directly related to 'vestment', and this was precisely what it originally meant, when first current in the seventeenth century. So Pepys records in his *Diary* on 16 February 1663: 'A priest was taken in his vests officiating somewhere in Holborne the other day'. But a more common usage was to refer to the former robe or gown worn by men, a top garment, or to a similar garment worn in eastern countries. For example, Sir Thomas Herbert, in his *Travels* (1634), notes of the Persians that: 'Their out Garment or Vest is commonly of Callico

quilted with Cotton', and Barham, in *The Ingoldsby Legends* (1842), tells how:

The slanting ray of the evening sun
  shone [. . .]
With fitful light on regal vest, and
  warrior's sculptured mail.

In a poetic sense, too, 'vest' could be used of a similar garment worn by women, which usage today may give a rather odd effect, as in Scott's early poem *Glenfinlas* (1801):

O gentle huntsman, hast thou seen [. . .]
A lovely maid in vest of green?

The next sense to appear, still in the same century, was that of 'waistcoat' (the vest begins its journey from outer man to inner!), with this usage still retained by tailors until quite recently. The original of this was the garment introduced by Charles II in 1666, and we must be grateful that Pepys recorded the event in his *Diary* entries for 8 and 15 October that year, respectively: 'The King hath yesterday, in Council, declared his resolution for setting a fashion in clothes [. . .] It will be a vest, I know not well how; but it is to teach the nobility thrift'; 'This day the King begins to put on his Vest, [. . .] being a long cassocke close to the body, of black cloth, and pinked with white silk under it, and a coat over it, and the legs ruffled with black riband like a pigeon's leg'. The modern 'vest' materialized only in the nineteenth century, as a unisex garment ('Cotton, [. . .] spun silk, merino, and Cashmere gentlemen's and ladies' vests', *Catalogue of the Great Exhibition*, 1851).

vet (subject someone to a physical check; verify a person's suitability for a particular post or position)
The word is the basic familiar contraction of 'veterinary surgeon' in verbal use. At first, in the late nineteenth century, the meanings were 'submit an animal to a medical examination or medical treatment' (by a 'vet'), and 'examine or treat a person medically'. Both these sense are still current (animals are 'vetted in' at a show, for example), but the latter usage is now somewhat dated. In the early twentieth century, the modern sense of 'vet' emerged, as applied to the checking of a person' suitability, fitness, trustworthiness, and so on,

mostly in a military, political or sporting contest. In *Traffics and Discoveries* (1904), Kipling wrote: 'These are our crowd [. . .]. They've been vetted, an' we're putting 'em through their paces'.

vice (tool with two jaws designed to grip objects firmly)
The earliest sense of 'vice' in English, in the fourteenth century, was 'winding staircase', this deriving from the French word *vis* meaning 'screw'. (Even today, the French for 'spiral staircase' is *escalier à vis*.) Wyclif even has such a staircase in his Bible translation of 1382, where I Kings 6:8 runs: 'Bi a vyce thei stieden vp into the mydil sowpynge place, and fro the mydil into the thridde' (Authorized Version of 1611: 'And they went up with winding stairs into the middle chamber, and out of the middle into the third'; the reference is to the building of Solomon's temple). In the fifteenth century, English 'vice' came to mean 'screw' itself, a sense that was current for some two hundred years, and somewhere at the end of this same century, or beginning of the next, the word finally acquired its modern meaning, referring to the screw that brings the two jaws together. In North America, the tool is still sometimes spelt 'vise', as a reminder of the word's original French source.

victim (person or animal that suffers death or severe treatment of some kind)
The word was first widely used in English by the Rhemish translators of the Bible in the second half of the sixteenth century, where 'victim' always referred to a living creature killed and offered as a sacrifice. Thus in the Rhemish New Testament of 1582, Mark 9:49 has: 'Euery victime shal be salted with salt' (Authorized Version of 1611: 'Every sacrifice shall be salted with salt'), and Acts 7:42 has: 'Did you offer victims and hostes vnto me?' (Authorized Version: 'Have ye offered to me slain beasts and sacrifices?'). The word then acquired its present meaning, applying to any 'sufferer', only in the seventeenth century, and even then it was not widely current until nearly 1800.

vindicate (uphold, justify)
In the sixteenth century, 'vindicate' meant 'set free', a sense that subsequently became widely current in the first half of the seventeenth century. Inigo Jones, in his monumental work (in more senses than one) *The Most Notable Antiquity of Great Britain, vulgarly called Stone-Heng, on Salisbury Plain, Restored by Inigo Jones* (1620–51), wrote that his aim was: 'To vindicate, as much as in me lies, the Founders of this venerable Antiquity from oblivion'. This usage became obsolete by the end of the eighteenth century. The present meaning evolved some hundred years earlier.

virgin (person, especially a girl, who has never had sexual intercourse)
In its earliest use in English, in the thirteenth century, 'virgin' was exclusively applied to an unmarried or chaste woman (probably a 'virgin' technically in the modern sense) who was also pious and 'steadfast in religion'. The word was thus a term of veneration or reverence, something on a par with 'martyr' or 'saint'. The reference in particular was to such 'virgins' of early Christian times as St Catherine and (in Wales) St Winifred (or Winefride, or Gwenfrewi). Another example is quoted by Robert Manning of Brunne in *Handlyng Synne* (1303):

And she ys callede Iustyne,
A martyr and an holy vyrgyne.

In the fourteenth century, the word acquired its present sense, but here, too, early usage almost always refers to the Virgin Mary. However, another contemporary meaning, perhaps now obsolete, was simply 'girl', 'young woman', especially one who probably was a virgin, or at any rate behaved and looked as if she was. An example of the usage comes in Shakespeare's *The Taming of the Shrew* (1596), where Katharina addresses the disguised Vincentio (her suitor):

Young budding virgin, fair and fresh and sweet,
Whither away, or where is thy abode?
Happy the parents of so fair a child.

Another comes in Dickens's *The Old Curiosity Shop* (1838): 'The beautiful virgin took another pinch [of snuff]'. Today, such poetic uses are rare, and the word usually has the factual sense as defined above.

vision (sight; something imagined that appears to be seen)
In the thirteenth century, 'vision' was the word for something that appeared to be seen other than by physical sight, such as a dream or when the mind was in a special state. Many such 'visions' were religious in nature, and several biblical characters such as Moses and Daniel experienced them. The sense is not obsolete, but the precise definition of what such a 'vision' is in psychological or even physical terms remains unsettled. In the fourteenth century, 'vision' came to be the word for something that is seen by the eye but that is not actually present, usually as a form of 'supernatural insight' when in a state of ecstasy. The last sense to arrive was the current one, simply 'faculty of sight', in the fifteenth century.

visit (go and see, whether for pleasure, interest or business)
The early senses of the word in English, from the thirteenth century, reflected the religious usage of Latin *visitare* in the Vulgate. They therefore usually relate to a 'visitation' by God to comfort or benefit a person, or to a specific 'visiting' of the sick or bereaved, to comfort them. Examples are frequent in the Bible, such as 'O Lord, thou knowest: remember me and visit me' (Jeremiah 15:15), and 'The Lord had visited his people' (Ruth 1:6). Similarly, of humans, 'To visit the fatherless and the widows in their affliction' (James 1:27), or, in the Prayer Book, 'When the sick person is visited'. In the fourteenth century, two apparently contradictory senses evolved: 'deal with severely', 'afflict', and 'go and see in a friendly way', 'call on'. The first of these is now almost obsolete, or at least highly stylized (or humorous, as 'I was visited by a tummy bug'). Again, it is widely found in the Bible, with the particular 'bad' sense arising from the fact that a 'visit' by God, although made for a person's good, might actually be in order to punish, and would thus be quite unpleasant. The use of 'visit' to apply to a place (as 'visiting an island') finally followed in the fifteenth century. The usage is well illustrated by the

first record we have of it, from *The Romaunt of the Rose* (1400):

> This knowe ye, sir, as wel as I,
> That lovers gladly wole visiten
> The places there her loves habiten.

volume (book, especially one of a series; size, bulk, capacity)
The origin of the word is in Latin *volumen*, 'roll', 'scroll' (compare 'revolve'), and in the fourteenth century, 'volume' was thus the term for a roll of parchment or the like that formed a book. Wyclif uses the word for rendering Deuteronomy 17:18 in his Bible translation of 1382: 'He shal discriue to hym a declaracioun of this lawe in a volym' (Authorized Version of 1611: 'He shall write him a copy of this law in a book'). It is the Authorized Version itself, in fact, that offers an even clearer example of the sense, in Psalm 40:7: 'In the volume of the book it is written'. The 'capacity' sense of 'volume' began to emerge in the sixteenth century, when the word was used first, of the size or bulk of a book (a now obsolete usage), then, in the seventeenth century, of the size of other objects. Compare **tome**.

vulgar (crude, gross, offensive)
Today, perhaps by association with some other words or sounds, the word itself almost seems 'vulgar'. However, originally, in the fourteenth century (although not commonly until the sixteenth), the meaning was simply 'ordinary', 'common'. An example of the use comes in John Lydgate's *Minor Poems* (1430):

> Isys [i.e. Isis] in Egipt fonde [founded] a diversite
> Of sundry lettres parted in tweyne;
> First to pristes, and to the comunalte
> Vulgar lettres he dide also ordeyne.

From the fifteenth century, 'vulgar' then came to mean 'vernacular', 'native' of a language, which was after all the 'ordinary' one for a particular people. Hence, in the Prologue to Caxton's translation (1483) of Geoffroi de la Tour l'Andri's *The Knyght of the Toure*, the statement that he has aimed: 'To translate & reduce this said book out of frenssh into our vulgar Englissh'. Related to this is the name 'Vulgate' for the fourth-century Latin version of the Bible translated by St Jerome, who himself spoke only 'vulgar Latin', that is, a 'popular' dialect of classical Latin that developed in the Roman empire. The modern sense 'coarse', 'unrefined' arose in the seventeenth century, since the 'common' people lacked refinement or culture. Compare the sense of 'common' itself, as used by some people (not always themselves 'common').

wade (walk through water)
The Old English verb *wadan*, that gave modern 'wade', meant simply 'go', and is indirectly related to Latin *vadere*, 'to go' (as in 'vade mecum'). An example of the usage is found in the *Scottish Legends of the Saints* (1375): 'As he towart me cuth [i.e. could] wad, a gredy wolf hynt me [seized me]'. A late text preserving this sense, too, is Richard Brathwait's *Barnabees Journal* (1638), where he bids farewell to:

Steepy wayes by which I waded,
And those trugs with which I traded.

The verb otherwise became naturally obsolete hardly later than the fifteenth century, and no example has been found of the Old English word meaning 'wade' in the modern sense, which itself developed from the thirteenth century.

waft (carry through the air)
The verb derives from a now obsolete word 'wafter', which was the term for an armed ship used as a convoy. Hence the original sense of 'waft', in the sixteenth century, was 'convoy', or 'convey safely through water'. The first of these meanings became obsolete only a hundred years or so later, but occurs, for example, in Edward Hall's *Chronicle* (1548), which tells how because 'certain

pyrates' were 'lurkyng at the Temmes mouthe': 'Thomas Lord Camois with certaine shippes of warre was appointed to wafte over the kyng [i.e. Henry IV]'. The second sense is still current, at least in poetical use, and in a suitable context you can still 'waft' things through the air, although perhaps less frequently through water. But Thomas Moore wrote in *Lalla Rookh* (1817):

Again she sees his pinnace fly,
Wafting him fleetly to his home.

However, 'waft' was not used of motion through the air until the eighteenth century, where the usage (a transference from water to air) is first recorded in Pope's *Pastorals* (1704):

Your praise the birds shall chant in
   evr'ry grove,
And winds shall waft it to the pow'rs
   above.

waif (abandoned or homeless child or animal)
As originally used, in the fourteenth century, 'waif' applied only to a piece of property that was found without an owner, not to a person. It could, however, be used of a stray animal. Such a piece of property went to the lord of the manor if still unclaimed after due notice had been given and a fixed period of time elapsed. The term was thus a legal one, and frequently occurred in the combination 'waif and stray', the latter specifically applying to the lost animal. Many 'waifs' were washed ashore as the result of a shipwreck, or were even whole ships, and the word is used in this sense by Charles Kingsley in *Hereward the Wake* (1866), where he refers to the country folk 'who were prowling about the shore after [i.e. in search of] the waifs of the storm'. It was thus only in the eighteenth century, that 'waif' came to apply to a homeless child, and this sense is first recorded in Cowper's poem *The Task* (1784):

'Twas hard, perhaps, on here and there
   a waif,
Desirous to return, and not receiv'd.

The charity organization now called the Church of England Children's Society was founded as the 'Waifs and Strays' Society in 1881 to provide for abandoned children.

wait (remain, stay, postpone doing something; serve at table)
The original sense of the verb was 'watch out', as when looking for an enemy or a spy (compare modern French *guetter* having this meaning). The usage first arose in the twelfth century, and is recorded down to the sixteenth. The 'hostile intent' implicit in 'wait' can be found, for instance, in Miles Coverdale's English Bible translation of 1535, in which he renders Obadiah 1:14 as follows: 'Nether shalt thou stone waytinge enymore at yᵉ corners of the stretes, to murthur soch as are fled' (Authorized Version of 1611: 'Neither shouldest thou have stood in the crossway, to cut off those of his that did escape'). The meaning 'remain', 'stay', came in the fourteenth century, with the sense 'postpone doing' ('wait and see') evolving only three hundred years after this. However, the 'serve at table' meaning is first found in the sixteenth century, with 'waiter' recorded from the fourteenth century, when it originally meant 'watcher', not gaining its current sense until the seventeenth century, after the verb.

walk (go on foot)
The verb acquired its common modern sense only in the thirteenth century. Before this, in Old English, *wealcan* meant either 'roll', 'toss' or 'move about', 'go' (generally). The first of these meanings gave the other, more specialized verb 'walk' meaning 'full cloth' (by beating and pressing it), and the corresponding agent noun of this, 'walker' (person who walks cloth), is the origin of the surname Walker. The 'roll' sense of 'walk' could apply to a person, as in these lines from *Twenty-six Political Poems* (1400), which is about as late as the usage is found:

Allas, I walke in a lake
Of dedly synne that doth me tene
[i.e. grieve].

In the sense 'go', the verb 'walk' could apply to things as much as people, and is found as late as the seventeenth century, with special uses applying to crime spreading and drink circulating. For example, in Nicholas

Breton's *Pasquils Fooles-Cappe* (1600) come the lines:

Wealth is a witch that hath a wicked charme,
That in the mindes of wicked men doth walke,

and Sir Walter Ralegh, in *The Discoverie of the [. . .] Empyre of Guiana* (1596), records: 'Wee found them all as drunke as beggers, and the pottes walking from one to another without rest'. The transitive use of 'walk' (as when 'walking' a dog or a horse) followed in the fifteenth century.

wallet (pocket book or container for banknotes, papers etc.)
In the fourteenth century, a 'wallet' was a bag holding goods for a journey, or a similar 'pack' or 'scrip', as carried by pedlars and pilgrims. The usage is recorded from Chaucer right down to the twentieth century, and so perhaps cannot be regarded as obsolete even yet. Dickens used the word, for example, in *The Old Curiosity Shop* (1840): 'The old man had forgotten a kind of wallet which contained the light burden he had to carry', and Robert Bridges' 'masque' *Demeter* (1904) also has the word:

Approach him with a gift: this little wallet.

(A stage direction follows: '(Giving a little bag of seeds)'). The better known sense of 'wallet', however, arose in American usage only in the nineteenth century. One of the earliest instances of the new sense comes in a short story by Nathaniel P. Willis, in his *Dashes at Life with a Free Pencil* (1845): 'Our several borrowings were thrust into a wallet which was sometimes in his pocket, and sometimes in mine, as each took the turn to be paymaster'.

wallop (beat, hit hard)
The verb is actually related to 'gallop', and this was its original meaning, from the fourteenth century down to the eighteenth. In *Generedes, a Romance* (1440) one finds the lines:

He founde anon
The kyng of kynggez vppe and down rideng
And he anon to hym com waloping.

In a poem of 1721 by the Scottish poet Allan Ramsay, too, one reads:

> And witches wallop o'er to France,
> Up in the air
> On my bony grey mare.

In the sixteenth century, 'wallop' came to be used for a bubbling or boiling sound, a usage that only recently became obsolete. However, Nathaniel Hawthorne has it in *Our Old Home* (1863): 'We beheld an immense pot over the fire, surging and walloping with some kind of a savory stew'. In the eighteenth century, the meaning progressed to describing any violent noisy movement, as of a lolloping clumsy animal. This usage is at least obsolescent today, yet occurs, for example, in Helen Mathers' *Tally Ho!* (1906): 'Sir George Freeling came walloping up on his big iron-grey horse'. Finally, the sense 'beat' arrived in the nineteenth century.

wan (pale, pallid)
This unusual word, which may perhaps be related to 'wane', originally meant not 'pale' but 'dark', 'dusky' in its identical Old English form. This usage is found down to the sixteenth century, although mainly in poetry, such as John Skelton's *Phyllyp Sparowe* (1529):

> With vysage wan,
> As swarte as tan.

The meaning 'pale' is first recorded in the early fourteenth-century *Cursor Mundi:*

> For lene he was, and wan the face.

The sense change is perhaps not so drastic as it appears if both shades, dark and pale, are regarded as 'livid', and as that of a sickly face, one that is literally 'off colour'.

wanton (uncontrolled, deliberately savage)
The word has gone through a number of now obsolete senses before arriving at its present meaning in the sixteenth century, with the only earlier usage still current that of 'lascivious', 'lewd', which dates from the fourteenth century. A hundred years earlier, when the word first entered the language, it meant 'undisciplined', 'rebellious', or otherwise, of children, 'naughty', 'unruly'. This

is found down to the seventeenth century, when it occurs in an account (1697) of the life of the Duke of Gloucester, referring to an incident that took place when he was still a small boy: 'The Dutchess of Northumberland came with several ladies of fashion to the Duke at Windsor, when unfortunately he was a little wanton, suffering some improper expressions to escape him'. In the fourteenth century, apart from the 'lascivious' sense that then arose, 'wanton' also came to mean 'capricious', 'sportive', as in the Prologue to Chaucer's *Canterbury Tales* (1386), describing the 'limiter', or friar who had a 'limited' area for his begging activities:

> A frere ther was, a wantowne and a mery,
> A lymytour, a ful solempne man [i.e. a 'grand' man].

In the sixteenth century, 'wanton' acquired the sense 'insolent'. 'When men get abundance, they soon grow wanton', wrote Jeremiah Burrowes, in *An Exposition of Hosea* (1643-52). The poetic sense of 'luxurious' also came in the sixteenth century, with overtones of 'decadent', as in Shakespeare's *Henry IV*, Part 2 (1597), where the Archbishop of York says:

> We are all diseas'd;
> And with our surfeiting and wanton hours
> Have brought ourselves into a burning fever.

Finally, and at almost the same time, the modern meaning developed.

wardrobe (cupboard for clothes)
The earliest meaning of the word was 'room for clothes', in the fourteenth century. This sort of 'wardrobe' was usually next to a bedroom, so was in effect a dressing room, which the term came to designate before it became obsolete in the nineteenth century. The earliest record of this usage is in Thomas Usk's *The Testament of Love* (1387-8): 'Jupiter hath in his wardrobe bothe garmentes of joye and of sorowe'. In the sixteenth to eighteenth centuries, the meaning was influenced by its French counterpart, *garderobe*, and came more to mean simply a room where valuables were

stored, rather than clothes. In his *Diary* entry for 25 January 1700, Evelyn thus records: 'In the wardrobe above they shew'd us fine wrought plate, porcelan, [etc.]'. The sense expanded somewhat in the fifteenth century to mean the whole department of a large house that was responsible for the clothes, with the word even designating the building where those entrusted with this office had their premises. Hence in Shakespeare's *Twelfth Night* (1601), Malvolio's remark: 'The lady of the Strachy married the yeoman of the wardrobe'. Also in this period, 'wardrobe' acquired the sense 'person's stock of clothes'. But it was only in the eighteenth century, that the 'wardrobe' became the 'clothes cupboard' that it is today, with the meaning really being a development of the earliest sense, 'room for clothes'.

watch (keep looking at, be on the alert for)
In Old English, 'watch' meant simply 'to be awake', whether naturally, as in the daytime, or by special intention, as at night. The latter sense is the one used by Milton in *Paradise Lost* (1667):

As when men wont to watch
On duty, sleeping found by whom they
  dread,
Rouse and bestir themselves ere well
  awake.

The meaning became obsolete shortly after this. The two main current senses, 'keep a lookout' and 'keep looking at', developed respectively in the thirteenth and fourteenth centuries.

weeds (mourning dress)
The word is little used now, but when it is, it is usually as 'widow's weeds' or some similar expression. In the singular, 'weed' in Old English meant simply 'garment' or, in a collective sense, 'clothing'. Both meanings were still current in poetry as late as the nineteenth century, with Tennyson's *In Memoriam* (1850), for example, containing the lines:

In words, like weeds, I'll wrap me o'er,
Like coarsest clothes against the cold,

and William Morris's *The Earthly Paradise* (1868–70), similarly has:

In face, in figure, and in weed,
She wholly changed before his
  wondering eyes.

The specific sense 'mourning garments' for 'weeds' emerged only in the sixteenth century.

weird (strange, uncanny, odd)
In Old English, as a noun, 'weird' (*wyrd*) meant 'fate', 'lot', 'destiny', and hence, also early, it was the name for one of the Fates, the three goddesses of classical mythology who were believed controlled the course of people's lives. Chaucer used the latter sense in *The Legend of Good Women* (1385):

The werdys that we clepyn [i.e. call]
  destene
Hath shapyn hire [her] that she mot
  nedis be [must needs be]
Pyetous sad.

From the noun, the word became an adjective in the related sense, 'shaping people's lives', in the fourteenth century, so that the 'weird sisters' were the three Fates before they were the three witches in Shakespeare's *Macbeth* (1605). The modern meaning dates from only the nineteenth century, with the use of the word familiar from poetry of the time (especially that of Shelley and Keats).

welkin (sky, heaven)

Hark, how all the welkin rings,
'Glory to the King of kings'.

These two lines were Charles Wesley's original opening couplet for his well known Christmas hymn of 1746, now beginning:

Hark! the herald-angels sing
Glory to the new-born King.

(The substitution was made, perhaps felicitously, by George Whitefield in 1753.) Wesley's words, together with similar poetic phrases such as 'make the welkin ring' and 'rend the welkin' are all we have left today of the Old English word that originally meant 'cloud' (compare modern German *Wolke* in this sense). This literal meaning became obsolete as early as the thirteenth century, however, although a secondary sense, 'sky', 'firmament' developed from the twelfth century, and this is the meaning that survives today, inasmuch as it survives at all. The original meaning thus faded from the language when the standard word became **cloud** (which see, for its own sense development).

well (healthy, fit)
As an adjective, 'well' originally meant 'happy', 'fortunate' in English, with the sense current from the thirteenth century to the nineteenth (latterly in old fashioned or deliberately stylish writing). In this usage, like many other adjectives, it often came after the noun, rather than before it, or at any rate with the verb inverted to follow its subject, as in the common 'well were we' or 'well was he'. An example comes in Henry Howard, Earl of Surrey's translation (1547) of Virgil's *Aeneid:*

And well were they whoes handes might touch the cordes.

In the fourteenth century, a sense 'prosperous' developed, now current only in such stock phrases as 'well to do' and 'well off'. This usage also became obsolete by the nineteenth century. Finally, the current meaning, 'having good health', evolved in the sixteenth century, in time for Shakespeare to use it regularly in his works.

wench (woman or girl, especially a buxom one)
Today, the word is used only humorously, and is regarded as having agreeably 'naughty' overtones (mainly through the verb 'to wench', meaning, of a man, 'chase the girls'). In the original sense of 'young woman', 'girl', however, from the thirteenth century, the usage was quite regular, with no colouring of the meaning, at least not to begin with. Thus in a sermon of 1380, Wyclif wrote: 'Christ came to the hous of this prince that the wenche lay deed inne' (see Luke 9:23 for the reference), and Shakespeare, too, used 'wench' as a standard word in *Antony and Cleopatra* (1606), where Charmian asks the Soothsayer: 'Prithee, how many boys and wenches must I have?'. After this, the word became increasingly common as a dialect term, and may still be current as such today. It was in the fourteenth century, however, that 'wench' first acquired its 'wanton' overtone, and that it

was first used to mean 'maidservant'. The 'wanton woman' usage comes, for example, in Coverdale's Bible translation of 1535, to render Isaiah 23:16: 'Take thy lute (saie men to her) and go aboute the citie, thou art yet an vnknowne wensche' (Authorized Version of 1611: 'Take an harp, go about the city, thou harlot that hast been forgotten'). Similarly, but in the sense 'maidservant', Tindale's translation of Mark 14:66 runs: 'There cam won of the wenches off the hyest preste' (Authorized Version: 'There cometh one of the maids of the high priest'). If either of these senses is still current, it is the latter, although only in a jocular or popularly commercial context, as mentioned. ('Wenches' serve at 'Elizabethan banquets' in late twentieth-century hotels and restaurants, for example, in a semi-serious attempt to indulge in the licence of 'merry England'.)

wife (married woman)
The current meaning dates from Old English times, when, however, the word also meant simply 'woman' (compare modern German *Weib* still in this sense). Today, the meaning survives only in compounds, such as 'housewife', 'midwife', and the now dated 'fishwife' and 'alewife'. The usage is found down to at least the sixteenth century, however, and Tindale chose the word to translate Revelation 17:6 in his English Bible of 1526: 'I sawe the wyfe dronke with the bloud of saynctes' (Authorized Version of 1611: 'I saw the woman drunken with blood of the saints'). After this, the sense passed increasingly into dialect use.

wince (shrink back involuntarily from pain, etc.)
The original meaning of the verb, in the thirteenth century, was 'kick restlessly' as of a horse. Thus in *Select English Works* (1380) Wyclif writes: 'A horce unrubbed, that has a sore back, wynses when he is oght [i.e. in any way] touched or rubbed on his rugge [back]'. This, therefore, is the sense in the well known words in Shakespeare's *Hamlet* (1603), when Hamlet comments during the Players' scene: 'Let the galled jade wince, our withers are unwrung'. (The 'galled jade', or irritated horse, is the Player King.) The modern meaning of 'wince'

followed much later, in the eighteenth century, and the earlier sense passed into dialect use, where it may still be current.

wink (close one eye briefly in greeting or as a mild provocation)
In Old English, *wincian* meant either 'close the eyes' generally or 'glance at meaningfully'. The first sense is found as recently as the nineteenth century, when it became obsolete. Before this, it occurs, for instance in Shakespeare's *Cymbeline* (1611), where Posthumus says to the First Gaoler: 'I tell thee, fellow, there are none want eyes to direct them the way I am going but such a wink and will not use them'. More recently, Cowper used the word in his poem *Tirocinium* (1784):

> To follow foolish precedents, and wink
> With both our eyes, is easier than to
> think.

The other sense, 'give a significant glance', is also obsolete, although it was similarly current down to the nineteenth century, and is found in Dickens's *Sketches by Boz* (1835): 'Ma having first nodded and winked to the governess to pull the girls' frocks a little more off their shoulders', Earlier, in Shakespeare's *Henry V* (1599), King Henry says to the Duke of Burgundy (regarding Katharine, the French king's daughter, whom he wishes to marry): 'Then, good my lord, teach your cousin to consent winking'. Burgundy replies: 'I will wink on her to consent, my lord, if you will teach her to know my meaning'. In the thirteenth century, 'wink' came to mean 'blink', a sense it can still have, although the present usage, indicating a greeting or implying a teasing, emerged only in the nineteenth century, when it is first recorded in Dickens.

winsome (pleasantly and openly attractive)
Old English *wynsum*, that gave the modern word, originally meant just 'pleasant', 'agreeable', with this sense found down to the fourteenth century. It is found in one of the latest texts of the period, the *Cursor Mundi*, which tells of:

> ...a wonsun thede [i.e. country],
> A land rinnand bath honi and milk.

The word then fell out of general use, but must have survived in local currency in Scotland and northern England, since it reemerged from there in the seventeenth century with the connotation 'attractive', 'handsome'. Burns has it in his poem *My Wife's a Winsome Wee Thing* (1792), and the usage soon spread to the literary and general language of the whole country.

wit (sound mind, imaginative use of intelligence to entertain, witty man)
The senses developed in the order given here, respectively, in the twelfth, sixteenth and seventeenth centuries. Originally, however, the Old English word (spelt identically) meant 'mind', 'understanding', 'sense'. All these meanings are now obsolete, with the exception of the last when in the plural (as in 'have one's wits about one' or 'live by one's wits'). In the sense 'understanding', for example, 'wit' occurs in Shakespeare's *A Midsummer Night's Dream* (1590), where Bottom, on waking from his sleep, says: 'I have had a dream, past the wit of man to say what dream it was'. In the sixteenth century, however, 'wit' meant 'wise man' before it meant 'witty man' a hundred years later, and although this sense is now obsolete, it is found, for example, in Dr Johnson's *The Lives of the English Poets* (1779–81), where he describes Milton as a 'scholar and wit' (meaning he was a learned person, not a witty one in the modern meaning). See also **witness**, and **witty** itself (below).

with (accompanying)
Can 'with' ever have had any other meaning? The answer is that it can and did. In Old English, *with* meant 'against', that is, denoted opposition. It is from this original meaning, in itself now obsolete, that today the preposition 'with' occurs (on the face of it paradoxically, if one thinks about it) with such 'opposing' verbs as 'compete', 'fight', 'quarrel' and 'struggle', and in such phrases as 'be at odds with' and even 'go to law with'. Old English *with* thus meant 'against', and the word that meant 'with' in the modern sense was *mid* (compare modern German *mit*). What is odd is that for some reason about the twelfth or thirteenth century, *with* acquired the sense of *mid*,

which thus gradually faded from the language, not surviving after about 1400.

witness (person who can testify to something seen or known to be true)
It is unusual to find '-ness' on a word describing a person, and it is much more usual to find it forming an abstract noun, such as 'goodness', 'lateness', 'helpfulness'. This is in fact its original use in Old English, when 'wit-ness' (as it were) actually meant 'knowledge', 'wisdom', with the suffix '-ness' added to 'wit' meaning 'reason', 'understanding' (see **wit** itself, above). The usage became obsolete in the fifteenth century, but Wyclif used 'witness' in this sense in his English Bible of 1382 to translate Proverbs 8:5: 'Vnderstondeth, yee litle childer, witnesse' (Authorized Version of 1611: 'O ye simple, understand wisdom'). However, Old English also had the modern meaning 'testimony' (as in 'bear witness'), and the transfer of sense to 'person who bears testimony' also took place before the fourteenth century. See also **witty**.

witty (cleverly amusing)
In Old English, 'witty' related specifically to 'wit', that is to reasoning and understanding, so meant 'wise', 'sensible'. The meaning is found down to the sixteenth century, and occurs, for example, in Reginald Pecock's *The Repressor of over much Blaming of the Clergy* (1449), where he says: 'Ech witti man muste graunte that the first principal conclusioun bifore sett is trewe'. In the fourteenth century, 'witty' progressed to meaning 'clever', 'ingenious', 'skilful'. The sense became obsolete only in the nineteenth century, but can be found, for instance, in Cowper's poem *The Task* (1784), where he is referring to London:

Show this queen of cities, that so fair
May yet be foul; so witty, yet not wise.

The modern usage is first recorded in Shakespeare's *Love's Labour's Lost* (1588), where Sir Nathaniel says to Holofernes: 'Your reasons at dinner have been sharp and sententious; pleasant without scurrility, witty without affection'. Compare **wit** and **witness** (above).

wizard (magician, man skilled in occult arts)
A 'wizard' is really a 'wise-ard', that is a philosopher or 'wise man'. This is what the word originally meant in the fifteenth century, with the sense current down to the nineteenth century. A typical example can be found in Spenser's *The Faerie Queene* (1596):

Therefore the antique wisards well invented,
That Venus of the fomy sea was bred.

The modern meaning of 'wizard', which cannot be said to be obsolete, then followed in the sixteenth century, when at first it often referred to the biblical 'Three Wise Men' or astrologers, and this usage is preserved in Milton's ode *On the Morning of Christ's Nativity* (1629):

The Star-led Wisards haste with odours sweet.

The use of 'wizard' to mean 'expert', 'champion' (as a 'wizard at chess') developed from the seventeenth century.

wold (area of upland or downs)
In Old English, *weald* or *wald* was a standard word for 'forest' (compare modern German *Wald*), and the term came to apply in particular to a raised or prominent forest on upland, and to a wooded upland itself. By extension, the sense then came to apply in the thirteenth century to a hill or area of downland, even where the wood had been cleared. After about 1500, however, the word fell out of general use and became restricted to the names of particular areas, such as the Lincolnshire Wolds, the Yorkshire Wolds or the Cotswolds, with the modern general use deriving from such place names only after about 1600, especially in poetic writing. In his poem *To J.S.* (1832), Tennyson wrote:

The wind, that beats the mountain, blows
More softly round the open wold.

worm (earthworm)
The present use of the word dates from the thirteenth century. Before that, in Old English, 'worm' (*wyrm,* later *wurm*) had a

range of meanings, from 'snake' or 'dragon' to 'maggot'. The first of these comes in Tindale's Bible translation of 1526, when in Acts 28:4 one reads: 'When the men off the countree sawe the worme hange on hys honde' (Authorized Version of 1611: 'And when the barbarians saw the venomous beast [i.e. a viper] hang on his hand'). The reference was frequently to the snake in the Garden of Eden, as personifying evil, and even as late as 1867, William Morris wrote, in *The Life and Death of Jason:*

> Therewith began
> A fearful battle betwixt worm and man.

The 'maggot' sense is still current, of course, but as 'snake' or 'serpent', 'worm' occurs, if at all, only in poetry.

worry (harass, pester, afflict mentally)
The Old English sense of 'worry' was 'strangle'! As recently as 1606 one can thus find recorded in the *Register of the Privy Council of Scotland* (although no later): 'He tuike the said compleiner be the throat and thought to have wirryed her or [i.e. before] she had awaked'. In the thirteenth century, 'worry' came to mean 'choke' (that is, on a mouthful of food). This sense fell out of use in the eighteenth century at the latest, but occurs in a folk ballad of 1715 which tells of a man who:

> . . . like a fool, did eat the cow,
> And worried on the tail.

From the fourteenth century, 'worry' came to mean 'seize with the teeth', as an animal at the throat of another (typically, a wolf or dog with a sheep, or a dog with a bone), and it was from this sense, still current, that the meaning 'harass' emerged in the sixteenth century, and 'afflict mentally' in the nineteenth. The concept has thus passed from literal to figurative, and the overall sense has modulated and become diffused over the centuries.

wrong (incorrect, mistaken)
The original meaning of 'wrong', in Old English, was probably 'crooked', 'twisted' ('probably' because early examples of the adjective have not been found). The sense can be seen in the following lines from Henry Parker's *A Compendiouse Treatise Dyalogue of Diues and Pauper* (1470):

> The bowe is made of ii. thynges,
> Of a wronge tree, and a right strynge.

(That is: A bow is made of two things: a crooked branch and a straight string.) This usage of 'wrong' is not recorded later than the seventeenth century, and even then in dialect or local use. In the thirteenth century, the meaning 'unjust', 'not morally right' developed, and a hundred years later, the wider sense of 'incorrect', 'mistaken'.

yawn (inhale deeply or a result of weariness or boredom)
The present sense of the verb is recorded no earlier than the fifteenth century. Before this, to 'yawn' meant to open the mouth wide, either when gaping, or when eating something. The 'gaping' sense is preserved by Shakespeare in *Coriolanus* (1607), where Coriolanus talks of 'woollen vassals' who are:

> Things created
> To buy and sell with groats, to show
> bare heads
> In congregations, to yawn, be still, and
> wonder.

This sense of 'yawn' is still current as applied to 'gaping' objects, such as a 'yawning' abyss or a 'yawning' gap (literal or figurative).

zest (keenness, gusto, 'spice', piquancy)
The word came into English from French in the seventeenth century, when it meant (as modern French *zeste* still means) 'orange peel', 'lemon peel', that is, as used for flavouring. This sense was current to the twentieth century, but is now only in specialist culinary use. John Wesley's *Primitive Physick* (1747) instructs: 'Pour into the Palm of the Hand a little Brandy, with some Zist of Lemon'. The addition of such peel to a drink gave it a special flavour or piquancy, and it was from this concept that the word acquired its modern sense in the eighteenth century, when 'zest' meant either 'piquancy' or 'gusto'. The former sense evolved first, at the beginning of the century, and is now perhaps less widely used than the second, which followed towards the close of the same eighteenth century. Hence (with the former meaning) the import of the word in Keats's *Ode to Fanny* (1819):

That sweet minor zest
Of love, your kiss.

zoology (science of animals)
The word was originally used, in the seventeenth century, to apply to the science of the means whereby medical remedies can be obtained from animals. The particular sense can be seen in the English title of a translation of Johann Schröder's *Zoologia: or the History of Animals, as they are Useful in Physick and Chirurgery* (1657). However, by the eighteenth century, the term had settled to its present meaning, and in Nathan Bailey's *English Dictionary* of 1726 'zoology' is defined as 'A Treatise concerning living Creatures'.

BIBLIOGRAPHY

Bartlett, John, *Bartlett's Familiar Quotations,* Little, Brown, Baston, 1980.

Baugh, Albert C., and Cable, Thomas, *A History of the English Language,* Prentice Hall, Englewood Cliffs, NJ, 1978.

Burchfield, Robert, *The English Language,* Oxford University Press, 1985.

Burchfield, Robert (ed.) *A Supplement to the Oxford English Dictionary,* Oxford University Press, Volume I (A-G), 1972, Volume II (H-N), 1976, Volume III (O-Scz), 1982.

Copley, J., *Shift of Meaning,* Oxford University Press, London, 1961.

Drabble, Margaret (ed.), *The Oxford Companion to English Literature,* 5th edn, Oxford University Press, 1985.

Foster, Brian, *The Changing English Language,* Macmillan, London, 1968.

Funk, Wilfred, *Word Origins and Their Romantic Stories,* Bell Publishing, New York, 1978.

Harvey, Sir Paul (comp. and ed.), *The Oxford Companion to English Literature,* 4th edn. revised by Dorothy Eagle, Clarendon Press, Oxford, 1967.

Heller, Louis, Humez, Alexander, and Dror, Malcah, *The Private Lives of English Words,* Routledge & Kegan Paul, London, 1984.

Hoad, T.F. (ed.), *The Concise Oxford Dictionary of English Etymology,* Clarendon Press, Oxford, 1986.

Hughes, Geoffrey, *Words in Time: A Social History of the English Vocabulary,* Basil Blackwell, New York, 1988.

Leech, G.L., *Semantics,* Longman, London, 1974.

Leith, Richard, *A Social History of English,* Routledge & Kegan Paul, London, 1983.

Lewis, C.S., *Studies in Words,* Cambridge University Press, 1974.

McDonald, James, *Wordly Wise,* Constable, London, 1984.

Matthews, C.M., *Words, Words, Words,* Lutterworth Press, Guildford, 1979.

Murray, James et al. (eds), *The Oxford English Dictionary,* Oxford University Press, 1933.

Onions, C.T. (ed.), with the assistance of G.W.S. Friedrichsen and R.W. Burchfield, *The Oxford Dictionary of English Etymology,* Clarendon Press, Oxford, 1966.

Onions, C.T. (rev. and ed.), *The Shorter Oxford English Dictionary,* Oxford University Press, 1972.

Ousby, Ian, *The Cambridge Guide to Literature in English,* Cambridge University Press, Cambridge, 1988.

The Oxford Dictionary of Quotations, Oxford University Press, 2nd edn 1953, 3rd edn 1979.

Picoche, Jacqueline, *Dictionnaire étymologique du français,* Robert, Paris, 1979.

Pinkerton, Edward C., *Word for Word,* Verbatim Books, Essex, Ct., 1982.

Potter, Simeon, *Changing English,* André Deutsch, London, 1969.

Samuels, M.L., *Linguistic Evolution: With Special Reference to English,* Cambridge University Press, 1972.

Shipley, Joseph T., *Dictionary of Word Origins,* Philosophical Library, New York, 1945.

Shipley, Joseph T., *In Praise of English: The Growth and Use of Language,* Times Books, New York, 1977.

Skeat, Rev. Walter W., *An Etymological Dictionary of the English Language,* Clarendon Press, Oxford, 1909.

Skinner, Quentin, 'Language and Social Change', in Michaels, Leonard and Ricks, Christopher (eds), *The State of the Language,* University of California Press, Berkeley and Los Angeles, 1980.

Strang, Barbara M.H., *A History of English,* Methuen, London, 1974.

Thody, Philip, and Evans, Howard, *Faux Amis and Key Words: A Dictionary-Guide to French Language, Culture and Society through Lookalikes and Confusables,* Athlone Press, London, 1985.

Trench, Richard Chenevix, *A Select Glossary of English Words Used Formerly in Senses Different from their Present,* 2nd edn, John W. Parker, London, 1859.

Trench, Richard Chenevix, *On the Study of Words,* edited with emendations by A. Smythe Palmer, Routledge, London, n.d. [*c.* 1910].

Waldron, R.A., *Sense and Sense Development,* André Deutsch, London, 1967.

Weekley, Ernest, *Words Ancient and Modern,* John Murray, London, 1926.

Weekley, Ernest, *More Words Ancient and Modern,* John Murray, London, 1927.

Williams, Raymond, *Keywords: A Vocabulary of Culture and Society,* Fontana, London, 1976.

Wyld, H.C., *A Short History of English,* John Murray, London, 1914.